AMNESTY INTERNATIONAL
REPORT 2002

UNITED STATES OF AMERICA
CANADA
ICELAND
IRELAND
UNITED STATES OF AMERICA
PORTUGAL
MEXICO
BAHAMAS
CUBA
MOROCCO
WESTERN SAHARA
HAITI
DOMINICAN REP.
BELIZE
JAMAICA
GUATEMALA
HONDURAS
SAINT KITTS AND NEVIS
ANTIGUA AND BARBUDA
MAURITANIA
DOMINICA
EL SALVADOR
NICARAGUA
SAINT VINCENT AND THE GRENADINES
SAINT LUCIA
BARBADOS
CAPE VERDE
GRENADA
SENEGAL
TRINIDAD AND TOBAGO
GAMBIA
COSTA RICA
GUINEA-BISSAU
GUINEA
VENEZUELA
PANAMA
SIERRA LEONE
LIBERIA
CÔTE D'IVOIRE
GUYANA
SURINAME
COLOMBIA
ATLANTIC OCEAN
KIRIBATI
ECUADOR
PACIFIC OCEAN
BRAZIL
PERU
BOLIVIA
SAMOA
PARAGUAY
URUGUAY
TONGA
ARGENTINA
CHILE

… the period January to December 2001
AMNESTY INTERNATIONAL
REPORT 2002

This report covers the period January to December 2001

CONTENTS

Preface/1
AI's appeals for action/2

PART 1
Foreword by Irene Khan/5
Introduction/9

PART 2
Afghanistan/25
Albania/27
Algeria/29
Angola/31
Argentina/34
Armenia/35
Australia/37
Austria/38
Azerbaijan/40
Bahamas/42
Bahrain/43
Bangladesh/44
Belarus/45
Belgium/47
Belize/49
Bhutan/50
Bolivia/51
Bosnia-Herzegovina/52
Brazil/55
Brunei Darussalam/57
Bulgaria/58
Burkina Faso/60
Burundi/61
Cambodia/64
Cameroon/65
Canada/67
Central African Republic/68
Chad/69
Chile/71
China/72
Colombia/76
Congo (Democratic Republic of the)/79
Côte d'Ivoire/82
Croatia/83
Cuba/85
Czech Republic/87
Dominican Republic/88
East Timor/89
Ecuador/90
Egypt/92
El Salvador/94
Equatorial Guinea/95

Eritrea/96
Ethiopia/98
Fiji/100
Finland/101
France/102
Gambia/104
Georgia/105
Germany/107
Ghana/109
Greece/110
Guatemala/112
Guinea/114
Guinea-Bissau/115
Guyana/117
Haiti/118
Honduras/120
Hungary/122
India/123
Indonesia/126
Iran/128
Iraq/131
Ireland/133
Israel and the Occupied Territories/134
Italy/137
Jamaica/139
Japan/140
Jordan/142
Kazakstan/143
Kenya/144
Korea (Democratic People's Republic of)/146
Korea (Republic of)/148
Kuwait/149
Kyrgyzstan/150
Laos/152
Latvia/153
Lebanon/154
Lesotho/157
Liberia/158
Libya/160
Lithuania/162
Macedonia/162
Malawi/165
Malaysia/165
Maldives/167
Mauritania/168
Mauritius/169
Mexico/170
Moldova/173
Morocco/Western Sahara/174
Mozambique/176

CONTENTS

Myanmar/177
Namibia/179
Nepal/180
New Zealand/183
Nicaragua/183
Niger/184
Nigeria/185
Oman/187
Pakistan/188
Palestinian Authority/190
Papua New Guinea/192
Paraguay/193
Peru/194
Philippines/196
Poland/198
Portugal/199
Puerto Rico/201
Qatar/202
Romania/202
Russian Federation/204
Rwanda/207
Saint Lucia/210
Saudi Arabia/211
Senegal/213
Sierra Leone/214
Singapore/217
Slovakia/218
Solomon Islands/219
Somalia/220
South Africa/222
Spain/224
Sri Lanka/227
Sudan/228
Suriname/231
Swaziland/231

Sweden/233
Switzerland/234
Syria/236
Taiwan/238
Tajikistan/239
Tanzania/240
Thailand/241
Togo/243
Trinidad and Tobago/244
Tunisia/245
Turkey/248
Turkmenistan/250
Uganda/251
Ukraine/253
United Arab Emirates/254
United Kingdom/255
United States of America/258
Uruguay/261
Uzbekistan/261
Venezuela/264
Viet Nam/265
Yemen/266
Yugoslavia (Federal Republic of)/268
Zambia/271
Zimbabwe/272

PART 3
What is AI?/279
AI in action/283
International and regional organizations/291
Selected international human rights treaties/295
Selected regional human rights treaties/300
Geneva Conventions and their Additional Protocols/304

PREFACE

Amnesty International (AI) is a worldwide movement of people campaigning for internationally recognized human rights.

AI is independent of any government, political ideology, economic interest or religion. It does not support or oppose any government or political system, nor does it support or oppose the views of the victims whose rights it seeks to protect. It is concerned solely with the impartial protection of human rights.

AI mobilizes volunteer activists in more than 140 countries and territories in every part of the world. There are more than 1,000,000 AI members and subscribers from many different backgrounds, with widely different political and religious beliefs, united by a determination to work for a world where everyone enjoys human rights.

AI's mission is to undertake research and action focused on preventing and ending grave abuses of the rights to physical and mental integrity, freedom of conscience and expression, and freedom from discrimination. In this context:

- it seeks the release of all prisoners of conscience. These are people detained for their political, religious or other conscientiously held beliefs or because of their ethnic origin, sex, colour, language, national or social origin, economic status, birth or other status — who have not used or advocated violence;
- it works for fair and prompt trials for all political prisoners;
- it opposes without reservation the death penalty, torture and other cruel, inhuman or degrading treatment or punishment;
- it campaigns for an end to political killings and "disappearances";
- it calls on governments to refrain from unlawful killings in armed conflict;
- it calls on armed political groups to end abuses such as the detention of prisoners of conscience, hostage-taking, torture and unlawful killings;
- it opposes abuses by non-state actors where the state has failed to fulfil its obligations to provide effective protection;
- it campaigns for perpetrators of human rights abuses to be brought to justice;
- it seeks to assist asylum-seekers who are at risk of being returned to a country where they might suffer serious abuses of their human rights;
- it opposes certain grave abuses of economic, social and cultural rights.

AI also seeks to support the protection of human rights by:

- cooperating with other non-governmental organizations, the UN and regional inter-governmental organizations;
- ensuring control of international military, security and police relations to prevent human rights abuses;
- organizing human rights education and awareness-raising programs.

AI is a democratic, self-governing movement. Major policy decisions are taken by an International Council made up of representatives from all national sections.

AI's national sections and local volunteer groups are primarily responsible for funding the movement. No funds are sought or accepted from governments for AI's work investigating and campaigning against human rights violations.

Amnesty International Report 2002

This report documents human rights issues of concern to AI during the year 2001. It also reflects the activities AI has undertaken during the year to promote human rights and to campaign against specific human rights abuses.

The core of this report is made up of entries on individual countries and territories, listed alphabetically. Each of these entries gives a summary of the human rights situation in the country or territory and describes AI's specific human rights concerns there. The absence of an entry on a particular country or territory does not imply that no human rights abuses of concern to AI took place there during the year. Nor is the length of individual entries any basis for a comparison of the extent and depth of AI's concerns.

A world map has been included in this report to indicate the location of countries and territories, and each individual country entry begins with some basic information about the country during 2001. Neither the map nor the country information or its absence may be interpreted as AI's view on questions such as the status of disputed territory, capital, population size or language. AI takes no position on issues other than human rights.

The later sections of the report contain some information about AI and its work during the year. The final section focuses on AI's work with intergovernmental organizations and includes information about which states are signatories or state parties to key international and regional human rights treaties and international humanitarian law.

Internet addresses

Reports published during the year are listed at the end of country entries. These are available on the AI website. The AI Index given in this report can be used to locate a document as follows: AI Index: ABC 63/004/2001
http://web.amnesty.org/ai.nsf/index/ABC630042001

Abbreviations for treaties

The following abbreviations have been used:

- UN Convention against Torture refers to the Convention against Torture and Other Cruel, Inhuman or Degrading Treatment or Punishment.
- UN Women's Convention refers to the Convention on the Elimination of All Forms of Discrimination against Women.
- UN Children's Convention refers to the Convention on the Rights of the Child.
- UN Convention against Racism refers to the International Convention on the Elimination of All Forms of Racial Discrimination.
- UN Refugee Convention refers to the Convention relating to the Status of Refugees.
- European Convention on Human Rights refers to the (European) Convention for the Protection of Human Rights and Fundamental Freedoms.

PREFACE

AI'S APPEALS FOR ACTION

The country entries in this report include numerous examples of human rights abuses that AI is dedicated to oppose. In response to these human rights abuses, AI urges those in authority in all countries where abuses occur to take the steps recommended below. More detailed additional recommendations relevant to particular situations are included where necessary in the specific country entry.

Recommendations to governments

Prisoners of conscience
AI calls for the immediate and unconditional release of all prisoners of conscience. Prisoners of conscience are people detained anywhere for their political, religious or other conscientiously held beliefs or because of their ethnic origin, sex, colour, language, national or social origin, economic status, birth or other status — who have not used or advocated violence.

Political prisoners
AI calls for all prisoners whose cases have a political aspect to be given a prompt and fair trial on recognizably criminal charges, or released.

AI calls for trials to meet minimum international standards of fairness. These include, for example, the right to a fair hearing before a competent, independent and impartial tribunal, the right to have adequate time and facilities to prepare a defence, and the right to appeal to a higher tribunal.

Torture and ill-treatment
AI calls on governments to take steps to prevent torture and ill-treatment. Such steps include initiating impartial, prompt and effective investigations into all allegations of torture and bringing to justice those responsible for torture.

Further safeguards against torture and ill-treatment which AI promotes include:
- clear policies that torture and ill-treatment will not be tolerated;
- an end to incommunicado detention, including giving detainees access to independent medical examination and legal counsel;
- outlawing the use of confessions extracted under torture as evidence in courts of law;
- independent inspection of places of detention;
- informing detainees of their rights;
- human rights training for law enforcement personnel;
- compensation for the victims of torture;
- medical treatment and rehabilitation for the victims of torture.

Prison conditions
AI calls on governments to ensure that prison conditions do not amount to cruel, inhuman or degrading treatment or punishment, in line with international human rights standards for the treatment of prisoners.

Death penalty
AI calls on governments to abolish the death penalty in law and practice.

Pending abolition, AI calls on governments to commute death sentences, to introduce a moratorium on executions, to respect international standards restricting the scope of the death penalty and to ensure the most rigorous standards for fair trial in capital cases.

Political killings and 'disappearances'
AI calls on governments to end extrajudicial executions and "disappearances". It calls for prompt, independent and effective investigations into such violations and for those responsible to be brought to justice.

AI calls on governments to:
- demonstrate their total opposition to extrajudicial executions and "disappearances" and make clear to security forces that these abuses will not be tolerated in any circumstances;
- end secret or incommunicado detention and introduce measures to locate and protect prisoners;
- provide effective protection to anyone in danger of extrajudicial execution or "disappearance", including those who have received threats;
- ensure that law enforcement officials use force only when strictly required and to the minimum extent necessary — lethal force should be used only when unavoidable to protect life;
- ensure strict chain-of-command control of all security forces;
- ban "death squads", private armies and paramilitary forces acting outside the official chain of command.

Unlawful killings in armed conflict
AI calls on governments engaged in armed conflict to adhere to provisions of international humanitarian law, including the prohibition of direct attacks on civilians and of indiscriminate attacks.

Asylum-seekers
AI calls on governments to ensure that no asylum-seekers are returned to a country where they might suffer violations of their fundamental human rights.

AI calls on governments to ensure that all asylum-seekers have access to a fair and impartial individual asylum determination, and to ensure that they are not arbitrarily detained or otherwise put under undue pressure.

Promote and respect human rights
AI calls on states to ratify international and regional human rights instruments without reservations, and calls on all governments to respect and promote the provisions of these instruments.

Recommendations to armed political groups
AI calls on armed political groups to respect fundamental standards of human rights and international humanitarian law, and to halt abuses such as the detention of prisoners of conscience, hostage-taking, torture and unlawful killings.

AI REPORT 2002
PART 1

FOREWORD

by Irene Khan, Secretary General

COUNTERING THE BACKLASH

"Your role collapsed with the collapse of the Twin Towers in New York". This blunt statement to AI delegates by a senior government official captured the challenge faced by the human rights movement following the events of 11 September 2001. Did the attacks on the USA and the reaction of governments and public opinion indeed make human rights and their advocates irrelevant? Has the "war against terrorism" meant a significant shift in states' obligations and interests to respect human rights and international humanitarian law?

Undoubtedly, the environment for human rights activism changed sharply after 11 September in some parts of the world, setting back the gains of many years. In some places, however, there was a sickening familiarity about the repression and abuse. Millions of people faced continuing human rights abuses throughout the year. Millions more were still suffering the effects of genocide and other atrocities committed in the past. Whether in the context of new threats or long-standing violations, the universality and indivisibility of international human rights were repeatedly challenged. The obligation to pursue justice, end impunity and instil accountability was frequently flouted.

As the "war against terrorism" dominated world news, governments increasingly portrayed human rights as an obstacle to security, and human rights activists as romantic idealists at best, "defenders of terrorists" at worst. But precisely because of these pressures, the role of human rights activists, far from diminishing, gained new urgency and importance.

Security and human rights

The shock, outrage and grief following the attacks of 11 September gave rise to strong public demand for the punishment of the perpetrators and the prevention of similar attacks. The fact that the tragedy unfolded on television screens across the world intensified the sense that no one was safe.

Governments, shaken by their vulnerability to unexpected violent attacks, responded with a wide range of legislative and other measures. Many rushed through laws formulating new crimes, banning organizations and freezing their assets, curbing civil liberties and reducing the safeguards against human rights violations. Regrettably, a number of these laws used definitions of "terrorism" which were dangerously broad and vague. For example, in some the proscribed conduct was not defined clearly, allowing the criminalization of peaceful activities. In South Korea, the government introduced an "anti-terror" bill criticized by human rights groups for limiting rights to freedom of expression and freedom of assembly. In Jordan, the authorities changed the Penal Code, expanding the definition of "terrorism", introducing loosely defined offences, restricting freedom of expression and expanding the scope of offences punishable by death. In India, a new Prevention of Terrorism Ordinance gave the police wide powers of arrest and provided for up to six months' detention without charge or trial for political suspects. It also provided for immunity from prosecution for government and army officials, as well as other paramilitary forces, for any action taken "in good faith" when combating "terrorism".

In some parts of the world, including countries where military forces have in the past been responsible for widespread repression and human rights violations, the aftermath of 11 September saw a resurgence in the powers of the military. More and more civilians were detained by the military and tried by military courts. Military forces, as well as unaccountable security and intelligence services, were increasingly involved in public security functions and in intelligence operations targeted at the civilian population. At the UN, the Security Council adopted resolution 1373, setting out a range of legislative and other measures for states to adopt to prevent and suppress "terrorism". The Security Council established a Counter-Terrorism Committee to assess states' progress, to which states are required to report. Neither the Security Council nor the Counter-Terrorism Committee reminded states of their UN Charter obligations to comply with international human rights or advised them how to do so. The call from the UN High Commissioner for Human Rights, AI and others to issue such guidance went unheeded, threatening a dangerous schism in the UN's dual obligation to maintain international security as well as promote international human rights.

The readiness of governments to trade human rights in the interest of security is nothing new. The doctrine of national security has been used frequently in the past to deny human rights. The difference this time lay in the uneasy realisation that it was not autocratic regimes but established democracies that took the lead in introducing draconian laws to restrict civil liberties in the name of public security. In the United Kingdom (UK), the government passed "emergency" legislation which provided for detention of foreign nationals without charge or trial, thereby creating a shadow criminal justice system without the essential safeguards of the formal system. Legislation was passed in the USA allowing for indefinite detention on national security grounds of non-US nationals facing deportation.

AI recognizes the right — indeed the duty — of states to protect their citizens, but we do not believe that human rights need to be sacrificed in order to achieve security. The dichotomy between security and human rights is false. International human rights standards oblige states to protect the public from harm. The rights enshrined in human rights treaties, such as the right to life and not to be subjected to torture, are

Amnesty International Report 2002

FOREWORD

another way of describing the idea of security that people expect their governments to ensure. They are not discrete rights, to be pursued without regard to other rights. In the key human rights treaties, such as the International Covenant on Civil and Political Rights, they are part of an integrated package of rights that states are obliged to respect. While some rights may be restricted in narrowly prescribed circumstances, other rights are absolute, even in times of public emergency.

We must turn the debate about security and human rights on its head – human rights are not an obstacle to security and prosperity, they are the key to achieving these goals. Human security comes only with human rights and the rule of law. Human rights are the basis for creating strong and accountable states, without which there can be no political stability or economic and social progress. The past year has shown more clearly than ever that if human rights are sacrificed in the search for peace and security, there will be no peace and no security. The challenge to states therefore is not security versus human rights, but rather to ensure respect for the full range of human rights.

Universality of human rights

The rights to life, physical and mental integrity, freedom from arbitrary detention, freedom of expression and freedom from fear and want are the inalienable rights of all human beings. One person's human rights cannot be founded on another person's loss of rights. But during 2001 a number of governments restricted the rights of foreigners or foreign-born nationals in the name of protecting the rights of citizens. In particular, governments around the world clamped down on irregular migration and further tightened asylum policies, undermining the rights of refugees and asylum-seekers and increasing the likelihood of abuse and exploitation of migrants.

European Union countries raised further obstacles to people fleeing in search of safety, for example by extending visa restrictions and returning more people to "safe" third countries. Australia, already subject to widespread criticism because of its treatment of asylum-seekers arriving by boat, used the 11 September attacks to justify its continuing policy of detaining asylum-seekers, including hundreds from Afghanistan. In late September it amended its laws to exclude certain off-shore Australian territories from the application of its refugee law in order to prevent boat people arriving there from lodging asylum claims under Australian law. It also removed some procedural safeguards and increased the indefinite detention of asylum-seekers. Such action by developed states undercut any moral authority they might have had to persuade developing countries such as Pakistan to receive refugees. When the bombing of Afghanistan began, many of those forced to flee found the borders of neighbouring countries closed.

In the "war against terrorism", the tendency has been to portray foreigners, particularly refugees and asylum-seekers, as "terrorists". In the year when the UN held its World Conference against Racism, Racial Discrimination, Xenophobia and Related Intolerance, it was particularly disturbing to see a refuelling of the fires of racism. Legislation and administrative decrees discriminating against foreigners fed people's fear of threats from abroad. The climate of suspicion fostered in the public's mind encouraged racism, xenophobia, intolerance and violence, intensifying the sense of isolation and injustice felt by many migrant or foreign communities. People were attacked in the USA, Canada, western Europe, parts of Asia and Africa, not for what they did but for who they were, simply for being a Muslim or Arab or Asian, or even for looking like a Muslim, Arab or Asian.

The application of double standards by powerful governments lent weight to those seeking to challenge the universality of human rights. The hypocrisy and selectivity of governments are not a new phenomenon in the human rights discourse, but they became even clearer in the drive to build an alliance in the "war against terrorism". Governments remained silent on abuses committed by those they counted or sought as allies. The same governments that denounced the human rights abuse of women by the *Taleban* government of Afghanistan remained silent about the plight of women in Saudi Arabia. Those who condemned human rights violations in Iraq did not protest against human rights violations by Russian troops in Chechnya, or by the authorities in Uzbekistan against Muslims who peacefully practise their faith outside state controls.

A number of governments jumped on the "anti-terrorism" bandwagon to stifle political dissent. The Chinese authorities intensified their crackdown on Uighur opponents of Chinese rule in the Xinjiang Uighur Autonomous Region, claiming that they were linked to international "terrorism". The Egyptian authorities clamped down on public gatherings and demonstrations, and sent an increasing number of civilians for trial by military courts. In Zimbabwe, where the government was increasingly suppressing the freedom of the press, the authorities labelled international journalists reporting on political opponents as supporters of "terrorists".

With the media spotlight on "anti-terrorism" measures in the west and the bombing campaign in Afghanistan, human rights violations and increased repression in other parts of the world went largely unnoticed and unaddressed. This exacerbated the unbalanced approach of the international community to human rights abuses.

If human rights priorities can be changed according to the interests of powerful states or the attention span of the international news media, the universality of human rights is undermined. This paves the way for cynicism, disbelief and ultimately wider disrespect for human rights. Today, more than ever before, human rights activists must resist the shifting agenda of powerful states. We must reject the subjective yardstick of "terrorism", by which states condemn the violence of their opponents and condone that of their

FOREWORD

allies. We must insist on applying only the objective standards of human rights and international law. No cause can justify the abuse of human rights, regardless of whether the abuses are committed by a government, an armed political group, international criminals or people acting in the name of religion.

Human rights activists will continue to insist that the universality and indivisibility of human rights must be upheld. At its most simple, all human beings deserve to enjoy all human rights. We take all human rights abuses seriously, whether they occur in a country in the headlines, or one remote from international attention. AI's members and supporters campaigned vigorously throughout 2001 against human rights abuses in countries such as Algeria, Colombia, Democratic Republic of the Congo, Indonesia, Israel and the Occupied Territories, Myanmar and Turkey. Guided by principles of impartiality, independence and international solidarity, we base our work on the values enshrined in the Universal Declaration of Human Rights and apply the same standards to all countries.

Justice for all

The inconsistency and hypocrisy of governments in the aftermath of the attacks of 11 September were particularly striking when it came to the question of bringing the suspected perpetrators to justice. AI called for justice for those who planned, committed and aided the attacks in the USA; those who might have violated international humanitarian law in the course of the war in Afghanistan; and those who abused human rights and international law throughout the 23 years of armed conflict in the country.

The attacks of 11 September were clearly gross abuses of human rights, which AI believes should be considered crimes against humanity. AI believes that the international dimensions of the attacks, and their seriousness, mean that the international community as a whole has an interest in seeing those responsible brought to justice in a process that upholds international fair trial standards, without the imposition of the death penalty. Our basic call has always been for justice, not revenge.

The US authorities announced that "military commissions" would be set up to try non-nationals suspected of involvement in "international terrorism", although US citizens and some others would continue to be tried in the criminal justice system. While the US government had not by the end of the year announced the rules under which these commissions would operate, information indicated that it was considering allowing secret evidence and anonymous witnesses. Furthermore, the commissions would be able to impose the death penalty, with no right of appeal. Such commissions would violate international standards of fair trial, including those in the Geneva Conventions. They would be discriminatory, applying only to foreign nationals.

However strongly we may feel about those who brutally destroyed thousands of lives on 11 September, we must be vigilant about the methods used to bring them to justice. In condemning those who blatantly disregard the most fundamental principles of human rights and humanity, governments must not debase those same values.

Within weeks of 11 September, the USA and its allies launched a sustained military campaign in Afghanistan. The campaign was an unprecedented response to acts believed to have been committed by an armed political group. Previously, the USA had used sanctions, diplomacy, negotiations and one-off reprisal attacks after "acts of terrorism".

As AI activists, our role is to scrutinize the conduct of war in order to protect human rights. The US-led bombing campaign against the *Taleban* in Afghanistan raised serious concerns about possible breaches of international humanitarian law. In particular, as civilian casualties mounted, doubts were raised about the proportionality of the force used. AI called on the US military to strengthen measures to minimize the risk to civilians and to investigate thoroughly reports of all incidents that appeared to breach the rules on the conduct of hostilities.

The rules of war are designed to protect not only civilians, but also imprisoned combatants. AI pressed for investigations into possible violations of international humanitarian law, including the deaths of hundreds of *Taleban* and *al-Qa'ida* prisoners in a fort near Mazar-e Sharif in November 2001. The circumstances of the incident, which reportedly involved United Front (Northern Alliance), UK and US forces, were unclear. The call by AI and other human rights groups for an urgent investigation by the parties to the conflict or by an international body was rejected.

In the plethora of calls for new methods to deal with new threats, it was striking how old were the methods used in Afghanistan. The pictures of B-52 planes and carpet bombing could have been taken from the Viet Nam war. Gross human rights abuses by forces armed, trained and supplied by other powers has been going on for decades. For many years too, AI has urged arms exporting countries not to supply weapons to those with appalling human rights records. In this crisis, we called for a halt to unconditional transfers of arms and expertise to all the warring parties in Afghanistan and for a moratorium on the use of cluster bombs, which leave numerous unexploded bomblets over a wide area.

When an interim political settlement in Afghanistan was under discussion, the issue of accountability for past violations was raised, with Afghan groups and others pressing for an end to impunity. This was hotly debated, but the issue of impunity was sacrificed in the pragmatic – and short-sighted – interests of reaching agreement. In countries such as Angola, Argentina, Cambodia and Sierra Leone, experience has shown that in the long run ignoring human rights abuses for reasons of political expediency does not pay off.

Condoning impunity as part of a political settlement today will not lead to stability or respect for human rights tomorrow. AI believes that the truth

FOREWORD

about past abuses must be established. There should be no amnesties or pardons for alleged perpetrators if such measures prevent the emergence of the truth, a judicial determination of guilt or innocence and full reparation to victims and their families. Human rights activists must renew their efforts to ensure that an effective permanent independent International Criminal Court is established as soon as possible and that all states agree to its jurisdiction. A situation where the powerful determine how justice will be done and to whom is wrong and cannot be sustained. For human rights activists, there can be no compromise between justice and impunity, no selective approach to accountability.

Indivisibility of human rights

The tragic events of 11 September have been a catalyst for discussions about grievances deeply felt by communities from which the alleged perpetrators came. The conflict between Israel and the Palestinians is the most obvious example. But beyond political conflicts, there are social and economic inequities arising from gross abuses of human rights, economic, social and cultural as well as civil and political. Respect for human rights must encompass not only the universality, but also the indivisibility of those rights.

Many of the world's poor have been bypassed by the benefits of globalization. The free market has not necessarily brought about a more socially conscious market. On the contrary, large pockets of poverty in the midst of prosperity heighten the sense of economic deprivation and social exclusion, creating a breeding ground for unrest and violence. Many people feel a deep sense of social injustice. Millions of Africans are denied affordable treatment for HIV/AIDS, and will die early deaths, although the drugs they need exist and are available to inhabitants of richer countries. Millions of people around the world are denied equal access to education, jobs and positions of influence because of their race or ethnic origin, gender or sexual orientation.

As globalization spreads, bringing greater wealth to some and destitution and despair to others, human rights activists must promote not just legal justice, but also social justice. An ethical approach to globalization can mean nothing less than a rights-based approach to development. We must struggle not only against torture, arbitrary detention and unfair trials, but also against hunger, illiteracy and discrimination if human rights are to be meaningful in developing countries.

When AI talks of a world of freedom and justice, we mean a world in which every person enjoys all of the human rights enshrined in the Universal Declaration of Human Rights and other international human rights standards. Our agenda has expanded in the face of human rights issues that demand our attention. In the future we will not only work on those civil and political rights that have formed the heart of our campaigning for decades, we will also mobilize to ensure that economic, social and cultural rights are respected.

Looking ahead

I began by underlining the urgency and importance of the challenges facing human rights activists in these difficult times. Let me end by highlighting the increased vulnerability of our front-line activists and those with whom we work. In 2001 human rights defenders, including AI members, suffered threats or attacks in many countries, including in the Democratic Republic of the Congo, Zimbabwe, Tunisia, Mexico, Colombia and Bangladesh. We must protect human rights defenders from attack or intimidation through mobilizing support around the world, taking practical measures to help individuals in danger and their families, and forming networks ready and able to respond at short notice.

We must not let fear win. We must not allow fundamental freedoms to be eroded or prejudice and intolerance to prevail. Universality and indivisibility of human rights are non-negotiable. There can be no trade-off between human rights and security, between justice and impunity. A human rights approach — an approach which puts the security of people, rather than states, first — may seem more difficult at first glance, but in these troubled times it is the only one that offers any real hope for the way forward.

INTRODUCTION

> "As with all victims of violent crime, human rights violations and abuses, the suffering of victims, survivors and the bereaved demands compassion and justice. We urge you to lead your government to take every necessary human rights precaution in pursuit of justice, rather than revenge, for the victims of this terrible crime."
>
> Letter from Irene Khan, Secretary General of AI, to US President George W. Bush, September 2001

Justice not revenge

Images of the 11 September attacks in New York, Washington and Pennsylvania reverberated around a shocked and disbelieving world. At least 3,000 people from more than 60 countries were killed. Amnesty International (AI) joined with countless others in offering condolences to the victims and condemning the attacks.

As people sought to make sense of what had happened, questions began to be asked about who was responsible for the attacks and why. And what should be the response?

US President George W. Bush and his administration soon pointed the finger at Osama bin Laden and the *al-Qa'ida* network as key players in the planning of the attacks, and attention turned to Afghanistan where Osama bin Laden was believed to have his base.

AI called on governments to bring to justice those responsible for the 11 September attacks and to ensure that they were tried in accordance with international human rights standards and were not at risk of being sentenced to death. It also called on states to ratify the Rome Statute of the International Criminal Court and to promote international judicial mechanisms.

On 7 October the USA, in collaboration with its coalition allies, began a sustained bombing campaign in Afghanistan as part of President Bush's declared "war on terrorism". By the end of the year, an as yet unknown number of Afghan civilians had been killed or injured or had their homes or property destroyed, in circumstances that led AI to call for investigations by competent authorities to determine whether violations of international humanitarian law had been committed.

AI urged governments to ensure that the use of force did not add to the human rights violations visited upon the Afghan population and that any military intervention was conducted with the highest regard for international humanitarian law. AI continued to call on Afghan groups to respect human rights and on other governments to use their influence to this end. It also continued to stress that governments should not send arms into Afghanistan which could be used to commit human rights abuses and called for a moratorium on the use of cluster bombs. AI expressed concern that specific US attacks may have breached international humanitarian law and called for an inquiry into the killings of more than 200 *Taleban* prisoners and others during incidents in a fort controlled by the United Front (commonly known as the Northern Alliance) in Mazar-e Sharif. US and United Kingdom (UK) forces were also present during these incidents. No inquiry had taken place by the end of the year.

In November, AI launched a forward-looking campaign to promote an agenda for human rights in Afghanistan. By December, US bombing, combined with renewed assaults by the United Front, had driven the *Taleban* from power and a new interim administration for Afghanistan was brokered by the UN in Bad Godesberg, Bonn, Germany. AI called on the international community to ensure that human rights were integrated into all discussions about the future of Afghanistan. The organization emphasized the vital importance of ensuring that those entrusted with leadership are committed to the protection of human rights and that women and ethnic and religious minorities are not discriminated against in the creation of government and institutions.

A group of women at a candlelight vigil in New York, USA, to commemorate the victims of the attacks of 11 September.

INTRODUCTION

AI has documented grave human rights abuses by combatants of all the various warring parties involved in the decades-long conflicts which have ravaged Afghanistan. While AI appreciates the need for national reconciliation after years of war and repression, it stressed that any future political agreement must ensure accountability for these abuses. Specific protection should be sought against retaliation and discrimination against ethnic and religious groups, and measures should be taken to combat discrimination against women. AI called for the demobilization of child soldiers, international protection for refugees, and a vigorous program of human rights institution-building. AI called for restrictions on arms supplies and for programs of disarmament and de-mining, adequately resourced and supported by the international community, to be included as important components of a political settlement.

Around the world, the 11 September attacks were followed by a wave of racist attacks directed at people because of their appearance. In North America, Europe and elsewhere, Muslims, Arabs and Sikhs were shot, stabbed and beaten. Mosques were sprayed with racist graffiti, attacked and burned down. Human rights defenders around the world called on their governments to ensure that a clear message was sent out that a backlash against people of Middle Eastern or Asian origin or against Muslims or other communities was totally unacceptable and would not be tolerated.

There was also growing concern towards the end of the year that governments were introducing draconian measures curtailing human rights and civil liberties. For example, the US authorities introduced legislation which enables the government to detain indefinitely foreign nationals facing deportation orders and to establish "military commissions", which lack fundamental guarantees for fair trial, to try foreign nationals. In the UK, the government derogated from Article 5(1) of the European Convention on Human Rights and introduced legislation to detain foreign nationals indefinitely without charge or trial. In Zimbabwe, political opponents of the government and those who published articles critical of the government's human rights record were accused of supporting "terrorism". At the end of 2001 the Zimbabwean government was in the process of introducing legislation to create a new crime of "terrorism", punishable by death; to punish with terms of imprisonment non-violent civil disobedience, criticism of the President and disturbing the peace; and to criminalize all journalism by those not licensed by the state. In India, a new ordinance was promulgated which gave the police wide powers of arrest and provided for up to six months' detention without charge or trial for political suspects. AI warned that these and similar measures taken by a number of governments would deny basic human rights to some of the most vulnerable people.

Governments have a responsibility to take steps to protect their citizens and to prevent future attacks. However, AI and other human rights organizations continued to stress that in addressing security concerns governments must ensure that internationally recognized safeguards to protect human rights are not infringed in any way. Governments must ensure that

"The world does not need a war against 'terrorism', it needs a culture of peace based on human rights and justice for all."
Irene Khan, Secretary General of AI

An Afghan asylum-seeker at Sangatte Red Cross Centre in northern France, home to up to 1,700 refugees and asylum-seekers in 2001. The centre, which is run by the French Red Cross, is housed in a vast hangar originally used to store building materials while the Channel Tunnel was under construction. During 2001, the UK government sought to have the centre closed, claiming that its location encouraged asylum-seekers to try to enter the UK. The centre was run on an "open door" policy, giving help to anyone who walked in through the front door.

INTRODUCTION

Protesters march to the Prime Minister's residence in Sydney, Australia, on the 50th anniversary of the UN Refugee Convention. The demonstrators demanded the closure of detention centres where asylum-seekers are held.

members of ethnic, religious or other minorities are not victimized. The principle of non-discrimination on grounds such as race, colour, ethnic origin, sex, language, religion and social status, which is repeated in virtually every major international human rights treaty, is the very bedrock of international law.

There were also fears that intergovernmental discussions on migration and asylum would focus on restrictive measures relating to countering "terrorism" rather than on refugee protection. AI stressed that all asylum-seekers should be allowed entry in order to have their claims assessed according to a fair and satisfactory procedure and on an individual basis, as stated in international refugee law. No one should be denied this right because the group they belong to is perceived as a possible security threat.

(For discussion of the challenges faced by human rights defenders in the wake of the 11 September attacks and AI's response, please see the Foreword by Irene Khan.)

Refugees

Shortly before the 11 September attacks, media attention highlighted the plight of a group of more than 430 mainly Afghan asylum-seekers stranded at sea off the coast of Australia. The asylum-seekers had been saved from drowning by the crew of a Norwegian freighter, the *Tampa*, when the ferry on which they were travelling sank on 26 August. The Australian and Indonesian governments refused to allow them to disembark and the passengers, who included 43 children, remained captive at sea for more than three weeks, first aboard the *Tampa* and then on an Australian troopship. The asylum-seekers remained on the *Tampa*, which was licensed for a crew of up to 50, for more than eight days, sheltering beneath tarpaulins on deck and in empty freight containers. The Australian authorities ordered the ship to leave Australian territorial waters.

While legal proceedings aimed at ensuring that the asylum-seekers would be released from their detention at sea and brought to Australia were continuing, the asylum-seekers were transferred onto the Australian troopship *Manoora*. Most were taken to the tiny impoverished island of Nauru to have their claims assessed; the rest were transferred to New Zealand. On Nauru, the asylum-seekers were held in sweltering conditions in a derelict sports ground in corrugated iron and wooden shelters, speedily constructed by the Australian military. There they remained at the end of the year surrounded by pinnacles of limestone and phosphate mine shafts and guarded by a private security firm. The asylum-seekers had survived a harrowing journey and now faced an uncertain future. As the survivors waited to hear the outcome of their applications for refugee status, their plight posed the question, had the world changed for them in the wake of the 11 September attacks and the increased global awareness of the plight of Afghanistan?

According to reports, 20 of those who found themselves stranded on the Tampa were from the village of Ejan in the Salang gorge in the northeast of Afghanistan, where living conditions were said to be so wretched that only 50 families remained in a village that once housed 500. Millions of people had sought refuge from a country which offers its people a life expectancy of 45, where every other child is malnourished, and where one in four children die before they reach the age of five. About 150,000 Afghans had applied for asylum in Western Europe during the past 10 years. The overwhelming majority of Afghan refugees, more than three million people, were living in Pakistan and Iran.

On 22 October, another boat sank while headed for Australia carrying some 400 asylum-seekers. More than 350 of the mainly Iraqi passengers were reported to have been drowned.

"You cannot complain about the huge number of people moving around the world if you are not prepared to give the money that is needed for solutions in the regions where the refugees come from."
Ruud Lubbers, UN High Commissioner for Refugees, interviewed for the BBC's *The World This Weekend*, quoted in *The Guardian* newspaper, 3 September 2001

Amnesty International Report 2002

11

INTRODUCTION

The rights of asylum-seekers and refugees were the subject of major international debate in 2001. AI was deeply concerned that asylum policy was increasingly focusing on how to keep people out rather than on how to effectively protect people fleeing war, civil upheaval and grave human rights abuses.

All too often the debate descended into populist diatribes which demonized and dehumanized some of the most vulnerable people in the world. In many industrialized countries, asylum-seekers were dubbed "bogus", "queue-jumpers" and "scroungers". Their plight was hidden behind headlines which screamed of "waves" and "floods" of immigrants. Rather than focus on what lay behind the movement of peoples across the world, governments and politicians resorted to tough talk of "crack-downs". The authorities colluded with sections of the press in manipulating misleading facts to stoke fears and attack political opponents who were accused of being "soft" on refugees.

Yet the desperate plight of the Tampa passengers must provoke questions about what it is that makes the risks inherent in such a journey seem less daunting than remaining at home.

2001 marked the 50th anniversary of the UN Refugee Convention. Since 1951, 141 states have become parties either to the Convention or its 1967 Protocol. Yet for many governments the pledge to honour the rights and protections set out in the Convention has remained mere rhetoric. AI urged all states to renew their commitment to the spirit and the letter of the 1951 Convention and called on those states that have not already done so to accede to the Convention and its Protocol.

One of the key principles spelled out in the Convention – the cornerstone of international refugee protection – is that no one should be forcibly returned to a country where they would be at risk of grave human rights violations. Yet governments continued to send people back to face imprisonment, torture, even execution.

In recent years governments have introduced policies which have effectively prevented people fleeing persecution from reaching safety and obtaining the protection to which they are entitled. Governments have sought to limit access to their territory, they have applied extremely harsh criteria for asylum and they have sought to fine transport companies for allowing people to travel without proper documentation. In short, protecting refugees has come a long way down their list of priorities, way behind keeping refugees away from their borders.

At the beginning of 2001 there were believed to be some 17 million refugees and asylum-seekers worldwide. The overwhelming majority of these – more than 70 per cent – live in the South, many in the world's poorest countries, and far from the scrutiny of the world's media.

In the Middle East no durable solution was found to the plight of more than 3,700,000 Palestinian and 100,000 Sahrawi refugees. Iran continued to host one of the largest populations of refugees, including more than 1,482,000 Afghan and 386,000 Iraqi refugees.

The scale of the refugee crisis in Africa is staggering. In the Democratic Republic of the Congo, where some 2.5 million people were believed to have died as a result of the fighting since 1998, deliberate reprisals against the civilian population remained a common reaction by all sides to military setbacks. By the end of 2001 as many as two million civilians were internally displaced, unable to support themselves and out of reach of humanitarian

Refugees in Katkama camp, southeastern Guinea, queue to register for transfer to camps in safer areas, February 2001.

INTRODUCTION

organizations. Many were facing starvation. Thousands of others had fled to neighbouring states. War continued to ravage Burundi, costing the lives of hundreds of unarmed civilians. All parties to the conflict continued to show a complete disregard for human rights. Hundreds of thousands of people remained internally displaced and people continued to flee the country in their thousands. In Sudan, the civil war, which has claimed some two million lives since 1983, has been characterized by mass human rights abuses, including abduction, rape and arbitrary killings. By 2001 some 4.5 million people were believed to be internally displaced within Sudan and some 500,000 were thought to have sought refuge abroad.

Sierra Leonean refugees fleeing vicious fighting marked by widespread killings, abduction, rape and amputation at home had sought safety in Guinea. By mid-2000 some 500,000 Sierra Leonean and Liberian refugees remained in Guinea; many had lived there for several years. Although Guinea is one of the world's least developed countries, the Guinean government agreed to host the refugees. While there had been some violence and tension over the previous decade, until September 2000 Guinea was a relatively safe and accommodating country of refuge. On 6 September 2000, the Revolutionary United Front (RUF), a Sierra Leonean armed group responsible for massive human rights abuses at home, reportedly attacked a village inside Guinea in the border area near Conakry. Following the attack, Guinea's President Lansana Conté made a speech, which was broadcast on radio, calling on Guineans to defend the country and repel the invaders. He accused refugees of assisting and supporting the attacks and said that refugees should be confined to camps and should return home. The speech was widely seen as a decisive turning point in national policy as regards refugees, implicitly encouraging the military and the Guinean public to go on the offensive against refugees in Guinea. In the aftermath, refugees were rounded up and detained, repeatedly harassed and attacked. Refugees and Guinean villagers were forced to flee from camp to camp and from village to village in a desperate attempt to avoid the fighting. Countless refugees were killed or abducted by rebels; others "disappeared" after being picked up by Guinean soldiers. Guinean men, women and children were abducted, raped and killed during incursions into Guinea by members of the RUF. During 2001, some 300,000 Guineans were forced to flee their homes.

In April AI called on the international community to protect hundreds of thousands of Sierra Leonean and Liberian refugees and Guinean civilians caught in the vicious fighting in Guinea. AI sought to draw the world's attention to the pressing need for adequate protection and assistance for refugees and displaced Guineans. The international community must ensure that UN agencies, aid organizations and the Guinean government have adequate resources to provide the assistance that is required.

The link between the flight of refugees and the failure to protect human rights could not be clearer. While government statements on refugee issues in much of the industrialized world focused on building ever greater barriers against refugees, AI sought to highlight the importance of tackling the causes of the fear and misery which force people to flee and how the failure to do so condemns millions of people to ever greater abuse and desperation.

Drawing by a former child combatant in Sierra Leone. AI is calling for international criminal tribunals and national courts to prosecute those who have recruited and used child soldiers. In 2001, more than 300,000 children were fighting in armed conflicts in more than 30 countries worldwide.

INTRODUCTION

The *intifada*

September 2001 saw the first anniversary of the al-Aqsa *intifada* (uprising) and an intensification of the human rights tragedy in Israel and the Occupied Territories.

In the 15 months to December 2001, more than 750 Palestinians were killed by Israeli security forces, the vast majority of them unlawfully when no lives were in danger. More than 220 Israelis, including 166 civilians, were killed by Palestinian armed groups and individuals. Many children were among the victims: more than 160 Palestinian and 36 Israeli children were killed. More than 18,000 other people were wounded, many maimed for life.

The Israeli authorities continued to respond to the *intifada* and the killing of Israeli civilians by firing upon and thereby wounding and killing Palestinians at demonstrations, checkpoints and borders, and by shelling residential areas and police stations. The Israel Defence Force openly carried out a policy of deliberately targeting and extrajudicially executing Palestinians said to be planning or to have carried out attacks; more than 40 Palestinians were assassinated in attacks in which more than 20 bystanders, including children, were killed. No killing in the Occupied Territories was properly investigated and the claims and counter-claims continued to reverberate.

In response to attacks on Israeli settlements, Israeli forces shelled Palestinian towns and cut off almost every Palestinian town and village from the outside world by army checkpoints or physical barriers of earth, concrete blocks or metal walls. Villages and districts of Palestinian towns and villages were put under curfew so that the residents could not leave home or go to work for days, weeks or even months. In the name of security, hundreds of Palestinian homes were demolished and Palestinians were barred from travelling along certain roads in the Occupied Territories.

The level of abuses committed by armed groups escalated. Palestinian armed groups shot deliberately at cars with Israeli number-plates travelling along the roads of the Occupied Territories and set off bombs in public places such as malls and restaurants, deliberately targeting civilians. Israeli settlers killed and attacked Palestinians with almost complete impunity.

> Since the signing in 1993 of the Oslo Agreement, which began the current peace process, AI has underlined the need to base peace negotiations on the human rights enshrined in international standards. It has reiterated its view that a major flaw in the process was that it was not founded on ensuring respect for and protection of human rights. Events in 2001 showed more clearly than ever that if human rights are sacrificed in the search for peace and security there will be no peace and security. Failure to uphold people's basic rights feeds hatred and perpetuates abuses. AI called for human rights to be put at the heart of the agenda for peace and for international observers, with a strong, transparent and public mandate to monitor respect for international human rights and humanitarian law, to be sent to the Occupied Territories.

A Palestinian boy plays by a wall sprayed with graffiti in Khan Yunis, Gaza Strip, April 2001. Since the latest *intifada* began in September 2000, violence has become a part of daily life in Israel and the Occupied Territories.

Amnesty International Report 2002

INTRODUCTION

Campaign against torture

At the same time as AI was striving to respond to the crises which dominated much of 2001, it also sought to remain true to its commitment to address long-term, persistent and chronic abuses of human rights in countries far from the glare of international scrutiny. The organization's worldwide membership continued to devote much of its energy to AI's global campaign against torture which was launched in October 2000 and continued throughout 2001.

As part of AI's global campaign against torture, AI members in Croatia called on the public to send postcards to their members of parliament, urging them to support AI's campaign. In January 2001, activists surrounded the parliament building with Torture Free Zone tape while inside 52 members of parliament pledged to "prevent torture from happening in any of my areas of responsibility and the areas of responsibility of the institution I represent by supporting the implementation of Amnesty International's 12-Point Program for the Prevention of Torture by Agents of the State". In May, on the 40th anniversary of AI, President Stjepan Mesić declared Croatia a Torture Free Zone.

A key focus for the campaign was the link between identity-based discrimination and torture and ill-treatment. In March, AI marked international women's day with the publication of a report, *Broken bodies, shattered minds: Torture and ill-treatment of women.* As the report shows, violence against women is sometimes carried out by agents of the state, such as police officers and prison guards or soldiers. Sometimes the perpetrators are members of armed groups fighting against the government. However, much of the physical, mental and sexual abuse faced by women is committed by people they know.

Violence against women is rooted in and reinforces discrimination. The failure by a state to ensure that women have equal opportunities for education, shelter, food, employment and access to formal state power is another facet of the state's responsibility for abuses against women. Making women's voices heard at all levels of government is essential to enable women to contribute to policies that counter abuses and combat discrimination.

Poor and socially marginalized women are particularly at risk of torture and ill-treatment. In many cases, racist and sexist policies and practices

AI and other non-governmental organizations hold a rally in Pakistan to celebrate International Women's Day, 8 March 2001.

Amnesty International Report 2002

INTRODUCTION

compound the violence they experience and increase their vulnerability to further violence. Social and cultural norms which deny women equal rights with men also render women more vulnerable to physical, sexual and mental abuse. The common thread is discrimination against women, the denial of basic human rights to individuals simply because they are women.

States have a duty to ensure that no one is subjected to torture or ill-treatment, whether by agents of the state or private individuals. Yet all around the world the authorities allow beatings, rape and other acts of torture to continue unchecked. AI's report set out a plan of action to combat the torture of women. This plan is based on an understanding that the patterns, methods, causes and consequences of the torture of women are decisively influenced by the victim's gender. It is also based on the framework of international human rights law which prohibits such abuses.

Lesbians, gay men and bisexual and transgender (LGBT) people all over the world face persecution and violence simply for being who they are. As part of its campaign against torture, AI sought to highlight the abuses suffered by members of the LGBT community at the hands of agents of the state and in the society at large. While the perpetrators and the settings of the abuses may vary, at the heart of all forms of homophobic violence are ignorance and prejudice within society, official discrimination and repression, and the impunity enjoyed by those responsible for such abuses.

However, human rights defenders have emerged in countries around the world, campaigning for an end to homophobic violence and to ensure equal dignity and rights for all. In June, AI launched a report, *Crimes of hate, conspiracy of silence: Torture and ill-treatment based on sexual identity*, as part of its contribution to growing international efforts to end these abuses. The report was launched in Buenos Aires, Argentina, in collaboration with members of the local LGBT community. At the time of the launch, AI reiterated its appeal to the Romanian authorities to repeal legislation which was discriminatory on the grounds of sexual orientation, and under which prisoners of conscience had been imprisoned. In June, the Romanian government adopted an emergency ordinance which abolished Article 200 of the Penal Code. In addition to prohibiting homosexual relations between consenting adults "if the act was committed in public or produced public scandal", Article 200 had made it an offence punishable by between one and five years' imprisonment "to entice or seduce a person to practise same-sex acts, as well as to form propaganda associations, or to engage in other forms of proselytizing with the same aim".

One of the main goals of AI's campaign against torture was the adoption in Europe of guidelines to prevent torture. In April 2001, the European Union (EU) adopted the Guidelines on the Prevention and Eradication of Torture in Third Countries. These guidelines marked a significant advance for human rights policy in the EU and provide the EU with practical tools to enable it to show its opposition to torture and other cruel, inhuman or degrading treatment or punishment.

AI members also campaigned to encourage governments to ratify the UN Convention against Torture, without reservations. During 2001, Lesotho, Nigeria, Saint Vincent and the Grenadines and Sierra Leone became states parties to the Convention.

Military, security and police transfers

One of the issues highlighted in AI's campaign against torture was the need to prevent "security" equipment and training which can easily be used to facilitate torture from reaching abusers around the world. In many countries, torturers rely on foreign

A group of transvestites protesting outside the central police station in Córdoba, Argentina, about the death in custody in February 2000 of Vanessa Lorena Ledesma following five days of incommunicado detention. LGBT activists campaigning for justice in the case have faced threats and harassment from the police.

INTRODUCTION

Poster showing Muhammad Ali in support of AI's campaign against electro-shock stun belts. Stun belts, which are worn by the prisoner for several hours at a time, work by remote control and can deliver a shock of 50,000 volts. AI believes that the use of stun belts constitutes cruel, inhuman or degrading treatment and that the manufacture, transfer and use of stun belts should be banned.

© AI

governments and companies to provide them with security equipment and training. Some governments directly sanction this torture trade; others prefer to turn a blind eye. Few have shown the political will to put an end to a trade whose profits are built on the suffering of countless victims of torture. In February AI published a report, *Stopping the torture trade*, which included new research showing that the number of companies worldwide known to be producing or supplying electro-shock equipment had risen from 30 in the 1980s to more than 130 by 2000. Since 1990, electro-shock devices have been used to torture or ill-treat people in prisons, detention centres or police stations in at least 76 countries in every region of the world. Modern high-voltage electro-shock weapons can be used to inflict great pain without leaving permanent marks on the victim's body. For this reason they have become the tools of choice for many torturers. AI called on governments to take steps to eradicate torture, such as suspending the use and export of electro-shock security equipment and introducing strict guidelines on the transfers of equipment which could be used to inflict torture or ill-treatment.

In July, the first ever UN Conference on the Illicit Trade in Small Arms and Light Weapons was held in New York, USA. An estimated 500,000 people, mostly unarmed civilians, are killed on average each year with small arms; many more are injured and left destitute. Despite this devastating toll, the number of factories making such arms continued to increase in countries which lack basic controls on the manufacture and transfer of small arms. AI joined with other non-governmental organizations (NGOs) in calling for a plan of action that would bring about real improvements in the lives of those suffering repression in war-torn countries. Campaigners called for, among other things, a legally binding international convention to control arms exports and a convention to regulate the shady world of arms brokers and traffickers. However, under pressure, especially from the USA, China and Russia, the UN Conference agreed a weaker Program of Action which focused on measures such as the marking and tracing of weapons — provisions which, by themselves, can have little effect. AI continued to argue that under existing international law, no government should authorize any transfer of small arms or light weapons to any country where there was a clear risk that they would be used by the likely recipients to commit gross human rights abuses, war crimes or crimes against humanity.

Racism – a global issue

AI has documented and campaigned against race-based violations of human rights throughout the world. In July, AI published a report, *Racism and the administration of justice*, which surveys some of the organization's work in this area over the past few years and includes recommendations to help states honour their international obligations to implement measures necessary to eradicate racial discrimination.

Unchecked racism can lead to tragedy on a massive scale. The world looked on in horror when in just 13 weeks up to one million people, most of them from the Tutsi ethnic group, were massacred in Rwanda in 1994. But the abuses which happen every day as a result in whole or in part of racism in the administration of justice rarely catch the headlines, even though the effects of such abuses continue to devastate millions of lives around the world every year. In India, some 160 million Dalits (formerly known as "untouchables") are vulnerable to a whole range of human rights abuses in the community and by officials because of their caste. A large number of these abuses are never investigated. Around the world an estimated 300 million indigenous people still face discrimination in almost every aspect of their lives and many are targeted for human rights abuses. Their vulnerability is enhanced by a lack of state protection.

Racism, to varying degrees and in various forms, infects virtually every country. Around the world, foreigners, including migrant workers and asylum-seekers, live in xenophobic environments, sometimes stirred up by the authorities and almost always reflected in the administration of justice. Increasingly, asylum-seekers are being detained for months or years while their claims for protection are examined.

The law and its administration, which should uphold the values of justice and equality, are among the primary forces in opposing the effects of racism. Yet justice systems all too often fail in this purpose and instead mirror the prejudices of the society they serve. Racial discrimination in the administration of justice

Amnesty International Report 2002

INTRODUCTION

Wagner dos Santos, a survivor and chief witness of the 1993 Candelária massacre in Rio de Janeiro, Brazil, visited AI's International Secretariat in December 2001 and spoke about the events surrounding the massacre. Eight street children were killed, and Wagner himself was shot and left for dead. He survived the shooting and testified against the police officers responsible, three of whom received long prison sentences. In 1995 he survived another attempt on his life by police officers. In September 2001, a deputy in the Rio de Janeiro state assembly said, "...as for 17-year-old children dying in Candelária, I've said before and repeat that if any more should die, I'll pay for their coffin and give a prize to whoever kills them." Another key witness of the massacre, Elizabeth Cristina de Oliveira Maia, was shot dead by a hooded gunman in September 2000.

© AI/Ayse Hassan

systematically denies certain people their human rights because of their colour, race, ethnicity, descent or national origin. AI's research in recent years has shown that members of ethnic or national minorities often suffer torture, ill-treatment and harassment at the hands of the police in disproportionately large numbers. In many parts of the world they face unfair trials and discriminatory sentencing which put them at increased risk of harsh punishments, including the death penalty.

> "[I]n the context of the 11th of September [this Declaration and Programme of Action from Durban] has become even more significant, even more relevant to exactly what we need to be doing. It requires that we address the evils of Islamophobia, anti-Arab sentiment, anti-Semitism, that we have concern for minorities, be they Roma, Sinti, travellers in Europe, be they African descendants in the Americas, the indigenous peoples, migrants, economic migrants, undocumented migrants, refugees, asylum seekers."
>
> Mary Robinson, UN High Commissioner for Human Rights, briefing to the press, Geneva 25 September 2001

AI's report was published to coincide with the third conference on racism organized by the UN – the World Conference against Racism, Racial Discrimination, Xenophobia and Related Intolerance – which was held in August and September in Durban, South Africa. A Declaration and Programme of Action, formulated on the basis of input from various preparatory meetings, was adopted at the Conference, although the placement of a number of paragraphs remained a matter of dispute at the end of the year.

Despite difficulties, the Conference succeeded in highlighting the extent of racism around the world. It also put the plight of groups such as Dalits, Palestinians, Roma, Tibetans, indigenous peoples and those facing multiple forms of discrimination – such as refugees, women and members of the LGBT community – forcefully on the world's human rights agenda. AI and other NGOs pledged that they would continue to campaign to ensure that governments do not forget their obligations to combat racism. All those committed to anti-racism must now work to ensure that this increased awareness is translated into concrete action that will make a real difference to people's lives.

Sihem Ben Sedrine, a journalist and human rights defender, was jailed on her return to Tunisia in June 2001. She had conducted a two-week tour of Europe during which she had openly criticized the human rights situation and lack of freedom of expression in Tunisia.
While she was in prison her husband and daughter travelled to the United Kingdom to collect AIUK's Special Award for Human Rights Journalism under Threat on her behalf.
Sihem Ben Sedrine was provisionally released in August after six weeks in prison. At the end of the year she was still facing charges of "spreading false information intended to undermine public order" and defamation of a Tunisian judge. She expressed her gratitude to AI and all those who had campaigned on her behalf.

© AI

Amnesty International Report 2002

INTRODUCTION

Impunity

AI has campaigned for many years, alongside other NGOs, for an end to impunity for the perpetrators of human rights violations and abuses.

AI's campaign against torture, for example, highlighted impunity – the failure to bring to justice those who commit serious abuses of human rights – as one of the key factors in perpetuating torture and made recommendations about how it could be overcome. Victims of torture have a right to see justice done, to have the truth about what happened to them acknowledged and to receive reparation. Yet, as AI's report, *End impunity: Justice for the victims of torture*, published in November, showed, the shameful fact is that justice is the exception not the rule. Most torturers commit their crimes safe in the knowledge that they will never face arrest, prosecution or punishment.

However, the tide seems to be turning, albeit slowly. More and more governments are recognizing the importance of bringing alleged perpetrators to justice, if not at home, then abroad.

The prosecution of offences which are serious crimes under international law within the jurisdiction where they occurred is, in an ideal world, the form of prosecution to be preferred. It is one of the best ways to demonstrate to civil society that justice is being done. It is often the most efficient way to collect evidence and testimonies. It is generally the most economical way for victims and witnesses to participate in criminal proceedings. Finally, it allows suspects to be tried in a legal system and in a language they and their lawyers know best.

Where justice at the place of the crime is not possible, other means to ensure justice need to be found. The last century saw the first modern use of *ad hoc* international criminal tribunals to supplement national courts. Such tribunals were established after the Second World War at Nuremberg and Tokyo and later for the prosecution of genocide, war crimes and crimes against humanity committed in the former Yugoslavia since 1991 and in Rwanda in 1994.

In June 2001, former President Slobodan Milošević was transferred to the custody of the International Criminal Tribunal for the former Yugoslavia (ICTY). This marked the first step towards ending the impunity enjoyed by senior political figures suspected of responsibility for massive violations of international law in the conflict in the former Yugoslavia. Slobodan Milošević had been in custody in Serbia since his arrest on 1 April 2001, under investigation for crimes including corruption and abuse of power. The former President had been indicted by the ICTY, along with four other former government officials, on 24 May 1999 on charges of crimes against humanity and violations of the law and customs of war committed in Kosovo by forces acting under their command, with their encouragement and with their support. Slobodan Milošević was also indicted on charges of crimes against humanity, grave breaches of the Geneva Conventions and violations of the laws and customs of war in both Croatia and Bosnia-Herzegovina; the Bosnia indictment also includes the charge of genocide.

In November 2000, a variation on this theme of establishing *ad hoc* international tribunals was repeated when the UN Secretary-General proposed that the UN Security Council establish an *ad hoc* Special Court in Sierra Leone which would be of mixed national and international jurisdiction and composition. Its applicable law would include international, as well as Sierra Leonean, law. Its judges, prosecutors and staff would be composed of Sierra Leonean nationals and people of other nationalities.

This "mixed tribunal" approach, with UN and national involvement, was also the format being

A mass grave in Liplje in the east of Bosnia-Herzegovina, November 2001. AI continued to campaign for those charged by the International Criminal Tribunal for the Former Yugoslavia with crimes committed in Bosnia-Herzegovina to be brought to justice.

INTRODUCTION

Teodoro Cabrera García (left) and Rodolfo Montiel Flores (right), environmental activists and former prisoners of conscience, were arrested in May 1999 by members of the Mexican army, kept in incommunicado detention and convicted on the basis of confessions extracted under torture. They were released in November 2001 by presidential decree following intense national and international pressure. No proper investigation into their torture had been carried out and the charges against them had not been dropped. Torture is widespread in Mexico, and victims include criminal suspects, political detainees and members of indigenous communities. Torture is frequently inflicted to secure confessions which are later used in court as evidence to convict the accused. In the vast majority of cases, those responsible for acts of torture go unpunished, contributing to a culture of impunity.

suggested in Cambodia and analogous to the international components in East Timor. In August 2001, the King of Cambodia signed a law, passed by parliament, allowing for the prosecution before a panel of both national and international judges of some former leaders of the Government of Democratic Kampuchea (Khmer Rouge). The Khmer Rouge ruled Cambodia between April 1975 and January 1979, years in which millions of Cambodians were victims of crimes against humanity, including torture and political killings. However, serious concerns remained because the law falls short of international law and standards.

The principle of universal jurisdiction allows states to investigate and try people suspected of crimes, including serious crimes under international law, irrespective of the nationality of the perpetrator, the nationality of the victim or the place where the crime was committed. There have been a number of cases of the exercise of universal jurisdiction in recent years. For example, in Belgium, four Rwandese nationals were convicted in 2001 of war crimes committed in the context of the 1994 genocide in Rwanda. Other criminal proceedings in the exercise of universal jurisdiction have been initiated against former heads of state such as Augusto Pinochet of Chile and Hissein Habré of Chad, as well as against officials still in power, such as Prime Minister Ariel Sharon of Israel.

The arrest of Augusto Pinochet in October 1998 in the UK transformed public awareness of the possibilities for overcoming impunity, both within Chile and internationally. Although he was returned to Chile in March 2000, efforts to prosecute him for human rights violations continued. The Santiago Appeals Court ruled that his parliamentary immunity should be lifted and in early 2001 he was taken into custody to stand trial on charges connected with a military operation in October 1973, known as the "Caravan of Death", in which 19 people "disappeared". By 2001 Augusto Pinochet was named as a suspect in 241 lawsuits. Although the Santiago Court of Appeals decided in July 2001 to suspend all charges as he was deemed unfit to stand trial – a decision which has been appealed – the Pinochet case continues to inspire all those fighting against impunity.

Another method for prosecuting people suspected of serious crimes under international law in the near future will be the permanent International Criminal Court. Seated in The Hague, in the Netherlands, this court will be a treaty-based body which will be established after 60 states have ratified the 1998 Rome Statute of the International Criminal Court. By December 2001, 48 states had already ratified and 139 states had signed the Statute and it was generally expected that the Court would be established in 2002. The Court will exercise jurisdiction over genocide, crimes against humanity and war crimes.

The death penalty

> "The state should not assume the right which only the Almighty has... to take a human life. That is why I can say firmly I am against Russia reinstating the death penalty."
> Russian President Vladimir Putin, July 2001

There were some important steps forward in 2001 in the worldwide trend towards abolition of the death penalty. In April the Eastern Caribbean Court of Appeal ruled that the mandatory death penalty was unconstitutional. In the words of Justice J. Saunders: "The mandatory death penalty robs those upon whom sentence is passed of any opportunity whatsoever to have the court consider mitigating circumstances even as an irrevocable punishment is meted out to them. The dignity of human life is reduced by a law that compels a court to impose death by hanging upon all convicted of murder, granting none an opportunity to have the individual circumstances of his case considered by the court that is to pronounce sentence." In May, Chile abolished the death penalty for ordinary crimes and replaced it with life imprisonment, and in June the Irish

INTRODUCTION

> By the end of 2001, 74 countries and territories had abolished the death penalty for all crimes. A further 15 countries had abolished it for all but exceptional crimes such as wartime crimes. At least 22 countries were abolitionist in practice: they had not carried out any executions for the past 10 years or more and were believed to have an established practice of not carrying out executions or had made an international commitment not to do so. Eighty-four other countries retained the death penalty, although not all of them passed death sentences or carried out executions during the year.

electorate voted to remove all references to the death penalty from the country's Constitution. Also in June, the first World Congress against the Death Penalty was held in Strasbourg, France. The Congress — which was organized by the NGO *Ensemble contre la peine de mort*, Together Against the Death Penalty, and hosted by the Council of Europe — was attended by former death-row prisoners from the USA and Japan, as well as by members of the European Parliament, the French National Assembly and numerous NGOs, including AI. The appeal for a worldwide moratorium on the death penalty with the goal of universal abolition was signed by the presidents of 15 national and international parliaments.

In the USA, five states — Arizona, Connecticut, Florida, Missouri and North Carolina — joined the 13 other states and the federal government which had enacted legislation prohibiting the use of the death penalty on defendants with mental retardation. However, in Texas, which has accounted for one third of executions in the USA since 1977, a bill prohibiting the execution of prisoners with mental retardation was vetoed by Governor Rick Perry. In 2001, one child offender was executed in the USA. Since the beginning of 1998, nine of the 14 known executions worldwide of child offenders — people who were under 18 at the time of the crime — have taken place in the USA. Two other executions of child offenders were recorded in 2001, one in Iran and one in Pakistan. In December, President Pervez Musharraf of Pakistan announced that the death sentences on around 100 young offenders would be commuted to terms of imprisonment.

China continued to defy the worldwide trend towards abolition and intensified its use of the death penalty in 2001. The number of executions increased dramatically after the Chinese government launched a national "strike hard" campaign against crime. Between April and July 2001 at least 1,781 people were executed — more than the total number of people executed in the rest of the world in the previous three years. More than

> In 2001 at least 3,048 people were executed in 31 countries. At least 5,265 people were sentenced to death in 68 countries. These figures include only cases known to AI; the true figures were certainly higher.
>
> The vast majority of executions worldwide were carried out in a tiny handful of countries. In 2001, 90 per cent of all known executions took place in China, Iran, Saudi Arabia and the USA.
> - In China, preliminary figures indicated that at least 2,468 people were executed, although the true number was believed to be much higher.
> - At least 139 executions were carried out in Iran.
> - In Saudi Arabia, 79 executions were reported.
> - Sixty-six people were executed in the USA.

A woman shouts as she hears the verdict before she is taken to be executed in Ghangzhou, China, in April 2001.

Amnesty International Report 2002

INTRODUCTION

4,015 people were sentenced to death during the year for crimes including embezzlement, fraud and bribery, as well as violent crimes. Many of those condemned to death were likely to have been tortured to extract confessions. Many executions took place after mass sentencing rallies in front of huge crowds in public squares and sports stadiums. Condemned prisoners were often shackled and humiliated by being paraded in public.

The future for AI

> "This dream of justice has brought together human rights activists from all cultural backgrounds, origins and walks of life. Our cultural diversity is the source of our strength, inspiration and determination... We need to find new ways of building international solidarity, to continue to transform despair into hope and compassion into action."
>
> Irene Khan, Secretary General of AI

AI's 25th International Council Meeting (ICM) took place at a time when the movement found itself at a crossroads. In August delegates from 72 countries came together in Dakar, Senegal, to discuss the changes that had taken place in the international political, economic and social landscape, including the human rights environment, in recent years. Uppermost in the delegates' minds was the need for a careful critical assessment of AI's strengths and weaknesses in order to ensure that the organization continues to be able to act effectively in defence of human rights. In particular, delegates debated ways to better embody within AI the principles of universality and indivisibility of all human rights. In an effort to underline the equal importance of civil and political rights and economic rights, delegates explored ways for AI to better integrate both sets of rights in its work, which until now has been largely confined to the sphere of civil and political rights. The revised definition of AI's mission encapsulates all AI's work to date, while providing a framework reflecting a view of human rights advocacy which encompasses a broader range of rights including economic, social and cultural rights, and greater flexibility:

> "AI's mission is to undertake research and action focused on preventing and ending grave abuses of the rights to physical and mental integrity, freedom of conscience and expression, and freedom from discrimination, within the context of its work to promote all human rights."

The nature of the human rights community itself has undergone enormous changes. The number of NGOs has increased dramatically in the past 10 years or so from around 6,000 to approximately 26,000. The development of global NGO networks comprising local, regional and international NGOs is one of the main human rights trends of the past decade. AI, which remains the largest international human rights organization with a membership base in every corner of the world, has sought to respond by greater participation in local and regional human rights networking and collective campaigning.

ICM delegates discussed how to ensure that the high quality of information for which AI is renowned is matched by greater strategic focus for its campaigns. They decided that AI should in future organize its campaigning work around a set of major thematic campaigns on key issues. Such thematic campaigns will, it is hoped, make it easier for AI members to link AI concerns with local issues, to promote strategic work on an issue spanning the movement, and to make the most of AI's expertise.

Human rights activists release 40 balloons in Trafalgar Square in London, United Kingdom, to celebrate AI's 40th anniversary.

> "Forty years on, Amnesty International has secured many victories. Its files are full of letters from former prisoners of conscience or torture victims thanking the organization for making a difference. Torture is now banned by international agreement. Every year more countries reject the death penalty. The world will soon have an International Criminal Court that will be able to ensure that those accused of the worst crimes in the world will face justice. The Court's very existence will deter some crimes.
>
> But the challenges are still great. Torture is banned but in two-thirds of the world's countries it is still being committed in secret. Too many governments still allow wrongful imprisonment, murder or 'disappearance' to be carried out by their officials with impunity.
>
> Those who today still feel a sense of impotence can do something: they can support Amnesty International. They can help it to stand up for freedom and justice."
>
> Peter Benenson, founder of AI, May 2001

AI REPORT 2002
PART 2

AFGHANISTAN

AFGHANISTAN
Chairman of the Interim Administration: Hamid Karzai (replaced President Burhanuddin Rabbani and the *Taleban*, headed by Mullah Mohammad Omar, in December)
Capital: Kabul
Population: 22.5 million
Official languages: Dari, Pushtu
Death penalty: retentionist

There were grave, systematic and widespread human rights abuses throughout the year. Violations of international humanitarian law were committed in the context of armed conflict between the *Taleban* and the National Islamic United Front for the Salvation of Afghanistan (United Front, commonly referred to as the Northern Alliance). Torture and cruel, inhuman or degrading treatment and punishment were inflicted by the *Taleban*. Women were denied basic rights including access to education and employment, and were subjected to systematic ill-treatment, such as beatings. The death penalty continued to be imposed. Forces of the United Front reportedly tortured, ill-treated, and executed some captured *Taleban* and *al-Qa'ida* fighters. Drought and internal conflict swelled the number of refugees and internally displaced people. The number of people fleeing their homes increased further in anticipation of, and during, the international conflict between *Taleban* and *al-Qa'ida* forces, and the US-led coalition. An unknown number of Afghan civilians were killed or injured during the bombing campaign by the USA and its coalition allies.

Background

For most of the year fighting continued between the *Taleban*, which had controlled over 90 per cent of the country, and the United Front, an armed alliance which supported the UN-recognized government headed by Burhanuddin Rabbani and opposed the *Taleban*. Ahmad Shah Masood, a key leader of the United Front was assassinated on 9 September.

Following the attacks in the USA on 11 September, a US-led coalition undertook action against Osama bin Laden and his *al-Qa'ida* forces, which the US government claimed were being sheltered by the *Taleban*.

On 7 October, US-led forces launched air strikes on Kabul, Kandahar and Jalalabad. Ground forces entered Afghanistan 13 days later. The US-led forces coordinated air strikes with the United Front and provided other assistance. By 11 November, the United Front had captured much of northern Afghanistan and on 13 November, defying international pressure to wait, United Front forces entered Kabul.

On 5 December, UN-brokered talks on Afghanistan culminated in the Bonn Agreement, which outlined the establishment of a six-month interim authority, established on 22 December, in preparation for the institution of an Emergency *Loya Jirga* (General Assembly) followed by a Constitutional *Loya Jirga* within 18 months. The Constitution of 1964 was made applicable pending the adoption of a new Constitution.

The population of Afghanistan faced severe food shortages, largely owing to a three-year drought. The World Food Programme estimated that four to five million people were at risk of starvation.

Women

While in power, the *Taleban* continued to impose restrictions on women's movement, employment and education, which were frequently enforced with cruel, inhuman or degrading punishment. Women were reportedly beaten if they were found outside their homes without a close male relative or clothed in a way that did not meet strict dress regulations.

After the collapse of the *Taleban*, there were concerns for the safety of the families of non-Afghan fighters in Afghanistan.

Following the Bonn Agreement, two female ministers were appointed to to the interim administration, and women's rights to education and employment were recognized.

Abuses against ethnic and religious minorities

Taleban forces targeted particular religious and ethnic minorities in mass killings and other attacks against civilians during military campaigns in central Afghanistan.

▭ In early January, following their recapture of Yakaolang district, *Taleban* forces reportedly detained and then killed at least 170 men from the Hazara ethnic minority, a predominantly Shia Muslim group. According to reports, this was a collective punishment against local residents whom the *Taleban* suspected of cooperating with United Front forces.

▭ In January, a *Taleban* edict declared that any Muslim converting to Judaism or Christianity and any non-Muslim trying to convert Muslims faced the death penalty. On 4 August, 24 Shelter Now International aid workers, including 16 Afghans and eight foreign nationals, were arrested. The foreign nationals were charged with proselytizing Christianity. The 16 Afghan aid workers escaped from Pul-e Charkhi prison near Kabul on 12 November. The foreign aid workers were released on 15 November following an anti-*Taleban* uprising.

Torture and ill-treatment

Torture was reported to be endemic in *Taleban* detention facilities. Thousands of people were reportedly held without charge or trial; many were subjected to cruel, inhuman or degrading treatment. Prison conditions continued to be poor, with concerns about the quality and quantity of food, inadequate medical treatment and overcrowding. Following the *Taleban*'s defeat in major cities, some prisoners broke out of *Taleban*-controlled prisons; others were released.

Men whose beard or hair length was found not to conform with *Taleban* regulations were beaten, often with metal cables. Other social regulations, such as prohibitions on playing cards and listening to music, were similarly enforced.

Unfair trials, the death penalty and other cruel judicial punishments

Under the *Taleban*, *Shari'a* (Islamic) Courts imposed cruel, inhuman or degrading punishments after trials that did not conform to international fair trial standards. The death penalty continued to be imposed. At least 51 people were executed, most of them publicly. At least 30 people were flogged, including 20 women. The majority were accused of committing adultery. At least three people had limbs amputated as punishment for theft; the true figure may have been much higher. Often these punishments were carried out in public.

◻ On 26 October, Abdul Haq, a former member of the *Mujahideen*, was captured by *Taleban* forces south of Kabul while reportedly on a mission to generate support for the return of the exiled King. He was summarily tried and executed on the day of his capture. His deputy, Sayed Hamid, was also executed.

Child soldiers

Both the *Taleban* and the United Front were responsible for the recruitment, including forced recruitment, of boys.

◻ A Hazara man from Kandahar reported that in November his 15-year-old son was turned back at the border with Pakistan by members of the *Taleban* who said that he should be fighting alongside *Taleban* forces. The whereabouts of the boy remained unknown at the end of the year.

Possible violations of international humanitarian law by US and allied forces

An as yet unknown number of Afghan civilians were killed or injured or had their homes or property destroyed during the bombing by the USA and its coalition allies. US officials admitted that a number of civilian targets were hit in error, but there was a lack of public information about whether necessary precautions had been taken to avoid civilian casualties. By the end of the year impartial observers had not been able to verify the circumstances in which civilians were reportedly killed, but reports from UN officials, humanitarian agencies and refugees raised serious concerns. AI requested information about specific attacks in which civilians had been killed or in which civilian objects had been damaged and called for an immediate and full investigation into possible violations of international humanitarian law. No response had been received from US officials by the end of the year. AI also called for a moratorium on the use of cluster weapons, which present a high risk of violating the prohibition of indiscriminate attack because of the wide area covered by the numerous bomblets released.

◻ On 8 October, four Afghan workers of the UN-funded de-mining agency Afghan Technical Consultants were killed when their offices in Kabul collapsed. The building had been hit during bombardment of the city by US forces.

◻ On 10 October US planes bombed what appeared to be a civilian radio station near Kabul. When asked about the attack, US Secretary of Defense Donald Rumsfeld replied that radio and television "were vehicles for the *Taleban* leadership and for *al-Qa'ida* to manage their affairs and that therefore they were certainly appropriate targets."

◻ On 29 December, it was reported that civilians were killed in two waves of US bombing of Qala-i-Niazi village near the eastern town of Gardez. A UN spokesperson reported that relatives identified 52 bodies, including 25 children. Although a US military spokesperson said that members of the *al-Qa'ida* and *Taleban* leadership were in the village, a UN spokesperson said that there was no evidence that either *Taleban* or *al-Qa'ida* fighters had been in the village when it was hit. Two of the houses hit had contained stored old ammunition, while three had been civilian residences. The ammunition dumps were reportedly unlocked and unguarded and it was unclear if actions other than bombing were considered as a way of addressing the situation.

There were serious concerns about the treatment and conditions of detention of thousands of captured *Taleban* and *al-Qa'ida* fighters who had been wounded or had surrendered and were being held by the United Front. There were reports that some of these soldiers, particularly non-Afghans, were summarily executed when they were captured, attempted to surrender, or were otherwise rendered *hors de combat*. There were also concerns about the treatment of *Taleban* and *al-Qa'ida* fighters who were held by the US forces on the ship *USS Bataan* and in detention facilities inside Afghanistan.

◻ Hundreds of *Taleban* fighters were reportedly killed, in unclear circumstances, during a United Front siege of the Sultan Raziya school in Mazar-e Sharif in November. According to some accounts, some of the *Taleban* troops who had sought refuge in the school were shot when they attempted to surrender. Subsequently, unarmed religious leaders attempting to persuade *Taleban* troops to surrender were reportedly shot dead by the *Taleban* troops.

◻ In November, hundreds of fighters were reportedly killed during clashes within Qala-i-Jhangi fort on the outskirts of Mazar-e Sharif where captured *Taleban* forces were held. In circumstances that remained unclear, fighting broke out between United Front forces and the detained *Taleban* fighters. US warplanes and United Front artillery then bombed the area. The United Front, the United Kingdom and the USA claimed that they had used the degree of force necessary to quell a prisoners' rebellion. Amid reports that some prisoners were found dead with their hands tied, AI called for an inquiry into what triggered the violence and the proportionality of the response.

◻ In December, General Jurabek, the commander-in-charge of a prison in Shibarghan in northern Afghanistan, told reporters that 43 prisoners had died from injuries or asphyxiation while they were being transported in shipping containers from Kunduz to Shibarghan. Others reported that the number of deaths was much higher.

Refugees and internally displaced people

The UN High Commissioner for Refugees (UNHCR) estimated that 3.5 million Afghan refugees were living in Iran and Pakistan prior to the US-led bombing campaign in Afghanistan. Since late 2000, the borders of Pakistan and Tajikistan had effectively been closed to fleeing Afghans. Iran also took measures to restrict the influx of new refugees during this period.

Throughout the year, there were serious concerns that the authorities in Pakistan were planning to forcibly return refugees to Afghanistan. Thousands of Afghan men living in Pakistan were reportedly detained by police; many were intimidated, beaten, and forcibly returned without access to any procedures. (See Pakistan entry.) In August, the government of Pakistan and the UNHCR agreed to a joint screening program for refugees in Jalozai and Nasir Bagh camps near Peshawar. This screening process was suspended after 11 September.

Approximately 10,000 refugees reportedly continued to remain on promontories in the Panj river, which forms the Tajikistan-Afghanistan border, without adequate shelter, food or drinking water.

After the events of 11 September, all neighbouring countries announced that they had closed their borders with Afghanistan in anticipation of a massive exodus of refugees. On 8 October, Pakistan announced that only the sick and infirm would be allowed to enter. There were serious concerns about the screening process used by Pakistan border guards as family members were separated from one another and many men were forcibly returned. Despite the official closure of the border, approximately 200,000 Afghan refugees entered Pakistan after 11 September. Many had fled because of the feared or actual consequences of the US-led bombing. Existing refugee camps did not adequately support the new arrivals and the UNHCR transferred many new refugees to eight newly established camps along the Afghanistan-Pakistan border where there were major security concerns.

At least 1.1 million Afghans were internally displaced prior to the US-led bombing as a result of the continuing drought and armed conflict. Following the events of 11 September, international assistance programs were severely reduced at the same time as the number of internally displaced people increased.

◻ The World Health Organization announced that 164 people, mostly children, reportedly died of cold and hunger in a four-week period from November to December in a camp for internally displaced people near Kunduz.

In October, the Iranian Red Crescent established two camps for displaced people – Mahkaki and Mile-46 – inside Afghanistan along the Iranian border, raising serious concerns about inadequate protection and security for those in the camps. By mid-November, these camps were militarized and controlled by the United Front. Approximately 10,000 people were afforded scant shelter in these overcrowded camps. Mahkaki camp was reported to have serious sanitation problems. In December, at least six people died because of the cold. (See Iran entry.)

AI country reports/ visits

Reports
- Afghanistan: Protect Afghan civilians and refugees (AI Index: ASA 11/012/2001)
- Afghanistan: Making human rights the Agenda (AI Index: ASA 11/023/2001)

Visits

AI delegates visited Pakistan in October, November and December to interview newly arrived Afghan refugees. In December, AI's Secretary General visited Pakistan and met President Pervez Musharraf to discuss concerns about the situation in Afghanistan.

ALBANIA

REPUBLIC OF ALBANIA
Head of state: Rexhep Meidani
Head of government: Ilir Meta
Capital: Tirana
Population: 3.1 million
Official language: Albanian
Death penalty: abolitionist for ordinary crimes

Detainees, including children, continued to be frequently ill-treated and sometimes tortured during arrest and in police custody, usually to force confessions. Further steps were taken to provide human rights training and to monitor human rights violations by police, and some police officers were dismissed or suspended from service after complaints of ill-treatment were made against them. Judicial proceedings against police officers accused of ill-treating detainees were infrequent, but there were several cases in which police officers were referred for trial and at least three police officers were reported to have been convicted by courts. Conditions in which detainees were held in police stations were often poor, with severe overcrowding.

Background

The national elections, held in June, were won by the governing Socialist Party. The elections were monitored by the Organization for Security and Co-operation in Europe (OSCE) and the OSCE Office for Democratic Institutions and Human Rights, which concluded that the conduct of the campaign, media coverage and election administration had improved compared with past elections. Various flaws were noted, however, including serious irregularities in the voting process in a limited number of zones, and instances of police interference. The main opposition party, the Democratic Party (DP), complained of election rigging and of instances of police violence, including an incident in the town of Kavaja during the pre-election campaign, when DP demonstrators were alleged to have been beaten by police. Organized crime, involving drugs trafficking, and the trafficking in women, children and would-be immigrants to countries in the European Union, continued to be a major problem despite measures to combat it. In October an International Anti-trafficking Centre was established in Vlora, to which Albania, Germany, Greece and Italy contributed.

Torture and ill-treatment

The torture and ill-treatment of detainees during arrest or subsequently in police stations was common.

In January Azgan Haklaj, a local DP leader in the northern district of Tropoja, filed a complaint alleging that masked police officers had beaten him with rifle butts while arresting him at his home on the night of 20 January, and had continued to beat and kick him while driving him to Tirana. He was detained on charges of "taking part in illegal demonstrations" and "violence against property", in connection with violent clashes between armed men and police in the town of Bajram Curri in November 2000. A forensic medical report confirmed he had injuries consistent with these allegations. The Ministry of Public Order stated that police officers had resorted to force only because he had violently resisted arrest; they denied his allegations that his wife and child had been ill-treated during his arrest. An investigation into the allegations had not been completed by the end of the year. Azgan Haklaj was released in July after gaining parliamentary immunity as a result of being elected a deputy in June.

In March Lorenc Çallo alleged that he was punched and kicked in the town of Pogradec by a police officer who wrongly suspected him of having fired a gun. The officer also hit him with a radio handset, injuring his left eye. Eyewitnesses and a forensic medical examination supported Lorenc Çallo's allegations.

Çlirim Proko, from the southern village of Lazarat, was arrested on 16 March in connection with an incident in September 2000 when a government minister was prevented from entering the village by a group of armed men. He was also accused of wounding a police officer. Several police officers reportedly took him from the police station in Gjirokastra and drove him into the hills outside the city, where they beat him. Bruising on his hands and the soles of his feet were reportedly visible to his lawyer and to a doctor who examined him nine days later.

Ill-treatment of minors

Local human rights organizations reported that police routinely ill-treated minors during arrest and detention in order to force them to confess to crimes. In March the Legal Clinic for Minors stated that almost all of the 45 minors they had interviewed during the previous six months who had been detained in custody or were serving sentences had been subjected to beatings in police stations.

In October the Albanian Human Rights Group (AHRG), which conducted interviews with 47 minors in two prisons (Vaqarr and Tirana 313), reported that all 47 alleged they had been ill-treated by police or prison guards. In one case, guards at Tirana 313 prison had beaten a group of seven minors who had repeatedly called for medical help for one of their cellmates who was ill. According to the AHRG, the marks of the beating were clearly visible on all members of the group, except for the sick child. The AHRG was also concerned that in Tirana 313 prison minors were held together with adult detainees.

Investigation of complaints against police

A number of senior police officers received training to provide human rights education to their subordinates. In March the Ministry of Public Order publicized legal provisions relating to the rights of citizens in their contacts with the police, including the right not to be subjected to torture or cruel, inhuman or degrading punishment. In September the Ministry opened a telephone complaints line and within the first month reportedly received 33 complaints, many of them from Tirana and Elbasan, alleging physical ill-treatment or verbal abuse. As a result, eight police officers were reportedly suspended from duty or dismissed for these or other abuses.

In July the Ombudsman's Office reported that in the past year it had investigated 153 complaints of police ill-treatment and had found 74 of them to be justified. As a result of its recommendations, the Ministry of Public Order dismissed two police officers and 10 others were transferred or demoted. A decision was pending in 11 other cases.

Despite the frequency of complaints of ill-treatment, few police officers were brought to trial.

In December 2001, penal proceedings were restarted against a police officer accused of beating and burning with a cigarette Ergest Shele, an 11-year-old orphan wrongly suspected of theft, in June 2000. In October 2001, the Ombudsman had called on the Prosecutor General to ensure that proceedings were reopened following a decision by a Saranda prosecutor to halt proceedings in December 2000.

Korça District Military Court tried three police officers from Elbasan alleged to have brutally ill-treated and injured Naim Pulaku in September 2000; one officer was found guilty of "abuse of office" and two others were acquitted. The Prosecutor's Office filed an appeal against this judgment. In December 2001 Naim Pulaku was again beaten and injured by two police officers, one of whom, he alleged, was the chief of police of Elbasan district, who was shortly afterwards dismissed from the police service and charged. At least two other cases involving allegations of torture and ill-treatment were referred to court for trial, including that of Ferit Çepi, who lost the sight of an eye after being tortured by police officers in November 2000.

Conditions of detention

Conditions in police cells were harsh, amounting in some cases to cruel, inhuman and degrading treatment. In March the AHRG reported the lack of space and poor food and hygiene at Gjirokastra police station. In March and October the Albanian Helsinki Committee (AHC) reported severe overcrowding at police stations in Fier, Korça, Vlora, Gramshi, Lushnja and Elbasan. In July Rrëshen police station was reportedly so crowded that detainees were forced to take turns to lie down to sleep.

AI country reports/visits

Report
- Albania: Torture and ill-treatment — an end to impunity? (AI Index: EUR 11/001/2001)

Visit
In March AI representatives visited Albania to conduct research.

ALGERIA

PEOPLE'S DEMOCRATIC REPUBLIC OF ALGERIA
Head of state: Abdelaziz Bouteflika
Head of government: Ali Benflis
Capital: Algiers
Population: 30.9 million
Official language: Arabic
Death penalty: retentionist

The conflict which has ravaged the country since 1992 continued; the level of violence and killings remained high. Hundreds of civilians, including women and children, were killed in targeted and indiscriminate attacks by armed groups which define themselves as "Islamic groups". Hundreds of members of the security forces, state-armed militias and armed groups were killed in attacks, ambushes and armed confrontations. Dozens of civilians were unlawfully killed by the security forces or by state-armed militias. These included more than 80 unarmed civilians shot dead by the security forces in the context of demonstrations in the northeastern region of Kabylia following the death in April of a schoolboy in the custody of the gendarmerie. A commission of inquiry established by the authorities to look into these events issued reports in July and December. No independent investigations were carried out into the thousands of other killings, massacres, "disappearances", abductions and reports of torture since 1992. Torture continued to be widespread. Reports of secret and unacknowledged detention continued to be received. Freedom of expression was threatened by new legislation. Over 100 people had their death sentences commuted to prison terms. The state of emergency imposed in 1992 remained in place.

Background

The authorities stated in October that the security forces had "neutralized" 20,000 "terrorists" since 1992, without specifying how many had been killed and how many apprehended. For the first time, the authorities gave an official figure for the number of active members of armed groups, estimating it to be between 700 and 800, of whom 300 to 400 were said to be armed. In the wake of the attacks on 11 September in the USA, the Algerian government declared strong support for UN-led measures against "terrorism" and pushed for the expulsion to Algeria of nationals living abroad whom it said it suspected of having links with armed groups.

The first detailed account by an ex-officer in the Algerian army about his experiences during the current conflict was published in France in February. In April, former Defence Minister General Khaled Nezzar cut short a visit to Paris to promote his memoirs after learning that three criminal suits for torture had been filed against him in France. These two events sparked renewed debate on the involvement of the various parties to the conflict in Algeria in the massive human rights abuses committed since 1992.

Floods in November left over 700 people dead and thousands more homeless, mostly in Algiers.

Negotiations between Algeria and the European Union concluded in December with the initialling of an association agreement which aims to deepen bilateral relations in the field of trade and other areas such as security and illegal immigration.

The official human rights body, the *Observatoire national des droits de l'homme,* National Human Rights Observatory, was dissolved and replaced in March by the newly established *Commission nationale consultative de promotion et de protection des droits de l'homme,* National Advisory Commission for the Promotion and Protection of Human Rights. The members of the new body were designated by President Abdelaziz Bouteflika in October. A national office for the families of the "disappeared" was opened in September by a national association campaigning on the issue of "disappearances".

Killings

Hundreds of civilians were killed by armed groups which define themselves as "Islamic groups" in both targeted attacks and indiscriminate bomb explosions. Often groups of up to some 25 civilians, including entire families, were killed in their homes in rural areas in the north by armed groups. Most killings took place outside the main cities and the perpetrators were routinely able to escape, even though some attacks were committed near army and security force checkpoints or outposts. For the first time in some two years, bomb attacks took place in Algiers. Hundreds of members of the security forces, state-armed militias and armed groups were killed in ambushes and armed confrontations. However, as a result of official restrictions on information about such incidents, it was often not possible to obtain precise details about the identity of the victims or the exact circumstances of their deaths.

Dozens of civilians were killed by the security forces in the context of waves of anti-government demonstrations which rocked the country throughout much of the year. The protesters were venting deep-seated anger at the authorities' apparent lack of concern about deteriorating socio-economic conditions for the majority of the population and use of repressive measures. In many demonstrations, growing demands for official recognition of the Berber language and culture were also expressed.

◻ Members of the gendarmerie and other security forces killed more than 80 unarmed civilians and injured hundreds of others in the context of demonstrations during April, May and June in the Berber-dominated northeastern region of Kabylia. The demonstrations followed the death in April of schoolboy Massinissa Guermah in the custody of the gendarmerie. Gendarmes reportedly fired on unarmed protesters standing more than 100 metres away from them and shot others in the back after dispersing them using tear gas. In several instances, protesters were reportedly pursued to their homes and shot dead inside. In all cases, the security forces appear to have used live ammunition.

In May President Bouteflika ordered the establishment of an official commission of inquiry to look into the events in Kabylia. The commission issued a preliminary report in July which concluded that the gendarmerie and other security forces had repeatedly resorted to excessive use of lethal force. A final report, published in December, expressed concern at the excessive powers held by the military authorities and at the fact that the commission had been unable to investigate further because many witnesses were too afraid to speak to them.

The authorities announced in October that those responsible for the killings would be brought to justice and that the victims or their families would receive just compensation. It was reported that some gendarmes were detained in connection with the events in Kabylia. However, by the end of the year, no member of the security forces was known to have been put on trial for unlawful killings or other human rights violations in the context of demonstrations in Kabylia.

Failure to establish truth and justice

No concrete action was known to have been taken by the authorities to clarify the fate of some 4,000 men and women who "disappeared" after arrest by members of the security forces or state-armed militias since 1993. Similarly, no steps were known to have been taken to investigate information provided by families about the alleged burial place of relatives who had been abducted and killed by armed groups, but whose bodies were never found. This was despite the pledges to the representatives of families of victims made by President Bouteflika and other government officials in recent years.

The government provided no information about the investigations which the authorities claimed had been carried out into the massive human rights abuses committed since 1992, including thousands of cases of extrajudicial executions, deliberate and arbitrary killings of civilians, torture and ill-treatment, and "disappearances". Some members of the security forces and militias were reportedly tried and sentenced during the year to prison terms on charges of murder and other crimes, but no concrete measures were known to have been taken to bring to justice the overwhelming majority of those responsible for human rights abuses committed by the security forces, state-armed militias or armed groups in 2001 or previous years.

In theory, since the expiry of the Law on Civil Harmony in January 2000, members of armed groups who give themselves up to the authorities no longer benefit from immunity from prosecution. However, reports continued to be received that members of armed groups who surrendered during 2001 appeared to be exempted from prosecution and were released without adequate inquiries being made by the authorities into what crimes they may have committed during their time as members of armed groups. Moreover, no investigations were known to have been carried out into the complaints made in 2001 or previous years that members of armed groups who had surrendered to the authorities were allegedly responsible for killings or abductions.

Victims and families of victims of unlawful killings, torture and "disappearance" committed by the security forces or state-armed militias since 1992 continued to be denied compensation. Families whose relatives had been abducted by armed groups and were presumed killed and who had filed complaints with the authorities also did not receive compensation. Women's associations continued to complain that victims of rape by armed groups did not benefit from rehabilitation, including medical and psychiatric care and other post-traumatic counselling, or from the compensation which other victims of armed groups had received.

Torture and secret detention

Torture remained widespread. Cases of secret and unacknowledged detention continued to be reported. The government and judicial authorities systematically denied all knowledge of the detainees until after they were brought to court or released. Many of those detained in this manner were subjected to torture or ill-treatment.

◻ Dozens of civilians, including children as young as 15, were reported to have been tortured or ill-treated following arrest by members of the security forces in the context of demonstrations during April, May and June in Kabylia. Beatings with fists, batons and rifle butts appear to have been common at the time of arrest and in detention. Some detainees alleged that, while in the custody of the gendarmerie, they were undressed, tied up with wire and threatened with sexual violence; others alleged that they were whipped or slashed with sharp implements.

Fayçal Khoumissi spent some 10 months in secret detention before his family learned that he was being held in El-Harrach Prison in Algiers. He had been arrested in November 2000 in the centre of the district of El-Harrach by four armed men in civilian clothes and travelling in an unmarked car. He was taken to a security force base, where he alleged that he was shot in both legs, given electric shocks to his ears and genitals, beaten with an iron bar on his back and genitals, and forced to swallow large amounts of dirty water through a cloth placed in his mouth. He was then treated in hospital before being presented before the judicial authorities and remanded in custody on charges related to "terrorism". His family only found out about his detention when they were contacted in September by a former detainee who had met Fayçal Khoumissi in prison and was subsequently released.

Legislative changes

Changes to the Penal Code, promulgated in June, threatened the right to freedom of expression. Penalties for defamation were increased. Amendments to the law prescribed prison terms of up to one year and fines of up to 250,000 dinars (approximately US$3,500) for individuals found guilty of defaming the President of the Republic or other state institutions such as the army, parliament or the judiciary, using the written or spoken word or an illustration. The editor and publisher of an offending article or illustration, as well as the publication itself, are also liable to be prosecuted. Punishments, including sentences of up to three years' imprisonment, were also introduced for anyone attempting to preach in places of prayer without authorization.

Changes to the Code of Penal Procedure, promulgated in June, significantly extended the legally permitted period of pre-trial detention. Those accused of "crimes considered to be terrorist or subversive acts" can now be held in pre-trial detention for a maximum of 32 months, twice the previous maximum, and those accused of a "transnational crime" for up to 56 months.

Death penalty

In October, 115 people had their death sentences commuted to prison terms by order of a presidential decree. The moratorium on executions declared in December 1993 remained in place.

International organizations

The UN Working Group on Enforced or Involuntary Disappearances, which asked in 2000 to visit Algeria, was not granted access to the country in 2001. Long-standing requests by the UN Special Rapporteur on extrajudicial, summary or arbitrary executions and the UN Special Rapporteur on torture to visit Algeria had not resulted in invitations by the end of the year.

At its 29th Ordinary Session, held in Libya, the African Commission on Human and Peoples' Rights expressed its "deep concern" at the killings in Kabylia and recommended that the "fight against impunity becomes a reality". In May the European Parliament adopted a resolution condemning the killing of peaceful demonstrators in Kabylia and expressing concern over legislative amendments relating to the press.

The International Committee of the Red Cross (ICRC) continued prison visits, resumed in 1999.

Having been given access to the country in 2000, AI and other international human rights organizations asked to visit again, but had not been allowed entry by the end of 2001.

AI country reports/visits
Reports
- Algeria: Amnesty International calls for a prompt and impartial investigation into the recent bloodshed in Kabylia (AI Index: MDE 28/005/2001)
- Algeria: Every killing must be urgently investigated (AI Index: MDE 28/007/2001)
- Algeria: Relatives of the "disappeared" violently dispersed (AI Index: MDE 28/010/2001)

ANGOLA

REPUBLIC OF ANGOLA
Head of state and government: José Eduardo dos Santos
Capital: Luanda
Population: 13.5 million
Official language: Portuguese
Death penalty: abolitionist for all crimes

Civil war continued throughout the year. Hundreds of unarmed civilians were indiscriminately and deliberately killed by government forces and by forces of the *União Nacional para a Independência Total de Angola* (UNITA), National Union for the Total Independence of Angola. UNITA forces mutilated civilians and abducted hundreds of children. In Cabinda, armed political groups continued to take Angolan and foreign nationals hostage. Thousands of people were displaced and faced severe hardship. Police used lethal force against demonstrators, killing two people and injuring at least nine others, and reportedly killed and tortured suspected criminals. The authorities detained people for exercising their rights to freedom of assembly and expression.

Background

The civil war, which entered a guerrilla phase in 2000 after government forces expelled UNITA from its strongholds, continued to devastate the country. The government continued to control an estimated 90 per cent of the country. There were increased attacks by

UNITA forces on villages and roads, killing thousands of unarmed civilians. UNITA also attacked towns close to Luanda. The provinces of Malanje, Uige and Kwanza Norte in the north and Huila in the south saw a greater number of UNITA attacks, which drove thousands of refugees into neighbouring countries. An increased number of civilians suffered death and injury from landmines laid by both sides.

Relations with neighbouring Namibia and Zambia became increasingly strained over the lack of security in border areas. Zambia repeatedly accused the Angolan armed forces of entering its territory in pursuit of UNITA troops. There were reports of Namibian troops fighting alongside the Angolan armed forces against UNITA.

The armed conflict and insecurity were responsible for the number of internally displaced people increasing by 300,000 during the year to an estimated total of four million and for a precarious humanitarian situation. Over half a million internally displaced people received humanitarian assistance. Of those, nearly 300,000 lived in camps.

The Catholic Church and a growing peace movement within civil society continued to press for dialogue and a negotiated peace settlement. Both sides to the conflict expressed willingness to enter talks but set preconditions deemed unacceptable by the other party. In the first half of 2001, thousands of prisoners, including those accused of crimes against the security of the state, were released under the terms of a November 2000 amnesty law.

In April and October the UN Security Council extended the mandates of the UN Office in Angola and the UN Monitoring Mechanism on Sanctions against UNITA, each time for six-month periods. The UN Monitoring Mechanism on Sanctions reported in March and October that sanctions against UNITA were effective despite violations by some countries.

In November the government announced that it would begin a gradual withdrawal of its troops — estimated at between 2,000 and 2,500 — from the Democratic Republic of the Congo. This withdrawal had not started by the end of 2001.

Armed conflict
Killings of unarmed civilians

The killing of hundreds of unarmed civilians, as well as other abuses including mutilations and torture, continued in violation of humanitarian law. It remained difficult to obtain independent confirmation of many of these reports.

UNITA was responsible for most of the numerous attacks on civilians, including aid workers, and for the abduction of hundreds of people.

▫ In one incident in January, UNITA soldiers reportedly killed Katondo Hedila, cut off the arms of Simeon Nghishongwa and castrated a third man. The three were Angolans living in Namibia who had crossed the border looking for their cattle.

▫ In August, UNITA forces were alleged to have attacked a passenger train in Zenza Itombe, Kwanza Norte province, killing over 200 people. After derailing the train with an anti-tank mine, UNITA soldiers reportedly shot dead the surviving passengers.

Government forces killed and tortured civilians suspected of collaborating with UNITA.

▫ In April, Friquixi Chapassa, the traditional chief in Cuango, Lunda Norte province, was reportedly put on a fire and burned by soldiers and beaten with a red-hot cutlass. He was suspected of collaborating with UNITA following attacks by UNITA forces in the area.

Abduction of children

UNITA abducted hundreds of children throughout the year. The youngest were used as porters and the girls as sex slaves, while the older boys were forced to join UNITA's fighting forces. Children who escaped, including some who had been abducted in previous years, said they had been forced to carry heavy loads for UNITA fighters and to undergo military training. One boy, who had been abducted with dozens of others during an attack on Dombe Grande, Benguela province in May, said that UNITA combatants had stabbed three boys to death.

▫ In May, UNITA abducted at least 30 children during an attack on Caxito, a town 60 kilometres from Luanda, in which 100 people were reportedly killed. A further 60 children and two adults were abducted from an orphanage on the outskirts of Caxito immediately after the attack. The 60 children were released four weeks later, following a national and international outcry. They had been made to carry heavy loads for 12 hours a day for the UNITA forces. Three of the children abducted in Caxito town escaped in August. However, the others remained in captivity at the end of 2001.

There were reports throughout the year that the Angolan armed forces continued forced recruitment of youths into the army, including many children under 15 years of age. There were, however, fewer than in previous years.

Cabinda

Fighting between government forces and the two armed factions of the *Frente para a Libertação do Enclave de Cabinda* (FLEC), Front for the Liberation of the Cabinda Enclave, intensified during the first half of the year as government forces launched an offensive to free hostages held by the two FLEC factions. All warring sides were responsible for human rights abuses and violations of humanitarian law. Government soldiers carried out attacks against civilians and reportedly burned villages and beat, raped and extrajudicially executed unarmed civilians suspected of supporting the FLEC.

▫ In May, government soldiers reportedly killed Abiniel Macaia, the chief of Seke-Mbanza village, his wife and children, and other villagers, before burning their homes and attacking other villages. In Sanda Massala village, soldiers allegedly killed the traditional chief, Alberto Kionga, and his family, and raped several women before killing them.

Both FLEC factions continued to take hostages to extort money, particularly from foreign companies. In February, *FLEC-Forcas Armadas de Cabinda* (FLEC-FAC), FLEC-Cabindan Armed Forces, ambushed the car in which doctor Bernardino Paulo Paim was travelling and took him hostage. He was released in May. In April and

June FLEC-FAC released three Portuguese hostages it had taken in March 2000. In March, FLEC-*Renovada*, FLEC-Renewed, took one Angolan and five Portuguese workers hostage for two months.

Other human rights violations
Death in police custody
The police were reported to have tortured and killed suspected criminals.

◻ Gomes Dinis Ribeiro was feared to have been shot dead at the Cazenga police station in Luanda in January. He had been accused of theft, arrested and reportedly severely beaten in front of his wife. She said that the police asked for payment to release him. After she came back with the money, she said that she heard shooting inside the police station and was told by police that her husband had escaped with a gun. Two days later, his body was found in the morgue with a bullet in his head and marks on his body apparently consistent with a severe beating. The official autopsy report attributed the cause of death to "clinical reasons". No independent investigation had been carried out by the end of 2001.

Use of lethal force
On two successive weekends in July, the police, including the Rapid Intervention Police and the Angola National Police and supported by armed forces units, forcibly evicted residents of the Boavista neighbourhood of Luanda and demolished their homes. On both occasions police officers fired into the crowds that resisted the eviction, killing Emílio Rafael and Andrade Jungo Jaime and injuring at least nine others, including António Samuel. Other protesters were bitten by police dogs. Fifteen people were arrested and brought to court within a week on charges of possessing firearms and disobeying police orders to disperse. No prosecution evidence was presented and the defendants were released pending further police investigation. Among those arrested was the coordinator of the Boavista residents, José Rasgadinho, who was again detained for a few days in September on charges of incitement to violence. This trial was also suspended for lack of evidence. By the end of 2001 the trials had not resumed and there had been no independent inquiry into the use of lethal force against the protesters.

Restrictions on fundamental freedoms
Restrictions on freedom of assembly, association and expression continued. As in previous years, restrictions were greater in the provinces where political activists and journalists were often harassed and prevented from carrying out their activities. Some were detained for short periods.

The police beat and arrested peaceful demonstrators. The authorities banned several planned demonstrations in Luanda on the grounds that the organizers had not obtained required authorizations and on security grounds following a UNITA attack on a town near Luanda.

◻ In January, the police used force to disperse a peaceful demonstration by the *Partido de Apoio Democrático e Progresso de Angola*, Angolan Party for Democratic Support and Progress, and arrested its President, Carlos Alberto de Andrade Leitão, and five other members. The demonstrators were demanding the resignation of President dos Santos and clarification of an arms sale scandal involving former French government officials. Two days later, the six detainees were tried and acquitted on charges of holding a demonstration within 100 metres of government buildings and failing to obtain the necessary authorizations to hold a demonstration.

Journalists and others who criticized the government continued to face detention and threats of violence, and journalists were prevented from carrying out their work and travelling outside the country.

◻ João Zaba, a bank employee, was arrested in March after he published an article on the Internet critical of the government's actions in Cabinda. He was convicted in May of crimes against the security of the state and incitement to violence, and sentenced to nine months in prison. He was conditionally released in September after serving half the sentence.

◻ Gilberto Neto, a journalist with the independent newspaper *Folha 8*, was arrested in July at Malanje airport. Two police officers escorted him and a foreign journalist, who was researching the economic effects of the war, back to Luanda. They were not detained but were interrogated twice at the Department of Criminal Investigation and accused of visiting Malanje without authorization. The police confiscated their identity documents and other belongings, which were later returned. A month later, immigration police at Luanda airport stopped Gilberto Neto from leaving the country, ostensibly because he had criminal charges pending against him from 1999, although he had been allowed to travel abroad in January. They confiscated his passport and had not returned it by the end of 2001.

ARGENTINA

ARGENTINE REPUBLIC
Head of state and government: Fernando de la Rúa was replaced in the last two weeks of December successively by Provisional Presidents Ramón Puerta, Adolfo Rodríguez Saá and Eduardo Camaño
Capital: Buenos Aires
Population: 37.5 million
Official language: Spanish
Death penalty: abolitionist for ordinary crimes
2001 treaty ratifications/signatures: Rome Statute of the International Criminal Court

There were numerous allegations of torture and ill-treatment of detainees by law enforcement and prison officers. Dozens of killings by police in disputed circumstances were reported. Important judicial decisions were made regarding past human rights violations, including those linked to "Operation Condor". Lawyers and human rights defenders were threatened and attacked.

Demonstrations
The political situation was dominated by civil unrest over government economic policies and attempts to restructure the economy. Public opposition to spending cuts triggered protests in Buenos Aires and around the country. Scores of demonstrators, including trade unionists and community leaders, were arrested. Some were charged and several alleged that they were tortured by members of the security forces.

In June, two people, including a minor, were killed and an unconfirmed number of people injured during violent confrontations between demonstrators and members of the *Gendarmeria Nacional* in the locality of General Mosconi, Salta Province. In July, a federal judge requested disciplinary proceedings against Mara Graciela Puntano, a lawyer acting on behalf of those arrested and allegedly tortured by members of the *Gendarmeria Nacional*. She had made a statement to the press about irregularities in the judicial investigation into these incidents and into the killing of Anibal Verón during a demonstration in 2000.

In December, demonstrations involving hundreds of thousands of people took place across the country as a result of the economic crisis. A state of siege was imposed for four days and hundreds of demonstrators were arrested. Over 30 people were killed during the demonstrations and there were reports of excessive use of force by the security forces. The crisis resulted in a change of administration.

Ill-treatment and torture
There were widespread reports of the torture and ill-treatment of detainees, including minors, in prisons and police stations. In August members of the judiciary published a declaration expressing their concern at the generalized and systematic use of torture during police investigations and the general treatment of detainees. The declaration also pointed out the lack of action by the judicial authorities in applying appropriate measures to prevent and punish torture.

In a separate resolution submitted to the judicial authorities, the Buenos Aires Province Appeal Court Defender recorded over 600 cases of torture in police stations and prisons between March 2000 and June 2001. Methods of torture included beatings, near-asphyxiation and electric shocks. The resolution also highlighted severe overcrowding, appalling sanitary conditions and obstruction of detainees' right of defence by members of the Buenos Aires Province Penitentiary Service.

Police violence and killings
Reports of killings by police officers in disputed circumstances continued to be received. In October, the Provincial Supreme Court issued a resolution which stated that at least 60 minors were killed by police in Buenos Aires Province between 1999 and 2000. Many of those killed had made complaints of threats or ill-treatment by members of the police. According to the non-governmental human rights organization *Coordinadora Contra la Represión Policial e Institucional* (Correpi), Association against Police and Institutional Repression, 60 people, including 14 minors, were killed between January and August 2001 by police. Relatives of victims campaigning for truth and justice were intimidated and threatened.

Past human rights violations
In September, the Under-Secretary for Human Rights publicly acknowledged that 15,000 people had "disappeared" during the military government (1976 to 1983).

During 2001, legal proceedings to clarify the fate of victims of "disappearances" and to bring those responsible to justice continued in Argentina and abroad. A number of important positive judicial decisions were made.

In a landmark decision, Federal Judge Gabriel Cavallo ruled in March that the Full Stop and Due Obedience laws, which granted immunity from prosecution for human rights violations committed under the military government, were unconstitutional and void. His ruling related to criminal prosecutions regarding the "disappearance" in 1978 of José Liborio Poblete Roa, his wife, Gertrudis Marta Hlaczik, and their daughter. In November, the Federal Appeals Court upheld the decision.

In June and July, a federal judge issued three judicial decisions indicting and requesting the arrest of a number of former members of the armed forces of Argentina, Chile, Paraguay and Uruguay for their involvement in a criminal plan characterized by a systematic pattern of forced disappearances known as "Operation Condor". In his decision the judge ordered the trial and preventive arrest of Jorge Rafael Videla. At the end of the year Jorge Rafael Videla was held under house arrest in connection with a case involving the kidnapping of children. The judge also requested the provisional arrest, pending requests for extradition, of former Chilean President Augusto Pinochet. In December, in a separate decision, the judge requested the provisional arrest pending requests for extradition of the former Bolivian President, Hugo Banzer Suárez.

Germany
In July, the Nuremberg prosecutor in Germany issued an international warrant for the arrest of former General Carlos Guillermo Suárez Mason and in October his extradition was requested for the suspected murder of Elisabeth Kasemann, a German national who was kidnapped and "disappeared" in Buenos Aires in March 1977.

However, in December, a presidential decree was issued stating that the Ministry of Foreign Affairs would reject all requests for extradition related to events that took place in Argentina.

Spain
In August, Claudio Scagliuzzi, a former member of the Argentine army intelligence service was arrested in Barcelona, Spain. His arrest pending extradition had been requested by an Argentine judge in the context of the investigation of "disappearances" that took place as part of "Operation Condor".

Human rights defenders threatened
Human rights lawyers in Mendoza Province representing families of victims of human rights violations and human rights activists in a number of provinces were subjected to further intimidation and attacks.

AI country reports/visits
Reports
- Argentina: *Amicus Curiae* brief on the incompatibility with international law of the Full Stop and Due Obedience Laws (AI Index: AMR 13/012/2001)
- Argentina: Vanessa Lorena Ledesma and repeated threats to other transvestites in the Province of Córdoba (AI Index: AMR 13/015/2001)

ARMENIA

REPUBLIC OF ARMENIA
Head of state: Robert Kocharian
Head of government: Andranik Makarian
Capital: Yerevan
Population: 3.7 million
Official language: Armenian
Death penalty: retentionist
2001 ratifications/signatures: European Convention on Human Rights and its Protocol No. 6 concerning the abolition of the death penalty; European Convention for the Prevention of Torture and Inhuman or Degrading Treatment or Punishment

There were persistent reports of torture and ill-treatment by state officials. The authorities continued to imprison conscientious objectors to compulsory military service. At least three death sentences were passed during 2001, and at least 30 men were under sentence of death at the end of the year, although the moratorium on executions continued. Delays in adopting the new draft criminal code held up important human rights reforms, such as abolition of the death penalty and the decriminalization of consensual sexual relations between men.

Torture and ill-treatment
Reports continued to be received of torture and ill-treatment by law enforcement officials, as well as of brutal treatment of army conscripts, known as "hazing". There were persistent allegations that law enforcement officials subjected people to torture and ill-treatment to obtain confessions and coerce testimony. There were concerns that investigations by the authorities into such allegations were not adequate.

Political activist Pogos Pogosian, aged 43, was reportedly found dead in the toilet of the "Aragast" café in Yerevan in the early hours of 25 September, 10 minutes after President Robert Kocharian had left the club. According to eyewitness accounts, Pogos Pogosian had approached the President as he was leaving and had verbally abused him, at which point some of the presidential bodyguards began to beat him. Pogos Pogosian was then reportedly taken to the toilet for a "conversation" by a member of the security team. On 27 September, it was announced that President Kocharian had suspended three of his bodyguards and had stated that the investigation into the incident must be impartial. One of the bodyguards was reportedly charged with manslaughter in November. AI urged the authorities to ensure that the investigation be impartial, thorough and effective, so that justice not only be done, but be seen to be done.

Prisoners of conscience
At least 27 men, all Jehovah's Witnesses, were reported to have been imprisoned during the year for their

conscientious objection to compulsory military service, and sentenced to terms of imprisonment ranging from one to three and a half years. Fourteen remained in prison at the end of 2001. The draft law on introduction of alternative civilian service remained under discussion.

A number of conscientious objectors were released early. At least 16 were reported to have been conditionally released from detention after serving part of their sentences but were required to report regularly to the police. Others were released under the terms of an amnesty. This amnesty reportedly did not apply to those convicted of the military crime of "desertion", who included conscientious objectors who had escaped after being forcibly conscripted.

Prosecution of member of religious minority

In September Levon Margaryan, a Jehovah's Witness, was acquitted of charges of "enticing minors into attending religious meetings of an unregistered religion" and "influencing members to refuse their civic duties". The case had been brought against him reportedly because children had attended meetings in the town where Levon Margaryan was a Jehovah's Witness elder. The defence maintained that parents had signed documents giving permission for their children to attend, and that the court case was an attempt to block the Jehovah's Witnesses officially registering in Armenia. Following an appeal by the prosecution against the acquittal, a trial was opened in November, which had not concluded by the end of the year. AI was concerned that the charges against him were brought to punish him for peacefully exercising his religious belief.

Political prisoners

The trial into the case of the 1999 armed attack in the Armenian parliament, in which eight people, including the Prime Minister and the Speaker of Parliament, were killed, opened in February in Yerevan. In previous years, AI had raised concerns about the fairness of the trials and conditions of detention of those detained in connection with the attack, such as allegations of torture and ill-treatment, difficulties in access to defence lawyers, lack of access to families and denial of access to independent medical practitioners. During the court hearings defendant Nairi Unanian repeated allegations that he was tortured during the pre-trial investigation, including being beaten with rubber batons. It was reported during court proceedings that an investigation into these torture allegations had opened in June 2000 and had concluded by the end of the month with a decision not to initiate criminal proceedings because of lack of sufficient evidence. There was widespread public and political support, including from the Prime Minister, for imposing the death penalty in this case, which led the Council of Europe to warn that Armenia would face suspension from the organization if any of the defendants was executed.

Death penalty

The draft new Criminal Code, under which the death penalty would be replaced by a maximum sentence of life imprisonment, had not been adopted by the end of 2001. At least three death sentences were passed during the year. In April, army servicemen Tsolak Melkonian, Levon Madilian and Artak Alekian were reportedly sentenced to death for killing eight people in July 2000 after deserting from their unit. In March, the Court of Appeal upheld the death sentences imposed on Armen Ter-Saakian and Alik Grigorian. There were no executions.

Council of Europe

Armenia entered the Council of Europe in January. Among its human rights obligations were: to ratify within a year of accession the European Convention on Human Rights and its Protocol No. 6 concerning the abolition of the death penalty, and the European Convention for the Prevention of Torture and Inhuman or Degrading Treatment or Punishment; to adopt within a year of accession the draft new Criminal Code, drawn up in 1997, thereby replacing the death penalty with life imprisonment, and decriminalizing homosexual relations between consenting adult men; and to adopt, within three years of accession, a law on alternative service, and in the meantime pardon all imprisoned conscientious objectors. By the end of 2001, Armenia had yet to fulfil any of these commitments.

The Council of Europe Secretary General instituted post-accession monitoring of Armenia's commitments relating to respect for democratic principles, rule of law and the observance of human rights. A report entitled "Cases of alleged political prisoners in Armenia and Azerbaijan" was submitted by independent experts to the Secretary General (see Azerbaijan entry). The experts gave detailed attention to only the two substantive cases in Armenia that had been raised with them. However, in the context of the Council of Europe's ongoing monitoring of this issue, AI raised with the Council of Europe its concerns about a number of other cases, including those of the defendants in the 1999 parliamentary shootings case (see above).

AI country reports/ visits
Reports
- Armenia: A positive step towards religious freedom (AI Index: EUR 54/008/2001)
- Concerns in Europe, January-June 2001: Armenia (AI Index: EUR 01/003/2001)

AUSTRALIA

AUSTRALIA
Head of state: Queen Elizabeth II, represented by Peter Hollingworth (replaced William Deane in June)
Head of government: John Howard
Capital: Canberra
Population: 19.3 million
Official language: English
Death penalty: abolitionist for all crimes

More than 1,800 asylum-seekers travelling by boat were intercepted by warships, arbitrarily detained and denied the right to claim asylum on the Australian mainland. About 600 possible asylum-seekers travelling by boat from Indonesia were turned back by the navy. Parliament passed legislation which reduced the government's accountability in the courts for actions taken to prevent asylum-seekers from arriving in Australia without valid travel documents.

Background

Australians celebrated 100 years of constitutional democracy, but critics lamented the lack of human rights guarantees in the Constitution.

In November, the government of Prime Minister John Howard was returned to power in elections dominated by the debate on asylum issues. Throughout much of the year, public discussion of human rights centred on the controversy over refugee rights. The government defended itself against strong international criticism over its refugee policy by stating that Australia seeks to prioritize refugees awaiting resettlement in other countries. However, it did not increase its annual intake of such refugees and refused entry into Australia to those awaiting resettlement from Indonesia.

Deaths in custody

Aborigines remained disproportionately represented at all stages of the criminal justice system. This was despite a Royal Commission into Aboriginal Deaths in Custody which 10 years earlier had recommended reducing indigenous overrepresentation in prison and police custody. In April, the Australian Institute of Criminology reported that during the past 20 years, indigenous people were between seven and 22 times more likely than other Australians to die in custody or in police operations.

In June, the state government of Western Australia confirmed that forensic tissue samples from the body of Stephen Wardle, missing since 1992, had been located. His controversial death within hours of being detained without charge at a police station was expected to be examined in 2002 by a Royal Commission of Inquiry into the Western Australia police service.

Asylum-seekers

In August, the federal government began developing a new policy to prevent people arriving by boat without valid travel papers from making asylum claims on mainland Australia. Warships and elite soldiers stopped so-called "boat people" from reaching the continent.

By December, Australian military and civilian authorities had transferred more than 1,700 asylum-seekers who had been intercepted at sea to remote islands in the Indian and Pacific Oceans. Almost all were then arbitrarily and indefinitely detained without independent review or any legal justification for their detention, in contravention of international law. The rest were either deported, or imprisoned in Australia on people-smuggling charges.

By 31 December, 1,118 Afghan and Middle Eastern asylum-seekers were detained on Nauru, in return for some US$15 million in aid from Australia. Australia funded the cost of their detention and the processing of their refugee claims in facilities run by the International Organisation for Migration (IOM). In October, the IOM set up an Australian-funded detention centre at the isolated Lombrum military base in Manus Island, Papua New Guinea, for another 216 asylum-seekers (see Papua New Guinea entry). The UN High Commissioner for Refugees (UNHCR) assessed more than 500 of the first asylum-seekers taken to Nauru, but declined subsequent requests to process other asylum-seekers transferred by Australia to other countries. The results of the processing was expected to be announced in 2002.

In December, the government suspended processing of asylum applications lodged by Afghans on grounds of persecution under the *Taleban*, but continued to detain them indefinitely without the right to seek release from detention in court.

◻ In October, a warship fired warning shots across a boat carrying asylum-seekers in an attempt to deter the boat from heading for Australia.

◻ The military forced some 600 asylum-seekers to leave Australian territorial waters. At least 356 others, including 70 children, drowned after their leaking boat sank on the journey from Indonesia to Australia. Some of them had close relatives among refugees already in Australia, while others had waited months to be resettled in another country after being recognized as refugees by the UNHCR. Ahmed al-Zalime, a refugee living in Australia whose three daughters drowned in the incident, was unable to visit his rescued wife in Indonesia, because Australian temporary refugee visas prohibit return to the country after any overseas travel. Another refugee was unable to retrieve his wife's body from Indonesia for the same reason.

◻ In August, 433 mostly Afghan asylum-seekers became the first of more than 2,500 people to be prevented from exercising their right to claim asylum in Australia. They were rescued from their sinking Indonesian boat by the crew of the Norwegian freighter *MV Tampa* off Australia's Christmas Island. The asylum-seekers were refused permission to land by both the Indonesian and Australian authorities and spent eight days in appalling conditions on board the *Tampa*. The Australian government denied access to a medical team sent by the organization *Médecins Sans Frontières* to provide humanitarian assistance to the asylum-seekers. Licensed and equipped for only 50 people, the *Tampa* sailed towards Christmas Island without Australian permission after sending a medical distress signal because of health problems among the asylum-seekers, some of whom threatened to jump overboard if returned to Indonesia. Armed Australian troops then boarded the *Tampa* and later transferred the asylum-seekers to an improvised detention centre in Nauru, an isolated South Pacific island state. In October, 131 of these asylum-seekers were flown to New Zealand which offered residency to those it assessed to be refugees.

Legislative changes
In September, Parliament hastily passed legislation aimed at curbing the smuggling of asylum-seekers into the country. Under the new legislation, people arriving at certain off-shore Australian islands were denied the right to claim asylum there. The laws created three classes of refugees whose rights and status depend on their manner of arrival in Australia. Recognized refugees on temporary visas were denied indefinitely permission to reunite with their children, spouse or other relatives living overseas, and more than 2,000 of them lost the right to seek permanent protection in Australia.

The laws also sought to narrow Australian interpretation of the 1951 UN Refugee Convention in a manner criticized by the UNHCR and non-governmental organizations. They widened the government's powers to arbitrarily detain asylum-seekers arriving without valid visas and to remove asylum-seekers to other countries for detention and determination of their refugee status. Australian courts can no longer hear cases against any government action or use of force to prevent the arrival of people, including asylum-seekers, suspected of trying to land without authorization.

Following elections in October, the newly elected Labor government of the Northern Territory amended controversial criminal legislation on mandatory minimum terms of imprisonment for both adults and juveniles convicted of offences involving damage to property. The amendments restore power to the courts to take into account the severity of an offence and other circumstances, and remove the requirement that repeat child offenders serve a minimum prison term irrespective of what damage they caused.

Conditions of detention
There were protests and riots in Australian immigration detention centres throughout the year. In October, the Western Australian Inspector of Custodial Services linked such riots to detention conditions, including unacceptable overcrowding, "disgracefully inadequate" medical services and a lack of accountability for detention staff.

In November, the Human Rights Commissioner launched a national inquiry into the situation of nearly 600 children detained as asylum-seekers in Australia; some had been held for as long as three years. In December, the Commission criticized detention conditions for asylum-seekers on Christmas Island, where it found women and children being held in a crowded sports hall without any separation from single men and with virtually no contact with the world outside. They were not allowed to use the telephone or send letters, read newspapers or listen to the radio, and were initially only allowed access to sunlight and fresh air for 20 minutes a day.

AI country reports/visits
Visit
In November, an AI delegate visited Australian-funded detention facilities on Nauru.

AUSTRIA

REPUBLIC OF AUSTRIA
Head of state: Thomas Klestil
Head of government: Wolfgang Schüssel
Capital: Vienna
Population: 8.1 million
Official language: German
Death penalty: abolitionist for all crimes

At least two gay men were imprisoned; they were prisoners of conscience. There were continuing allegations that police officers had ill-treated detainees and used excessive force. The European Committee for the Prevention of Torture and Inhuman or Degrading Treatment or Punishment (CPT) published the report of its 1999 visit to Austria. A date was set for the trial of three police officers in connection with the death of the deportee Marcus Omofuma in 1999. A man died in questionable circumstances in prison. In the aftermath of the attacks on 11 September in the USA, there were discussions about tightening up Austria's asylum procedures and alien legislation.

Unequal age of consent
There was heightened debate within Austrian society surrounding Article 209 of the Criminal Code. This sets the legal age of consent for heterosexuals and lesbians at 14 years of age, but that for gay men at 18. Gay men convicted of contravening Article 209 faced up to five years' imprisonment.

On 24 August, Vienna-Neustadt Regional Court sentenced a 36-year-old gay man to 15 months' imprisonment, of which 14 months were suspended, for having consensual sexual relations with his 17-year-old boyfriend. The state prosecutor's office contested the verdict, reportedly on the grounds that it was too lenient, and on 23 October, Vienna's Court of Appeal sentenced the 36-year-old man to a further four months' imprisonment.

◻ A gay man was arrested on 14 February, accused of having consensual sexual relations with a 15-year-old adolescent. The man remained in pre-trial detention until 27 February when a judge at Vienna Regional Criminal Court, which had issued the original arrest warrant and had authorized his detention thereafter, ordered his release, instructing him to pay compensation. At the end of the year this ruling was being contested by the state prosecutor's office.

Allegations of police ill-treatment

Allegations that police ill-treated detainees and used excessive force persisted. In June, the CPT published the report of its third visit to Austria in September 1999, reflecting a number of AI's concerns. On the basis of its fact-finding visits to a number of police jails, police stations and gendarmerie posts, the CPT recorded a number of complaints of police ill-treatment, although "... compared with the allegations received during earlier visits [in 1990 and 1994] the instances were less numerous and the ill-treatment less serious". Nevertheless, the CPT stated that the continuing allegations of ill-treatment clearly warranted vigilance on the part of the authorities. The majority of the complaints of ill-treatment encountered by the CPT during its 1999 visit were made by foreign nationals who alleged that they had been punched, kicked and slapped, especially while handcuffed. Police ill-treatment was most commonly alleged to have occurred at the time of arrest.

◻ In May, Vienna's Independent Administrative Tribunal upheld the allegations of a 25-year-old demonstrator, referred to as Martin P. in the Austrian news media, that he was ill-treated by police officers on 4 February during an anti-government demonstration, during which there were some reports of violence. A photographer from the *Austrian Press Association* had photographed the incident, reportedly clearly capturing on film several police officers repeatedly striking Martin P. with their batons as he lay on the ground.

◻ In July, the Independent Administrative Tribunal in Vienna stated that police officers subjected a detained demonstrator to a "humiliation ritual" by cutting off a 30cm piece of his hair with a knife, after knocking him to the ground. AI received several reports that police officers used excessive force against demonstrators or, in some cases, ill-treated them during an anti-government demonstration on 22 February in Vienna during which there were a significant number of violent incidents.

Safeguards against ill-treatment

In its report of its 1999 visit, the CPT made several recommendations to strengthen safeguards against ill-treatment. Most notably, any medical examination of a detainee should not take place within hearing or seeing distance of police officers, unless this is specifically requested by the doctor. In addition, people suspected of a crime should have the right of access to legal counsel from the moment of their arrest, a right not always accorded in Austria.

Death of Marcus Omofuma

March 2002 was set as the start-date for the trial of the three police officers accused of the ill-treatment of Marcus Omofuma which resulted in his death. The 25-year-old Nigerian asylum-seeker died on 1 May 1999 after being gagged and bound during his forced deportation from Vienna to Nigeria, via Sofia, Bulgaria. In May the results of a third autopsy conducted by a German specialist were made public and appeared to reinforce the findings of an initial autopsy conducted in Bulgaria shortly after the death, that Marcus Omofuma had died of asphyxia as a result of being gagged.

Abusive restraint techniques

A 56-year-old prisoner, referred to as Ernst K. in the Austrian news media, died in Krems-Stein prison during the night of 15/16 June. At the time of his death Ernst K.'s hands and legs had reportedly been strapped to the sides of his bed. The decision was made to restrain him after he reportedly experienced psychological difficulties. He was reportedly left completely immobilized until the following morning when prison officials found him dead, reportedly as a result of an obstruction to the intestines.

AI country reports/visits

Report
- Concerns in Europe, January-June 2001: Austria (AI Index: EUR 01/003/2001)

Visit
An AI delegate visited Austria in April and met representatives of non-governmental organizations and lawyers.

AZERBAIJAN

REPUBLIC OF AZERBAIJAN
Head of state: Heydar Aliyev
Head of government: Artur Rasizade
Capital: Baku
Population: 8.1 million
Official language: Azeri
Death penalty: abolitionist for all crimes
2001 treaty ratifications/signatures: (first) Optional Protocol to the International Covenant on Civil and Political Rights; Optional Protocol to the UN Women's Convention; European Convention for the Prevention of Torture and Inhuman or Degrading Treatment or Punishment; European Convention on Human Rights; Protocol No. 6 to the European Convention on Human Rights concerning abolition of the death penalty

At least two men died in detention, allegedly as a result of torture and ill-treatment. Demonstrators and political activists were detained for short periods of time, and some reportedly ill-treated in detention. As respect for media freedoms generally decreased, criminal defamation legislation was used to stifle apparently legitimate criticism of public officials. In the disputed region of Karabakh, conscientious objectors continued to face imprisonment.

Background

In January parliamentary elections were held again in constituencies where the results of the November 2000 ballots had been annulled owing to irregularities in the electoral process. Some opposition parties boycotted the elections. Observers for the Organization for Security and Co-operation in Europe (OSCE) reported that, despite improvements, there were again serious irregularities. These included stuffing of ballot boxes, multiple voting, a failure to follow counting procedures and artificially inflated turn-out figures.

Little progress was made in peace talks with Armenia, held under the auspices of the OSCE's Minsk group, regarding the status of the disputed region of Nagorno-Karabakh, where a ceasefire has been in place since 1993.

Torture and ill-treatment

Allegations of torture and ill-treatment by law enforcement officials persisted, in spite of Azerbaijan's commitments to uphold international and domestic laws and procedures prohibiting such practices. There were reports of ill-treatment by police, including of journalists, at several anti-government demonstrations. The UN Special Rapporteur on torture concluded in a report of his visit to Azerbaijan in May 2000 that torture or similar ill-treatment remained widespread.

▭ It was reported that on 12 May police officers in uniform and in plain clothes beat and injured at least eight journalists covering an unauthorized demonstration in Baku of an estimated 2,000 supporters of the opposition Democratic Party of Azerbaijan (ADP) who were demanding the release of political prisoners. They included Suleiman Mamedli, editor-in-chief of *Hurriet*, the ADP newspaper, who was reportedly beaten and briefly detained. According to reports, two newspaper journalists, Seimur Verdizade and Raghim Gadinov, were beaten by men in civilian clothing who broke their cassette recorders, and correspondents from Russian and Turkish television channels were assaulted and prevented from filming.

Deaths in custody

There were allegations that police ill-treatment had led to at least two deaths in custody.

▭ Ilgar Javadov, a 28-year-old oil company engineer, died following his detention at police station No. 9 in Baku's Sabail District on 13 May. His relatives reported that he died in the early hours of 13 May after being severely beaten by police officers and sustaining injuries such as fractures to the right arm, ribs and spine, and bruising to the legs and body. His lawyer reportedly said that a forensic examination had proved the cause of death was the beating. Official police sources reportedly said that he fell while trying to escape through a second-floor window of the police station and died before the ambulance arrived. Other reports indicated that three police officers were charged with incitement to suicide, later amended to "exceeding official powers with the use or threat of force", and that they were released from custody following a court hearing held at short notice in Sabail District. Demands by Ilgar Javadov's relatives for his body to be exhumed and for an autopsy to establish the exact cause of death had received no response by the end of 2001.

Conditions of detention

Reports suggested that conditions of detention in Gobustan Strict Regime Prison, where many political prisoners were detained, amounted to cruel, inhuman and degrading treatment.

▭ One political prisoner, Alakram Alakbar oglu Hummatov, was said to be held in a cell without ventilation, with an electric light permanently switched on and in temperatures of up to 44°C.

Possible prisoners of conscience

Criminal defamation charges were apparently used to intimidate and silence critics of the government.

▭ In September, four journalists were convicted on criminal defamation charges. Shakhbaz Khuduoglu, editor-in-chief of *Milletin Sesi* newspaper, was sentenced to six months' imprisonment and correspondent Gulnaz Qamberli to three months' imprisonment, suspended, after Ramiz Mehdiyev, Head of the Presidential Administration, complained about an article that *Milletin Sesi* had published about him. Elmar Huseynov, publisher of *Bakinsky Bulvar* newspaper, was sentenced to six months' imprisonment, and Bella Zakirova, editor-in-chief, to a six-month suspended sentence, after publishing an article alleging racketeering by officials. The two sentenced to imprisonment were released under a presidential pardon in October but investigations against them, and two other journalists investigated in connection with these cases, reportedly remained open at the end of the year.

UN Human Rights Committee

In November the UN Human Rights Committee released observations and comments on Azerbaijan's second periodic report to the Committee under the International Covenant on Civil and Political Rights. The Committee noted some positive developments, such as the transfer of the jurisdiction over detention facilities from the Ministry of the Interior to the Ministry of Justice and the abolition of the death penalty in 1998. It also expressed concern at a number of issues, including continuing reports of torture and other cruel, inhuman or degrading treatment; the failure to ensure application of international standards to prevent torture; reports that detainees' rights of access to legal counsel, medical advice and family visits were not always respected; prison overcrowding; and the use of criminal libel law to harass journalists.

The Committee also raised concerns that there was no independent mechanism for investigating complaints against police officers and prison guards and that new legislation regulating the legal profession could compromise lawyers' independence. Among other things, it recommended the establishment of an independent body to investigate complaints of abuses by law enforcement officials and initiate proceedings against those found responsible, and the institution of independent inspections of detention facilities.

Council of Europe

On joining the Council of Europe in January, Azerbaijan undertook a number of human rights obligations. The Secretary General instituted post-accession monitoring of Azerbaijan's commitments. They included ratifying, within a year of accession, the European Convention on Human Rights and its Protocol No. 6 concerning the abolition of the death penalty, and the European Convention for the Prevention of Torture and Inhuman or Degrading Treatment or Punishment. By the end of 2001, Azerbaijan had signed but not ratified these instruments. Another commitment was to adopt within one year a law on an ombudsperson. The procedure of appointment of the post in the law adopted by the Azerbaijani parliament in December failed to meet international standards.

In February the Council of Europe appointed independent experts to inquire into reports by human rights organizations of political imprisonment in Azerbaijan and Armenia. In October the experts reported that, on the basis of objective criteria, the case law of the European Court of Human Rights and Council of Europe standards, at least 17 prisoners could be defined as political prisoners in Azerbaijan.

Six were released under a presidential amnesty in August. The prison term of one was reduced in December. However, domestic non-governmental organizations said that hundreds more remained in detention, including 11 determined as political prisoners by the independent experts.

Nagorno-Karabakh

There were allegations of torture and unfair trial in the self-proclaimed Nagorno-Karabakh Republic, which is not recognized by the Azerbaijani authorities. The death penalty was retained but no death sentences or executions were reported.

Torture and unfair trial

In February, the Supreme Court of Nagorno-Karabakh sentenced former Defence Minister Samvel Babaian to 14 years' imprisonment for organizing an assassination attempt on Arkady Ghukasian, President of the self-proclaimed Republic, in March 2000. He was said to have been beaten severely and drugged following his arrest, and he retracted in court a statement he had made to police in April, reportedly under duress. A number of others convicted with him were reportedly sentenced to terms ranging from suspended prison sentences to up to 14 years in prison. Some were said to have been severely ill-treated and to have had inadequate access to their defence lawyers. The verdict was upheld on appeal in March by the board of the Supreme Court.

Prisoners of conscience

At least three young men were detained pending trial for conscientious objection to compulsory military service. All three were convicted of "evasion of military development call-up", and two were given custodial sentences. They had reportedly been released by the end of 2001.

AI country reports/ visits
Report
- Concerns in Europe, January-June 2001: Azerbaijan (AI Index: EUR 01/003/2001)

BAHAMAS

COMMONWEALTH OF THE BAHAMAS
Head of state: Queen Elizabeth II, represented by Orville Turnquest
Head of government: Hubert Alexander Ingraham
Capital: Nassau
Population: 0.3 million
Official language: English
Death penalty: retentionist

Prisoners continued to be held in conditions which amounted to cruel, inhuman and degrading treatment. There were reports of ill-treatment and brutality. A child was reported to have been raped in prison by other inmates. Death sentences continued to be imposed by the courts; no executions were carried out. At least 22 people remained on death row, including one woman. There was continued concern that asylum-seekers were returned to their countries of origin without access to a full and fair determination procedure, in violation of international standards.

Death penalty
At least 22 people, including one woman, remained on death row at the end of the year, according to official figures. Remanded prisoners continued to be held on death row with convicted prisoners.

Eddison Thurston, a death-row inmate, died in March in Fox Hill prison. In October a coroner's inquest jury found that he had committed suicide in his cell, and returned a verdict of gross negligence on the part of the prison service.

Prison conditions
There was continued concern that conditions within prisons constituted cruel, inhuman and degrading treatment. Reports persisted of severe overcrowding and of prisoners being locked in their cells for nearly 24 hours a day.

Reports of serious diseases among inmates and of inadequate medical treatment exacerbated fears about conditions of detention in prisons. In July, 100 prisoners were reported as having contracted tuberculosis, although the Ministry for National Security later stated that only 10 cases had been confirmed. Although the Ministry of Health announced in July that all inmates would be tested for tuberculosis, a doctor at Fox Hill prison complained in August that he had been refused permission by the prison authorities to carry out the tests.

Children continued to be detained with adults, putting them at risk of sexual and physical abuse.

International concern was expressed in October about reports that a 17-year-old inmate had been raped in August by three other inmates in Fox Hill prison. The acting prison superintendent publicly denied the allegations. The incident was still being investigated by police officers attached to the prison at the end of the year.

Asylum-seekers
Asylum-seekers from Haiti and Cuba continued to be forcibly returned without prior access to a full and fair determination procedure, in violation of international law. Many were also held in detention. In July several asylum-seekers died attempting to reach the Bahamas after the boat they were travelling in was shipwrecked.

In July AI urged the government of the Bahamas to ensure that Haitian nationals seeking asylum would be granted full and fair access to refugee determination procedures. The government replied that it believed that the majority of undocumented Haitian nationals attempting to enter the Bahamas were "economic migrants" and not genuine political refugees. The government stated that it used a systematic procedure, approved by the regional officer for the UN High Commissioner for Refugees (UNHCR), for the processing of undocumented foreign nationals. AI's request for further information about these procedures had not received a response by the end of the year.

Police ill-treatment
There were several reports alleging ill-treatment of detainees by police officers.

In April, two children and two men were allegedly ill-treated by police following their detention without charge by unidentified officers. All four suffered serious bruising resulting from beatings at the time of arrest and during their three-day detention by officers of the Criminal Investigations Department. Police allegedly placed plastic bags over their heads to try to obtain confessions.

BAHRAIN

STATE OF BAHRAIN
Head of state: Shaikh Hamad bin 'Issa Al Khalifa
Head of government: Shaikh Khalifa bin Salman Al Khalifa
Capital: al-Manama
Population: 0.7 million
Official language: Arabic
Death penalty: retentionist

Significant steps were taken in 2001 to promote and protect human rights. All political prisoners and detainees were released and the State Security Court and state security legislation were abolished. Bahraini nationals who had been forcibly exiled or prevented from entering the country were allowed to return without conditions. An Ethiopian woman remained under sentence of death.

Background
In February the Amir declared a general amnesty as a result of which all political prisoners and detainees were released. Among those released were four prisoners of conscience — 'Abd al-Wahab Hussain, Sayyid Ibrahim 'Adnan al-'Alawi, Shaikh Hassan Sultan and Hassan 'Ali Mshaima' — who had been held without charge or trial since 1996.

In February, the authorities announced that 108 Bahraini nationals who had been forcibly exiled or prevented from entering the country would be allowed to return. This was later extended to all Bahraini nationals living abroad, without conditions. Some, like 'Abdul Rahman al-Nu'aimi, had lived in forced exile for more than 30 years.

In the same month, the State Security Court was abolished and the 1974 Decree Law on State Security Measures was repealed. These measures had allowed the Ministry of the Interior to detain people without charge or trial for up to three years.

The authorities granted Bahraini citizenship to scores of stateless people living in Bahrain and Bahraini nationals who had lived in forced exile abroad. By the end of the year, 7,000 others were said to have applied for citizenship.

In February, Bahraini men and women voted by a majority of 98.4 per cent in favour of a proposed National Charter. The Charter provided for the establishment of an elected parliament with legislative powers, in addition to the appointed *Shura* (Consultative) Council, and for Bahrain to become a constitutional monarchy. Elections for the second chamber were due to be held before the end of 2003. The Charter also included reference to the protection and promotion of human rights, freedom of expression, the right of women to vote and stand for election, as well as the setting up of non-governmental organizations, an independent judiciary and a constitutional court. A committee headed by the Crown Prince, was set up to activate the National Charter. One of the committee's tasks was to review Bahraini legislation, including the Press and Publications Law, Trade Unions Law and the 1989 Law on Social and Cultural Societies and Clubs, and to submit recommendations to the government.

Human rights and political developments
In March the non-governmental Bahraini Human Rights Society (BHRS) was officially registered. A previous request to set up the organization made in August 2000 had been rejected by the authorities. The BHRS was reported to have helped 39 people who had been forcibly exiled during the 1980s and 1990s to recover their Bahraini citizenship in July.

In August the Amir ordered the setting up of a Supreme Council of Women and in November, 16 women members were appointed to the Council. Among the Council's key aims was the development and promotion of women's rights.

During the year scores of political opponents of the government who had been living abroad returned to the country. Many gave interviews to the local media and organized seminars where political, social and human rights issues were debated. Specific concerns were raised about freedom of the press and equal job opportunities.

Political movements of various tendencies emerged in the form of associations, some of which were officially recognized. In September, the Association for National Democratic Action became the first association to be officially registered under the leadership of 'Abdul Rahman al-Nu'aimi. The Progressive Democratic Forum and the Islamic National Reconciliation Association were recognized in October and November respectively.

Freedom of expression
In November a legal action was initiated by the Ministry of Information against Hafidh al-Shaikh, a freelance journalist, for "attempting to undermine national unity" and "violating press and publications laws". Hafidh al-Shaikh was banned from writing in the local press and from travelling abroad. The Ministry's action was taken reportedly in connection with articles that he had written for the foreign press, in which he criticized Bahrain's strong support for the bombing campaign in Afghanistan by the USA and its allies. In December Hafidh al-Shaikh began legal proceedings against the Ministry of Information to challenge the ban.

Torture and ill-treatment
In December, two people from al-Manama, Mohammad al-Sayyid Hashim Sa'id al-'Alawi, aged 23, and Hussain Ghulum Hassan 'Ali Murad, aged 21, were said to have been subjected to beatings by police officers at al-Hura Police Station. They were detained for two days before they were released on bail. The reasons for their detention were unclear.

Intergovernmental organizations
In July, Bahrain submitted its report on implementation of the UN Children's Convention. UN-sponsored

seminars and workshops on racism and on human rights education and awareness were organized by the BHRS and the Human Rights Committee, which was set up within the *Shura* Council in 1999. In October, delegates of the UN Working Group on Arbitrary Detention (WGAD) visited Bahrain, held talks with government officials and others, visited prisons and met former detainees. The WGAD was due to report its findings at the UN Commission on Human Rights session in April 2002.

Death penalty
Yoshork Dostazudi, a 21-year-old Ethiopian woman sentenced to death for murder in 2000, remained under sentence of death at the end of the year.

AI country reports/ visits
Visits
AI delegates visited Bahrain in March and held talks with the Amir, the Crown Prince and government officials. AI visited the country again in November.

BANGLADESH

PEOPLE'S REPUBLIC OF BANGLADESH
Head of state: Badruddoza Chowdhury (replaced Shahabuddin Ahmed in November)
Head of government: Begum Khaleda Zia (replaced Sheikh Hasina in October)
Capital: Dhaka
Population: 140.4 million
Official language: Bangla
Death penalty: retentionist

Political violence in advance of elections resulted in about 150 deaths. There were high levels of violence against minorities, particularly Hindus. Impunity for perpetrators of human rights violations was widespread. Religious groups sought to overturn a landmark High Court judgment which banned *fatwas*, religious edicts most often issued against women. Women continued to be subjected to violent attacks in their homes and communities. Three executions were carried out, the first for over three years.

Political developments
A caretaker government took power in July to organize parliamentary elections in October. The Bangladesh Nationalist Party (BNP), formerly Bangladesh's main opposition party, won more than two thirds of the seats in alliance with three other parties including *Jamaat-e-Islami*. BNP leader Begum Khaleda Zia was sworn in as Prime Minister in October. The unopposed presidential nominee, Badruddoza Chowdhury, was declared President in November.

In the run-up to the elections, there were violent clashes between BNP and Awami League supporters in which about 150 people were killed and thousands injured. The former ruling party, the Awami League, alleged that the elections were rigged and boycotted Parliament.

Violence against minorities
Following the elections, hundreds of Hindu families were reportedly subjected to violent attacks, including rape, beatings and the burning of their property. They were allegedly attacked by BNP supporters because of their perceived support for the Awami League. In November, a prominent member of the Hindu community was killed while hundreds of families reportedly fled to India. The police failed to take effective measures to protect the community; some arrests were made but most assailants were not brought to justice. No information was provided about an official investigation into the atrocities, promised in November and December. In response to a petition in November by the legal aid organization, *Ain-o-Salish Kendra*, the High Court gave the government one month to explain why it did not protect Hindus. No explanation was provided by the end of the year.

On 22 November, Shahriar Kabir, a prominent writer and journalist, was detained by police on his return from India. In December, he was charged with sedition but the authorities did not make public the evidence to support the charge. His detention appeared to be solely because he had been investigating the situation of Hindus who fled persecution in Bangladesh. He was still held in Dhaka Central Jail under the Special Powers Act at the end of 2001.

Other minorities suffered attacks. In June, 10 people were killed and more than 20 wounded in a bomb explosion in a church in Baniarchar, Gopalgonj district. Violent clashes between tribal inhabitants and Bengali settlers continued to be reported in the Chittagong Hill Tracts. Three women from the Jumma minority were allegedly raped in May by army personnel; no one was known to have been brought to justice.

Women's rights
Women continued to be subjected to violent attacks, including rape. Dozens reportedly died in dowry-related murders. Acid attacks left many severely scarred. The authorities rarely provided adequate protection or means of redress. The failure of the police to investigate and take legal action against perpetrators of violence against women engendered a climate of impunity.

By launching an appeal to the Supreme Court, religious groups sought to overturn a landmark High Court judgment in January which banned *fatwas*, which were often used to repress women's rights.

Torture and prison conditions
Widespread beatings and other ill-treatment by the police and the armed forces persisted with impunity. At least 30 people reportedly died in custody as a result of torture. The authorities appeared to ignore torture allegations. The new government promised in October to repeal the Special Powers Act and the Public Safety Act but continued to use them to detain people for long periods without charge or trial.

Thousands of people awaited trial in overcrowded prisons. In July large numbers of people were detained during a drive to recover unlawful weapons, forcing prisoners to have to take turns to lie down to sleep.

Death penalty
Two men were hanged in February, marking a resumption of executions after more than three years. Another man was hanged in November. At least 20 people were sentenced to death in 2001.

▭ In the latest ruling in April, the death sentences of 12 army officers, accused of the killing of Sheikh Mujibur Rahman and his family, were upheld by the High Court. Four of those convicted were detained in Bangladesh.

AI country reports/visits
Report
- Bangladesh: Attacks on members of the Hindu minority (AI Index: ASA 13/006/2001)

Visit
AI delegates visited Bangladesh in March to take part in an AI-organized human rights defenders seminar.

BELARUS

REPUBLIC OF BELARUS
Head of state: Alyaksandr Lukashenka
Head of government: Gennady Novitsky (replaced Vladimir Yermoshin in October)
Capital: Minsk
Population: 10.1 million
Official languages: Belarusian, Russian
Death penalty: retentionist
2001 treaty ratifications/signatures: UN Refugee Convention and its Protocol

No progress was made in clarifying the spate of possible "disappearances" in Belarus in 1999. At least two long-term prisoners of conscience were held and hundreds of people were detained for their peaceful opposition activities. There were further allegations of ill-treatment of detainees, particularly members of the opposition. Human rights defenders faced harassment and intimidation. Executions of people sentenced to death continued to be carried out in secret and without prior notification to the relatives.

Background
President Alyaksandr Lukashenka was re-elected in September. There were serious concerns about the fairness of the elections and the outcome was disputed by Belarus' opposition as well as many foreign governments. The pre-election period was marred by numerous accounts of arbitrary action on the part of the state aimed at stifling the peaceful activities of the opposition. Police raided the offices of election-monitoring organizations and independent newspapers and confiscated office equipment and election materials. People were arbitrarily detained; some faced continued persecution after the election because of their opposition activities.

Possible 'disappearances'
▭ No progress was made in determining who was responsible for the abduction and apparent killing in 1999 of several prominent political opponents of President Lukashenka. The former Minister of the Interior, Yury Zakharenko; the first secretary chairman of the dissolved parliament, the 13th Supreme Soviet Viktor Gonchar; and his companion, Anatoly Krasovsky, apparently "disappeared" in May and September 1999. The investigations conducted by the Belarusian authorities into the possible "disappearances" repeatedly drew domestic and international criticism for their lack of impartiality and transparency.

There were reports in June that two officials of the Prosecutor General's Office assigned to investigate the possible "disappearances" fled to the USA, where they obtained asylum. They alleged that officials in President Lukashenka's immediate circle of appointees had employed the elite *Almaz* police group to eliminate a number of members of Belarus' opposition.

◻ The trial of four men accused of abducting and killing the *Russian Public Television* cameraman, Dmitry Zavadsky, in July 2000, began in Minsk on 24 October 2001. Two of the accused men were reported to be past and present members of the elite *Almaz* police group, linked to a spate of other possible "disappearances" in the country. The trial, which was held behind closed doors, was still continuing at the end of the year.

Prisoners of conscience

◻ On 18 June, 43-year-old Professor Yury Bandazhevsky was sentenced by the Military Collegium of the Belarusian Supreme Court in the city of Gomel to eight years' imprisonment in a strict penal colony with confiscation of property. He was convicted on charges of taking bribes from students seeking admission to the Gomel Medical Institute, of which he was the former rector. However, his conviction was widely believed to be related to his outspoken criticism of the Belarusian authorities' reaction to the Chernobyl nuclear reactor catastrophe of 1986. International and domestic trial observers considered that not only was the basis of Yury Bandazhevsky's conviction extremely weak, but his right to a fair trial had been repeatedly violated.

◻ Andrey Klimov, a 36-year-old deputy in the dissolved parliament and political opponent of President Lukashenka, remained imprisoned in Minsk. He had been sentenced in March 2000 to six years' imprisonment with confiscation of property on charges of corruption. However, the real reason for his imprisonment was believed to be his opposition activities.

◻ On 5 February, Vladimir Koudinov was released in an amnesty after serving four years in prison. He had originally been sentenced to seven years' imprisonment in August 1997 on charges of bribing a police officer. Vladimir Koudinov had taken an active role in attempting to impeach President Lukashenka for dissolving parliament in November 1996.

Torture and ill-treatment

In January the UN Special Rapporteur on torture stated in his report that he shared the concerns about Belarus expressed by the UN Committee against Torture in November 2000. Among the concerns were numerous continuing allegations of torture and other cruel, inhuman or degrading punishment or treatment, particularly affecting political opponents of the government and peaceful demonstrators; and the pattern of failure of the authorities to promptly and impartially investigate such allegations and prosecute alleged perpetrators.

Detention of protesters

There were numerous reports that people were detained for exercising their rights to freedom of expression and peaceful assembly. Several opposition activists were detained for up to 15 days. Detainees often alleged that police officers either used unnecessary force to detain them or ill-treated them.

◻ Throughout 2001 a significant number of activists of the newly emerged youth pro-democracy and human rights organization, ZUBR, served periods of imprisonment after being detained on account of their peaceful protest activities. On 21 April, 33 young people were detained during a peaceful anti-presidential event in Gorky Park in Minsk. Fourteen of the 33 youths remained in detention at Okrestina detention centre in Minsk until 25 April when they were brought before a court, which sentenced them to three days' imprisonment for taking part in an unauthorized demonstration. They were released immediately as the sentence was applied to the days they had been detained prior to trial.

Harsh conditions of detention

Protesters detained during peaceful demonstrations frequently complained about the conditions in which they were held. Conditions in places of detention and prisons fell well below international standards and often amounted to cruel, inhuman and degrading treatment.

◻ On 12 June, 60-year-old prisoner of conscience Valery Schukin, a veteran human rights defender, independent journalist and member of the dissolved parliament, began a three-month prison sentence for his opposition activities. He served his sentence in Zhodino prison where, upon arrival, officials forcibly shaved off his long beard using a blunt razor. Twenty days of the sentence were spent in isolation in a punishment cell after Valery Schukin reportedly attempted to inform other prisoners of their rights.

Human rights defenders

Individuals engaged in the defence and promotion of human rights faced considerable obstacles in the course of their work, which appeared to be part of a deliberate campaign by the Belarusian authorities to frustrate and undermine their activities.

In February the UN Special Rapporteur on the independence of judges and lawyers, published the report of his visit to Belarus in June 2000. The report commented on the lack of independence of the judiciary in Belarus and on the pressure exerted on certain human rights lawyers. The report stated that: "[l]awyers must be allowed to practise their profession without any harassment, intimidation, hindrance or improper interference from the Government or any other quarter."

Death penalty

Death sentences continued to be imposed in Belarus. Owing to the veil of secrecy surrounding information about the death penalty, which continued to be classed as a state secret, no reliable figure could be obtained regarding the number of executions.

AI country reports/visits

Reports
- Belarus: Briefing for the UN Committee against Torture (AI Index: EUR 49/002/2001)
- Belarus: In the spotlight of the state — human rights defenders in Belarus (AI Index: EUR 49/005/2001)

- Belarus: Professor Yury Bandazhevsky — prisoner of conscience (AI Index: EUR 49/008/2001)

Visits
AI delegates visited Brest, Gomel, Minsk, Mogilov and Vitebsk in February and March.

BELGIUM

KINGDOM OF BELGIUM
Head of state: King Albert II
Head of government: Guy Verhhofstadt
Capital: Brussels
Population: 10.3 million
Official languages: Dutch, French, German
Death penalty: abolitionist for all crimes

There were new allegations that criminal suspects were ill-treated by law enforcement officers and that asylum-seekers were ill-treated during forcible deportation operations. By the end of 2001 no one had been brought to justice in connection with the death in 1998 of an asylum-seeker who was asphyxiated after gendarmes pressed a cushion over her face during forcible deportation. There was concern that the treatment of detained child asylum-seekers, who included unaccompanied minors, was not in line with international standards on the treatment of children. There was also concern that new administrative measures introduced to accelerate asylum procedures had eroded access to fair and impartial refugee determination procedures. The level of prison overcrowding, together with understaffing, prompted strikes by prison guards. Four Rwandese nationals were convicted in Belgium of war crimes committed in Rwanda in 1994. A parliamentary inquiry concluded that members of the Belgian government and other Belgian participants were "morally responsible" for the circumstances leading to the assassination of Patrice Lumumba in 1961, seven months after he became the first democratically elected prime minister of the newly independent African state of Congo, but found no evidence that they had ordered his "physical elimination".

Police ill-treatment
On the streets and in police stations
There were further allegations of ill-treatment and racist abuse by police officers. In its annual report to parliament in March, the Standing Police Monitoring Committee recorded an exponential increase in the number of complaints made against law enforcement officers, including scores relating to physical assault, threats, and verbal, including racist, abuse. It said that such complaints rarely resulted in criminal sanctions. The Centre for Equal Opportunities and Opposition to Racism recorded for the second year running a decrease in the number of complaints of racism and discrimination concerning law enforcement officers, but nevertheless indicated receipt of dozens of complaints against officers, around a third of which related to ill-treatment.

During its third visit to Belgium carried out in November, the European Committee for the Prevention of Torture and Inhuman or Degrading Treatment or Punishment (CPT) reviewed the measures taken by the authorities in response to the recommendations made after its previous visits regarding the introduction of certain fundamental safeguards against ill-treatment in the custody of law enforcement officers, including the right of immediate access to a lawyer.

Emily Apple, a British citizen detained in the context of demonstrations during a European Union summit in Brussels in December, complained to the Belgian authorities that, while leaving a demonstration, a group of men, whom she later learned were plainclothes police officers, hit her around the head and kicked her legs from under her, forcing her to lie face down on the pavement. After being handcuffed and photographed she was informed that she and others had been detained after failing to obey an order to disperse. She claimed that no such order had been given and that she was held in a police station until the early hours of the next morning, together with some 20 other women. She said all of them were detained during demonstrations and denied access to lawyers. She was released without charge, after being subjected to verbal abuse by police officers.

An army colonel from the Republic of the Congo alleged that, while attending a training course with the Belgian armed forces, he saw police ill-treating and harassing black African men during identity checks on the Brussels metro. He claimed that when he intervened he was himself assaulted and detained, along with an army colleague, a co-national. He said that they were held overnight in police cells, handcuffed throughout, given no explanation for their detention and then released without charge. Belgian army authorities indicated that one of them had visible injuries following the incidents. The police stated that the two men had shown violence towards the Belgian police officers carrying out the identity checks.

During deportation and in detention facilities
There were reports that police officers subjected some foreign nationals who were resisting deportation to physical assault, death threats and racist abuse, and deprived them of food and drink for many hours.

In some instances deportees were reported to have received inadequate medical attention for injuries incurred during deportation operations. There were also allegations that dangerous restraint methods, which restricted breathing, were sometimes used to subdue deportees. These allegations included using material to cover the mouth, thus blocking the airway. Some official investigations into such allegations appeared inadequate or subject to delays, with complainants often at risk of deportation while investigations were still under way.

In October, after it emerged that police officers were being paid a special allowance for acting as escorts during deportation operations but received only half the allowance if the operation had to be abandoned before the deportee left the country, fears were expressed that the practice could encourage use of excessive force by police. The Minister of the Interior stated that he favoured the same allowance being paid to all escorting officers, whatever the outcome of the operation.

The CPT stated that during its November visit it examined in detail "the procedures and means applied during the repatriation by air of foreign nationals."

☐ Ibrahim Bah, an asylum-seeker from Sierra Leone, alleged that he was subjected to physical assault, excessive force, dangerous restraint methods, threats and verbal abuse during several unsuccessful attempts to deport him between January and May. He alleged that during such attempts in April and May, police officers kicked and beat him while he was bound hand and foot, exerted heavy pressure on his carotid artery, used their legs and a cushion to press down heavily on his ribcage and forced a handkerchief into his mouth. Individuals who visited him after these deportation attempts reported that he displayed visible injuries. Medical reports issued by a privately hired doctor who examined Ibrahim Bah concluded that the overall symptoms and injuries recorded were consistent with his allegations and, following an examination the day after the final attempt in May, prescribed further examinations and medication. A member of parliament who visited him in prison 10 days later reported that he had still not received any of the prescribed treatment. The Minister of the Interior responded that Ministry-appointed doctors had examined Ibrahim Bah five days after the final attempt in May but had recorded no particular injuries or evidence of deliberate medical neglect. He said that a report by the General Inspectorate of Police concluded that police had scrupulously respected prescribed procedures and that the allegations could not be proved. Following his release from prison, although still liable to deportation, Ibrahim Bah lodged a criminal complaint about his treatment.

☐ A letter addressed to the Prime Minister in October by over 50 members of parliament expressed concern about allegations made by Mohamed Konteh, another asylum-seeker from Sierra Leone, who claimed he suffered ill-treatment, threats and racist abuse during numerous attempts to deport him between June and October. He said that police officers used various methods to cover his mouth, and that during one attempted deportation he was beaten until he defecated involuntarily, then tied up inside a blanket, wearing his soiled garments, and left in this condition for several hours. Individuals, including members of parliament, who visited him while in detention following failed deportation attempts, reported that he displayed visible injuries, and a medical report issued by a privately hired doctor in October recorded injuries consistent with some of his allegations. There was no indication of official steps being taken to investigate the allegations.

Semira Adamu

Criminal proceedings had still not been concluded in connection with the death in 1998 of Semira Adamu, a Nigerian national, who died after gendarmes pressed a cushion over her face during a deportation operation. In December 2000, the Brussels Public Prosecutor's Office had requested that three of the escorting gendarmes be charged with manslaughter but not with violation of Belgian anti-racism legislation, as had been requested by civil parties to the proceedings. In April 2001, a Brussels court heard part of the submissions of the various parties to the proceedings and further hearings were scheduled for May. However, by then Semira Adamu's relatives had lodged a new criminal complaint with the Public Prosecutor's Office against another four gendarmerie officers, including the colonel in charge of the airport deportation unit and a gendarme who filmed the deportation operation without intervening. Further hearings before the court were postponed and the proceedings were still open at the end of the year.

Universal jurisdiction

Legislation enacted in 1993 and 1999 made specific provision for Belgian courts to exercise universal jurisdiction over war crimes in international and non-international armed conflict, genocide and crimes against humanity, including torture.

In the context of this legislation, between 1998 and the end of the year, criminal complaints, some of which were still pending declarations of admissibility, had been lodged with Belgian courts against several leaders and prominent members of past and present administrations in over 15 foreign states.

In June, following Belgium's first trial based on universal jurisdiction, the Brussels Court of Assizes convicted four Rwandese nationals resident in Belgium of war crimes committed in the context of the 1994 genocide in Rwanda and sentenced them to between 12 and 20 years' imprisonment. One of the accused was found guilty of some charges and not guilty of others. The other three accused, including two Roman Catholic nuns, were convicted of all charges and subsequently entered appeals against their sentences. AI publicly welcomed the judgment as a significant step in the fight against impunity and called on Belgium not to weaken its universal jurisdiction legislation in any way.

AI country reports/visits
Report
- Concerns in Europe, January-June 2001: Belgium (AI Index: EUR 01/003/2001)

BELIZE

BELIZE
Head of state: Queen Elizabeth II, represented by Colville Young
Head of government: Said Musa
Capital: Belmopan
Population: 0.2 million
Official language: English
Death penalty: retentionist
2001 treaty ratifications/signatures: UN Convention against Racism

There were several reports of torture and killings in disputed circumstances by police officers. Four people were sentenced to death and two others saw their sentences commuted. No one was executed. Five trade unionists were expelled from the country, reportedly because of their union activities. Their expulsion orders were subsequently revoked by Prime Minister Said Musa.

Killings in disputed circumstances

Several reports of police shootings in disputed circumstances were received in 2001. In some cases an investigation was announced, but the outcome was not known at the end of the year.

George Michael Hyde, whom police apparently suspected of drug dealing, was shot by police in October after he refused to stop at a roadblock at the entrance to Benque Viejo Town. The police claimed that George Michael Hyde had fired at them and was killed when they returned fire. The family contested this version as there were no bullets holes in the car, there was no blood on the front seat and he had bruises on his face.

A police officer shot 18-year-old Frederick Reynolds in an apparent revenge attack. Frederick Reynolds had testified against the officer in a case about police brutality. Police claimed that the officer's gun went off accidentally, hitting Frederick Reynolds. However, a witness already in custody stated that he saw the officer throw Frederick Reynolds into the vehicle and begin beating him. The officer then reportedly pulled out a gun and shot Frederick Reynolds in the chest. By the end of the year, the Police Department had sent all statements to the Director of Public Prosecutions for the investigation, but no report had been made public.

Torture and ill-treatment

Human rights organizations, lawyers and journalists reported that ill-treatment and torture by the security forces were widespread, but were often not reported because victims feared reprisals.

Seventeen-year-old Francis Westby was said to have been brutally beaten by police during arrest on 23 July. A witness said that the police hit Francis Westby several times, pushed his head into a pool of water and continued to beat him as they escorted him to their vehicle. The Police Internal Affairs Unit opened an investigation, but the outcome was not known at the end of the year.

Prisons

Prison conditions reportedly remained very poor. Among the main concerns were insanitary conditions, partly as a result of overcrowding, and reports that minors were in some cases imprisoned with adults. People convicted and sentenced to periods of up to three months' imprisonment can be held in district police stations, where conditions were said to be poor. The Penal System Reform (Alternative Sentences) Bill 2001, due to be enacted in January 2002, lists a number of minor offences for which offenders can be sentenced to a community service order rather than imprisonment. This was part of an effort to reduce the prison population.

Corporal punishment

Corporal punishment continued to be inflicted. The punishment was reinstituted in prisons in February 2000.

Frederick Arzu and John Elijio each received four lashes with a tamarind whip on 4 September for escaping from jail.

Death penalty

In February in Barbados, the Caribbean Community (CARICOM) states signed an historic agreement establishing the Caribbean Court of Justice (CCJ) to replace the Judicial Committee of the Privy Council (JCPC) in London, United Kingdom, as the final court of appeal for Belize and the Commonwealth Caribbean. The CCJ had not been set up by the end of the year.

The last execution in Belize took place in 1985. However, 13 people remained on death row at the end of 2001. During 2001, four men were sentenced to death. Two others sentenced to death in 1993 and 1994 had their sentences commuted to life in prison, in accordance with previous JCPC jurisprudence regarding individuals who have spent five or more years on death row.

Trade unionists

On 5 September the Minister of Immigration issued an expulsion order against five banana workers and trade unionists. The men had recently been fired from their jobs, allegedly because of their trade union activities. On 6 September, four of the men, two Belizean nationals and two permanent residents, were expelled to Honduras. One day later the Prime Minister revoked the order and the four men were allowed to return to Belize.

BHUTAN

KINGDOM OF BHUTAN
Head of state: King Jigme Singye Wangchuck
Head of government: Khandu Wangchuk (replaced Yeshey Zimba in August)
Capital: Thimphu
Population: 0.6 million
Official language: Dzongkha
Death penalty: abolitionist in practice

A team of Bhutanese and Nepalese officials began verifying the status of the almost 100,000 Nepali-speaking people from southern Bhutan living in refugee camps in eastern Nepal. It was intended that the process would identify those eligible for return to Bhutan, nearly 10 years after most had left or been forced to leave. A possible prisoner of conscience was arrested and at least 65 political prisoners from southern and eastern Bhutan continued to serve long prison sentences.

Background
The Trade and Industry Minister, Khandu Wangchuk, took office as Chairman of the Council of Ministers in August. The National Assembly of Bhutan passed the Civil and Criminal Procedure Code. The codification was part of an ongoing process to strengthen the rule of law. In December, a committee was appointed to draft a Constitution for Bhutan.

There was tension in the refugee camps in Jhapa and Morang districts, in eastern Nepal, attributed to the slow progress of the verification process and the killing in September of the leader of a political party in exile, the Bhutan People's Party. The Bhutan Independent Students' Revolutionary Army, a previously unknown group, claimed responsibility for the killing.

UN Convention on the Rights of the Child
The UN Committee on the Rights of the Child considered the report submitted by Bhutan in June and expressed concern about the impact on children of reported discrimination against the Nepali-speaking community in the south. It also recommended the government consider the establishment of an independent national human rights institution.

Nepali-speaking refugees
On 26 March a joint verification team, comprising officials from the governments of Bhutan and Nepal, began interviewing 12,500 Nepali-speaking people living in Khudunabari, one of seven refugee camps run by the UN High Commissioner for Refugees (UNHCR) in eastern Nepal. This followed an agreement between the two governments which had been reached at the meeting of the Ministerial Joint Committee (MJC) in December 2000. Each family head was required to complete a form giving details of the family, thus "validating" relationships. There was concern about the slow progress of the verification. The verification process in Khudunabari camp was completed on 12 December, representing approximately 12.5 per cent of the total refugee population.

Although at the August meeting of the MJC in Thimphu both governments agreed to accelerate the verification process, by the end of the year the team had not been increased as proposed, and the number of those interviewed had not increased substantially. No agreement was reached during talks on 6 November between the Foreign Secretaries of both countries on the categorization of the people in the refugee camps. The government of Bhutan rejected Nepal's proposal that the four categories agreed in 1993 should be reduced to two (Bhutanese and non-Bhutanese).

International non-governmental organizations expressed concern that no efforts had been made to establish an independent monitoring or referral body for cases in dispute, and no third party, such as the UNHCR, had been given an active role in monitoring and facilitating the process.

There were continuing reports of the resettlement of northern and eastern Bhutanese people on land formerly belonging to Nepali-speaking southern Bhutanese people now living in the refugee camps. Discrimination was alleged against Nepali-speaking Bhutanese when seeking work, business licences or permission to travel abroad.

Detention of possible prisoners of conscience
Damber Pulami, a refugee living in Timai refugee camp in Jhapa district, Nepal, was arrested and detained by police on 26 May at Kamikhola, Sarbhang district. Damber Pulami was believed to be a member of the youth wing of the Bhutan People's Party. He had reportedly gone to Bhutan to monitor resettlement in the district.

Fifteen political prisoners, including possible prisoners of conscience, arrested during demonstrations in eastern Bhutan in 1997, continued to serve long prison sentences. In addition, an estimated 50 prisoners arrested around 1990 in southern Bhutan remained in prison. None had been given permission to appeal against their sentences.

Religious intolerance
In April, several members of the small Christian community were reportedly harassed and warned against practising their faith in public.

BOLIVIA

REPUBLIC OF BOLIVIA
Head of state and government: Jorge Quiroga Ramírez (replaced Hugo Banzer Suárez in August)
Capital: La Paz
Population: 8.5 million
Official language: Spanish
Death penalty: abolitionist for ordinary crimes

Ill-treatment of detainees by members of the armed forces continued to be reported. Excessive use of force and killings by members of the security forces in disputed circumstances occurred in El Chapare region and during demonstrations. Human rights defenders continued to suffer attacks and harassment, including death threats.

Background
In August, Vice-President Jorge Quiroga Ramírez was sworn in as President following the resignation of President Hugo Banzer Suárez. During both administrations the issues of economic restructuring and the increasing militarization of El Chapare region led to violent confrontations between demonstrators and members of the security forces. In December an Argentine federal judge requested the provisional arrest, pending requests for extradition, of former President Hugo Banzer Suárez for his alleged involvement in a criminal plan characterized by a systematic pattern of forced disappearances known as "Operation Condor".

Suppression of demonstrations
There were reports that the security forces ill-treated peaceful protesters, and may have used excessive force to break up demonstrations. In April, a number of people, including women, were beaten during a march for "People's Life and Sovereignty". Several participants, including members of the *Asamblea Permanente de Derechos Humanos* (APDH), Permanent Human Rights Assembly, were arbitrarily detained by the security forces. Journalists who tried to cover the events were attacked. Several deaths were recorded. Organizers were repeatedly harassed. Oscar Olivera, a spokesman for the mobilizing committee of the march publicly expressed his concern at a list reported to be circulating of people, including himself, who were to be "eliminated". There was no information on investigations reportedly initiated into these incidents.

During the march the police tried to disperse the crowd by throwing tear gas canisters, allegedly causing the deaths of two people. The police reportedly claimed that they had acted in response to being stoned by the crowd but this version was disputed by witnesses.

◻ Ezequiel Daniel Vela Cuba, was reportedly killed by a tear gas canister which witnesses said was fired at point-blank range.

Killings in El Chapare
Several people were killed during operations by the security forces to eradicate coca-leaf crops which often appeared to involve excessive use of force. There were reports that investigations into the incidents had been initiated under the military justice system.

◻ Ramón Pérez was killed in September when members of the police and army Joint Task Force fired at a group of six journalists he was taking to visit a military camp in Loma Alto.

◻ In October Nilda Escobar Aguilar died during confrontations near Isarzama between peasants and members of the Joint Task Force after being hit by a tear gas canister.

Human rights defenders
Attacks on and harassment of human rights defenders and members of their families were reported during the year.

◻ In January, a member of the *Unidad Móvil para el Patrullaje Rural* (UMOPAR), Mobile Rural Patrol Unit, shot at two representatives of the Ombudsperson's Office in El Chapare as they approached the community of Nuevo Tacaparí, Cochabamba department, to investigate reports of human rights violations. The District Attorney's Office reportedly opened an investigation.

Members of APDH continued to be targets of harassment.

◻ Waldo Albarracín, national president of APDH, and his family received death threats in February and March.

◻ The arrest of Adalberto Rojas, regional president of APDH in Santa Cruz, was ordered by a provincial prosecutor investigating the arrests of students.

Refugees
Several political refugees and immigrants from Peru reported discrimination and harassment by the security forces. Many feared being returned to Peru where they claimed they would face ill-treatment.

◻ Rumaldo Juan Pacheco Osco and his wife, Fredesvinda Tineo Godos, were detained in La Paz in February by officials of the Bolivian *Servicio Nacional de Migración*, National Migration Service, and handed over, together with their three children, to the Peruvian police. In Peru the couple were reportedly transferred to the *Sala Nacional Corporativa*, National Corporative Court, which deals with cases of "terrorism". They were eventually released.

Intergovernmental organizations
In May the UN Committee against Torture examined Bolivia's initial report on the implementation of the UN Convention against Torture. In its concluding observations and recommendations, the Committee noted the lack of human rights training provided to law enforcement officials and members of the armed forces. It also noted the number of complaints by detainees of torture and other cruel, inhuman or degrading treatment, on many occasions resulting in deaths, and the impunity for alleged perpetrators

arising from the slow pace and inadequacy of investigations into complaints. The Committee was concerned at the lack of effective action by the authorities to eradicate these practices and, in particular, the gross dereliction of duty on the part of the Public Prosecutor's Office and the courts. It also noted the excessive and disproportionate use of force and of firearms by the police and the armed forces in suppressing mass demonstrations.

AI country reports/ visits
Reports
- Bolivia: A summary of Amnesty International's concerns presented to the Bolivian Minister of Justice and Human Rights (AI Index: AMR 18/006/2001)
- Bolivia: Torture and ill-treatment – Amnesty International's concerns (AI Index: AMR 18/008/2001)

BOSNIA-HERZEGOVINA

BOSNIA-HERZEGOVINA
Head of state: three-member rotating presidency – Beriz Belkić, Živko Radišić and Jožo Križanović
President of the Muslim/ Croat Federation of Bosnia-Herzegovina: Karlo Filipović
President of Republika Srpska: Mirko Šarović
Head of national government: Zlatko Lagumdžija (replaced Božidar Matić in June)
Capital: Sarajevo
Population: 4.1 million
Official languages: Bosnian, Croatian, Serbian
Death penalty: abolitionist for ordinary crimes
2001 treaty ratifications/ signatures: Second Optional Protocol to the International Covenant on Civil and Political Rights, aiming at the abolition of the death penalty

Refugees and internally displaced persons increasingly returned to their pre-war municipalities, including over 80,000 "minority returnees" whose ethnic group since the war formed a minority in their place of return. Tens of thousands of potential returnees were unable to gain access to their pre-war homes. In practice many returns were not sustainable as returnees lacked physical security and suffered discrimination in access to employment, education and social welfare. The International Criminal Tribunal for the former Yugoslavia (the Tribunal) issued precedent-setting judgments and new indictments for serious violations of international humanitarian law. However, investigations and prosecutions of war crimes and other human rights violations in domestic courts were few and problematic. The suspected perpetrators overwhelmingly remained at large and often in positions of power. There were continued reports of police ill-treatment, for which few police officers were apparently brought to justice.

Background
Under the 1995 Constitution, enshrined in the Dayton Peace Agreement, the country is made up of two largely autonomous entities, the Federation of Bosnia and Herzegovina (Federation) and the Republika Srpska (RS), as well as the autonomous district of Brčko. The High Representative, appointed by the UN Security Council to oversee implementation of the Dayton Peace Agreement, exercises wide legislative and executive powers.

The results of the November 2000 general and RS presidential elections were implemented in the first half of 2001. The Federation government was inaugurated in March. A national government was formed in February under the leadership of Božidar Matić, who resigned in June and was replaced by Zlatko Lagumdžija.

In March, the *Hrvatski narodni sabor* (HNS), Croatian National Congress, representing Bosnian Croat political parties, led by the Bosnian *Hrvatska demokratska zajednica* (HDZ), Croatian Democratic Union, proclaimed "interim autonomy" for the Federation cantons and municipalities which had a significant Bosnian Croat population. The HNS justified its initiative by arguing that Bosnian Croat interests were threatened by amendments to the Federation Constitution and new electoral rules. In response, the High Representative dismissed a number of Bosnian Croat Federation and state officials, who had withdrawn from Federation and state governments. In April and May several thousand Croatian police officers and Federation armed forces officers and soldiers defected to the interim administration, many allegedly after intimidation. In May and June, agreement was reached between the Federation authorities and officers loyal to the HNS, and Bosnian Croat soldiers returned to their barracks. In July Ante Jelavić, the former Bosnian Croat member of the state presidency, and six other Bosnian Croat politicians were charged with endangering the constitutional integrity of the Federation. Their trial was continuing at the end of 2001.

The Constitutional Commissions of both Federation and RS parliaments continued to draft amendments to their respective Constitutions to bring them into line with decisions by the Constitutional Court in 2000. Neither entity had fully implemented the decisions, which granted equal rights and status to the Bosniac, Croat and Serb peoples throughout the country, by the end of 2001.

Return of refugees and displaced persons
According to the UN High Commissioner for Refugees (UNHCR), the number of refugees and displaced people

registered as having returned to their pre-war homes increased substantially. They included over 80,000 minority returns. Progress was partly due to the improved implementation of property legislation by local authorities, although the overall implementation rate was still just 40 per cent. Thousands of potential returnees to the RS — where only 20 per cent of claims had been settled — were unable to return to their pre-war housing.

Returnees faced physical violence and damage to their property, in particular in the RS, as well as discrimination in access to employment, education and social welfare. The failure to protect returnees and to investigate and prosecute attacks against them — despite the available evidence and the extensive support provided to the local police by the International Police Task Force (IPTF) — created a climate of impunity which deterred others from returning.

▫ In May an estimated 2,000 Bosnian Serb protesters violently disrupted a rebuilding ceremony for the 16th century *Ferhad paša* mosque in Banja Luka, which had been destroyed in the war. They assaulted and injured scores of Bosniacs attending the ceremony — many of them pre-war inhabitants of the city — while Bosnian Serb police failed to take adequate measures to protect people from violence. An injured 60-year-old Bosniac man later died as a result. Police reportedly filed criminal reports against 19 people for their involvement in the attacks, but no one had been charged or tried for organizing the violence by the end of 2001.

The return process was also frustrated by a widening gap in funding by donor governments for reconstruction; at the end of 2001, over 20,000 destroyed housing units remained in need of funding. At the end of the year UNHCR urged donor governments to provide humanitarian aid to enable some 5,000 returnee families to remain over the winter season.

In many municipalities, unauthorized building on socially owned land continued, often with the aim of ensuring that displaced persons remained in the municipality to provide electoral support for authorities hostile to minority returns.

▫ In Bratunac in eastern RS, such building continued despite pressure by the Organization for Security and Co-operation in Europe and the High Representative. In June the High Representative removed from post the mayor and another local official for contravening his April 2000 decision on the allocation of socially owned land.

▫ Stabilization Forces (SFOR) obstructed the return of several hundred Bosnian Serbs by using public and private land and property on a firing range near Glamoč in the Federation. The legal basis on which SFOR occupied and used the land remained unclear and AI questioned SFOR's insistence that they were under no legal obligation to compensate landowners. In June some pre-war inhabitants were allowed to return to part of the site, but in October SFOR Headquarters said they could provide no guarantees that anyone could return to villages inside the range.

Impunity
International Criminal Tribunal for the former Yugoslavia

Nine trials of men suspected of grave violations of international humanitarian law during the war were conducted before the Tribunal. Verdicts were reached in five cases.

▫ In February, three Bosnian Serb men were convicted in a precedent-setting verdict that rape and sexual enslavement were crimes against humanity. Two of the accused were convicted of keeping scores of Bosniac women and girls in captivity, and raping and otherwise abusing them.

▫ In August, in the Tribunal's first verdict of genocide, General Radislav Krstić was convicted of participation in the planning and execution of mass killings after the fall of the UN protected area of Srebrenica in July 1995.

The Tribunal Prosecutor issued several new indictments for crimes committed by all three sides during the war.

▫ In August and September, four high-ranking commanders of the former Army of Bosnia-Herzegovina were charged with war crimes against Croatian and Serb civilians in central and southern Bosnia. They voluntarily surrendered to the Tribunal's custody upon learning of the charges against them.

▫ Three Bosnian Serb army officers were indicted for their participation in crimes against Bosniacs after the fall of Srebrenica.

▫ In October charges were publicized against a Bosnian Croat army commander for his involvement in the mass killings of Bosniac civilians in Ahmići in central Bosnia. He subsequently surrendered to the Tribunal's custody.

▫ In November Slobodan Milošević, former President of the Federal Republic of Yugoslavia, who had been surrendered to the Tribunal in April, was additionally indicted for genocide, crimes against humanity and war crimes committed in Bosnia-Herzegovina.

▫ In December the Prosecutor unsealed the indictments of two Bosnian Serbs who had been charged with crimes against humanity and war crimes committed in Foča prison against Bosniac detainees; they had been charged jointly with Milorad Krnojelac who was standing trial at the end of the year.

The Tribunal took custody of 13 people suspected of war crimes. SFOR units arrested two, Dragan Obrenović and Vidoje Blagojević, but failed to apprehend any other suspects.

Domestic prosecutions

The police and judiciary in the Federation and RS remained largely incapable of conducting proceedings for war crimes and human rights violations committed during and after the war. The entities also failed to cooperate in order to proceed with such prosecutions. In the few trials that were conducted, there were consistent indications that courts were not impartial and independent, that investigations were not thorough and that victims and witnesses were not protected.

▫ In April the Mostar Cantonal Court acquitted four Bosnian Croat former military police officers charged with war crimes against Bosniac prisoners of war in 1993. Two of them were tried *in absentia*. During the trial, which started in November 2000, the court appeared biased in favour of the accused. It ruled in one instance that no credible evidence had been submitted that one defendant had been in a command position despite a large amount of documentation, including from the Office of the Prosecutor at the Tribunal. It held that a commander was not criminally responsible for his failure to prevent war crimes by his subordinates or for not punishing subordinates for such crimes. The court ruled that, although one of the accused was present in his capacity of commander during the torture of some victims, and refused one victim's request for help, this conduct did not constitute a war crime. This ruling directly contradicted the Protocol Additional to the Geneva Conventions (Protocol I), as well as jurisprudence of the Tribunal. Prosecution witnesses were reported to have changed their testimony out of fear of reprisals by the accused, who remained in positions of influence.

▫ In October and November the IPTF Commissioner removed nine high-ranking officers from the Prijedor and Omarska police forces after receiving information that they had served as interrogators and had held command functions in local detention camps where war crimes had been committed. The IPTF recommended that the RS authorities launch criminal investigations; by the end of 2001 no action had been taken.

▫ The Sarajevo judicial authorities reportedly failed to conduct prompt, impartial and thorough investigations into crimes against Serb civilians and prisoners of war in Sarajevo during the war, despite extensive evidence presented to them. This included evidence presented to the Supreme Court in 2000 in an appeal by Edin Garaplija, a former intelligence officer, against his conviction in connection with the detention of a former member of a paramilitary unit suspected of such crimes.

Outstanding cases of 'disappearances'

According to the International Committee of the Red Cross, tens of thousands of people were still missing after the war. Many of those who "disappeared" were presumed killed by members of armed forces or paramilitary groups, including over 7,000 Bosniac men and boys detained and killed in mass executions by the Bosnian Serb army in Srebrenica in July 1995. Entity and regional authorities continued to withhold information from relatives which could lead to establishing the fate of missing persons. A new forensic laboratory in Tuzla, run by the International Commission for Missing Persons, started work in May and another in Sarajevo in December, with the aim of accelerating the identification process by DNA analysis.

▫ There was progess in the case of Father Tomislav Matanović and his parents, who "disappeared" after being detained by Bosnian Serb police in September 1995. The RS government had made no attempt to ascertain their fate despite a binding decision by the Human Rights Chamber in 1997 to do so. In November 2000, under pressure from the UN Mission in Bosnia-Herzegovina, it opened an investigation. In April investigators reported that Father Matanović's car had been in the possession of the Prijedor police since his "disappearance". In September the investigative team acknowledged for the first time that Father Matanović and his parents had been illegally detained, and their bodies were found in a well near Prijedor. In May and December the IPTF Commissioner removed several suspected police officers from post.

Arbitrary detentions

▫ In the Federation, at least a dozen people suspected of acts of "terrorism" were detained, incommunicado and without charge, by SFOR for up to two weeks, after which some were handed over to local police; most of these detentions took place in the aftermath of the 11 September attacks in the USA. They were denied access to legal counsel or to a court to challenge the legality of their detention. Nobody was known subsequently to have been charged.

▫ In October, Federation police forces reportedly deported two dual Bosnian-Egyptian nationals to Egypt at the request of the Egyptian authorities and without formal extradition proceedings. The two men had criminal proceedings pending against them before local courts and AI expressed concern that Federation authorities had not obtained guarantees from Egypt that they would not be subjected to torture.

AI country reports/visits

Report
- Concerns in Europe, January-June 2001: Bosnia-Herzegovina (AI Index: EUR 01/003/2001)

Visits
In April and October AI delegates visited the country to carry out research into minority returns, unresolved "disappearances", unfair trials and arbitrary detentions and deportations.

BRAZIL

FEDERATIVE REPUBLIC OF BRAZIL
Head of state and government: Fernando Henríque Cardoso
Capital: Brasília
Population: 172.6 million
Official language: Portuguese
Death penalty: abolitionist for ordinary crimes
2001 treaty ratifications/signatures: Optional Protocol to the UN Women's Convention

The use of torture and ill-treatment remained widespread and systematic throughout the criminal justice system, at point of arrest, in police stations and prisons as well as in juvenile detention centres. In several states, large-scale rioting occurred in prisons and juvenile detention centres, primarily as a result of chronic problems in the penal system and cruel, inhuman or degrading prison conditions. Police officers and "death squads" linked to the security forces were responsible for numerous killings of civilians, including children, in circumstances suggesting that they were extrajudicial executions. Land reform activists, environmentalists and indigenous peoples in rural areas were killed or assaulted by military police or gunmen hired by local landowners. Human rights defenders continued to be threatened and attacked. Important trials of human rights violators took place. However, most of those responsible for human rights abuses continued to benefit from impunity.

Background

Urban crime continued to be a serious problem throughout the country. Violence, often drug-related, claimed large numbers of victims especially in the major cities. There was widespread public pressure for more repressive policing. Strikes by police in several states demonstrated high levels of discontent over pay and conditions.

Major corruption scandals were widely reported in the press. Investigations into corruption and malpractice led to the resignation of three senators, including the current and former Presidents of the Senate. Throughout the country individuals who investigated or denounced official corruption were reportedly threatened and attacked.

Torture and ill-treatment

The use of torture and ill-treatment by members of the civil and military police, prison guards and members of the armed forces continued. It was used to extract confessions, to humiliate and control detainees and, increasingly, to extort money. The number of police investigations of torture allegations rose, but convictions under the 1997 Torture Law remained low.

In April the UN Special Rapporteur on torture described torture and ill-treatment as "widespread and systematic" in a report to the UN Commission on Human Rights of his visit to Brazil in August and September 2000. The report cited 348 cases of torture, and highlighted the failures in the criminal justice system which allowed impunity for perpetrators of torture. In May the government submitted its initial report to the UN Committee against Torture, 10 years after it was due. The Committee recognized the report as frank and transparent but criticized the extent of torture and the failure of the authorities to punish those responsible.

The federal government launched a publicity campaign against torture in October and launched a national free-phone service, operated by a non-governmental organization (NGO), to receive anonymous reports of torture. The 518 reported cases of torture received in the first month included torture by the civil and military police and members of the public prosecution service. The government also announced the setting-up of a national commission to investigate torture allegations and make recommendations on steps to end torture and impunity. While this campaign was recognized as an important first step, many NGOs, including AI, feared that it did not go far enough towards implementing the UN recommendations and ensuring the implementation of the necessary reforms to end the impunity enjoyed by those responsible for acts of torture.

◻ In September, 17 detainees were allegedly tortured at the "Belem 2" *Centro de Detenção Provisorio* (pre-trial detention centre) in São Paulo by guards who accused them of planning an escape attempt. They were reportedly hooded for three consecutive nights, taken from their cells and beaten for periods of up to 45 minutes each, and given minimal medical attention for their injuries. The Prisons Administration Secretariat informed AI that initial forensic examinations could not substantiate these claims, although detainees stated that the examinations had been cursory.

◻ In October Francisco das Chagas Gomes de Sousa, 26 years old, was illegally detained at the 10th Police Station in Teresina, in the state of Piauí, by members of the civil police. He was released five days later with extensive bruising and cuts, a dislocated knee and coughing blood, allegedly as a result of torture by named police officers. He died the next day in hospital. Members of the federal police subsequently found torture instruments at the police station, ascertained that most of the 800 people held there in the previous year had been arbitrarily detained without notification to the judicial authorities, and received many accounts of torture and extortion by civil police officers. Their report was sent to the federal public prosecution service.

Conditions of detention and deaths in custody

Prisoners in police stations, pre-trial detention centres, prisons and juvenile detention centres, continued to suffer from cruel, inhuman or degrading conditions. Severe overcrowding, illegal detention of convicted prisoners in pre-trial facilities, poor sanitary and health provisions, under-trained and poorly paid staff, coupled with the existence of powerful prison gangs, often led to violent confrontations and riots. State authorities in more than 10 states, usually assisted by military police "shock troops", quelled riots in prisons, police stations and juvenile detention centres. The worst took place in São Paulo in February, when coordinated riots broke out in 29 detention centres throughout the state, and 16 detainees were killed, the majority by other inmates.

There were many reported deaths in custody resulting either from excessive use of force by guards and police officers, lack of medical care or violence between detainees. Attempts to resolve prison problems, such as the project to build more manageable prisons in São Paulo, were hampered by, among other problems, the judiciary's increased use of prison sentences for minor offences. In a state which already held over 40 per cent of the national prison population, 800 extra detainees a month had to be absorbed by the system.

◻ In October AI delegates visited two police stations in Belo Horizonte, in Minas Gerais, which lacked medical and sanitation facilities and where extreme overcrowding of police cells was caused by the illegal detention of convicted prisoners. In the Drugs and Narcotics Police Station, overcrowding had reached 1,000 per cent, with 280 detainees — 80 per cent of them convicted prisoners — held in a space designed for 28. Detainees there were held in small, dark cells and allowed out for one hour every two weeks; some were forced to use disposable plates as toilet facilities. Detainees in both police stations reported being tortured. Those in the Robbery and Theft Police Station reported that guards had used electric shocks, fired guns into their cells, hosed them with cold water as well as other forms of torture.

◻ In October heavily armed members of the military police entered the *Complexo Penitenciário do Estado do Amapá*, the Amapá state penitentiary, in Macapá and reportedly shot a prisoner in the head. The prisoner was awaiting trial on charges of attacking a military police officer. The police officer allegedly responsible said that he had fired in self-defence. According to reports, witnesses saw the prisoner being ordered to kneel before he was shot, but were prevented from approaching or informing the prison director the next day by military police officers who reportedly fired at and injured two detainees and beat and kicked two others.

Extrajudicial executions and 'death squads'

Members of both military and civil police continued to be responsible for numerous deaths, often in situations which indicated excessive use of force or extrajudicial execution. In São Paulo, the police ombudsman's office received reports of 481 police killings, the majority by military police, over the whole year. This was considerably higher than the 364 reported in 2000. "Death squads" continued to act with impunity in many states, with the participation or collusion of the police. In the state of Bahia, the State Human Rights Commission reported that "death squads" largely made up of off-duty military and civil police had killed 159 people in the city of Salvador in the first seven months of the year. In several states, human rights defenders, as well as politicians, journalists and environmentalists, were victims of death threats or extrajudicial executions, often after they had been investigating or denouncing official corruption.

◻ On 7 January Luís Gustavo Romano's father reported him missing to the police. He had heard rumours that his son and Paulo Bezerra dos Santos, both 16 years old, had been involved in a shoot-out with members of the military police in Jabaquara in the city of São Paulo. According to witnesses, the two youths were beaten and arrested on the street before being driven off in a police car. On 8 January the body of Luís Gustavo was found at a crossroads and that of Paulo dos Santos in a wood. According to reports both youths had been shot and at least one of the bodies showed signs of a beating. Police later stated that they had been caught attempting to steal a car and were killed in an exchange of gunfire. A number of military police officers were arrested, accused of killing the youths.

Violence over land rights

Land activists suffered harassment and attacks at the hands of military police carrying out evictions. The Pastoral Land Commission reported that by September at least 73 land activists had received death threats and 25 had been killed by hired gunmen, often acting with the apparent acquiescence of the police and local authorities.

In the south of Pará state, which continued to be a focus of extreme land-related violence, slave labour and impunity, at least nine land activists were killed. Following a visit to the region, members of the Federal Commission of Human Rights reported that private security firms were openly offering their services as hired killers.

◻ On 9 July José Pinheiro Lima was killed, with his wife and 15-year-old son, by two gunmen in their house near the town of Marabá, in the south of Pará. He was a leading member of the rural workers trade union in Marabá which had been acting for 120 families whose legal right to unfarmed land was being contested by a local landowner. Two men suspected of ordering the killings were detained but were released after a few days. One of the men suspected of carrying out the killings was arrested but escaped from police custody in December. Police investigations had made no further progress by the end of 2001.

Indigenous peoples were also targets for threats, assaults and killings in the context of land disputes. At least 10 indigenous people were killed by police or by gunmen hired by landowners, acting with the knowledge or acquiescence of the authorities, and many more received death threats.

◻ Caught in an ambush, Xucuru chief Francisco de Assis Santana, also known as Chico Quelé, was killed on 23 April. He was shot twice with a 12-bore shotgun, in Pesqueira, Pernambuco state. Chico Quelé was on his way to meet members of FUNAI (the government's indigenous office) to discuss the indemnity payments to be made to local landowners whose land was to be demarcated as indigenous land. The Federal Police have stated that they were investigating the possibility of internal conflicts among the Xucuru as the main motives for the killings. However, according to information received by AI, there are strong indications that a local landowner may have been responsible for ordering the killing. The landowner is also suspected of having ordered the killing of Francisco de Assis Araújo, known as Chicão Xucuru, in May 1998.

Impunity
The slow pace of Brazilian justice has allowed many human rights abusers to go unpunished. However, under sustained pressure from human rights activists, some long-standing cases came to trial.

Carandiru
In June Colonel Ubiratan Guimarães, a former high-ranking military police officer, was convicted on charges in connection with the massacre of 111 detainees in the Carandiru detention centre following a riot in 1992. In a historic decision, the jury found him to be responsible for São Paulo's military police "shock troops" and that the troops entered the prison with the prior intention of committing as much harm as possible. He was sentenced to 632 years' imprisonment, but was released pending hearing of his appeal. A further 105 military policemen were awaiting trial for their part in the massacre at the end of 2001. The São Paulo authorities later announced their intention to close Carandiru prison by early 2002.

Ticuna
In May, 13 men were convicted of ordering or carrying out an attack on around 100 Ticuna Indians at Capacete Creek in the state of Amazonas in 1988, in which 14 people died, including six children. They were sentenced to between 15 and 25 years' imprisonment. A number of the accused were tried in their absence. These were the first convictions for genocide handed down by a court in the state of Amazonas.

Eldorado dos Carajás
In June the retrial of 153 military police officers charged with aggravated homicide was again postponed. They were charged with killing 19 land activists protesting on a road in the south of Pará state in 1996. New forensic evidence produced by the prosecution was not accepted by the court and further tests were carried out by court-appointed specialists. Members of the prosecution team complained that the judge did not give sufficient grounds for rejecting the evidence and testimony of their specialist, and appealed against the decision. A date for the retrial had not been set by the end of 2001.

AI country reports/ visits
Reports
- Brazil: Commentary on Brazil's first report to the United Nations Committee against Torture (AI Index: AMR 19/016/2001)
- Brazil: "They Treat Us Like Animals", Torture and ill-treatment in Brazil: Dehumanization and impunity within the criminal justice system (AI Index: AMR 19/022/2001)
- Brazil: "People End Up Dying Here" – Torture and ill-treatment in Brazil: Summary report (AI Index: AMR 19/027/2001)
- Brazil: "They Treat Us Like Animals" – Appeals Cases: Torture in Brazil (AI Index: AMR 19/024/2001)

Visits
AI delegates attended the UN Committee against Torture in Geneva in May, and visited Brazil and launched a report on torture in October.

BRUNEI DARUSSALAM

BRUNEI DARUSSALAM
Head of state and government: Sultan Haji Hassanal Bolkiah
Capital: Bandar Seri Begawan
Population: 0.3 million
Official language: Malay
Death penalty: abolitionist in practice

Three prisoners of conscience were detained for nine months for alleged "subversive" activities related to their peaceful Christian beliefs. More than 20 others were reported to have been questioned, with some detained for over three weeks. Amendments to press laws introduced a series of restrictions to press freedoms. Death sentences continued to be passed and a number of people convicted of criminal offences were reportedly subjected to corporal punishment.

Background
The monarch, Sultan Haji Hassanal Bolkiah, continued to exercise a wide range of executive powers, holding the offices of Prime Minister, Defence Minister, Finance Minister and head of the police. Under the 1962 state of emergency, constitutional provisions safeguarding fundamental liberties remained suspended. The sole remaining opposition party, reported to have less than 200 members, was largely inactive.

Arrests under the Internal Security Act (ISA)
The ISA allows the Minister of Home Affairs, on the orders of the Sultan, to detain any person deemed to be a threat to national security. The Minister is empowered to sign two-year detention orders, renewable indefinitely. ISA detainees are denied their rights to a trial, to legal counsel and to be presumed innocent. During prolonged interrogation, while held in isolation and denied access to lawyers, family members

and independent medical attention, ISA detainees are at risk of ill-treatment or torture.

☐ Three men, Yunus Murang, Freddie Chong and Malai Taufick, were arrested under the ISA in December 2000 and held for nine months. The three prisoners of conscience, all reportedly Christians linked to the Borneo Evangelical Church Mission, were accused of "cult" activities which sought to convert "by deception" members of the country's majority Muslim community and so threatened inter-religious harmony. According to reports, the three detainees were subjected to intense psychological pressure, including threats of indefinite detention without trial, unless they confessed to "subversive" activities or cooperated in a process of Islamic re-education. At least one detainee was reported to be have been held for two months in a darkened cell. The three were released in October after signing a statement regretting their "past involvement in subversive activities", taking an oath of allegiance to the Sultan and pledging not to repeat their alleged wrongdoings.

More than 20 others, Christians and Muslims, were reported to have been temporarily detained during related investigations by Internal Security Department police in early 2001. At least four of these detainees, including three Christian women, were held for over three weeks. Upon release the detainees were subject to restrictions including reporting regularly to the police and attending religious education programs.

Restrictions on press freedom

The government introduced amendments to existing press laws that were criticized as a threat to press freedom and the right to freely hold and peacefully express one's opinions. Under the amendments, all newspapers are required to apply for an annual publishing permit, issued solely at the discretion of the Minister of Home Affairs without the right of judicial review. Those publishing without a permit are liable to a fine or up to three years' imprisonment. The legislative changes also empowered the Minister to charge journalists with the crime of maliciously publishing "false news", punishable by a fine or up to three months' imprisonment or both. The Minister has the power to ban the sale of foreign publications and to suspend media outlets. Government permission is also required for the provision of funds from foreign sources for newspapers or journalists in Brunei.

Death penalty and corporal punishment

In October, Mohd Omar bin Abdullah, a Malaysian citizen convicted of drugs trafficking, had his death sentence confirmed by the Appeal Court. No executions were known to have been carried out since 1957. Unconfirmed reports stated that at least one person may have been executed in recent years, but no relevant government statistics were published.

Caning remained mandatory for drug-related and other criminal offences including vandalism. People convicted of criminal offences were reportedly caned during 2001.

BULGARIA

REPUBLIC OF BULGARIA
Head of state: Petar Stoyanov
Head of government: Simeon Saxe-Coburg-Gotha (replaced Ivan Kostov in July)
Capital: Sofia
Population: 7.9 million
Official language: Bulgarian
Death penalty: abolitionist for all crimes
2001 treaty signatures/ratifications: Optional Protocol to the UN Children's Convention on the involvement of children in armed conflict

Reports of ill-treatment and torture by law enforcement officials were widespread. Very few of the suspected perpetrators were brought to justice. Many of the victims, some of whom were minors, were Roma. Law enforcement officials continued to use firearms in circumstances prohibited by international standards, resulting in deaths and injuries. Conditions in many institutions for adults with mental disabilities amounted to cruel, inhuman and degrading treatment. Restrictions on the right to freedom of expression continued to be imposed. An organization of ethnic Macedonians was prevented from holding a peaceful assembly.

Torture and ill-treatment by police

Numerous incidents of police ill-treatment and torture were reported. At least one person died in suspicious circumstances following an incident in which he was beaten by police officers.

☐ In January, police officers in Sofia searching for a murder suspect apprehended Mehmed Mumun (also known as Milotin Mironov), who reportedly tried to evade a police check. Police reportedly kicked him all over his body after he had been immobilized on the ground. Mehmed Mumun lost consciousness and died before he could receive emergency medical treatment. A spokesman for the Ministry of the Interior later claimed that Mehmed Mumun had resisted arrest and had to be handcuffed. Following an investigation into his death, two officers were charged; their trial was continuing at the end of the year.

The vast majority of those who complained about police torture and ill-treatment alleged that following their arrest they were not allowed to contact their lawyer or inform members of their family of their whereabouts, and that they were denied medical treatment.

☐ In July, Veska Voleva, a lawyer, intervened in the eviction of a family from an apartment in Sofia. Two police officers handcuffed her, dragged her down the stairs and took her to the 9th Regional Police Department. In a barred holding cell she was reportedly slapped and kicked all over the body for about 15 minutes by five officers, and then handcuffed to an iron bar for between two and three hours. She was held for 24 hours in a bare cell where she slept on the cement floor. Her requests to contact her family and to be medically examined were denied.

Only a few of the reported perpetrators were brought to justice. Even then, the investigations appeared to be unnecessarily prolonged and hampered by the suspected perpetrators who, it was reported, frequently harassed witnesses.

◻ In January, two former police officers from Nikopol were sentenced to five and six years' imprisonment respectively for the beating of a detainee who died in November 1994 from injuries suffered as a result of ill-treatment. The incident had been observed by a witness who kept silent about it for a year because he was threatened by the police officers.

Roma

There were reports of police torture and ill-treatment of members of the Romani community throughout the year. Many of the victims were minors. The Human Rights Project, a local non-governmental organization, investigated over 90 complaints of serious human rights violations suffered by Romani victims. In the majority of reported cases complaints were filed with the military prosecutors. However, investigations frequently appeared not to be conducted in a thorough and impartial manner.

◻ In May, a 16-year-old youth was apprehended in Stara Zagora by a man, who introduced himself as a police officer, in front of the house where the youth had picked some plums from a tree. He was handcuffed and taken into the officer's house where he was reportedly punched, kicked and beaten with a truncheon all over his body. The officer then reportedly pointed a gun at the boy's head and asked his wife: "What shall I do with his body after I have killed him?" Shortly afterwards the youth's parents arrived and the youth was released. That evening he was treated for contusions to the chest, head and face.

◻ In February, Nikolay Nikolovov was reportedly beaten with a truncheon by a police officer in Pavlikeni Regional Police Department who questioned him about the theft of a hi-fi system. On the same day he was examined by a forensic medical expert who noted weals 12 to 15 centimetres long on his arms, back and right thigh. In June the Military Prosecutor of Tarnovo decided not to initiate a criminal investigation against the officer because his conduct was considered to be of a "clearly insignificant degree of social danger".

Use of firearms by police

There were numerous reports of police shootings which breached internationally recognized standards. The authorities failed to address adequately this pernicious human rights problem. At least three people were killed in such incidents. In February, Emanuil Yordanov, then Minister of the Interior, reportedly stated that he would re-examine all provisions concerning the use of firearms by both police officers and civilians, but it was only for the latter that proposals were formulated. He also ordered that all police officers undergo psychological examinations within a three-month period and that there should be stricter internal inspections within the Ministry of the Interior. However, it appeared that these measures had little effect.

Conditions in homes for adults with mental disabilities

People with mental disabilities placed in state institutions for permanent care were subjected to conditions which amounted to cruel, inhuman and degrading treatment. Social homes, the official title for such institutions, were typically located in remote areas. Residents were housed in unsuitable, dilapidated quarters with extremely poor standards of hygiene and with no signs that residents were permitted any personal belongings. They were sometimes subjected to cruel forms of restraint and seclusion. These institutions were often inadequately staffed by untrained personnel. The medical care available was usually inadequate and resources for rehabilitation non-existent. In some homes the lack of adequate medical care, heating and food appeared to contribute to deaths. Autopsies were seldom carried out to establish the cause of death and no criminal investigations appear to have been initiated to establish the responsibility for grossly negligent care of people with a mental disability.

◻ In the Sanadinovo home for mentally disabled women, those who "misbehaved" were held in a cage made of two brick walls with iron bars and wire on the remaining two sides. In October, an AI delegate witnessed six women being held in this 3m x 1.5m space. They looked withdrawn and vacant and appeared non-aggressive. The cage was full of urine and faeces and the women were covered in filth. One woman was naked from the waist down and many sores were visible on her skin. It was not possible to establish how long anyone would be subjected to this form of seclusion as no records of this appeared to be maintained.

Freedom of expression

Several people peacefully exercising their right to freedom of expression were detained on charges of "hooliganism".

◻ In January, four men and a minor were detained in Sofia after they had held a banner at a public ceremony with the slogan "Out NATO supporters!" on which the NATO emblem had been altered to resemble a swastika. After the ceremony President Petar Stoyanov reportedly stated: "This is blasphemy! It is high time that we took decisive measures against such ruffians..." The protesters were taken to a police station where they were held until the following day. An investigation was opened on the orders of the Prosecutor before the Supreme Court of Cassation who considered that the protesters had committed an offence of "hooliganism". However, the charge was dismissed by the Sofia County Court in April.

◻ In September, the Pleven County Court quashed on appeal the conviction of Aleksandar Kandjov. He had been sentenced to four months' imprisonment, suspended for three years, for aggravated hooliganism because he had organized the signing of a petition in which the Minister of Justice was described as "top idiot of the judiciary". Aleksandar Kandjov had been held in custody for four days following his arrest in July 2000.

OMO 'Ilinden'
In March, the Blagoevgrad Public Prosecutor initiated a criminal investigation for incitement to racial or national hatred in connection with leaflets distributed by the United Macedonian Organization "Ilinden" (OMO "Ilinden"), calling on the residents of the region to declare themselves in the census as Macedonians. However, no one had been charged by the end of the year.

In July, police prevented OMO "Ilinden" activists from holding a peaceful assembly to commemorate a national anniversary. Three activists filming the police action were detained for three hours before being released without charge. In October the European Court of Human Rights ruled that the authorities had violated the right to freedom of assembly and association when they prohibited OMO "Ilinden" activists from holding similar commemorative meetings in the period between 1994 and 1997.

AI country reports/visits
Report
- Bulgaria: Disabled women condemned to "slow death" (AI Index: EUR 15/002/01)

BURKINA FASO

BURKINA FASO
Head of state: Blaise Compaoré
Head of government: Ernest Yonli
Capital: Ouagadougou
Population: 11.9 million
Official language: French
Death penalty: abolitionist in practice
2001 treaty ratifications/signatures: Optional Protocol to the UN Women's Convention; Optional Protocol to the UN Children's Convention on the involvement of children in armed conflict

A member of the security forces was indicted for the extrajudicial executions of four people, including a leading investigative journalist, in 1998. The government set up a national human rights commission.

Background
Tens of thousands of Burkina Faso nationals who faced growing hostility in Côte d'Ivoire returned to Burkina Faso in the early months of 2001, putting the country's economy under increased pressure.

There were concerns about Burkina Faso's role in the diamonds for arms trade linked to large-scale human rights violations in Liberia and Sierra Leone.

National human rights commission
In late October the government created a national human rights commission with a brief to raise awareness of human rights and to organize human rights education.

Impunity
In early February an officer of the *Régiment de la sécurité présidentielle*, the presidential security force, was indicted on charges of murder and arson in connection with the deaths in December 1998 of Ernest Zongo, Ablassé Nikiema, Blaise Ilboudo and Norbert Zongo, a leading investigative journalist. An independent Commission of Inquiry had recommended in May 1999 that the officer be prosecuted. No further progress was recorded on this case following the indictment.

President Blaise Compaoré announced a controversial national day of reconciliation at the end of March to ease the ongoing national and international tension about the slow progress of investigation and prosecution in cases of human rights violations. The family of Norbert Zongo and the widow of Thomas Sankara, the former Head of State killed in unclear circumstances in the coup which brought the current President to power in October 1987, refused to take part in the ceremonies.

In October, during a visit by President Compaoré to France, *Reporters sans Frontières*, a non-governmental organization working for freedom of the press, tried to initiate a prosecution against him on charges of crimes against humanity in connection with the alleged extrajudicial execution of Norbert Zongo. The French prosecutors refused to open a suit against President Compaoré.

In January, one of the suspects who had been named by the May 1999 Independent Commission of Inquiry investigating the death of Norbert Zongo, died in hospital after several months of illness. He was one of three members of the *Régiment de la sécurité présidentielle* convicted of causing the death by torture in January 1998 of David Ouédraogo, chauffeur of François Compaoré, presidential adviser and brother of the President. A potential key witness in the case of the death of Norbert Zongo, he was serving a 20-year prison sentence at the time of his death.

AI country reports/ visits
Reports
- Burkina Faso: Amnesty International welcomes progress in the Norbert Zongo Case (AI Index: AFR 60/001/2001)
- Burkina Faso: The long and dangerous fight for justice — West African human rights defenders under attack (AI Index: AFR 60/003/2001)

BURUNDI

REPUBLIC OF BURUNDI
Head of state and government: Pierre Buyoya
Capital: Bujumbura
Population: 6.5 million
Official languages: Kirundi, French
Death penalty: retentionist
2001 treaty ratifications/ signatures: Optional Protocol to the UN Women's Convention; Optional Protocol to the UN Children's Convention on the involvement of children in armed conflict

War continued to ravage the country throughout the year despite a peace agreement signed in August 2000. Hundreds of unarmed civilians were killed by government soldiers and members of armed opposition groups, and hundreds of thousands of people remained internally displaced. People continued to flee the country in their thousands. Scores of detainees were arrested and held incommunicado in unauthorized detention centres. Many people were tortured. Others were feared to have "disappeared". Thousands of people, including children, remained in detention without trial from previous years, some since 1994. Most perpetrators of human rights abuses continued to benefit from impunity. At least 40 death sentences were passed; no executions were reported. The activities of human rights groups and humanitarian organizations were hindered by the conflict and by government and military authorities and armed opposition groups.

Background
Conflict continued throughout the year between the two main armed political movements not party to the August 2000 peace agreement, and government forces. In February, the armed opposition group the *Forces nationales de libération* (FNL), National Liberation Forces, attacked and occupied parts of Bujumbura for nearly two weeks. Armed opposition and government forces continued to be involved in the war in neighbouring Democratic Republic of the Congo (DRC). There were repeated allegations that the Rwandese army was operating in Burundi and of links between Rwandese and Burundian Hutu-dominated armed opposition groups. The report of the UN Panel of Experts on the Illegal Exploitation of Natural Resources and Other Forms of Wealth of the DRC, submitted to the UN Security Council in April, accused Burundi of involvement in illegal exploitation, as well as transport and exportation of minerals and other natural resources from the DRC. The government denied the allegations.

In the first half of the year, implementation of the peace agreement continued to stagnate. Attempted coups took place in April and July, apparently led by junior officers opposed to the peace agreement. After months of diplomatic activity it was announced in July that the first period of a transitional government to be set up under the terms of the peace agreement would commence on 1 November. It was to be led by the incumbent President, assisted by a vice-president nominated from the main Hutu-dominated opposition party, the *Front pour la démocratie au Burundi* (FRODEBU), Front for Democracy in Burundi. The announcement led to an increase in political tension, including a second attempted coup, and further fighting. Major issues left outstanding from the peace negotiations were not resolved by the end of the year. These included involving both main armed opposition groups in peace talks, negotiating a cease-fire and reform of the army. In September, foreign military observers arrived in the country to review the situation in advance of a proposed international peace-keeping force and to act as a special protection unit for returning political leaders from exile.

The transitional government came to power in November.

Abuses in conflict areas
Both the armed forces and armed opposition groups continued to show complete disregard for human rights and to act with apparent impunity. The use of unpaid but armed *Gardiens de la Paix* (government militias) increased. Human rights violations, including torture, were attributed to them.

Government forces and militias

Government forces were responsible for indiscriminate violations against the Hutu civilian population. They carried out hundreds of extrajudicial executions, including of children, and deliberately destroyed and looted property. The attacks were often in reprisal for activities of the armed opposition, but also indicated that the Hutu population in general continued to be regarded by government forces as both hostile and complicit with the armed opposition. There was a marked increase in the unlawful and indiscriminate killing of unarmed civilians by the armed forces around the inauguration of the transitional government.

◻ Between 30 October and 4 November, at least 93 civilians, including Stanislas Manirakiza, Marc Ndarubayemwo, Cécile Minani, and Madame Moshi and her four children, are reported to have been massacred by government forces at Maramvya, Mutimbuzi commune in Rural-Bujumbura province. The killings were apparently in reprisal for an incident the previous day in which combatants, believed to belong to the FNL, fired at a government army vehicle and attacked a military post in Maramvya. Soldiers opened fire indiscriminately on people as they worked in the fields, before bayoneting to death others who had taken refuge in their homes.

Armed opposition groups

The main armed opposition groups, the *Conseil national pour la défense de la démocratie-Forces pour la défense de la démocratie* (CNDD-FDD), National Council for the Defence of Democracy-Forces for the Defence of Democracy, and the FNL, were not bound by the peace agreement. Initiatives aimed at negotiating a cease-fire or entering into peace talks were unsuccessful. Members of both groups deliberately and unlawfully killed and abducted scores of people whom they suspected of collaborating with the government administration or armed forces. Ambushes were conducted by armed opposition groups in which scores of civilians were killed, often caught in the cross-fire. Armed opposition groups repeatedly robbed, raped and intimidated local civilian populations and forced people to carry looted possessions or ammunition. Hundreds of children were abducted in Burundi and forcibly recruited by the CNDD-FDD in November; hundreds of others were recruited throughout the year from refugee camps in Tanzania. Humanitarian aid workers were also targeted.

◻ Eight civilians were killed by the FNL between 20 and 28 July. All were peasant farmers from Masama, Kabezi commune, Rural-Bujumbura province, and two belonged to the *Gardiens de la Paix*. The men were reportedly accused by the FNL of collaboration with government forces.

◻ On 6 November, 18 civilians, including eight children, were killed by the CNDD-FDD at Munini, Bururi province, southern Burundi, apparently in reprisal following CNDD-FDD clashes with the armed forces.

Arbitrary arrest and detention without trial

Despite the introduction in January 2000 of a revised Code of Criminal Procedure, suspects continued to suffer arbitrary detention, often in poor conditions, as well as torture and "disappearance". Those arrested on suspicion of links with the armed opposition, including children, were often held incommunicado by the military in unauthorized places of detention.

◻ Salvator Ndagijimana, aged 14, was arrested with two others by soldiers in Bujumbura on 15 June on suspicion of collaboration with an armed opposition group and involvement in the murder of a local government official. On 20 June his older brother, Juvénal Ndayisenga, was arrested while trying to take food to Salvator and subsequently detained at the *Groupement d'intervention*, Intervention Squad, a paramilitary unit in Bujumbura frequently accused of torturing detainees. He was reportedly tortured before being released without charge after several days of incommunicado detention. His family were initially denied information about his whereabouts. Salvator Ndagijimana and his two co-defendants were beaten, stabbed and whipped in military custody. They remain in Mpimba central prison awaiting trial.

Torture and ill-treatment by the security forces

Torture and ill-treatment were routine immediately after arrest, sometimes resulting in death. Torture methods included having their arms tied tightly behind their backs for long periods and being bayoneted and whipped. Several prisoners died as a result. According to a report published in August by the Burundian Association for the Defence of Prisoners' Rights, of a total prison population of around 8,500, approximately 4,500 detainees were tortured or ill-treated at the time of their arrest. Cases were rarely investigated.

◻ On 12 June, a man called Birahwe was arrested for fighting by the *Gardiens de la Paix*, apparently on the orders of a government official in Minago, Bururi province, who allegedly ordered the *Gardiens* to "administer a correction". He was reportedly taken to an unofficial lock-up in Minago and beaten with gun butts. He was released three days later but died at home from his injuries shortly afterwards.

Political trials/investigations

Major trials remained in progress during the year. New political cases were investigated but trials had not started, including the following:

◻ At least 11 people were arrested in January in connection with a machine-gun attack on a civilian aircraft landing at Bujumbura airport in December 2000. The plane landed safely. Four men remained in detention in Mpimba central prison awaiting trial at the end of the year. Three of the 11, who were provisionally released or remained at liberty, were also awaiting trial on related charges. Two others were released unconditionally and one man, Safari, reportedly "disappeared" after being questioned at the *Groupement d'intervention* and later died. The group were held, mostly incommunicado, in various gendarmerie and police stations in Bujumbura while the case was investigated by a government Commission of Inquiry, and two brothers, Bernard and Barnabé Barayegeranije, were tortured at the *Groupement d'intervention*. The government blamed the attack on the FNL, which denied responsibility.

◻ A Commission of Inquiry into the attempted coup of 18 April submitted its report to the Minister of Justice in May. A total of 54 people charged in connection with the attempt were awaiting trial by the Military Court of Appeal at the end of the year.

◻ Following a second coup attempt in July, 103 people were remanded in custody, including seven civilians. Their trial, also by the Military Court of Appeal, had not started by the end of the year.

During the investigations into both coup attempts, detainees were held in incommunicado detention for several weeks. Some could face the death penalty if convicted.

Political trials relating to 1993 crisis

Trials continued of people charged in connection with the massacres of Tutsi civilians in October and November 1993, following the assassination of the then President, Melchior Ndadaye. Concern remained that trials, before civilian courts, fell far short of international standards for fair trial, in particular due to the denial of the right to appeal and the use of statements extracted under duress or torture. Thousands of Hutu, many of them supporters of FRODEBU, remained in detention awaiting trial. However, few, if any, members of the security forces or Tutsi civilians were arrested and prosecuted by the Tutsi-dominated judiciary for their part in the reprisal killings of thousands of Hutu civilians.

◻ In November 2000, the African Commission on Human and People's Rights requested the reopening of the case against Gaëtan Bwampamye, convicted of participation in the 1993 massacres and sentenced to death after an unfair trial in 1997, on the grounds that his rights to legal assistance and equality before the law had been violated. However, at the end of 2001, no action appeared to have been taken. He is currently held in harsh conditions in Bururi prison.

Journalists arrested and ill-treated

Journalists were arrested in what appeared to be an increasing pattern of harassment. In March, the government issued a press statement in which it called on private and state media to "respect the code of conduct, morality and the law" and warned that failure to do so would be severely punished. President Buyoya reportedly warned journalists against "playing the enemy's game". Following these statements, several journalists were harassed, ill-treated and arrested.

◻ Gabriel Nikundana and Abbas Mbanzumutima, both journalists from the independent radio station *Bonesha FM+*, were arrested and briefly detained in Bujumbura in March by members of the *Documentation nationale*, National Intelligence Agency. The arrests followed the broadcast of an interview with the spokesperson for the FNL, which was then occupying parts of Bujumbura.

Arrests of opponents to the peace process

Demonstrations against the peace process were organized by a number of groups, including the Tutsi self-defence association *PA Amasekanya* and the *Parti pour le redressement national* (PARENA), National Recovery Party, the party of former President Jean-Baptiste Bagaza and other Tutsi-dominated political parties. The authorities prevented some demonstrations from taking place, and scores of PARENA members were detained for short periods. Diomède Rutamucero, president of *PA Amasekanya*, was briefly detained on several occasions.

Impunity

The authorities failed to bring to justice members of the security forces suspected of serious human rights violations. In September a military court sentenced a soldier convicted of grievous bodily harm to 18 months' imprisonment for killing a Hutu member of the National Assembly in December 1999. He was also fined 1,000 Burundian francs (approximately US$1). The killing appeared to have been an extrajudicial execution.

Death penalty

At least 40 people were sentenced to death during 2001, all by civilian courts and mostly after conviction for offences relating to the 1993 crisis. Civilians sentenced to death by civilian courts do not have the right to a full appeal. No death sentences were reported to have been passed by military courts. Over 440 people remained under sentence of death. No executions were reported.

Refugees

Over 12,000 Burundians fled to neighbouring Tanzania which already hosted nearly 400,000 Burundian refugees in camps close to the border. Several thousand refugees returned to Burundi from Tanzania. Hundreds of thousands of people remained displaced within the country. A tripartite voluntary repatriation agreement between Burundi, Tanzania and the UN High Commissioner for Refugees (UNHCR) was signed in September, although the UNHCR cautioned that the situation was still not conducive to mass repatriation.

AI country reports/visits

Reports
- Burundi: Memorandum to the transitional government: an opportunity to confront torture and impunity (AI Index: AFR 16/043/2001)
- Burundi: Preparing for peace, one year on (AI Index: AFR 16/037/2001)
- Burundi: Between hope and fear (AI Index: AFR 16/007/2001)

CAMBODIA

KINGDOM OF CAMBODIA
Head of state: King Norodom Sihanouk
Head of government: Hun Sen
Capital: Phnom Penh
Population: 13.4 million
Official language: Khmer
Death penalty: abolitionist for all crimes
2001 treaty ratifications/signatures: Optional Protocol to the UN Women's Convention

Hundreds of refugees from Viet Nam crossed the border into Cambodia after unrest in their home provinces in February. Cambodia's ability and willingness to protect them was limited, and scores were forced back across the border. Following the attack by an armed political group in Phnom Penh in November 2000, and the arrests that followed, dozens of people were brought to trial, in proceedings which fell short of international standards for fairness. Many were sentenced to long prison terms. A law allowing for the establishment of a mixed international and domestic tribunal to try those most responsible for the grave human rights violations during the period of Khmer Rouge rule (1975-1979) was signed by the King, but raised serious human rights concerns. Political activists were subjected to threats, harassment and attacks, especially in rural areas, ahead of local elections planned for 2002.

Refugees

In March, groups of ethnic minority refugees from the Central Highlands of Viet Nam crossed into Ratanakiri and Mondulkiri provinces, seeking protection following unrest in Viet Nam in February. The Cambodian authorities were contacted by their Vietnamese counterparts, who requested that all such people be returned to Viet Nam by the Cambodian provincial police. An initial group of several dozen refugees were swiftly resettled in the USA, but scores of others continued to cross the border, some of whom were forced back to the Vietnamese side by the Cambodian authorities (see Viet Nam entry). Initial government statements indicated that the refugees would not be granted permission to stay in the country, and no camps would be allowed in the border areas. As a state party to the 1951 UN Refugee Convention and its 1967 Protocol, Cambodia is obliged to ensure protection for all refugees on its territory. In April the UN High Commissioner for Refugees (UNHCR) was granted permission to work in the affected provinces and later to establish safe sites for the refugees. Attempts to arrange an agreement with the Cambodian and Vietnamese authorities over voluntary repatriation of the refugees failed in July, when the Vietnamese refused to grant the UNHCR access to the Central Highlands. Following trials in Viet Nam in September dozens more refugees arrived in Cambodia seeking protection. At the end of the year around 1,000 refugees remained in Ratanakiri and Mondulkiri.

▫ In May, Dien Y Lien, his wife, Maria Nam Linh, and their five children were detained by the Cambodian police in Mondulkiri province and were forced across the border into the custody of the Vietnamese authorities, where Dien Y Lien was reportedly detained and beaten.

Arrests and trials

Dozens of people remained in detention awaiting trial following the attack in Phnom Penh in November 2000 by the Cambodian Freedom Fighters (CFF) group, which left at least eight people dead and resulted in scores of arrests. Two high-profile trials were held, with most of the defendants found guilty of charges ranging from "terrorism" to raising an illegal armed force. A new wave of arrests began in September, and dozens of new CFF suspects were in detention awaiting trial by the end of the year.

▫ In June, the trial of 32 suspects (two of whom were tried *in absentia*) took place in Phnom Penh, amid intimidating security arrangements. Family members, journalists and human rights monitors were initially denied access to the courtroom, while heavily armed police, soldiers and military police with dogs patrolled the area. Defendants were held in pre-trial detention for longer than the six months permitted under Cambodian law, and lawyers for some of the accused were prevented from holding pre-trial confidential meetings with their clients, undermining the right to a fair trial. The majority were sentenced to long prison terms, including life imprisonment, which is not a codified punishment under Cambodian law.

Khmer Rouge cases

In January, the National Assembly passed a law allowing for the establishment of a mixed international and domestic tribunal to bring to justice those suspected of responsibility for the gross human rights violations during the period of Khmer Rouge rule. The Senate also approved the law, but in February the Constitutional Council, which has responsibility for ensuring that all new laws comply with Cambodia's Constitution, called for changes because the law referred to punishments laid down in the 1956 Penal Code. These included the death penalty, which was abolished in the 1993 Constitution. After months of delay, the revised law was passed by the National Assembly and Senate in July. It was approved by the Constitutional Council in August, and swiftly signed by the King. In January the UN had also raised concerns about the law in a detailed letter to the Cambodian government, pointing out among other issues where the law fell short of international standards for fairness. The revised version of the law did not address the majority of these concerns, and this was duly highlighted by the UN's legal office. In November, the Prime Minister complained that the UN was causing delays in the process, and stated that the

Cambodian side would proceed without the organization if necessary.

◻ Two Khmer Rouge suspects arrested in 1999 remained in detention in Phnom Penh's military detention facility throughout the year.

Political violence and intimidation
Local elections were scheduled for early 2002, and the voter registration process and identification of candidates took place during 2001. There were scores of complaints of harassment and intimidation of activists from the opposition Sam Rainsy Party (SRP). Ten likely candidates from the SRP and the National United Front for an Independent, Neutral, Peaceful and Cooperative Cambodia (FUNCINPEC) parties were killed during the year in attacks which may have been politically motivated. Official investigations blamed the deaths on personal disputes and witchcraft, but investigations by independent monitors suggested a political motive in some of the killings.

◻ In July Meas Soy, a FUNCINPEC prospective local election candidate, was shot dead at his house in Kampong Chhnang province. Police in the province suggested that the killing might have been related to a personal dispute, but independent investigators found no evidence to support this. One suspect was acquitted and released by the provincial court in November, when the judge ruled there was insufficient evidence against him.

Intergovernmental organizations
The Special Representative of the UN Secretary-General on Human Rights in Cambodia visited the country three times during the year, highlighting among other issues the weak judicial system and its effect on human rights protection. He reported to both the UN Commission on Human Rights and the UN General Assembly, both of which adopted resolutions requesting that reports be submitted to their next sessions.

AI country reports/visits
Reports
- Cambodia: Fear of forcible repatriation (AI Index: ASA 23/001/2001)
- Cambodia: Judiciary on trial (AI Index: ASA 23/005/2001)

Visit
An AI delegation visited Cambodia in August and met the King.

CAMEROON

REPUBLIC OF CAMEROON
Head of state: Paul Biya
Head of government: Peter Mafany Musonge
Capital: Yaoundé
Population: 15.2 million
Official languages: French, English
Death penalty: retentionist
2001 treaty ratifications/signatures: Optional Protocol to the UN Children's Convention on the involvement of children in armed conflict

Criminal suspects continued to be extrajudicially executed by the special security forces. Under strong national and international pressure, the government took steps to investigate some of the killings but no results of investigations were published. Throughout the year human rights defenders continued to be ill-treated and intimidated by the security forces. Offices of several human rights organizations were targeted for arson and burgled in Douala and Maroua. In October the security forces killed three people when dispersing peaceful demonstrations in North-West Province. Leading members of the Southern Cameroons National Council (SCNC) were arrested and held for two months without trial. Eighteen detainees sentenced to long prison terms after an unfair trial in 1999 remained held; some were in a critical state of health.

Background
In preparation for the Franco-African Summit held in Yaoundé in January, the authorities banned meetings announced by civil society groups intending to address the government's human rights record. The World Bank appointed an International Advisory Group to monitor the upholding of international human rights standards and the use of revenue and loans in connection with the construction of the Chad-Cameroon Petroleum Development and Pipeline Project. The territorial dispute with Nigeria over the oil-rich Bakassi Peninsula remained unresolved. Opposition parties continued to challenge the government about the elections supervisory body, the *Observatoire national des élections*, expressing particular concern about its powers and composition, and its perceived lack of independence.

Extrajudicial executions
Faced with accusations of condoning large-scale extrajudicial executions carried out by the *Commandement opérationnel* (CO), a special security force set up in 2000, the government announced steps in January to restructure the force. After a brief period during the Franco-African Summit when no extrajudicial executions were alleged, reports again increased after January. In April, following growing public protests, the government conducted an internal

inquiry; eight security officials were arrested. They remained in detention at the end of the year. No findings of the inquiry were made public, and the CO continued to be reportedly responsible for the extrajudicial execution of criminal suspects.

◻ On 23 January, nine youths were arrested by security forces from the Bépanda Omnisports neighbourhood in Douala, suspected of stealing a neighbour's cooking gas bottle. The nine were subsequently transferred to a detention facility in Bonanjo-Douala belonging to the CO. They were last seen there by relatives on 26 and 27 February. There was no later information about their whereabouts and they were believed to have been killed by security forces.

Excessive use of force

Security forces continued to use excessive, sometimes lethal, force in operations to disperse demonstrations and suppress freedom of expression. Tension mounted in the English-speaking South-West and North-West provinces as arrests continued of activists from the SCNC, a group supporting independence for those provinces.

◻ At least three people were killed and nine injured on 1 October after gendarmerie and police used firearms to disperse a peaceful demonstration in Kumbo, North-West Province.

◻ Eighteen leading members of the SCNC were arrested in October and detained for nearly two months without trial.

Human rights defenders and journalists

Human rights defenders and journalists continued to be harassed for denouncing human rights violations and commenting on actions by the security forces. Steps taken in May in Belgium by political and civil society groups to prosecute President Paul Biya for crimes against humanity were followed by a growing number of incidents of repression and harassment against human rights defenders. The offices of the *Action des Chrétiens pour l'abolition de la torture* (ACAT), Action by Christians for the Abolition of Torture, were targeted in a failed arson attack which caused damage to adjacent offices. The offices of the Maroua-based *Mouvement pour la Défense des Droits de l'Homme et des Libertés* (MDDHL), Movement in Defence of Human Rights and Freedom, were burgled. In August, Abdoulaye Math, president of the MDDHL, was arrested and intimately body-searched. Documents relating to human rights violations were taken from him and were not returned.

◻ Jean-Marc Soboth, editor of the Douala-based newspaper *La Nouvelle Expression* was arrested and questioned by police about an article published on 24 September which discussed plans by the authorities to counter demonstrations planned for 1 October. He was released without charge the next day.

◻ On 26 April, five men, four of them activists from the *Collectif national contre l'Impunité*, National Collective against Impunity, were arrested while on their way to a meeting. They were released without charge after three days.

◻ After lodging a complaint with the regional military tribunal in April, a relative of Luc Bassilekin, who was killed reportedly by members of the CO in Douala in October 2000, was harassed, his private possessions were searched and documents stolen after his office was burgled. No progress on the case was reported by the end of 2001.

Political prisoners

Eighteen prisoners, convicted in 1999 after an unfair trial of charges including murder and robbery in connection with armed attacks in North-West Province in March 1997, remained held in Yaoundé. Most suffered from serious health problems as a result of poor prison conditions and prolonged confinement in darkness. They continued to be denied access to adequate medical treatment.

Releases

In March, Frederik Ebong Alobwede, Chief Otun Ayamba, James Sabum and three other SCNC activists were released after 14 months' detention without trial. Maurice Tchambou, a member of the MDDHL, was released in December. He had been first arrested in 1999 by the *Brigade anti-gang*, a special security force.

AI country reports/visits

Reports

- Cameroon: The government must throw more light on the "disappearance" of nine children in Douala (AI Index: AFR 17/002/2001)
- Cameroun: Justice pour les victimes du Commandement opérationnel – des ONG internationales se mobilisent pour obtenir la vérité sur les exactions des derniers mois (AI Index: AFR 17/004/2001)
- Cameroon: Security forces must respect human rights in reaction to political demonstrations (AI Index: AFR 17/009/2001)

Visits

Despite repeated requests to visit the country, the Cameroonian authorities failed to grant visas to AI delegates.

CANADA

CANADA
Head of state: Queen Elizabeth II, represented by Adrienne Clarkson
Head of government: Jean Chrétien
Capital: Ottawa
Population: 31 million
Official languages: English, French
Death penalty: abolitionist for all crimes

There were sporadic reports of the use of excessive force by police officers. The Supreme Court ruled against extradition on charges that carry the death penalty unless assurances had been obtained that capital punishment would not be applied.

Police brutality

In April, police used excessive force against demonstrators during the Summit of the Americas in Quebec City. Eyewitnesses observed the use of tear gas against protesters who were not involved in violent behaviour or posing any threat to property or the police. Tear gas was fired directly at individuals and into private property for no apparent reason. Plastic bullets were used in situations where the safety of police officers and the integrity of the Summit were not threatened. Police used an electro-shock device on a peaceful demonstrator who had refused police instructions to move. Some of those under arrest were reportedly denied prompt legal representation and were held in overcrowded cells for prolonged periods. No independent inquiry into the allegations had been convened by the end of the year.

The trial of the four police officers for the manslaughter of Otta Vass, who was beaten to death in Toronto in August 2000, had not taken place by the end of 2001. A further hearing on the case was scheduled for June 2002.

In November the Saskatchewan provincial government announced the establishment of a commission of inquiry into indigenous peoples and the justice system. There had been allegations that for a number of years some members of the Saskatoon City Police had routinely abandoned "troublesome" members of the indigenous community in areas far from the population centre, where they were at risk of dying of hypothermia.

An investigation into the deaths of two indigenous men, Rodney Naistus and Lawrence Wegner, near Saskatoon, did not result in criminal charges. The two men had been found frozen to death in the outskirts of the city in early 2000.

In September, the two police officers charged in connection with the abandonment of an indigenous man, Darrell Night, in freezing temperatures in January 2000, were acquitted of the charges of assault, but convicted of unlawful confinement. Both officers were sentenced to eight months' imprisonment and were dismissed from the police force.

AI continued to call for an independent inquiry into the 1995 shooting by Ontario Provincial Police of Dudley George, an indigenous man involved in a land claims protest. During the year the organization supported the call for a coroner's inquest into the death.

Death penalty

In February, the Supreme Court of Canada issued a landmark decision on Canadian extradition procedures in potential death penalty cases. Ruling in the case of two Canadian citizens facing extradition to the USA, the Supreme Court unanimously held that the Canadian Minister of Justice is now constitutionally required to seek and obtain extradition assurances against the death penalty "in all but exceptional cases".

In March, Glen Sebastian Burns and Atif Ahmad Rafay, who had been arrested in Canada for the 1994 murder of Atif Ahmad Rafay's parents and sister in Washington state, USA, were returned to stand trial after Washington state authorities provided assurances that neither man would face the death penalty if convicted.

Refugees

A new Immigration and Refugee Protection Act was adopted in November which could result in certain groups of people being sent to a country where they could be at risk of torture or being removed from Canada without getting access to any form of risk review. The Act was set to enter into force in June 2002.

In January, Haroun M'Barek, whose application for asylum had been denied, was sent back to Tunisia in spite of information that was presented to the authorities that he would face torture upon being returned. In 1996 a Tunisian court had sentenced him *in absentia* to 12 years' imprisonment, following an unfair trial, for "attempting to interfere with the welfare and security of people and goods" and "creating a gang of wrongdoers". Haroun M'Barek was arrested on his return to Tunisia and reportedly tortured. No investigation was known to have been carried out into his allegations of torture. In March, he was sentenced to three years' imprisonment. He was released in May, pending a new trial. He was able to return to Canada in September after the Tunisian authorities agreed to issue him a passport.

Anti-Terrorism Act

The Anti-Terrorism Act was adopted in December. Although the Act focuses on bringing individuals accused of certain offences to justice, there were concerns that it undermined the right to a fair trial and might disproportionately impact on certain ethnic and religious communities.

AI country reports/ visits
Visit
An AI delegate monitored the policing of the Summit of the Americas in Quebec City in April.

CENTRAL AFRICAN REPUBLIC

CENTRAL AFRICAN REPUBLIC
Head of state: Ange-Félix Patassé
Head of government: Martin Ziguélé
Capital: Bangui
Population: 3.8 million
Official Language: French
Death penalty: abolitionist in practice
2001 treaty ratifications/signatures: Rome Statute of the International Criminal Court

Following a coup attempt in May, the human rights situation deteriorated. Hundreds of people were extrajudicially executed. Scores of detainees, many of whom were prisoners of conscience, were unlawfully detained. Some detainees were tortured and ill-treated in police and gendarmerie cells. Tens of thousands of people fled from the violence to neighbouring countries. Freedom of the press and freedom of assembly were restricted. At least two people were sentenced to death. No executions were reported.

Background

A failed coup took place on 28 May, reportedly led by General André Kolingba, former Head of State from 1981 to 1993, leader of the main opposition party and a member of the Yakoma ethnic group. In the weeks following, Bangui became the scene of considerable violence as government forces loyal to President Ange-Félix Patassé regained control with the support of troops from Libya, other foreign governments and an armed opposition group in the Democratic Republic of the Congo, the *Mouvement pour la libération du Congo* (MLC), Movement for the Liberation of the Congo.

Soldiers suspected of being involved in the coup attempt, and civilians from the Yakoma ethnic group suspected of supporting them, were summarily executed. The government subsequently said that human rights violations had been carried out by uncontrollable members of the security forces. No one was brought to justice for these violations. In August, a judicial commission of inquiry was established by the government to investigate killings of members of the armed forces and civilians by the soldiers involved in the coup attempt. Those killed included General François Bédaya N'Djadder and other members of the presidential guard. There was no investigation into killings by government and allied forces.

Fighting erupted again in Bangui in early November, when army chief General François Bozize was dismissed and government troops tried to arrest him for alleged coup plotting. He was banned from speaking to the news media and the church of which he was a leading member was shut down by the authorities. He and his supporters subsequently fled to Chad. During the fighting civilians, including women and children, were reportedly killed by stray bullets and shrapnel.

Extrajudicial executions

Hundreds of unarmed civilians and Yakoma soldiers suspected of involvement in the coup attempt were unlawfully killed and extrajudicially executed during and after the coup attempt. Others were killed in the following weeks as they returned to their places of work after the coup attempt at the request of the authorities. Occasional extrajudicial executions were continuing at the end of 2001.

▫ On 30 May the nine-year-old nephew and two other relatives of Théophile Touba, a Yakoma former member of parliament and university professor, were reportedly killed by members of the Presidential Guard. On 31 May, Théophile Touba was arrested by the Presidential Guard and accused of involvement in planning the coup attempt. On 1 June his body, showing signs of torture, was found in front of President Patassé's official residence.

▫ A Yakoma teacher at the University of Bangui, Evrard Wanguia-Bickot, his 18-year-old son, Romaric Wangui-Bickot, and his 30-year-old cousin, Olivier Kongbeya, were reportedly shot dead by Presidential Guards on 6 June as Evrard Wanguia-Bickot was returning to Bangui after having fled.

▫ On 12 June, two gendarmes, Patrice Igawe Ngobetene and Zoe-Virginie Yembimon, who was said to have been pregnant, and a gendarmerie captain — all Yakoma — were reportedly killed by Presidential Guards when they returned to work.

Detentions and ill-treatment

Political detainees were subjected to ill-treatment throughout the year.

▫ Abdoulaye Aboukary Tembeley, a leading human rights defender, was arrested in February after criticizing President Patassé in a newspaper article and allegedly beaten severely at the National Gendarmerie headquarters.

By late September more than 100 civilians and military personnel had been detained on the recommendations of the commission of inquiry investigating killings of members of the armed forces in the coup attempt. Most had not been charged or tried by the end of 2001. Many of those arrested, who included lawyers, priests and other prominent figures, appeared to be prisoners of conscience detained solely on account of their ethnic identity. Detainees were held in police and gendarmerie cells in harsh and overcrowded conditions.

▫ Jean-Jacques Demafouth, Minister of Defence at the time of the coup attempt, was arrested on 26 August and accused of involvement in the coup plot. He was still detained, incommunicado and without charge or trial, at the end of 2001.

▫ In September Zarambaud Assingambi, a lawyer, was reportedly beaten in the street by police officers, apparently in connection with an article he had written for the newspaper *Le Citoyen* questioning the legitimacy of the commission of inquiry. He was detained without charge for three months, and was released on 12 December.

☐ Serge Wafio, First Vice-President of the National Assembly, was detained in early November. He continued to be detained without charge at the end of the year.

Refugees
Some 30,000 mostly Yakoma civilians and members of the armed forces fled to the neighbouring Democratic Republic of the Congo and northern Republic of the Congo to escape reprisals following the coup attempt. In July, the government closed the border in an attempt to prevent fleeing soldiers using territory in the Democratic Republic of the Congo as a base for rebel military activity.

Most refugees were without basic humanitarian assistance and at risk of malnutrition and exposure for more than six months. In December, despite continuing human rights violations and insecurity, the government started preparations to repatriate refugees from the Democratic Republic of the Congo.

Death penalty
Two men were sentenced to death after being convicted of murdering the Libyan Ambassador in August 2000. The sentence was confirmed in September by the Court of Cassation.

No executions took place.

AI country reports/visits
Statement
- Central African Republic: Government should stop all extrajudicial executions (AI Index: AFR 19/005/2001)

CHAD

REPUBLIC OF CHAD
Head of state: Idriss Déby
Head of government: Nagoum Yamassoum
Capital: N'Djaména
Population: 8.1 million
Official languages: French, Arabic
Death penalty: retentionist

Armed conflict continued in the north of the country. There were reports of human rights violations against the civilian population as a whole, and of suspected members or sympathizers of armed or political opposition movements in particular. These included the torture and ill-treatment of civilians by government forces. At least one death resulted from possible excessive use of force by members of the security forces in the context of presidential elections in May. Two political leaders were ill-treated and scores of opposition supporters briefly detained. Freedom of expression continued to be threatened and human rights defenders worked in a climate of intimidation and danger.

Background
In May President Idriss Déby was re-elected. Opposition candidates alleged that the election was marred by fraud and intimidation and called for the results to be annulled. The results were, however, confirmed by the Constitutional Court. On 30 May the government banned gatherings of more than 20 people. However, political protests continued and the Chadian security forces responded with excessive use of force.

An armed opposition group, the *Mouvement pour la Démocratie et la Justice au Tchad* (MDJT), Movement for Democracy and Justice in Chad, continued to operate in northern Chad. Human rights violations by government troops, particularly during counter-insurgency operations against the MDJT, were reported. These included extrajudicial executions of unarmed civilians as well as suspected MDJT supporters or combatants; torture, particularly in military barracks; the destruction of villages; and the use of detainees as forced labourers. However, lack of access to the area made independent verification difficult.

Over 200 people were killed in intercommunal violence in eastern Chad in June.

Presidential elections
A number of serious human rights violations took place following the May presidential elections.

☐ An opposition supporter, Brahim Selguet, was fatally wounded by police gunfire at the house of an opposition leader on 28 May and died hours later. Police from the *Compagnie d'action rapide police*, Rapid Action Police Company, had arrived at the house to halt a meeting of opposition presidential candidates and their supporters. The presidential candidates were briefly detained. Although the government promised an investigation, by the end of the year none was known to have taken place and the exact circumstances of Brahim Selguet's killing remained unclear. Several other opposition supporters who had gathered at the house were beaten.

◻ On 11 June, the security forces used excessive force to disperse scores of women who had gathered outside the French embassy in N'Djaména in a peaceful protest against the conduct of the presidential election and in order to deliver a statement to the embassy. Anti-riot police threw a number of tear gas canisters at the protesters. Jacqueline Moudeina, a lawyer for the *Comité International pour le Jugement de Hissein Habré*, International Committee for the Trial of Hissein Habré, an international coalition of human rights organizations, was seriously injured. Members of the security forces reportedly asked for Jacqueline Moudeina to be pointed out to them before throwing a tear gas grenade in her direction. A senior member of the security forces searching for her reportedly twice visited the medical centre where she was receiving treatment. Thirteen other women were also injured, one seriously.

Arrests

Scores of opposition supporters were arbitrarily detained. At the end of May, following the presidential elections, leading opposition members, including candidates in the presidential elections, were arrested and briefly detained on two occasions, accused of incitement to violence and civil disobedience.

◻ In May, eight people including Alain Nadjimangar, Serge Béré and Moïse Mbaïlo were arrested in Moundou and later transferred to the civil prison in Ndjaména. Moïse Mbaïlo was provisionally released a month later, but the others remained in detention at the end of the year, charged with membership of an armed group.

'Disappearances'

◻ Abel Karim Abbo Seleck "disappeared" after being taken from his home in N'Djaména on 26 June 2001 by two men believed to be members of the Chadian security forces. There was no official confirmation of his arrest, although he was rumoured to be held at the *Agence nationale de sécurité*, National Security Agency. He may have been arrested on suspicion of having links with the Chadian armed opposition. His whereabouts remained unknown at the end of the year.

◻ There was mounting evidence that at least six members of the MDJT were held in secret detention centres. In December 2000, seven members of the MDJT were presented on television shortly after their arrest in a counter-insurgency attack in Tanoua. In January 2001, the Chadian authorities stated that Yaya Labadri, one of those arrested, had died in detention as a result of wounds sustained during the December attack. The whereabouts of the other six detainees remained unknown at the end of the year.

Torture and ill-treatment

The government failed to take action to address the continuing pattern of torture and ill-treatment in police and military custody.

◻ Ibrahim Adoum, reportedly died on 11 July as a result of ill-treatment in police custody in Abéché.

◻ A woman, who was arrested and briefly detained, alleged that she was made to undress and was tied in a position known as "*arbatachar*", which involves tying the victim's arms behind the back, causing intense pain and sometimes resulting in paralysis.

Hissein Habré

At the end of the year, 40 individual and two collective complaints were under investigation. The complaints had been lodged by the *Association des Victimes des Crimes et Répressions Politiques au Tchad*, Chadian Association of Victims of Political Repression and Crime, against members of the *Direction de la documentation et de la sécurité*, Directorate of Documentation and Security, a security service that was answerable directly to former President Hissein Habré. The complaints related to "crimes of torture, murder and enforced disappearance". In May the N'Djaména Constitutional Court had ruled that, although a special court to try Hissein Habré and his collaborators, provided for in a 1993 law, had never been established, the ordinary courts had jurisdiction over the cases. (See Senegal entry.)

Attacks on freedom of expression

There were further attacks on freedom of expression and on the freedom of the press.

◻ Michaël Didama, acting editor of the newspaper *Le Temps*, received a six-month suspended sentence after being found guilty of defamation in January. He was also ordered to pay substantial damages. The complaint against Michaël Didama was lodged by one of President Déby's nephews after *Le Temps* alleged that a number of attempted coups had been carried out by relatives of President Déby. The offices of *Le Temps* were also visited in January by members of the armed forces, apparently angry at an article which reported on the death toll in clashes in the north of the country. The visit appeared to be an attempt to intimidate *Le Temps* employees.

AI country reports/ visits
Reports
- Chad: Violent crack-down on peaceful protesters (AI Index: AFR 20/001/2001)
- Chad: The Habré legacy (AI Index: AFR 20/004/2001)

CHILE

REPUBLIC OF CHILE
Head of state and government: Ricardo Lagos
Capital: Santiago
Population: 15.4 million
Official language: Spanish
Death penalty: abolitionist for ordinary crimes
2001 treaty ratifications/signatures: Second Optional Protocol to the International Covenant on Civil and Political Rights, aiming at the abolition of the death penalty; Optional Protocol to the UN Children's Convention on the involvement of children in armed conflict; Protocol to the American Convention on Human Rights to Abolish the Death Penalty

Police were accused of using excessive force to break up peaceful demonstrations; scores of protesters were arrested and reportedly ill-treated. Long-standing land disputes led to increasing tension between indigenous groups and the police. Judicial efforts, both in Chile and abroad, continued to clarify past human rights violations.

Background
New legislation and penal reforms were introduced during the year. These included the abolition of the death penalty for ordinary crimes, which became law in May, and the gradual implementation of the new Code of Penal Procedure in the II, III and VII regions. The Code was expected to be implemented in the Santiago Metropolitan area in 2004.

Judicial and government initiatives to deal with the issue of "disappearances" during the years of military rule continued. These included the appointment of special judges to investigate some 150 cases and the submission of information by the armed forces to President Ricardo Lagos, containing the names of 180 people arrested between 1973 and 1976 and 20 unidentified victims. The information stated that most of the victims had been thrown into the sea, rivers and lakes in Chile. The information was handed over to the President of the Supreme Court for the Chilean courts to initiate investigations. Human rights organizations were highly critical of the information provided which was considered inadequate and, in a number of cases, contradicted well-documented evidence.

Ill-treatment and excessive use of force
Carabineros (uniformed police) reportedly used excessive force in a number of incidents including when dispersing peaceful demonstrations. Scores of protesters were reportedly subjected to ill-treatment during arrest and while detained in police stations in Santiago.

□ Andrea Martina Olivares Díaz was arrested in March with some 30 others during a peaceful demonstration. She was dragged into a police vehicle where she was insulted, fondled repeatedly and pinched. She was kept in detention for several hours at the 3rd Police Station where she was not allowed to eat, drink or use the lavatory. She was not informed of the reasons for her arrest and was forced to sign some documents before being released.

□ In April, Marta Alban Ochoa was arrested by *Carabineros* while participating in a demonstration against human rights violations in Peru. She and several other people were allegedly dragged into a van, beaten and insulted. She was held at the 19th Police Station in Providencia where she was eventually allowed to see the doctor about her injuries. She was subsequently released.

Indigenous peoples
Long-standing land conflicts in southern regions generated increasing tension between police and members of indigenous groups. Police reportedly used excessive force during demonstrations and police operations.

□ In January, during a peaceful land rights demonstration in the VIII region, *Carabineros* and plainclothes police reportedly fired rubber bullets and tear gas at protesters and beat many others. Abraham Santi, a Mapuche member of the Pascual Coña indigenous community, was shot in the right eye. It was unclear whether an investigation had been opened into this incident.

□ In May, members of the *Policía de Investigaciones*, Investigation Police, fired on people queueing at a social security office in Tirua, VIII Region; most were Mapuche indigenous people. Officers were apparently trying to make an arrest. Four people were injured. An investigation was reportedly initiated into the shootings.

□ In October, members of the Lafkenche indigenous community in the VIII region, tried to perform a religious ceremony in an area belonging to a timber company which has been officially claimed by the community. After being stopped from entering the area by *Carabineros*, they tried to return home but were surrounded by members of the security forces, including *Carabineros*, who held them there for several hours. The officers fired into the air and harassed community members. The community lodged a complaint to the regional authority.

Other incidents
In November, Gladys Marín, Secretary General of the Communist Party, and scores of Communist Party members were beaten by *Carabineros* during an eviction at the party headquarters in Santiago. Those arrested were subsequently released without charge and an investigation was reportedly initiated into the incident.

Developments concerning past human rights violations
There were developments both inside Chile and abroad in relation to judicial investigations into past human rights violations.

Augusto Pinochet
In January, former President Augusto Pinochet was placed under house arrest in Chile, accused of being the perpetrator of "kidnapping and/or aggravated

homicide" committed in 1973 against 75 victims of a military operation known as the "Caravan of Death". In March, the Santiago Appeals Court rejected an appeal to dismiss the indictment but decided to end the house arrest, reducing the charges against him from that of "perpetrator" to one of "covering up" these crimes. In July, the Sixth Chamber of the Santiago Appeals Court "suspended temporarily", on health grounds, all legal proceedings affecting Augusto Pinochet. In August, the Supreme Court decided to consider the legal action filed by the prosecution lawyers against the temporary suspension of the case, on the grounds that judges had reached their decision by invoking articles of the new Code of Penal Procedure which was not in force in the Santiago Metropolitan area. The case was still pending before the Chilean courts at the end of the year.

Argentina: 'Operation Condor'
Criminal investigations were opened in Argentina into the secret conspiracy by military governments of the Southern Cone countries —Argentina, Bolivia, Brazil, Chile, Paraguay and Uruguay— known as "Operation Condor", to forcibly return exiles to the countries from which they had escaped to face torture, "disappearance" and, often, murder.

In June and July, an Argentine federal judge issued two judicial decisions indicting a number of former officials in connection with a plan "dedicated to illicit acts" involving the systematic "enforced disappearance of people". A number of former Uruguayan military officers were indicted and Argentine, Paraguayan and Chilean former military officers, including former Chilean President Augusto Pinochet, former head of Chilean intelligence Manuel Contreras and former Colonel Pedro Espinoza, were named. In his July decision, the judge requested the preventive detention, pending a request for extradition, of Augusto Pinochet.

The Prats investigation
In May, an Argentine judge requested that Chile extradite former President Augusto Pinochet for the murder of Chilean General Carlos Prats and his wife, who were killed in Buenos Aires in 1974. In August, the Chilean Supreme Court rejected the request for extradition and for permission for the judge to interrogate Augusto Pinochet concerning the killings. In October, five members of the former *Dirección de Inteligencia Nacional* (DINA), National Intelligence Directorate, were arrested in Chile in connection with the killings. The case of Carlos Prats and his wife was also included in the Argentine investigation regarding Operation Condor.

AI country reports/ visits
Reports
- Chile: Legal brief on the incompatibility of Chilean decree law No. 2191 of 1978 with international law (AI Index: AMR 22/002/2001)
- Chile: Testament to suffering and courage – the long quest for justice and truth (AI Index: AMR 22/014/2001)

CHINA

PEOPLE'S REPUBLIC OF CHINA
Head of state: Jiang Zemin
Head of government: Zhu Rongji
Capital: Beijing
Population: 1.3 billion
Official language: Mandarin Chinese
Death penalty: retentionist
2001 treaty ratifications/ signatures: International Covenant on Economic, Social and Cultural Rights; Optional Protocol to the UN Children's Convention on the involvement of children in armed conflict

Serious human rights violations increased in 2001. Thousands of people remained arbitrarily detained or imprisoned across the country for peacefully exercising their rights to freedom of expression, association or belief. Thousands of others were detained during the year. Some were held without charge or trial under a system of administrative detention; others were sentenced to prison terms after unfair trials under national security legislation. Torture and ill-treatment remained widespread and appeared to increase against certain groups. A "strike hard" campaign against crime led to a massive escalation in death sentences and executions. The limited and incomplete records available at the end of the year showed that at least 4,015 people were sentenced to death and 2,468 executed; the true figures were believed to be far higher. In the autonomous regions of Xinjiang and Tibet, freedom of speech and religion continued to be severely restricted. Repression of Muslim ethnic groups suspected of nationalist activities increased.

Background
The authorities continued to show willingness to adhere on a pro-forma level to the international human rights regime, but pursued domestic policies which resulted in serious human rights violations on a large scale, undermining efforts by some groups and institutions to strengthen the rule of law and the protection of human rights. Faced with growing social unrest and public criticism of official corruption and economic inequalities, the government responded with both containment and reforms. It imposed new restrictions on the media and cracked down on groups and individuals deemed a threat to the "stability" or "unity" of the country.

In February China ratified the International Covenant on Economic, Social and Cultural Rights, but placed a reservation on the right to freely form trade unions. In May the government signed a Memorandum of Understanding with the International Labour Organisation (ILO) aimed at setting up a program of cooperation, including raising public awareness about international labour standards. Amendments to the Trade Union Law were adopted in October with the stated aim of strengthening the right to form trade unions, but the All China Federation of Trade Unions remained the only permitted union.

At the UN Commission on Human Rights in April, China again blocked debate on its human rights record by using a procedural motion "not to take action". In August the UN Committee on the Elimination of Racial Discrimination (CERD) made 15 recommendations to China, including giving full effect in its domestic legislation to the provisions of the International Convention on the Elimination of All Forms of Racial Discrimination; punishing all acts of racial discrimination; reviewing legislation and practices that might restrict minorities' right to freedom of religion; ensuring respect for the economic, social and cultural rights of minority populations; and providing statistics, by nationality and region, about detention, imprisonment, torture, death sentences and executions.

China formally joined the World Trade Organization (WTO) in December. Officials had previously announced that China was reviewing some 2,300 laws and regulations for its forthcoming entry into the WTO, and that transparency in law-making and policy decisions was to be increased. An official said in October that the Chinese people would have a greater say on laws and regulations "except those concerning national security".

In late October China's parliament ratified two treaties on terrorism and "separatism": the International Convention for the Suppression of Terrorist Bombings, adopted by the UN General Assembly in 1998; and the Shanghai Treaty on Fighting Terrorism, Separatism and Extremism, under which China and five other members of the Shanghai Cooperation Organization — the Russian Federation, Kazakstan, Kyrgyzstan, Tajikistan and Uzbekistan — agreed to cooperate to crack down on "terrorism", "separatism" and "extremism", including "separatist" activity by ethnic Uighurs from China in Central Asia.

Labour and rural protests

Labour unrest and rural discontent continued. There were many reports of workers' protests against lay-offs, redundancy terms, management corruption and delayed welfare payments. Farmers protested in response to excessive taxes, corruption by local officials and increased poverty. Some protests were met with excessive use of force by police, and some protesters were detained.

▫ Police fired at farmers protesting against high taxes in Yuntang, Jiangxi province, in April, killing two men. One of the alleged protest leaders, Su Guosheng, was arrested. His fate was unknown at the end of 2001.

People continued to be imprisoned solely for trying to organize free trade unions, striking or speaking out on labour issues. Some were sent to "re-education through labour" camps, others sentenced to prison terms or forcibly detained in psychiatric hospitals.

▫ Cao Maobing, a labour activist at a silk factory in Funing, was released in July after seven months' detention in Yancheng No. 4 Psychiatric Hospital. He alleged that he was forcibly given drugs and electric shocks. He was detained at the hospital after he led a strike and talked to foreign journalists.

▫ In July, three labour activists were reportedly sentenced to terms of imprisonment by Tianshui People's Intermediate Court in Gansu province for "subverting state power" after they published a journal that campaigned for workers' rights. Yue Tianxiang received 10 years' imprisonment; Guo Xinmin and Wang Fengshan each received two years.

Repression of spiritual and religious groups

The campaign against groups branded as "heretical organizations" continued. There was mounting evidence that the authorities were permitting the use of violence against *Falun Gong* practitioners as one of the means to eradicate the group. Reports of torture and deaths in custody increased. Around 200 *Falun Gong* practitioners allegedly died in custody as a result of torture. Hasty cremations of the victims hampered investigations into such cases. Others continued to suffer arbitrary detention, unfair trials and imprisonment. Some were held in unregistered detention places, officially described as "study classes", and subjected to coercion to renounce their beliefs. Members of Christian groups were also arrested and some sentenced to long prison terms.

▫ Zhang Min, a *Falun Gong* practitioner from Yilan county, Heilongjiang province, was reportedly arrested on 5 December for handing out *Falun Gong* leaflets. She died six days later, after police reportedly tortured her. Officials reportedly told her family that she had died of a heart attack, although she had no previous history of heart disease.

Dissidents, human rights defenders and reformers

Dissidents, human rights defenders and advocates of reform were arrested and imprisoned. Many were held on charges relating to "state secrets" vaguely defined offences widely used to repress dissent.

▫ Veteran labour activist Li Wangyang was sentenced to 10 years' imprisonment on 20 September for "incitement to subvert state power". He was arrested in May after demanding compensation for ill-treatment in prison. He had been sentenced to 13 years' imprisonment in 1990 for involvement in the 1989 pro-democracy movement, but had been released early in 2000 because of his poor health.

Restrictions on the media and the Internet

Further restrictions were placed on the media and the use of the Internet. A new punishment system was introduced to allow the authorities to close down any publication which violated the restrictions three times. Several newspapers and magazines were closed and journalists dismissed for publishing stories on politically "sensitive" issues. The authorities set up official websites to monitor public views, but continued to crack down on people using the Internet to disseminate information deemed to be sensitive. Among those detained were journalists trying to expose official corruption: some were reportedly held on trumped-up criminal charges.

☐ In June Liu Weifang, an essayist who posted his writings on the Internet, was sentenced to three years in prison on subversion charges by a court in the Xinjiang Uighur Autonomous Region.

Tiananmen Square anniversary

The authorities continued to refuse to hold a public inquiry into the widespread killings and arrests by the security forces during the suppression of the 1989 pro-democracy movement and protests in Tiananmen Square. No one was held to account for the thousands of people killed, injured or arbitrarily detained. The authorities also failed to review the cases of those still imprisoned in connection with the protests for "counter-revolutionary" offences which by 1997 were no longer crimes under national law.

Torture and ill-treatment

Torture and ill-treatment continued to be widespread, occurring in many state institutions – from police stations to drug rehabilitation centres – as well as in people's homes or workplaces. The victims included all types of detainees and prisoners, as well as bystanders to protests, people involved in disputes with officials, migrant workers, vagrants and women suspected of prostitution. The perpetrators included police officers and security officials, tax collectors, judges and prosecutors, birth control officials, village and party officials. Common methods of torture included kicking, beating, electric shocks, hanging by the arms, shackling in painful positions, and sleep and food deprivation.

☐ Zhang Shanguang, serving a 10-year sentence at a prison factory in Hunan province, was reportedly beaten by guards and put in solitary confinement after he circulated a petition in March demanding an end to torture and long working hours. The petition described appalling conditions at the Hunan No. 1 Prison and punishments amounting to torture for prisoners who complained or could not do the heavy work required. The 47-year-old former teacher and labour activist, convicted in 1998 of "endangering state security" because he spoke out on radio about peasant and worker unrest, was reportedly beaten severely during pre-trial detention. He was subsequently reported to have contracted tuberculosis, been denied medical care and forced to do heavy physical labour in shackles.

In July a Chinese periodical reported that torture was still being used routinely by police and investigating prosecutors to extract confessions. It quoted an independent study by China's parliament, carried out in six cities and provinces between 1997 and 1999, which uncovered 221 cases of confessions extracted under torture that had led to the deaths of 21 criminal suspects.

There was concern that the new "strike hard" anti-crime campaign in April would lead to an increase in the torture of criminal suspects and other targeted groups such as alleged "ethnic separatists" in the Xinjiang Uighur Autonomous Region.

Administrative detention and unfair trials

According to official sources, some 260,000 people were administratively detained in "re-education through labour" camps in early 2001, a substantial increase on the number officially reported in 1998. The use of this form of arbitrary detention increased particularly against *Falun Gong* practitioners and during the "strike hard" campaign against crime. Among other victims were political dissidents, members of Christian religious groups, and people accused of "disturbing public order", including prostitutes.

Many criminal and political detainees were denied access to legal representation and other rights associated with fair trial. Political trials continued to fall far short of international fair trial standards, with verdicts and sentences decided by the authorities before trial and appeal hearings usually a formality. Those charged with offences related to "state secrets" had their legal rights restricted and were tried *in camera*.

☐ Yang Zili, a computer engineer, was arrested in March for designing a website that contained essays promoting democracy and political reforms. On the morning of 28 September he was brought before Beijing's First Intermediate People's Court, along with three others, facing charges of "subverting state power". The hearing ended in the early afternoon. A request by the defence to summon three witnesses who had allegedly given evidence against the accused was turned down by the presiding judge. No verdict had been given by the end of the year.

The death penalty

The death penalty continued to be used extensively, arbitrarily, and frequently as a result of political interference. In the weeks after intensification of the "strike hard" campaign, a record number of people were sentenced to death and executed, many after apparently summary trials. From April to early July, AI recorded 2,960 death sentences and 1,781 executions, a rate of executions not seen since a previous "strike hard" campaign in 1996. Executions were carried out for non-violent crimes such as bribery, pimping, embezzlement, tax fraud, selling harmful foods, as well as drug offences and violent crimes. By the end of the year, with the limited records available, AI had recorded 4,015 death sentences and 2,468 executions, although the true figures were believed to be much higher. Execution was by shooting or lethal injection and sometimes occurred within hours of sentencing. Many executions took place after mass sentencing rallies in front of vast crowds in public areas. At least one rally was reportedly broadcast live on state television.

☐ On 20 April, over 200 people were executed in a single day after rallies held across China, including 55 executed in Chongqing municipality alone. Official media reports said the rallies were to "wipe out evil".

Asylum-seekers

Hundreds, possibly thousands, of North Korean refugees and asylum-seekers in northeast China were arrested and forcibly repatriated during the year, denying them access to any refugee determination procedures, in breach of the principles embodied in the 1951 UN Refugee Convention to which China is a state party. CERD expressed concern that they were systematically refused asylum and returned, even in cases where the UN High Commissioner for Refugees had recognized them as refugees. It recommended that China guarantee and ensure equal treatment of all refugees and asylum-seekers, and adopt measures to implement objective criteria for the determination of refugee status.

Xinjiang Uighur Autonomous Region (XUAR)
Gross violations of human rights continued in the XUAR, including arbitrary and summary executions, torture, arbitrary detention and unfair political trials. Particularly targeted were Uighurs, the majority ethnic group among the predominantly Muslim local population. Thousands of political prisoners were believed to be held in the region.

▫ Jur'at Nuri and Abduhalik Abdureshit, both Uighurs, were executed on 9 January in Gulja (Yining) for alleged opposition activities. They had been convicted in July 1999 of "separatism" and illegal possession and carrying of arms, ammunition and explosives. Their trial was grossly unfair, with the convictions based primarily on confessions extracted under torture.

The intensification of the "strike hard" anti-crime campaign led to a wave of executions of alleged Uighur nationalists. Officials in the XUAR said that a major aim of the campaign was to eliminate "separatism" and "illegal" religious activities. Many suspected "separatists" were reportedly detained. Some were sentenced to prison terms or death.

▫ At the end of April, 30 Uighurs were reportedly sentenced to death for alleged involvement in "separatism" and "illegal" religious activities.
A new wave of executions, of people labelled as "separatists" or "terrorists" by the authorities, took place after the 11 September attacks in the USA. A "political re-education campaign" for imams in charge of mosques in the XUAR, which was initiated in March, intensified after 11 September. Restrictions on religious practice were also placed on schools and other institutions during the holy month of Ramadan.

Tibet Autonomous Region
Human rights violations against Tibetan Buddhists and nationalists continued in Tibet. Over 250 prisoners of conscience, many of them monks and nuns, were known to remain imprisoned. The "patriotic education campaign", launched by the Chinese authorities in 1996 to control monasteries and nunneries and undermine the influence of the exiled Dalai Lama, continued, as did restrictions on religious freedom which had been extended to the population at large in recent years. Some monasteries and nunneries were closed down by the authorities, and monks and nuns expelled. Reports continued of torture and ill-treatment of detainees and harsh prison conditions. Many Tibetan prisoners suffered health problems because of poor food and sanitation, harsh working conditions or beatings. Arbitrary arrests and unfair trials also continued.

▫ Migmar, a Tibetan woman, was reportedly sentenced to six years' imprisonment in May by Lhasa Intermediate People's Court after being arrested by Public Security Bureau officials while watching a video of the Dalai Lama at her home.

Inner Mongolia Autonomous Region
Mongolian intellectuals continued to be imprisoned on charges of "separatism" for trying to promote their culture and ethnic identity, for criticizing government policies, and for raising human rights issues.

▫ Hada, a former general manager of a bookshop in Huhehot city, and Tegexi, a former regional government official, continued to serve prison sentences of 15 and 10 years respectively for involvement in "separatist" activities. They were convicted in 1996.

Hong Kong Special Administrative Region
Discussions about an extradition agreement with mainland China and a "subversion" law continued to raise controversy. Frequent demonstrations were held against government policies or during international economic forums. There were reports of police abusing their powers to arrest protesters without sufficient legal grounds under the controversial Public Order Ordinance and of the use of excessive force.

Members of the *Falun Gong*, a registered society in Hong Kong despite being banned in China, were arrested at peaceful demonstrations and alleged that they were victims of police violence.

In September a magistrate ruled that police had abused their powers when arresting three protesters during the visit of China's President Jiang Zemin. Ng Kwok-hung, Sunny Leung Chun-wai and Wan Shu-nam, all members of the Hong Kong Alliance in Support of the Patriotic Democratic Movement in China, were acquitted of assaulting police.

AI country reports/ visits
Reports
- People's Republic of China: Tiananmen 12 years on – the Tiananmen mothers campaigning for accountability (AI Index: ASA 17/001/2001)
- People's Republic of China: Torture – a growing scourge in China: time for action (AI Index: ASA 17/004/2001)
- People's Republic of China: "Striking harder" than ever before (AI Index: ASA 17/022/2001)
- People's Republic of China: Human rights in China in 2001 – A new step backwards (AI Index: ASA 17/028/2001)
- People's Republic of China: The plight of Zhang Shanguang and others – "a legal system in tatters" (AI Index: ASA 17/033/2001)

Visit
In May, two AI delegates attended a European Union-China expert seminar in Beijing on the death penalty and the right to education.

COLOMBIA

REPUBLIC OF COLOMBIA
Head of state and government: Andrés Pastrana Arango
Capital: Santafé de Bogotá
Population: 42.3 million
Official language: Spanish
Death penalty: abolitionist for all crimes

Colombia's internal conflict continued to escalate. Systematic and gross abuses of human rights and international humanitarian law persisted. Paramilitary groups acting with the active or tacit support of the security forces were responsible for the vast majority of extrajudicial executions and "disappearances"; many of their victims were tortured before being killed. Armed opposition groups were responsible for violations of international humanitarian law, including arbitrary or deliberate killings. More than 300 people "disappeared" and more than 4,000 civilians were killed outside of combat for political motives by the armed groups. Over 1,700 people were kidnapped by armed opposition groups and paramilitary forces. All parties to the conflict were responsible for the forced displacement of large numbers of civilians. The security situation of those living in conflict zones, particularly human rights defenders, trade unionists, judicial officials, journalists, members of Afro-Colombian and indigenous communities and peasant farmers, continued to worsen. Evidence emerged of the strong links between the security forces and the paramilitaries. Judicial and disciplinary investigations advanced in several high-profile cases, implicating high-ranking officials in human rights violations, but impunity remained widespread.

Escalating conflict

The intensifying internal conflict affected most areas of the country. Nariño Department saw an intensification of the conflict. Paramilitary forces managed to establish several bases in the region, despite the heavy presence of the armed forces, and carried out a series of incursions into several communities unhindered. Most of the victims of human rights abuses were civilians. Hundreds of massacres, the majority by army-backed paramilitaries, were reported in different parts of the country and over 300,000 civilians were forcibly displaced. Guerrilla attacks on security force bases continued to place civilian communities at considerable risk. Guerrilla and paramilitary forces continued to use child combatants.

Peace process

Peace talks initiated in 1999 between the government and the *Fuerzas Armadas Revolucionarias de Colombia* (FARC), Revolutionary Armed Forces of Colombia, failed to make substantive progress. Agreement was reached for a limited exchange of combatants.

In September, a Commission of Eminent People presented a report with proposals to advance the peace talks. These proposals included recommendations to agree to a truce, to combat paramilitary forces and put an end to kidnapping. On 5 October the government and the FARC agreed to analyse the Commission's recommendations. However, the peace talks stalled once again when the government rejected a series of FARC demands. At the end of November contacts between the government and the FARC resumed.

Peace talks between the government and the armed opposition group *Ejército de Liberación Nacional* (ELN) National Liberation Army failed to progress. On 7 August, President Andrés Pastrana announced that the government was suspending peace talks with the ELN. The following day the government removed political status from the ELN. In November talks to explore restarting contacts between the government and the ELN were held in Cuba. In December the government formally reopened peace talks with the ELN.

Paramilitaries

There was a marked increase in the numbers of paramilitaries captured by the security forces. However, the Office of the Attorney General often failed to receive adequate support from the armed forces. Many arrest warrants issued were not carried out. Furthermore, many of those arrested were reportedly released or escaped from security force bases.

Paramilitaries were able to continue to carry out massacres of civilians unhindered.

▫ In April, over 40 civilians were massacred in the Alto Naya region, Cauca Department, by paramilitaries who were able to enter the region despite the heavy presence of the III Brigade of the Colombian Army and despite repeated warnings, including precautionary measures issued by the Inter-American Commission on Human Rights of the Organization of American States, to the authorities of an imminent paramilitary incursion.

Armed forces

Reports were received of direct security force complicity in human rights violations, sometimes in joint operations with paramilitaries. Judicial and disciplinary investigations into human rights violations committed by paramilitaries operating in unison with the security forces continued to implicate high-ranking military officers.

▫ Criminal investigations were reportedly opened on six paramilitaries and several members of the armed forces in relation to the massacre in January in Chengue, Sucre Department. More than 100 armed men from the paramilitary group *Autodefensas Unidas de Colombia* (AUC), United Self-Defence Groups of Colombia, had attacked the hamlet of Chengue. They picked out 25 people from a list and hacked them to death with machetes, or shot them. Before they left, the paramilitaries set fire to the hamlet and reportedly seized 10 of the villagers, six of them children; their whereabouts remained unknown at the end of the year.

Humanitarian organizations trying to get into the area to help survivors were reportedly turned back by troops of the First Marine Infantry Unit. In July the Office of the Procurator General opened formal disciplinary investigations against eight members of the armed forces. Judicial investigations into the possible involvement of military personnel in the massacre were also under way in 2001.

Armed opposition groups

Armed opposition groups were responsible for numerous abuses including the arbitrary and deliberate killing of hundreds of civilians. Journalists, indigenous leaders and politicians were among those members of civilian society particularly targeted by guerrilla forces for opposing their policies or exposing their abuses. Scores of civilians were wounded or killed in the course of indiscriminate and disproportionate attacks against military targets.

◻ In February, seven young trekkers were killed in the Puracé Natural Park, Cauca Department, following their abduction by FARC forces of the XIII Front. In March the FARC admitted responsibility for the massacre. In November AI wrote to the FARC leadership raising this and other cases of abuses, but no reply had been received by the end of the year.

◻ Pablo Emilio Parra Castañeda, the manager of a radio station in Tolima Department, was killed on 27 June, reportedly by members of the FARC who accused him of being an informant.

◻ ELN guerrillas of the María Cano Front killed a 73-year-old member of the indigenous community of Katío Tegual La Po in the municipality of Segovia, Antioquia Department.

◻ On 15 May, ELN guerrillas entered the Campo Dos area, Tibú Municipality, Norte de Santander Department. They threatened several members of the civilian population, accusing them of collaborating with the army, and killed Francisco Javier Rola and Luis Burgos.

Kidnapping

2001 saw continued high levels of kidnappings and hostage-taking. Guerrilla forces were responsible for an estimated 60 per cent of around 3,000 kidnappings. Paramilitaries also increasingly resorted to hostage-taking and were responsible for an estimated eight per cent of reported kidnappings. Hostages held by guerrilla forces were killed during confrontations with the security forces.

◻ On 24 September, Consuelo Araújo Noguera, a former Minister of Culture and the wife of the Procurator General, was kidnapped, together with 24 other people, by the 59th Front of the FARC, in Patillal, near Valledupar, Cesar Department. The majority of the hostages were released by 25 September. Consuelo Araújo Noguera was killed by the FARC on 30 September.

◻ Timothy Parks, a British citizen who was being held hostage by the ELN, was killed on 28 October during an armed confrontation between the ELN and the armed forces in Chocó Department.

The FARC and the ELN agreed to end collective kidnappings in October and December respectively.

Plan Colombia

There was continuing concern that Plan Colombia, a controversial US, mainly military, aid package, was contributing to the escalating human rights crisis.

In the south of the country, intensification of the conflict and human rights abuses led to large-scale forced displacement in areas in which US-funded anti-narcotics battalions were operating. FARC forces also committed human rights abuses in these areas. There were reports that paramilitary activity intensified in several regions where fumigations, ostensibly of illicit drug cultivation, were taking place or where US-funded units were operating.

◻ There were reports that between September 2000 and April 2001 at least 7,000 people had fled Putumayo Department to Ecuador and another 8,000 were internally displaced as a result of Plan Colombia fumigations and the military operations by both sides in the conflict.

Persecution of human rights defenders, social activists and other civilian sectors

Attacks and threats against national human rights organizations intensified throughout the year. Groups targeted for abuses included peasant farmers; Afro-Colombian and indigenous communities living in conflict zones or areas of economic interest; those campaigning for socio-economic alternatives or seeking to protect land rights, including trade unionists, community leaders and environmental activists; and those exposing violations of human rights and international humanitarian law, including human rights defenders, journalists and judicial officials.

At least 10 journalists were killed and many others were threatened by either guerrilla or paramilitary forces.

There was a significant increase in attacks against trade unionists. By November over 140 had been killed, the majority by paramilitaries. Investigations into the attempted murder of trade union leader Wilson Borja Díaz in December 2000, for which national paramilitary leader Carlos Castaño immediately admitted responsibility, implicated several active and retired security force officers.

◻ Human rights worker Yolanda Cerón, director of a human rights organization linked to the Roman Catholic Church in Tumaco, Nariño Department, was killed on 19 September by gunmen thought to be paramilitaries. Her death followed repeated threats against human rights defenders in Tumaco and the killing in August of Pepe Zabala and Angela Andrade in Tumaco Municipality. Both were members of the Multi-Ethnic People's Movement of the Nariño Pacific Coast, which had faced repeated paramilitary threats in 2000. Immediately after the killing of Yolanda Cerón, members of the national non-governmental human rights organization *Sembrar* received a death threat at their Bogotá offices.

mines. The authorities failed to investigate or take measures to prevent these shootings.

⛶ Eighteen-year-old Mukeba Muchuba was shot in the head by a MIBA guard on 16 September; his speech was severely impaired as a result of his injury.

⛶ Dibua Brinch was shot dead, reportedly by a Zimbabwean soldier, near the village of Luamuela on 12 October.

Neither was known to have been armed or to have posed any threat to life.

Torture

The security forces and armed political groups backed by the government tortured unarmed civilians suspected of supporting opposition forces or to settle personal scores. Journalists were particularly targeted. Methods included whippings and beatings with belts or metal tubes. Conditions of detention often amounted to cruel, inhuman or degrading treatment.

⛶ In February Rachel Chakupewa and her niece, Marie Muzingwa, were reportedly beaten by members of the security forces at the Hotel Okapi in Kinshasa, where the funeral ceremony of a relative of President Kabila was taking place. The two women were accused of attempting to poison relatives of President Kabila. They were detained for several days by the *Garde spéciale présidentielle*, Special Presidential Guard, at the presidential residence and subsequently at a security service detention centre known as the *Groupe Litho Moboti* (GLM) in Kinshasa. During the night of 6/7 February, Rachel Chakupewa was reportedly whipped for several hours by five soldiers and beaten with a metal tube until she was bleeding and unconscious.

⛶ Guy Kasongo Kilembwe, editor-in-chief of the satirical newspaper *Pot-Pourri*, was reportedly beaten at the time of his arrest in February and while held in detention without charge, mostly incommunicado, for a month. He was said to have been whipped, beaten with metal bars and threatened with death because his newspaper had criticized the then Minister of the Interior.

⛶ Anne-Marie Masumbuko Mwali was reportedly beaten with belts and a piece of wood at the GLM detention centre while being interrogated, during three separate arrests in March, about the alleged role of her husband, former army major Janvier Bora Kamwanya, in the murder of President Kabila.

Many of those arrested in connection with alleged coup attempts in late 2000 and April 2001 and the assassination of President Kabila were tortured. At least two people arrested in connection with the assassination died as a result of their torture.

⛶ Pierre Ngbutene died on the night of 13/14 April while in the custody of the security service known as the *Détection militaire des activités anti-patrie* (DEMIAP), Military Detection of Unpatriotic Activities, in Kinshasa, reportedly as a result of torture.

⛶ On 9 September Koyese Swako died of septicaemia, apparently caused by a lung infection contracted through repeated blows to the chest during torture, also in DEMIAP custody. In neither case were any steps taken to bring the perpetrators to justice.

Political prisoners

As many as 100 civilians and soldiers, accused of involvement in the alleged coup attempt of October 2000 and the assassination in January of President Laurent-Désiré Kabila, were detained without charge in detention centres in Kinshasa and the southeastern province of Katanga. Human rights defenders were also detained as prisoners of conscience and ill-treated in an attempt to intimidate them and prevent them from carrying out their work.

⛶ Golden Misabiko Baholelwa, president of the Lubumbashi branch of the *Association africaine de défense des droits de l'homme* (ASADHO), African Association for the Defence of Human Rights, was tortured while detained without charge from February to September. He was questioned in particular about an ASADHO communiqué which denounced the executions in November 2000 of eight alleged coup conspirators.

⛶ Guy Maginzi, a member of the Lubumbashi-based *Centre des droits de l'homme*, Human Rights Centre, was detained for several days in February after he exchanged greetings with Golden Misabiko Baholelwa at N'djili airport as the latter was being transferred from Lubumbashi to Kinshasa. He was reportedly whipped and beaten on the soles of his feet at the GLM detention centre.

⛶ N'sii Luanda Shandwe, president of the *Comité des observateurs des droits de l'homme* (CODHO), Committee of Human Rights Observers, was arrested in June and detained by DEMIAP agents. He was held at the Kinshasa Penitentiary and Re-education Centre before being released without charge in September.

Journalists

Journalists were particularly targeted for arrest and ill-treatment in a continued clamp-down on freedom of expression.

⛶ In March, Trudon Kiomba Shesha, a journalist with the Kasai-Oriental province newspaper *Congo Wetu*, was reportedly beaten by police officers after the newspaper accused the provincial governor of xenophobia and improper sale of land.

⛶ Kinshasa newspaper journalists Washington Lutumba of *Le Potentiel* and Jules-César Mayimbi of *Forum des As* were arrested in March and April respectively on libel charges after publishing allegations that flour delivered to the southwestern province of Bas-Congo may have been unfit for human consumption. Jules-César Mayimbi did not receive any medication for tuberculosis while in detention and both men had to rely entirely on their families for food. They were provisionally released in May and had not been tried by the end of 2001.

Areas controlled by armed political groups and foreign forces

Unlawful killing of civilians, arbitrary and unlawful detentions, and torture, including rape, continued to be inflicted by Congolese armed political groups, particularly the RCD-Goma and the RCD-ML, as well as their allies among Rwandese and Ugandan troops present in the DRC. Very few perpetrators were held to account by the commanders or foreign governments responsible.

Unlawful killings
Armed political groups and foreign troops killed hundreds of unarmed civilians in eastern DRC.

The collapse of the coalition between the RCD-ML and the MLC reportedly resulted in the killings of hundreds of unarmed civilians in the northeast of the country.

◻ In January, in reprisal for earlier killings of several dozen members of the Hema ethnic group by Lendu fighters, armed Hema combatants, supported by Ugandan soldiers, killed as many as 250 unarmed civilians, most of them Lendu, in the northeastern town of Bunia.

◻ In February, 15 unarmed civilians on a bus to Nyamirera, Bunyakiri territory, South-Kivu, were shot and killed by *mayi-mayi* combatants.

◻ Between April and July, MLC combatants and Ugandan troops, contesting control of coltan mines with *mayi-mayi* near Butembo in North-Kivu, reportedly killed several hundred unarmed civilians and burned homes.

◻ On 13 September RCD-Goma and Rwandese troops, firing to disperse a peaceful demonstration held in Bukavu over non-payment of civil service salaries, shot dead Ombeni Bahati, a student.

Persecution of human rights defenders
Human rights defenders, investigating human rights abuses by armed political groups and their foreign backers, were targeted.

◻ Jules Nteba Mbakumba, of the *Elimu* Association, fled in August to neighbouring Burundi from Uvira, South-Kivu, controlled by the RCD-Goma and its Rwandese and Burundian allies, after several of his colleagues were detained by RCD-Goma and accused of distributing leaflets for the *mayi-mayi*. In October he was arrested by the Burundian authorities, returned to the RCD-Goma in DRC, and detained at a Rwandese military camp at Kavimvira near Uvira, where he was reportedly bound and severely beaten. He was subsequently transferred to a detention centre in Goma where he was still being held at the end of 2001.

◻ Juma Pili Rumanya, a member of the *Héritiers de la Justice*, was shot dead on 29 October by men in military uniform in Uvira, South-Kivu. It was suspected that he had been targeted because of a call by his group for the release of Jules Nteba.

◻ Norbert Kisanga, a journalist, was reportedly beaten during six days' detention in October by the *Direction de sécurité et de renseignements* (DSR), Directorate for Security and Intelligence, the RCD-Goma security police. His newspaper, *Les Coulisses*, had reported that RCD-Goma officials were involved in importing counterfeit textiles.

Detention and torture
Critics of RCD-Goma and foreign troops in eastern DRC were detained and subjected to torture, including rape, in private houses, shipping containers and pits. Many detainees accused of supporting the DRC government or its allies were only released after payment.

◻ In August Pastor Claude Olenga Sumaili, of the Roman Catholic Church's Justice and Peace Commission in Kisangani, was stripped and beaten for several hours by members of the DSR. He had reportedly voiced support in a radio broadcast for the demilitarization of Kisangani.

◻ Mami Mwayuma was shot dead on 7 August after she rejected an RCD-Goma soldier's advances in Kisangani. The soldier was reportedly arrested and tried by a military court; the outcome was unknown.

◻ In September, two sons of businessman Bakana Meso, aged about 17 and 30, were accused of links with the DRC government and detained overnight in Bukavu by the DSR until their father paid US$500.

Impact of economic activities
Hundreds of civilians were reportedly forced by combatants of armed political groups and their foreign backers to work in mines, including in the Masisi territory, North-Kivu. Miners and mineral dealers were frequently detained and subjected to beatings and other forms of ill-treatment, sometimes to force them to work harder or to extort money or diamonds. In some areas, members of armed political groups used violence, including torture and other forms of ill-treatment, to force civilians to leave their homes and to seize their land for mining activities.

◻ Mashini Lofofo, Albert Lukumbura and Sherif Mbayi were detained in August by members of the RCD-Goma, reportedly in an attempt to force them to sell diamonds to RCD-Goma officials at a low price. They were released in November after intervention by visiting AI delegates.

AI country reports/visits
Reports
- Democratic Republic of Congo: Deadly conspiracies? (AI Index: AFR 62/004/2001)
- Democratic Republic of Congo: Rwandese-controlled east – Devastating human toll (AI Index: AFR 62/011/2001)
- Democratic Republic of Congo: Torture – a weapon of war against unarmed civilians (AI Index: AFR 62/012/2001)
- Democratic Republic of Congo: Memorandum to the Inter-Congolese Dialogue – Amnesty International's recommendations for a human rights agenda (AI Index: AFR 62/030/2001)

Visits
In October AI delegates visited Kinshasa, Mbuji-Mayi and Lubumbashi to gather information about human rights violations in areas controlled by the government, and held talks with government authorities. In October and November AI delegates visited eastern DRC to gather information about human rights abuses there.

CÔTE D'IVOIRE

REPUBLIC OF CÔTE D'IVOIRE
Head of state: Laurent Gbagbo
Head of government: Pascal Affi N'Guessan
Capital: Yamoussoukro
Population: 16.3 million
Official language: French
Death penalty: abolitionist for all crimes

Despite some unrest following an alleged coup attempt in January, political tension reduced significantly compared to the previous year. In March, municipal elections were held peacefully with the participation of the opposition party, the *Rassemblement des Républicains* (RDR), Republican Assembly. The RDR had boycotted the October and December 2000 presidential and legislative vote after its leader, Alassane Ouattara, was barred from standing in the polls because his Ivorian nationality was challenged. In December, a national forum aimed at resolving political and ethnic problems concluded that Alassane Ouattara should be given Ivorian nationality papers. President Laurent Gbagbo took official note of this recommendation and said that the issue should be dealt with by the courts. There appeared to be a marked lack of willingness by the authorities to investigate the serious human rights violations committed by security forces during the previous two years.

Background
Public debate continued on the concept of nationality following the introduction of a new Constitution in July 2000 which stipulated that presidential candidates must be born of Ivorian parents and have never held another nationality. This focused attention on Alassane Ouattara and his right to stand for presidential and legislative elections. The debate led to land disputes between migrants, mostly from Burkina Faso, who had lived for decades in Côte d'Ivoire, and local people who challenged the right of foreigners to own land. Despite calls from the authorities to end these disputes, several deaths resulted and more than 1,000 people from Burkina Faso returned to their country of origin.

Possible prisoners of conscience
Several leaders of the RDR were arrested or remained detained for several months before being acquitted or provisionally released. They appeared to have been prisoners of conscience.

In January, Jean-Jacques Béchio, the RDR foreign affairs adviser, was arrested without a warrant by members of the security forces and severely ill-treated (see below). He was charged with plotting against the state. The security forces alleged that weapons were found in his home. He was provisionally released in May but the charges were believed to remain.

In July, two RDR leaders, including Aly Coulibaly, party spokesman, were acquitted of "complicity in the destruction of private and public property and disrupting public order". They had been arrested in December 2000 and held for five months.

Torture and ill-treatment
Torture and ill-treatment of both civilians and military by the security forces were reported following the alleged coup attempt in January. No inquiry appeared to have been conducted into the allegations.

Jean-Jacques Béchio was arrested in January and taken to a building in the Presidency compound. He was threatened with death and severely beaten by up to eight members of the security forces before being provisionally released.

Military accused of attempted coup
Following the alleged coup attempt in January, up to 50 people, mostly members of the military, were arrested and detained without trial on charges of plotting to overthrow the government. Most remained in detention at the end of the year.

In October, six military, including captain Fabien Coulibaly, the *aide-de-camp* of former Head of State General Gue, were arrested and charged with "threatening state security and plotting an assassination". They were all provisionally released 10 days after their arrest; their trial had not begun by the end of the year.

In March, a special military court sentenced General Lansana Palenfo, a former government minister, to one year's imprisonment for conspiring to overthrow General Gue. Another defendant, General Abdoulaye Coulibaly, was acquitted. In July, General Palenfo was released after the Supreme Court cancelled all legal proceedings against him on the grounds that the military tribunal sentencing him did not have the authority to try a government minister.

Harassment of journalists
Several journalists were briefly detained, harassed or threatened during the year. Security forces broke into the premises of a newspaper, apparently in search of weapons.

In January, Mohammed Junior Ouattara, a well-known reporter working for the French news agency *Agence France Presse*, was arrested by several police officers in plain clothes and accused of involvement in the attempted coup. He was released without charge five days later.

In February, police broke into the printing office of the independent newspaper *Le Jour*, in search of "weapons and mercenaries". They made death threats against the newspaper's financial director, Biamari Coulibaly, who was not on the premises.

Impunity
Despite firm public commitments by the government to bring to justice security force members responsible for the serious human rights violations during the previous two years, most of the violations were not

independently investigated. A legal action was launched in Belgium by an association of some 150 Ivorian victims against current and former government leaders, including President Gbgabo, for crimes against humanity.

◻ In August a military trial acquitted eight gendarmes (paramilitary police) of charges of homicide and murder in relation to the Youpougon mass grave. In October 2000, 57 bodies were found in a mass grave in Youpougon, on the outskirts of Abidjan. Investigations by the UN and non-governmental organizations, including AI, concluded that the massacre had been committed by gendarmes. At the trial, the military prosecutor recommended life sentences for the eight gendarmes but the trial concluded that there was a lack of evidence. It was conducted in a highly tense atmosphere, and many witnesses failed to appear because they feared for their safety. Although the military prosecutor said that he would appeal against the acquittal, it was unclear at the end of the year whether an appeal had been lodged.

◻ Despite a report ordered by President Gbagbo which confirmed that women had been raped in December 2000 in the presence of security forces who did nothing to protect them, no independent investigation was opened to bring to justice those responsible. Other serious cases of torture and sexual violence committed by the security forces in December 2000 remained uninvestigated.

AI country reports/ visits
Visit
An AI delegation visiting Côte d'Ivoire in June met government officials, including President Gbagbo, and carried out research into the human rights situation.

CROATIA

REPUBLIC OF CROATIA
Head of state: Stjepan Mesić
Head of government: Ivica Račan
Capital: Zagreb
Population: 4.7 million
Official language: Croatian
Death penalty: abolitionist for all crimes
2001 treaty ratifications: Optional Protocol to the UN Women's Convention; Rome Statute of the International Criminal Court

Croatia continued to suffer the legacy of the 1991-1995 armed conflict, particularly impunity for war crimes and other violations of human rights. Significant progress was made in cooperation with the International Criminal Tribunal for the former Yugoslavia (the Tribunal). The domestic criminal justice system improved its record in investigating and prosecuting war crimes committed by both Croats and Croatian Serbs, although not all proceedings were conducted thoroughly and impartially. Return of the country's pre-war Serb population continued to be marred by discriminatory laws and political obstruction. Allegations that law enforcement officials ill-treated detainees were not investigated promptly and thoroughly.

Background
In March amendments to the Croatian Constitution abolished the upper chamber of Parliament (*Sabor*), the Chamber of Deputies. The incumbent government coalition of six parties narrowly won municipal elections in May, while the opposition *Hrvatska demokratska zajednica* (HDZ), Croatian Democratic Union, gained significant support. In October Croatia signed a Stabilization and Association Agreement with the European Union, which was ratified in December by the European Parliament.

In November the Ministry of the Interior announced that some 38,000 files compiled on individuals by the security services would be made accessible in the state archives. During 10 years of HDZ rule (1990-2000), many journalists and opposition politicians were placed under surveillance, which was apparently unlawful because it was not justified by reasons of national security or the prevention or detection of crime. However, administrative and legal procedures prevented those responsible from being brought to account.

Human Rights Committee
In March, AI briefed the Human Rights Committee prior to its examination of Croatia's initial report under the International Covenant on Civil and Political Rights. In April, the Committee requested that Croatia report back on measures taken to investigate and prosecute those responsible for human rights violations after

army offensives in 1995, and to provide more information on the application of the 1996 Amnesty Law which, the Committee feared, allowed perpetrators of human rights violations to escape accountability. It also recommended measures to facilitate the return of refugees and displaced persons.

Investigations and prosecutions for war crimes
International Criminal Tribunal for the former Yugoslavia
Cooperation improved with the Tribunal. Croatian army General Rahim Ademi was surrendered to its custody in August, after his indictment for war crimes against Croatian Serb civilians in 1993 had been unsealed. However, Croatia failed to surrender former Croatian army General Ante Gotovina, charged with war crimes committed during army operations in 1995. The Tribunal Prosecutor criticized the government for allowing him to escape arrest despite being informed about his indictment before it was unsealed. In November Bosnian Croat Pasko Ljubičić, indicted for war crimes in central Bosnia, gave himself up to Croatian police and was subsequently surrendered to the Tribunal.

In October, the Tribunal Prosecutor charged the former President of the Federal Republic of Yugoslavia (FRY), Slobodan Milošević, with war crimes and crimes against humanity committed in Croatia. Also named in the indictment were 15 other Serb and Croatian Serb men, all former officials and armed forces officers. The indictment covered the murders of hundreds of non-Serbs, the illegal detention of thousands of people, many of whom were tortured or ill-treated, and the expulsion of over 170,000 others from Serb-occupied areas.

Domestic prosecutions
At least six trials of Croatian army and police officers charged with human rights violations against Croatian Serbs during the war continued or commenced before Croatian courts. They included retrials of people whose earlier acquittals had been quashed by the Supreme Court.

However, prosecutions progressed slowly and the criminal justice system remained ill-equipped to investigate and prosecute these sensitive cases thoroughly and impartially. In July the government proposed a law to set up an independent prosecution office which would take over the investigation and prosecution of war crimes. By the end of 2001, the draft law had not yet been introduced into Parliament.

◻ In March, police investigated the torture and subsequent "disappearance" of scores of Serb and Montenegrin prisoners in the *Lora* military prison in Split during the war. In September, seven former military police officers suspected of these crimes were arrested. In October a former detainee was reportedly threatened and photographed by war veterans at Split County Court while waiting to be questioned by the investigative judge. Anonymous threats were reportedly also received by the Split County Public Prosecutor. In December the Dalmatia-Split County Prefect visited the seven suspects in prison and publicly expressed hopes that they would be freed, compromising the independence of judicial proceedings.

Scores of criminal proceedings continued against Croatian Serbs charged with human rights violations, many in the absence of the accused. At least 300 — and possibly hundreds more — international arrest warrants were issued, most of them for Croatian Serb suspects believed to be abroad. Many concerned individuals convicted *in absentia* and on the basis of insufficient evidence. In May AI reiterated its recommendation that Croatia establish a system analogous to the Rules of the Road procedure in Bosnia-Herzegovina. Under this procedure domestic courts must refer potential war crimes cases to the Tribunal prosecutor for an independent assessment.

◻ In March a warrant was issued for the arrest of Edita Radjen-Potkonjak, a Croatian Serb dental nurse. In 1995 she had been convicted and sentenced to 15 years' imprisonment after a trial *in absentia*, with 25 others, in connection with mass executions of Croatian civilians in 1991. Her conviction appeared to have been based on hearsay evidence from one witness.

Allegations of ill-treatment by law enforcement officials
Investigations into several reports that detainees were ill-treated by prison officers and did not receive immediate or adequate medical treatment were not conducted promptly and thoroughly.

◻ In June Tomica Bajšić, a detainee under investigation in Karlovac District Prison, went into a coma, allegedly as a result of ill-treatment or excessive use of force. He was reportedly denied immediate medical care following his collapse. In August the government said there was no evidence of ill-treatment but that an investigation into the conduct of personnel at the prison was ongoing. However, the outcome of any investigation was not known to have been made public by the end of 2001.

Refugee returns
According to estimates by the Organization for Security and Co-operation in Europe, less than one third of the 300,000 Croatian Serbs who fled the country during the war had returned to the country. Official government statistics listed around 10,000 people as having returned from the FRY and the Republika Srpska in 2001, a significant decrease from 2000.

The return of property belonging to Croatian Serbs remained slow. Local housing commissions failed to implement promptly the provisions of the Return Programme, which allowed the temporary occupant to remain if no alternative accommodation was available. By contrast, in eastern Slavonia, the local authorities applied different legislation, allowing them to evict Croatian Serbs occupying houses belonging to Croats, without having provided the former with alternative housing. In August the government issued instructions requiring housing commissions to tackle the problems of illegal and double occupation of property belonging to returnees.

However, in November the government said it was under no obligation to restore the tenancy rights of Croatian Serbs. In 1995, tens of thousands lost their right to rent socially owned apartments for life and were consequently unable to return to their pre-war homes. Many Croatian Serbs had also lost tenancy rights as a result of unfair civil proceedings, or after being illegally and violently evicted.

AI country reports/visits
Report
- Concerns in Europe, January-June 2001: Croatia (AI Index: EUR 01/003/2001)

CUBA

REPUBLIC OF CUBA
Head of state and government: Fidel Castro Ruz
Capital: Havana
Population: 11.2 million
Official language: Spanish
Death penalty: retentionist

A number of prisoners of conscience were released in 2001, but several new arrests indicated that the Cuban authorities had not renounced curbs on the peaceful exercise of freedom of expression, association and assembly. Short-term detention and other forms of harassment continued to be used to repress the activities of journalists, political activists and others. An unofficial moratorium on executions was said to be in force. No executions were reported during 2001, although the courts continued to hand down death sentences. The four-decades-old embargo against Cuba by the USA continued to contribute to a climate in which fundamental rights were denied. However, for the first time the USA sold agricultural commodities to Cuba in the wake of a hurricane in November. Both countries denied that this signified a change in overall relations. In November, UN General Assembly members voted overwhelmingly to condemn the embargo, for the 10th consecutive year.

Background
After 75-year-old President Castro fainted briefly during a speech in June, speculation grew about his eventual successor as Head of State. President Castro addressed the issue openly and publicly reiterated his choice of his brother Raúl Castro Ruz, First Vice-President and head of the armed forces, as head of a collective leadership structure following his own eventual departure from office.

UN Commission on Human Rights
After unprecedented campaigning, in April the UN Commission on Human Rights again passed by a narrow margin a Czech Republic-sponsored resolution on the situation in Cuba. A resolution critical of Cuba's record had been passed annually since 1992, with the exception of 1998. This year's text was more conciliatory towards Cuba; while stopping short of condemnation of the US embargo, it stated for the first time that UN member states should "take steps to improve the economic condition of the Cuban people." The subsequent detention for nearly three weeks of two prominent Czech citizens on subversion charges was regarded by some as retaliation for the resolution. The two men were released after signing statements admitting that they had unwittingly broken Cuban law by meeting dissidents at the behest of a US-based organization.

Relations with the USA
In July the US House of Representatives voted to ease travel restrictions to Cuba, but President George W. Bush expressed his opposition to the proposed measure. In October, US lawmakers cut the relevant language from the bill, then before the Senate, thereby avoiding the issue for this year.

On the legal front, the US authorities released US$ 90 million in frozen Cuban assets in February as compensation to the families of three pilots shot down in February 1996 by Cuban jets. In June a US federal jury convicted five Cubans of working as agents for a Cuban espionage ring which had allegedly infiltrated military installations and Cuban exile groups in Florida. By the end of the year, four of them had been sentenced to prison terms ranging from 15 years to life. In September a US Defense Department intelligence analyst was arrested on charges of passing national defence secrets to Cuba; the Cuban government denied any knowledge of this. In September a retired Cuban immigrant living in Miami was arrested on charges of torturing Cuban political prisoners with electric shocks when he worked in a Havana psychiatric hospital several decades earlier.

Prisoners of conscience
The Cuban state continued to imprison critics for the peaceful exercise of their rights to freedom of expression, assembly and association. Limitations on these fundamental freedoms remained codified in Cuban law. A number of releases raised hopes that Cuba might be easing these restrictions and bringing its laws and practices into line with international standards. However, new arrests indicated that such hopes were premature. At the end of 2001 at least seven prisoners of conscience were held in Cuba.

In May, José Orlando González Bridón, Secretary General of the *Confederación de Trabajadores Democráticos de Cuba*, Cuban Confederation of Democratic Workers, was sentenced to two years' imprisonment for "spreading false news against international peace". This was apparently in retaliation for an article he wrote accusing the

Amnesty International Report 2002

authorities of negligence in a domestic violence case. In September his sentence was reduced to one year by the highest court in Cuba, and he was released in November.

Detention without trial
A number of dissidents were held in detention for several months without trial before being released. They were prisoners of conscience.

⌕ Trade unionist Pedro Pablo Alvarez Ramos, General Secretary of the *Consejo Unitario de Trabajadores Cubanos* (CUTC), United Cuban Workers Council, was released in January after three months in prison without trial. He had been arrested in October 2000 by state security agents, apparently to prevent him from participating in the first national convention of the CUTC on 20 and 21 October 2000. Several other prominent trade unionists were briefly detained before the convention.

⌕ Leonardo Miguel Bruzón Avila was detained in December 2000 during a wave of arrests intended to prevent dissidents from participating in activities to commemorate the 52nd anniversary of the Universal Declaration of Human Rights. Leonardo Bruzón, president of the *Movimiento Pro Derechos Humanos 24 de Febrero*, 24 February Human Rights Movement, was reportedly held in the Technical Investigations Department, where he said he was handcuffed to the bars of a punishment cell while standing almost knee-high in water for four days. He was released on 1 February. He was rearrested in September after opening an "independent library" for children in his home; his family was threatened with eviction. He was released without charge after four days.

Medical concerns for detainees
There were continuing concerns about prisoners' lack of access to adequate medical care. The country's stock of medicines and materials was adversely affected by the US embargo. However, there were concerns that in some cases care was deliberately withheld from prisoners of conscience or other political prisoners as an additional punishment.

⌕ The family of Marcelo Amelo Rodríguez, aged 52, who died in custody in May after suffering from chest pains, accused prison officials of not giving him access to adequate treatment. Marcelo Amelo had been imprisoned in 1993 for rebellion and released in June 2000 after completing his sentence. He was later rearrested on different charges. There had been concerns about his health for several years.

⌕ Prisoner of conscience Nestor Rodríguez Lobaina was reportedly confined in close quarters with prisoners suffering from active pulmonary tuberculosis in Combinado de Guantánamo Prison, thereby putting him at risk of infection. Nestor Rodríguez was serving a sentence of six years and two months after having been convicted in February 2000 of "disrespect", "public disorder" and "damage".

⌕ Political prisoner Jorge Luis García Pérez went on hunger strike in April to protest at the lack of medical attention for various health problems. He ended his hunger strike after nearly one month, after the authorities allowed him to be examined by a lung specialist.

Continuing harassment of dissidents
The Cuban authorities continued to try to discourage dissent by harassing suspected critics of the government. Suspected dissidents were subjected to short-term detention, frequent summonses, threats, eviction, loss of employment and restrictions on movement. Harassment was at times carried out by state security agents or police officers, as well as by members of local groups such as the *Brigadas de Respuesta Rápida*, Rapid Response Brigades, or the *Comités de Defensa de la Revolución*, Committees for the Defence of the Revolution, set up in 1991 and 1960 respectively to discourage crime and dissident activities.

There were several incidents of verbal assaults against dissidents, most often by unidentified attackers. In some cases the homes of suspected dissidents were attacked by individuals throwing rocks or bottles, and in a few instances dissidents were said to have been punched or kicked by unidentified assailants in attacks that they believed were related to their political views or activities.

⌕ Rafael León Rodríguez, coordinator of the *Proyecto Demócrata Cubano*, Cuban Democratic Project, one of the organizations belonging to the *Mesa de Reflexión de la Oposición Moderada*, Table of Reflection of the Moderate Opposition, was reportedly evicted from his home in July following an apparent bureaucratic error. In spite of protests, Rafael León Rodríguez' home and belongings had not been returned to him by the end of the year. This led to concerns that the move was intended as punishment for his dissident activities.

⌕ Activists attempting to collect signatures for the *Proyecto Varela*, a petition for a referendum on legal reform, were subjected to threats, short-term detention, summonses, confiscation of materials and other forms of harassment by state security agents, police and other officials in a number of locations. At the end of November project organizers reported that they had collected over 2,500 voters' signatures; the law requires 10,000 signatures in order for a referendum to be held.

Death penalty
There were indications of a change in government policy on executions; no executions were reported to have been carried out in 2001. However, the death penalty was not legally abolished and in December the legislature reportedly reaffirmed its use against those convicted of the crime of "terrorism", the definition of which was said to have been expanded under new legal provisions. Courts continued to hand down death sentences. According to the *Comisión Cubana de Derechos Humanos y Reconciliación Nacional*, Cuban Commission for Human Rights and National Reconciliation, a non-governmental organization, approximately 50 prisoners remained on death row at the end of 2001.

AI country reports/visits
Reports
- Cuba: Prisoner of Conscience José Orlando González Bridón (AI Index: AMR 25/006/2001)
- Cuba: Medical Letter Writing Actions – Insufficient medical care for Jorge Luis García Pérez [Antúnez] (AI Index: AMR 25/003/2001 and AI Index: AMR 25/005/2001)
- Cuba: Medical Letter Writing Action – Political prisoners in need of medical attention (AI Index: AMR 25/004/2001)

Visits
AI last visited Cuba in 1988. The government did not respond to AI's requests to be allowed into the country.

CZECH REPUBLIC

CZECH REPUBLIC
Head of state: Václav Havel
Head of government: Miloš Zeman
Capital: Prague
Population: 10.3 million
Official language: Czech
Death penalty: abolitionist for all crimes
2001 treaty ratifications/signatures: Optional Protocol to the UN Women's Convention; Optional Protocol to the UN Children's Convention on the involvement of children in armed conflict

The authorities failed to conduct thorough and impartial investigations into reported cases of arbitrary detention and police ill-treatment. Roma who were subjected to racist violence were frequently inadequately protected by police officers.

Inadequate investigations
Investigations continued into reports that dozens of people suspected of involvement in anti-globalization demonstrations in Prague on 26 and 27 September 2000 had been arbitrarily detained and ill-treated by police. Investigations into complaints of criminal behaviour by police officers were carried out by the Inspectorate of the Ministry of the Interior. There were concerns that the investigations could not be considered independent and impartial as both those conducting investigations and those being investigated were under the control of the same authority — the Ministry of the Interior.

⬜ The Environmental Law Service, a non-governmental human rights organization based in Brno, filed 27 criminal complaints on behalf of victims of human rights abuses. The Inspectorate of the Ministry of the Interior decided to investigate only three cases of police ill-treatment. All other complaints were referred to the Department of Inspection and Complaints of the Police Presidium which investigates alleged misdemeanours by officers. The Department failed to establish that any police officer was responsible for a misdemeanour in connection with the September demonstrations.

The Inspectorate of the Ministry of the Interior's investigations reportedly confirmed that police in two Prague police stations may have ill-treated detainees. In one case, forensic experts established that a tooth and two of the 10 bloodstains found in the police station belonged to a Polish national. He was one of the very few victims questioned in the course of the investigation. He was able to identify one of the police officers he believed was responsible for ill-treating him. However, the Inspectorate was still unable to establish the identity of any of the perpetrators.

The conduct of the Inspectorate in these investigations was consistent with its persistent failure to promptly and impartially investigate allegations of torture and ill-treatment in previous years. The failure to bring to justice those responsible for human rights violations contributed to an atmosphere in which police officers felt they could commit abuses with impunity.

In May the UN Committee against Torture recommended that the Czech authorities "ensure the independence and thoroughness of investigations of all allegations of ill-treatment in general, and in connection with the IMF/World Bank meeting in September 2000 in particular, and to provide the Committee in its next periodic report with information on the findings and measures taken, including prosecutions and compensation to victims, as appropriate".

In July, the UN Human Rights Committee, reviewing the Czech Republic's compliance with the International Covenant on Civil and Political Rights, concluded, among other things, that the current system of investigating complaints against the police "lacks objectivity and credibility and would seem to facilitate impunity for police involved in human rights violations".

Roma
There were numerous reports that the police failed to protect Roma from attack or to effectively investigate violent assaults against them. Where prosecutions did take place, the courts tended to convict those responsible for racist attacks of lesser offences.

⬜ In April a group of about 45 skinheads reportedly attacked a group of some 20 Romani men with baseball bats in a bar in Nový Bor in the north of the country. The group of mainly Czech and German youths were celebrating the anniversary of Hitler's birth. Although eight Roma were said to have been injured in the attack, according to reports no one had been charged with any criminal offence by the end of the year.

⬜ Ota Absolon, a 30-year-old man of Romani origin, was stabbed to death in July in Svitavy, East Bohemia. The young man charged with this attack had a long record of previous convictions for violent crimes. He had, for example, been given a suspended sentence in 1997 for stabbing another Romani man in the stomach. Apparently that offence had not been considered by the court to be a racially motivated attack, which would have carried a stiffer penalty. More recently he had been convicted of another violent crime. The judge allowed him to remain at liberty pending the outcome of his appeal against this most recent conviction, reportedly because he considered that the young man would not commit any further offences.

In May the UN Committee against Torture expressed concern about the "continuing incidents of discrimination against Roma, including by local officials, and particularly about reports of degrading treatment by the police of members of minority groups, continuing reports of violent attacks against Roma and the alleged failure on the part of police and judicial authorities to provide adequate protection, and to investigate and prosecute such crimes, as well as the lenient treatment of offenders". Similar concern was expressed in July by the Human Rights Committee.

AI country reports/ visits
Report
- Czech Republic: Arbitrary detention and police ill-treatment following September 2000 protests (AI Index: EUR 71/001/2001)

DOMINICAN REPUBLIC

DOMINICAN REPUBLIC
Head of state and government: Hipólito Mejía
Capital: Santo Domingo
Population: 8.5 million
Official language: Spanish
Death penalty: abolitionist for all crimes
2001 treaty ratifications/signatures: Optional Protocol to the UN Women's Convention

The pattern of unlawful killings by security forces, noted in previous years, continued in 2001. Although a growing number of such cases were tried by civilian courts, the majority continued to be heard before police or military tribunals. There were reports of ill-treatment of criminal suspects in police stations. Prisons remained severely overcrowded, with at least half the total number of prisoners in pre-trial detention.

Background
On 23 March, the UN Human Rights Committee reviewed the Dominican Republic's fourth periodic report on its implementation of the International Covenant on Civil and Political Rights. The Committee's recommendations focused on illegal killings by security forces, police and military courts, torture and cruel, inhuman or degrading treatment, prison conditions and treatment of suspected Haitians. The national Commission for the Reform and Modernization of the Armed Forces and the Police, set up in 2000, continued its review of police tribunals. The military were given increased policing functions, with the creation of new riot and anti-terrorism units within the armed forces.

Killings and excessive use of force
Killings in disputed circumstances by police and military continued. Some appeared to be extrajudicial executions. In many cases, the authorities alleged that the victims were killed in exchanges of gunfire with criminal suspects, but this version was often disputed in witness testimony and other evidence.

On 29 September, a police officer repeatedly shot Pedro Manuel Contreras, aged 19, in his family's house. He then reportedly dragged the body into the street where he continued to shoot at it. When Pedro Manuel Contreras' mother tried to intervene she was held at gunpoint by two other officers. According to an official complaint lodged by the family on 24 August, a month before the killing took place, they had requested a local non-governmental organization to intervene with the authorities to provide protection for their son, as he had received several death threats from the same police officer who shot him. The officer was suspended from his post.

Demonstrations
Demonstrations against police brutality and electricity blackouts took place across the country throughout the year, during which several demonstrators were killed and many were injured or arrested. In some instances the military were sent to help police the demonstrations.

On 13 February, hundreds of doctors and other medical personnel participating in a protest march in Santo Domingo against new social security measures were fired at by police in an attempt to disperse the marchers and prevent them from reaching the National Congress building. Several doctors reportedly received wounds from rubber bullets or pellets, and others were beaten and kicked.

Police tribunals
The Commission for the Reform and Modernization of the Armed Forces continued its review of police tribunals. Both the police and the military were governed by their own codes of justice, which dictated whether members were to be tried by police or military rather than civilian courts. The Supreme Court of Justice was considering a petition, initiated by seven civil society organizations, demanding that police tribunals be declared unconstitutional. In a step widely perceived as positive, by June civil prosecutions had begun against seven police officers accused of shooting civilians.

Forced repatriation

Forced repatriations continued to be carried out throughout the year of those of Haitian origin and Dominicans suspected of being Haitian because of their colour.

Father Ruquoy, a Belgian priest and human rights activist, continued to denounce ill-treatment of Haitian sugar workers, in particular the increasing numbers of arrests and forced deportations by the army. After he testified at the Inter-American Court of Human Rights in August 2000, Father Ruquoy became the victim of anonymous death threats and attacks, and was threatened at knife point in his home in April 2001.

On 16 January, soldiers opened fire with machine guns on a lorry transporting Haitians across the border at Lascahobas. Two passengers, Théodore Alexandre and Telvi Jean, died later from bullet wounds, and an unspecified number of people were injured.

Following the attacks in the USA on 11 September, there were reports of harassment, arrest and detention of people believed to be Muslim or of Middle Eastern origin. s

Prison conditions

Severe overcrowding and poor conditions reportedly continued in the majority of the country's prisons. Skin diseases were rampant and contagious diseases such as tuberculosis were of major concern. Medical care was inadequate. Water and sanitary conditions were sub-standard in many prisons, contributing to intestinal and other health problems. The government announced that the standard and quality of food in prisons would be improved, and that an automated information system to record prisoner numbers and details would be introduced.

Torture and ill-treatment

Reports of beatings of detainees in prison and police detention continued to be received. There were several reports of killings of detainees, by military or police guards, generally in the context of escape attempts or prison riots.

Several activists were detained on 18 June, the day before a national day of protest against cuts in the national electricity supply and the economic measures introduced by the government, and to call for the removal of the chief of police. Víctor Gerónimo was allegedly beaten by three police officers, and Fernando Peña was said to have been beaten about the head by a police officer, causing damage to his right eye. The complaint subsequently lodged by the men was rejected by the district prosecutor on the grounds that it did not identify those responsible by name.

AI country reports/ visits
Report
- Dominican Republic: UN Human Rights Committee's recommendations must be implemented (AI Index: AMR 27/003/2001)

EAST TIMOR

EAST TIMOR
Capital: Dili
Population: 0.8 million
Death penalty: abolitionist for all crimes

East Timor's transition to independence continued with the election of a Constituent Assembly, the appointment of an all-Timorese government and the drafting of a new Constitution. The first ruling against suspects on trial for crimes against humanity committed during 1999 was handed down in December. However, the newly established justice system remained fragile and was unable to respond fully to the demands placed upon it. The rule of law was undermined by the use of processes outside the official justice system, including traditional law, which did not always meet international standards, and there were indications that some individuals benefited from impunity. The incomplete legal and institutional framework also impacted on the rights to protection of vulnerable groups, including refugees returning from Indonesia, members of the Muslim and ethnic-Chinese communities, and women and children.

Background

In a process which observers considered to have been free and fair, 16 political parties contested elections on 30 August for the 88-member Constituent Assembly. A "Second Transitional Government" was subsequently appointed by the UN Transitional Administrator and was supervised by a Council of Ministers, although overall authority for government remained with the UN Transitional Administrator.

The mandate of the UN Transitional Administration in East Timor (UNTAET) was expected to be extended to 20 May 2002, the date set for East Timor's independence. A reduced UN presence after independence was endorsed by the UN Security Council although final plans had not been agreed.

The Constitution

The Constituent Assembly began deliberations on East Timor's draft Constitution, in a process which was scheduled to be completed in early 2002.

Criminal justice system

New regulations adopted by UNTAET on legal aid as well as the prison and police services signalled progress in establishing a legal framework to protect human rights. However, some important legislation had not been drafted, and other legislation dating from the occupation by Indonesia which fell short of international human rights standards had not been reviewed. Provisions in the UNTAET Regulation on the Transitional Rules of Criminal Procedure which did not conform to human rights standards were also not amended.

By the end of the year only one of East Timor's four district courts was fully functioning. Rulings were not always consistent with human rights standards. Lack of capacity and inexperience within the public defenders service meant that in some cases detainees did not have access to lawyers for weeks or months.

Judicial independence was threatened by direct interference in the working of the courts, including by political officials, and by incidents of physical threats against members of the judiciary. A code of ethics for the judiciary was drafted, but not yet adopted, and no effective, independent and impartial judicial overview mechanism had been established. Efforts to resolve the problem of unlawful detentions resulting from expired detention orders were only partially successful.

Lack of confidence in the formal criminal justice system contributed to a reliance on alternative, non-judicial mechanisms, including traditional law. Crimes such as rape and domestic violence were among those being resolved through such unregulated processes. Without guidelines or effective monitoring, such practices were applied inconsistently and vulnerable groups were at risk of discrimination and other human rights abuses.

Investigations and trials of past violations

By the end of the year, over 30 indictments had been issued by the UNTAET Serious Crimes Unit, responsible for the investigation and prosecution of cases relating to the 1999 violence. They included indictments for crimes against humanity. The first sentence in a serious crimes case was delivered on 25 January when a former militia member was sentenced to 12 years' imprisonment for murder. Hearings in the first crimes against humanity case began in July. The judgment, delivered in December, found 10 defendants guilty and they were sentenced to up to 33 years and four months in prison. One suspect, a member of *Kopassus*, Indonesia's Special Forces Command, was still at large in Indonesia. He was among a number of individuals indicted by the Serious Crimes Unit who were in Indonesia and who had not been transferred to East Timor for trial.

Despite some progress, problems within the Serious Crimes Unit, such as poor management and lack of experienced staff and resources, continued to impact on the speed and quality of its work as well as on relations with local human rights organizations. Capacity to hear serious crimes cases was increased in November with the addition of a second panel of judges, but some concerns remained about the fairness of the trials. The work of the Serious Crimes Unit was also hampered by lack of cooperation from Indonesia (see Indonesia entry).

A regulation establishing a national Commission for Reception, Truth and Reconciliation was adopted in June. The selection process for Commissioners began in September.

Protection of vulnerable groups

Cases of assault, illegal detention and threats by unofficial security groups and others against refugees returning from Indonesia were reported during the year and were not always effectively addressed by the authorities.

The legal status of minority groups such as the Muslim and ethnic Chinese communities had not been resolved and they continued to be at risk of discrimination, including violent attacks. In Baucau, the mosque was destroyed during disturbances in March.

The legal and institutional framework to protect and promote the rights of women and children remained inadequate. High levels of domestic violence, lack of access by women to the criminal justice system and gender bias in court proceedings were yet to be adequately addressed.

AI country reports/visits
Report
- East Timor: Justice – past, present and future (AI Index: ASA 57/001/2001)

Visit
AI delegates visited East Timor in March.

ECUADOR

REPUBLIC OF ECUADOR
Head of state and government: Gustavo Noboa Bejarano
Capital: Quito
Population: 12.9 million
Official language: Spanish
Death penalty: abolitionist for all crimes

Torture and ill-treatment, including death in custody, remained a concern. Dozens of people were killed in circumstances suggesting that they may have been extrajudicially executed. Threats against human rights defenders, as well as lawyers and witnesses in human rights cases, were frequent. Impunity remained institutionalized. There were serious concerns that lesbian, gay, bisexual and transgender people suffered persecution and violence.

Background

Widespread protests continued against the government's economic program, which included extensive privatization of state-owned enterprises and designating the official currency as the US dollar. A state of emergency was declared for several weeks in February. Many trade unionists, indigenous people, students and community leaders were arrested by police, allegedly without arrest warrants, and detained for several days without being charged.

Indigenous people

In early February security forces in Tena violently evicted a group of indigenous people from the Puerto Napo church where they had assembled peacefully in opposition to the government's economic policies. Three civilians were shot dead and at least a dozen injured in what appeared to be excessive use of force by the police. Witnesses alleged that the security forces opened fire on the demonstrators. Relatives of those killed during the demonstrations received financial compensation from the authorities.

More than 3,000 indigenous people, including at least 350 children, took part in a demonstration at a university in Quito. They were allegedly intimidated and harassed by the police, who attempted to disperse them with tear gas.

Following these mass demonstrations the government offered to hold talks with indigenous organizations to discuss their concerns.

Plan Colombia

The US-backed principally military aid package known as Plan Colombia came into force (see Colombia entry) amid serious concerns about its possible impact on Ecuador as the conflict in Colombia spilled across the border. The large numbers of refugees entering Ecuador early in 2001 exacerbated these fears but the influx had reduced by the end of the year.

Cocaine processing laboratories as well as camps allegedly used by the Colombian armed opposition and paramilitary groups were discovered in Sucumbíos province. There was a high number of kidnappings in the region, particularly foreign oil workers. Indigenous groups fled the area and became internally displaced. They were alleged to have been threatened by unidentified Colombian armed groups from across the border, and also feared retaliation from security forces seeking the kidnappers.

Intimidation of human rights defenders

There were continued reports of threats and harassment of those working on human rights.

▫ A number of human rights defenders and organizations received a series of death threats from a group called "White Legion", who accused them of being "shelters and recruitment centres for national and international subversion".

▫ Teresa Gladys Pita Bravo and Gino Cevallos Gonzales, the mother and lawyer of Elías Elint López who, together with Luis Alberto Shinin Laso, "disappeared" in 2000 after having been detained by the police in Tungurahua province, received threats in June and July. These stated that the two would suffer the same consequences if they continued with judicial proceedings against the police officers charged with the "disappearances".

Possible extrajudicial executions

Allegations continued that police officers were carrying out extrajudicial executions, particularly in Guayaquil where some 26 people were found dead in the city's outskirts during the first 10 months of the year. All had been shot in circumstances suggesting extrajudicial execution. Many appeared to have been tortured before being killed. One human rights organization stated that 65 bodies have been found in the area since 1999.

▫ Joffre Aroca Palma was reportedly detained on 27 February by a police patrol in Guayaquil. His body was found abandoned some hours later with a gunshot wound to the chest.

Impunity

Concern remained that cases of human rights violations involving members of the security forces were not resolved promptly, impartially and independently. Many were brought before police courts where the vast majority of those accused of human rights violations are not convicted.

▫ Eight police officers were charged with the "disappearance" in November 2000 of Elías Elint López and Luis Alberto Shinin Laso (see above). Their case was being heard before a police court.

▫ Six police officers were charged with the killing of Pedro Ashanga Akintua and his son Germán Akintua Chup in December 2000. The two were reportedly shot dead at point blank range after being stopped with their families by 20 police officers on the road in Morona Santiago province. Their case was being heard before a police court.

Torture and ill-treatment

Torture and ill-treatment, including death in custody, remained a serious concern.

▫ Luis Alfredo Redrobán was detained in April by police in Pillaro, Tungurahua province. He reportedly died at the police station after being severely beaten by officers.

Lesbian, gay, bisexual and transgender people

Lesbian, gay, bisexual and transgender people were victims of grave human rights violations throughout the year. AI documented cases of intimidation and death threats, torture and ill-treatment, and of attempted extrajudicial execution as well as of arbitrary arrest of people who had been detained on grounds of their sexuality.

AI country reports/visits

Reports
- Ecuador: Torture and "disappearance" of Elías Elint López and Luis Alberto Shinin Laso (AI Index: AMR 28/008/2001)
- Ecuador: Continued torture and ill-treatment of lesbian, gay, bisexual and transgender people (AI Index: AMR 28/009/2001)

Visits

AI visited Ecuador in April and June, to conduct research and to launch a report on the torture and ill-treatment of lesbian, gay, bisexual and transgender people.

EGYPT

ARAB REPUBLIC OF EGYPT
Head of state: Muhammad Hosni Mubarak
Head of government: 'Atif Muhammad 'Ubayd
Capital: Cairo
Population: 69.1 million
Official language: Arabic
Death penalty: retentionist
2001 treaty ratifications/signatures: African Charter on the Rights and Welfare of the Child

At least 27 prisoners of conscience were sentenced to prison terms of up to seven years. At the end of the year, 47 prisoners of conscience, including 21 people imprisoned in previous years, remained held. Thousands of suspected supporters of banned Islamist groups, including possible prisoners of conscience, remained in detention without charge or trial; some had been held for years. Others were serving sentences imposed after grossly unfair trials before military courts. Torture and ill-treatment of detainees was widespread. Prison conditions amounting to cruel, inhuman or degrading treatment were reported. At least 67 people were sentenced to death and at least four were executed.

Background
Elections to Egypt's Upper House began in mid-May and took place over a period of several weeks. The ruling National Democratic Party won the vast majority of seats. Scores of alleged members of the banned Muslim Brothers organization were arrested, particularly in the run-up to the elections.

Following the attacks in the USA on 11 September, the Egyptian authorities arrested several people suspected of having links with militant Islamist groups; they included people who had been forcibly deported to Egypt. The authorities also clamped down on public gatherings and demonstrations.

Freedom of expression and association
Prisoners of conscience were sentenced to up to seven years' imprisonment. At least 21 prisoners of conscience, including political activists and members of religious groups, sentenced in previous years remained in prison. Among them were 15 alleged Muslim Brothers sentenced in 2000 to up to five years' imprisonment after an unfair trial.

Civil society institutions such as political parties, non-governmental organizations, professional associations and trade unions, and the news media continued to face legal restrictions and government control. In July, an administrative court ruled that the authorities should no longer obstruct the registration of the Egyptian Organization for Human Rights.

In June, the Cairo office of the Sudanese Human Rights Organization was closed by the Egyptian authorities. The Sudanese authorities had allegedly demanded the closure of the office which had operated for some years in Egypt.

The Egyptian authorities imposed a ban on the activities of two political parties and maintained bans on other parties, including the suspension of party newspapers, imposed in previous years.

Human rights defenders
In May the Supreme State Security Court in Cairo sentenced Saad Eddin Ibrahim, a prominent human rights defender and Director of the Ibn Khaldun Center for Development Studies, to seven years' imprisonment. Three fellow human rights defenders who also worked at the Center were sentenced to two-year prison terms. The main charges against them were in connection with European Union funded projects aimed at promoting participation in elections. In a joint statement the UN Special Representative on Human Rights Defenders and the UN Special Rapporteur on the independence of judges and lawyers declared that the conviction "will have a chilling effect on the activities of other human rights defenders in Egypt".

Freedom of religion
People continued to be at risk of detention, trial and imprisonment in violation of their right to freedom of religion.

☐ More than a dozen alleged members of the Baha'i faith, most from the Sohag Governorate, were arrested between January and April and detained for several months. In February the UN Special Rapporteur on religious intolerance noted that "Baha'is are not allowed to meet in groups, especially for religious observances, and their literature is destroyed".

☐ In January, Salah al-Din Muhsin, a writer, was convicted of "offending religion" in several of his publications and sentenced to three years in prison after an unfair trial before the (Emergency) State Security Court for Misdemeanours in Giza.

☐ In June, feminist writer Nawal El-Saadawi appeared before a Personal Status Court in Cairo after a private complaint had been filed against her accusing her of apostasy. The complaint was linked with comments she made on religious issues which were published in the Egyptian weekly newspaper, *al-Midan*. In July the court rejected the complaint.

Imprisonment for alleged sexual orientation
In July, the trial of 52 allegedly gay men was opened before the (Emergency) State Security Court for Misdemeanours in Cairo; this Court permits no right of appeal. All the defendants were charged with "habitual debauchery" while two faced additional charges of "contempt of religion". They were reportedly tortured or ill-treated while held in pre-trial detention; all the defendants were forcibly subjected to anal examinations. In November the Court sentenced 23 of the defendants to between one and five years' imprisonment. They were imprisoned for their alleged sexual orientation; 22 were prisoners of conscience.

☐ A 17-year-old boy was convicted in September of charges of "habitual debauchery" and sentenced to three years' imprisonment — the maximum sentence allowed —

by the Cairo Juvenile Court. In December, his sentence was reduced on appeal to six months.

Unfair trials

Hundreds of people were tried or referred for trial before exceptional courts, such as state security courts, established under emergency legislation. They faced a variety of charges, including membership of illegal organizations, contempt for religion, publishing obscene material, habitual debauchery, espionage and corruption. The procedures of these courts fell far short of international standards for fair trial. For example, defendants did not have the right to a full review before a higher tribunal.

◻ In September, the (Emergency) Supreme State Security Court began the retrial of Sharif al-Filali who was charged with spying for Israel. He had been acquitted of the same charges by a different panel of the same court in June. However, President Mubarak refused to ratify the acquittal and ordered a retrial.

◻ In September the (Emergency) State Security Court for Misdemeanours in Cairo sentenced the editor-in-chief of *al-Naba'a* newspaper, Mamduh Mahran, to three years' imprisonment on charges including insulting a religion and holy places, spreading false information, and publishing pictures which violate public morals. The charges related to an article published in June about a former Coptic monk. The article included photographs of alleged sexual activities in a monastery and led to widespread protests by the Coptic community in Egypt against the publication of the article, which was considered offensive.

◻ In October, President Mubarak decreed that more than 250 people would be tried in two separate cases before the Supreme Military Court in connection with their alleged affiliation with armed Islamist groups. The majority of the defendants had been detained for several years without charge or trial.

◻ In November, President Mubarak ordered that 22 alleged members of the Muslim Brothers should be tried before a military court. They had been detained in connection with alleged preparations for political activities opposing military intervention in Afghanistan by the USA and its allies.

Detention under emergency legislation

Following the attacks in the USA in September, several people suspected of being affiliated to militant Islamist groups were arrested under provisions of the emergency legislation. Thousands of suspected members or sympathizers of banned Islamist groups arrested in previous years, including possible prisoners of conscience, continued to be administratively detained without charge or trial.

More detainees were allowed visits by their relatives. However, prison conditions remained poor. Scores of detainees were reportedly suffering from diseases caused or exacerbated by the lack of hygiene and medical care, overcrowding or poor food. Thousands of political detainees continued to be denied the right to visits by lawyers and family members.

Torture and ill-treatment

Torture continued to be widespread in detention centres throughout the country. The UN Special Rapporteur on torture concluded that "torture is systematically practised by the security forces in Egypt, in particular by State Security Intelligence". The most common methods reported were electric shocks, beatings, suspension by the wrists or ankles and various forms of psychological torture, including death threats and threats of rape or sexual abuse of the detainee or a female relative. Torture victims came from all walks of life and included political activists and people arrested in criminal investigations.

◻ Saif al-Islam Mohammad Rashwan was detained for several days in May at a branch of the State Security Intelligence in Giza, suspected of membership of the Muslim Brothers. He was reportedly given electric shocks, beaten and suspended from a horizontal pole.

◻ Fifteen-year-old Rania Fathi 'Abd al-Rahman was detained in April for one day, together with other family members in a neighbourhood in the north of Cairo in connection with a criminal investigation. While held at the police station of Shubra al-Khaima's first precinct she was reportedly subjected to torture, including electric shocks. The Association for Human Rights and Legal Assistance reported that a family member was intimidated and harassed after filing a torture complaint. No investigation had been initiated by the end of the year.

Local human rights organizations

Local human rights organizations filed numerous complaints on behalf of torture victims and published several reports. In September the Human Rights Center for the Assistance of Prisoners received a communication from the Ministry of the Interior in response to its report documenting the cases of more than 1,000 torture complaints filed over the past two decades.

Deaths in custody

In January the UN Special Rapporteur on torture commented on communications received from the Egyptian authorities regarding cases of deaths in custody in previous years. He expressed concerns about the persistence of explanations of the cause of death such as "sharp drop in blood pressure". He concluded that such symptoms were generally provoked by prior factors such as trauma or malnourishment. Several security officers were given prison sentences in connection with deaths in custody in previous years.

Harassment of victims and their relatives

Victims of torture and their relatives who filed complaints with the authorities continued to report harassment by security agents.

◻ In May relatives of Fathi 'Abd al-Mun'im, who had died in 1994 in police custody in Helwan in circumstances suggesting that torture had caused or contributed to his death, were harassed and reportedly ill-treated by police officers. Fathi 'Abd al-Mun'im's widow, Sammah Hamid Ali, was arbitrarily detained for three days at Helwan police station. The harassment was apparently linked to the forthcoming trial of a police officer accused of Fathi 'Abd al-Mun'im's murder.

Impunity
Hundreds, if not thousands, of complaints of torture, some relating to deaths in custody, lodged over the past two decades by victims, relatives, lawyers and human rights organizations had still not been investigated.

Forcible return
There were reports that several Egyptian nationals forcibly returned to Egypt were held in incommunicado detention for weeks or even months. People suspected of having links with Islamist organizations were returned from several countries, including Bosnia-Herzegovina, Azerbaijan, Sweden and Saudi Arabia.

In December, the Swedish authorities forcibly returned two Egyptian asylum-seekers – Muhammad Muhammad Suleiman Ibrahim el-Zari and Ahmed Hussein Mustafa Kamil Agiza – after rejecting their applications for asylum in an unfair procedure. At the end of the year, the two men remained held in incommunicado detention in Egypt and were at risk of human rights violations, including torture and unfair trial.

Death penalty
The death penalty continued to be used extensively. At least five women and 62 men were sentenced to death by criminal courts during 2001 and at least one woman and three men were executed.

Intergovernmental organizations
In January the UN Committee on the Elimination of Discrimination against Women expressed concerns regarding insufficient measures for the "prevention and elimination of violence against women, including domestic violence, marital rape, violence against women in detention centres and crimes committed in the name of honour."

In January the UN Committee on the Rights of the Child expressed concerns about child labour in Egypt, in particular in the agricultural sector. The Committee noted that many children work "long hours in dusty environments, without masks or respirators, receiving little or no training on safety precautions for work with toxic pesticides and herbicides."

AI country reports/ visits
Reports
- Egypt: Torture remains rife as cries for justice go unheeded (AI Index: MDE 12/001/2001)
- Egypt: Imprisonment of human rights defenders (AI Index: MDE 12/016/2001)
- Egypt: Torture and imprisonment for actual or perceived sexual orientation (AI Index: MDE 12/033/2001)

Visits
In July AI organized a training seminar for human rights defenders from North Africa in Cairo, in conjunction with local human rights organizations. AI delegates also visited Egypt in July.

EL SALVADOR

REPUBLIC OF EL SALVADOR
Head of state and government: Francisco Flores
Capital: San Salvador
Population: 6.4 million
Official language: Spanish
Death penalty: abolitionist for ordinary crimes
2001 treaty ratifications/signatures: Optional Protocol to the UN Women's Convention

Impunity in two prominent past cases of human rights violations underlined long-standing concerns. There was a new attempt to reinstate the death penalty. There were serious problems in various government institutions, including the Office of the Human Rights Procurator and the judiciary.

Background
More than 1,000 people died in two massive earthquakes which devastated the country in January and February. Infrastructure and thousands of homes were destroyed, further deteriorating the living conditions of already impoverished communities.

Profound public concern persisted at the high levels of criminal activity, such as kidnappings for ransom in which several victims died, including children. Organizational problems within the judiciary undermined public confidence. The Attorney General's Office found that the qualifications of dozens of professionals working within the judicial system were irregular, and there were also allegations of corruption among officials. By the end of the year the Supreme Court of Justice had not taken steps to remove inadequately qualified incumbents, including judges, prosecutors and lawyers.

Impunity
Impunity for past human rights violations continued to be a serious concern.

In January the Court of Appeal in San Salvador stayed proceedings against six people accused of ordering the killings in 1989 of six Jesuit priests, their housekeeper and her daughter. All the accused were in high-ranking civilian and military posts at the time. This ruling was the result of an appeal against the dismissal of the case in December 2000 on the grounds that criminal responsibilities had lapsed since the crime had been committed more than 10 years previously. The Third Magistrate's Court of San Salvador had indicated at that time, however, that the accused could have been prosecuted as the 1993 Amnesty Law would not have benefited them.

AI argued that the statute of limitations did not apply in this case because the human rights violations committed in El Salvador between 1980 and 1991, including these killings, constituted crimes against humanity which, according to international law, are not subject to such limitations. In November several non-governmental organizations initiated the process for this case, and that of Archbishop Oscar Arnulfo Romero, murdered in 1980, to be examined by the Inter-American Court of Human Rights.

Death penalty
In July a new attempt was made to reinstate the death penalty, which had been abolished in 1983 for all but some crimes under military law. The move was initiated as a result of public concern at the increase in the crime rate. However, the Legislative Assembly approved instead an increase to the length of sentences for murder, kidnapping and rape from 35 to 75 years' imprisonment.

Office of the Human Rights Procurator
In July, the Legislative Assembly elected Beatrice Alamanni de Carrillo as Human Rights Procurator. There was serious concern that the functions of the Office had stagnated during the more than one year's delay in her appointment, apparently as a result of political partisanship within the selection process. AI made several appeals to the Legislative Assembly to proceed with the election and to support rather than undermine the Office of the Human Rights Procurator, one of the cornerstones of the 1992 peace accords.

National Civil Police
There were reports of an improvement in the performance of the *Policía Nacional Civil* (PNC), National Civil Police, and consequently in its perception by the public. More crimes were solved and there were fewer complaints about the police. A large number of people responsible for kidnappings were reportedly arrested by PNC members. However, reports persisted of involvement by PNC members in human rights violations and criminal activities, including kidnappings.

◻ In October a man died reportedly as a result of a beating by police officers. He had allegedly been causing a disturbance and police came to his house to investigate. He was handcuffed and beaten and, according to forensic evidence, died as a result. Five police officers were charged with causing his death; three were arrested and brought to trial and two evaded arrest. Further proceedings were pending at the end of the year.

Updates
The *Asociación Pro-Búsqueda de Niñas y Niños Desaparecidos*, Association for the Search for Disappeared Children, continued its efforts to locate children separated from their families during the armed conflict of 1980 to 1992 and reunite them with their families. In November Moisés Morán, aged 27, met his family for the first time since 1981. The *Asociación* persisted with its requests to the government to create an official commission to locate children who had "disappeared" in the conflict.

AI country reports/visits
Reports
- El Salvador: Peace can only be achieved with justice (AI Index: AMR 29/001/2001)
- El Salvador: Legislative Assembly must support, not undermine the Office of the Human Rights Procurator (AI Index: AMR 29/005/2001)
- El Salvador: The death penalty is a retrograde step and does not work (AI Index: AMR 29/007/2001)

EQUATORIAL GUINEA

REPUBLIC OF EQUATORIAL GUINEA
Head of state: Teodoro Obiang Nguema Mbasogo
Head of government: Candido Muatetema Rivas (replaced Angel Serafin Seriche Dougan in February)
Capital: Malabo
Population: 0.5 million
Official languages: Spanish, French
Death penalty: retentionist

Around 50 members of the Bubi ethnic group sentenced after unfair trials in 1998 remained imprisoned throughout 2001; many appeared to be prisoners of conscience. Most were detained in poor conditions hundreds of kilometres from their families on whom they relied for food and medical assistance. The authorities harassed the few journalists who continued to defend their right to freedom of expression. Harassment of peaceful political opponents continued, but to a lesser extent than in previous years as opposition political parties were weakened by internal divisions, apparently encouraged by the government and ruling party.

Background
In February, following accusations of corruption against several members of the former government, the President appointed a new Prime Minister, but many of the key ministers remained in post.

In September the government held a meeting of the 13 officially recognized political parties to reassess a 1997 political pact aimed at monitoring elections and free access to the media for all political parties. After their boycott of municipal elections in 2000 because of electoral irregularities by the authorities, opposition parties stepped up their demands for increased access to the official news media. The news media had remained under government control since the return to multi-party democracy in 1992.

UN Commission on Human Rights
In April the UN Commission on Human Rights examined the report of the UN Special Representative on

Equatorial Guinea who had been denied access to the country on three occasions in 2000. The Commission urged the government of Equatorial Guinea to respect freedom of movement, association and expression. It called on the authorities to adhere to the UN Convention against Torture and to ensure that the jurisdiction of military courts, which had frequently tried civilians, was strictly limited to military offences committed by military personnel. The Prime Minister, who led the official delegation to the UN Commission session, announced during the session that Equatorial Guinea would ratify the Convention against Torture, but this commitment had not been fulfilled by the end of the year.

In November, the UN Special Representative on Equatorial Guinea was finally allowed to visit the country for the purposes of monitoring the human rights situation.

Harsh treatment of Bubi prisoners

Some 50 prisoners from the Bubi ethnic group continued to be held throughout the year. About 30 of them had been transferred to Evinayong, some 500 kilometres east of Malabo, in 2000; the rest remained in the main prison in Malabo. They had been convicted of offences including "treason, terrorism and the illegal possession of explosives" in 1998 after an unfair military trial. Many appeared to be prisoners of conscience, arrested solely on account of their ethnic origin.

Most were tortured in pre-trial detention and held for two years in extremely harsh conditions. Their conditions improved gradually as they were allowed to work outside the prison during the day. However, their families continued to face difficulties in overcoming the obstacles of distance and cost in order to visit them and bring them food and medicine, vital support given that prison food was inadequate and medical treatment practically non-existent.

Freedom of expression and association

Freedom of association continued to be restricted by the authorities, notably in the field of human rights. The government continued to give no response to applications for the registration of human rights organizations made in previous years. As a result, there were no groups monitoring human rights violations inside the country.

Harassment of peaceful political opponents continued, but to a lesser extent than in previous years. Opposition political parties, undermined by years of repression and internal dissension and defections, often engineered by the ruling party, found it increasingly difficult to mobilize their supporters.

In February, the authorities shut down the premises of the country's only journalists' association, the Equatorial Guinea Press Association. The authorities refused to give any reason for this move. The Association, which was registered in 1997, brought together journalists from the private and government-owned press in a country in which there were no regularly published newspapers.

In May, Pedro Nolasko Ndong, President of the Equatorial Guinea Press Association, was briefly detained at Malabo airport on his way back from a seminar in Namibia on freedom of expression. The security forces confiscated documents, including information on the human rights situation in Equatorial Guinea, before releasing him.

ERITREA

ERITREA
Head of state and government: Issayas Afewerki
Capital: Asmara
Population: 3.8 million
Official languages: English, Arabic, Tigrinya
Death penalty: retentionist
2001 treaty ratifications/signatures: International Covenant on Economic, Social and Cultural Rights; UN Convention against Racism

The authorities used repressive measures to deal with an upsurge in public dissent in the latter part of 2001. At least 80 people were detained including 11 former senior party officials and at least 24 journalists. The independent press was suspended in September and remained so at the end of the year. Student leaders were arrested and thousands were kept in harsh conditions during their compulsory summer work program; at least two died as a result. Allegations of detentions and extrajudicial executions of political opponents were difficult to verify.

Background

The mandate of the UN Mission in Ethiopia and Eritrea (UNMEE), created under the 2000 Algiers Agreement which ended the war with Ethiopia, was extended to March 2002. In May, the UN arms embargo on Eritrea and Ethiopia was lifted. On a number of occasions throughout the year, UNMEE complained that the authorities were restricting their movement on some roads both inside and leading into the UNMEE-monitored Temporary Security Zone, a buffer zone inside Eritrea. The government said it required prior notification if UNMEE wanted to move outside the Zone or into restricted military areas. Both Eritrea and Ethiopia alleged that the other's forces illegally entered the Zone on a number of occasions. The Boundary and Compensation Commissions, instituted under the Algiers Agreement, were established. Although both sides began to repatriate prisoners of war in early 2001, disagreements led to a considerable slowing down of the process by the end of the year.

In August the Chief Justice was sacked after complaining of government interference in the judicial process.

In September the Italian Ambassador was expelled after he raised European Union concerns about recent arrests. The Eritrean authorities said they had called for his removal before this. All European Union member states recalled their representatives in October for consultation. All except the Italian Ambassador returned in November.

By the end of 2001, regulations allowing for the formation of political parties had been shelved and an electoral law had not been ratified. Elections due in December were not held.

Refugees and returnees

Tens of thousands of refugees returned to Eritrea in 2001, including at least 25,000 from Sudan. Hundreds of people internally displaced by the war began to return to their homes. Hundreds of Eritreans were voluntarily repatriated from Ethiopia under the auspices of the International Committee of the Red Cross (ICRC). However, in June the ICRC complained that 722 Eritreans were involuntarily repatriated from Ethiopia; the Ethiopian authorities said they had returned willingly.

Armed opposition

Eritrea continued to support political and armed opposition groups in Ethiopia, and Ethiopia continued to support such groups in Eritrea. It was difficult to obtain information on the activities in Eritrea of the Alliance of Eritrean National Forces, which included the Eritrean Liberation Front-Revolutionary Council, supported by Ethiopia, and the Eritrean Islamic Salvation Movement, supported by Sudan. It was impossible to verify allegations by these groups of killings, torture and detentions of their supporters by government forces.

Students

Thousands of students taking part in the compulsory student work program in August and September were forced to work in extremely harsh conditions which led to the deaths from heat-stroke of at least two students. The government said it regretted the deaths, but no investigation was known to have been carried out nor steps taken to improve conditions.

Semere Kesete, a student leader from Asmara University, was arrested in July following his public criticism of some elements of the program. He remained in incommunicado detention without charge or trial at the end of the year.

Attacks on government critics

In June the government denied reports that around 15 journalists had been arrested. It said they were carrying out military service. There were fears that regulations concerning military conscription may have been applied to silence critics of the government.

At least 80 people were arrested in September. The independent press was suspended by the government for "not abiding by the press law" and remained closed at the end of the year.

On 18 and 19 September, 11 senior officials in the ruling People's Front for Democracy and Justice were arrested. They had written an open letter in March to fellow party members accusing the government of acting in an "illegal and unconstitutional" manner. They remained in incommunicado detention without charge or trial at the end of the year.

At least nine journalists were arrested following the suspension of the independent press; they remained in incommunicado detention without charge at the end of 2001.

Detention without trial and unfair trials

There were continuing allegations that many people, particularly those suspected of having links with Eritrean armed opposition groups, were being held without charge or trial for political reasons. Scores of people were also reported to remain in detention throughout 2001, awaiting trial by the Special Court. Trials before the Special Court continued to fall short of international fair trial standards, with trials conducted behind closed doors and no rights to defence counsel or of appeal to a higher or independent court.

In June, the government reported that Ermias Debesay, a former ambassador to China, had been convicted by the Special Court of theft, embezzlement and abuse of power, and sentenced to seven years' imprisonment. It was alleged that his conviction was politically motivated.

Dozens of Eritrean officials of the former Ethiopian government in Eritrea were believed to be still serving prison sentences, imposed after unfair trials, for human rights abuses.

AI country reports/visits
Report
- Eritrea: Growing repression of government critics (AI Index: AFR 64/001/2001)

ETHIOPIA

FEDERAL DEMOCRATIC REPUBLIC OF ETHIOPIA
Head of state: Girma Wolde-Giorgis (replaced Negasso Gidada in October)
Head of government: Meles Zenawi
Capital: Addis Ababa
Population: 58.8 million
Official language: Amharic
Death penalty: retentionist

At least 31 people were killed and over 3,000 arrested during rioting in April. Armed conflict continued within Ethiopia between government forces and Oromo and Somali opponents; many human rights violations by government troops were reported. Suspected rebel supporters were detained, tortured and extrajudicially executed. Several thousand remained in detention; some had been held for years without charge or trial. Journalists, human rights activists, demonstrators and other critics of the government were arrested. Most were held without trial, although some received unfair trials. During local elections in March, April and December scores of opposition party supporters were subjected to intimidation, beatings and arbitrary arrest. The trials of officials of the former military government on charges including genocide and extrajudicial executions proceeded slowly. Several death sentences were imposed; no executions were reported.

Background

The mandate of the UN Mission in Ethiopia and Eritrea (UNMEE), created under the 2000 Algiers Agreement which ended the war with Eritrea, was extended to March 2002. In May, the UN arms embargo on Eritrea and Ethiopia was lifted. Both Ethiopia and Eritrea alleged that the other side illegally entered the UNMEE-monitored Temporary Security Zone, a buffer zone inside Eritrea, on a number of occasions throughout the year. UNMEE reported occasional restrictions on freedom of movement imposed on the Ethiopian side. The Boundary and Compensation Commissions, instituted under the Algiers Agreement, were established. Although both sides began to repatriate prisoners of war in early 2001, disagreements led to a considerable slowing down of the process by the end of the year.

In March internal conflict within the Tigray People's Liberation Front (TPLF), the dominant party of the ruling coalition, led to the expulsion of 12 members of its Central Committee. A number of regional and security officials were dismissed and some were arrested. Over the following months many key officials left the TPLF. In May Kinfe Gebre-Medhin, who was in charge of internal security in the government, was assassinated. Eighteen people, including two of those recently expelled from the TPLF, were arrested in May for corruption. In June, President Negasso Gidada was removed from the Central Committee of his party and in October, when his presidential term expired, he was replaced by Girma Wolde-Giorgis.

Prime Minister Meles Zenawi was reappointed in September as Chair of the ruling coalition, the Ethiopian People's Revolutionary Democratic Front, and formed a new cabinet.

Although legislation had been passed in July 2000 allowing for the formation of a national human rights commission and ombudsman's office to be established in 2002, nominating committees had not been established for either body by the end of 2001.

Refugees and returnees

Hundreds of people internally displaced by the war began to return to their homes. Thousands of Ethiopians were voluntarily repatriated from Eritrea under the auspices of the International Committee of the Red Cross (ICRC). However, in June the ICRC complained that 722 Eritreans were involuntarily repatriated from Ethiopia; the Ethiopian authorities said they had returned willingly.

Internal and regional armed conflicts

The government continued to face long-running armed opposition in the Oromo region from the Oromo Liberation Front (OLF), and in the Somali region from the Ogaden National Liberation Front (ONLF) and its ally *al-Itihad*, an Islamist group with ties to Islamist groups in Somalia. Many human rights abuses were reported in the context of these two conflicts, particularly by government troops against civilians suspected of supporting the rebels.

Ethiopian government troops remained in Somalia's Gedo, Bay and Bakol regions, supporting particular local Somali factions.

April riots

On 10 April, police violently dispersed students at Addis Ababa University who were peacefully protesting on their campus against restrictions on their academic freedoms. Over 40 students were injured and the situation on campus remained tense during the following week.

On 17 April, the authorities ordered the students to return to their classes or face expulsion. According to reports, a group of protesters supporting the students then began to throw stones at a police post next to the University. The police retaliated violently and two days of rioting ensued, which resulted in the deaths of at least 31 people. The police used live bullets and admitted to excessive use of force. However, investigations into the riots did not appear to be independent or impartial and no police officers had been brought to justice by the end of the year.

Around 3,000 people, including students, opposition party members, human rights activists and newspaper vendors, were arrested. Most were released without charge over the following months. In November the government announced that it had sentenced 326 of the 1,114 people still detained to prison terms of between four and 10 months for theft and destruction of property. A further 531 were on bail pending trial at the end of the year.

Many of those released complained of ill-treatment during detention and at least two people reportedly died in detention. Demonstrations held outside Addis Ababa in support of the students were violently disrupted by police and at least seven people were arrested and detained without charge for weeks. Many students, mainly from Addis Ababa University, fled to Kenya and Djibouti.

⎕ Mesfin Wolde Mariam, former Secretary General of the Ethiopian Human Rights Council (EHRCO), and Dr Berhanu Nega, a supporter of EHRCO, were arrested in Addis Ababa on 8 May. The two men were charged with "organizing themselves under an underground political party ... with a view to changing the Constitution through illegal means" and "incitement to violence". They were released on bail in June. Their trial began on 4 December, but was adjourned until April 2002. The offices of EHRCO were shut down for 10 days and searched by police following the arrests.

Detentions without charge or trial
In July the Ministry of Justice stated that 600 people in the Oromo region were in detention without trial, most since 1999, primarily as a result of failures in police investigation. However, the number of those detained was feared to be much higher as, in the Oromo and Somali regions in particular, thousands of detainees arrested over the previous eight years continued to be detained without charge or trial.

Political trials
Hundreds of people were arrested for political reasons. Most were detained without charge or trial; the authorities failed to allow access to or to give information on the whereabouts of some detainees. They included prisoners of conscience and others who, although ostensibly detained on suspicion of having links with armed opposition groups, particularly the OLF and ONLF, may in fact have been detained for their non-violent political activities.

⎕ In May, 28 of a group of 60 Oromos being tried together in Addis Ababa were released. They had been arrested in 1997 and charged with armed conspiracy with the OLF. Those released included seven founding members of the Human Rights League, and journalists, including Tesfaye Deressa, Solomon Namara, Garoma Bekele and Tilahun Hirpasa, all of whom then fled the country. Trials for the remaining 32, including one other member of the League, were continuing at the end of 2001.

⎕ Appeal hearings began in October for Taye Wolde-Semayat, President of the Ethiopian Teachers Association and a prisoner of conscience. He had been sentenced in 1999 to 15 years in prison for "armed conspiracy". Appeal hearings were still ongoing at the end of the year.

Torture
Political prisoners reportedly continued to be tortured and ill-treated. Torture took place during unlawful and incommunicado detention in official and unofficial places of custody. Allegations of torture made by prisoners were not investigated by officials. Prison conditions were generally harsh and medical treatment was inadequate.

Dergue trials
Trials continued of former officials of the government of Mengistu Haile-Mariam (known as the Dergue). They were charged with genocide and other crimes against humanity. Over 2,200 other former officials remained in prison awaiting trial. Scores were convicted and sentenced to prison terms, many were acquitted and at least five were reportedly sentenced to death. In March the Special Prosecutor for the trials said they would be finished in 2004.

Arrests and harassment of critics
Scores of government critics were harassed and arrested throughout the year. Police arrested journalists from the privately owned media on the grounds that articles criticizing the government were false or a threat to security. Dozens of journalists were taken in for questioning and released on bail with charges pending. Several fled the country after repeated court appearances and police summonses. Many were prisoners of conscience.

⎕ In August the Ethiopian Women Lawyers Association was suspended by the Ministry of Justice for six weeks, ostensibly for operating beyond its jurisdiction. The suspension followed a television program in which members of the Association criticized the government.

Killings by government forces
Scores of people, including suspected rebel supporters, were reportedly killed by government forces during 2001 in what appeared to be extrajudicial executions or indiscriminate use of force.

Death penalty
Several people were sentenced to death for murder. No executions were reported.

AI country reports/visits
Reports
- Ethiopia: Fear for safety/Use of excessive force by security forces (AI Index: AFR 25/006/2001)
- Ethiopia: Freedom of expression and association under attack (AI Index: AFR 25/012/2001)

FIJI

REPUBLIC OF THE FIJI ISLANDS
Head of state: Ratu Josefa Iloilo
Head of government: Laisenia Qarase
Capital: Suva
Population: 0.8 million
Official languages: English, Fijian, Fiji Hindi
Death penalty: abolitionist for ordinary crimes

Respect for constitutional human rights and the rule of law were ignored because of political considerations. The military's efforts to assist a return to democracy and the rule of law were hampered by the impunity effectively enjoyed by perpetrators of torture and extrajudicial executions. Non-governmental organizations (NGOs) suffered selective restrictions under emergency powers.

Political situation

Human rights issues were often at the centre of public debate on the country's efforts to return to democracy and the rule of law. On several occasions, the government condemned those who publicly criticized its policies, and political prisoners often received particularly harsh treatment. Thousands of Fijians of ethnic Indian origin (known as Indo-Fijians) emigrated. In December, it was recommended that Fiji be readmitted to the Councils of the Commonwealth, and by the end of the year, most international sanctions had been lifted.

Following the government's failure to win its appeal against a High Court ruling in a major human rights case, President Ratu Josefa Iloilo paved the way for fresh elections which began in August. The elections created a new parliament which reflected Fiji's ethnic divisions, while the restoration of political dominance to indigenous Fijians reflected the principal aim of the coup of May 2000. In September, the President appointed caretaker Prime Minister Laisenia Qarase to form a new government. His party entered into a coalition with coup leader George Speight's nationalist indigenous Fijian party. George Speight won a seat in parliament while facing treason charges in court, but was later denied parliamentary status. Almost all ministers in the new government were indigenous Fijians; a court challenge against the ethnic imbalance in the government was pending at the end of the year.

Ongoing constitutional uncertainty and fears of politically motivated violence continued to hamper efforts to rebuild political stability. Many Indo-Fijians feared a repeat of post-coup racist violence. Some Indo-Fijians were threatened with reprisals after being called to give evidence in court against ethnic Fijians accused of looting or driving them from their homes. For much of the year, the police and military personnel maintained an increased presence in some of the areas worst affected by post-coup racist violence. However, some police posts visited by AI lacked vehicles and communication facilities to respond promptly to security threats. In December, the military confirmed that an elite squad to combat internal security threats was being set up to replace the disbanded Counter Revolutionary Warfare (CRW) unit which was involved in the coup. Some senior police officers, local community leaders and government officials worked to reduce ethnic tension and helped to foster reconciliation at a local level. An unknown number of Indo-Fijian coup victims returned to their homes and tried to rebuild farms and businesses.

The rule of law

Confidence in the justice system was damaged by friction within the judiciary, government criticism of judges and apparent attempts to minimize judicial challenges against the post-coup authorities. In March, five international judges rejected a government appeal against a landmark High Court human rights ruling that the 1997 Constitution was still in place after the coup, and that the post-coup government was illegal. Interim Prime Minister Laisenia Qarase promised to abide by the Court of Appeal's judgment, but his ministers were reappointed as a caretaker government, pending elections. The Court also ruled that decrees which restricted people's rights were invalid if they violated the Constitution, but the authorities rejected calls to repeal them. Chandrika Prasad, a displaced Indo-Fijian farmer who had won the original court challenge, fled Fiji after his family received threats of reprisals.

The judiciary's independence was undermined by the interim Attorney-General's public criticism of judges in political cases, and by moves to prevent such cases from being heard by judges who had upheld the Constitution after the coup. In April, the Chief Justice banned five members of the Fiji Law Society from his court because they criticized him for assisting the post-coup authorities in their efforts to abolish the Constitution and to allow racial discrimination.

Human rights restrictions

The military-backed government repeatedly claimed that it had normalized the security situation; however, it continued to use emergency powers to maintain restrictions on human rights, particularly on the freedoms of assembly and expression, until November. In June, the caretaker government cancelled the charity status of the Citizens Constitutional Forum, a multi-ethnic NGO, after it filed constitutional challenges against the government in court. Days later, Reverend Akuila Yabaki, Director of the Forum and Chairperson of the national NGO Coalition of Human Rights, was dismissed from the Methodist Church Ministry. The Church's president was later appointed to the Senate by the Prime Minister.

Impunity

Court proceedings against suspected coup rebels were marked by delays, encouraging an atmosphere of impunity. The trial of coup leader George Speight was expected to start in 2002. Cases against others suspected of having taken part in the coup were adjourned, or collapsed after a state prosecutor and key witnesses failed to appear in court. Soldiers involved in the rebel takeover of military and police stations on Vanua Levu island were reportedly discharged with a fine of US$4.

A military court martial began in August against 15 former members of the disbanded CRW unit for their alleged role in an attempted mutiny in November 2000. Several of them alleged serious ill-treatment after their initial arrest, and some individual officers offered a traditional form of apology to the families of the victims. The police criticized the military for lack of cooperation in preparing murder charges against soldiers suspected of beating to death at least four CRW suspects. When the military faced court proceedings over its treatment of CRW detainees, the government issued a decree granting the military and the police immunity for human rights violations and other acts committed "in good faith" during post-coup operations. The military denied that the decree covered torture, but did not bring suspected torturers to justice.

AI reports/visits
Visit
AI delegates visited Fiji for research purposes in May.

FINLAND

REPUBLIC OF FINLAND
Head of state: Tarja Halonen
Head of government: Paavo Lipponen
Capital: Helsinki
Population: 5.2 million
Official languages: Finnish, Swedish
Death penalty: abolitionist for all crimes

Eleven imprisoned conscientious objectors to national service legislation were considered prisoners of conscience. There were allegations of discriminatory treatment by the police.

Conscientious objection
Under the 1998 Military Service Law, the length of alternative civilian service remained punitive. All conscientious objectors were required to perform 395 days of alternative civilian service; most recruits who perform military service serve for 180 days. Most conscientious objectors who refused to perform alternative service were sentenced to 197 days' imprisonment. The Ministers of Labour and of Foreign Affairs stated that their ministries would continue to work for a reduction in the length of alternative civilian service. However, the Minister of Defence restated his commitment to maintaining the status quo.

Prisoners of conscience
Eleven conscientious objectors became prisoners of conscience during 2001. All were convicted of a "non-military service crime" and most of them were sentenced to 197 days' imprisonment. The majority refused alternative service because of its discriminatory length. Some were total objectors who held pacifist convictions.

Allegations of racism
There was concern about reports of racism and discriminatory practices by police towards Somali nationals in Hakunila in the city of Vantaa.

Farah Muhamed, a refugee from Somalia, was sentenced to four years' imprisonment on 5 January by Vantaa District Court. He was convicted of attempted manslaughter after an incident in September 2000 in which the car he was driving hit and ran over a white man. Farah Muhamed claimed that his conviction was the result of racist and prejudicial behaviour by the police during the course of their investigations. He stated that the incident happened when he panicked while trying to escape from a gang of white men who were charging at his car wielding a baseball bat and an axe. There were reports that the investigating police had ignored evidence and eyewitness accounts of the incident. On appeal, Farah Muhamed's sentence was reduced to two and a half years' imprisonment. A further appeal was lodged with the Supreme Court. Farah Muhamed was released on 19 December 2001.

AI country reports/visits
Report
- Concerns in Europe, January-June 2001: Finland (AI Index: EUR 01/003/2001)

FRANCE

FRENCH REPUBLIC
Head of state: Jacques Chirac
Head of government: Lionel Jospin
Capital: Paris
Population: 59.5 million
Official language: French
Death penalty: abolitionist for all crimes
2001 treaty ratifications/signatures: Protocol Additional to the Geneva Conventions of 12 August 1949, and relating to the Protection of Victims of International Armed Conflicts

Incidents of police brutality were reported. Asylum-seekers and undocumented foreign nationals were among the alleged victims. Children alleged ill-treatment and there was concern about children being isolated in holding areas. Some reports related to the ill-treatment of foreign nationals in overseas departments or territories. Poor conditions for detainees in police custody incurred strong criticism. The judicial resolution of certain cases of fatal police shootings aroused further serious concerns about the impunity of officers. AI called on the government to face up to its judicial obligations in respect of torture and summary executions of Algerians during the Algerian war of independence. Several judicial inquiries were opened into allegations of human rights violations during the war, but some were closed shortly afterwards.

Ill-treatment of asylum-seekers

There were numerous reports that police ill-treated asylum-seekers allegedly resisting deportation. Individuals described how, while handcuffed, they had been slapped, beaten with truncheons or dragged along the ground. In March a preliminary judicial inquiry was opened after a report was sent to the prosecutor of Bobigny by a Ministry of Foreign Affairs (MAE) official, stationed at the newly opened holding area of ZAPI 3 at Roissy-Charles de Gaulle Airport. The official stated that he saw Blandine Tundidi Maloza, a woman from the Democratic Republic of the Congo, lying on the waiting room floor. Her legs were covered with "wounds tinged with blood that were clearly recent". The woman claimed that the injuries were caused by a police officer kicking her, pulling her backwards and dragging her over the ground by her hair while she resisted attempts to put her on a flight to Douala, Cameroon. Her application for asylum was later accepted.

There was concern about the isolation of children in holding areas. In June, two children, aged three and five, were reportedly separated from their parents and held at Roissy for four days. A 14-year-old girl of Congolese origin was held at ZAPI 3 for 10 days, separated from her mother and in the presence of male as well as female adults.

In October, Cameroonian national Eric Nguemaleu was allegedly hit with a plastic truncheon while officers tried to put him on a flight to Douala. Medical examinations showed a number of injuries and bruising. In early November he was released from ZAPI 3 by order of the Paris Appeal Court, which concluded that he had not been given prompt medical attention while at the holding area.

Ill-treatment of other foreign nationals

A number of foreign nationals alleged that they were ill-treated at borders or in overseas departments or territories such as French Guiana and Saint-Martin (Guadeloupe).

In February, Malian national Baba Traoré was arrested by frontier police as he was travelling by train from Spain to Paris to renew his passport. Baba Traoré, who had valid work and residence papers for Spain, and was resident in the Canary Islands, claimed that he was punched in the left eye at the police station in the town of Hendaye. Shortly afterwards he was handed over to Spanish police officers, and on the same day underwent urgent surgery on his eye. Medical reports stated that his eye had been severely damaged by a "direct blow". Baba Traoré lodged a complaint with the public prosecutor of Bayonne.

In August, Koneisi Geddeman, an undocumented national from Suriname, was reportedly severely injured in French Guiana after being repeatedly kicked and beaten in the stomach and head while he was handcuffed and lying on the ground. He was pursued by National Police officers in Cayenne after fleeing when asked for his papers, and was allegedly beaten by up to six officers, both in the street and in the police station, where he was also head-butted. He was held for several hours in a cell without medical care and started to vomit after drinking water. Koneisi Geddeman was subsequently admitted to hospital in Cayenne, where he reportedly remained for several weeks after undergoing surgery.

Ill-treatment of minors

The Court of Nanterre opened an inquiry into the alleged serious police ill-treatment of a minor who required urgent surgery for removal of a testicle after being held in police custody in July. According to reports, 16-year-old "Yacine" was taken to Asnières police station, in the Paris area, where he initially resisted attempts to handcuff him and insulted officers. He was taken into a corridor where, although handcuffed, he was punched, kneed and kicked. Contrary to the law, his mother was not immediately informed about his arrest, despite requests by "Yacine".

Allegations of police ill-treatment were made in June by a group of children of African, North African and Macedonian Rom origin in the Goutte d'Or area of Paris. One of the children, 12-year-old "Ahmet", told AI that he had been struck on the head after being taken to the Goutte d'Or police station in connection with an alleged theft. The children said they had also been insulted, threatened and racially abused.

CPT report

In July the European Committee for the Prevention of Torture and Inhuman or Degrading Treatment or Punishment (CPT) published its report on a visit in May 2000 to various police stations, holding areas and prisons. The CPT observed that most allegations of police ill-treatment involved the National Police and consisted principally of individuals being punched, kicked, violently pushed to the ground and handcuffed too tightly. The CPT also noted allegations of ill-treatment inflicted on foreign nationals at airports during attempts to deport them. The CPT observed that conditions of detention, notably in National Police establishments, were incompatible with human dignity, and often "repulsively dirty".

Prolonged isolation of prisoners

In January AI called on the government to take immediate steps to resolve the situation of members of the former armed group *Action directe* (Direct Action), whose health was reported to have deteriorated alarmingly as a result of prolonged periods of isolation since their arrest in 1987. At least two, Georges Cipriani and Nathalie Ménigon, had reportedly suffered breakdowns in mental and physical health. AI noted that there was evidence that the treatment of the prisoners had fallen short of international standards which seek to minimize the detrimental effects of isolation.

Two *Action directe* prisoners, Jean-Marc Rouillan and Joëlle Aubron, went on hunger strike in January to draw attention to the plight of Georges Cipriani and Nathalie Ménigon. The hunger strike was called off after a number of assurances were given by the prison authorities, including the provision of appropriate health care.

Effective impunity

There was continued concern that delays and obstacles to trials of some police officers contributed to a climate of impunity.

◻ Ten years after Youssef Khaïf, a young man of Algerian origin, was shot and killed while attempting to flee in a stolen car, a police officer charged with his death was acquitted by the Yvelines Court of Assizes in September. The killing of Youssef Khaïf occurred in June 1991 at Mantes-la-Jolie, Yvelines department, during the disturbances which followed the death in custody of 18-year-old Aïssa Ihich that May. Although the prosecutor excluded the defence argument of legitimate defence, and accepted the officer's guilt, he requested only a suspended prison term as a "nominal sentence".

The officer's trial took place only after a series of legal obstacles had been overcome. The family of Youssef Khaïf intended to appeal to the European Court of Human Rights against the acquittal.

◻ The trial of those implicated in the death in custody of Aïssa Ihich in May 1991 also took place after 10 years' delay. Aïssa Ihich died from an asthma attack after being severely beaten while lying on the ground. In March 2001, two police officers were sentenced by the Correctional Court of Versailles to suspended 10-month prison terms for acts of violence. The prosecutor had requested that the officers be found not guilty. A doctor was given a 12-month suspended prison sentence for involuntary homicide by negligence after deciding that Aïssa Ihich's condition was not incompatible with the prolongation of custody sanctioned by the prosecutor. An appeal by the officers and doctor was heard in December by the Appeal Court of Versailles, when the prosecutor argued that the police officers should be found not guilty but that the sentence against the doctor should be upheld. The Court's decision was deferred until February 2002. The case was notable for its role in reforming the rules governing police custody.

◻ In January the Appeal Court of Aix-en-Provence confirmed the order of an investigating judge not to proceed against police officers in connection with the death by asphyxia while under prolonged restraint of Mohamed Ali Saoud in Toulon in 1998. The victim's family, who had joined proceedings as a civil party, appealed to the Court of Cassation.

◻ In December, the Court of Appeal of Orléans closed the case against a police officer for the shooting, in the back of the neck, of 16-year-old Abdelkader Bouziane in 1997. An investigating judge, and the Court of Appeal of Paris, had earlier rejected the officer's argument of "legitimate defence" and decided that he should be tried in a court of assizes. In March the Court of Cassation had annulled this decision.

Algerian war: torture and killings

In a book published in May, General Paul Aussaresses, a high-ranking French military officer during the Algerian war of independence from 1954 to 1962, admitted not only that he had personally taken part in torture and summary executions, claiming that they had been necessary, but maintained that the French government of the time had been directly implicated in them. AI called the claims extremely serious and urged the authorities to open a full and prompt investigation. While condemning the actions of General Aussaresses, by the end of the year the government had continued to resist calls for such an investigation.

In May and June a number of legal proceedings against General Aussaresses and others were initiated by groups and individuals. In July and September an investigating judge refused to act on judicial complaints filed against General Aussaresses by two human rights organizations for "crimes against humanity". However, in November, General Aussaresses appeared before a Paris correctional court for "complicity in apology for war crimes". Judgment was deferred until January 2002.

Initial steps were taken to officially commemorate the massacre of Algerians in Paris 40 years before, when a plaque was mounted on the Pont Saint-Michel to the memory of "the many Algerians killed during the bloody repression of the peaceful demonstration of 17 October 1961". Inauguration of the plaque by the Mayor of Paris in October was hotly contested by some police unions and politicians. The precise number of Algerians who drowned after being thrown into the Seine by police officers, or were killed in police stations, on the night of 16 October 1961 still remained unclear but up to 200 were thought to have lost their lives.

Update
In September the Correctional Court of Toulouse sentenced a police sergeant to a three-year suspended prison term for involuntary homicide for the fatal shooting of 17-year-old Habib Ould Mohamed in December 1998. The officer was also barred from pursuing a career in the police force. The Court concluded that, although he had not fired his weapon deliberately, he had committed an "astonishing series of reckless actions, blunders and professional errors" which had resulted in the minor's death. Habib Ould Mohamed, who was not armed, was shot during an attempted arrest and died in the street. The firing of the weapon was not reported, as required by law, and no serious attempt was made by the police patrol involved to assist Habib Ould Mohamed, whose body was later discovered by a passer-by.

AI country reports/visits
Report
- Concerns in Europe, January-June 2001: France (AI Index: EUR 01/003/2001)

GAMBIA

REPUBLIC OF THE GAMBIA
Head of state and government: Yahya Jammeh
Capital: Banjul
Population: 1.3 million
Official language: English
Death penalty: abolitionist in practice
2001 treaty ratifications/signatures: African Charter on the Rights and Welfare of the Child

Human rights defenders, journalists and opposition supporters were arbitrarily detained and beaten. Members of the security forces accused of using excessive lethal force which resulted in the deaths of at least 14 people and the ill-treatment of scores of others in 2000 were granted immunity from prosecution. Civilians and members of the security forces charged with plotting to overthrow the government continued to be held without trial; the trial of one member of the security forces concluded with his conviction. Freedom of expression and of the press remained under attack. No new death sentences were passed.

Background
Legislation restricting political activities was lifted in July. However, President Jammeh was reported as warning against "disturbing the peace or the stability of the nation", saying that anyone who did so "would be buried six feet deep". Other restrictive legislation severely limiting freedom of expression remained in force.

President Jammeh won presidential elections, contested by five candidates, in October. Politically motivated murder charges brought against one of the candidates did not prevent his candidacy. His trial had not concluded at the end of the year. The electoral campaign was marred by violence between rival supporters, as well as targeted attacks on opposition leaders, reportedly by government supporters. President Jammeh's electoral victory was followed by a further crack-down on the independent media, opposition supporters and human rights defenders.

Prisoners of conscience
Human rights defenders and opposition supporters were arbitrarily detained. Freedom of expression remained under threat as journalists from the privately owned independent media were arrested, beaten and harassed.

In April, Dudu Kassa Jatta, a member of the Youth Wing of the opposition United Democratic Party (UDP), was detained incommunicado by the National Intelligence Agency (NIA), the security police, at their headquarters in Banjul. He was held for nearly two weeks before being released without charge. He had recently contributed to an article published in the *Daily Observer* in which he criticized President Jammeh.

In August, Alhagie Mbye, a reporter with *The Independent* newspaper, was detained for three days by the NIA, without charge or trial and incommunicado, following publication of an article about reports of an attempted coup. He was again detained incommunicado by the NIA for nine days in November after an article in the United Kingdom-based *West Africa* magazine, for which he was a correspondent, alleged electoral fraud in the presidential elections.

Mohamed Lamin Sillah, Secretary General of AI Gambia, was detained incommunicado for five days at the NIA headquarters in October, apparently in connection with his human rights work. Although he was released without charge, he was required to report on a regular basis to the NIA.

Around 40 opposition supporters were arrested in October following the presidential elections. The majority were held incommunicado by the NIA before being transferred to police custody and subsequently released on bail. Seven were charged in connection with election violence.

Impunity
In January, the government responded publicly to a report, submitted to it in September 2000, of the findings of a Commission of Inquiry into the deaths of at least 14 people and the ill-treatment of scores of others during demonstrations in April 2000. The report itself was not published. The Commission of Inquiry found security force officers largely responsible for the deaths and recommended their prosecution. It also recommended that student leaders could be prosecuted for their role in organizing the demonstrations. The government announced that it

would not prosecute any of those responsible in the interests of "reconciliation", and introduced a law to grant immunity from prosecution to members of the security forces involved in the demonstrations, which was enacted by Parliament as the 2001 Indemnity Amendment Act and signed into law in May.

◻ In March, a teacher sued the authorities for compensation for injuries he received, allegedly in an assault by the security forces. In July the High Court referred the case to the Supreme Court for interpretation of the constitutionality of the 2001 Indemnity Amendment Act. In December the Supreme Court ruled that the case should be heard by the High Court. A High Court ruling was pending in another complaint for damages for unlawful detention and assault related to the demonstrations.

◻ The demonstrations had been in part to protest at the death of a secondary school student, Ebrima Barry, allegedly as a result of being tortured by Brikama Fire Service personnel. Seven Fire Service officers arrested in connection with his death were tried and acquitted in March 2001 on the grounds that the charges against them had not been proved beyond reasonable doubt.

Detention of suspected coup plotters

◻ Out of five members of the armed forces extradited from Senegal in 1997 to face charges in connection with an attack on Kartong military post in July 1997, four had still not been charged or tried by the end of 2001. The fifth was released after successfully challenging the legality of his detention, reportedly in late 2000 or early 2001.

◻ Lieutenant Landing Sanneh, detained since January 2000 on suspicion of taking part in an alleged coup attempt, was sentenced in September to 16 years' imprisonment with hard labour after trial by court martial. The defence alleged numerous procedural irregularities and that some of the evidence against him had been extorted under duress. An appeal had not been heard by the end of 2001.

◻ Court hearings started in the trial of two armed forces officers and four others, arrested in June 2000 and charged in December 2000 with involvement in an alleged coup plot. Charges against a seventh man were withdrawn in December. The trial had not concluded by the end of 2001.

Torture and ill-treatment

In July, Omah Bah, court reporter with *The Independent* newspaper, was beaten by soldiers when he attempted to attend the trial of Lieutenant Sanneh at Yundum Army Barracks, Banjul. Although an officer intervened and senior officers dissociated themselves from the attack, those involved were not known to have been disciplined.

Female genital mutilation continued to be widely practised and not prohibited by specific legislation. Campaigners against it were denied access to state-controlled media.

Death penalty

Death sentences imposed on three men in 1999 were confirmed by the Court of Appeal. They had been convicted of treason in connection with the 1997 attack on Kartong military post. An appeal by the state to the Supreme Court, against the decision by the Court of Appeal in October 1997 to commute the sentences, from death to life imprisonment, of four men convicted in 1997 in connection with an armed attack on Farafenni military camp in 1996, had not been heard by the end of 2001. No new death sentences were known to have been passed.

Intergovernmental organizations

In October, a working group of the UN Human Rights Committee considered, under a special procedure, Gambia's compliance with its reporting obligations under the International Covenant on Civil and Political Rights because of its failure to submit regular reports.

Also in October, the UN Committee on the Rights of the Child considered Gambia's initial report, in which the government acknowledged that there was no standard definition of a child in Gambian legislation and that it had not defined a minimum age at which a child could be enrolled in the armed forces, bear criminal responsibility or be married.

AI country reports/ visits
Statements
- Gambia: Justice not impunity (AI Index: AFR 27/001/2001)
- Gambia: Amnesty International demands the release of the head of its Gambian section (AI Index: AFR 27/007/2001)
- Gambia: Secretary General of AI Gambia released but concern remains (AI Index: AFR 27/008/2001)

GEORGIA

GEORGIA
Head of state and government: Eduard Shevardnadze
Capital: Tbilisi
Population: 5.2 million
Official language: Georgian
Death penalty: abolitionist for all crimes
2001 treaty ratifications/signatures: Protocol No. 12 to the European Convention on Human Rights

There were numerous allegations of torture and ill-treatment in custody. Two people died in custody in circumstances suggesting torture or ill-treatment may have contributed to their deaths. The authorities failed to investigate allegations adequately and bring those responsible to justice. Attacks against members of non-traditional religions continued unabated. Prison conditions were often extremely harsh. In the disputed region of Abkhazia, conscientious objectors to military service continued to face imprisonment. Abkhazia retained the death penalty but no new death sentences were passed and there were no reported executions.

Background
President Eduard Shevardnadze dismissed the entire government on 1 November. His action followed mass protests over an attempted raid two days earlier by Ministry of State Security personnel on the offices of the independent television channel *Rustavi-2*. The raid was widely interpreted as an act of political intimidation and rekindled debate over the freedom of the media in Georgia, an issue which had come to the fore in July following the murder of Giorgi Sanaya, a well-known journalist with *Rustavi-2*.

The disputed regions of Abkhazia and South Ossetia remained out of the control of the Georgian authorities and peace talks to regulate their status made little progress. Fighting flared up in October in the Kodori Gorge in Abkhazia between armed groups, said to include Georgian and Chechen fighters, and the Abkhaz forces. In November, Georgian authorities claimed that the Russian military bombed the Pankisi Gorge, a border region where the Russian authorities accused the Georgians of sheltering Chechen fighters.

Torture and ill-treatment
Reports of torture and ill-treatment in detention, particularly in order to extract confessions, continued. Allegations persisted that police and investigators obstructed detainees' access to defence lawyers and independent medical personnel, and that complaints of torture and ill-treatment were not pursued impartially or with vigour.

◻ On 16 November, Zezva Nadiradze was arrested in the village of Samtavisi in Kaspisky region. Police officers in Tbilisi reportedly tortured him with electric shocks to his genitals, burned him with a cigarette and beat him, in an attempt to force him to confess to a robbery. One officer allegedly attempted to rape him. On 19 November, a medical examination reportedly found bruises, burns and abrasions. At the first court hearing, the judge ordered his release because of his injuries. The criminal case against him remained open. Following a television report about the case, a criminal investigation was opened into his allegations. No one had been charged by the end of 2001.

◻ Revaz Bzishvili, a traffic police inspector sentenced in July 2000 to two years' imprisonment for "exceeding his authority" in connection with the death in 1999 of David Vashaqmadze, was released in February, nine months early. The court ordered his release on the grounds of "exemplary behaviour when in detention." David Vashaqmadze had been stopped by officers in November 1999 in Tbilisi and reportedly been beaten so severely by them that he died in hospital two days later.

Deaths in custody
Two people died in police custody: one after a fall from a window in unclear circumstances during police interrogation, the other after reportedly being severely beaten by police.

◻ Gia Chichaqua died in January, reportedly six hours after being taken into custody. According to reports police beat him with truncheons during interrogation in Ozurgeti, western Georgia. Reports cited Gia Chichaqua's wife as stating that four drunken policemen, who said they were acting on the orders of their superiors, took him into custody for questioning about a theft. A television report quoted the police chief as saying that Gia Chichaqua died suddenly and that there were no traces of violence on his body. It also cited an unidentified official as saying: "As he was giving evidence, he suddenly felt unwell and died." No independent post-mortem examination was known to have been performed. A police officer was reportedly detained in January in connection with the death, but no one was known to have been brought to trial by the end of the year.

Human rights defender
On 4 May the head of Isolation Prison No. 5 in Tbilisi threatened to "physically annihilate" Nana Kakabadze for criticizing conditions in pre-trial detention. Nana Kakabadze, a member of the non-governmental human rights organization Former Political Prisoners for Human Rights, had given an interview to the newspaper *Alia* after visiting the prison on 2 May. She commented that while most cells in isolation prisons were overcrowded, some were empty. The head of the prison telephoned her at her organization's office, apparently incensed at what he believed was an implication that empty cells were kept for rich prisoners able to bribe officials for the privilege of avoiding extreme overcrowding. The Minister of Justice is reported to have verbally reprimanded the head of the prison within hours of the threat.

Attacks on members of religious minorities
Members of minority religions, such as Evangelical Christians, Jehovah's Witnesses and Pentecostalists, were attacked by radical supporters of the Orthodox Church. In the majority of cases, police officers reportedly failed to take action to protect the victims of such attacks, and in some cases they allegedly took part in the violence themselves. Basil Mkalavishvili and another alleged leader of these attacks, Petre (or Gia) Ivanidze, were charged on 3 September in connection with the attacks, but on minor charges which did not involve serious physical assault. Further attacks continued to be reported. For example, on 28 September, a group of around 100 people reportedly set up a roadblock on a main road leading out of Tbilisi towards the town of Marneuli, where a Jehovah's Witness convention was due to be held that day. The Jehovah's Witnesses had reportedly informed the authorities in advance of the convention and received guarantees from the police that proper measures would be taken to protect their right of assembly. However, according to the Jehovah's Witnesses, police stood aside and watched as the group stopped the buses carrying Jehovah's Witness delegates, dragged men, women and children outside, and kicked and punched them and beat them with

clubs. Up to 40 people were said to have been injured, around 12 seriously. Police also allegedly stood by and watched as the group looted and set fire to the convention site, and confiscated film and a video camera from the Jehovah's Witnesses.

UN Committee against Torture

In May the Committee against Torture reviewed Georgia's second periodic report on its implementation of the UN Convention against Torture.

The Committee expressed concern that the failure to launch prompt, impartial and full investigations into all the numerous allegations of torture, as well as the lack of sufficient efforts to prosecute alleged offenders, resulted in a state of impunity for the perpetrators of torture and ill-treatment.

The Committee also stated that certain powers of the procuracy and the way in which this institution functions gave rise to serious doubts about its objectivity and the existence of an independent mechanism to hear complaints. It also stated that prison conditions were unacceptable and that provisions for detainees' access to a lawyer, to a doctor of their own choice, and to family members were inadequate. The Committee also expressed its concern about instances of mob violence against religious minorities, and the failure of the police to intervene and take appropriate action to bring the perpetrators to justice.

The Committee welcomed legislative reform aimed at safeguarding human rights, and the transfer of the prison service from the control of the Ministry of the Interior to the Ministry of Justice.

Abkhazia

In a meeting in Yalta in March, the Georgian and Abkhaz sides formally restated their commitment to creating the necessary conditions for the safe and voluntary return of refugees and internally displaced people to the disputed region. However, the region, in particular the southern district of Gali, remained volatile, and high levels of crime and lawlessness added to the insecurity of the local population.

In October there was a serious outbreak of hostilities between armed groups, said to include Georgian and Chechen fighters, and the Abkhaz forces. Reports of casualties were difficult to verify, although estimates were that about 60 members of armed groups, 16 Abkhaz troops, and at least 21 civilians had been killed. These casualties were in addition to those killed when a UN helicopter was shot down over the Gulripsh district of Abkhazia. There were nine unarmed people on board.

Human rights defenders

According to reports, Abri Dzhergeniya, then Abkhaz Procurator General, stated on 15 May that a Georgian citizen currently living in Bryansk in the Russian Federation had been identified as the main suspect in the murder of Zurab Achba, a legal assistant to the UN Human Rights Office in Abkhazia who was shot dead in Sukhumi in August 2000. Abri Dzhergeniya stated that the suspect was wanted by the Russian police and that two other suspects had been detained in connection with Zurab Achba's death but had not been charged with murder. There were allegations that some official structures were implicated in the killing of Zurab Achba.

Death penalty

No death sentences were reported to have been passed during the year. At least 15 death sentences were believed to have been passed since Abkhazia declared independence in 1992. The *de facto* moratorium on executions remained in force.

Prisoners of conscience

One person, Elgudzha Tsulaya, was known to be in prison during the year for refusing on religious grounds to perform compulsory military service. He had been sentenced to four years' imprisonment in October 2000 by the Military Court for desertion, reportedly in connection with steps he had taken earlier in the year to avoid forcible conscription, on the grounds that military service was incompatible with his religious beliefs. No alternative civilian service was available in 2001.

AI country reports/visits

Report
- Concerns in Europe, January-June 2001: Georgia (AI Index: EUR 01/003/2001)

Visits
In March, an AI delegate visited Tbilisi and met state officials and representatives of non-governmental organizations. In April, an AI delegate visited Abkhazia and met representatives of the *de facto* authorities.

GERMANY

FEDERAL REPUBLIC OF GERMANY
Head of state: Johannes Rau
Head of government: Gerhard Schröder
Capital: Berlin
Population: 82 million
Official language: German
Death penalty: abolitionist for all crimes

There were further allegations that police officers had ill-treated detainees. A man died after officials forcibly administered an emetic substance to him. It was not known whether criminal charges would ensue in relation to the death of the Sudanese asylum-seeker Aamir Ageeb in 1999. No criminal or disciplinary proceedings were taken against police officers who shot dead a mentally disabled man in 2000. Law enforcement officers in four federal areas (*Länder*) were reportedly conducting trials of electro-shock stun gun technology. There were concerns about the use of an abusive restraint technique in a

Berlin prison. The International Court of Justice in the Hague ruled in favour of Germany against the USA in connection with the execution of Karl and Walter LaGrand in the USA in 1999.

Intergovernmental organizations

In March the UN Committee on the Elimination of Racial Discrimination reviewed Germany's 15th periodic report on steps the authorities had taken to implement the UN Convention against Racism. Among the Committee's main concerns were "... repeated reports of racist incidents in police stations as well as ill-treatment inflicted by law enforcement officials on foreigners, including asylum seekers, and German nationals of foreign origin". The Committee urged Germany to strengthen existing educational measures for officials who have contact with foreign nationals and German nationals of foreign origin.

Allegations of police ill-treatment

Allegations of ill-treatment of detainees by police officers persisted. Complainants stated that they were repeatedly kicked and punched, most commonly at the time of arrest.

 Police officers of the Special Deployment Command were alleged to have ill-treated 49-year-old Josef Hoss while arresting him on 8 December 2000 in the North Rhine-Westphalian town of St.Augustin. Josef Hoss alleged that masked police officers dragged him from his van and proceeded to hit him with their batons and fists and to kick him after he was thrown to the ground and handcuffed. He suffered multiple injuries as a result of his alleged ill-treatment, including two fractured ribs and numerous abrasions and bruises to his face, head, body and limbs. Throughout 2001 his lawyer repeatedly called for an investigation into the incident and attempted to obtain compensation for the injuries Josef Hoss sustained.

 In April, Rottweil District Court in Baden-Württemberg reportedly upheld the convictions of two police officers for ill-treating a 28-year-old man. They had detained the man as he was leaving his house in Rottweil in February 1999, after reportedly mistaking him for a criminal suspect they were pursuing. One of the police officers grabbed hold of the man while the other police officer repeatedly hit him with his torch; the two officers were given suspended prison sentences respectively of nine and 14 months. The victim required hospital treatment for his injuries.

Death in police custody

A 19-year-old Cameroonian asylum-seeker, referred to as Achidi J. in the German news media, reportedly suffered a cardiac arrest and fell into a coma in a Hamburg hospital on 9 December after medical personnel and officials forcibly administered an emetic substance to him. He died in hospital four days later on 13 December. He had been arrested on suspicion of possessing illegal drugs. An investigation into his death had not been completed by the end of the year.

Death during forced deportation

A significant development came to light in the investigation into the death of 30-year-old Aamir Ageeb, a Sudanese asylum-seeker who died in late May 1999 during his forced deportation from Frankfurt-am-Main airport to Khartoum via Cairo, Egypt. In late July the weekly current events magazine, *Der Spiegel*, reported that Aamir Ageeb died of asphyxia as a result of being restrained in his airplane seat, with his head and upper body forced forwards onto his knees by the three accompanying police officers. As a result of the pressure applied to his upper body, several of his ribs were reportedly broken. At the end of the year, it was not known whether the investigation into the death had been concluded.

Police shooting

It was reported that no criminal or disciplinary action would be taken against two police officers who shot at a man 21 times, hitting him eight times, on 20 September 2000. The fatal shooting took place in a wooded area near the town of Ulm. At the time of the shooting the 28-year-old victim, who had wandered off from a care home for the mentally disabled where he was a resident, was in possession of a plastic toy gun. There were concerns that the police officers appeared to have used little restraint in discharging their firearms in apprehending a suspect who had not returned fire.

Electro-shock stun technology

Police forces in the four German *Länder* of Baden-Württemberg, Bavaria, Berlin and North Rhine-Westphalia reportedly conducted trials of electro-shock stun gun technology in 2001. Among the devices being tested were M-26-type taser guns which shoot two wire-trailing darts with hooks through which a high-voltage electric shock can be delivered. AI was concerned at the possible future deployment of electro-shock stun gun technology by the authorities in the four *Länder*, in the absence of a full and independent investigation into the medical effects of such weaponry.

Abusive restraint technique

There was concern about a report that a 46-year-old Somalian prisoner in Tegel prison in Berlin had been chained by the ankle to a fixed point in his cell for several weeks at the start of the year. The Berlin authorities confirmed the report in late March, stating that the measure had been unavoidable because of the prisoner's disruptive behaviour. He had repeatedly struck the door of his cell and all attempts to dissuade him from doing so were said to have failed. The prisoner was transferred to a psychiatric clinic in Berlin in late February on the basis of expert medical opinion, which ruled that he was unfit to be held in prison.

International Court of Justice

On 27 June the International Court of Justice in the Hague ruled in favour of Germany against the USA in a case involving the execution of two men in 1999. The Court declared that the USA was in breach of its obligation under the 1963 Vienna Convention on Consular Relations to Germany and two German nationals because it failed to inform them of their right to seek consular assistance upon their arrest. The two German citizens, brothers Karl and Walter LaGrand, had been convicted of committing a murder during a robbery in Arizona in 1982 and were executed in Florence prison, Arizona, in February and March 1999. Germany was only informed of their conviction in 1992 by the brothers themselves.

AI country reports/ visits
Report
- Concerns in Europe, January-June 2001: Germany (AI Index: EUR 01/003/2001)

GHANA

REPUBLIC OF GHANA
Head of state and government: John Kufuor
Capital: Accra
Population: 19.7 million
Official language: English
Death penalty: retentionist

Five political prisoners held since 1994 were released. Legislative provisions on criminal libel and sedition were repealed. Proposals for a Reconciliation Commission were debated. There were prosecutions in continuing cases of female genital mutilation.

Background
In January John Kufuor, leader of the New Patriotic Party (NPP), took office as President, ending the 19-year rule of Jerry John Rawlings, initially at the head of a military government and from 1993 a civilian one.

Treason trials
In March court proceedings were discontinued in the case of four men sentenced to death for treason in 1999. Sylvester Addai-Dwomoh, Kwame Alexander Ofei, Kwame Ofori-Appiah and John Kwadwo Owusu-Boakye, imprisoned since September 1994, had been convicted of plotting to overthrow the government. They were reported to have suffered ill-treatment in custody following their arrest.

Karim Salifu Adam, an NPP member and former army officer imprisoned since May 1994 and awaiting retrial on treason charges, was released in July after the government filed to discontinue the prosecution at the High Court in Accra. Following his arrest, he had reportedly been tortured after he refused to implicate leading opposition politicians in an alleged coup plot.

Criminal libel and sedition laws
In July, Parliament repealed the laws of criminal libel and sedition. The widely acclaimed decision removed a legacy of colonial rule used particularly in the last decade to arrest, try and imprison journalists and other members of civil society for alleged defamation of members of the government, officials and their associates.

Reconciliation Commission
Soon after the change of government, public and parliamentary debate started about the terms of reference, powers and composition of a Reconciliation Commission. Although its composition and powers had not been finalized by the end of 2001, there was broad agreement with the government proposal, in a bill introduced in Parliament in July, that the Commission should receive complaints and make recommendations about human rights violations committed between independence from British colonial rule in 1957 and the end of military rule in 1993.

Women's rights
Although female genital mutilation has been a criminal offence in Ghana since 1994, it is still practised on girls and young women in some parts of the country. There were prosecutions in a few cases.

In November a 70-year-old woman from western Ghana was charged with carrying out female genital mutilation on four girls, aged between 14 and 16 years, who had reportedly sought protection in a local church. Other elders in the community were briefly detained on suspicion of abetting the offence. No trial had taken place by the end of the year.

A proposal for a bill on domestic violence was publicly discussed but not put before Parliament.

GREECE

HELLENIC REPUBLIC
Head of state: Constantinos Stephanopoulos
Head of government: Constantinos Simitis
Capital: Athens
Population: 10.6 million
Official language: Greek
Death penalty: abolitionist for ordinary crimes

There were numerous allegations that police had ill-treated detainees. A Rom and an Albanian citizen were shot dead by police officers in unrelated incidents. Serious concerns continued about failures to bring to justice police responsible for ill-treatment and other human rights violations. In the first half of the year undocumented migrants and asylum-seekers under deportation orders continued to be detained for months without judicial review; in June a law was introduced setting the maximum period of detention at three months, but some detainees were held beyond that time. As increasing numbers of undocumented foreign nationals arrived in the country, there were reports that some were being denied the right to apply for asylum, and concerns persisted about their conditions of detention. Legal proceedings continued against people for exercising their rights to freedom of expression and religion. Conscientious objectors continued to face trial.

Background
Under amendments to the Constitution adopted in January, the death penalty was abolished except for "serious offences committed in time of war and related to it". An interpretative note was added to the Constitution which allowed for legislation permitting conscientious objectors to military service to perform alternative civilian service.

Intergovernmental organizations
In May the UN Committee against Torture considered Greece's third periodic report submitted under the Convention against Torture. The Committee made specific recommendations concerning the use of force by police, and concerning harsh conditions of detention. Similar concerns and recommendations were among those presented in reports by the European Committee for the Prevention of Torture and Inhuman or Degrading Treatment or Punishment in its reports on earlier visits to Greece, which were finally published in September, together with government responses.

Ill-treatment
Allegations persisted that police had ill-treated detainees. Some detainees reported that they were sexually humiliated by police officers. Alleged victims were often undocumented migrants and asylum-seekers, foreign workers and Roma.

☐ In February a 16-year-old Albanian, Refat Tafili, was arrested in Athens during a police operation to identify and expel foreign nationals lacking residence and work permits. Refat Tafili was allegedly pushed to the ground and repeatedly kicked. After being taken to a police station, he became ill and was promptly released. Relatives took him to hospital where he underwent an operation for a ruptured spleen. A week later he was rearrested at the hospital and detained at a police station pending deportation; after five days in unhygienic conditions of detention, he was readmitted to hospital with an infection and internal bleeding. Following intervention by the Ombudsman his appeal against imminent deportation was granted. A criminal investigation into his complaints of ill-treatment had not been completed by the end of the year.

☐ In May, two brothers, Panayiotis and Giorgos Skouteris, were arrested in Athens; a police officer reportedly forced one of them to publicly lower his trousers to be searched for drugs, and hit him when he protested. No drugs were found, but the officer later allegedly threatened to plant drugs on them if they challenged his version of the incident.

☐ In June a group of some 160 possible asylum-seekers, many of Kurdish origin, arrived in Crete. At least 16 of them were reportedly beaten by coastal guard forces; doctors who examined them found severe bruising and other injuries consistent with their account. One man further alleged that a coastguard had attempted to rape him with a truncheon. An administrative investigation was undertaken by the Port Authority, and disciplinary proceedings were subsequently begun against an officer and five coastguards for the "irregular performance" of their duties. In November, four were punished with between 30 and 50 days' imprisonment, and two received lesser penalties. A criminal investigation had not been completed by the end of the year.

Killings by police
Two men were shot dead by police officers in the Athens area in separate incidents. Marinos Christopoulos, a Rom, aged 21, was shot and killed in October, and Gentjan Celniku, aged 20, an Albanian citizen, in November. In both cases, the police officers concerned claimed that their guns had fired accidentally. They were charged with murder and released on bail; one of them was returned to service. Investigations into these deaths had not been completed by the end of the year.

Investigations and impunity
Criminal and other investigations into complaints of ill-treatment by police were slow, and official figures indicated that police officers enjoyed almost complete *de facto* impunity. In March government officials stated that between 1996 and 2000, 163 complaints of ill-treatment had resulted in administrative investigations, and that criminal investigations had been opened into 52 of these cases. In that period no police officer was convicted of ill-treatment and only 24 officers had been disciplined. These figures appeared

not to include a small number of convictions of police officers for inflicting "bodily harm" on detainees.

◻ In October AI observed a trial in Patras at which a police officer was acquitted of charges under Article 137A of the Penal Code of beating and injuring two young Roma in 1998 at Mesolonghi police station to force them to confess to crimes. Lazaros Bekos and Lefteris Koutropoulos, then aged 17 and 18 respectively, had been arrested for attempted theft. The court found no causal link between the officer's conduct and the boys' injuries. In earlier administrative proceedings the officer had been fined for failing to prevent the boys from being ill-treated by another officer, although the senior police officer who carried out the administrative investigation concluded in 1999 that the two officers had "behaved with exceptional brutality".

◻ In October an appeals court in Athens ruled that Vasilis Athanasopoulos, a plainclothes police officer, was guilty of having caused grievous bodily harm to Melpo Koronaiou, but reduced his sentence of 30 months' imprisonment imposed in 1999 (and suspended pending appeal) to a sentence of 15 months' imprisonment suspended for three years. Vasilis Athanasopoulos had been found to have caused serious injuries to Melpo Koronaiou when he kicked her face and head after she had been knocked to the ground by police during a demonstration in Athens in 1995.

Refugees

There were concerns that the authorities were impeding the applications of some possible asylum-seekers. There were reports that many undocumented migrants, including possible asylum-seekers, arriving via Turkey from third countries, were detained by police and forcibly returned to Turkey without observing due procedures for deportation. In November Greece and Turkey signed a protocol allowing for the reciprocal return of migrants from third countries. Greece stated this would not be applied to asylum-seekers. However, soon afterwards there were reports that boats carrying migrants were being turned back in mid-sea to Turkey, without examining if any of the passengers would want to seek asylum or were refugees entitled to protection. In October it was reported that police were frequently serving administrative deportation orders on arriving migrants, requiring them to leave the country within 30 days, without giving them the chance to apply for asylum.

Detention of undocumented migrants and asylum-seekers

The numbers of undocumented foreigners arriving in the country increased. According to official figures, between January and the end of September some 205,000 undocumented migrants, the majority Afghans and Kurds from Iraq, were arrested for illegal entry and residence in the country. They and others were detained without judicial review, sometimes for months, pending deportation or a decision on their asylum request. However, a law came into effect in June making it illegal to hold such persons in excess of three months, and providing for the right to challenge their detention in court. Scores continued to be held illegally. On 28 June the human rights organization Greek Helsinki Committee appealed to the Ombudsman on behalf of 10 men, including several asylum-seekers, who remained in detention, although they had already been held for between three and 12 months. Following the intervention of the Ombudsman, they and some 60 other foreigners illegally detained in Attica were released.

The conditions of detention of many foreigners held pending deportation were reported to be often inhuman and degrading, with severe overcrowding and lack of hygiene.

Freedom of expression and religion

People continued to face legal proceedings for peacefully exercising their rights to freedom of expression and religion.

◻ In February a court in Athens convicted Sotiris Bletsas, a member of the Society for Aromanian (Vlach) Culture, of "distributing false information liable to cause public alarm" and sentenced him to a fine and 15 months' imprisonment suspended for three years. He was found guilty of distributing a leaflet at a 1995 festival which listed minority languages in European Union member states, including Aromanian and several other languages in Greece. However, in December he was acquitted on appeal.

◻ In January a court in Lamia sentenced Mehmet Emin Aga to four months' imprisonment, a penalty replaced by a fine, on charges of "usurpation of the function of a Minister of a known religion".

The charges related to religious messages he had distributed to Muslims in Xanthi, signed as the Mufti of Xanthi. Mehmet Emin Aga is not recognized by the state in this function, although in 1990 he was elected to this position by local Muslims. Later in the year he was acquitted at four other trials (twice in the first instance and twice on appeal) on 12 other counts for the same offence. Legal proceedings against him continued.

Conscientious objectors

Provisions of the law on conscription fell short of international standards. Alternative civilian service continued to be of discriminatory and punitive length. The appeal hearing of conscientious objector Lazaros Petromelidis was due to be heard in June, but was postponed. There were also complaints about delays and lack of coordination in the services dealing with applications for conscientious objector status.

AI country reports/visits
Reports
- Greece: The alleged ill-treatment of two young Roma, Theodoros Stephanou and Nikos Theodoropoulos, by police on the island of Cephalonia (AI Index: EUR 25/005/2001)
- Greece: Sweep Operation – The alleged ill-treatment and torture of 16-year-old Refat Tafili, an Albanian citizen (AI Index: EUR 25/010/2001)

Visit

AI visited Greece to observe two trials and carry out research.

GUATEMALA

REPUBLIC OF GUATEMALA
Head of state and government: Alfonso Portillo
Capital: Guatemala City
Population: 11.7 million
Official language: Spanish
Death penalty: retentionist

Little was done to implement the 1996 Peace Accords. Recommendations in post-Accord reports by the Guatemalan church and the UN-sponsored Historical Clarification Commission, to address massive abuses perpetrated during the civil conflict by the Guatemalan military, civil patrols and military commissioners, were also virtually ignored. In June, three armed forces officers were sentenced to long prison terms for the 1998 extrajudicial execution of Bishop Juan José Gerardi. Non-governmental human rights organizations, journalists, members of the judiciary, witnesses and others involved in efforts to bring perpetrators to justice faced continuing obstacles and threats. Widespread corruption exacerbated citizens' loss of faith in the law, which in turn encouraged lynchings. Death sentences were passed; there were no executions.

Background

When President Alfonso Portillo took office in January 2000, he promised to implement the Peace Accords, dismantle the "parallel" power structure impeding human rights protection and prosecution of perpetrators, and abolish the notorious Presidential Chiefs of Staff Unit (EMP), implicated in some of the most egregious abuses.

His failure to implement these promises appeared to reflect his loss of power within his own party to retired General Efraín Ríos Montt, former head of state and current President of Congress, who was responsible in the early 1980s for counter-insurgency campaigns in which tens of thousands of non-combatant indigenous men, women and children were massacred, often after torture including rape. General Ríos Montt and other military officers reportedly continued to operate a parallel power structure, obstructing efforts to bring human rights violators to justice and ensuring positions of influence for former military officials with dubious human rights records.

International concern

The deteriorating human rights situation in Guatemala brought resolutions of concern and visits from representatives of international monitoring mechanisms.

▢ The UN Special Rapporteur on the independence of judges and lawyers visited Guatemala in May 2001 to investigate threats and attacks, including the killings of seven lawyers between October 2000 and February 2001 and the lynching of a judge (see below). He found no improvement in the human rights situation and expressed regret that Guatemala had largely ignored recommendations made following his 1999 visit.

The human rights community under siege

Human rights advocates, judicial personnel, witnesses and survivors, involved in cases against security officials responsible for human rights violations, suffered almost daily death threats and intimidation. Anti-impunity activists had important data stolen, and reported electronic surveillance and tampering with computerized records.

▢ Supporters of the *Asociación Justicia y Reconciliación* (AJR), Association for Justice and Reconciliation, and the *Centro para Acción Legal en Derechos Humanos* (CALDH), Centre for Legal Action in Human Rights, were threatened and assaulted. In February, soldiers and former members of civil patrols — adjuncts to the military during Guatemala's civil conflict — reportedly threatened AJR communities to dissuade surviving witnesses from testifying in a suit against former officials in General Ríos Montt's administration, subsequently filed in June. Threats were directed at CALDH staff and villagers involved in gathering evidence. The AJR, which brings together survivors of massacres perpetrated during the administrations of General Romeo Lucas García (1978-1982) and General Ríos Montt (1982-1983), had filed in 2000 a suit for genocide against General Lucas García and former officials in his administration, with the support of CALDH. In April 2001, CALDH employees were assaulted by government supporters brought into the capital to confront demonstrators calling for General Ríos Montt to be tried for illegally altering liquor tax legislation. In July, a community leader from a village involved in AJR's first suit was shot and killed.

▢ In May the director of the association Families of the Detained and "Disappeared" in Guatemala (FAMDEGUA) and her driver were briefly abducted by armed men, despite the presence of security personnel "protecting" them following previous attacks. They were questioned about FAMDEGUA's work and threatened. FAMDEGUA actively promotes exhumations and the prosecution of perpetrators of massacres.

Conviction in the case of Bishop Gerardi

In June, after protracted international pressure, three armed forces officers charged with the murder of Bishop Gerardi were convicted and sentenced to 30 years' imprisonment. President Portillo had promised that those responsible would be brought to justice. The case was regarded as a test for the justice system's capacity to tackle sensitive human rights cases and the verdicts and sentences were widely hailed. However, those convicted immediately appealed and doubts were raised about their culpability. The case against other officers allegedly involved was left open.

The cost of pursuing justice in this case was high. Three witnesses and six other potential witnesses, indigents sleeping outside the Bishop's home on the night of the murder, were killed. Dozens of others suffered threats and harassment, including staff of the Archbishop's Human Rights Office, formerly headed by Bishop Gerardi and responsible for the exhaustive report which he spearheaded on abuses during the conflict, as well as lawyers, prosecutors and judges involved in the case. A number, including three prosecutors, were forced to flee abroad.

Petitions through the Inter-American human rights system

Some organizations and individuals have sought reparations and government acknowledgement of abuses through the Inter-American human rights apparatus. In 2000 "friendly settlements" had been agreed, between the Guatemalan government and plaintiffs under the aegis of the Inter-American Commission on Human Rights (IACHR), in which the government had accepted generalized state responsibility for abuses. In May the government dismissed the official who had negotiated the agreements with the IACHR and later his deputy. While in most cases the settlements did not assist prosecution of perpetrators in the Guatemalan courts or timely payment of agreed compensation, the dismissals appeared to reflect the army's dissatisfaction at this approach.

The Dos Erres massacre

Compensation by the government was agreed in May and announced in December to the relatives of some 350 men, women and children massacred — the women after mass rape — in 1982 at Dos Erres, El Petén, by the Guatemalan army and their civilian adjuncts. Relatives and human rights groups, who have long struggled for justice in the face of threats and abuses, welcomed the payments but continued to insist that the perpetrators be brought to justice. They named as responsible a government minister reportedly involved in training those responsible and four officers still in active service. Although in March 2000 arrest orders were issued for nine soldiers, in April 2001 the Constitutional Court provisionally stayed their implementation on the grounds that an Appeal Court decision was still pending on whether they were immune from prosecution under a 1996 amnesty law.

Myrna Mack

In March, the IACHR filed the case of anthropologist Myrna Mack, extrajudicially executed in 1990, before the Inter-American Court of Human Rights. A decision was expected in 2002. The IACHR accepted the case as the complainant, the victim's sister Helen Mack, had been impeded in efforts to pursue domestic remedies and there had been unjustified delays. Myrna Mack was reportedly murdered because her study on the displacement of Guatemala's indigenous peoples by the army's counter-insurgency policies was highly damaging to the government.

In 2000 Helen Mack had agreed to explore "friendly settlement", dependent upon conclusion of legal proceedings against those responsible within a reasonable period, and Guatemala had accepted institutional responsibility for Myrna Mack's murder and agreed compensation. However, official monitors had indicated that Guatemala was not fulfilling the agreements and asked that proceedings continue within the Inter-American system. An EMP sergeant was convicted of the murder in 1993, but progress in the trial of three officials charged with planning the killing was delayed by frequent defence appeals.

People who have struggled to bring to justice those responsible for her murder continued to be targeted. Five employees of a foundation set up in her name were threatened in April. They included retired Peruvian General Rodolfo Robles, who had testified on the likely reaction of the Guatemalan military to human rights inquiries at trials in connection with the murders of both Myrna Mack and Bishop Gerardi. In October Matilde Leonor González, a historian with a social science research institute co-founded by Myrna Mack, was threatened and followed, apparently because of her findings that the military manipulated local power structures to incite mob violence and lynchings.

Universal jurisdiction in Spain

The Rigoberta Menchú Foundation was awaiting a decision in 2001 on its appeal against a December 2000 ruling by the Spanish High Court that it did not currently have jurisdiction to hear the Foundation's 1999 suit against eight former Guatemalan officials, including General Ríos Montt, for genocide and other crimes against humanity. Since filing the suit, Nobel laureate Rigoberta Menchú and her colleagues have reported harassment and death threats.

Corruption-related abuses

Journalists reporting on corruption, and staff of official environment and natural resources protection agencies, have been targeted. Widespread impunity has encouraged criminal alliances of officials, business, the security forces and common criminals to control legal and illegal industries including oil extraction and refining, drugs and arms trafficking, money laundering, car theft rings, illegal adoptions, kidnapping for ransom, illegal logging and other proscribed use of state-protected lands.

▫ In February, an employee of the National Forestry Institute was shot and killed in Alta Verapaz Department, apparently in retaliation for his efforts to control illegal logging and contraband trade in protected precious woods.

Lynchings

The UN Verification Mission in Guatemala reported that around 347 lynchings took place between 1996 and mid-2001. In over 97 per cent of cases, no one had been brought to justice. While many were perpetrated by citizens alarmed at rising crime, who took the law into their own hands to eliminate perceived wrongdoers, some "spontaneous" lynchings were reportedly planned and instigated for other reasons.

▫ In March Judge Alvaro Hugo Martínez was lynched in Alta Verapaz, reportedly because of his inquiries into local corruption and efforts to crack down on car theft rings controlled by powerful local and national figures.

AI country reports/visits
Reports
- Guatemala: Human rights community under siege (AI Index: AMR 34/022/2001)
- Guatemala: Open letters to Presidents Portillo and George W. Bush (AI Index: AMR 34/030/2001)
- Guatemala: Submission to Param Cumaraswamy, Special Rapporteur of the UN Commission on Human Rights on the independence of judges and lawyers (AI Index: AMR 34/032/2001)

Visits
An AI delegation in May and June collected human rights data, raised concerns with government officials and demonstrated support for the anti-impunity efforts of Guatemala's beleaguered human rights community. AI's Guatemala Trial Observers Project monitored the trial relating to the murder of Bishop Gerardi.

GUINEA

REPUBLIC OF GUINEA
Head of state: Lansana Conté
Head of government: Lamine Sidimé
Capital: Conakry
Population: 8.3 million
Official language: French
Death penalty: retentionist

Hundreds of refugees and internally displaced Guinean civilians were killed, beaten, raped and abducted in attacks on refugee camps by armed political groups. Refugees were also extrajudicially executed, arrested and tortured by the Guinean security forces. After more than 17 years without executions, at least seven people were executed and 22 others were sentenced to death. Prisoners of conscience were released, including one opposition leader.

Background
Armed clashes between the security forces and armed groups from neighbouring countries, which had intensified from September 2000, decreased after April.

A new Constitution was approved after a referendum in November which was boycotted by the opposition. It removed the limitation of a presidential mandate to two terms in office, which will allow President Conté, who came to power in a coup in 1984, to stand for re-election. The new Constitution extended the presidential term from five to seven years. It also lifted an age limit of 70 for presidential candidates, which would have barred President Conté from standing for re-election when his term expires in 2003.

Legislative elections, postponed from June 1999 and due to be held in December, were again postponed. The government said that this was to allow further consultation with political parties.

Attacks on refugees
Following an upsurge of violence against Sierra Leonean and Liberian refugees in Guinea in September 2000, hundreds were killed, beaten, raped and abducted in early 2001 in continued attacks on refugee camps, as well as on refugees living in rural areas and towns. Hundreds of thousands of refugees and Guineans remained displaced within the country in the early months of the year. Most refugees were subsequently relocated to new camps.

Abuses by armed political groups
Alleged perpetrators of abuses were armed political groups, including the Revolutionary United Front (RUF) from Sierra Leone and others from Guinea and Liberia.
▢ On 9 March RUF forces and other armed political groups attacked refugee camps in the Nongoa area, about 30km from Guékédou. Nabie Sillah was shot and killed after he fled with his wife and baby from the attack. His family survived.
▢ Mabinte Bangura fled from Koundo Lengo Bengo Camp with nine children following the attacks in Nongoa. An unidentified armed group severely beat her 17-year-old son, Sorie Bangura, and abducted her 15-year-old daughter, Salaymatu Bangura.

Violations by government forces
Refugees were killed, tortured and arbitrarily detained by Guinean soldiers, the local Guinean civilian population and Guinean civil defence groups, apparently in an effort to drive them out of the country. Many refugees detained at military checkpoints were forced to pay bribes to gain their freedom.
▢ On 11 March, in the aftermath of the attacks on refugee camps in Nongoa, medical worker Fayia Johnson was accused of being a member of the RUF. Soldiers arrested him and took him to Nongoa prison. The following day his family received a message that the body should be retrieved, and found him on the ground outside the prison with his throat cut.

Abuses against civilians
In sporadic attacks on villages and towns by armed political groups from Sierra Leone and Liberia in the early part of the year, particularly in southern Guinea, an unknown number of civilians were reported to have been killed, raped, beaten and abducted. Many areas were occupied by armed political groups or were the sites of protracted fighting between various forces. Thousands of villagers lost their property and belongings, which were looted or destroyed.

Excessive use of force
Shortly before the constitutional referendum, the security forces routinely used excessive force against peaceful demonstrators. Leaders of opposition parties were briefly detained, and tear gas was used to disperse protesters in Conakry. In November demonstrators

were reportedly arrested and beaten in the northeastern town of Kankan.

In December, three people were reportedly shot and several injured when the security forces fired on students protesting about study conditions in Koundara in the northwest and Mali in the north. A legal complaint was filed against a police officer who allegedly ordered the beating of photographer Mamadou Cellou Diallo during a strike by students in Conakry in December.

Release of prisoners of conscience
Three prisoners of conscience — Alpha Condé, an opposition leader, and two others — were released from prison in May after being granted a presidential pardon. They had been sentenced to prison terms after their conviction in September 2000, with seven others, on charges of threatening the security of the state. Their trial before the State Security Court did not meet international standards for fair trial. Alpha Condé was officially banned from all political activity in Guinea because of his criminal record.

Death penalty
Executions resumed for the first time since 1984. Four people were executed in February and three others in April. Twenty-two people were sentenced to death in July. They had been convicted of murder after 33 people died in clashes over a land dispute in Konissérédou in April 2000.

International initiatives
The international community was slow to react to the deteriorating situation in Guinea or to protect civilians from widespread human rights abuses. In particular, the UN High Commissioner for Refugees (UNHCR) in Guinea was not provided with the financial or political support necessary to effectively implement its protection mandate. The UNHCR and other agencies struggled to arrange the transfer of refugees from volatile border areas to safer locations. The report in March of a UN inter-agency mission of representatives from 13 UN departments and agencies, including the UNHCR and the World Food Programme, noted insecurity, instability and a potential for further deterioration of the situation in the region.

AI country reports/ visits
Reports
- West Africa: Guinea, Liberia and Sierra Leone – A human rights crisis for refugees and the internally displaced (AI Index: AFR 05/005/2001)
- West Africa: Guinea and Sierra Leone – No place of refuge (AI Index: AFR 05/006/2001)

Visits
AI delegates visited Guinea in February and March to interview refugees and internally displaced people. They also met the Minister of Territorial Administration.

GUINEA-BISSAU

REPUBLIC OF GUINEA-BISSAU
Head of state: Kumba Ialá
Head of government: Alamara Nhasse (replaced Faustino Fadut Embali in December, who replaced Caetano N'Tchama in March)
Capital: Bissau
Population: 1.2 million
Official language: Portuguese
Death penalty: abolitionist for all crimes

The government failed to investigate reports of human rights violations including extrajudicial executions. Allegations of attempted coups resulted in the arrest of dozens of people, including security personnel and refugees from the Casamance region of neighbouring Senegal. Political detainees were held for long periods without charge or trial in harsh conditions. The authorities attempted to curb freedom of expression and journalists were briefly detained for criticizing the government. The independence of the judiciary came under attack.

Background
2001 saw continuing political instability in Guinea-Bissau. The coalition government collapsed in January and a minority government was formed by the *Partido de Renovação Social* (PRS), Social Renewal Party.

The border with Senegal was militarized in January following increased incursions by the *Mouvement des forces démocratiques de Casamance* (MFDC), Movement of Democratic Forces of Casamance, a Senegalese armed opposition group seeking independence for the Casamance region. Dozens of people, reportedly including civilians, were killed in the fighting between the armed forces of Guinea-Bissau and the forces of the MFDC.

After a long internal battle within the ruling PRS, Prime Minister Caetano N'Tchama was dismissed in March and replaced by Faustino Fadut Embali, who announced that the government's program would centre on the restoration of peace along the northern border with Senegal. He also announced plans to end impunity for human rights abuses by strengthening the justice system, making it more accessible, and ensuring respect for the independence of the judiciary.

There were frequent calls for the resignation of the government which came under increased criticism for its handling of the economy. In April the government announced that several million US dollars, earmarked to pay the salaries of public employees, had disappeared from the Treasury.

Civil servants, including teachers, went on strike to demand payment of their salaries. In February the police responded violently to students demonstrating against the teachers' strike. In August the police also beat demonstrators calling for the resignation of a minister following the death of his lover in disputed circumstances.

In October the mandate of the UN Peace-building Support Office in Guinea-Bissau (UNOGBIS) was extended until December 2002.

In December, the authorities announced that they had foiled an attempted coup. The government was dismissed and Alamara Nhasse was appointed Prime Minister. A new government was formed composed entirely of members of the PRS.

The judiciary under attack
The independence of the judiciary came under increasing attack from the government.

◻ In September all senior Supreme Court judges were dismissed in violation of the Constitution which stipulates that the Higher Council of Magistrates is the only body with the authority to appoint and dismiss Supreme Court judges. Magistrates and prosecutors went on strike for over a month demanding the judges' reinstatement. In November, Emiliano Nosolini dos Reis and Venancio Matins, President and Vice-President respectively of the Supreme Court, were arrested and detained without charge or trial despite widespread international protests. No reason was given for their continued detention although it was suggested that it was in connection with money which allegedly went missing from the Supreme Court during their period in office. However, their dismissal and subsequent arrests appeared to be politically motivated and in response to court rulings which had displeased the government.

Impunity
Attempts initiated in 2000 to tackle impunity suffered a set-back. The authorities failed to carry out investigations into human rights violations.

◻ Three security officers, sentenced to long terms of imprisonment in August 2000 for human rights violations committed during the armed conflict in 1998 and 1999, were reported not to be serving their sentences, although they had not benefited from an amnesty or pardon. The authorities failed to clarify why they were still at liberty.

◻ The authorities failed to investigate the death of Brigadier Ansumane Mané following an alleged coup attempt in November 2000, reportedly in a confrontation with soldiers loyal to President Kumba Ialá. Reports suggested he had been extrajudicially executed.

◻ In January a 28-year-old man called Mama was killed in the village of Sancoma near the border with Senegal. According to reports, soldiers and border police officers dragged him from his home and shot him dead in front of his father's house. No inquiry into this case had been carried out by the end of the year.

Detention without charge or trial
Political detainees were held for long periods without charge or trial.

◻ Over 100 military officers arrested in November 2000 were detained without charge or trial until their release on bail in June 2001. They had been held in severely overcrowded conditions which lacked sanitation facilities and several contracted serious diseases as a result. One, Colonel Baba Djasi, died in February from typhoid. Under the conditions of their bail they were not allowed to leave Bissau and had to report to the court or police authorities daily. No charges had been brought against them by the end of the year.

At least 30 of these soldiers, including former Vice-Chief of Staff of the Army Almane Alam Camará and former Chief of Staff of the Navy Mohamed Laminé Sanhá, were rearrested in December following allegations of their involvement in an alleged attempted coup. They remained detained without charge at the end of the year.

In February, allegations of attempted coups resulted in the arrest of dozens of people, including security personnel and refugees from Casamance accused of belonging to the MFDC. Most were released soon after arrest. However, others were held for several months without charge or trial. Some were held incommunicado.

◻ In February Sene Djedjo, Sidi Djedjo, Ibo Djata, Laminé Sambú and Aliou Candé were arrested in their homes by the security police and accused of belonging to the MFDC. They were held incommunicado for at least two weeks in an underground cell without light or ventilation. They were released without charge in July.

Freedom of expression and assembly
There were attempts to inhibit freedom of expression and assembly, and the police reportedly used excessive force against demonstrators.

◻ In February the Rapid Intervention Police (PIR) appeared to use excessive force to disperse a demonstration by students in Bafatá. They used tear gas and beat students.

Journalists were harassed and briefly detained for publishing articles critical of the government or organizing radio debates deemed sensitive by the authorities. Two independent newspapers — *Diário de Bissau* and *Gazeta de Notícias* — were closed down by the authorities in October, allegedly because they did not have licences.

◻ In March, a high-ranking military officer interrupted a debate about the alleged attempted coup of November 2000 on the independent radio station *Rádio Bombolom*. He reportedly accused the radio station of fomenting instability and threatened to bomb it in the event of renewed internal armed conflict.

◻ João de Barros, owner and director of the *Diário de Bissau*, and Athizar Mendes, a journalist at the paper, were arrested in June after publication of an article criticizing the government's mishandling of the economy. They were charged with defamation and released on bail after two days. João de Barros was re-detained for two days in November.

Updates
◻ Ten prisoners of conscience, including opposition leader Fernando Gomes who was briefly detained in

November 2000, remained under restrictive bail conditions, pending charges.

☐ Between January and March, six people who had been detained since the end of the 1998-1999 armed conflict were tried on charges of treason and collaborating with the enemy and were acquitted. They included Brigadier Humberto Gomes, the former Chief of Staff of the Armed Forces, and his deputy, Lieutenant-Colonel Afonso Te.

AI country reports/visits
Reports
- Guinea-Bissau: Human rights violations since the armed conflict ended in May 1999 (AI Index: AFR 30/011/2001)
- Guinea-Bissau: Attack on the independence of the judiciary (AI Index: AFR 30/014/2001)

Visit
AI delegates visited Guinea-Bissau in March.

GUYANA

REPUBLIC OF GUYANA
Head of state: Bharrat Jagdeo
Head of government: Samuel Hinds
Capital: Georgetown
Population: 0.7 million
Official language: English
Death penalty: retentionist

There were frequent reports of killings in circumstances suggesting that they were extrajudicial executions. Torture and deaths in custody were also reported. Prison conditions were poor, with allegations of ill-treatment and overcrowding. President Bharrat Jagdeo announced that the recommendations of a review of the police force, prisons and the justice system would be considered by the government. Death sentences continued to be imposed. No executions were carried out. Approximately 23 people, including two women, remained on death row at the end of the year.

Background
Following general elections in March, the People's Progressive Party/Civic was returned to office for a third consecutive term. The elections were followed by political violence in some areas, including Georgetown and East Coast Demerara. In April President Jagdeo and the leader of the opposition People's National Congress/Reform (PNC/R) committed themselves to working to reduce ethnic tension and unrest.

Institutional reforms
Legislation to establish a parliamentary commission on human rights was presented to the National Assembly. Proposals included the monitoring of Guyana's compliance with international human rights treaties, and initiatives for human rights education.

Police shootings
Frequent reports were received of killings by police in circumstances suggesting that they were extrajudicial executions. In June, members of the PNC/R submitted a parliamentary motion calling on the President to establish an inquiry into the police force.

☐ Shazad Bacchus, aged 15, Azad Bacchus and Faddil Ally, aged 18, were beaten and shot by members of the Berbice Anti-Smuggling Squad (BASS) in circumstances suggesting extrajudicial execution. According to relatives, Shazad Bacchus was arrested and beaten by BASS officials at his uncle's home before being taken to hospital with injuries to his face and body. BASS officials are alleged to have opened fire on a minibus the three were travelling in as they left the hospital. Witnesses alleged that the three were subsequently dragged from the bus and killed. The Minister for Home Affairs stated that an investigation into the killings would be forwarded to the Director of Public Prosecutions. The findings had not been released by the end of the year.

In August Saif Ghani and Steven Angel were shot dead and four others were injured after police opened fire on an estimated 400 people who were protesting against the killings at the BASS headquarters.

Torture and deaths in custody
Reports continued of torture and ill-treatment by the police.

☐ In May Anthony Brumesh died in Aurora police lock-up in disputed circumstances. Witnesses alleged that he had been beaten and slammed against the wall by a police officer and had been denied medical attention. An autopsy was said to have revealed the cause of death as a fractured skull and haemorraging. No response to AI's request for information on investigations had been received by the end of the year.

Investigation and prosecution of police abuses
☐ On 27 November, the High Court quashed a verdict given earlier in the month by a coroner's inquest that the police should be held criminally responsible for the death of Mohammed Shafeek, who died in Brickdam police lock-up in September 2000. Two police officers had allegedly held Mohammed Shafeek by his hands and feet, thrown him against a concrete wall and refused him medical attention. One witness was allegedly intimidated by being arrested, held in incommunicado detention, beaten around the head and tortured, including by mock executions.

☐ In September the Chief Justice ordered the Commissioner of Police and Chief Magistrate to ensure that an inquest be held by 2 October into the fatal shootings in July of Antoine Houston, Steve Grant and John Bruce by members of the police Special Target

Squad, in circumstances suggesting that they were extrajudicial executions. The inquest had not started by the end of the year. An autopsy report on Antoine Houston revealed that he had been shot seven times, including once in the back of the head at close range.

Prisons

Conditions and overcrowding in prisons remained severe, amounting in some cases to cruel, inhuman and degrading treatment.

In July, prisoners at Camp Street prison staged a protest, alleging that they had been beaten by members of the police specifically brought in for this purpose. In a further protest in August, 22 inmates complained about the inadequate provision of food and hygiene facilities, lack of medical treatment and ill-treatment.

International organizations

In October, the Inter-American Commission on Human Rights ruled that a petition in connection with the alleged "disappearance" of Franz Britton in January 1999 was admissible.

HAITI

HAITI
Head of state: Jean Bertrand Aristide (replaced René Préval in February)
Head of government: Jean Marie Chérestal (replaced Jacques Edouard Alexis in February)
Capital: Port-au-Prince
Population: 8.3 million
Official languages: French, Creole
Death penalty: abolitionist for all crimes

Seven years after Haiti's return to constitutional order in 1994, many of the important human rights gains made in that time were in danger. Following the February inauguration of President Jean Bertrand Aristide, there were repeated indications that the police and justice systems were becoming more politicized. The President's June announcement of a "zero tolerance" policy towards crime was followed by an increase in killings by police in disputed circumstances; in "popular justice" killings of suspected criminals; and in attacks by increasingly intolerant partisans of the ruling party *Fanmi Lavalas* (FL) on perceived opponents, including human rights defenders and journalists. Tensions were exacerbated by an attack in July on several police stations by unidentified and heavily armed assailants, and another such attack in December on the National Palace. The investigation into the murder in April 2000 of prominent radio journalist Jean Dominique and his radio station guard Jean Claude Louissaint was repeatedly obstructed.

Background

Haiti became further isolated from the international community as disputes continued over the validity of the 2000 elections, despite negotiations facilitated by the Organization of American States (OAS). Seven FL senators, whose victories had been contested, resigned in an unsuccessful effort to resolve the conflict. In addition to the closure in February of the UN field mission, present since 1993, the UN's Independent Expert on Haiti stepped down and was not replaced. Haiti's precarious economic situation worsened with the decision by the European Union to freeze aid to the country. The USA cut off bilateral aid, giving only to non-governmental organizations (NGOs). In November the US Congressional Black Caucus wrote to President George W. Bush to protest at the impact of the measures on the poorest country in the Western hemisphere. The OAS reactivated the group of governments called "Friends of Haiti", expanding it to 14 members.

The opposition coalition named a parallel "provisional president", who called for a return of the notorious Haitian Armed Forces (FADH) disbanded by President Aristide in 1995. In March several hundred former soldiers demonstrated in support. In response, an organization of coup victims petitioned for a constitutional amendment to formally abolish the FADH, and presented the Senate with over 100,000 signatures in October.

On 28 July heavily armed men, reportedly claiming to be former members of the FADH, attacked police stations in Port-au-Prince and the Central Plateau and killed five police officers. Following the attacks, a former soldier was killed in disputed circumstances in Hinche and dozens of people were arrested, although all were subsequently released. For several hours on the morning of 17 December, more heavily armed men took possession of the National Palace in Port-au-Prince; in the course of the attack and the subsequent pro-government mob violence more than 10 people, including an assailant and two police officers, were killed. FL partisans burned four offices belonging to opposition parties, as well as an NGO office and homes belonging to several opposition figures. Journalists attempting to cover the events received death threats, and several radio stations were forcibly closed by pro-FL mobs. Investigations were reportedly opened into both attacks and their aftermath, although no results were made public.

Freedom of expression

At a press conference held in January, FL supporters threatened violence against certain key opposition politicians, as well as journalists and religious figures whom they accused of undermining the party. One of the speakers was later questioned by the Public Prosecutor but no further action was taken. In October, human rights defenders from two NGOs, the National

Coalition for Haitian Rights and the Platform of Haitian Human Rights Organizations, reported that they had received death threats which they believed were linked to their publicizing of human rights violations and partisan behaviour by the police. The failure by the police to halt mob violence against journalists and opposition figures following the December attack on the National Palace, or to arrest any perpetrators, was perceived as further evidence of growing intolerance and of the impunity enjoyed by government supporters.

Attacks on journalists

There was a series of attacks against journalists, most frequently by the police or pro-government crowds.

◻ On 12 October, *Radio Haïti Inter* journalist Jean Robert Delciné was assaulted and threatened by police officers after investigating the alleged killing of Mackenson Fleurimon (see below) by police officers in Cité Soleil. The police inspector implicated refused to respond to summonses from the prosecutor and from the force's internal investigative unit.

◻ On 3 December, the news director of *Radio Echo 2000*, Brignol Lindor, was hacked to death in Petit Goave by a mob which included members of a pro-FL organization. Several days before, the FL assistant mayor had called for "zero tolerance" against Brignol Lindor, whom he accused of supporting a rival party. Although several of the perpetrators admitted to the murder, warrants issued had not been executed by the end of 2001.

◻ Following the attack on 17 December on the National Palace, many reporters and radio stations were targeted for attack by pro-government crowds. Several, including a *Radio Métropole* correspondent in Gonaives, were attacked in the street as they tried to cover events. Radio stations *Signal FM* and *Caraïbes FM* were surrounded and threatened by crowds, and the latter had windows broken and vehicles damaged on their premises. Other stations such as *Métropole*, *Vision 2000* and *Kiskeya* curtailed their coverage after receiving telephone threats. Up to 10 journalists were reported to have fled the country due to attacks and threats received during this period.

Jean Dominique investigation

The April 2000 killings of respected Radio Haïti Inter journalist Jean Dominique and station guard Jean Claude Louissaint continued to dominate the political scene as human rights groups, journalists, churches, elected officials and grassroots groups across the political spectrum collectively pressed for the perpetrators to be brought to justice. During a visit in March to the radio station, the President publicly committed his efforts to ensuring full and impartial justice in the case, and declared a "National Press Day" on the anniversary of the deaths.

In spite of such public support, numerous death threats reportedly received by the investigating judge were seen as attempts to intimidate them into dropping influential people from the investigation. The judge resigned briefly, citing insufficient attention to his security and lack of adequate resources. The Inter-American Commission on Human Rights requested that the Haitian government undertake precautionary measures to protect him for a period of six months.

In response to the prosecutor's request for supplementary information, the judge formally requested in August that the parliamentary immunity of a sitting FL senator be lifted. The request remained pending before the Senate at the end of the year. Arrest warrants for prominent FL activists who had failed to respond to the judge's summons were not acted upon by the police, in spite of repeated opportunities to do so; the activists only appeared before the judge after a delay of several months, reportedly after urging from the President. The investigation was further hampered by the failure of the police to heed the judge's recommendations regarding protection of a key suspect; the man was killed by a mob in Léogâne shortly after his arrest in November. The local police commissioner was briefly detained following this incident.

Haitian National Police

Nearly all senior police officials were replaced following President Aristide's inauguration. The post of Inspector General of the police internal oversight unit was filled after nearly a year's vacancy. There were reports of ill-treatment, particularly of suspected criminals during arrest. The police were accused of excessive use of force in some crowd-control situations, while in others, such as mob violence in the wake of the attack on 17 December, they reportedly failed to intervene at all.

In response to rising public concern about crime levels, the President announced in June a "zero tolerance" policy towards law-breakers. NGOs reported a subsequent increase in killings of alleged criminal suspects. Several were reportedly attributed to police officers, and others were by crowds carrying out "popular justice".

◻ On 11 October Mackenson Fleurimon, aged 16, was reportedly shot dead by the police in the Cité Soleil neighbourhood of Port-au-Prince. Family members and witnesses claimed that police officers killed him after failing to find his brother, whom they suspected of gang activity. A police inspector and a commissioner were questioned by prosecutors on 18 October, but the former apparently went into hiding rather than respond to further summonses. A warrant was issued for his arrest.

Justice system

There was growing concern about the lack of independence of the justice system, partly due to public awareness of obstacles to the Jean Dominique investigation. The Ministry of Justice expressed hope that the reconstitution in October of the *Cour de Cassation*, the highest court in Haiti, after a long period of inactivity, could reinforce independence by serving as a channel for appeals against improper decisions. However, incidents of elected officials and party loyalists pressurising judges continued at every level.

◻ In March, a former justice of the peace in Maissade was threatened, and a member of his family assaulted, by the local mayor and armed supporters. Several of these were reportedly arrested, but freed after the mayor and his group visited the police station to demand their release. The judge was forced to go into hiding.

☐ In Hinche, also in March, the local mayor and his armed group burst into the court and physically assaulted two justices of the peace, whom they reportedly accused of not being FL supporters. The mayor was later arrested but the Minister of the Interior reportedly intervened to obtain his release. The mayor was replaced, reportedly by presidential decree, in December.

Overcoming impunity

Efforts to bring to justice those responsible for past human rights violations continued.

☐ Little progress was made regarding an appeal to the *Cour de Cassation* against the guilty verdict in the trial in 2000 of those accused of the 1994 Raboteau massacre. In June, immigration officials arrested Carl Dorelien, a former Haitian army colonel, as he attempted to enter the USA. He had been found guilty in November 2000 in Haiti of involvement in the massacre and sentenced *in absentia* to life imprisonment.

☐ On 26 May former military general Prosper Avril was arrested by riot police in Port-au-Prince. Prosper Avril, who had been head of security under former President Jean Claude Duvalier, led Haiti following a military coup in 1988 until March 1990, a period marred by serious human rights violations. He was arrested on a warrant dating from 1996, on charges of torture, assault and illegal arrest. State security charges were also filed against him. The case was assigned to an investigating judge.

In September President Aristide announced that the documents confiscated by US troops from military and paramilitary headquarters in 1994 had been returned to Haiti. It was not clear if the documents were intact. Victims' groups and legal groups working on past cases pressed for access to the files, which they believed could be useful in prosecuting those responsible for past human rights violations.

Prisons

A crisis in the country's prisons was acknowledged as delays in the criminal justice system meant that of a prison population of over 4,000, some 80 per cent were held in pre-trial detention. The Ministry of Justice convened a seminar on criminal justice in May to discuss possible remedies. In September, two investigating magistrates and three substitute prosecutors were permanently assigned to the National Penitentiary in Port-au-Prince to try to resolve the situation of the pre-trial detainees among its 2,000 inmates. Despite reduced budgets for prisoners, improvements were made to prison administration and the provision of food. Over 100 new prison guards were trained and deployed.

Killings of detainees

On the night of 15/16 November, at least four prisoners were reportedly killed in the National Penitentiary as specialized police units attempted to break up a riot. Around a dozen inmates were believed to have been wounded. According to press reports, the riot was sparked by the beating to death of a detainee by prison guards. The Minister of Justice announced the formation of an investigative commission into the incident, made up of police and justice officials; no report was made public by the end of the year.

AI country reports/visits

Reports
- Haiti: Human rights challenges facing the new government (AI Index: AMR 36/002/2001)
- Haiti: Steps forward, steps back – human rights 10 years after the coup (AI Index: AMR 36/010/2001)

Visit
AI delegates visited Haiti in October.

HONDURAS

REPUBLIC OF HONDURAS
Head of state and government: Carlos Flores Facussé
Capital: Tegucigalpa
Population: 6.6 million
Official language: Spanish
Death penalty: abolitionist for all crimes

A community leader was killed amid continued threats to human rights defenders. Formal criminal charges were brought against several and they faced a campaign to discredit their work. Demonstrators were injured as a result of excessive use of force by the police in breaking up demonstrations. Members of indigenous groups faced renewed attacks, including killings, beatings and ill-treatment by the police and unjustified criminal charges. There were reports of ill-treatment in prisons, and conditions amounted to cruel, inhuman or degrading treatment.

Background

The general election was held in November. The opposition National Party won and Ricardo Maduro was elected President.

Little headway was made to address the serious institutional problems affecting the police force and the judiciary, and public confidence in them remained low. Although the Ministry of Security approved plans to dismiss national police members who had committed crimes, including human rights violations, in the course of their work, no official investigations were carried out into the actions of former officers. The judiciary faced accusations of corruption and inefficiency. A new system to elect members to the Supreme Court was established with the aim of making it more independent.

The crime rate remained high and kidnappings for ransom increased. Youth gangs known as "*maras*" were assumed to be responsible for many crimes. Deaths of *maras* members were often attributed to inter-gang conflicts but there was also concern that they could have been victims of "social cleansing" by individuals allegedly acting with the consent or complicity of the police.

Human rights defenders

Human rights defenders faced threats, attacks and criminal charges as a result of their work. Certain government authorities attempted to discredit their activities by making public statements alleging that they were protecting criminals.

☐ Peter Marchetti, a US citizen and Jesuit priest who worked on land issues with the Aguán Peasant Movement, was threatened in June by gunmen who went to his church. Both Peter Marchetti and Santos Figueroa, another human rights defender who was also threatened, had been active in efforts to bring to justice those responsible for the death of Carlos Escaleras, an environmental activist and politician shot dead in October 1997 in Tocoa, Colón department. As a result of the threats Peter Marchetti was forced to leave the country.

☐ Carlos Roberto Flores, a community leader and environmental activist, was shot dead on 30 June by security guards outside his home in El Ocotal, Gualaco, Olancho department. He was among a group of local activists opposed to the construction of a hydroelectric dam in the region. Charges were filed against five security guards and arrest warrants were issued in August. By the end of the year they had not been arrested. Many others in the area, including the mayor of Gualaco, had been intimidated and threatened, some with death. In July, a demonstration protesting at the killing of Carlos Roberto Flores and the failure of the authorities to protect the local population was dispersed with tear gas, water cannons and batons. There were some arrests but all those detained were later released. Human rights defenders were among 22 people against whom police later initiated criminal proceedings before the First Criminal Court in Tegucigalpa. Charges included contempt, disobedience and assault. There was no progress in the proceedings against the 22 who, if imprisoned, would have been considered prisoners of conscience by AI.

Indigenous groups

In November José Roberto Isidro, a Chorti, was shot dead by police during a demonstration over land rights in Ocotepeque department. The September 2000 agreement in which the authorities made a number of commitments to indigenous groups was not fully honoured. In particular, an agreed program to investigate the killing of indigenous and black people in previous years was not set up and a large majority of cases remained unresolved. Members of indigenous groups were among those injured in July when police dispersed demonstrations protesting at the killing of Carlos Roberto Flores (see above).

Update

In July Salvador Zúñiga was one of the 22 people who had criminal charges filed against them following the July demonstration (see above). However, he was not in Tegucigalpa at the time but at home in La Esperanza, 200km away. This was perceived by indigenous groups and others as further harassment by the authorities. He had been harassed and intimidated in June 2000 for his activities on behalf of indigenous people.

Impunity

There was no significant progress in the investigation or judicial proceedings regarding cases of "disappearance" in the 1980s. The office of the Special Human Rights Prosecutor in the Attorney General's Office organized exhumations in a specific location but no remains of known "disappeared" people were found. No investigations were begun into more recent cases, including deaths of street children and other young people believed to be *maras* members.

☐ In April AI asked the authorities to take advantage of the return to Honduras of José Barrera, a former member of the armed forces, to initiate an investigation into past "disappearances". In September the Special Human Rights Prosecutor in the Attorney General's Office filed charges against José Barrera of providing false evidence. This step was taken after he had retracted a statement he made in 1987 regarding the involvement of military personnel in human rights violations as well as certain "disappearance" cases, including that of José Eduardo López who was arrested and tortured in 1981 and who "disappeared" in 1984.

National police

The police force was responsible for human rights violations against peaceful demonstrators and others. In June a group of members of the Aguán Peasant Movement were demonstrating in favour of rights to land in the former *Centro de Entrenamiento Militar* (CREM), Military Training Centre, when the police and riot police dispersed them using live ammunition, tear gas and batons. Sixteen people were injured, some suffering bullet wounds. In June Trinidad Sánchez was shot dead when the police went to his house to arrest him. There was no evidence that he presented a danger to the police. By the end of the year no one had been brought to justice in these cases.

Prisons

There were reports that prisoners were beaten and kept in conditions which amounted to cruel, inhuman or degrading treatment. Prisons were severely overcrowded and often insanitary, causing health problems to inmates.

AI country reports/visits

Reports

- Honduras: José Eduardo López: 20 years later – it is time for justice (AI Index: AMR 37/002/2001)

- Honduras: Stop the impunity. Agreements with indigenous peoples should be honoured now (AI Index: AMR 37/001/2001)
- Honduras: Much remains to be done in terms of human rights (AI Index: AMR 37/011/2001)

Visits
AI delegates visited Honduras in July and August to hold talks with government authorities and meet local organizations and activists.

HUNGARY

REPUBLIC OF HUNGARY
Head of state: Ferenc Mádl
Head of government: Viktor Orbán
Capital: Budapest
Population: 9.9 million
Official language: Hungarian
Death penalty: abolitionist for all crimes
2001 treaty ratifications/signatures: Rome Statute of the International Criminal Court

There was continued concern about ill-treatment of detainees by police. There were reports that Roma were both ill-treated by the police and inadequately protected by them from racist attacks. Large numbers of Afghan refugees and asylum-seekers were segregated from and subjected to greater restrictions than other foreign nationals.

Ill-treatment
In March the Hungarian government permitted the publication of the report of the European Committee for the Prevention of Torture and Inhuman or Degrading Treatment or Punishment (CPT) on its visit to Hungary in December 1999. The CPT delegation had heard a number of allegations of physical ill-treatment by the police, particularly during its visit to police stations in Budapest, Debrecen and Hajdúhadház. The great majority of complainants alleged that they had been struck with truncheons, punched, kicked or slapped by police officers. Foreign nationals, juveniles and Roma seemed to be particularly at risk of such ill-treatment.

The CPT reiterated several recommendations already made in its report on a visit in 1994, concerning detainees' rights to notification of custody, access to a lawyer and information on rights; the use of force by police officers; and medical examination of people in police custody. The CPT also expressed concern "with the practice followed by police officers of formally advising detained persons who have manifested their wish to register a complaint that to defame a police officer is a criminal offence; such a practice could easily discourage a person who has been ill-treated by the police from lodging a complaint". The CPT also expressed concern at the continuing overcrowding in prisons and at some aspects of the treatment of prisoners who were considered dangerous, such as the routine shackling of prisoners when they left their cells and prolonged isolation. The Hungarian government did not fully agree with the CPT that police violence continued to be a serious problem in Hungary. In reply to a CPT request, the Ministry of the Interior provided information regarding the number of complaints and criminal proceedings in 1999 against police officers which was at variance with information on the Database of the Unified Police and Prosecutorial Criminal Statistics. For example, the Ministry stated that 133 complaints had been received concerning interrogation under duress and ill-treatment, whereas the total number of such complains in 1999 appears to have been 1,068.

Roma
In February, around 80 police officers raided a Romani settlement in Bag, Pest County, during a wake. They are said to have indiscriminately assaulted the mourners attending the funeral, as well as other people whose houses they searched in an aggressive manner. According to one report, eight people, who were detained during the raid, were released after four hours without being questioned or charged with any criminal offence.

Although the police stated that the motive for their action was to apprehend several suspects, there were indications that the raid may have been intended to intimidate László Vidák, a Romani man who had filed a complaint alleging that he had been beaten by police officers during interrogation in October 1999. One of the officers who had ill-treated him also participated in the police action in February 2001 during which László Vidák was again said to have been severely beaten by police and required four days of hospital treatment.

In April, four police officers were convicted in connection with the ill-treatment of László Vidák in 1999 and three were given suspended sentences.

In May the police in Kalocsa reportedly failed to protect five young Romani men from racist violence and then failed to act upon their complaint. The five men described how they were subjected to racist abuse and threats by the driver of a jeep while a police officer looked on. As the Romani men continued their journey, they found the road blocked by the jeep while a police patrol car was parked some distance away. The driver of the jeep then chased the Romani men and reportedly shot at them several times with what was believed to be a shotgun. Later the same day, the Romani youths tried to report the incident to the police and went to four police stations in the region but none of the officers they spoke to would accept their complaint or take other appropriate action.

Five days later one of the Romani men, Pál Sztojka, went once again to a police station and recorded the response of the officer on duty. When Pál Sztojka said he wanted to report a shooting the officer reportedly replied: "And you have not been shot dead? That is too bad... There was a police officer there and he didn't shoot you?" The officer then threatened to hit Pál Sztojka. When an investigation was subsequently initiated into the incident some of the Romani victims reported that they were harassed by officers who threatened to have them investigated on suspicion of theft. The investigation met with repeated obstacles from the authorities. A decision to close the investigation without charging anyone was under appeal at the end of the year.

Afghan asylum-seekers

In September the authorities transported non-Afghan refugees and asylum-seekers from the Debrecen refugee reception centre to other reception centres in the country and transferred all Afghan refugees and asylum-seekers from the other centres to Debrecen. By October, Debrecen, which was guarded by armed border guards, housed 812 Afghan nationals.

Afghan asylum-seekers and refugees had their freedom of movement restricted in a discriminatory way which contravened both national and international human rights law. Under Hungarian law asylum-seekers must reside in designated reception centres which they are not allowed to leave for more than 24 hours without special permission. Additional restrictions can only be imposed on the basis of a court ruling or an administrative order which is subject to a judicial review. However, none of the Afghan refugees and asylum-seekers were allowed to leave Debrecen reception centre for two weeks following an order of the Office for Immigration and Naturalization.

AI country reports/visits
Report
- Concerns in Europe, January-June 2001: Hungary (AI Index: EUR 01/003/2001)

INDIA

REPUBLIC OF INDIA
Head of state: Kocheril Raman Narayanan
Head of government: Atal Bihari Vajpayee
Capital: New Delhi
Population: over 1 billion
Official language: Hindi
Death penalty: retentionist

People from socially and economically marginalized sections of society continued to be particularly vulnerable to torture and ill-treatment by both the police and non-state actors. The numbers of deaths in custody among members of these groups remained high, while their access to redress continued to be difficult despite the existence of progressive legislation. Human rights defenders continued to be harassed by both the police and non-state actors, and some of their activities were labelled "anti-national" by the government. Excessive force was often used by law enforcement officers while policing peaceful demonstrations. Inter-caste and inter-religious tensions were often politically exploited, leading to several violent incidents throughout the country in which the police were believed to have taken a partisan role. Security concerns were addressed by the government through proposals for new and particularly stringent special legislation intended to grant wide powers of arrest and detention to law enforcement personnel. The criminal justice system continued to be extremely slow, under-resourced and to provide weak safeguards for the accused. Law enforcement officers were allowed *de facto* impunity both inside and outside areas of armed conflict. Impunity was encouraged by provisions in most existing security legislation, by political protection and by slow judicial proceedings and lack of implementation of findings by commissions of inquiry.

Background
The Bharatiya Janata Party (BJP)-led National Democratic Alliance continued in office throughout the year, despite recurring tensions between the BJP and some of its allies. State elections were held in five states in May. Their results reflected a growing importance in state-level politics of caste and regional parties respectively in the northern and in the southern states. Tensions between the Hindu and Muslim communities continued to be fuelled by different political groups, and clashes between the police and some Muslim groups intensified after the government declared its support for the bombing campaign in Afghanistan which followed the attacks in the USA on 11 September. In Kashmir, human rights abuses continued to be committed both by armed groups, and police and security forces on a large scale. An average of 100

civilians were killed there each month. Tensions between India and Pakistan on the issue of the support to armed groups in Kashmir became a subject of international debate in the context of the bombing campaign in Afghanistan by the USA and its allies. These tensions further increased, leading to a military build-up on the border between the two countries, following an attack on the Union Parliament on 13 December by members of an armed group. In the northeast, a cease-fire between the National Socialist Council of Nagaland (Issac-Muivah) and the central government was extended in July for one year. Violent protests led by non-Naga organizations in the neighbouring state of Manipur prevented the cease-fire being extended beyond Nagaland, as initially proposed.

Special legislation

Calls by the USA for a "global campaign against terrorism" following the attacks in the USA on 11 September provided a context for several initiatives by the Indian government to tighten security legislation in the country. A new Prevention of Terrorism Ordinance (POTO) was promulgated in October, giving the police wide powers of arrest and providing for up to six months' detention without charge or trial for political suspects. As the Ordinance was not discussed in Parliament during the winter session, it was repromulgated in December. Human rights organizations were concerned that some provisions were not consistent with the rights to freedom of expression and association set out in international human rights standards. Similar "anti-terrorism" bills were adopted or under examination in several states, including West Bengal, Karnataka and Andhra Pradesh. In November the Foreign Contribution (Management and Control) Bill 2001 was drafted. The Bill was intended to replace the Foreign Contributions Regulation Act and to curb the flow of foreign funds to both "terrorist" groups and non-governmental organizations.

The authorities continued to use the lapsed Terrorist and Disruptive Activities Act (TADA) to detain people in Jammu and Kashmir by linking them to ongoing cases filed before 1995. Hundreds of people remained in detention under the TADA, despite Supreme Court orders for a review of all cases.

Impunity

In August, government officials proposed granting amnesties to police officers facing trial for committing human rights abuses in their official capacity during the period of militancy in Punjab between 1984 and 1994. These proposals were neither officially confirmed nor withdrawn by the end of the year.

The government failed to act on recommendations made by several commissions of inquiry after identifying the involvement of police and security forces in human rights violations. The recommendations of the Shrikrishna Commission, concerning the communal riots which took place in Mumbai in 1992 and 1993 following the destruction of the Babri mosque in Ayodhya, were implemented extremely slowly. Seventeen police officers had been issued with charge-sheets by the end of the year for having taken sides with violent Hindu groups during the riots which claimed 1,788 lives. Similarly, the recommendations of the Pandian Commission on the unlawful killings in April 2000 of protesters at Barakpore, Jammu and Kashmir, were not implemented by the government. The report itself was not made public. Special security laws, including the Armed Forces (Special Powers) Act, the POTO and the National Security Act, as well as the Protection of Human Rights Act, continued to retain provisions granting virtual impunity for government officials and army officers committing abuses while acting in their official capacity.

Discrimination

Socially and economically marginalized sections of society such as women, *dalits*, *adivasis* (tribal people) and religious minorities continued to suffer abuses as a result of discrimination by both the police and non-state actors. Their access to justice remained limited, despite the existence of some progressive pieces of legislation, as the criminal justice system tended to reproduce in its functioning the gender, caste and class discrimination exisiting in the society.

Discrimination against members of *dalit* communities received international attention when the issue was discussed during the UN World Conference against Racism (WCAR), held in South Africa in September. However, the final declaration of the WCAR did not acknowledge discrimination based on "work and descent" as a form of racism.

Since the attacks in the USA of 11 September and on the Union Parliament in December, the Muslim community became increasingly vulnerable to victimization by both the state and some Hindu political groups. Tensions between the police and Muslim groups erupted into rioting in different parts of the country, including Lucknow and Malegaon. Tension also escalated in connection with the intensification of the Vishwa Hindu Parishad's campaign for the reconstruction of the Ram temple in Ayodhya, at the site of a mosque destroyed by Hindu rioters in 1992.

Human rights defenders

Harassment of human rights defenders by both state officials and other groups and individuals remained a constant feature throughout the year. There were reports of beatings, shootings and the use of excessive force by the police to try to prevent human rights defenders organizing peaceful protests against the government and non-state actors. Organizations assisting tribal communities to prevent their land being taken for industrial projects were particularly targeted. Several activists had false charges brought against them in an attempt to discredit their work. The government initiated inquiries into cases of suspected abuses against human rights defenders, but charges were rarely brought and investigations were often little more than a formal exercise.

◻ Four *adivasis* (tribal people) were killed in April when police opened fire on a peaceful meeting in Mehndikheda, Madhya Pradesh, held to discuss allegations of abuses of the rights of *adivasis* by local police and forest officials. An administrative inquiry set up to investigate the killings fell short of international standards for an independent and impartial inquiry. Its report had not been made public by the end of the year.

◻ Azam Ali, District Secretary of the Nalgonda branch of the Andhra Pradesh Civil Liberties Committee (APCLC), was killed in February by unidentified gunmen while on his way to a meeting to commemorate the death of the Joint Secretary of the APCLC, who was killed in November 2000. Despite the immediate establishment of a judicial inquiry into the killing, its report was not made public by the end of the year. Harassment of other members of the APCLC, including death threats, continued unchecked.

The Special Representative of the UN Secretary-General on Human Rights Defenders had not been invited to visit the country by the end of the year.

Torture and ill-treatment

Torture by both state agents and non-state actors remained widespread throughout the country. Members of marginalized sections of society were particularly vulnerable. The National Human Rights Commission reported that 127 people had died in police custody between April 2000 and March 2001.

◻ On 26 October Raja Ram was reportedly arrested with his two brothers after a neighbour had called the police because of a dispute. The three men, belonging to the *dalit* community, were allegedly beaten with sticks and rods at the Mariyaon police station in Lucknow. Raja Ram was hung upside down and water was poured into his nose. The three were released on bail after the police reportedly filed the case under section 151 of the Indian Penal Code (preventive detention) in order to legalize the arrests. Raja Ram died on 29 October. A case was filed for murder against five police officers. However, the Lucknow police authorities allegedly denied any responsibility, arguing that Raja Ram died because of disease.

By the end of 2001 India had not ratified the UN Convention against Torture, which it had signed in October 1997, nor had national legislation been drafted to enable its ratification. Therefore, no code or law specifically forbids torture as a criminal offence. Several provisions introduced by the POTO were believed to facilitate the use of torture in police custody.

The UN Special Rapporteur on torture was not granted access to the country by the end of the year, despite repeated requests.

Human rights commissions

There were no indications of progress by the government in considering amendments recommended in 2000 by the National Human Rights Commission (NHRC) to the Protection of Human Rights Act 1993. The NHRC thus continued to be unable to investigate allegations of human rights violations committed by members of the army or paramilitary forces, as well as incidents which took place more than a year before a complaint was made. In September, the NHRC attended the World Conference against Racism and took an independent view from the government, in favour of the inclusion of caste discrimination as a form of racism.

In November the NHRC announced its opposition to the enactment of the POTO, judging it to be "draconian" and superfluous, and considering the existing laws sufficient to deal with "terrorism" if properly enforced.

State human rights commissions (SHRCs) were created in Maharashtra and Chattisgarh in July, bringing to 12 the number of states having an SHRC. Difficult working conditions, including lack of resources, continued to be reported by some SHRCs.

Abuses by armed groups

There were continued reports of abuses by armed groups in many states, including torture and deliberate killings of civilians. In areas of armed conflict, such as Jammu and Kashmir and the northeast, hundreds of non-combatants, including children, were killed in indiscriminate violence. Conflicts in the states of Bihar, Andhra Pradesh and parts of Madhya Pradesh, Orissa and West Bengal, involving different factions of the *naxalite* (armed left-wing) groups and the police, claimed many civilian lives.

Death penalty

At least 16 people were sentenced to death in 2001. It was not known if any executions were carried out, nor how many prisoners were held on death row. The government of India does not publish statistical information about the implementation of the death penalty.

Legislation to extend the use of the death penalty to crimes of rape remained pending. The Explosive Substances (Amendment) Bill 1999, which extends the scope of the death penalty by making the possession of lethal explosives a capital offence, was passed by parliament at the end of the year. The POTO provides for the death penalty for "terrorist" offences which result in death. The concern that this would lead to an increase in the number of death sentences was heightened by the fact that provisions of the Ordinance made unfair trials more likely.

AI country reports/visits
Reports
- India: Words into action – recommendations for the prevention of torture (AI Index: ASA 20/003/2001)
- India: The battle against fear and discrimination – the impact of violence against women in Uttar Pradesh and Rajasthan (AI Index: ASA 20/016/2001)
- India: Time to act to stop torture and impunity in West Bengal (AI Index: ASA 20/033/2001)
- India: Briefing on the Prevention of Terrorism Ordinance (AI Index: ASA 20/049/2001)

INDONESIA

REPUBLIC OF INDONESIA
Head of state and government: Megawati Sukarnoputri (replaced Abdurrahman Wahid in July)
Capital: Jakarta
Population: 215 million
Official language: Bahasa Indonesia
Death penalty: retentionist
2001 treaty ratifications/signatures: Optional Protocol to the UN Children's Convention on the involvement of children in armed conflict

The human rights situation in the provinces of Aceh and Papua deteriorated during the year and hundreds of cases of extrajudicial execution, "disappearances", torture and unlawful arrests were reported. Human rights defenders were among the victims. Peaceful independence activists were tried and were among the first prisoners of conscience to be convicted since 1998. Armed independence groups in both provinces were also responsible for committing abuses. Elsewhere, deaths and injuries resulted from excessive force used by the military and police, including against striking workers, protesters and in areas of religious and ethnic conflict. Impunity continued; there were no credible investigations into allegations of human rights violations. The appointment of a new President in July did little to forward progress on legal, judicial and other human rights reform. The death penalty was applied.

Background
Political conflict, which effectively paralysed the government for the first half of the year, culminated in July in the impeachment of the first democratically elected President in over four decades. Abdurrahman Wahid was succeeded by the Vice-President, Megawati Sukarnoputri. The process of human rights reform and efforts to resolve some of Indonesia's most intractable conflicts were obstructed by political infighting both before and after the impeachment.

Legal and judicial reform
Although judges were appointed to serve in new courts to deal with gross violations of human rights, the courts had not been established by the end of the year. There was concern that the right to fair trial in the new human rights courts would be jeopardized because relevant legislation had not been amended and that legislation for a witness/victim protection program had not been enacted.

Long-standing government commitments to amend the Criminal Code were not fulfilled and provisions which contravened basic rights, including rights to freedom of expression and assembly, continued to be applied. Existing legal safeguards to protect the rights of detainees were frequently ignored.

Prisoners of conscience and unfair trials
Independence activists in Papua and Aceh, as well as labour and political activists, were among at least 13 people who were sentenced to terms of imprisonment for the peaceful expression of their views. Several were found guilty of crimes under the "Hate-sowing Articles" of the Criminal Code prohibiting the "spreading of hatred" against the government, which had been used extensively in the past to suppress dissent but which had fallen out of use in recent years. Prisoners of conscience and others were convicted after unfair trials. Defendants were routinely denied access to legal representation and some were coerced into making confessions, including through torture.

◻ Mixilmina Munir and Aris Wardoyo, activists with the student group City Forum (*Forkot*), were sentenced to five months' imprisonment in November for peacefully protesting against increases in fuel prices. The two were found guilty of defying police orders.

◻ Four students from Papua were found guilty in August of "spreading hatred" against the government for their role in a peaceful demonstration in support of Papuan independence outside the Netherlands Embassy in Jakarta in December 2000. Hans Gobay, Mathius Rumbrakuk, Luan Wenda and Yosep Wenda were initially interrogated without lawyers and subjected to torture and ill-treatment. They were denied medical treatment in detention for injuries sustained as a result of beatings upon arrest. They were sentenced to three months and 25 days' imprisonment.

Impunity
Resistance by the authorities to bringing perpetrators of human rights violations to justice continued to prevail and the vast majority of allegations of human rights violations were not investigated. The cases that were investigated did not result in trials. Thousands of cases of past violations remained unresolved.

The National Commission on Human Rights (*Komnas HAM*) investigated several cases but none had resulted in prosecutions by the end of the year. In May a team headed by *Komnas HAM* reported that members of the Police Mobile Brigade (Brimob) and the local police in Papua were responsible for violations including the unlawful detention and torture of around 100 people in Abepura in December 2000. Two of the detainees died from their injuries. Local police officials, who refused to cooperate with the inquiry team, were also reported to have intimidated witnesses.

A report published by *Komnas HAM* in February on inter-religious conflict in the Moluccas stated that over 3,000 people had been killed since January 1999. The report also found that the government had failed to protect the civilian population and that the security forces were also responsible for human rights violations.

There was no progress on bringing to trial cases in Aceh which the government-appointed Independent Commission to Investigate Violence in Aceh had recommended in 1999 should be prioritized for investigation and prosecution. Four civilian suspects accused of unlawfully killing three members of a humanitarian organization, the Rehabilitation Action for Torture Victims, in Aceh in December 2000, escaped from police custody in March. Four military suspects in the same case remained in custody but had not been charged by the end of the year.

The establishment of an *ad hoc* Human Rights Court for the Tanjung Priok case, in which scores of people were killed or had "disappeared" when the security forces opened fire on Muslim demonstrators in 1984, was approved by the President but had not been set up.

Past human rights violations in East Timor
Despite repeated government commitments to begin trials of cases of serious crimes committed in East Timor around the popular consultation on independence of 30 August 1999, the *ad hoc* Human Rights Court on East Timor had not been established by the end of 2001.

The effectiveness of the Court was undermined by limits placed on its jurisdiction even before it had been established. A Presidential Decree, issued in August 2001, gave the court jurisdiction over only the two months of April and September 1999, and over only three of East Timor's 13 districts. There was no indication that the government was willing to review the decree to ensure that suspects in all cases of serious crimes, including crimes against humanity, committed throughout East Timor during 1999 could be brought to justice. In the meantime, senior police and military officials who had been named as suspects in the investigations had not been charged and remained in active service.

Investigators with the UN Transitional Administration in East Timor (UNTAET) continued to be denied access to witnesses and other evidence in Indonesia. Indictments against suspects in Indonesia, including members of the military, had been issued by UNTAET by the end of the year but none had been transferred to East Timor for trial. (See East Timor entry.)

Repression of pro-independence movements
Repression of pro-independence movements intensified during the year. In Aceh, dialogue between the government and the armed opposition Free Aceh Movement (GAM) broke down and in April new security operations, involving both the police and the military, were launched against GAM. Local human rights groups claimed that some 1,500 people were killed during the year. Scores of cases of unlawful detention, "disappearances" and torture, including rape, were also reported. Many of the violations resulted from reprisals against civilians for GAM attacks on the security forces. Operations by the security forces against the independence movement in Papua also resulted in dozens of cases of unlawful killings, "disappearances", torture and other violations. Houses and means of livelihood were also destroyed in both provinces as a form of collective punishment for attacks by armed opposition groups against the police and military.

◻ On 9 August workers and their families at the PT Bumi Flora Plantation in East Aceh were ordered from their homes by unidentified men. At least 31 people, including children, were believed to have been shot dead. Although the military and GAM accused each other, evidence collected by local human rights monitors indicated that the military may have been responsible. No one was brought to justice.

◻ Four people were believed to have been killed on 3 May when members of Brimob opened fire on them as they were boarding a boat in Wasior, Papua. Eighteen others, including Musa Kuluwa and Mandinus Yikwa, who suffered gunshot wounds, were kicked and beaten before being arrested. The group was brought to trial, accused of "attempting to commit separatism" and rebellion. The trial continued.

Leading figures in the pro-independence movements in both Papua and Aceh were imprisoned. Muhammad Nazar, chair of the Information Centre for a Referendum on Aceh (SIRA), was sentenced to 10 months' imprisonment in March for "spreading hatred" against the government. He was released in October after serving his sentence. The head of SIRA's Jakarta branch, Faisal Saifuddin, was also charged with "spreading hatred". His trial began in November but had not concluded by the end of the year. Both were prisoners of conscience.

Political leaders, together with other leading members of civil society, were also among the victims of unlawful killings. In Papua, Theys Eluay, chairman of the civilian umbrella independence group, the Papua Presidium Council (PPC), was found dead in his vehicle in November. He and four other members of the PPC had been on trial for their peaceful pro-independence activities. The military repeatedly denied any involvement in the killing but this was strongly contested by local human rights groups. A police investigation indicated that members of the Special Forces Command (*Kopassus*) were responsible. Five parliamentarians were killed in Aceh during the year. These cases had not been thoroughly investigated; the identity of the perpetrators was not established.

Human rights defenders
An increasing number of cases of human rights violations against human rights defenders were documented, mainly in Aceh and Papua. The violations included extrajudicial executions, unlawful arrests and torture, although threats and other forms of harassment by the police and military were also commonplace. Several activists were accused of, and in one case formally charged with, defamation and other offences for publicizing human rights violations by the security forces. In Aceh, GAM was also responsible for intimidating human rights activists.

◻ Indra P. Keumala and Hepi Suaidi, from the Commission for Disappearances and Victims of Violence (*Kontras*) and the People's Crisis Centre (PCC) respectively, were detained at a military checkpoint in July in Southeast Aceh District as they were returning from investigating reports of the killing of around 100 people in Central Aceh District by members of military and militia groups. The two were slapped, kicked and beaten with rifle butts. Their fingers were burned with cigarettes and they were doused in water containing human excrement. They were released without charge two days later.

Refugees

Security conditions, including the continued presence of armed militia, did not permit the return to West Timor of the UN High Commissioner for Refugees (UNHCR), which had evacuated the province in September 2000 after the murder of three of its staff by members of East Timorese pro-Indonesia militia. Despite the absence of a formal repatriation process, some 18,000 refugees returned to East Timor during the year. Concerns remained about the safety of the remaining 75,000 refugees who had been in West Timor since September 1999 when they fled the post-referendum violence in East Timor or were forcibly expelled.

Death penalty

Gerson Pandie and Fredrik Soru were executed by firing squad in May in the first known executions since 1995. At least 10 people were sentenced to death during the year, bringing to 40 the total number of people known to be under sentence of death. According to AI's information, this was the highest number of sentences passed in one year for the last 10 years.

Intergovernmental organizations

In November, in its concluding observations on Indonesia's first periodic report on the implementation of the UN Convention against Torture, the UN Committee against Torture expressed concern about the high number of allegations of torture committed by members of the security forces; numerous attacks against human rights defenders, sometimes resulting in death; the climate of impunity resulting from failure to bring to justice individuals suspected of carrying out acts of torture; and the inadequate legal and institutional framework for protection against torture.

A technical assistance program with the office of the Attorney General was suspended by the UN Office of the High Commissioner for Human Rights in August pending the amendment of the presidential decision to extend the jurisdiction of the *ad hoc* Human Rights Court on East Timor.

AI country reports/visits

Reports
- Indonesia: Comments on the law on Human Rights Courts (Law No. 26/2000) (AI Index: ASA 21/005/2001)
- Indonesia: Briefing on the current human rights situation in Indonesia (AI Index: ASA 21/006/2001)
- Indonesia: Amnesty International briefing on the deteriorating human rights situation in Aceh for participants in the ASEAN Regional Forum (AI Index: ASA 21/020/2001)
- Indonesia: Commentary on Indonesia's first report to the UN Committee against Torture (AI Index: ASA 21/048/2001)

Visit
AI delegates visited Indonesia in February and met government and other officials.

IRAN

ISLAMIC REPUBLIC OF IRAN
Leader of the Islamic Republic of Iran: Ayatollah Sayed 'Ali Khamenei
President: Hojjatoleslam val Moslemin Sayed Mohammad Khatami
Capital: Tehran
Population: 71.4 million
Official language: Persian (Farsi)
Death penalty: retentionist

Scores of political prisoners, including prisoners of conscience, were arrested and others continued to be held in prolonged detention without trial or following unfair trials. Some had no access to lawyers or family. In a continuing clamp-down on freedom of expression and association, led by the judiciary, scores of students, journalists and intellectuals were detained. At least 139 people, including one minor, were executed and 285 flogged, many in public.

Background

President Khatami, the incumbent candidate, won the presidential election in June in a comprehensive victory seen by many as a reaffirmation of a reform agenda. He made public appeals to the judiciary to respect the constitutional rights of parliamentarians and citizens.

There were increasing indications of social, regional and ethnic disquiet and unrest. In July clothing and shoe factory employees protested, including in front of parliament, over unpaid wages. In the same month, disturbances occurred when Tehran officials attempted to destroy unauthorized housing. In August an announcement that the government planned to divide Khorasan province led to riots in Sabzevar in which three people reportedly died. Thousands of people were detained in October following public disorder after international football matches in Tehran. In July, student groups marked the anniversary of a raid by the security forces on student dormitories in Tehran in 1999, when at least one student was allegedly killed and others were ill-treated.

Drought and conflict in Afghanistan in 2001 increased the numbers seeking refuge in Iran. Protests in July over social conditions and lack of employment resulted in attacks on Afghan refugees in Falavarjan, central Iran. The authorities introduced restrictions on the employment of Afghans and more than 100,000 were repatriated during 2001. In October, following the bombing of Afghanistan, Iran closed its borders with the country and built refugee camps in Afghanistan near the Iranian border (see Afghanistan entry).

There were unconfirmed reports that the People's Mojahedin Organization of Iran, an armed political group, ill-treated its own members at a base in Iraq. The reports were denied by the organization but it failed to provide substantive information to allay AI's concerns.

IRA

Detention of prisoners of conscience

In March and April, the Revolutionary Court ordered the arrest of at least 60 academics, journalists and intellectuals associated with the *Milli Mazhabi* (national-religious trend), notably the *Nehzat-e Azadi*, Iran Freedom Movement. Some were released within days and many others between May and October. In November, at least 26 detainees were publicly accused by the judiciary of "acts against national security" and "seeking to overthrow the state by illegal means", vaguely worded charges which could attract long prison sentences. In November, trial proceedings against at least 12 members of the *Nehzat-e Azadi* were initiated with the reading of a 500-page indictment. The trials had not started by the end of 2001, but at least six other detainees — including Dr Habibollah Payman and Dr Reza Raiss-Toussi — remained in detention without charge at the end of the year. The trial of Alireza Alijani and Ezzatollah Sahabi (see below) was scheduled to start in January 2002.

In March over 150 parliamentarians issued an open letter expressing concern about the arrests. The detainees' families repeatedly protested at the arrests to the judiciary, the Islamic Human Rights Commission and the parliamentary Article 90 Commission, and in June they demonstrated outside UN offices in Tehran.

▭ Arrested in March, Mohammad Bastehnegar was held incommunicado until May. His wife informed parliamentarians that he was threatened with death and the arrest of his family if he did not write a confession, and that he appeared to have been drugged.

The Berlin conference trials

In January, verdicts were announced after unfair trials which took place between October and December 2000 of at least 15 participants at an academic conference in April 2000 in Berlin, Germany, about recent cultural and political developments in Iran.

They faced vaguely worded charges including "undermining national security [by] promoting the aims of hostile and subversive groups", "propaganda against the state" and "insulting Islam". Following closed and unfair trials before the Revolutionary Court, which failed to meet international standards for fair trial, at least eight were sentenced to custodial sentences.

The verdicts of the appeals heard in November dropped the charges related to "state security", but upheld reduced sentences in connection with "propaganda". As a result, in December, some individuals were acquitted, some sentences were reduced and others converted to fines.

▭ Following eight months' detention, journalist Akbar Ganji was sentenced to 10 years' imprisonment, reduced on appeal in May to six months. In July, while still in custody, he was reportedly placed in solitary confinement. New charges were brought against him and, after a further trial, he was convicted and sentenced to six years' imprisonment. Allegations he made at his trial in November 2000 of ill-treatment in custody were not investigated.

▭ Human rights lawyer Mehrangiz Kar and publisher and women's rights activist Shahla Lahiji, who were both detained for several months, were sentenced to four years' imprisonment, reduced to fines on appeal.

▭ Translators Khalil Rostamkhani and Saed Sadr were sentenced to nine (reduced to eight on appeal) and 10 years' imprisonment respectively, to be served in cities far from their homes and families.

▭ Journalist Ezzatollah Sahabi, aged 70, and student leader Ali Afshari were sentenced to four and six years' in prison, reduced to one year and six months, respectively, following appeal verdicts in December. Both had already served the sentences as they were detained in December 1999. They were held incommunicado for prolonged periods and at unauthorized detention centres. In May they reportedly made "confessions" after being denied access to legal representation. In a letter to the Revolutionary Court, Ali Afshari's family said that his harsh conditions of detention amounted to torture. In August new charges were reportedly brought against him. Immediately following his release on 29 December, Ali Afshari was sentenced to an additional 12 months in prison in connection with student demonstrations in July 1999 and it was reported that "new" charges were being prepared against him. Ezzatollah Sahabi was not released and faced additional charges and was scheduled to be tried in January 2002.

▭ Researcher Hojjatoleslam Hasan Yousefi Eshkevari was unfairly tried in the Special Court for the Clergy where he faced additional charges including defamation, heresy, being "at war with God" and "corruption on earth". The verdict was not announced but he was widely reported to have been sentenced to death. Following domestic and international condemnation, the Head of the Special Court for the Clergy, which convicted him, admitted that the trial was flawed. In November it was reported that his sentence had been reduced to two and a half years' imprisonment and removal of his status as a cleric.

Freedom of expression

At least 30 parliamentarians were interrogated and arrested by judicial officials and sentenced in connection with allegations of defamation, slander and spreading false information, although only one was imprisoned by the end of the year. In October President Khatami expressed concern to the head of the judiciary about the trials of parliamentarians.

▭ In March, Fatemeh Haqiqatjou was briefly detained by the judiciary. In July she and Davoud Solemani were questioned in court about statements made in their capacity as deputies. On 26 December, an appeal court reduced to 17 months a prison sentence handed down to Fatemeh Haqiqatjou in August for, among other charges, "propaganda against the state". She had not been imprisoned by the end of the year.

▭ In September, Shahrbanou Angane Amani, deputy for Urumiye, appeared before the Disciplinary Court for Government Employees in connection with "false reports and deceitful information" she had reportedly provided to a newspaper.

▭ On 9 December, an appeal court reportedly upheld a seven-month prison sentence passed on

Amnesty International Report 2002

parliamentarian Mohammad Dadfar. He was charged with "insulting top security officials" as well as "spreading lies". The verdict had not been carried out by the end of the year.

Publications were suspended for indeterminate periods by the judicial authorities, including the Special Court for the Clergy, and journalists were detained or sentenced to prison terms. Only two of the more than 50 publications closed in previous years were permitted to reopen. In November, the Supreme Council of the Islamic Revolution, an unelected body with legislative powers in the field of culture and education, announced that the state would take control of all Internet service providers over the next two years.

The human rights debate

The human rights debate was invigorated in April with the hosting of the Asia-Pacific regional conference of the UN World Conference against Racism. Scores of the burgeoning number of Iranian non-governmental organizations took part, including human rights and women's groups.

Parliamentary deputies increasingly voiced human rights concerns. In January, a parliamentary delegation visiting prisons expressed concern at reports of physical and psychological torture taking place at four unofficial detention centres outside the control of the prison authorities. In April, over 150 parliamentarians wrote an open letter to the head of the judiciary calling for an end to arbitrary arrests and "lawlessness". In June, Tehran deputies called for greater recognition of women's rights. In July many deputies called for a speedier investigation into the 1999 raid on student dormitories. Also in July, the speaker of the house wrote to the Leader asking for clemency for students detained in riots in 1999.

In May parliament passed a law defining and limiting the scope of political crimes. In June, however, it was rejected by the Council of Guardians, the highest legislative assembly, and sent back to parliament. Also in June, parliamentarians won the right to scrutinize the working of state television and radio. A bill for the reform of the Revolutionary and General Courts was introduced in November but was rejected by the Council of Guardians on 26 December. In November, parliament repealed Article 187 of the Law on the Third Economic, Social and Cultural Development Plan which gave the judiciary powers to license lawyers and to control entry into the legal profession and candidacies for the Bar Association's board.

Parliament's Article 90 Commission, constitutionally charged with investigating citizens' complaints, became the main avenue for raising cases of human rights violations and issued several reports. In one report in January, it stated that there was "no legal justification" for the imprisonment of four journalists. They included Akbar Ganji (see above) and Emaddedin Baqi, sentenced to three years' imprisonment in 2000, partly in connection with a newspaper article questioning the place of the death penalty in public life. In August the Commission criticized the detention of about 60 national-religious activists (see above).

Death penalty and cruel, inhuman and degrading punishments

At least 139 people, including one minor, were executed, at least two by stoning and one by beheading. At least 285 individuals were flogged. The true figures may have been considerably higher.

A surge in public executions and floggings between July and September provoked intense debate on the role of such punishments, which have often been carried out on young people and occasionally minors.

In October journalist Fatemeh Govara'i was sentenced to six months' imprisonment and 50 lashes for an interview she gave to a newspaper. She appealed against the sentence.

Impunity

Some officials involved in extrajudicial executions in previous years were convicted and sentenced to death, while others were acquitted or pardoned after trials which failed to meet international standards.

In January, 15 former Ministry of Intelligence officials were convicted in connection with the murders of three writers and two political activists in 1998 in a case known as the "serial murders". Three were sentenced to death, five to life imprisonment and seven to prison terms of between two and 10 years. In August the Supreme Court overturned the verdict and ordered a re-examination of the case. By the end of the year, there were no further developments. The defendants were not accorded full rights of defence, since at least two serving or former Ministry of Intelligence officials summoned as witnesses for the defence were excused from participating in the trial.

Intergovernmental organizations

In August a report by the Special Representative of the UN Commission on Human Rights on the situation of human rights in Iran drew particular attention to human rights abuses in pre-trial detention and to economic, social and cultural rights. A UN General Assembly resolution in December reflected these concerns, calling on the government to "implement judicial reform speedily". The General Assembly also called on the authorities "to ensure that people are not punished for exercising their political freedoms".

Communications with the government

The government responded to several cases raised by AI but failed to address substantive issues. A memorandum on AI's concerns and recommendations was sent to the government for comment, but no reply was received by the end of the year.

AI country reports/visits
Report
- Iran: A legal system that fails to protect freedom of expression and association (AI Index: MDE 13/045/2001)

IRAQ

REPUBLIC OF IRAQ
Head of state and government: Saddam Hussain
Capital: Baghdad
Population: 23.6 million
Official language: Arabic
Death penalty: retentionist

Scores of people, including possible prisoners of conscience and armed forces officers suspected of planning to overthrow the government, were executed. Scores of suspected anti-government opponents, including people suspected of having contacts with opposition groups in exile, were arrested. The fate and whereabouts of most of those arrested, including those detained in previous years, remained unknown. Several people were given lengthy prison terms after grossly unfair trials before special courts. Torture and ill-treatment of political prisoners and detainees were systematic. The two Kurdish political parties controlling Iraqi Kurdistan detained prisoners of conscience, and armed political groups were reportedly responsible for abductions and killings.

Background

Iraq remained under stringent economic sanctions imposed by UN Security Council resolutions since 1990 which reportedly resulted in severe hardship for the civilian population and a humanitarian crisis. In May the US government submitted a British-drafted resolution for a new sanctions regime, "smart sanctions", to the other permanent members of the UN Security Council. The proposal included lifting restrictions on imports of civilian goods while keeping in place controls on military imports and Iraqi oil revenues. The USA and United Kingdom (UK) wanted the resolution to be adopted by the Security Council before June, when the six-month phase of the "oil-for-food" program ended. However, the Russian Federation opposed the proposal and asked for more time to study the details. The vote was postponed indefinitely and the "oil-for-food" program was extended twice, in July and November.

In April the UN Commission on Human Rights adopted a resolution strongly condemning "the systematic, widespread and extremely grave violations of human rights and of international humanitarian law by the Government of Iraq, resulting in an all-pervasive repression and oppression sustained by broad-based discrimination and widespread terror." The Commission extended for a further year the mandate of the UN Special Rapporteur on Iraq.

Civilian deaths resulting from air strikes by US and UK forces against Iraqi targets inside the "air exclusion zones" were reported during the year. In February, for the first time in more than two years, US and UK forces bombed targets in Baghdad, outside the air exclusion zones. According to the Iraqi government, a man and a woman died as a result of these attacks and more than 20 people were injured. US officials said that the attacks were in retaliation for increased Iraqi anti-aircraft activities in the air exclusion zones and that the targets included Iraqi radar and command posts. The Iraqi government said that, on 19 June, 23 people were killed and 11 wounded after US and UK warplanes attacked a football pitch in Tel Afr, west of Mosul in northern Iraq. US officials denied this claim and stated that no missiles were dropped by US and UK forces on that day in that area. In January AI requested a visit to Iraq to investigate reports of civilian killings following US and UK air strikes. In March the government turned down the request without giving any specific reason.

Death penalty

The death penalty continued to be applied extensively. In November the Revolutionary Command Council, the highest executive body in the country, issued a decree to provide the death penalty for the offences of prostitution, homosexuality, incest and rape. The decree also stated that those convicted of providing accommodation for the purposes of prostitution would be executed by the sword. Women and men were reportedly beheaded in the last two years for alleged prostitution and procuring prostitutes, usually without formal trial and sometimes for political reasons.

Scores of people, including possible prisoners of conscience, were executed. The victims included army officers suspected of plotting to overthrow the government or of having contacts with opposition groups abroad, and suspected political opponents, particularly Shi'a Muslims suspected of anti-government activities.

In March, three air force officers, Sa'eed 'Abd al-Majid 'Abd al-Ilah, Fawzi Hamed al-'Ubaidi and Fares Ahmad al-'Alwan, were executed by firing squad.

Also in March, army officer Major-General Tariq Sa'dun was executed, reportedly for criticizing the government.

In May, two Muslim clerics, 'Abd al-Sattar 'Abd al-Ibrahim al-Musawi and Ahmad al-Hashemi, were executed in Baghdad, reportedly for publicly accusing the government of being behind the murder of Ayatollah Mohammad Sadeq al-Sadr in 1999. The two were said to have been arrested at the end of 2000.

In July, two lawyers, Mohammad 'Abd al-Razzaq al-Hadithi and Karim al-Shammari, were reportedly sentenced to death by a special court for alleged anti-government activities. The two were among a group of lawyers interrogated in June about the distribution of leaflets critical of the lack of independence of the judiciary. It was not known whether the sentences were carried out.

In October, 23 political prisoners, mainly Shi'a Muslims, were reportedly executed in Abu Ghraib prison. Three of them, 'Abd al-Hamid Naji Taleb, Riyadh Fathi Jassem and Fares Talal Hatem, were said to have been accused of murdering a security officer in Saddam City in Baghdad in June.

Arrests and incommunicado detention

During the year scores of people were arrested for their suspected anti-government activities or simply because of their family relationship to people sought by the authorities. Many were held in incommunicado detention without charge or trial.

◻ In March Hussam Mohammad Jawad, a 67-year-old retired medical doctor, and his brother-in-law Iyyad Shams al-Din, aged 63, were arrested by the authorities, reportedly to put pressure on Su'ad Shams al-Din, a medical doctor and the wife of Hussam Mohammad Jawad, to return to the country. Arrested in June 1999 and tortured, she had subsequently fled abroad. The two men were reportedly released in May.

◻ In August, 22 people were arrested in Ramadi and Kut, allegedly for suspected anti-government activities. At the end of the year their fate and whereabouts remained unknown.

Long prison sentences after unfair trials

Trials before special courts, always conducted *in camera*, continued to fall far short of internationally recognized standards for fair trial. Military officers or civil servants lacking adequate training and independence were the judges. Access to government-appointed lawyers remained severely restricted and occasionally confined to the day of the trial.

◻ In April, four people — 'Issam Mahmoud, a retired army officer, Basil Sa'di al-Hadithi, a university lecturer, Khairi Mohammad Hassan and 'Imad Mohammad Hassan — were sentenced to life imprisonment by a special court in Mosul, reportedly on charges of attempting to form a political grouping. No information was available regarding their place of imprisonment.

◻ Also in April an Iraqi nuclear scientist, Hussain Isma'il al-Bahadli, was sentenced to 31 years' imprisonment by a special court. The charges were not made public.

Torture and ill-treatment

Political prisoners and detainees were subjected to systematic torture. The bodies of many of those executed had evident signs of torture. Common methods of physical torture included electric shocks or cigarette burns to various parts of the body, pulling out of fingernails, rape, long periods of suspension by the limbs from either a rotating fan in the ceiling or from a horizontal pole, beating with cables, hosepipe or metal rods, and *falaqa* (beating on the soles of the feet). In addition, detainees were threatened with rape and subjected to mock execution. They were placed in cells where they could hear the screams of others being tortured and were deliberately deprived of sleep.

◻ In March 'Abd al-Wahad al-Rifa'i, a 58-year-old retired teacher, was executed by hanging after he had been held in prison without charge or trial for more than two years. He was suspected of having links with the opposition through his brother who lived abroad. His family in Baghdad collected his body from the Baghdad Security Headquarters. The body reportedly bore clear marks of torture, with the toenails pulled out and the right eye swollen.

◻ In July, two men, Zaher al-Zuhairi and Fares Kadhem 'Akla, reportedly had their tongues cut out for slandering the President, by members of *Feda'iyye Saddam*, a militia created in 1994 by 'Uday Saddam Hussein, the President's eldest son. The amputations took place in a public square in Diwaniya City, south of Baghdad.

Iraqi Kurdistan

In the two provinces in northern Iraq controlled by Kurdish political parties, a new government was formed in January in the area controlled by the Patriotic Union of Kurdistan (PUK). The former Prime Minister, Kosrat Rassul, resigned for health reasons and was replaced by Barham Ahmad Salih. Local council elections were held in May in the area controlled by the Kurdistan Democratic Party (KDP). The KDP reportedly won all seats.

A number of bombs exploded at offices of the UN and international non-governmental organizations in Kurdistan, resulting in considerable material damage. Kurdish officials blamed the Iraqi security services for these bomb attacks.

In September many members of the Islamic Unity Movement in Kurdistan, whose stronghold is the Halabja area, broke away to set up a new Islamist group called *Jund al-Islam* (Soldiers of Islam). The new group immediately declared a "holy war" against non-Islamist parties and heavy fighting broke out between its members and PUK forces sent to the Halabja area. Dozens were killed on both sides. Armed forces of *Jund al-Islam* reportedly beheaded and mutilated a number of PUK prisoners in Kheli Hama village. Further fighting gave PUK forces control of Halabja and drove *Jund al-Islam* fighters into the mountains near the Iran-Iraq border.

The PUK issued a general amnesty in October for members of *Jund al-Islam*, urging them to return under the authority of the regional government. The amnesty did not include those responsible for the assassination of Faranso Hariri (see below) and the massacre at Kheli Hama village.

Political arrests

◻ In April Youkhana Yalda Khaie, a 32-year-old Assyrian Christian landowner from the Duhok area, was arrested by the KDP. He was held in solitary confinement, blindfolded, and allegedly subjected to torture before he was released in September. He was accused of having links with the Turkish opposition group, the Kurdish Workers' Party (PKK). However, his family said that the real reason for his arrest was to expropriate his land and prevent him from raising funds to build a church.

◻ In June, five members of the Iraqi Workers' Communist Party (IWCP) — Karwan Najm al-Din, Kamran Hussain, Falah Ahmad, Ribwar Jalil and Alan Najm al-Din — were arrested by the authorities in PUK-controlled Sulaymania. They were alleged to have opened a newspaper office without authorization. The five were released at the end of July without charge.

◻ Hashim Zebari, a journalist writing for the independent Kurdish newspaper *Hawlati*, and two other people were arrested in July in Dohuk, in the KDP-controlled area. They were held for a few weeks and then released. The reason for the arrests was not known.

Assassination and abduction by armed groups

◻ In February Faranso Hariri, the Governor of Arbil and member of the KDP's Central Committee, was shot dead by unidentified gunmen while driving his car in Arbil. Scores of people were arrested and interrogated in connection with the assassination. The KDP later blamed armed Islamists belonging to the Islamic Unity Movement of Kurdistan who, it alleged, later joined *Jund al-Islam*.

◻ Dr Ribwar 'Omar Nouri, the director of a hospital in Halabja, was abducted on 22 September by armed men belonging to *Jund al-Islam* to put pressure on the PUK to release an arrested *Jund al-Islam* member. Dr Nouri was freed 20 days later, after the PUK had released the *Jund al-Islam* member.

◻ Bistun Muhye al-Din Hama Sharif was abducted on 5 September by *Jund al-Islam*. He was held for three days and reportedly tortured before he was released. The reason for his abduction was said to be his membership of a left-wing political group.

AI country reports/visits
Report
- Iraq: Systematic torture of political prisoners (AI Index: MDE 14/008/2001)

IRELAND

IRELAND
Head of state: Mary McAleese
Head of government: Bertie Ahern
Capital: Dublin
Population: 3.8 million
Official languages: Irish, English
Death penalty: abolitionist for all crimes

Following a referendum in June, the Irish Constitution was amended to remove the death penalty and to accept the jurisdiction of the International Criminal Court. By the end of the year the government had still failed to pass legislation to incorporate the European Convention on Human Rights into domestic law. The bill was deferred pending consultation. In July the national Human Rights Commission was established in law and began to function. The Review of the Offences Against the State Act(s), set up by the government as part of its undertakings under the Multi-Party Agreement, had not issued its final report by the end of the year. AI called on the government to provide leadership in combating racism effectively.

Shootings by the security forces: updates

◻ In April a parliamentary sub-committee began an inquiry into the killing in April 2000 of John Carthy. However, it was quickly suspended and had not restarted by the end of the year. John Carthy was shot by the police Emergency Response Unit (ERU) after he had barricaded himself in his home in Abbeylara, Co. Longford. The sub-committee was formed to examine publicly the internal police report into the shooting; it was given powers to compel oral and written evidence. At the end of April, nine ERU members sought exemptions from giving evidence. In May, 36 police officers were given leave by the High Court for judicial review, arguing that the sub-committee was undertaking an inquiry into the shooting incident, thus going beyond its terms of reference.

Two police representative bodies joined the family of John Carthy and civil liberties campaigners in calling for an independent public judicial inquiry as the only means of establishing the full circumstances of the killing.

◻ At a June inquest, the jury returned a finding — rather than a verdict — that John Morris had died in 1997 from a bullet wound to the head. The family of John Morris and their counsel withdrew from the proceedings some days before the conclusion, because key documents had not been disclosed to them.

Prisons

There was concern about reports that some aspects of the treatment of detainees who suffer from mental illness may be cruel, inhuman and degrading. These concerns increased following a report in April by the Irish Penal Reform Trust on the treatment of offenders with mental illness, which focused on the effects of solitary confinement. AI wrote to the government in August stating that its concerns included the lack of explicitly stated criteria for the imposition of solitary confinement; conditions in isolation cells; and the prolonged periods spent in solitary confinement.

Policing

There was concern that the introduction of video-recording of police interviews into 200 stations had not yet been implemented by the end of the year. In October the government announced that it will introduce an independent system for dealing with complaints made against *Gardaí* (police).

Dublin/Monaghan bombings

The Independent Commission of Inquiry into the 1974 bombings in Dublin and Monaghan, which resulted in 33 deaths and many injuries, continued to collect evidence about the circumstances of the bombings. The relatives were concerned that the United Kingdom government had not provided full evidence to the Commission.

Refugees

Among AI's concerns were: the grounds for, and prescribed places of, detention of asylum-seekers and those awaiting deportation; the lack of legal representation at first instance; the excessive use of accelerated procedures; and the proposed introduction of carriers' liability legislation which may obstruct asylum-seekers' effective access to Ireland's asylum procedure. AI also expressed concern that an agreement concluded by the government with Nigeria in September relating to the return of each other's nationals contained no specific provision that the receiving state would protect returnees against ill-treatment.

AI country reports/visits
Report
- Concerns in Europe, January-June 2001: Ireland (AI Index: EUR 01/003/2001)

ISRAEL AND THE OCCUPIED TERRITORIES

STATE OF ISRAEL
Head of state: Moshe Katzav
Head of government: Ariel Sharon (replaced Ehud Barak in March)
Official languages: Hebrew, Arabic
Death penalty: abolitionist for ordinary crimes
2001 treaty ratifications/signatures: Optional Protocol to the UN Children's Convention on the involvement of children in armed conflict

More than 460 Palestinians were killed during 2001 by the Israeli security forces; most were unlawfully killed. Among the victims were 79 children and 32 individuals targeted for assassination. More than 2,000 Palestinians were arrested for security reasons. There were widespread reports of police brutality. Palestinian detainees frequently reported that they were tortured or ill-treated during interrogation. At the end of the year at least 40 people were under administrative detention. At least 33 conscientious objectors were imprisoned during 2001. Hundreds of Palestinians from the Occupied Territories were tried before military courts in trials whose procedures fell short of international standards. Collective punishments against Palestinians included closures of towns and villages, demolition of more than 350 Palestinian homes and prolonged curfews. Palestinian armed groups killed 187 Israelis, including 154 civilians.

Background

Prime Minister Ariel Sharon took office in March, leading a coalition government. Israeli colonies, generally known as settlements, in the Occupied Territories continued to be maintained and sometimes expanded. The General Security Service (GSS), which interrogates most Palestinian detainees, was renamed the Israeli Security Agency (ISA).

Intifada

The *al-Aqsa intifada* (uprising) continued throughout 2001.

From January onwards, the Israeli Defence Forces (IDF) went increasingly on the offensive, invading Palestinian areas, including areas under full Palestinian Authority (PA) control. The Oslo peace process had defined three areas in the West Bank: Area A, where the PA held responsibility for civil affairs and internal security, while Israel was responsible for external security; Area B, where the PA held responsibility for civil affairs while Israel had overriding responsibility for security; and Area C, where Israel has sole responsibility for civil affairs and security.

Palestinian houses, especially those close to borders or settlements, were frequently destroyed without warning and orchards and agricultural or industrial installations were destroyed. Most of the towns and villages in the Occupied Territories were closed by physical barriers or by army checkpoints during 2001.

The IDF used heavy weaponry, including tanks, F16 fighter aircraft and naval gunships, to shell randomly Palestinian areas from where Palestinians had opened fire.

Palestinians were killed unlawfully by the Israeli security forces. Israeli security forces killed some Palestinians during gun battles. Palestinian armed groups killed Israeli security force personnel and deliberately targeted Israeli civilians.

In August, the IDF assassinated Mustafa Zibiri (also known as Abu 'Ali Mustafa), the leader of the People's Front for the Liberation of Palestine (PFLP). In October, in reprisal, members of the PFLP killed Rehavam Ze'evi, who had just resigned as Minister of Tourism. Following the killing the IDF reoccupied six Palestinian towns.

The Commission of Inquiry set up by the Fifth Special Session of the UN Commission on Human Rights in October 2000 reported in February. In April a fact-finding committee set up by the Sharm al-Shaykh summit in October 2000 presented its report, known as the Mitchell Report. Recommendations included calls on the Israeli government to freeze settlements, lift closures, ensure that the security forces stopped destroying Palestinian homes and ensure that any response to Palestinian gunfire minimized danger to the lives and property of Palestinian civilians. The report called on the PA to prevent Palestinian gunmen from using Palestinian populated areas to fire on Israeli populated areas and to arrest the perpetrators of attacks. A number of attempted cease-fires failed.

Unlawful killings

Israeli security forces killed more than 460 Palestinians, including 79 children. The vast majority were killed unlawfully, when the lives of others were not in imminent danger, during demonstrations, during shelling of residential areas and at checkpoints. At least 32 Palestinians were deliberately targeted in extrajudicial executions which also killed 15 bystanders. IDF and other Israeli security forces using high-velocity ammunition and rubber-coated metal bullets killed and wounded demonstrators throwing stones or Molotov cocktails. Ammunition used against Palestinians included mortars, grenade launchers and artillery shells, including shells containing flechettes (5cm-long steel darts).

☐ Fatima Abu Jish was killed in January as she was returning to her village of Beit Dajan from the hospital in Nablus where she worked as a receptionist. The IDF fired at her car which was in a queue of cars slowly travelling along a track through the fields because an IDF barrier had blocked the road to the village. The IDF first stated that soldiers had been firing in response to shots. It then admitted that no shots had been fired at the checkpoint. The IDF then claimed that a soldier had fired at the wheels of Fatima Abu Jish's car and that disciplinary procedures would be taken against him. No reason was given why one car in a convoy should have been targeted.

☐ Two Bedouin women and a child were killed in June in the Gaza Strip when an Israeli tank shelled their tent with a 120mm shell filled with up to 2,000 flechettes. Three other artillery shells exploded in the same area, wounding other Bedouin and killing sheep. The IDF initially said it was responding to gunfire, but later said that the killings had been a "mistake".

☐ Jamal Mansur and Jamal Salim were assassinated in Nablus when the IDF fired two missiles from an Apache helicopter in July. Six other people, including two children aged six and 11 who were playing outside the building, were also killed. Jamal Mansur and Jamal Salim were *Hamas* leaders who ran the Palestinian Centre for Information.

Arrests

At least 2,000 Palestinians, including about 100 from Israel and more than 1,900 from the Occupied Territories, were arrested during 2001. Several of those arrested were prisoners of conscience. More than 90 Palestinians were arrested during raids into Area A. Palestinians arrested were frequently held in prolonged incommunicado detention without access to lawyers or family.

☐ In May Israeli security forces arrested Samer Fawzi Awartani, Administrator of the Rafidiya Hospital in Nablus, on his return from a conference in the United Kingdom where he had discussed medical problems during the *intifada*. He was held in Petah Tikva Detention Centre. The High Court of Justice twice rejected petitions to allow him access to an attorney and he only had access to a lawyer after 22 days in incommunicado detention. He was a prisoner of conscience. In June an administrative detention order was issued against him for "endangering state security". However, he was later released without charge after 51 days' detention.

Police brutality

Palestinians frequently suffered verbal or physical abuse from members of the Israeli security forces. Security force personnel who carried out attacks on Palestinians benefited from impunity in all but the most high-profile cases.

Torture and ill-treatment

There were numerous allegations of torture and ill-treatment by the ISA. Victims included Palestinian citizens of Israel and Palestinians from the Occupied Territories. Many of the latter were held in prolonged incommunicado detention for 20 days and sometimes for up to 70 days.

☐ Muna 'Ubayd, a teacher and a Palestinian citizen of Israel, was arrested in August. She was held for 27 days in solitary detention in the Petah Tikva Detention Centre, apparently suspected of having had contacts with *Hizbullah*. During her interrogation she was reportedly manacled or tied to a chair, her blouse was pulled and she was thrown several times against the wall. She said she was frequently insulted and was threatened with the rape of her mother. She was also subjected to loud noise in a cell which was constantly lit. During her detention she was transferred three times for several hours to hospitals and to a psychiatric hospital. She was only able to meet her lawyer after 10 days' incommunicado detention. She was charged with "having relations with a terrorist organization" and released in September on bail; no trial had taken place by the end of the year.

Administrative detention

At least 70 administrative detention orders were issued; by the end of the year the number of those in administrative detention had risen from 12 to 40. Among them were six Palestinian citizens of Israel and Lebanese nationals placed in administrative detention under Israeli law. Administrative detainees are held without charge or trial or any right to full appeal.

☐ Two Lebanese nationals, Shaykh 'Abd al-Karim 'Ubayd and Mustafa al-Dirani, abducted from Lebanon in 1989 and 1994 respectively, continued to be held in secret detention as hostages without access to the International Committee of the Red Cross.

Conscientious objectors

At least 33 Jewish and Druze citizens of Israel who refused to perform military service or to serve in the Occupied Territories were sentenced to terms of imprisonment of up to four and a half months. They were prisoners of conscience.

Unfair trials

Hundreds of Palestinians were tried by military courts in trials which did not meet international standards for fair trial.

☐ Sana' Amer, aged 14, was arrested in February in Hebron, accused of planning to stab a settler. She alleged that she was punched during her arrest. She was held in the Moscobiyyeh Detention Centre in Jerusalem for 19 days and was only allowed one visit from her father. She was tried before the Military Court in July. Her legs were bound throughout the trial and she was handcuffed when the judge left the room. She appeared not to have a clear understanding of the judges' questions, but was sentenced to one year's imprisonment with an additional four-year sentence suspended for five years. She was released in November, a month after she became eligible for parole.

Political prisoners

At the end of the year, 2,200 Palestinians were held on political charges; some were allegedly ill-treated. Palestinian children held at Abu Kabir Detention Centre alleged that they were beaten, sexually abused and insulted by fellow prisoners; for several months families were not allowed to visit them in prison. More than 1,000 political detainees in Megiddo Prison were held in tents in overcrowded conditions. All prisoners suffered from a lack of family visits because of Israeli government restrictions on Palestinian movement.

House demolitions

The Israeli authorities destroyed Palestinian houses for alleged security reasons, as punishment, and as part of a discriminatory planning policy which prohibits the building of Palestinian houses while freely allowing Israelis to construct settlements. At least 350 Palestinian houses were destroyed in the Gaza Strip, East Jerusalem and the West Bank during 2001.

Closures and curfews

The Israeli authorities maintained strict closures on most of the Palestinian areas of the Occupied Territories. The Gaza Strip was surrounded by a high wire fence and throughout the year most Gazans were forbidden from entering Israel, the West Bank and Jerusalem. Some Palestinian areas of the Gaza Strip were barred to non-residents. In the West Bank roads to Palestinian towns and villages were repeatedly closed by earth barriers, concrete blocks and deep trenches. Palestinians from the West Bank were barred from entry into East Jerusalem except with special permission. Palestinians were barred from travelling along certain roads in the Occupied Territories. Although regulations required IDF soldiers to allow medical emergencies through, these were often ignored and at least 29 people died after delays impeded their access to hospitals.

☐ Fatima 'Abed Rabbo, a woman in labour, was turned back twice in October as she tried to cross checkpoints to go from al-Walaja to hospital in Bethlehem, 3km away. Soldiers only allowed her through as the baby was being born; attempts to save the baby in hospital failed.

Killings by armed groups

A total of 187 Israelis, including 154 civilians, were deliberately killed by Palestinian armed groups. At least 36 of those killed were children. The main armed groups involved in attacks were *Fatah,* the dominant political force in the PA, *Hamas,* Islamic *Jihad* and the PFLP. Others were killed by new groups whose organization and affiliation remained vague. *Hamas* and Islamic *Jihad* frequently carried out attacks in crowded places, apparently to target the maximum number of Israeli civilians.

☐ A total of 21 people were killed, including 12 children, and 84 injured when a Palestinian suicide bomber blew himself up among a group of young people waiting outside a disco near the Dolphinarium in Tel Aviv in June. *Hamas* claimed responsibility for the bombing.

United Nations

The UN Committee against Torture considered Israel's third periodic report in November. The Committee's conclusions raised concerns about continuing torture and administrative detention, and stated that Israel's policy of closures and demolitions of Palestinian homes may amount to cruel, inhuman or degrading treatment.

Geneva Conventions

In December a meeting of High Contracting Parties to the Geneva Conventions reaffirmed the applicability of the Fourth Geneva Convention to Occupied Palestinian Territory and called on Israel, the Occupying Power, to refrain from carrying out grave breaches of the Geneva Conventions such as wilful killings and extensive destruction and appropriation of property not justified by military necessity.

AI country reports/ visits

Reports
- Israel/Occupied Territories: State assassinations and other unlawful killings (AI Index: MDE 15/005/01)
- Israel/Occupied Territories: Broken lives – a year of *intifada* (AI Index: MDE 15/083/2001)

Visits
AI delegates visited Israel and the Occupied Territories in January, February, March, July and September. In March AI's Secretary General visited the area in order to launch a human rights agenda for peace.

ITALY

ITALIAN REPUBLIC
Head of state: Carlo Azeglio Ciampi
Head of government: Silvio Berlusconi (replaced Giuliano Amato in June)
Capital: Rome
Population: 57.5 million
Official language: Italian
Death penalty: abolitionist for all crimes

There were further reports of excessive use of force and ill-treatment, sometimes amounting to torture, by law enforcement and prison officers. Several detainees and prisoners died in disputed circumstances. Hundreds of people suffered human rights violations during policing operations surrounding mass demonstrations. In violation of its international obligations, Italy refused to implement an international warrant issued by the International Criminal Tribunal for Rwanda (ICTR) for the arrest of a Rwandese national apparently indicted for genocide and crimes against humanity. One of three men convicted in 1995 of participating in a politically motivated murder in 1972, following criminal proceedings of questionable fairness, remained in prison, serving a 22-year sentence and awaiting the outcome of a petition against Italy lodged with the European Commission of Human Rights.

Background

General elections in May brought to power the centre-right House of Freedoms alliance, led by Silvio Berlusconi. The new government included the leader of the radical right-wing National Alliance party as Deputy Prime Minister, and the leader of the anti-immigration and formerly pro-secessionist Northern League as a minister with responsibility for devolution of power to the regions and institutional reform.

The new Prime Minister, who was involved in a number of criminal investigations relating to his vast business interests, and other government members repeatedly accused the judiciary of left-wing bias and of pursuing politically motivated prosecutions. Public tension between the government and the magistracy escalated in December after the government announced its intention of bringing about far-reaching reforms in the judicial system within six months. Although the excessive slowness and inefficiency of the judicial system was widely recognized, there were fears that some of the projected reforms might erode the constitutional separation of powers between the executive and the judiciary.

Ill-treatment and excessive use of force by law enforcement officers

Allegations that law enforcement officers subjected criminal suspects to physical assault, excessive force and racist abuse persisted, together with reports of shootings, sometimes fatal, in disputed circumstances.

In March, five youths, three of them Albanian, lodged a criminal complaint against Pistoia police officers and a discotheque bouncer. They alleged that, following a verbal argument with the bouncer, they were detained by police officers outside the discotheque and taken to a police station where they were assaulted by at least five officers and the bouncer. One detainee needed hospital treatment to a broken nose, a burst ear-drum and a damaged testicle as a result. The police officers had lodged a complaint accusing the youths of insulting them and causing them bodily harm. The officers claimed that they had detained the youths inside the discotheque and had intervened to stop a brawl between them and the bouncer inside the police station. Five officers were subsequently charged with causing bodily harm, falsifying evidence and calumny; one was additionally charged with verbal abuse and unlawful detention. In December, after plea bargaining, three officers received sentences ranging between 11 and 14 months' imprisonment, while two were committed for trial.

In April, three *carabinieri* officers were placed under criminal investigation on suspicion of murder. Inhabitants of Ladispoli reported seeing Tunisian national and illegal immigrant Edine Imed Bouabid getting into a *carabinieri* vehicle in March, some 30 minutes before his corpse was discovered near a motorway. Autopsy and forensic examinations apparently established that he had died after receiving three blows from a heavy object, fracturing his skull.

Demonstrations

There were reports of law enforcement officers using excessive force during large street demonstrations in Brescia, Naples and Genoa, and subjecting numerous peaceful demonstrators, including minors, to gratuitous assaults, including beatings with batons and arbitrary detention. Other violations of fundamental human rights were also reported.

Over 200,000 people participated in anti-globalization demonstrations surrounding a G8 summit held in Genoa in July. The vast majority protested peacefully but some demonstrations degenerated into violence, resulting in significant injuries to people and extensive damage to property. By the end of the summit, hundreds of people had been injured; over 280, many of them foreign nationals, had been detained; and one Italian protester had been shot dead by a law enforcement officer performing his military service in the *carabinieri* force.

Some protesters with apparently peaceful intent were not allowed to enter Italy and proceed to Genoa, thus violating their rights to freedom of expression and assembly.

There were well-documented reports of law enforcement officers indiscriminately assaulting non-violent protesters, and journalists and medical personnel working in a professional capacity and clearly identifiable as such. During an overnight raid carried out on a building legally occupied by the Genoa Social Forum (GSF), the umbrella group which had coordinated the demonstrations, officers inflicted beatings resulting in injuries to some 62 people, some of them requiring urgent hospitalization.

Dozens of people were subjected to arbitrary and illegal arrest and there were numerous allegations of law enforcement and prison officers subjecting individuals to cruel, inhuman and degrading treatment inside detention facilities. Detainees were systematically denied the rights to have their relatives promptly notified of their whereabouts, and to prompt access to lawyers and, in the case of foreign nationals, to consular officials.

While welcoming the prompt initiation of a number of criminal investigations into the treatment of people on the streets, during the raid on the GSF centre and in detention facilities, AI believed these were unlikely to provide an adequate response. In September a parliamentary fact-finding investigation into the Genoa events ended its work in disagreement and acrimony. No effective independent commission of inquiry, as advocated by AI, had been established by the end of the year.

Torture and ill-treatment in prisons

Numerous criminal proceedings into alleged ill-treatment, in some cases amounting to torture, and into deaths in disputed circumstances were opened or continued. Excessive delays in bringing offending officers to justice persisted, contributing to an apparent climate of impunity. A background of chronic prison overcrowding persisted, often accompanied by reports of inadequate medical assistance, poor sanitation and other connected problems including high rates of suicide and attempted suicide.

In February, 10 people, including prison officers and medical personnel employed at Potenza Prison, were put under criminal investigation in connection with possible charges of actual and grievous bodily harm and falsification of medical certificates. A criminal investigation had opened in August 2000, after Tbina Ama, a Tunisian prisoner, had climbed onto the prison roof to protest against a beating he alleged prison staff had inflicted on him the previous day. A forensic examination carried out at the Public Prosecutor's request concluded that the injuries he displayed were consistent with his allegations. Tbina Ama committed suicide in May 2001.

In October a magistrate began examining the Public Prosecutor's request for 95 people to stand trial, following a criminal investigation into allegations that on 3 April 2000 over 40 inmates of Sassari prison, Sardinia, were subjected to cruel, inhuman and degrading treatment, in some cases amounting to torture, by dozens of prison officers employed in various Sardinian penal institutions. The accused also included the former director of Sassari prison, the former regional director of Sardinian prisons, various doctors employed in Sassari and two other Sardinian prisons — Macomer and Oristano — as well as the directors of these two prisons.

Universal jurisdiction over crimes against humanity

In July the Chief Prosecutor of the ICTR expressed disappointment at Italy's refusal to implement an international warrant for the arrest of a Rwandese national resident in Italy on the grounds that, under Italy's domestic legislation, there was no legal basis to carry out any such arrest. The individual had been indicted by the ICTR on charges of genocide and crimes against humanity and his arrest was requested as a preliminary step in his transfer to the ICTR. AI called on Italy immediately to fulfil its international obligations and ensure that any perpetrators of serious human rights violations were brought to justice. A bill on cooperation with the ICTR, put forward by the government in August, was still awaiting final parliamentary approval at the end of the year.

In February the Supreme Court of Cassation annulled a Rome Appeal Court ruling of September 2000 which had ordered the release of former Argentine military officer Jorge Olivera. He had been arrested in Rome in August 2000, on an international warrant issued by France, for the abduction and torture of a French citizen in Argentina in 1976, during the period of military rule. Full examination of a French extradition request was still pending when the appeal court ordered his release on the grounds that the crimes of which he was accused were subject to a statute of limitations. Jorge Olivera immediately returned to Argentina.

Five more Argentine officers were under criminal investigation for the abduction and murder of three Italian citizens in a secret detention centre in Argentina during the years of military rule. In June, the Italian judiciary made an unsuccessful request for the extradition from Argentina of one of the officers. Further criminal investigations were under way into complaints of human rights violations committed against Italian citizens as a result of past collaboration between the security forces of Argentina and those of several other South American countries.

AI country reports/ visits
Reports
- Italy: Letters to the Italian government concerning the G8 policing operation (AI Index: EUR 30/008/2001)
- Italy: G8 Genoa policing operation of July 2001 — a summary of concerns (AI Index: EUR 30/012/2001)
- Concerns in Europe, January-June 2001: Italy (AI Index: EUR 01/003/2001)

JAMAICA

JAMAICA
Head of state: Queen Elizabeth II, represented by Howard Felix Cooke
Head of government: Percival James Patterson
Capital: Kingston
Population: 2.6 million
Official language: English
Death penalty: retentionist

Reports of police brutality and excessive use of force continued. At least 148 people were killed by the police, many in disputed circumstances. Detention without charge or trial and ill-treatment were reported. Conditions of detention frequently amounted to cruel and inhuman treatment. At least 50 people were on death row at the end of the year. Twenty-seven people, including two soldiers, were killed in disturbances in Kingston in July.

Background
The economic situation remained dire with large sections of society living below the poverty line. Jamaican society continued to suffer from an extremely high level of violence. In 2001, 1,139 people were reportedly murdered, including 15 police officers. Hundreds of people living in areas of West Kingston were forced to flee their homes because of political violence.

Brutality by the security forces
At least 148 people were killed by the police, and four by the Jamaica Defence Force. Many of these killings appeared to be extrajudicial executions. There were continuing reports of unlawful arrest and detention, and of ill-treatment, possibly amounting to torture, in police custody.

There were dozens of reports of ill-treatment, possibly amounting to torture, and extrajudicial executions by members of the Crime Management Unit, a specialist police unit. In October, the Commissioner of Police announced an immediate internal investigation into the management and activities of the unit. The internal investigation was completed in November, but the findings had not been made public by the end of the year. In December, the Commissioner of Police announced that he was satisfied with the Unit's performance and would be seeking additional equipment and training for members of the Unit.

In March, seven young males aged between 15 and 20 were killed during an operation led by the Head of the Crime Management Unit on a house in Braeton in circumstances suggesting they had been extrajudicially executed.

Approximately 60 police officers went to the house in the early morning, allegedly after receiving information that two of the youths had been involved in the murder of a police officer and a headmaster. The police claimed that they returned fire from outside the house after coming under heavy gunfire and that the youths were subsequently found bleeding heavily inside the house, and were removed to hospital. Local residents claimed the youths were beaten before being summarily executed, one at a time, having been forced to plead for their lives.

A pathologist, sent by AI, observed the autopsies and noted that six of the seven youths had been shot in the head, with at least one shot fired at close range, and concluded that it was "highly unlikely" that the shooting occurred in the manner suggested by the police and that the pattern of gunshot wounds was "more consistent" with the theory that the men were shot from inside the house.

In July the Director of Public Prosecutions ordered an inquest into the killings. The Coroner's Court was due to convene in January 2002, following three adjournments.

In July at least 27 people, including two members of the security forces, died and over 50 were injured following disturbances allegedly sparked by a Crime Management Unit raid in Tivoli Gardens, West Kingston. Local residents maintained that many of those killed were shot indiscriminately and that others were deliberately targeted by the security forces. Film of soldiers and police officers firing automatic weapons while holding the guns above their heads was shown several times on television. The incident led to disturbances around the island. In October, a three-person Commission of Inquiry, headed by a retired Supreme Court Judge from Canada, began investigating the events. There were concerns that aspects of the inquiry failed to conform to international standards. Civilian witnesses were unwilling to testify; some alleged that they had been intimidated by police. Counsel to the inquiry were refused an independent investigator, thereby forcing the inquiry to rely on statements and evidence collected by the police, who were themselves under investigation. Following the limitation of their right to cross-examine witnesses, lawyers acting for the leader of the opposition Jamaican Labour Party left the inquiry. The inquiry was continuing at the end of 2001.

Prolonged detention without trial
Many prisoners continued to be held for prolonged periods without being brought to trial.

In March, Ivan Barrows, aged 76, was released from prison after being held for 29 years without trial. He had originally been charged with breaking a window but was deemed unfit to plead at the time because of mental illness. The Commissioner of Prisons told the press that Ivan Barrows had been deemed fit to plead in 1998 but offered no explanation as to why he was incarcerated for a further three years.

Torture and ill-treatment in detention
In January, the Minister of National Security and Justice committed the government to the reintroduction of hard labour for prisoners.

Conditions in prisons and other places of detention were harsh and in many cases amounted to cruel, inhuman and degrading treatment. Serious disease was commonplace.

☐ The report by the Commission of Inquiry into disturbances in St Catherine's District Prison in May 2000, during which approximately 300 prisoners were beaten, was published in March. Evidence submitted by military and prison personnel conflicted with that given by the prison medical officer and inmates. The Commissioner found that the extent of injuries suffered by inmates was out of proportion to the threatened harm to soldiers and officers. He concluded that inmates were taken from their cells and beaten and that prison personnel discharged firearms into prisoners' cells. The Commissioner made a number of recommendations, including replacing batons with electro-shock weapons. However, his recommendations did not address the issue of bringing officers responsible for human rights violations to justice. The report noted the severe overcrowding and lack of adequate facilities in the prison which held 1,302 inmates in accommodation designed for 800.

Investigations and prosecutions

In May, a police officer was charged with murder in connection with the fatal shooting of 13-year-old Janice Allen in March 2000. Members of her family reportedly received death threats on several occasions following repeated visits by the police to the family's residence. In November the Commissioner of Police announced an investigation into the threats. The trial had not concluded by the end of the year.

In May, a Coroner's Inquest held that all police involved in the fatal shooting of Patrick Genius should be held criminally responsible. However, the Director of Public Prosecutions had made no ruling regarding criminal charges by the end of 2001. Patrick Genius was shot dead by police on 13 December 1999 in Kingston.

In October, three police officers convicted of murder in October 1999 had their sentences reduced on appeal to 10 years in prison with hard labour. The appeal court found them guilty of the lesser charge of manslaughter. They had been convicted of beating David Black to death in 1995 and dumping his body at sea.

Death penalty

At least two people were sentenced to death in 2001, bringing the number of people on death row to 50. No death warrants were issued and in June the Attorney General publicly stated that it was unlikely that executions would resume in the near future because of recent legal rulings.

Threats to human rights defenders

Human rights defenders continued to be threatened.
☐ In August, journalist and human rights lawyer Hilaire Sobers received a death threat that appeared to be connected to his weekly human rights column in the *Jamaican Observer*. The author of the death threat also made references to AI and local human rights activists.

AI country reports/ visits
Reports
- Jamaica: Killings and violence by police – how many more victims? (AI Index: AMR 38/003/2001)
- Jamaica: Police killings – appeals against impunity (AI Index: AMR 38/012/2001)
- Jamaica: The Braeton Seven – report on the observation of seven autopsies in Jamaica (AI Index: AMR 38/009/2001)

Visits
In March, AI sent a pathologist to Jamaica to observe the autopsies of seven youths killed by police. In April, AI's Secretary General held talks with members of the Jamaican cabinet, the Commissioner of Police, the Public Defender and the Chairman of the Police Public Complaints Authority. In October, AI delegates visited Jamaica and observed the Commission of Inquiry into the July violence in West Kingston.

JAPAN

JAPAN
Head of government: Koizumi Junichiro (replaced Mori Yoshiro in April)
Capital: Tokyo
Population: 127.3 million
Official language: Japanese
Death penalty: retentionist

There were two executions and more than 100 prisoners remained under sentence of death. Prisoners and pre-trial detainees continued to be ill-treated and arbitrarily punished under a harsh prison regime. The refugee recognition system remained secretive and arbitrary and failed to meet international standards as set out under the UN Refugee Convention.

Background

Koizumi Junichiro was appointed Prime Minister in April. The ruling coalition secured 78 of 121 seats contested in Upper House elections in July. The new government planned reforms to reverse long-term economic decline.

For the first time since 1945, legislative amendments passed by the Diet in October allowed the armed forces greater scope to participate in international conflicts. In September, the Prime Minister's Office initiated an Anti-Terrorism Special Measures Bill, aimed at widening the scope of operations by the defence forces, the Self Defence Forces (SDF), in foreign territories; strengthening international cooperation in gathering information on "terrorism"; and restricting the entry of immigrants and monitoring of immigrants, including asylum-seekers. The authorities appeared to adopt a policy targeting specific groups on the basis of their nationality. Many Afghan asylum-seekers were reportedly detained and questioned from September, apparently in anticipation of the Bill's enactment.

Death penalty
At least 10 death sentences were passed. Two executions were carried out. Asakura Koujiro and Hasegawa Toshihiko were executed in December. Asakura Koujiro, 66 years old, was executed in Tokyo Detention Centre and Hasegawa Toshihiko was executed in Nagoya Detention Centre. At least 118 prisoners remained on death row.

Conditions on death row remained cruel, inhuman or degrading. Many prisoners had been held in solitary confinement for a decade or more, with limited contact with the outside world and no contact with other prisoners. They remained at risk of execution at only a few hours' notice and denied the opportunity of contacting relatives or lawyers.

Cruel, inhuman or degrading treatment
By the end of 2001 Japan had not submitted its initial report to the UN Committee against Torture, due in July 2000 and a requirement following its accession to the UN Convention against Torture in 1999.

Ill-treatment of prisoners
The *Daiyo Kangoku* system of pre-trial detention, which had been criticized by the UN Human Rights Committee, continued. Suspects may be held up to 23 days in police detention and interrogated for lengthy periods. There were no legal regulations governing police interrogation procedures and no access to court-appointed lawyers for suspects before they were charged. Many detainees were allegedly misled into believing they would be freed on admission of guilt, and convictions were frequently based on improperly induced confessions.

Asylum-seekers
Of the 353 people who applied for asylum, 26 were recognized as refugees and 67 were granted special permission for residence. The refugee recognition process remained arbitrary; rejections were not fully explained and did not take into account risks faced by asylum-seekers if deported. There were reports of ill-treatment of asylum-seekers, including the denial of access to medical care, in immigration detention centres, where many were detained for long periods.

☐ Nine Afghan men who had applied for refugee status between August and September were detained in Tokyo Detention Bureau on 3 October. Their applications for temporary release were assigned to the Tokyo District Court. In November Judge Fujiyama Masayuki, sitting in District Court Section 3, suspended the implementation of the detention order on five of the group whose appeal was heard in his court, and they were released after 40 days of detention. For the first time, a judge in a Japanese court had given precedence to the 1951 UN Convention relating to the Status of Refugees over Japanese immigration laws. However, this decision was subsequently overturned by the Tokyo High Court on 28 November. The five were subsequently diagnosed as suffering from acute traumatic stress disorder. The other four asylum-seekers had their applications turned down by Tokyo District Court Section 2, and their appeals to revoke a written detention order were rejected by the Tokyo High Court. The four were detained at the East Japan Immigration Centre in Ibaragi Prefecture. The Immigration Bureau issued a notice of refusal of refugee status to all nine on 26 November.

Asylum-seekers were held in prolonged detention in immigration detention centres while their requests were being considered.

☐ A Sudanese national remained in detention at the West Japan Immigration Centre following his arrest in mid-2000 for "overstaying" his visa. He alleged that he was denied adequate access to medical facilities despite complaining of pain in his knee and heel. He suffered a serious infection in his foot, and severe depression as a result of his prolonged detention.

☐ "Shayda", an Iranian gay activist, was detained at the Tokyo Immigration Detention Centre for 19 months. After making an application for refugee status in April 2000, he had been arrested for "overstaying" in May 2000. His application was subsequently rejected by the Ministry of Justice despite fears for his life if deported to Iran, where homosexuality was punishable by death. He was finally granted "provisional release" in November.

Private security staff attached to the Landing Prevention Facility (LPF) in Narita International Airport reportedly abused detainees held there. Many potential asylum-seekers were among those detained and were often deported after being denied adequate access to lawyers and information about refugee determination procedures. Detainees were held virtually incommunicado in windowless rooms.

☐ Hasan Cikan, a Kurdish refugee detained in the LPF after he declared his intention to apply for refugee status, only escaped deportation because his family contacted a lawyer and human rights organizations. They ensured that evidence that he was at risk of further political imprisonment in Turkey was considered.

Impunity
Former President of Peru Alberto Fujimori, who resigned his presidency and remained in Japan after a visit in November 2000, was formally charged with murder before the Supreme Court of Justice in Peru in September. He was alleged to be jointly responsible for the murder of 15 people in 1991 at Barrios Altos, Lima, and the "disappearance" and murder of nine students and a university professor in Lima in 1992. The Japanese government, in apparent recognition of his Japanese nationality, said that requests for his extradition would be refused. By the end of 2001, the Japanese government had not adopted a clear position on its responsibilities under the UN Convention against Torture to investigate or prosecute charges against him. (See Peru entry.)

AI country reports/visits
Visit
An AI delegation visited Japan in October to carry out research.

JORDAN

HASHEMITE KINGDOM OF JORDAN
Head of state: King 'Abdallah bin Hussein
Head of government: 'Ali Abu Ragheb
Capital: Amman
Population: 5.1 million
Official language: Arabic
Death penalty: retentionist

Hundreds of people, including prisoners of conscience, were arrested for political reasons. There were reports of torture and ill-treatment of detainees by members of the security services. Trials of most of those charged with political offences continued to be heard before the State Security Court whose procedures did not meet international fair trial standards. Around 13 people were sentenced to death and at least nine people were executed. There were at least 19 cases of family or "honour" killings. Three people linked to Islamist groups remained in forcible exile.

Background

Unauthorized public meetings were banned in August under temporary legislation. In October, in the wake of the attacks in the USA on 11 September, a provisional law broadened the definition of "terrorism" and allowed for the freezing of suspects' bank accounts. Further interim amendments to the Penal Code were introduced expanding the number of offences carrying the death penalty, restricting freedom of expression, and giving the Prime Minister discretion to refer more cases to the State Security Court, including those relating to the "national economy". The amendments were approved by King 'Abdallah following the dissolution of parliament prior to elections scheduled for 2002.

Arrests and incommunicado detention

Hundreds of people were arrested for political reasons. During September and October scores of people were arrested on suspicion of involvement with Islamist groups, and demonstrations supporting the Palestinian *intifada* and protesting against the bombing campaign in Afghanistan by the USA and its allies. Some of those arrested were held incommunicado at the General Intelligence Department (GID) detention centre. Most were later released without charge.

▫ Dozens of people, including prisoners of conscience, were detained around September. They were reportedly arrested by the GID in connection with a rally on 28 September to mark the anniversary of the Palestinian *intifada*. All were released without charge by the end of November. All were held incommunicado, three for up to 60 days including 'Ali 'Abdallah and 'Abd al-Karim al-Hasanat who stated that they were punched, slapped and kicked during interrogation by police and GID officers. They were reportedly deprived of sleep for a number of days and held in solitary confinement until their release without charge on 26 November.

▫ In October, three students were reportedly beaten by university campus guards in connection with a demonstration in Jordan University in protest against the bombing campaign in Afghanistan. They were hospitalized and later arrested at the hospital by police officers. They were held for about two days and released without charge.

Torture and ill-treatment

Reports continued to be received of torture and ill-treatment by members of the security forces and prison services. Some victims were reportedly tortured while held in incommunicado detention by the GID. There were also reports of beatings by members of the police and other security services.

▫ Ra'ed Muhammad Hijazi remained in prison at the end of the year; his trial was continuing. He had been arrested in October 2000 after being extradited from Syria and held incommunicado in the GID detention centre for up to three weeks. He alleged that during that time his life was threatened and he was beaten with sticks and cables. He said that he signed "confessions" under duress relating to alleged membership of *al-Qa'ida* (the Base) and to conspiring to bomb tourist sites in Jordan. He was reportedly beaten intermittently in prison until early 2001. At a court hearing in May a doctor testified that there was bruising on his body. During a hearing in September a doctor confirmed that he had treated Ra'ed Muhammad Hijazi for severe pneumonia possibly caused by damp and poorly ventilated prison conditions.

▫ In January, 'Ali Abu Sukkar, a member of the unauthorized Anti-Normalization Committee, a sub-committee of Jordanian professional unions which opposes relations with Israel, was arrested by armed security agents. He was reportedly beaten to the floor and shackled while a gun was held to his head. Eight members of the Committee were charged with libel and membership of an illegal organization. 'Ali Abu Sukkar and 'Ali Hattar were also charged with possession of explosives. All were released on bail after about two weeks and their case was referred to the State Security Court. In October, the case was dropped.

▫ Thirteen men arrested in early 2001 and charged with offences in connection with alleged membership of the Islamist group *Tanzim al-Khalaya*, Cells Organization, were brought to trial before the State Security Court around July. They were reportedly tortured and ill-treated during interrogation by the GID, including by being beaten on the soles of their feet (*falaqa*), deprived of sleep for prolonged periods, made to remain in a sitting position without a chair and blindfolded. They were held incommunicado in solitary confinement. According to reports, the interrogation period lasted for over a month.

Unfair trials

Political prisoners continued to be tried before the State Security Court, a court which invariably used panels of military judges and failed to provide adequate safeguards for fair trials.

⌮ During a retrial in July before the State Security Court, nine alleged members of the Islamist group *Jama'at al-Islah wa'l-Tahaddi,* Reform and Challenge Group, accused of bomb attacks during 1998, were sentenced to life imprisonment despite allegations that their confessions were made under torture. No proper investigation was ever carried out into these allegations. The nine had been sentenced to life imprisonment in 1999 by the State Security Court, following a flawed trial; the verdict had been overturned by the Court of Cassation in April 2001.

Death penalty

At least nine people were executed and at least 13 people were sentenced to death, some after unfair trials.

⌮ In May Ra'ed 'Abdallah Najib Abu-Shamma and Basim 'Abdallah Najib Abu-Shamma were sentenced to death for murder following an unfair trial. The Court of Cassation upheld the death sentences against the two men even though one of the judges reportedly refused to sign the decision on the grounds that the trial was unfair.

Family or 'honour' killings

There were at least 19 family or "honour" killings during 2001. During December, the government amended Article 340 of the Penal Code to prevent exemption from penalty for men who murder their wives or female relatives on grounds of adultery. However, the Article still allows for the reduction of the penalty if the victim is found in an "adulterous situation". The reduction of the penalty is now also allowed for women who kill husbands found in an "adulterous situation" at home.

⌮ In May the Criminal Court reduced the sentence imposed on Nidal Mahmud for the murder of his sister, Huwayda, in April to one year's imprisonment. Nidal Mahmud had initially been sentenced to seven and a half years' imprisonment. Following a review by the Court of Cassation, his case had been returned to the Criminal Court for consideration under Article 98 of the Penal Code which reduces sentences for crimes committed in a "fit of rage" caused by unlawful or dangerous acts on the part of the victim. Huwayda had previously spent three years in protective custody after being raped.

Forcible exile

Three of the four leaders of the Islamist organization *Hamas* remained in forcible exile. A fourth, Ibrahim Ghosheh, was allowed to return from Qatar at the end of June on condition he agreed to refrain from activities in the name of *Hamas.*

KAZAKSTAN

REPUBLIC OF KAZAKSTAN
Head of state: Nursultan Nazarbayev
Head of government: Kasymzhomart Tokayev
Capital: Astana
Population: 16.1 million
Official language: Kazak
Death penalty: retentionist
2001 treaty ratifications/signatures: Optional Protocol to the UN Women's Convention

Death sentences continued to be passed and at least 30 people were reported to have been executed; no official statistics on the application of the death penalty were published. Members of the Uighur ethnic minority faced continued harassment.

The death penalty

No comprehensive official statistics on the application of the death penalty in Kazakstan had been published since 1998. However, at least three death sentences were imposed and at least 30 people were reported to have been executed. According to a report on Kazak Commercial Television in 2000, between 40 and 60 executions were carried out in the country each year.

Relatives of prisoners on death row were often treated by the authorities in a manner which could cause unnecessary distress and itself constituted cruel, inhuman and degrading treatment. The families were usually not informed of the date of execution. They also did not have the right to receive the body of their relative; the bodies of executed prisoners were buried in unmarked graves in an undisclosed location. In past years there were also reports that in some cases the family was not informed of the prisoner's death until some months after the execution.

There were reports that courts, including the Supreme Court, continued to admit evidence based on coerced confessions and to base convictions primarily on such evidence. There was particular concern that people may have been sentenced to death and executed on the basis of confessions made as a result of torture.

Torture and ill-treatment

Torture and ill-treatment of criminal suspects remained widespread.

The government responded to some of the concerns raised by the UN Special Rapporteur on torture on a number of cases of alleged ill-treatment by law enforcement officers. One of the cases raised was that of Irina Cherkasova, who alleged that she had been tortured in police custody in 1999 in order to force her to confess to a murder charge. The government admitted that Irina Cherkasova had stated in both her initial trial and during her appeal hearing at the Supreme Court that she had been tortured in detention, but claimed that her allegations had been carefully investigated. According to the government her interrogation had been carried out in accordance with the law and in the presence of her lawyer.

Harassment of Uighurs
Members of the Uighur population throughout Central Asia were increasingly accused of sympathizing with, and even supporting, banned Islamist opposition movements. Uighurs were frequently arbitrarily arrested, tortured and ill-treated by the authorities in Central Asia, and some were forcibly deported to China, where they faced ill-treatment, torture and the death penalty (see China entry). There were concerns that the harassment of Uighurs would intensify in the wake of the attacks in the USA on 11 September.

Nurpolat Abdullah, a 30-year-old Uighur with Australian citizenship, was tried on charges of "forming and leading a criminal organization"; "terrorism"; "illegally storing ammunition, explosives or explosive devices"; and "concealing a serious crime".

Supporters of Nurpolat Abdullah maintained that he was innocent, that the criminal case against him was fabricated, and that the real reason for his arrest was his ethnic origin. Nurpolat Abdullah had reportedly been arrested at his home in Almaty on 2 October 2000 following a police operation against a banned underground Uighur organization. Four Uighurs were shot dead by the police in the same raid. Before and after this operation, police were reported to have searched the homes of numerous local Uighurs. Several independent sources accused the police of having used excessive force.

Killing of human rights defender
On 9 June the body of 44-year-old Dilbirim Samsakova, a prominent Uighur activist, was discovered near a water reservoir outside Almaty. She had been missing since 24 May. She had reportedly been hit on the head with a blunt object. There were concerns that Dilbirim Samsakova's murder was politically motivated and that she was killed because of her ethnic origin and her high-profile activities in support of Uighurs.

Dilbirim Samsakova was the chairwoman of Nuzugum Foundation which she set up to provide assistance to Uighur women and children from Xinjiang Uighur Autonomous Region (XUAR) in China and from Central Asia. She was also a member of an organization based in Germany campaigning for the independence of XUAR. Dilbirim Samsakova played an active role in defending the rights of Uighurs. For example, in March 2001 she travelled to Osh in Kyrgyzstan to assist four Uighur men from XUAR who had been charged with terrorism and murder in relation to a 1998 bomb explosion in Osh which killed four people. She acted as translator and legal adviser for the accused during a retrial in March (see Kyrgyzstan entry).

AI country reports/visits
Report
- Central Asia: No excuse for escalating human rights violations (AI Index: EUR 04/002/2001)

KENYA

REPUBLIC OF KENYA
Head of state and government: Daniel arap Moi
Capital: Nairobi
Population: 31.3 million
Official languages: English, Swahili
Death penalty: retentionist
2001 treaty ratifications/signatures: UN Convention against Racism

Death sentences continued to be imposed; no one was executed. At least 18 people were killed by police in circumstances suggesting they may have been extrajudicially executed. Torture remained widespread. Scores of prisoners of conscience were arrested and detained. Police used violence to disperse peaceful demonstrations by human rights groups, opposition politicians, environmental activists and others. Security officials committed violations with impunity.

Background
The Constitutional Review Commission, established in 1997 to amend the Constitution before elections scheduled for 2002, engaged in a nationwide consultative process. In May its membership was increased in response to concerns that it was not representative and that it would amend the Constitution to increase presidential powers and extend the current limit of two terms in office for the President. The 12-member Commission had been appointed by the President. He appointed a further 12 members nominated by *Ufungamano*, a civil society group composed of religious faiths and opposition groups not already represented on the Commission.

The ruling party, the Kenya African National Union (KANU), continued discussions about a future merger with the National Development Party led by Raila Odinga, who was appointed a minister in the KANU government. This ensured KANU's continued dominance in Parliament.

A prominent KANU Member of Parliament and occasional outspoken critic of the government, Tony Ndilinge, was shot dead in suspicious circumstances in Nairobi in August. The motive for his killing had not been established by the end of the year, but it was reported that he had twice expressed fears for his safety. In by-elections in July and in November for his seat, several opposition party supporters were the targets of a campaign of violence by government supporters.

In August Parliament rejected the Constitution of Kenya (Amendment) Bill, part of a package of measures aimed at tackling corruption, in part because it provided an amnesty for those involved in economic crimes before 1997. As a result, some donors, including the International Monetary Fund (IMF) and the World Bank, suspended aid and economic conditions in

Kenya deteriorated. Passage of the Bill was required for the re-establishment of the Kenya Anti-Corruption Authority (KACA), a key precondition for the release of 15.5 billion Kenyan shillings (US$200 million) by the IMF. As a result of the failure to re-establish the KACA, the government set up a new Anti-Corruption Unit within the police force to continue investigations begun by the KACA.

Violence continued during the year in the southwestern region, between members of the Kisii and Maasai ethnic groups. Scores of people were killed in the clashes. In April, the government offered an amnesty for small arms in the northeastern region, in an attempt to reduce cattle rustling, which had not been successful in attracting a significant number of weapons by the end of the year.

Death penalty

At least 26 people were sentenced to death in 2001. No one was executed.

In June, President Moi reportedly called for the death penalty to be introduced for those who knowingly and deliberately infected others with HIV/AIDS. Earlier in June the government, which declared AIDS a national disaster in 1999, passed legislation to allow the import and manufacture of generic medicines used in the treatment of HIV/AIDS. By the end of 2001 it was estimated that about 2.2 million Kenyans were HIV positive.

Allegations of killings and ill-treatment

Allegations of killings and ill-treatment by police officers and prison warders remained widespread.
Prison warders

◻ On 2 April more than 200 prison warders from GK Prison in Eldoret reportedly attacked villagers from Ngomongo, Eldoret, including women and children, in revenge for the murder of one of their colleagues by people they suspected lived in the village. According to reports, at least one villager was killed in the attack and more than 50 people injured. There was no investigation into the incident.

◻ The government-appointed Standing Committee on Human Rights released a report in June which concluded that six prisoners from King'ong'o prison, Nyeri, Central Province, were killed by prison warders in September 2000. The report accused the prison authorities of attempting to cover up the killings by claiming that the prisoners died while trying to escape, and criticized the government's handling of the case. None of the warders involved had been brought to justice by the end of the year.
Police
At least 18 people were reportedly killed by police in suspicious circumstances.

◻ On 25 July, seven men ordered off a bus by police just outside Nairobi and ordered to lie on the ground, were reportedly shot in the back by officers after three firearms had been taken from them. Although the police publicly said the incident would be investigated, no investigation was known to have been initiated by the end of the year.

◻ Police reportedly killed two members of the *Mungiki* religious group in a forest on the outskirts of Nairobi. They were reported to have been taking part in shooting practice in the forest when they were shot by the police. No investigation had taken place into the incident by the end of the year.

◻ On 1 October, six prisoners were reportedly killed by other inmates at Thika police station, near Nairobi. A post-mortem conducted in the presence of human rights activists concluded that such severe injuries could not have been inflicted without weapons. Three inmates were charged with murder and six police officers with negligence for allegedly ignoring prisoners' pleas for help. No independent investigation into the circumstances of the deaths had been carried out by the end of 2001.

◻ An investigation was carried out by US police following widespread allegations of government involvement in the death of a human rights defender. In April, the US Federal Bureau of Investigation (FBI) reported its conclusion that Father Kaiser, a Roman Catholic priest who died in August 2000, had committed suicide. The FBI had been called in to assist with the investigation because Father Kaiser was a US national whose death was widely regarded as suspicious. Human rights, religious and other groups disagreed with the findings, believing that he was killed because of his criticisms of the government.

Freedom of expression and association

Numerous meetings and peaceful demonstrations organized by human rights, religious, environmental and other groups were broken up, sometimes violently, by police.
Human rights defenders

◻ On 20 October, 71 members and supporters of the lobby group Release Political Prisoners, commemorating Kenyatta Day in the compound of their offices, were arrested. Police reportedly used excessive force to break up the peaceful gathering and beat a number of people. The men were taken to Kamiti Maximum Security Prison and the women to Langa'ta Prison. They were charged two days later with "unlawful assembly" before being released on 26 October on bail of 30,000 Kenyan shillings (approximately US$385) each. On 23 November the charges against them were withdrawn.
Disruption of rallies
There were repeated police attacks on rallies held by both opposition and civil society groups. In May President Moi said that police should videotape all political rallies. He repeatedly called for churches and non-governmental organizations to stay out of politics and in particular out of the constitutional review process.

Scores of opposition members of parliament and political leaders were arrested and briefly detained.

◻ In February, police violently prevented two peaceful rallies by a cross-party lobby group, *Muugano wa Mageuzi*, Movement for Change, from taking place in Kisii and in Kisumu town in the west of Kenya. In Kisii the police used tear gas and batons to disperse protesters, scores of whom were injured and many more arrested. In Kisumu scores of people were injured when police used tear gas and batons against supporters and local residents. Subsequent clashes between police and protesters continued into the next day, when nine people were arrested and charged with incitement to violence and possession of illegal weapons. The outcome of their trial, which reportedly began in September, was not known.

Attacks on environmental activists
Environmental activists, including members of parliament, were briefly detained and had rallies disrupted by the police, sometimes violently.

On 7 March, Wangari Maathai, Member of Parliament and coordinator of the environmental Greenbelt Movement, was arrested while gathering signatures from the public for a petition to oppose the cutting down of 167,000 acres of forest. She was released the next day after being charged with convening an illegal rally. The case against her did not proceed.

On 7 July she was again detained, with opposition Member of Parliament James Orengo and a number of opposition activists, following a tree-planting ceremony to commemorate the killing of protesters against one-party rule in 1990. The police, armed with anti-riot gear, used batons and tear gas to disperse the gathering, which had been authorized. The police gave no reasons for the arrests, which occurred hours before James Orengo was due to address an opposition rally. The two members of parliament were detained for a few hours, and the other detainees overnight, before being released without charge.

On 16 July Nixon Sifuna, a lawyer, was briefly detained at Eldoret police station and his life reportedly threatened by police in an attempt to stop him pursuing a case through the courts. Two days earlier he had won a preliminary injunction from the High Court to halt the felling of government-owned forest in the area and had requested a police escort from the court after receiving anonymous threats.

Prison conditions
Conditions in prisons remained harsh, and torture and ill-treatment remained widespread. Despite pledges by senior prison officials to make prisons more accessible, local and international organizations continued to be refused access to prisoners. The majority of deaths in custody were caused by infectious diseases resulting from severe overcrowding, insanitary conditions, inadequate medical care and shortages of food, clean water, clothing and blankets.

Women
Women continued to be beaten and raped in their homes in Kenya, and marital rape was not prohibited in law. A bill that would increase protection for women from domestic violence, the Domestic Violence (Family Protection) Bill, introduced in Parliament in 2000, had not been debated by the end of 2001.

The practice of female genital mutilation remained widespread in Kenya. Groups opposed to the practice continued to campaign intensively for it to be prohibited.

In January, the Centre for Human Rights and Democracy, a local human rights organization in Eldoret in the west of Kenya, successfully defended the rights of two minors to restrain their father from subjecting them to forcible female genital mutilation.

AI country reports/ visits
Report
- Kenya: Ending the cycle of impunity (AI Index: AFR 32/011/2001)

Visits

AI delegates visited Kenya in August and September.

KOREA
(DEMOCRATIC PEOPLE'S REPUBLIC OF)

DEMOCRATIC PEOPLE'S REPUBLIC OF KOREA
Head of state: Kim Jong Il
Head of government: Hong Song Nam
Capital: Pyongyang
Population: 22.4 million
Official language: Korean
Death penalty: retentionist
2001 treaty ratifications/ signatures: UN Women's Convention

The government of the Democratic People's Republic of Korea (North Korea) continued to refuse access to independent human rights observers. North Korea remained heavily dependent on humanitarian aid as the food crisis deepened following severe flooding. Reports of public executions continued to be received. Freedom of religion was severely restricted. The UN Human Rights Committee made a number of recommendations in response to the submission by the government under its obligations as a party to the International Covenant on Civil and Political Rights. This was the first submission by the North Korean government in 16 years.

Background
Visits to the People's Republic of China and the Russian Federation by Chairman Kim Jong Il signalled the continuing efforts by the government to consolidate relations with both countries. Chinese President Jiang Zemin visited North Korea in September, the first Chinese Head of State to do so since China's normalization of relations with the Republic of Korea (South Korea) in 1992.

Relations between North and South Korea improved in September. However, ministerial talks in November failed to reach any significant agreements. The government expressed anger at the decision by the government of South Korea to put its military and police on alert following the attacks in the USA on 11 September. As North Korea accused South Korea of introducing more armoured vehicles into the demilitarized zone, established in 1953 at the end of the Korean War, there were reports in late November of an exchange of gunfire in the area.

Contacts between North Korea and the European Union (EU) continued with a visit in May by the Prime Minister of Sweden, European Commissioner Chris Patten and EU High Representative Javier Solana. In June, a North Korean delegation visited Brussels to discuss human rights issues with the EU.

Humanitarian crisis

The need for sustained humanitarian aid to North Korea became increasingly urgent as chronic food shortages continued. The crisis was exacerbated by severe flooding in the eastern provinces in October which left many people dead and some 60,000 homeless; continuing problems surrounding the distribution of food aid were highlighted by reports that between July and September none was distributed. In July the head of the Supreme People's Assembly, Kim Yong-nam, visited Viet Nam to discuss food aid. The Third International NGO Conference on Humanitarian Assistance to North Korea, held in South Korea in June, discussed practical obstacles to the crisis, such as the lack of fertilizers and other materials, insufficient energy supplies and inadequate transport.

Refugees

The number of North Koreans forcibly repatriated by the Chinese authorities increased sharply; many went into hiding in China to avoid being sent back. Information reaching AI suggested that almost three quarters of the North Korean refugees in China were women. There were reports that many were targeted by organized gangs, repeatedly raped and forced into prostitution.

Reports were also received of a crack-down on North Koreans who crossed the border into China. Chinese police were said to have increased checks on people's homes and to have offered rewards of up to 2,000 yuan (US$240) to Chinese citizens who gave information about North Korean refugees. At the end of July there were reports that some 50 North Koreans were being forcibly returned every two days from the border town of Lonjing (Jilin province) and that several hundred were detained awaiting repatriation in the border cities of Tumen (Jilin province) and Dandong (Liaoning province) in China. There were concerns that they had been tortured and imprisoned on their return to North Korea.

☐ The crack-down on North Koreans was reported to have intensified after a widely publicized incident in June when North Korean refugee Jang Gil-suh and his family sought asylum in the Beijing office of the UN High Commissioner for Refugees. The Chinese authorities allowed the family of seven to leave China for a third country on humanitarian grounds, and they were granted asylum in South Korea at the end of June 2001. They were part of a group of 17 who arrived in China in March 2000. Jang Gil-suh's mother, Jang Son-mi, was feared to have been arrested in China and forcibly returned to North Korea in March 2000 and there were fears for her safety.

Death penalty

North Koreans fleeing to China reported that public executions were being carried out. In July, North Korea reported to the UN Human Rights Committee that a 30-year-old man, Chu Su-man, had been publicly executed in Hamhung City in 1992 after "unanimous requests" by local people. The North Korean government had initially acknowledged the execution in a letter to AI in 1993, but denied it two years later, saying that there had been a mistake in translation.

In its report to the Committee, North Korea said that it had cut the number of capital offences from more than 30 to five: conspiracy against state power, high treason, terrorism, anti-national treachery and intentional murder. The Committee expressed serious concern that, apart from the crime of intentional murder, these were essentially political offences, and so vaguely worded that the death penalty could be applied to a wide range of peaceful political activities.

Recommendations by the UN Human Rights Committee

In its conclusions to the second periodic report submitted by North Korea in July, the Committee made a number of recommendations, including that the government take appropriate measures to ensure that constitutional and legislative provisions are amended to ensure the impartiality and independence of the judiciary; that amendments be made to relevant clauses of the criminal code concerning offences where the death penalty may be applied; that executions be suspended while the government takes steps to abolish the death penalty; that regular access be permitted to international human rights organizations; that every case of torture and ill-treatment be investigated by an independent body; and that conditions in places of detention be improved and that they be opened to independent, international bodies.

Religious persecution

Reports continued to be received that people attempting to practise their religion, especially Christians, were severely impeded by the authorities. In its recommendations in July, the UN Human Rights Committee expressed serious concern about the restrictions, and requested that the authorities take practical measures "to guarantee freedom of exercise of religion by the community".

It was feared that several thousand Christians were being held in labour camps where they reportedly faced torture, starvation and death. In October, the Director General of the External Relations Department of the EU stated that the North Korean response to his queries on the reported persecution of Christians and on human rights issues was "inconclusive" and "tentative".

KOREA
(REPUBLIC OF)

REPUBLIC OF KOREA
Head of state: Kim Dae-jung
Head of government: Lee Han-dong
Capital: Seoul
Population: 47.7 million
Official language: Korean
Death penalty: retentionist

Despite promises and high expectations of improvements, the government failed to bring about major changes in the field of human rights. While there was a reduction in the number of people detained under the National Security Law (NSL), short-term detentions, especially of trade union leaders, continued to be reported. There were no executions. A National Human Rights Commission Act was passed in May and a 11-member National Human Rights Commission was established in November. Prisoners enjoyed better access to relatives, lawyers, correspondence and newspapers. However, many prisons still lacked adequate heating and ventilation. There were allegations that those who appealed against their sentences or complained of ill-treatment in prisons were subjected to arbitrary harsh punishments. Some 1,600 conscientious objectors to the military service, mostly Jehovah's Witnesses, were reported to be serving prison sentences of up to three years. An Anti-Terrorist Bill was introduced in the National Assembly at the end of the year, despite criticism from opposition parties and human rights activists.

Background
Persistent economic difficulties and a lack of direction in the "Sunshine Policy," which calls for improvements in relations with the Democratic People's Republic of Korea, resulted in a decline in popularity of the Kim Dae-jung government. The ruling Millennium Democratic Party (MDP) led by President Kim Dae-jung performed badly in the National Assembly elections in October leading to President Kim stepping down as the chairman of the MDP. A motion of no-confidence in Lim Dong-won, widely regarded as the architect of the "Sunshine Policy", was passed by 148 votes to 119 by the National Assembly in September and was followed by the resignation *en masse* of the Korean cabinet. The "Sunshine Policy" lost further momentum with the failure of inter-Korean ministerial talks on 14 November. The talks broke up without setting a date or venue for future meetings, dashing hopes for the reunion of families separated by the Korean War and halting progress on economic relations.

Lack of legal reforms
Expected legal reforms did not take place. Despite promises by President Kim in 1998, when he took charge as President, to abolish the "poisonous clauses" of the National Security Law (NSL), the NSL had not been amended by the end of 2001 and at least 38 people were detained under the NSL. The vaguely worded clauses of articles of the NSL, the Security Surveillance Law, the Obstruction of Official Duty Act (OODA) and the Anti-Demonstration Law (ADL) remained in force, providing ample legislative discretion for law enforcement officials to detain activists expressing views opposed to the government's policies. Trade union leaders were subjected to short-term detention in an attempt to suppress their rights to freedom of expression and association. The NSL, the OODA and the ADL gave law enforcement officials the power to prohibit trade union activists from demonstrating in most public spaces. At least 600 trade unionists were detained under this legislation.

◻ Park Kyung-soon, who was sentenced to seven years' imprisonment under the NSL for reportedly leading the Youngnam Committee, remained in Pusan prison throughout the year. He was a prisoner of conscience and was suffering from cirrhosis of the liver. In July 1998, 15 members of the Youngnam Committee had been arrested and charged with membership of "an anti-state organization" under Article 3 of the NSL. However, they were later convicted of "participating in enemy-benefiting activities" under Article 7 of the NSL. While 12 of the defendants were released, Park Kyung-soon and two other men were sentenced to prison terms; the two others had since completed their sentences.

◻ In June, Ch'oe Jin-su's appeal against his two-and-a-half-year sentence was rejected. He was one of five people sentenced to terms of imprisonment in 2000 under the National Security Law for organizing and participating in the People's Revolutionary Party (*Minhyukdang*), which was accused of being "an anti-state organization". An appeal by Im T'ae-yol, who had also been sentenced to two years and six months' imprisonment, was pending at the end of 2001. Shim Jae-ch'un, Ha Young-ok and Kim Kyung-hwan were serving sentences of between three and a half and eight years' imprisonment.

Death penalty
A bill to abolish the death penalty was supported by 155 of the 273 members of the National Assembly. The bill was being considered by the Standing Committee for the Judiciary and Legislation at the end of the year. No executions had taken place since President Kim Dae-jung came to power in February 1998. Despite the apparent existence of a *de facto* moratorium on executions, death sentences continued to be imposed on people convicted of serious crimes. At least 51 prisoners were on death row at the end of 2001. Prisoners sentenced to death were reportedly handcuffed at all times during the first year after the sentence was passed.

National Human Rights Commission
The National Human Rights Commission (NHRC) Act was passed in May 2001 and the NHRC was established

in November amid hopes that it could lead to better monitoring of human rights issues, including potential improvement of prison conditions. The NHRC will be composed of 11 commissioners, including at least four women.

However, there are concerns that the NHRC lacked adequate investigative powers. It cannot investigate petitions which have been completed, are under investigation by other investigative agencies, or where remedies are being pursued through other procedures. The NHRC cannot compel national agencies to provide evidence. The National Human Rights Commission Act does not provide for exemption from liability for defamation suits in the course of their duties for NHRC for commissioners and staff. There were also concerns about the possible politicization of the selection process for commissioners.

Conscientious objectors

More than 1,600 conscientious objectors to military service, mostly Jehovah's Witnesses, were serving sentences of up to three years' imprisonment at the end of the year. All Korean men are expected to serve 26 months in the military. Over 500 conscientious objectors were believed to be imprisoned every year. After completing their prison sentences, conscientious objectors were not considered eligible for public office, or for travel to many countries.

Prison conditions

Lack of heating was a serious concern given that prisoners were sometimes held in temperatures as low as -20°C. Overcrowding and lack of access to medical care were also of concern.

There were reports of harsh and arbitrary punishments being imposed, especially on prisoners who appealed against their sentences or complained of ill-treatment in prison. These included prolonged solitary confinement for up to 60 days; some prisoners were kept handcuffed during this period. Death-row prisoners were reportedly handcuffed at all times during their first year in prison and were forced to eat with their hands tied behind their back.

Refugees

The UN High Commissioner for Refugees (UNHCR) was given permission by the government to establish an office in Seoul. Since the Republic of Korea signed the UN Refugee Convention and its 1967 Protocol in 1992, 104 people had applied for refugee status. Most were turned down or voluntarily withdrew their applications. In February, 26-year-old Tadasse Deresse Degu became the first person to be granted refugee status. However, the refugee recognition process was not transparent and asylum-seekers reportedly had no legal right to seek asylum. There was continuing concern that asylum-seekers were at risk of being returned to countries where they could face serious human rights violations.

KUWAIT

STATE OF KUWAIT
Head of state: al-Shaikh Jaber al-Ahmad al-Sabah
Head of government: al-Shaikh Sa'ad al-'Abdallah al-Sabah
Capital: Kuwait City
Population: 1.9 million
Official language: Arabic
Death penalty: retentionist

More than 40 political prisoners, including prisoners of conscience, continued to be held; they had been convicted in manifestly unfair trials since 1991. The fate of more than 70 people who "disappeared" in custody in 1991 remained unknown. At least five men were sentenced to death. Two men and a woman were executed. Scores of men suspected of spying and other security offences were arrested in September and October. There were reports of torture.

Martial Law – 10 years on

The majority of human rights violations related to the period of martial law following the withdrawal of Iraqi forces in February 1991. Ten years later, despite the recommendations by the UN Human Rights Committee in 2000, the government had still not addressed most of these violations, including the imprisonment of prisoners of conscience, unresolved extrajudicial executions and "disappearances", and political prisoners sentenced after manifestly unfair trials in the Martial Law and State Security Courts. Prisoners of conscience Ibtisam Berto Sulaiman al-Dakhil and Fawwaz Muhammad al 'Awadhi Bseiso, among others, continued to be held despite worldwide appeals for their release.

Arrests

There were reports that, in the wake of the 11 September attacks in the USA, the security forces carried out arrests targeting people suspected of links with the *Taleban* or *al-Qa'ida* in Afghanistan. Dozens of detainees were reportedly held incommunicado without charge or trial and were feared to be at risk of torture.

◻ In September, an official from the Ministry of the Interior confirmed reports that four Iraqi nationals suspected of spying had been arrested in Kuwait and had "confessed" to activities endangering state security.

◻ Five Kuwaiti nationals were arrested on 26 September; two of them had reportedly returned from Afghanistan, two from Chechnya and one from Pakistan.

◻ A group of more than 50 Kuwaiti nationals was arrested on 10 October prior to their reportedly imminent departure for Pakistan.

◻ Four Kuwaiti nationals who returned from Afghanistan on 15 December were reportedly arrested and interrogated about their suspected connections with *al-Qa'ida*. They were believed to remain in detention at the end of the year amid unconfirmed reports that they might be handed over to the US authorities for further questioning.

Torture
A Kuwaiti national was arrested in October and reportedly confessed to the shooting on 10 October of Luc Ethier, a Canadian national resident in Kuwait. However, his lawyer alleged that the confession had been obtained under torture during interrogation. He was released on 6 November. In early November the authorities announced the names of seven Philippine men and women, including the widow of Luc Ethier, who had reportedly confessed to responsibility for the murder. There were allegations that the confessions may have been obtained under torture.

Women's political rights
Women activists continued their struggle through the courts to win the right to vote. Seven legal challenges to the legitimacy of the electoral law, which denies women the right to vote, were rejected by the Constitutional Court on procedural grounds. An administrative court rejected three new cases by women contesting the constitutionality of the existing electoral laws. The cases were rejected on the grounds that they were intended to result in referral to the Constitutional Court.

Non-governmental organizations
In August, journalist Nasser al-Abdali announced the formation of the Kuwait Society for the Advancement of Democracy. It reportedly comprised 13 members of the National Assembly and 50 others, including lawyers, journalists and former members of the National Assembly. The group submitted an application to the government for official recognition, but this had not been granted by the end of the year. One of several other groups awaiting official recognition was the Kuwait Society for Human Rights.

Bidun (stateless people)
In June, the National Assembly passed legislation allowing a maximum of 2,000 *Bidun* to apply for citizenship before the end of the year. However, the First Deputy Prime Minister and Minister of Foreign Affairs reportedly stated in July that the government would not grant citizenship rights to more than 600 *Bidun* and that it was not obliged to grant such rights annually. This was in stark contrast to the recommendations of the UN Human Rights Committee, which called upon the government to ensure that all persons living in Kuwait, including *Bidun*, enjoyed all rights without discrimination.

Freedom of expression
A Kuwaiti woman writer, 'Alia Shu'aib, was charged with offending public decency for attempting to publish her academic research into sexual orientation. She was found not guilty following a trial in November.

Death penalty
Two men and a woman were hanged. Kadeer Kaleeja, a 24-year-old Indian domestic worker convicted of strangling her employer in 1999, was the first woman to be executed in Kuwait for over 10 years. Five men were sentenced to death. The Court of Appeal upheld the death sentences against three men convicted of attempting to smuggle drugs, and a fourth man convicted of murder.

'Collaboration' trial
In March the Court of Cassation commuted the death sentence against Ala' Hussein 'Ali to life imprisonment, citing as reasons "his good behaviour and his age as well as his decision to return to Kuwait from Norway voluntarily". A former colonel in the Kuwaiti army, he had been sentenced to death for heading the so-called provisional government during the Iraqi occupation in 1990.

KYRGYZSTAN

KYRGYZ REPUBLIC
Head of state: Askar Akayev
Head of government: Kurmanbek Bakiev
Capital: Bishkek
Population: 5 million
Official languages: Kyrgyz, Russian
Death penalty: retentionist

Human rights defenders, including journalists, faced continued harassment. One prisoner of conscience was released from prison. Members of the Uighur ethnic minority were at risk of forcible deportation to China. At least 10 death sentences were passed during the year.

Background
As a result of heightened security measures following the attacks in the USA on 11 September, detentions of suspected members of banned Islamic organizations increased and ethnic tensions were exacerbated. At least 50 members of *Hizb-ut-Tahrir* (Party of Liberation) were reportedly convicted after unfair trials on charges of distributing leaflets and inciting national, racial or religious intolerance; dozens more were detained. The majority of the detentions reportedly took place in southern regions, bordering Uzbekistan, and the majority of those detained were apparently ethnic Uzbeks. Relatives of those arrested alleged that they were targeted because of their ethnic origin.

Prisoner of conscience
On 20 March the Supreme Court turned down an appeal against his September 2000 conviction by Topchubek

Turgunaliev, leader of the opposition *Erkindik* (Liberty) party and chairman of the independent human rights organization Guild of Prisoners of Conscience. The Supreme Court upheld the November 2000 decision by Bishkek City Court to reduce his 16-year prison sentence to six years on appeal.

In January and again in July, 60-year-old Topchubek Turgunaliev was moved from a labour colony outside Bishkek to a prison hospital, reportedly to receive treatment for a deteriorating heart condition. He was released from prison on 20 August after being granted a special presidential pardon.

Topchubek Turgunaliev had been convicted on charges connected with an alleged plot to assassinate the President; seven others were also convicted in the trial. He had consistently denied the charges and alleged that the case against him was fabricated by the Ministry of National Security (MNS) in order to punish him for his peaceful opposition political activities.

Harassment of human rights defenders

The authorities continued to harass a number of independent newspapers and human rights organizations, as well as several individual human rights defenders and independent journalists.

☐ On 13 March Tolekan Ismailova, the leader of the Coalition of NGOs for Democracy and Civil Society, was attacked by an unidentified assailant as she left her home. She was hit over the head and lost consciousness. Human rights sources alleged that she had been deliberately targeted by the authorities to frighten her into stopping her activities to promote and monitor human rights.

☐ On 27 June the office of the Kyrgyz Committee for Human Rights (KCHR) in Osh was temporarily shut down by the MNS. Noomagan Arkabaev, the KCHR coordinator for Osh Region, was detained and charged with "public appeals for the violent overthrow of the constitutional order". During the search of the KCHR office, MNS officers claimed to have discovered leaflets which called for the overthrow of the President. The KCHR alleged that the real reason for the arrest of Noomagan Arkabaev was because he had prepared articles for publication accusing the director of the MNS of Osh Region of corruption. He was released from detention on 18 July on medical grounds when his health sharply deteriorated as a result of a hunger-strike.

Political prisoner

On 22 January Bishkek Military Court sentenced Felix Kulov, the chairman of the opposition *Ar-Namys* (Dignity) party, to seven years' imprisonment on reportedly fabricated and politically motivated charges of abuse of authority while serving as a Minister of National Security.

In August 2000 Bishkek Military Court had cleared Felix Kulov of the same charges. In September 2000, after the prosecution had lodged a protest against his acquittal, the Board of the Kyrgyz Military Court ruled that the verdict should be reconsidered, and ordered a retrial in Bishkek Military Court under a new presiding judge. Felix Kulov's supporters had alleged that his arrest and the criminal case brought against him had been intended to disqualify him from running in the October 2000 presidential elections.

In July the Supreme Court rejected Felix Kulov's appeal against the verdict. He was also facing new charges of embezzlement and abuse of office while he was governor of Chui Region and mayor of Bishkek.

Fear of forcible deportation

In January, China and Kyrgyzstan signed an agreement on cooperation, including on mutual extradition, of "criminals hiding on their territories". According to unofficial sources, Kyrgyzstan had been actively cooperating with China in tracing Uighur separatists from Xinjiang Uighur Autonomous Region in the People's Republic of China, living in Kyrgyzstan; Chinese State Security officers were reported to have regularly visited Bishkek where they detained or assisted the Kyrgyz authorities in arresting Uighurs. AI feared that Uighurs extradited to China would be at risk of torture and possibly the death penalty for alleged "separatist" activities.

☐ In March, four Uighurs, two of them Chinese citizens, were sentenced to death after being accused of having caused bomb explosions which killed four people in the city of Osh in 1998. In September the Supreme Court confirmed their death sentences. Supporters of the men claimed that they had nothing to do with the bombings, but rather that they had been targeted and prosecuted because of their ethnic origin. Due to a moratorium on executions in Kyrgyzstan the men were not in immediate danger of being executed. However, there was a danger that China might request the extradition of the two Chinese nationals.

Death penalty

In June the military court of Batken garrison sentenced to death two members of the banned Islamic Movement of Uzbekistan (IMU) (see Uzbekistan entry). The men, one Russian and one Tajik, were captured by Kyrgyz troops during military operations against IMU detachments in Batken Region in August 2000. They were accused of being mercenaries and were charged among other offences with terrorism, hostage-taking, banditry and premeditated murder, the latter being the only charge to carry a possible death sentence. Unofficial sources reported that although the prosecution had failed to provide evidence that the two men had themselves killed any Kyrgyz soldiers, they were nevertheless held responsible for murders committed by their organization. The Military Court of Kyrgyzstan upheld their death sentences in November.

AI country reports/visits
Report
- Central Asia: No excuse for escalating human rights violations (AI Index: EUR 04/002/2001)

LAOS

LAO PEOPLE'S DEMOCRATIC REPUBLIC
Head of state: Khamtay Siphandone
Head of government: Bounyang Vorachit (replaced Sisavat Keobounphanh in March)
Capital: Vientiane
Population: 5.4 million
Official language: Lao
Death penalty: retentionist

Freedom of expression, association and religion continued to be severely restricted. Strict controls on information prevented adequate international and local monitoring of the human rights situation. At least three prisoners of conscience and two political prisoners remained in cruel, inhuman or degrading conditions of detention. People continued to be arrested and harassed for their Christian beliefs. The fate of protesters arrested in October 1999 and November 2000 remained unknown. The death penalty was introduced for drug trafficking offences.

Background
The five-yearly congress of the ruling Lao People's Revolutionary Party in March resulted in President Khamtay Siphandone retaining leadership and an expansion of the political bureau to include three new members. Bounyang Vorachit was appointed Prime Minister, and several other ministerial changes were approved by the National Assembly.

A program of legal education was carried out to mark the 10th anniversary of the promulgation of the Lao Constitution in August 1991. In April, legislation was amended to provide the death penalty for drug offences involving the manufacture and/or trafficking of more than 500g of heroin or 10kg of amphetamines.

The authorities continued to ask for the extradition from Thailand of a group of 28 men alleged to be members of an armed opposition group involved in an armed attack on customs and immigration offices in Champassak province in July 2000.

Political prisoners
Official secrecy about political imprisonment continued, and the collection of independent and impartial information was seriously hampered by lack of access by independent human rights monitors and of freedom of expression. No information was made public about protesters arrested in 1999 and 2000, and their whereabouts and fate remained unknown. These included five members of the "Lao Students Movement for Democracy of 26 October 1999", arrested in October 1999. Thongpaseuth Keuakoun, Khamphouvieng Sisaath, Seng-Aloun Phengphanh, Bouavanh Chanhmanivong and Keochay were among a group of people who had attempted to publicly call for respect for human rights, the release of political prisoners, a multi-party political system and elections for a new National Assembly. Sinh Keotha, a woman arrested in connection with the same demonstration, was believed to have been released, while her brother, Sinh Sanay, remained in detention. At least 15 people arrested in November 2000 following a demonstration in Champassak province remained unaccounted for.

▫ Khamtanh Phousy, a prisoner of conscience detained since 1996, remained in Prison Camp 7, in a remote area of Houa Phanh province. A former army officer who converted to Christianity, he was sentenced to seven years' imprisonment on what were believed to be politically motivated charges. No information was available about the situation of two other political prisoners believed to be still held in Prison Camp 7. Sing Chanthakoumane and Pangtong Chokbengboun, detained for "re-education" and held without charge or trial since 1975, had been sentenced to life imprisonment after an unfair trial in 1992.

▫ Prisoners of conscience Feng Sakchittaphong and Latsami Khamphoui, both aged 61, remained in Prison Camp 7. Both men are former government officials who were arrested in 1990 after advocating peaceful political and economic change. In 1992 they were sentenced to 14 years' imprisonment under national security legislation following an unfair trial. Conditions of detention were extremely harsh. They continued to be held in darkness, and to be denied adequate food and medical care. Visiting rights for their families were severely restricted.

▫ In November, five foreign nationals, including a member of the European Parliament, were arrested after staging a protest in Vientiane to commemorate the second anniversary of the attempted demonstration on 26 October 1999. They were tried after two weeks, each given a two-year suspended sentence for anti-government propaganda, and immediately deported.

Religious persecution
Despite official denials, arrests and harassment of members of small unauthorized Christian churches continued. The majority of reported incidents took place in villages in the provinces. Churches were closed by the authorities and people who refused to renounce their faith in writing were imprisoned. Although several Christians previously detained in the provinces of Savannakhet, Luang Prabang and Attapeu were released, at least 30 remained in prisons around the country. These included Seuat, Khamthorn and Dam, arrested in November 2000 and held in Savannakhet City Jail; and Thongchan, Nhot and See arrested in Oudomsay province in 1999 and sentenced to 15, 12 and 12 years' imprisonment respectively. At least eight new arrests took place. In some cases people were held for short periods, while others were serving long sentences. It was reported that people released from prison were subjected to restrictions on movement by local authorities.

▫ Three Christian pastors were arrested in May in Bolikhamsai province after their church was closed down because they refused to sign a document renouncing their faith. Siaye Wang, aged 40 with six children, Tongkhue Wue, aged 43 with five children, and Yiaprie Wue, aged 31 with six children, were believed to be in poor health since their arrest because they were held in stocks and not given adequate food.

Torture and ill-treatment
AI continued to receive reports of extremely poor conditions of detention and the use of cruel, inhuman or degrading treatment. These included the prolonged use of stocks, deprivation of light, confinement in small cells, and inadequate provision of food, water and medication.

AI country reports/visits
Visit
In February AI representatives met a Lao government representative in France. A request to visit the country was refused.

LATVIA

REPUBLIC OF LATVIA
Head of state: Vaira Vike-Freiberga
Head of government: Andris Berzins
Capital: Riga
Population: 2.4 million
Official language: Latvian
Death penalty: abolitionist for ordinary crimes

There were reports of torture and ill-treatment of people deprived of their liberty by officials and allegations of ill-treatment of children. Draft legislation to introduce a civilian alternative to military service was under consideration.

Torture and ill-treatment
The report of the first visit of the European Committee for the Prevention of Torture and Inhuman or Degrading Treatment or Punishment (CPT) to Latvia in January and February 1999 was made public in November 2001. The report stated that "[t]he delegation received a considerable number of recent allegations of physical ill-treatment of persons detained by members of the police force in Latvia", most commonly at the time of arrest and during interrogation. The CPT noted that "[i]n some cases, the ill-treatment alleged — severe beating, asphyxiation using a plastic bag or a gas mask, strangulation using a guitar wire, infliction of electric shocks, in the course of questioning — could be considered as amounting to torture".

UN Committee on the Rights of the Child
In January the UN Committee on the Rights of the Child reviewed Latvia's initial report on steps the authorities had taken to implement the UN Children's Convention, to which Latvia became a state party in 1992. Among the Committee's main concerns was the lack of data and appropriate measures, mechanisms and resources to prevent and counteract violence within the family, including the sexual abuse of children. The Committee recommended, among other things, that "cases of domestic violence and ill-treatment and abuse of children, including sexual abuse within the family, be properly investigated within a child-friendly inquiry". In addition, the Committee issued a number of recommendations relating to the sexual exploitation and trafficking of minors, including programs to prevent and combat the phenomena and to rehabilitate and reintegrate the victims.

Conscientious objection
A working group established in 2000 submitted a draft law introducing a civilian alternative to military service to the Ministry of Defence in June 2001. This was referred to the Latvian government, the Cabinet of Ministers, for approval in July. However, the Cabinet of Ministers rejected the draft law in late August, requesting that amendments be made to it. By the end of 2001 the amended draft law had still not been submitted to parliament for approval. There was concern that the draft law would force conscientious objectors to undertake an alternative service of two years in length, twice as long as military service.

National human rights institutions
In February 2001 the Latvian National Human Rights Office published its annual report for the year 2000, which highlighted a number of concerns relating to the protection and promotion of human rights in the country. Recurring concerns expressed in the report included conditions in short-term police detention centres, which frequently amounted to "inhumane treatment" and were "degrading for human dignity". In addition, the office believed that prolonged periods in pre-trial detention violated the right to a trial within a reasonable time.

AI country reports/visits
Report
- Concerns in Europe, January-June 2001: Latvia (AI Index: EUR 01/003/2001)

LEBANON

LEBANESE REPUBLIC
Head of state: Emile Lahoud
Head of government: Rafiq al-Hariri
Capital: Beirut
Population: 3.6 million
Official language: Arabic
Death penalty: retentionist

Scores of suspected members and supporters of two unauthorized opposition groups — the Lebanese Forces (LF) and the Free Patriotic Movement (FPM) — were arrested during 2001. Most were arrested after demonstrations or other peaceful activities calling for the withdrawal of Syrian troops from Lebanon. At least 70 were referred for trial before criminal or military courts. Hundreds of suspected members and supporters of Israel's former proxy militia, the South Lebanon Army (SLA), continued to be tried in summary hearings before the Military Court. There were reports of torture and ill-treatment. At least eight people were sentenced to death; there were no executions. *Hizbullah*, the organization that played the leading role in the armed resistance to Israeli occupation in south Lebanon, continued to hold four Israeli hostages.

Background

Local elections were held in south Lebanon, the areas occupied by Israel from 1978 to 2000, for the first time in about four decades. *Amal* and *Hizbullah*, the two organizations with strongholds in the south, won a majority of seats.

In June a new Code of Criminal Procedures (CCP) was approved by parliament, but was returned to parliament by President Emile Lahoud with some reservations. Parliament approved the bill without amendments in July. However, the amendments suggested by the President were approved following a special parliamentary debate in August. The amended CCP allows the security forces to arrest and detain suspects for up to four days before bringing them before a judge, but maintains new guarantees provided for in the new law, such as immediate access of the accused to lawyers, doctors and family.

There were concerns and heated debates about prison conditions. The Parliamentary Committee for Human Rights undertook visits to several prisons where they found serious overcrowding and conditions that could amount to inhuman and degrading treatment. Among other things, the new CCP was designed to help reduce the prison population by limiting the period of pre-trial detention for all offences.

In July, the Lebanese Parliament repealed law No. 302 of 1994 which had expanded the scope of the death penalty, abolished judges' discretion to consider mitigating factors, and made capital punishment mandatory for certain offences, including political crimes. It was widely believed that the repeal of this law would limit the use of the death penalty, and might impact positively on outstanding death sentences. Several human rights non-governmental organizations campaigned tirelessly for the abolition of the death penalty and lobbied lawyers, parliamentarians and government officials.

The future of Lebanese-Syrian relations and the continued presence of Syrian troops in Lebanon was a recurrent topic of discussion during the year among church leaders and political groups. Demonstrations calling for the withdrawal of Syrian troops were organized by Christian-based opposition groups such as supporters of former military leader General Michel 'Aoun. Scores of people were arrested for taking part in unauthorized demonstrations and membership of unauthorized political groups, or on charges of "staging a conspiracy" and "harming Lebanon's relations with a friendly state".

Syrian troops were reported to have completed a partial redeployment of their forces, withdrawing some of their checkpoints in and around Beirut. Press reports set the number of Syrian troops in Lebanon during the year at between 30,000 and 35,000 soldiers.

Arrests

Hundreds of people were arrested for political reasons. They included members and supporters of the LF and the FPM, which support exiled former military leader General Michel 'Aoun.

☐ Four LF supporters were arrested in April following a sit-in protest held in the village of Becharreh, some 95km northeast of Beirut, against the continuing imprisonment of LF leader Samir Gea'gea'. Bechara Touq, Georges Sukkar, Hanna Rahmeh and Charbel Sukkar were reportedly held for three days at the Ministry of Defence detention centre before being released without charge.

☐ Over 200 members of the LF, the FPM, and the National Liberal Party were detained following a wave of arrests targeting these groups in August. They were reportedly detained because of their involvement in unauthorized political activities. The arrests were carried out by Lebanese Military Intelligence in different locations, including Beirut. Arrests were reportedly carried out without warrants. Both the Prosecutor General and the Minister of the Interior promised to investigate violations committed by officers during these arrests, but no report was made public during the year. Among the detainees were Tawfiq al-Hindi and Nadim Latif, leading members of the LF and FPM respectively, and scores of young men and women, including students and teenagers. Most of the detainees were subsequently released, some 77 of them on bail. Sixteen detainees were reportedly sentenced to prison terms ranging from one week to one month on charges of distributing leaflets "harming the reputation of the Syrian army" and "defaming the President of the Republic". However, Tawfiq al-Hindi and two journalists — Antoine Bassil, a Beirut reporter for the *Middle East Broadcasting Corporation*, and Habib Younes, editorial secretary of the newspaper *al-Hayat* in Beirut — were charged with "collaboration" with Israel. All three were held in Rumieh prison. They were formally indicted in December and referred to the Military Court on two separate but interrelated cases on charges that carry the death penalty. Their trials were continuing at the end of the year.

☐ Elie Kayruz and Salman Samaha, suspected LF members who were arrested during the wave of arrests in August, remained in custody until November, when they were released on bail. They were also referred to the Military Court on charges of withholding information. They were possible prisoners of conscience.

☐ Daniel Ahmad Samarji and Bilal Ali 'Uthman were arrested in October in Tripoli, northern Lebanon, in connection with a leaflet denouncing the US bombing in Afghanistan. The leaflet was signed by a previously unknown organization, *Jaysh al-Shari'a* (the army of *Shari'a*). The two were referred to the Military Court, accused of planning acts of violence.

Freedom of expression
There were reports of intimidation of journalists and other media workers.

☐ In March the *Lebanese Broadcasting Corporation International* (LBCI) was temporarily occupied by security forces following a dispute over censorship between shareholders, two of whom were government ministers. Nine employees were arrested. The incident was sparked by the refusal of the LBCI Director and majority shareholder, Michel Daher, to accept the appointment by other shareholders of a censor. The occupation ended after two days and the employees were released, apparently following an agreement among the shareholders; the idea of a censor was dropped.

☐ Raghida Dargham, a Lebanese-American journalist and UN correspondent for the newspaper *al-Hayat*, was indicted by the Military Court with "collaboration with the enemy". Raghida Dargham was reported to have taken part in a discussion panel in Washington, USA, with an Israeli official. Her trial before the Military Court was scheduled to begin in November. However, the charges against her were reportedly dropped on account of a letter she sent to the Military Prosecutor explaining the incident.

Unfair trials
Hundreds of political prisoners were tried before the Military Court in summary proceedings and hearings that fell short of international fair trial standards. Dozens were tried before the Justice Council whose verdicts are not subject to judicial review.

☐ The trials of former SLA members and alleged "collaborators" with Israel continued during 2001. Most were sentenced to prison terms ranging from several weeks to three years on charges of providing information to the SLA or Israeli intelligence services or entering Israel. A few were sentenced to between seven and 15 years' imprisonment. Dozens were sentenced *in absentia* to death or terms of imprisonment. Over 3,000 suspected SLA supporters and "collaborators" with Israel had been sentenced since the beginning of the trials in June 2000.

☐ The trial of Islamist activists allegedly linked to the Sunni-based *'Usbat al-Ansar* and involved in the clashes with the Lebanese security forces in the Dinnyah plateau in February 2000, started before the Justice Council in April 2001 and was continuing at the end of the year. At least 24 defendants appeared in court charged with participating in or aiding the Islamist group. The rest were tried *in absentia*. Defendants stated in the court that they had been subjected to torture and ill-treatment during interrogation to extract confessions (see below). In October, *'Usbat al-Ansar* was listed by the USA as one of 27 "terrorist" organizations whose bank accounts were to be frozen.

Torture and ill-treatment
There were reports of torture and ill-treatment. Methods of torture reported included kicking, beating and the *balanco* (hanging by the wrists, which are tied behind the back). There were continuing concerns that allegations of torture were not adequately investigated.

In August, in response to widespread public concern, the Lebanese authorities appointed a judge from the Prosecutor General's Office to investigate allegations of torture and ill-treatment of women in pre-trial detention.

☐ When Ihab al-Banna, a defendant in the Dinnyah trials (see above), appeared before the Justice Council in April he told the court that he and his co-defendants had been subjected to torture including beatings while in detention and after being transferred to Rumieh prison. He also alleged that detainees were denied medical care despite suffering from scabies. The Prosecutor General stated in court that his Office would duly investigate these allegations and, if proved, take legal measures against the perpetrators. The findings of such an investigation were not made public, but the Office of the Prosecutor General stated that the allegations could not be substantiated.

☐ Ahmad Muhammad 'Alyan and his niece, Huyam 'Ali 'Alyan, were both arrested in March, suspected of "collaboration" with Israel. They were taken to the Ministry of Defence detention centre where they were held incommunicado for weeks and reportedly subjected to torture and ill-treatment. Both were reported to have been forced to sign confessions. Both Huyam 'Ali 'Alyan and Ahmad Muhammad 'Alyan suffered ill-health as a result of their ill-treatment. According to a medical report Huyam 'Alyan suffered bruises on her arms and wrists, consistent with the use of violence and Ahmad 'Alyan suffered from back pain and had marks on his wrists, apparently resulting from the prolonged use of handcuffs.

Human rights defenders
Kamal al-Batal, the director of the human rights group Multi-initiative on Rights: Search, Assist, Defend (MIRSAD), was convicted in March by the Military Court of "tarnishing the reputation of the *police des moeurs*

[vice squad police]". Kamal al-Batal appealed against the verdict and at the hearing in July, attended by an AI observer, the Military Court of Cassation acquitted him of all charges.

Death penalty
At least eight people were sentenced to death. No one was executed during the year.

'Disappearances'
A Commission of Inquiry to investigate the fate of the thousands of Lebanese who went missing or "disappeared" during the civil war (1975 to 1990) started its work in February. The Commission was headed by the Minister of State for Administrative Development and was composed of members representing various judicial and security authorities: the Prosecutor General, the Director of State Security, the Director of General Security, the Director of Military Intelligence, the Director of Internal Security Services, and a lawyer representing the Beirut Bar Association. The Commission was reported to have received information on at least 700 cases from relatives of "disappeared" people by the end of 2001. The mandate of the Commission was said to have been extended for a further six-month term. In December a group of non-governmental organizations held a joint press conference to campaign on the issue of the "disappeared".

Hostages
In October 2000, *Hizbullah* captured three Israeli soldiers — Binyamin Avraham, Omar Su'ad and Adi Avitan. The three soldiers were seized while on a military patrol in the Israeli-occupied Shab'a Farms area on the southeastern border of Lebanon. A week later an Israeli reserve colonel, Elhanan Tenenboim, was abducted, apparently in Europe. None of the four had had access to the International Committee of the Red Cross (ICRC) nor were they known to have sent or received any messages from their families. The four Israelis were believed to have been held as "bargaining chips" to be exchanged for Lebanese nationals held as hostages by Israel, such as Sheikh 'Abd al-Karim 'Ubayd and Mustafa al-Dirani, as well as Lebanese and Arab prisoners held in Israel. In October, the Israeli authorities stated that three of the four hostages were believed dead. *Hizbullah* refused to confirm this information.

Refugees
Around 350,000 Palestinian refugees remained in Lebanon. They continued to be subjected to discriminatory legislation and policies, particularly as regards access to education, employment, housing and health care.

Hundreds of other refugees and asylum-seekers, mostly Iraqi and Sudanese nationals, continued to be detained by the Lebanese authorities on the grounds of illegal entry and residence in Lebanon. Detainees were reported to have staged a hunger strike in May and June to protest at their continued detention and at the pressure being put on them to accept "voluntary" repatriation. Scores of asylum-seekers, including those recognized as refugees by the UN High Commissioner for Refugees (UNHCR) in Beirut, were deported. There were reports of ill-treatment.

Giman Hamdan Ladu Kuku, a Sudanese national recognized as a refugee by the UNHCR, was deported to Sudan via Syria in March; his wife and son remained in Lebanon. There were fears that he would be at risk of human rights violations in Sudan.

Muhammad Hasan al-Khafaji, a 14-year-old stateless person born to an Iraqi father, was arrested in September at a checkpoint in Tyre, south Lebanon. He was sentenced to two weeks' imprisonment for illegally entering Lebanon, but remained held in Rumieh prison despite serving his prison term. Muhammad Hasan al-Khafaji, his father and his sister were recognized as refugees by the UNHCR office in Beirut and were awaiting resettlement. Muhammad Hasan al-Khafaji was among at least 180 Iraqi refugees and asylum-seekers deported to northern Iraq in December.

Ibrahim al-Taj Hussein Zaydan, a Sudanese asylum-seeker, was shot dead in March by an officer of the Lebanese General Security as he attempted to evade arrest. Members of the Lebanese General Security were apparently searching for suspected illegal immigrants in the Beirut neighbourhood of al-Awza'i and reportedly arrested 10 Sudanese nationals in the same raid. A letter received from the Lebanese General Security stated that the killing was accidental, but AI continued to call for a thorough an impartial investigation into the incident.

AI country reports/ visits
Reports
- Lebanon: Refugees and asylum-seekers at risk (AI Index: MDE 18/002/2001)
- Lebanon: Unfair trial of a human rights defender (AI Index: MDE 18/008/2001)
- Lebanon: Torture and ill-treatment of women in pre-trial detention — a culture of acquiescence (AI Index: MDE 18/009/2001)
- Lebanon: Amnesty International welcomes repeal of death penalty law (AI Index: MDE 18/010/2001)

Visits
AI delegates visited Lebanon several times during the year for research, meetings with government officials and non-governmental organizations, and to participate in activities organized by the AI regional office in Beirut. An AI delegation led by AI's Secretary General met President Lahoud in December.

LESOTHO

KINGDOM OF LESOTHO
Head of state: King Letsie III
Head of government: Pakalitha Bethuel Mosisili
Capital: Maseru
Population: 2.1 million
Official languages: Sesotho, English
Death penalty: retentionist
2001 treaty ratifications/signatures: UN Convention against Torture

There were continuing reports of torture and ill-treatment of suspects in criminal investigations and use of excessive force by police against striking workers. However, there were also indications that the government made new commitments to reform police training and operations. The judicial commission of inquiry into political unrest in 1998 recommended that there should be no general amnesty for those responsible for incidents of violence.

Background

Tensions within the ruling Lesotho Congress for Democracy party became clear in October when the Deputy Prime Minister, Kelebone Maope, and some supporting members of parliament left the party. They formed the Lesotho People's Congress and joined other political parties on the opposition benches in the parliament. The government announced that elections would take place in 2002, following the adoption of a new electoral system.

The government-appointed judicial commission of inquiry into the civil disturbances of 1998 presented its findings to the Prime Minister in October. The report, which the Prime Minister presented to parliament in November, included recommendations that there should be no general amnesty, that some opposition party supporters and members of the security forces should be investigated for possible prosecution, and that recruitment and training for the security forces should be reformed. The Prime Minister announced that some opposition leaders may be charged with treason for their alleged role in the unrest.

In July, a government delegation presented its report to the UN Committee on the Rights of the Child on its implementation of obligations under the UN Children's Convention.

Torture and ill-treatment in custody and excessive use of force

There were a number of reports that criminal suspects were tortured by police during 2001. Detainees alleged that they were suffocated with rubber tubing and beaten, including on the soles of the feet. Women who were victims of rape and domestic violence reported that they were ill-treated and humiliated by police when they tried to make complaints.

▫ An employee of a firm where an armed robbery had occurred was arrested in February and accused by police of being an accomplice. In a sworn affidavit she alleged that she was forced to partially undress and was suffocated with rubber tubing while her hands were bound. She was threatened with sexual abuse and beaten with a heavy blunt object on her back and buttocks. Medical evidence indicated bruising and other injuries consistent with her allegations.

▫ Motlamisi Kalaka, aged 24, was arrested by police in June and accused of theft. He was detained at Morija police station for over two days in crowded and poor conditions. He was forced to lie naked on his stomach with his ankles and wrists tied together and suffocated with rubber tubing. He was also beaten on the soles of his feet and a rope was tied tightly around his neck. A medical report completed the day after Motlamisi Kalaka's release confirmed injuries to his neck and feet. He was not charged with any offence.

Reports were received that the police used excessive force, including during an incident in October when police whipped striking workers in the streets of Maseru.

However, the government demonstrated a commitment to eradicate torture and ill-treatment by acceding to the UN Convention against Torture in November.

AI action

In June AI appealed to the government to ensure investigations were undertaken in specific cases involving alleged incidents of torture, ill-treatment and excessive use of force by law enforcement officers. The Minister of Home Affairs replied with information on the investigation of the cases raised, but denied the alleged human rights violations.

AI country reports/visits

Visit
An AI delegate visited Lesotho in November to conduct research on human rights protection and policing. The delegate met police and government officials, diplomatic contacts and non-governmental organizations, and interviewed victims of human rights violations.

LIBERIA

REPUBLIC OF LIBERIA
Head of state and government: Charles G. Taylor
Capital: Monrovia
Population: 3.1 million
Official language: English
Death penalty: retentionist

The human rights situation deteriorated significantly throughout the year as armed conflict continued. Widespread abuses against civilians were carried out by both the Liberian security forces and the Liberians United for Reconciliation and Democracy (LURD), an armed opposition group based in Guinea. Government forces were responsible for extrajudicial executions, unlawful detention, torture including sexual violence, forced labour and forcible recruitment of civilians. LURD forces carried out summary executions, abductions and torture including rape of civilians. Tens of thousands of civilians fled the fighting. Impunity for the security forces continued and punishment of those responsible for abuses was rare. A crack-down by the security forces on university students led to illegal detention and torture including rape. Press freedom was curtailed by the intimidation and detention of journalists. The jailing of two lawyers was followed by a lawyers' strike. Human rights defenders and critics of the government remained at risk.

Background

Armed conflict continued throughout the year in Lofa County in northern Liberia between government security forces and the armed opposition group based in Guinea, LURD, which has claimed responsibility for armed attacks on Liberian territory since July 2000. Early in the year Liberia blamed Guinea for providing military and financial support to LURD forces. A high number of civilian deaths and massive displacement has resulted from both direct and indirect attacks on civilians.

In May the UN Security Council with strong support from the USA and the United Kingdom imposed sanctions after a UN panel of experts published a report in December 2000 which contained evidence of the Liberian government's support for rebel forces in Sierra Leone, including by military training and weapons transfers, and its involvement in the trafficking of diamonds from rebel-held areas in Sierra Leone. Compliance was monitored by the UN panel of experts between April and October. In November it published evidence of continuing cooperation between the Sierra Leonean rebel group, the Revolutionary United Front (RUF), and the Liberian security forces, and of links between the timber trade and arms trafficking. The UN Peace-building Support Office in Liberia (UNOL) continued to remain silent on human rights issues.

In July the European Union opened consultations on human rights with the Liberian government under the Cotonou Agreement. In November members of the Liberian government made commitments to address key human rights issues.

In August the UN Committee on the Elimination of Racial Discrimination raised concerns about extrajudicial killings, allegations of torture, including rape, and the lack of accountability of perpetrators for these abuses.

A proposal by the Economic Community of West African States (ECOWAS) to send a peace-keeping force to the areas of Guinea and Sierra Leone which border Liberia was rejected. Under pressure from ECOWAS, the UN and civil society groups from the three countries, a dialogue between Liberia, Sierra Leone and Guinea began in August.

Violations by the Liberian security forces

Civilians throughout Liberia were subjected to human rights violations committed by the Liberian security forces with nearly absolute impunity.

There were large-scale violations in the context of the war in Lofa County. These included suspected massacres, extrajudicial executions, forcible recruitments into the armed forces, arbitrary detention and torture, including rape.

Extrajudicial executions

In Lofa County, men and boys were reported to have been extrajudicially executed by the security forces on suspicion of backing armed opposition groups. Unlawful killings of civilians by the security forces appeared to have been carried out with the acquiescence of the Liberian authorities which took no action to bring perpetrators to account.

☐ In late June, after Anti-Terrorist Unit (ATU) officers entered Gilima, a town in upper Lofa County near Kolahun, they rounded up and "screened" approximately 50 people. Twenty-five were accused of backing the rebels and taken away by the ATU. Later, fleeing civilians allegedly saw the bodies of at least 10 of those taken away by the ATU, on the side of a road near Kolahun. The victims had been blindfolded and some had their hands tied behind their backs. Eyewitnesses provided consistent accounts linking their deaths to the ATU.

Illegal detention and torture

Thousands of men and boys were arbitrarily detained as "dissidents" in dozens of illegal detention centres, held incommunicado and tortured. They were sometimes held for weeks in holes in the ground. The main detention centres were at the Gbatala military base and at the Liberia Petroleum Mining Company in Bong County, throughout Monrovia in police cells and at the presidential Executive Mansion.

☐ In May over 100 men and boys in Bong County in northern Liberia were arrested as suspected dissidents. They were subsequently detained at Gbatala military base for periods of up to a month and reportedly tear gassed, had acid thrown at them, denied water and starved. Several reportedly died as a result.

☐ On several occasions in June and July, ATU and police forces reportedly entered a camp for internally displaced people in Bong County, fired in the air, seized men and boys and took them to Gbatala military base where they were severely ill-treated.

Sexual violence

Sexual violence, including rape, continued against hundreds of women and girls. Caught in areas of fighting or fleeing the fighting, they were detained at military checkpoints and gang-raped. Victims included girls of 12 years old. Women were raped on suspicion of backing dissidents, being related to them or being spies. They were also raped while forced into sexual slavery by soldiers at detention centres or in private homes. They were reportedly beaten, kicked or stabbed with bayonets when they resisted rape, and threatened with reprisals if they attempted to lodge a complaint.

The scale of rapes suggested that sexual violence was used as a weapon of war, to instil terror among the civilian population. Victims in some cases identified senior security officers as rapists. The impunity that the security forces enjoyed for rape and other human rights violations continued to be a key factor in allowing rape and other forms of sexual violence to reach alarming proportions.

◻ In early June a 17-year-old woman was seized in Vahun district by an ATU officer, detained and gang-raped repeatedly over 10 days. When she was released, her life was threatened if she told anyone.

Human rights abuses by the armed opposition

LURD forces reportedly committed human rights abuses against civilians. Members of the LURD were reported to have deliberately killed and tortured, including by raping women, unarmed civilians suspected of supporting government forces.

◻ In late June a 29-year-old man was captured by the LURD while trying to flee the fighting. His hands were tied behind his back. He was detained for several days with two other men and a woman. He reportedly witnessed the deliberate shooting and killing of the two other men on the orders of a high-ranking officer. The woman was reported to have been raped. Both the woman and the man eventually escaped.

Internally displaced people

There was massive displacement of tens of thousands of civilians within Liberia and over the borders to Guinea and Sierra Leone to escape the fighting and human rights abuses. At least five camps had to be created to accommodate the fleeing populations from Lofa County. According to estimates from humanitarian agencies, in April and May as many as 30,000 fled from upper Lofa County to Bong County; in August and September up to 20,000 from Lofa County to Cape Mount County and Gbopolu County, and in November and December up to 20,000 were re-displaced to Bomi County and Monrovia when fighting broke out near Gbopolu.

Internally displaced people were particularly vulnerable to abuses by the Liberian security forces. The government took no action to stop these violations.

◻ In April and May, as many as 15,000 fleeing civilians were halted for several weeks at the St Pauls River on the border between Lofa and Bong Counties by the Liberian security forces. Civilians were subjected to violations such as torture, including rape, and forced recruitment into the security forces. There were reportedly numerous deaths from starvation, disease and insanitary conditions. Some people tried to cross the river and drowned. The international humanitarian agencies and the Liberian government agency responsible for internally displaced people were denied access to them by the security forces. In late May the international community organized trucks to bring the people across the river in a three-week operation.

Liberian refugees in the region

Early in the year Liberian and Sierra Leonean refugees in camps in Guinea came under attack from LURD forces, the RUF and the Guinean security forces. Refugees along the border in Guinea were relocated to camps further from the border. Some were forcibly repatriated to Liberia. Thousands fled to Sierra Leone where they faced abuses in areas controlled by the RUF.

At least 5,000 Liberian refugees fled to Sierra Leone as a result of the Lofa County conflict in the second half of the year. Several thousand more were reportedly in eastern Sierra Leone, along the Liberian border, and had not been registered as refugees by the end of 2001.

Human rights violations outside conflict areas

The security forces continued to enjoy impunity for human rights violations to a large extent. There were no investigations into reports of deaths in police custody or the misuse of lethal force.

◻ In November, two Nigerian nationals reportedly died in custody as a result of torture after being arrested on suspicion of stealing jewellery from a deputy government minister. The deputy minister and members of the security forces were subsequently arrested. No charges had been brought but they remained in detention at the end of 2001.

◻ In December, a 14-year-old boy in Gbarnga, Bong County, was shot dead by police who subsequently said that he was an armed robber. The Director of Police announced that the officer had been suspended from duty and that an investigation would be held; it had not started by the end of the year.

Threats to critics of the government

Attacks on journalists, human rights defenders, lawyers and opposition politicians continued. Others were forced to flee the country.

◻ In February Joseph Bartuah, Abdullah Dukuly, Jerome Dalieh and Bobby Tapson, four journalists from the privately-owned newspaper *The News*, were arrested and charged with espionage after publication of a report criticizing the delayed payment of civil service salaries. In March, dozens of university students and professors were whipped and severely beaten by the security forces during a peaceful protest in Monrovia against the arrests. More than 40 students were arrested. Some were released shortly afterwards without charge, with visible marks of beatings, and at least seven women students were reported to have been raped repeatedly in detention. At least 17 were released over the next three weeks after widespread public protests. In April the university suspended student leaders; most of them fled the country.

◻ In April Francis Massaquoi, Minister of Youth and Sports and former leader of the Lofa Defence Force, an armed group active in the civil war, was killed in unexplained circumstances in Lofa County. Reports suggested that he might have been killed because his political influence with government forces in the area was perceived to be a threat to the government.

◻ In September Thompson Ade-Bayor, head of Liberia Watch for Human Rights, was illegally detained without charge or trial for 10 days after criticizing the security forces in a published article. The Liberian police reportedly paid fellow inmates to hang him by his feet and beat him.

◻ In October Emmanuel Wureh, president of the National Bar Association, was imprisoned for a week after he was found in contempt of court for alleged insulting remarks during court proceedings. Leading Bar Association members Marcus Jones and Ismail Campbel announced a lawyers' boycott in protest and were themselves arrested. The House of Representatives subsequently asked the Minister of Justice to charge them with contempt of the Legislature and to detain them until they apologized to the House and retracted their protest. The legal basis for this process and their detention was unclear. Emmanuel Wureh was released in November and the other lawyers in December.

Most opposition leaders remained outside the country. Others remained in prison or were threatened.

◻ Raleigh Seekie, an opposition leader charged with treason with 14 others in August 2000, was still in prison awaiting trial at the end of 2001. Others charged with him had not been arrested.

◻ In April veteran politician Togba-Nah Tipoteh said that he and other politicians had received threats for criticizing the international community for giving financial assistance to the government.

AI country reports/visits
Reports
- Liberia: War in Lofa County does not justify killing, torture and abduction (AI Index: AFR 34/003/2001)
- Liberia: Killings, torture and rape continue in Lofa County (AI Index: AFR 34/009/2001)
- Liberia: Lack of justice for students, victims of torture, including rape (AI Index: AFR 34/010/2001)

Visits
AI delegates visited Liberia in February and November to carry out research into the human rights situation.

LIBYA

SOCIALIST PEOPLE'S LIBYAN ARAB JAMAHIRIYA
Head of state: Mu'ammar al-Gaddafi
Capital: Tripoli
Population: 5.4 million
Official language: Arabic
Death penalty: retentionist

Dozens of political prisoners were released, but hundreds, including prisoners of conscience and possible prisoners of conscience, remained in jail, many without charge or trial. Around 150 alleged political opponents were brought to trial on charges of membership of an illegal organization. The verdict in the trial of two Libyans charged with the Lockerbie bombing was handed down; one was acquitted and the other was sentenced to life imprisonment. The trial of six Bulgarians and a Palestinian accused of infecting children with the HIV virus was continuing at the end of the year. The fate of people who "disappeared" in previous years remained unclear.

Background
Freedom of expression remained severely restricted; Libyan law prohibits the formation of political parties and criticism of the political system. The national media continued to be strictly controlled by the government.

Prisoners of conscience and political prisoners
At the end of August the Gaddafi International Foundation for Charity Association (GIFCA), headed by Saif al-Islam Gaddafi, son of Colonel Mu'ammar al-Gaddafi, announced the release of dozens of political prisoners on the occasion of the 32nd anniversary of the revolution which brought Colonel Gaddafi to power. The GIFCA published a list of 107 released prisoners including more than 20 men who had been detained since a crackdown in 1984 on government opponents following an attack on the Bab al-'Aziziya Barracks in Tripoli. There were further releases of political prisoners in mid-September. The authorities continued to claim that there were no political prisoners in Libya.

However, hundreds of political prisoners arrested in previous years, including prisoners of conscience, remained in detention, many without charge or trial.

◻ Libya's longest serving political prisoner, Ahmad al-Zubayr Ahmad al-Sanussi, was released in August. Ahmad al-Zubayr Ahmad al-Sanussi was imprisoned for 31 years after being accused of involvement in an attempted coup in 1970, and had been held for many years in solitary confinement.

◻ 'Omran 'Omar al-Turbi, a dentist married with two children, was released in August after 17 years in prison. He had been arrested in 1984 along with hundreds of other suspected members of the National Front for the Salvation of Libya and held without charge or trial.

▢ Five prisoners of conscience, including Muhammad 'Ali al-Akrami and 'Abd al-Rahman al-Azhari, who were arrested in 1973 and convicted of membership of the prohibited Islamic Liberation Party, continued to serve life sentences in Abu Salim Prison.

Political trials
Groups of individuals were sentenced by courts whose procedures continued to fall short of international standards for fair trial.

Trial of alleged political opponents
In March the trial began of some 150 professionals, including engineers, doctors and university lecturers. Most had been arrested in June 1998 on suspicion of supporting or sympathizing with the Libyan Islamic Group, which is banned in Libya. This organization is not known to have used or advocated violence. The defendants were kept incommunicado until the opening of the trial. For several months after the opening of the trial, relatives were denied access to the detainees in prison and the defendants were reportedly denied the right to choose their legal counsel.

HIV trial
The trial of seven medical workers, comprising six Bulgarians and one Palestinian, before the People's Court was continuing at the end of the year. They had been charged in February 2000 with deliberately infecting 393 Libyan children with the HIV virus.

The defendants said that their confessions had been extracted under torture. The defendants stated, including in court, that they had been beaten with electric cables and subjected to electric shocks. No investigation was carried out into these allegations.

The Court reportedly refused to allow virology experts to testify as requested by the defence. The indictment said that the acts were part of an attempt to destabilize the Libyan state. At a summit on AIDS/HIV in Nigeria in April, Colonel Gaddafi delivered a speech suggesting that the defendants had infected the children under the orders of US or Israeli intelligence services.

Trials of Libyan nationals abroad
Lockerbie trial
In January, the verdict was handed down in the trial in the Netherlands of two Libyans charged with planting a bomb on Pan Am flight 103 which exploded over the town of Lockerbie in the United Kingdom in December 1988, killing 270 people. Al-Amin Khalifa Fhimah was acquitted. Abdel Basset Ali al-Megrahi was convicted and sentenced to life imprisonment. His appeal was due to be heard in 2002.

The UTA airliner bombing
France's highest court, the *Cour de Cassation*, ruled that Colonel Gaddafi could not be prosecuted in connection with the UTA airliner bombing in September 1989 in which 170 people died. The court overturned the appeals court ruling that Colonel Gaddafi did not enjoy diplomatic immunity as a head of state.

The 1986 Berlin disco bombing
In November a Berlin court found that members of the Libyan secret service had planned the 1986 bombing of the *La Belle* disco in Berlin, Germany, in which two US soldiers and a Turkish woman were killed and more than 230 others injured. A Libyan diplomat, a Palestinian staff member of Libya's diplomatic representation in East Berlin and another Palestinian and his German wife were sentenced to between 12 and 14 years' imprisonment in connection with the bombing.

Torture and ill-treatment
There were further reports of torture and ill-treatment from previous years where no impartial and thorough investigations had been conducted.

▢ In October the Ethiopian Human Rights Council, an Ethiopian non-governmental organization, wrote to the Libyan authorities calling for an investigation into the alleged torture in 1997 of eight Ethiopian prisoners; they reported that they had been subjected to electric shocks.

'Disappearances'
Several cases of people who "disappeared" in previous years remained unresolved.

▢ Relatives of Imam Moussa al-Sadr, a prominent Iranian-born Shi'a cleric living in Lebanon who "disappeared" during a visit to Libya in 1978, filed a complaint in a Lebanese court against the Libyan authorities.

▢ No concrete action was known to have been taken by the Libyan authorities to clarify the fate of Mansur Kikhiya, a Libyan human rights activist and opposition political activist who "disappeared" in December 1993 in Cairo. There were reports that Mansur Kikhiya was handed over to the Libyan authorities and executed in January 1994.

Death penalty
Death sentences were imposed on at least eight people convicted of criminal charges. No executions were known to have been carried out.

▢ In May, two Libyans, a Ghanaian and four Nigerians were sentenced to death, one *in absentia*, by the Tripoli People's Court. They had been found guilty of "plotting against the policy of Libya and its leading role in Africa, undermining the aim of the Libyan Jamahiriya of creating a united African entity, and disturbing public order". The Nigerians and the Ghanaian were also convicted of "the murder of Libyan citizens and theft". The trial followed racist attacks which took place in September 2000 in which dozens of sub-Saharan Africans were killed. The Libyan authorities gave assurances that those convicted in this trial would have the right to appeal.

AI country reports/visits
Visit
Two AI delegates attended the 29th Ordinary Session of the African Commission on Human and Peoples' Rights held in Tripoli in April, and met Libyan government authorities and members of civil institutions. Repeated requests from AI to send trial observers received no response from the Libyan authorities.

LITHUANIA

REPUBLIC OF LITHUANIA
Head of state: Valdas Adamkus
Head of government: Algirdas Mikolas Brazauskas (replaced Rolandas Paksas in July)
Capital: Vilnius
Population: 3.7 million
Official language: Lithuanian
Death penalty: abolitionist for all crimes

There were reports of torture and ill-treatment by officials of people deprived of their liberty and allegations of ill-treatment of children.

Torture and ill-treatment
The report of the first visit of the European Committee for the Prevention of Torture and Inhuman or Degrading Treatment or Punishment (CPT) to Lithuania in February 2000 was made public in October 2001. During the 10-day visit the CPT inspected various places where people are deprived of their liberty, including police stations, police detention centres, prisons and a detention centre for foreign nationals.

The CPT stated that while it appeared that there had been a marked improvement in the treatment of detainees by police, "... a significant proportion of the persons interviewed alleged that they had been ill-treated while in police custody". The alleged ill-treatment consisted mainly of slaps, punches, kicks and blows and mostly occurred before, during and after interrogation. The CPT noted: "[i]n certain cases, the ill-treatment alleged – e.g. partial suffocation by placing a rubber gas mask over the person's face and severe beating – could be qualified as torture."

The CPT also received frequent allegations of the use of excessive force by police officers during arrest. It recommended that a very high priority be given to the professional training of police officers of all ranks, emphasizing that ill-treatment was incompatible with the Lithuanian Constitution and international human rights standards, and that the authorities should make it clear to police officers that ill-treatment of detainees would be dealt with severely.

No allegations of torture and relatively few allegations of ill-treatment were heard from inmates in the prisons visited by the CPT. However, the CPT considered that improvements could be made regarding the material conditions of imprisonment, such as the quality of health care and prisoners' access to work, education and recreational activities. Overcrowding was cited as a significant problem.

Children
In January the UN Committee on the Rights of the Child reviewed Lithuania's initial report on steps the authorities had taken to implement the UN Children's Convention, to which Lithuania became a state party in 1992. Among the Committee's main concerns was the widespread use of corporal punishment within the family as well as in institutions such as schools. The Committee recommended that measures be taken to prohibit the use of corporal punishment in these contexts and to raise awareness of the harmful effects of corporal punishment. It also recommended that the authorities ensure that cases of domestic violence and ill-treatment of children, including sexual abuse, were properly investigated.

The Committee also expressed deep concern about the lack of data, consistent policies and rehabilitation and reintegration programs for child victims of trafficking. It urged the authorities to take greater steps to fully implement their national program against the commercial sexual exploitation and sexual abuse of children.

MACEDONIA

THE FORMER YUGOSLAV REPUBLIC OF MACEDONIA
Head of state: Boris Trajkovski
Head of government: Ljubčo Georgievski
Capital: Skopje
Population: 2 million
Official language: Macedonian
Death penalty: abolitionist in practice
2001 treaty ratifications/signatures: Optional Protocol to the UN Children's Convention on the involvement of children in armed conflict

The human rights situation deteriorated as fighting between Macedonian security forces and ethnic Albanian armed groups escalated in the first part of the year. There were reports of unlawful killings by both sides. Allegations of torture and ill-treatment by police became more frequent. There were also reports of ill-treatment and hostage-taking by groups of both ethnic Albanians and of Macedonians. More than 170,000 people were displaced from their homes at some point during the year and many were not able to return. After a peace agreement in August, the fighting tapered off and continued at a lower level.

Background
Fighting between the Macedonian security forces and an ethnic Albanian armed group, the National Liberation Army (NLA), escalated from the start of 2001. The NLA said it was seeking greater rights for ethnic Albanians and an end to discrimination. The government claimed that the NLA was made up of Albanians from Kosovo who were trying to gain territory, and attempted to defeat them militarily. In mid-August, when the country was on the brink of much

wider conflict, mediators appointed by the USA and European Union (EU) helped the leaders of the four main political parties to reach an agreement. The framework agreement, negotiated in Ohrid, included reforms aimed at addressing discrimination against the Albanian minority. In return, the NLA agreed to disarm (assisted by a NATO force called "Essential Harvest") and disband. There was also an understanding that there would be an amnesty from prosecution for NLA members except those who had committed serious war crimes. By the end of September, NATO had collected more than the agreed number of 3,300 weapons from the NLA, and an NLA spokesperson then declared that it had been disbanded.

Implementation of the framework agreement required parliament to amend the Constitution. This was delayed by strong opposition from ethnic Macedonians to what they perceived to be concessions towards ethnic Albanians. Displaced Macedonians wanted the Macedonian police to re-establish full control of villages in which their homes were located before they would return. However, ethnic Albanians in those areas wanted the amnesty to be confirmed first, as they were said to be afraid of police brutality and arrests of former NLA members. The international community tried to reassure both sides and to push forward the peace process with the promise of aid for reconstruction and up to 200 monitors from the Organization for Security and Co-operation in Europe and the EU protected by a new NATO force ("Amber Fox").

Violations by the security forces

On 12 August, following the deaths of eight Macedonian soldiers in an anti-tank mine explosion, Macedonian special police forces entered the nearby village of Luboten. According to journalists and a representative of the non-governmental organization Human Rights Watch who visited the site shortly afterwards, the special police summarily killed six civilians and ill-treated more than 100 others whom they arrested. The Ministry of the Interior claimed that the dead were armed and had been killed during exchanges of fire. The International Criminal Tribunal for the former Yugoslavia announced an investigation into this incident.

Numerous reports of shelling of villages under NLA control by the army and police indicated that the actions may have been indiscriminate. Civilians, including children, were killed and injured. Government sources asserted that civilians were being kept in the villages as human shields for the NLA. Others argued that villagers feared arbitrary arrest, ill-treatment and ethnic cleansing at the hands of the Macedonian security forces if they left their homes.

Arbitrary arrest, torture and ill-treatment

Police continued to ill-treat people during arrest and in detention. AI's longstanding concern about police ill-treatment was confirmed in a report by the European Committee for the Prevention of Torture (CPT). This followed a visit in May 1998, and was published with the government's response in October 2001. The Ministry of the Interior reported that several training courses on human rights had been held for police officers and senior officials and that steps were being taken to strengthen the rights of detainees. However, there was little evidence of these measures having practical effect on the ground. There were numerous allegations of ethnic Albanians being brutally beaten, particularly by police reservists hastily mobilized during the conflict. The CPT made a further visit to Macedonia in October 2001, including unannounced visits to several police stations in the disputed area. Its findings were not available by the end of the year.

Ethnic Albanians were detained arbitrarily and ill-treated at police checkpoints, in police raids on their homes or when trying to escape from NLA-controlled villages being shelled by the security forces. Allegedly, following arrest, men were beaten repeatedly while being interrogated about the NLA. Some were released without charge. Others were charged with "terrorism", or possessing explosives, or having weapons without a licence. Victims reported that they had been ill-treated by regular police, special police, reservists and by paramilitary units allegedly armed by the Ministry of the Interior. It was frequently claimed that the perpetrators of ill-treatment wore masks or covered the heads of their victims to avoid identification. There were also concerns that trials of people charged following interrogations were conducted in a manner that may have been unfair.

The framework agreement included provisions to increase the recruitment of ethnic Albanian police officers to serve in areas with a majority ethnic Albanian population. However, this step would not directly address the problems of other ethnic groups, particularly Roma, who have also been victims of ill-treatment at the hands of the police.

Police allegedly failed to provide protection during riots by ethnic Macedonians in Bitola and Prilep during which mosques, homes and businesses owned by ethnic Albanians and other Muslims were vandalized and burned. The riots followed the deaths of soldiers and police officers from these towns in NLA ambushes in April, June and August.

⌑ At least 34 men from Poroj and Germo near Tetovo were stopped at roadblocks by police on 6 April. They were beaten and kicked by police officers while being transported to Tetovo and Skopje police stations, at the police stations and during interrogation about the NLA. Almost all were released without charge. Z.Z. of Poroj, one of nine men interviewed by AI in June, had a medical report which confirmed injuries consistent with being beaten with fists, shoes, metal pipes and a baseball bat. Most of those interviewed said they would not make a complaint, fearing that it would lead to further assaults, or would be futile.

⌑ On 10 June, two ethnic Albanian officers of the Macedonian army were allegedly taken from their homes by police and subjected to racial slurs and physical ill-treatment. This included being tied to a table and denied drinking water, in one case for most of the day and in the other for 48 hours. They said they were questioned about giving information to the NLA, then released without charge. When interviewed by AI representatives a week later, both still had visible injuries and one was confined to bed. One of the officers initiated legal proceedings against the authorities for torture and breaches of the code of criminal procedure, but the case had not been heard by the end of the year.

🗁 The Albanian Ombudsman took up the case of 20 Albanian nationals arrested, beaten and then expelled from Macedonia in June. A hospital report from Peshkopi on one of the men described injuries consistent with his claim that he had been struck with a metal helmet. However, the Macedonian Ombudsman endorsed the reply from the Ministry of the Interior which accepted that the men had been detained and expelled, but denied that physical force was used against them.

Abuses by the NLA

NLA attacks were initially targeted at police and soldiers. The government claimed that one of these attacks, which killed four police officers and four soldiers in Vejce in April, was a crime against humanity because the bodies were mutilated. The International Criminal Tribunal for the former Yugoslavia announced an investigation into this case.

Between June and August, as clashes became more intense and the NLA moved into areas inhabited by ethnic Macedonians, civilians were kidnapped and ill-treated. The NLA took control of a number of villages near Tetovo, Skopje and Kumanovo whose residents were ethnic Macedonians, and frightened them into fleeing their homes. Among those allegedly killed by the NLA was an elderly man, Boris Magdenovski, who was shot, as ethnic Macedonians fled from Brezno. Five road workers were abducted on 7 August and, according to reports, physically ill-treated, sexually abused and threatened with death before being released.

Dozens of ethnic Macedonians were kidnapped. While many were released after a short time, 12 people apparently remained missing after the NLA released 14 others in late September. In October, reports suggested that the 12 may have been killed and buried in mass graves near Neproshten. The case was referred by the Macedonian government to the International Criminal Tribunal for the former Yugoslavia for investigation.

Amnesty

One of the key elements of the peace process was a commitment by President Boris Trajkovski to NATO that there would be an amnesty from prosecution for NLA members who had not committed war crimes and who voluntarily laid down their arms. The delay in clarifying and formalizing this amnesty became a major political issue as debates continued about the Ohrid agreement. During December, 64 people were released from prison, mainly from pre-trial detention, as a result of pardons from the President, but at least 24 others remained in detention in connection with conflict-related issues.

There was concern about the effects of any amnesty which would prevent the emergence of the truth and subsequent accountability before the law for people reasonably suspected of serious human rights abuses or breaches of international humanitarian law.

Refugees and the displaced

Over 170,000 people were displaced at some time between March and August and over 50,000 remained displaced within Macedonia and in Kosovo by the end of September. People who left their homes were mainly from villages which fell under the control of the NLA.

Between March and July around 65,000 ethnic Albanians from the areas caught in the conflict went to Kosovo to escape NLA control or the shelling of their villages by Macedonian security forces. Some of them, according to the UN High Commissioner for Refugees (UNHCR), experienced problems crossing the border without documents or had to bribe border guards. A return agreement was signed by UNHCR and the Macedonian government in April to facilitate the return of people without proper documents.

Tens of thousands of ethnic Macedonians reported being driven out of their homes by armed opposition forces and were displaced to other parts of Macedonia. Many of those from areas where they were in a minority did not return home. In mid-December around 18,680 people in total remained displaced.

Both ethnic groups said they feared that ethnic cleansing tactics, familiar from other parts of former Yugoslavia, were being used against them. There were numerous reports of homes being vandalized and burned once they were left empty. Some people moved to areas where their ethnic group was in a majority, exchanging properties rather than returning home.

AI country reports/ visits
Reports
- Macedonia: Collecting blows – the alleged ill-treatment of Roma in Šašavarlija (AI Index: EUR 65/008/2001)
- Macedonia: A durable peace depends on respect for human rights (AI Index: EUR 65/005/2001)

Visits
AI representatives visited Macedonia in June and in November to interview victims of human rights violations and to meet local human rights activists.

MALAWI

REPUBLIC OF MALAWI
Head of state and government: Bakili Muluzi
Capital: Lilongwe
Population: 11.6 million
Official languages: Chichewa, English
Death penalty: retentionist

Police used tear gas and live ammunition against a demonstration, killing one student. Journalists were assaulted, threatened and arrested for publishing articles critical of the government. Parliament petitioned to remove three High Court judges from office after they made rulings either perceived to be politically biased or which challenged the supremacy of Parliament.

Background
Amid popular protests, the ruling United Democratic Front (UDF) party stepped up its campaign for constitutional changes to allow President Bakili Muluzi to run for a third term. Religious leaders denounced "state-sponsored violence" aimed at silencing government critics, including the church. Malawi's Human Rights Commission reported that political violence, ethnic intolerance and other forms of human rights violations rose some 60 per cent over the previous year.

Excessive use of force
Police continued to use excessive force, using tear gas and live ammunition to disperse peaceful demonstrators. Torture by police officers continued, but only a few cases came to public attention.

In November, popular reggae musician Evison Matafale died in police custody three days after police arrested him for writing an allegedly seditious letter to President Muluzi. The death led to protests in several towns and cities. President Muluzi appointed a commission to investigate the death, although its composition was questioned by civil society groups. In December, police used tear gas and live ammunition in Zomba against unarmed demonstrators protesting in front of parliamentarians at the death of Evison Matafale. Police officers fatally shot Faikizo Phiri, and seriously injured one other demonstrator. A government inquiry into the death was initiated.

Journalists
Journalists suffered threats and reprisals for publishing articles critical of the government.

In February, police arrested five journalists from the *Daily Times* newspaper for publishing articles considered "false and the work of alarmists". President Muluzi later ordered that the charges be dropped. Newspaper editor Martines Namigha and the owner of a printing press were briefly arrested in May on similar charges. In August, UDF officials allegedly threatened journalist John Saini for writing articles critical of the party.

Judicial independence threatened
In a move that undermined judicial independence at the highest levels, parliamentarians voted in November to impeach three High Court judges for "incompetence" or "misbehaviour" after each of them had made rulings in separate cases perceived to be politically biased or which challenged the government. The parliamentary motion flouted an earlier High Court ruling by Justice Bathiel Chiudza Banda, who had ordered that the impeachment proceedings be halted until a constitutionally mandated investigation had concluded.

MALAYSIA

MALAYSIA
Head of state: Raja Tuanku Syed Sirajuddin (replaced Sultan Salahuddin Abdul Aziz Shah in December)
Head of government: Mahathir Mohamad
Capital: Kuala Lumpur
Population: 22.6 million
Official language: Bahasa Malaysia
Death penalty: retentionist

Opposition activists and suspected Islamic "extremists" were arrested and detained without trial under the Internal Security Act (ISA) and were at risk of torture or ill-treatment. Peaceful demonstrations were dispersed with excessive force and protesters arrested, detained and ill-treated. Students and academics faced penalties for peaceful political activity. Politically motivated prosecutions were pursued against opposition figures. A number of judicial decisions and the activities of the Human Rights Commission of Malaysia were perceived as bolstering respect for human rights principles.

Background
The ruling *Barisan National* (National Front) coalition continued to dominate the political scene and won 60 of 62 seats in the November state elections in Sarawak. Peaceful public assemblies and demonstrations were forcibly dispersed by police throughout the year. From April, after Prime Minister Mahathir Mohamad stated that the government would break from international human rights norms to preserve national stability, a series of opposition activists and suspected Islamic "extremists" were detained without trial under the ISA. A coalition of opposition parties and civil society groups formed to campaign against the detentions.

Following the attacks in the USA on 11 September, the government justified past use of the ISA and announced it may amend it and other laws to combat "terrorism".

Detention without trial under the ISA

The ISA allows the detention without trial for up to two years, renewable indefinitely, of any person considered by the authorities to be a potential threat to national security or public order. ISA detainees reported that they were subjected to intimidation and intense psychological pressure, at times amounting to torture. In the initial period of police investigation, detainees were held in solitary confinement and denied access to lawyers, family members and independent doctors. Isolated and induced to fear for the well-being of their families, the detainees were threatened with indefinite detention unless they cooperated and "confessed".

☐ Three members of the minority Shia Muslim community reportedly remained in detention during most of 2001. The reasons for their detention were not made public. They were among six members of the community who were arrested under the ISA from late 2000.

Keadilan activists and others

In April a human rights defender and nine political activists, mostly senior members of the opposition *Parti Keadilan Nasional*, National Justice Party, were arrested under the ISA and accused of planning to overthrow the government by "militant" means including violent demonstrations. No evidence to support these allegations was made public.

The detainees were prisoners of conscience. In June, four of them were released while six others, Tian Chua, Mohamad Ezam Mohd Nor, Haji Saari Sungib, Badrul Amin Bahron, Lokman Nor Adam and Hishamuddin Rais, were served with two-year detention orders. Badrul Amin Bahron was released in November, but was rearrested in December and charged with breaking the terms of a restriction order barring him from political activity and severely limiting his freedom of movement and association.

PAS members and others accused of Islamic 'extremism'

In August, 10 men, including at least seven members of the main opposition party *Parti Islam seMalaysia* (PAS), Islamic Party of Malaysia, were arrested under the ISA and accused of links with a local Islamic "extremist" group, *Kumpulan Mujahidin Malaysia* (KMM), Malaysia Mujahidin Group. Reported KMM members were alleged by the government to have received religious and military training in Afghanistan and to have planned to violently overthrow the government in order to set up an Islamic state.

After being held incommunicado for over 50 days, nine of the detainees were served with two-year detention orders. In October, six other men, mostly religious teachers at Islamic schools, were also detained and held incommunicado for over three weeks. Five of them were subsequently served with two-year detention orders. The authorities linked all these arrests to the detention under the ISA in June of at least six alleged Islamic "extremists" accused of various crimes, including murder, bank robberies and the bombing of a church and a Hindu temple. By the end of the year, at least seven other alleged Islamic militants, accused of having links with "international terrorism", were detained under the ISA as arrests continued.

Freedom of assembly

The authorities continued to impose restrictions on the right of peaceful assembly and association. A series of demonstrations against the ISA, or in support of political reform and Anwar Ibrahim (see below), were dispersed by police, at times with excessive force. Protesters were arrested and assaulted, held in remand for up to 14 days and charged with illegal assembly. Permits for public assemblies were issued or refused arbitrarily and selectively, and in July police issued a ban on all public political rallies.

Students and academics engaging in demonstrations and other political activity also faced penalties under the Universities and University Colleges Act. In June, following the arrest for illegal assembly of seven students who participated in a peaceful demonstration, a number of the students were expelled or suspended from their universities. In July, two students involved in peaceful campaigning against the ISA were arrested and detained incommunicado under the ISA for 10 and 23 days respectively.

☐ In August a schoolteacher was charged with sedition for setting an examination question to discuss the effectiveness of the Malaysian judiciary.

☐ In October the authorities announced that 61 university lecturers had been dismissed, transferred or issued with warnings for alleged "anti-government activities".

The judiciary

In late 2000 the newly appointed Chief Justice, Mohamad Dzaiddin Abdullah, pledged to address a decline of public confidence in the independence and effectiveness of the judiciary. In February the Kuala Lumpur Bar Committee submitted a memorandum listing a series of defects in the administration of justice and proposing reforms. In March the Chief Justice recommended limits on the size of defamation awards to avoid unjustified curbs on freedom of speech.

☐ In May a High Court upheld the habeas corpus petition of two people detained under the ISA and ordered their release after ruling that their detention was unlawful. The Court affirmed fundamental constitutional principles and urged parliament to review the relevance of the ISA. The police appealed against the ruling. Habeas corpus petitions by other ISA detainees were rejected and remained under appeal before the Federal Court at the end of the year.

☐ In June the Federal Court quashed a conviction for contempt of court previously upheld by the Court of Appeal against Zainur Zakaria, one of Anwar Ibrahim's defence lawyers. He had filed an affidavit in court in

1998 alleging that two public prosecutors had attempted to fabricate evidence against his client.

Prosecution of opposition figures
Selective and politically motivated prosecutions were threatened or pursued against opposition figures.

▭ In March Mohamad Ezam Mohd Nor, leader of the youth branch of *Keadilan*, was arrested and charged under the Sedition Act for allegedly planning violent demonstrations. In April he was detained without trial under the ISA. In October a court dropped charges against him of participating in an illegal assembly in April. In November Mohamad Ezam Mohd Nor went on trial under the Official Secrets Act for distributing allegedly classified documents about official corruption to journalists in 1999.

▭ Prisoner of conscience Anwar Ibrahim lodged an appeal against his sentence of nine years' imprisonment on charges of sodomy, imposed after an unfair trial in 2000. The sentence was being served consecutively with a six-year sentence for alleged abuse of power, which remained under appeal before the Federal Court at the end of the year.

National Human Rights Commission
In April the Human Rights Commission of Malaysia (*Suhakam*) submitted its first annual report to parliament, detailing the activities of its working groups, including those addressing law reform, human rights education and complaints. Initial recommendations included ratification of major international human rights instruments, review of restrictive laws including the ISA, and constitutional changes to combat gender discrimination. In April *Suhakam* called for the release of recently arrested ISA detainees and asserted their right to a trial. In July it reported on the arbitrary and selective application of laws restricting freedom of assembly, and recommended specific legislative amendments and enhanced liaison between the police and public assembly organizers.

In August *Suhakam* issued the findings of a public inquiry into the dispersal of a peaceful demonstration in November 2000. *Suhakam* found the police were responsible for human rights violations including excessive use of force during dispersals, assaults on detainees and delays in the provision of medical care; it gave detailed recommendations for reform of police policy and practice.

The government pledged to study some of *Suhakam*'s recommendations. However, its responses to *Suhakam*'s findings during the year were frequently dismissive and included public statements that its reports were "biased" and "idealistic".

Death penalty and corporal punishment
Four people convicted of murder and a man convicted of drugs trafficking were executed by hanging. At least three people were sentenced to death, and at least 159 were reported to be on death row. Caning, a cruel, inhuman or degrading punishment, was imposed throughout 2001 as an additional punishment to imprisonment.

AI country reports/visits
Reports
- Malaysia: Students penalized for political activities (AI Index: ASA 28/016/2001)
- Malaysia: Human rights under threat – the Internal Security Act and other restrictive laws (AI Index: ASA 28/031/2001)

Visits
An AI delegate visited Malaysia in April to conduct research and met relatives of those detained under the ISA.

MALDIVES

REPUBLIC OF MALDIVES
Head of state and government: Maumoon Abdul Gayoom
Capital: Malé
Population: 0.3 million
Official language: Maldivian Dhivehi
Death penalty: abolitionist in practice

Prisoners of conscience continued to be held. A bill on the protection of the rights of detainees was reportedly defeated in parliament.

Background
As in previous years, no political parties were allowed to function. On 28 February, 42 people including academics, intellectuals, businessmen and three members of parliament, handed a petition to the Minister of Home Affairs requesting permission to set up the Maldivian Democratic Party (MDP). By the end of the year, permission had not been granted and a number of signatories had been detained.

Prisoners of conscience and political prisoners
▭ Umar Jamaal, Mohamed Latheef, Abdul Hannan and Abdul Aziz were reportedly detained by National Security Service personnel for several weeks in December 2000 and January 2001. Their detention was believed to have been related to their support for a bill before parliament on the protection of the rights of detainees. The bill was reportedly defeated. The four men were warned on their release against making public statements about their detention.

▭ Abdulla Shakir, a member of parliament for Malé and leading petitioner for the MDP, was arrested on 18 July. His whereabouts remained unknown until his release several days later.

▭ Mohamed Nasheed, member of parliament for Malé and a prominent petitioner for the MDP, was arrested on 8 October and held incommunicado for several weeks. On 8 November, he was reportedly sentenced to be banished for two and a half years on charges of theft of unspecified "government property" although the real motive appeared to be political. Mohamed Nasheed was not permitted a lawyer or to speak in his own defence.

AI action
Throughout the year AI called upon President Maumoon Abdul Gayoom to confirm that the rights of those seeking to establish the MDP would be respected and that they would not be harassed by government officials. In June the Ministry of Information, Arts and Culture stated in a letter that "the government of Maldives does not arrest or detain people for the exercise of their freedom of expression, which is a right granted to its citizens by the Constitution of the Maldives".

MAURITANIA

ISLAMIC REPUBLIC OF MAURITANIA
Head of state: Maaouiya Ould Sid 'Ahmed Taya
Head of government: Cheikh El Avia Ould Mohamed Khouna
Capital: Nouakchott
Population: 2.7 million
Official language: Arabic
Death penalty: retentionist
2001 treaty ratifications/signatures: UN Women's Convention

Three members of an opposition party were convicted on politically motivated charges after an unfair trial. The government continued to deny the existence of slavery. Human rights organizations, including those campaigning against slavery, remained illegal, and freedom of expression remained limited. Female genital mutilation was reported to be widespread and no specific legislation was enacted prohibiting the practice. No steps were taken by the government to investigate massive human rights violations committed during the late 1980s and early 1990s. One death sentence was passed.

Background
Local and parliamentary elections were held in October, with the ruling party maintaining a large majority. Two political parties remained banned since 2000, following an increase in political tension and demonstrations. Political opponents continued to be harassed and freedom of expression was limited. Human rights organizations, including those campaigning against slavery, continued to operate without authorization, leaving human rights defenders liable to prosecution under law for "administer[ing] associations which are functioning without authorization".

Slavery and similar practices
Further evidence emerged to suggest that, despite official abolition in 1981, slavery or practices analogous to slavery and related practices, continued. Evidence also showed continued discrimination based on slave-related status. Although the government strenuously denied that slavery existed, few practical measures seemed to have been implemented to eradicate it. Precise data was not available on the extent of the practice.

Unfair trial of a political opponent
The arrest and detention of three members of the opposition *Front populaire mauritanien* (FPM), Popular Mauritanian Front, including its leader, Mohamed Lemine Chbih Ould Cheikh Melaïnine, was the latest example in a pattern of harassment of political opponents.

Mohamed Lemine Chbih Ould Cheikh Melanine, Mokhtar Ould Haïbetna and Bouba Ould Hassena, were convicted on 14 June by Aioun criminal court on charges of conspiracy to commit acts of sabotage and "terrorism". AI considered them to be prisoners of conscience.

The lawyers for the three men alleged numerous serious irregularities in investigation and trial proceedings, and initially withdrew from the case in protest. During the trial, both prosecution witnesses were dismissed as unreliable. Lawyers had already objected to their testimony as the two men were originally arrested with Mohamed Chbih and were then presented as prosecution witnesses by the police. One of the two men acknowledged in court that he was a police informant. Their incriminating testimony formed the bulk of the evidence against Mohamed Chbih. The three defendants stated that their signed statements had been obtained under duress. Following demonstrations in support of Mohamed Chbih by FPM supporters, the Supreme Court ruled on 13 May that the case should be transferred from Nouakchott to a court some 800km away in the town of Aioun.

Two people who had applied to observe the trial were refused permission, although a representative of the Senegalese *Rencontre africaine pour la défense des droits de l'homme*, African Assembly for the Defence of Human Rights, was permitted to attend.

The sentence was confirmed by the cassation chamber of the Supreme Court in December. At the end of the year, the three men remained in Aioun prison, where conditions were known to be very harsh and whose remote position posed difficulties for family support.

Freedom of expression further attacked

The pattern of repression of freedom of expression and harassment of members of the press continued.

▫ In April, Mohammed Lemine Ould Ba, the Mauritanian correspondent for *Radio France Internationale*, was banned by the government from working with a foreign media organization. The reason for the ban, which had not been lifted by the end of the year, was not clear.

Death penalty

One man was sentenced to death after being convicted of murder.

Intergovernmental organizations

In September, the European Parliament passed a resolution on Mauritania calling for the immediate and unconditional release of Mohamed Chibh and his two co-detainees, for the right of free expression to be guaranteed and for immediate steps to be taken to end slavery.

The UN Committee on the Rights of the Child considered the initial report of Mauritania in September. The Committee expressed concern that the report did not mention human rights issues such as female genital mutilation and slavery. It also said that insufficient resources were being used to tackle the effect of poverty on children, particularly in rural areas, and expressed concern at evidence of discrimination against minorities.

AI country reports/visits
Statement
- Mauritania: Prisoners of conscience sentenced to five years in prison (AI Index: AFR 38/005/2001)

Visits
AI made several requests seeking authorization to visit Mauritania to discuss human rights issues, including slavery, with government authorities. Despite apparent initial openness, no firm reply was received and the organization was not able to visit the country.

MAURITIUS

REPUBLIC OF MAURITIUS
Head of state: Cassam Uteem
Head of government: Anerood Jugnauth
Capital: Port Louis
Population: 1.2 million
Official language: English
Death penalty: abolitionist for all crimes
2001 treaty ratifications/signatures: Optional Protocol to the UN Women's Convention; Optional Protocol to the UN Children's Convention on the involvement of children in armed conflict

At least four detainees were reported to have died in police custody as a result of torture or other cruel, inhuman and degrading treatment. Others alleged torture and ill-treatment by police at the time of arrest. The government established a National Human Rights Commission in April which opened investigations into allegations of police torture, but international standards for such inquiries appeared not to have been met.

Deaths in police custody

There were at least four deaths in custody as a result of torture or other cruel, inhuman and degrading treatment. Neither these nor cases from previous years were investigated under open and thorough procedures.

▫ Josian Kersley Bayaram died on 21 July in prison in Pointe aux Cannoniers, after his arrest for alleged drunkenness. An official autopsy concluded death by asphyxiation. His family disagreed with the police statement that he had committed suicide by hanging, objecting that there was no trace of strangulation on his neck but that there were deep wounds under his left eye and on his left forearm. They filed a complaint to the Police Complaints Bureau and to the National Human Rights Commission but were not informed of any progress in the investigations. They had the body exhumed two months after burial for a private autopsy.

Torture and ill-treatment

Several detainees accused police officers of torture or ill-treatment to extract confessions or as punishment for juvenile and petty criminal suspects.

▫ Cehl Meeah, leader of the *Hizbullah* opposition party, who was held as part of a murder inquiry, alleged that in December 2000 police officers beat him, inserted needles into his fingernails and sexually abused him in an attempt to extract confessions. Investigations into his allegations by the Criminal Investigation Division of the police and the National Human Rights Commission were not completed at the end of the year. Police officers reportedly admitted beating him, but refused to cooperate with the investigations.

AI country reports/visits
Statement
- Mauritius: Amnesty International calls for independent investigation of torture complaints (AI Index: AFR 39/001/2001)

MEXICO

UNITED MEXICAN STATES
Head of state and government: Vicente Fox Quesada
Capital: Mexico City
Population: 100 million
Official language: Spanish
2001 ratifications/signatures: Inter-American Convention on Forced Disappearance of Persons
Death penalty: abolitionist for ordinary crimes

A leading human rights defender was murdered and many others received death threats. New legislation on indigenous rights failed to resolve the conflict in Chiapas. Arbitrary detention and torture remained widespread. There were reports of "disappearances" and extrajudicial executions. Impunity for such crimes remained the norm. Pressure increased for full and effective investigations of past human rights violations. More military personnel were assigned posts in the Attorney General's Office. Intense international and national pressure led to the release of two prisoners of conscience, but their convictions were not overturned nor their torturers brought to justice. Another prisoner of conscience remained in prison. At the end of the year the Senate approved the ratification of a number of international human rights treaties. Ratification of the Rome Statute of the International Criminal Court remained pending.

Background
On taking office in December 2000, President Fox, of the *Partido Acción Nacional*, National Action Party, made commitments to end the impunity which characterized much of the previous 70-year rule of the *Partido Revolucionario Institucional*, Institutional Revolutionary Party. In March the Foreign Minister made unprecedented pledges to combat human rights abuses, including by ratifying and incorporating into national law all outstanding international human rights treaties and by inviting all international human rights mechanisms to visit Mexico. However, by the end of the year, these international commitments had not resulted in effective improvement in human rights protection and reports of human rights violations remained widespread.

On taking office, President Fox had appointed as Attorney General of the Republic a serving army general who was also a former chief military prosecutor with a record of failing to prosecute military officials accused of human rights abuses. In 2001, at least 13 other military officials were given senior posts in the Attorney General's Office. No effective mechanism existed to carry out independent judicial investigations into the frequent reports of human rights violations committed by the military or agents of the Attorney General's Office or the Offices of State Attorney Generals. Pre-election proposals to reform the administration of justice did not materialize and the increasing role of the military in the Attorney General's Office raised serious concerns about the willingness of the government to tackle impunity.

The new position of Minister for Public Security was created with responsibility for the *Policía Federal Preventiva* (PFP), Federal Preventive Police, and prisons. Thousands of serving military personnel were transferred directly into the PFP.

In February the Mexican government authorized the extradition to Spain of an Argentine citizen accused of crimes against humanity during the military dictatorship in Argentina. At the end of the year the final decision of the Mexican courts on whether to allow his extradition was still pending.

Human rights defenders and journalists
There were numerous reports of harassment of human rights defenders and journalists in many different states. They were the victims of death threats, surveillance operations, smear campaigns and physical attacks. The authorities consistently failed to act to bring those responsible to justice, contributing to a worsening security climate.

On 19 October, Digna Ochoa, a human rights lawyer who had worked with the *Centro de Derechos Humanos "Miguel Agustín Pro Juárez"* (PRODH), Human Rights Centre "Miguel Agustín Pro Juárez", was shot and killed in her office in Mexico City. A death threat was left next to her body warning members of the PRODH that they would face the same fate. Digna Ochoa had worked on high-profile cases in which members of the military and the Attorney General's Office were accused of serious human rights violations. The authorities had repeatedly failed to identify and bring to justice those responsible for a series of threats and attacks against Digna Ochoa and the PRODH. Inconsistencies in the initial investigation into her murder raised concern that vital evidence may have been lost. A week after Digna Ochoa's murder, five other prominent human rights defenders in Mexico City received death threats. The authorities promised to protect human rights defenders and to bring those responsible for the murder and the threats to justice. Investigations into the murder and threats were continuing at the end of the year.

Over the year, members of the *Centro de Derechos Humanos "Fray Bartolomé de las Casas"* (CDHFBC), "Fray Bartolomé de Las Casas" Human Rights Centre in Chiapas State, reportedly suffered harassment and threats, including an attempted ambush by gunmen on the road to San Cristobal in August, e-mail threats and unidentified individuals requesting, both at the CDHFBC and at travel agencies, details of the travel arrangements of CDHFBC members.

◻ In October, Abel Barrera of the *Centro de Derechos Humanos de la Montaña "Tlachinollan",* Montaña Centre for Human Rights "Tlachinollan", Guerrero State, received a death threat after following up on investigations into previous threats against him. Despite commitments to investigate the new threat, the authorities failed to take appropriate action.

Chiapas State

As part of President Fox's commitment to reach an early negotiated settlement to the conflict in Chiapas with the *Ejército Zapatista de Liberación Nacional* (EZLN), Zapatista National Liberation Army, there were troop withdrawals in the conflict zone and many EZLN sympathizers were released from custody. In April, expectations of an early solution to the conflict receded after Congress modified and approved an indigenous rights bill which failed to meet agreed principles. Indigenous and human rights organizations across the country condemned the bill as a violation of Mexico's international obligations on indigenous rights. The EZLN withdrew from negotiations.

Indigenous communities continued to suffer intimidation and attack by paramilitary or "armed civilian" groups. Despite this, a number of internally displaced people returned to their communities.

◻ In February a paramilitary group reportedly forced six Tzotziles indigenous families off their land in the municipality of Chenalhó, Chiapas. The special unit of the Attorney General's Office set up in 1999 to investigate paramilitary groups failed to prosecute those responsible for this and other crimes.

◻ In November several of those who were reportedly responsible for organizing the 1997 massacre of 45 members of the indigenous community of Acteal were acquitted by a federal judge and released.

Arbitrary detention, torture and ill-treatment

Arbitrary detention, torture and ill-treatment continued to be commonly used by federal, state and municipal police forces and military personnel carrying out policing operations. Legislation preventing and punishing such abuses remained inadequate and was seldom invoked. The courts routinely failed to challenge prosecution evidence reportedly extracted under torture, or to investigate those allegedly responsible. There were reports of prison conditions amounting to cruel, inhuman or degrading treatment.

◻ In May, in the town of Miguel Aleman, Tamaulipas state, José Antinio Garcia Sandoval was dragged from his house by the municipal *Policía Preventiva,* Preventive Police, after a dispute with a neighbour. He was beaten, kicked and repeatedly struck in the face. He was held incommunicado for 24 hours and threatened with reprisals if he reported the incident. Two official medical examinations failed to identify his serious injuries, which included fractured ribs.

Although he lodged a complaint with the State Attorney General's Office and the State Human Rights Commission, no action was reportedly taken.

◻ In December, PFP agents in Tijuana, Baja California state, detained two migrant workers, Filiberto Girón Cisneros and Enrique Rey Buenrostro, and reportedly tortured them to extract confessions to trafficking illegal migrants. The two were subsequently hospitalized for their injuries and lodged official complaints. The PFP officers responsible were reportedly detained pending an investigation.

'Disappearances' and extrajudicial executions

Federal and state police were reportedly responsible for the "disappearance" of at least three people in police operations. The whereabouts of the victims remained unknown at the end of the year. A reform to the federal penal codes codifying the crime of "disappearance" was passed.

There were reports of extrajudicial executions by the members of the security forces in various states, including Chihuahua. The authorities reportedly failed to take prompt and effective action to bring those responsible to justice.

◻ In June, Faustino Jiménez Alvarez was reportedly detained by members of the *Policía Judicial del Estado,* State Judicial Police, in Tierra Colorada, Guerrero state. The local authorities failed to establish his whereabouts and officers accused of participating in his "disappearance" remained on active duty while under investigation; they fled the state before charges were filed. Faustino Jiménez Alvarez' fate had not been clarified by the end of the year.

Prisoners of conscience

◻ In November Rodolfo Montiel Flores and Teodoro Cabrera García, two peasant environmental activists, were released on "humanitarian grounds" by order of the President. The two men had been detained in 1999 for their peaceful activism and signed false confessions under torture by the military. They were then tried and sentenced by the courts and in July 2001 their appeal had been rejected by the courts. On their release, the authorities did not acknowledge their innocence or take steps to bring to justice those responsible for their torture.

◻ Another prisoner of conscience, Brigadier General José Francisco Gallardo, spent his eighth year in custody. An appeal to the civilian courts to compel the authorities to comply with the recommendation of the Inter-American Commission on Human Rights calling for his immediate release, was postponed after the authorities repeatedly failed to provide the courts with the requested documents. The Commission took the case to the Inter-American Court of Human Rights. At the end of the year the Court issued a resolution requiring the Mexican State to guarantee the safety of the General and summoning the parties to the Court to analyse the case.

Impunity

Relatives of the many hundreds of "disappeared" from the last three decades continued their campaign to learn the fate of their relatives and to put pressure on the judicial authorities to investigate and prosecute all those responsible for the "disappearances". New photographic evidence of the 1968 Tlatelolco square massacre emerged which increased pressure for investigations into the case to be reopened. President Fox failed to keep his pre-election promise to establish a Truth Commission to look at these and other unresolved cases of past human rights violations such as extrajudicial executions.

In November the *Comisión Nacional de Derechos Humanos* (CNDH), National Human Rights Commission, produced a report on 532 reported "disappearance" cases dating from the 1970s and 1980s. In response the President ordered the creation of a Special Attorney to investigate these crimes.

Military courts failed to effectively investigate or prosecute military officials accused of human rights violations, and prevented cases being heard by the civilian courts. CNDH officials stated that army anti-drug operations were a major source of complaints of human rights violations.

In March the military sealed off the village of Guardados de Abajo, Tamaulipas state, in a joint anti-narcotics operation with the federal police. Military personnel reportedly broke into houses and carried out arbitrary detentions, reportedly torturing several of those detained. Human rights defender Mauro Cruz of the organization *Centro de Estudios Fronterizos y de Promoción de los Derechos Humanos*, Centre for Border Studies and the Promotion of Human Rights, was threatened by soldiers when he tried to enter the area.

An Amnesty Law in Oaxaca state resulted in the release of many of the scores of indigenous people detained in the Loxicha region over the last four years on suspicion of links with an armed opposition group. Many of the detainees were reportedly held incommunicado and tortured to extract confessions which were later used to prosecute them for ordinary crimes. Despite recommendations by the Oaxaca State Human Rights Commission, those responsible for the torture had not been brought to justice.

In November the bodies of eight murdered women were discovered in Ciudad Juarez, Chihuahua state. Since 1993, over 200 women have "disappeared" or been murdered in Ciudad Juarez. According to reports, the authorities consistently failed to investigate these crimes effectively, to bring all those responsible to justice, or to take adequate measures to protect women in the area.

There were several reports of attacks on gay men, some fatal, in a number of states. The authorities of Yucatán and Colima states reportedly failed to act promptly to investigate these crimes or bring those responsible to justice.

Intergovernmental organizations
The first phase of the Technical Co-operation Program between the government and the UN High Commissioner for Human Rights was implemented. Training of medical and forensic experts in assessing torture was a priority; independent evaluation of the phase was critical. In May the UN Special Rapporteur on the independence of judges and lawyers visited Mexico to examine the judicial system.

The government agreed to reopen unresolved cases with the Inter-American Commission on Human Rights. It invited a Commission delegation to visit in July to assess, along with non-governmental organizations, victims and relatives, how to secure compliance with outstanding Commission recommendations. By the end of 2001, expectation of progress on many of these cases had not been fulfilled.

At the end of the year the Senate approved the ratification of a number of international human rights instruments. Steps were also taken to recognize the competence of the UN Human Rights Committee and the Committee against Torture and other treaty-body committees to receive individual complaints. Ratification of the Rome Statute of the International Criminal Court remained pending.

AI country reports/ visits
Reports
- Mexico: Torture cases – calling out for justice (AI Index: AMR 41/008/2001)
- Memorandum to the Government of Mexico (AI Index: AMR 41/015/2001)
- Mexico: Justice betrayed – torture in the judicial system (AI Index: AMR 41/021/2001)
- Mexico: Silencing dissent – an update on the case of General Gallardo (AI Index: AMR 41/037/2001)
- Mexico: Daring to raise their voices (AI Index: AMR 41/040/2001)

Visits
AI delegates visited Mexico on three occasions, including in March when the then Secretary General of AI met President Fox and other senior members of the administration.

MOLDOVA

REPUBLIC OF MOLDOVA
Head of state: Vladimir Voronin (replaced Petru Lucinschi in April)
Head of government: Vasile Tarlev (replaced Dumitru Braghiș in April)
Capital: Chișinău
Population: 4.3 million
Official language: Moldovan (Romanian)
Death penalty: abolitionist for all crimes

Arbitrary detention and ill-treatment by police continued to be reported. Conditions of detention in many police lock-ups and prisons amounted to cruel, inhuman or degrading treatment. At least three political prisoners remained imprisoned in the self-proclaimed Dnestr Moldavian Republic (DMR).

Background

Moldova remained the poorest country in Europe with close to 80 per cent of its population living below the poverty line.

Elections in February were won by the Party of Moldovan Communists and Vladimir Voronin, the party leader, was inaugurated as President in April. In June, Ombudsman Alexei Potinga stated in his annual report that violations of human rights were widespread. In July, trafficking in people was made a criminal offence. Between 600,000 and one million Moldovans, 70 per cent of whom were women, had reportedly left the country since independence in 1991. An alarming number of women and minors have been trafficked for sexual exploitation. Russian military withdrawal from the DMR, agreed at the 1999 Istanbul Summit of the Organization for Security and Co-operation in Europe (OSCE), was completed in November 2001. However, no progress was reported in the negotiations between the Moldovan government and the DMR authorities on the status of the breakaway region.

Torture and ill-treatment

There were reports that many criminal suspects were ill-treated, and in some cases tortured, in police lock-ups in order to extract confessions. Detainees, including minors, were frequently denied access to a lawyer and prevented from informing their families of their whereabouts. It was also reported that medical treatment was withheld from people injured as a result of ill-treatment. Relatively few complaints were lodged by the victims, who feared reprisals or that their grievances would not be addressed effectively. Some victims who did lodge complaints were harassed by police officers.

☐ In April 2001, 19-year-old Andrei Dascal was apprehended by several police officers, one of whom accused him of stealing his wife's necklace. Andrei Dascal was taken to a brewery where police officers and security guards reportedly beat him all over his body. He was then put in the boot of a car and taken to Ciocana police station. At the first court hearing, he was observed walking with the aid of crutches. His statement about the beating by the police was apparently not taken into consideration by the court.

☐ Aurel Paduret had lodged a complaint about police ill-treatment after he was severely beaten by trainee police officers in Chișinău in March 2000. Two officers were charged in connection with his complaint. In September 2001, after one of the hearings in the trial of the officers, Aurel Paduret was arrested by colleagues of the accused and held in detention for 72 hours. He was interrogated for some five hours during which time a lawyer working for the Moldovan Helsinki Committee, a local human rights organization, who was with Aurel Paduret at the time of the arrest, was not allowed to assist him because police claimed that they were questioning him "as a witness" and so were not obliged to allow a legal representative to be present. Aurel Paduret was eventually released following a court order.

Conditions in detention

The authorities failed to improve conditions of detention. There was particular concern about the conditions in which people were held while awaiting trial and sentencing, often for prolonged periods. Overcrowding and poor sanitary conditions in police lock-ups and pre-trial detention facilities often amounted to cruel, inhuman or degrading treatment.

☐ As of November, 106 minors were held pending trial in Chișinău Prison Number 3. Each of the cells held more people than there were beds available. The young people were not provided with any educational or recreational program and were only allowed access to a 25m^2 concrete yard for one hour a day. At least six of the detainees, one of whom was suffering from tuberculosis, had been held in these conditions for over 16 months. Many of them were poorly clothed and barefoot. In only a few exceptional cases were they allowed a family visit before sentencing.

☐ In the women's section of Chișinău Prison Number 3, the authorities reportedly claimed that a cell measuring 2.5m x 1.5m designed for solitary confinement was no longer in use. However, in October, a visiting human rights monitor reported that she saw a woman who had been detained in the cell for 10 days, the maximum allowed by prison regulations. The cell, which adjoined the shower room, was extremely humid.

Political prisoners in the DMR

Ilie Ilașcu, who had been convicted of murder in 1993 by a court in the DMR in the trial of the so-called "Tiraspol Six", was released in May. The six men had been convicted of "terrorist acts", including the murder of two DMR officials in 1993. Alexandru Leșco, Andrei Ivanțoc and Tudor Petrov-Popa remained in prison. In July the European Court of Human Rights ruled that their application against their conviction was admissible. The men had said that they were not convicted by a competent court, that the proceedings leading to their conviction were not fair and that their prison conditions were in breach of the European Convention on Human Rights.

MOROCCO/ WESTERN SAHARA

KINGDOM OF MOROCCO
Head of state: King Mohamed VI
Head of government: Abderrahmane Youssoufi
Capital: Rabat
Population: 30.4 million
Official language: Arabic
Death penalty: retentionist

The process of compensating victims of "disappearance" and arbitrary detention in previous years and their families continued. However, the authorities failed to clarify the cases of several hundred people, most of them Sahrawis, who "disappeared" between the 1960s and early 1990s. Fifty-six political prisoners, including prisoners of conscience, were released in a royal pardon. However, some 30 others sentenced after unfair trials in previous years remained in detention. Dozens of human rights defenders and over a hundred members and sympathizers of a banned Islamist association were sentenced to prison terms following demonstrations in December 2000; the human rights defenders were later acquitted. The failure to bring those responsible for human rights violations to justice remained a major concern.

Background

King Mohamed VI made several new appointments to key administrative positions, including the post of Minister of the Interior and nine new regional governorships. Many of the new officials were recruited from the business community, rather than from within the politico-administrative sector, as had traditionally been the case.

In April, a decree was enacted reforming the structure and mandate of the *Conseil consultatif des droits de l'homme* (CCDH), Human Rights Advisory Board. Changes introduced by the decree included expanding the Board's mandate to allow it to examine individual cases of human rights violations and to increase the representation of non-governmental organizations on the Board. In December, a new institution was created to deal with complaints from citizens who considered they had been unjustly treated by the authorities.

In March, King Mohamed VI announced the creation of a royal commission responsible for revising the *moudawana* (personal status code) which discriminates against women.

The UN Mission for the Referendum in Western Sahara (MINURSO) proposed a controversial new initiative to end the deadlock in the process designed to lead to a referendum on the sovereignty of Western Sahara. The proposed initiative would radically change the criteria for those eligible to vote. However, there was no agreement on whether or not the initiative should be implemented.

Impunity

The process continued of compensating victims of "disappearance" and arbitrary detention and their families. According to the authorities, by the end of 2001, compensation had been awarded in a total of over 700 cases where claims had been submitted to the arbitration commission, established in 1999. Many families continued to distrust the process, insisting that compensation was only one element in the process of providing full redress for victims of past human rights violations. The CCDH gave assurances to AI that receiving compensation would not prevent victims or their families from subsequently seeking legal redress through the courts.

However, despite the authorities' stated commitment to address all past human rights violations, no additional steps were taken to adequately resolve the cases of grave abuses committed between the mid-1960s and the early 1990s, notably the "disappearance" of several hundred people, the majority of them Sahrawis. The deaths of scores of "disappeared" had still not been acknowledged by the authorities by the end of 2001; their families had not been told the whereabouts of the remains or received the bodies for burial. Among them were some 70 Sahrawis who "disappeared" in the secret detention centres of Agdz, Qal'at M'gouna and Laayoune between 1976 and 1991. Investigations to establish responsibility for the grave and systematic human rights violations which occurred in the past were not known to have been opened and the perpetrators, including those responsible for gross violations over long periods, were not brought to justice.

In June retired security agent Ahmed Boukhari disclosed information relating to the "disappearance" of Mehdi Ben Barka, a leading Moroccan political opposition activist, who was abducted in Paris, France, in 1965. Ahmed Boukhari alleged that Mehdi Ben Barka died while being interrogated in a villa south of Paris by Moroccan security agents and that his body was then flown back to Morocco and dissolved in acid.

Ahmed Boukhari was twice unable to appear as a witness at a French judicial inquiry into the kidnapping of Mehdi Ben Barka. He was unable to attend a September hearing after he was sentenced in Morocco to one year's imprisonment, reduced on appeal to three months, for writing bad cheques. In December, he was again unable to attend after he was sentenced to three months' imprisonment in a new trial for defamation of three Moroccan officials, whom Ahmed Boukhari had implicated in involvement in grave human rights violations. The handling and timing of the case suggested that the Moroccan authorities were trying to prevent him from testifying. By the end of 2001, no judicial investigation had been launched in Morocco into alleged state involvement in the death of Mehdi Ben Barka.

Prisoners of conscience and political prisoners

The Moroccan authorities released 56 political prisoners, including prisoners of conscience, following a royal pardon in November.

◻ Morocco's longest serving prisoner of conscience was released. Mohamed Daddach, a Sahrawi, had been arrested in 1979 and was serving a life sentence for trying to desert from the Moroccan security forces into which he had reportedly been forcibly enlisted.

◻ Three Sahrawi prisoners of conscience, Brahim Laghzal, Cheikh Khaya and Laarbi Massoudi, serving four-year prison sentences imposed in 2000 for "threatening state security", were released. The charges related to their alleged connections with the *Frente Popular para la Liberación de Saguia el-Hamra y Río de Oro*, Popular Front for the Liberation of Saguia el-Hamra y Rio de Oro (known as the Polisario Front). Salek Bahaha ould Mahmoud, who was sentenced to four years' imprisonment on a similar charge in a separate trial in 2000, was also released.

Other releases involved people who had been imprisoned following trials since 1999 in connection with demonstrations in September 1999 in the cities of Laayoune and Marrakech which were violently suppressed by the security forces. They had been sentenced, following unfair trials, to prison terms of up to 15 years for, among other things, destruction of property and looting. Allegations that dozens of the protesters had been tortured in detention were not investigated by the courts during their trials.

However, some 30 political prisoners, including a prisoner of conscience, sentenced after unfair trials since the 1970s continued to be detained.

◻ Prisoner of conscience Mustapha Adib, a Moroccan Air Force captain, charged with indiscipline and dishonouring the army, remained in prison. On 21 February, the Supreme Court confirmed a two-and-a-half year prison sentence against him. He had been unfairly tried in 2000 following the publication of an article in a French newspaper which quoted him as denouncing corruption in the Moroccan armed forces.

Political opponents of the government faced intimidation and harassment when exercising their legitimate rights to freedom of expression and association.

◻ The first trials of approximately 130 members and sympathizers of the banned Islamist organization *al-'Adl wa'l-Ihsan*, Justice and Charity, began at the end of January in several cities around Morocco. Most of the defendants were charged with participating in an unarmed gathering liable to disturb public order in connection with demonstrations in December 2000 which were violently dispersed by the security forces. During the year, dozens of people were sentenced to prison terms of up to one year; appeals were still pending at the end of the year.

Human rights defenders

Dozens of human rights defenders were sentenced to prison terms as a direct consequence of their work. Others were prevented from carrying out their work.

◻ On 16 May, 36 human rights defenders were each sentenced to three months' imprisonment and a fine of 3,000 dirhams (around US$300) for organizing an unauthorized demonstration on 9 December 2000. On 21 November 2001, the Court of Appeal in Rabat acquitted them. The trial of the human rights defenders, who included men and women from prominent local human rights organizations, followed calls by the *Association marocaine des droits de l'homme* (AMDH), Moroccan Association for Human Rights, for the authorities to shed light on past human rights abuses. Just days before the demonstration, the AMDH had written to the Moroccan parliament asking for an independent inquiry into the alleged participation of 16 senior Moroccan officials in the torture and "disappearance" of opposition activists. Following the acquittal, the AMDH published an extended list adding 29 new names.

Journalists

Restrictions on freedom of expression continued to be imposed. Journalists were punished for work deemed to be critical of the authorities. Foreign journalists were expelled from the country, certain editions of foreign and domestic publications were banned and Moroccan journalists were sentenced to prison terms.

◻ On 1 March, a Casablanca court sentenced two journalists working for the Moroccan weekly *Le Journal Hebdomadaire* — Aboubakr Jamai and 'Ali 'Amar — to three and two months' imprisonment respectively and a fine of 20,000 dirhams (approximately US$2,000) in addition to damages of two million dirhams (approximately US$200,000). The two men were charged in connection with a series of articles which accused the current Minister of Foreign Affairs of embezzlement while he was Moroccan ambassador to the USA in the late 1990s.

Polisario camps

Freedom of expression, association and movement continued to be restricted in camps near Tindouf in southwestern Algeria controlled by the Polisario Front. Those responsible for human rights abuses in the camps in previous years continued to enjoy impunity. The Polisario authorities failed to hand over perpetrators still resident in the camps to the Algerian authorities to be brought to justice, and the Moroccan authorities failed to bring to justice the perpetrators of abuses in the Polisario camps present on Moroccan territory.

AI country reports/visits
Report
- Morocco/Western Sahara: Freedom of assembly on trial (AI Index: MDE 29/011/2001)

Visits
AI delegates visited Morocco in April and June and were granted an audience with King Mohamed VI in June.

MOZAMBIQUE

REPUBLIC OF MOZAMBIQUE
Head of state: Joaquim Alberto Chissano
Head of government: Pascoal Mocumbi
Capital: Maputo
Population: 18.7 million
Official language: Portuguese
Death penalty: abolitionist for all crimes

Two police officers were convicted of homicide for their involvement in the deaths by suffocation of more than 80 detainees in a police cell in November 2000. However, the authorities failed to investigate allegations of extrajudicial executions and torture following demonstrations in November 2000. Scores of people arrested in connection with the November 2000 demonstrations received trials which were unfair. One other remained in detention awaiting trial.

Background

Political tension continued for most of the year. This focused around allegations by the opposition coalition *Resistência Nacional Moçambicana-União Eleitoral* (RENAMO-UE), Mozambican National Resistence-Electoral Union, of irregularities during the December 1999 elections and around the killing of scores of people, mainly RENAMO-UE members, during civil unrest in November 2000.

In an attempt to restore stability, President Joaquim Alberto Chissano and RENAMO's President, Afonso Dhlakama, held several meetings between January and March to discuss RENAMO's demands for governorships in those provinces where it had obtained a majority in the elections. However, no agreement was reached and the talks collapsed in March.

A parliamentary commission of inquiry, set up to investigate the violence surrounding the November 2000 demonstrations organized by RENAMO in protest at the 1999 election results and subsequent deaths in detention, stalled in January and had not reported its findings by the end of 2001.

No compensation was paid to victims of human rights violations. In February, RENAMO deputies disrupted debates in the National Assembly in protest at its refusal to discuss constitutional reform and a suggestion that RENAMO deputies accused of instigating the November 2000 violence have their right of immunity from prosecution withdrawn. Immunity was not lifted and parliamentarians were not prosecuted.

In March, the Procurator General published a report in which he denounced corruption within the criminal justice system, including the judiciary and the police. The retraining and restructuring of the police force continued throughout the year, as did efforts to remove corrupt officers from the force. About 200 police officers had been dismissed for misconduct and abuses of power by the end of 2001.

Abuses by police

There were further reports of abuses by the police, including beatings and extortion.

In September and again in December, former emigrants to the former German Democratic Republic were severely beaten by members of the Rapid Intervention Police. Several hundred returnees demonstrated outside the Ministry of Labour to demand payment of benefits obtained while working abroad and to which they said they were entitled. No investigation into these incidents was known to have taken place by the end of the year.

Impunity

In July, two police officers were convicted of homicide in connection with the deaths of more than 80 detainees in November 2000. The detainees had died of suffocation in police custody in Montepuez, Cabo Delgado province. Charges against three other officers were withdrawn. However, according to reports, the authorities had not carried out thorough and impartial investigations into these and other reports of deaths in custody. The victims' families did not receive compensation.

There were no investigations into other human rights violations, including into the use of lethal force during the demonstrations in November 2000 and alleged torture and extrajudicial executions afterwards.

Political trials of RENAMO supporters

At the beginning of 2001, 80 mostly RENAMO supporters were in detention in connection with the November 2000 demonstrations. Eleven of them were serving sentences of up to six months' imprisonment after being convicted of charges such as theft, civil unrest and disobeying the authorities. Further arrests of suspected RENAMO members continued in January and February when at least 20 people were arrested in Cabo Delgado province for allegedly participating in the November 2000 demonstrations.

Scores more were tried in 2001. Most of them were tried in January on charges of theft, civil unrest and disobeying the authorities, and were sentenced to periods of imprisonment ranging from one to six months, as well as fines. A further 29 detainees were tried in December.

Most trials fell short of international fair trial standards. They were presided over by judges who in most cases were not legally trained or independent of the government, some being the local representatives of the ruling *Frente de Libertação de Moçambique* (FRELIMO), Mozambique Liberation Front. Most defendants reportedly did not have access to defence lawyers and some were appointed FRELIMO officials to act for them. They were denied the right to appeal against their conviction or sentence. The courts failed to investigate their allegations of torture.

In June, five men arrested in November 2000 in Montepuez — João Maulana Catae, José dos Santos Pintainho, Latifo Alimo, Rodrigues Virgílio Bacar and Secundino Manuel Cinquenta — were convicted of armed rebellion, illegally occupying a police station and releasing prisoners. They were sentenced to 20 years' imprisonment after a trial which appeared to be unfair. They told the court that they had been tortured in detention and had made some of their first statements under duress or coercion. The court made no investigation into these allegations and admitted their statements in evidence.

◻ Rita António was arrested in Montepuez, Cabo Delgado province, in November 2000 and subsequently charged with participating in demonstrations and in the mutilation of the genital organs of a police officer. She was reportedly tortured several times in detention. At her trial in December, the court did not investigate her allegations that she had made some statements to police only under duress; the statements were admitted in evidence. She was convicted and was awaiting sentence at the end of the year.

AI country reports/visits
Visit
An AI delegate visited Mozambique in November and December.

MYANMAR

UNION OF MYANMAR
Head of state and government: General Than Shwe
Capital: Yangon
Population: 48.4 million
Official language: Burmese
Death penalty: retentionist

In January the Special Envoy of the UN Secretary-General for Myanmar announced that a confidential dialogue had been taking place since October 2000 between the ruling State Peace and Development Council (SPDC) and Daw Aung San Suu Kyi, leader of the opposition National League for Democracy (NLD). The dialogue was believed to have continued for most of 2001. However, Aung San Suu Kyi remained under *de facto* house arrest, although international delegations were permitted to visit her. Some 1,600 political prisoners arrested in previous years remained in prison. Almost 220 people were released. Three people were sentenced to death for drug trafficking. Extrajudicial executions and forced labour continued to be reported in the ethnic minority states, particularly Shan and Kayin states.

Background
As in previous years, the army continued to engage in skirmishes with the Karen National Union, the Karenni National Progressive Party, and the Shan State Army-South (SSA-South). Small numbers of combatants in two Mon armed groups also engaged in skirmishes with the SPDC. Sixteen cease-fire agreements negotiated in previous years between the SPDC and various ethnic minority armed opposition groups were maintained.

The International Labour Organisation (ILO) High Level Team visited the country in September and October and the newly appointed UN Special Rapporteur on Myanmar visited in April and October.

Political developments
In February General Tin Oo, a senior SPDC leader, was killed in a helicopter crash. His post of SPDC Secretary II remained vacant at the end of the year. In November, seven ministers were removed from their posts, some of them reportedly for corruption. Ten of the 12 regional military commanders were removed from their positions.

The contents of the dialogue between the SPDC and Aung San Suu Kyi were not revealed but were believed to remain at the confidence-building stage rather than focusing on future political arrangements. Ethnic minorities were not included in the talks as both sides stated that the time was not right for a trilateral dialogue. The frequent attacks in the government-controlled media on Aung San Suu Kyi's character and on the NLD in general ceased. The NLD generally refrained from public statements critical of the government. In August the NLD publicly called for the release of Aung San Suu Kyi and all other political prisoners. Some NLD township offices in Yangon and Mandalay Divisions were allowed to reopen.

Political imprisonment
◻ U Shwe Saw Oo, U Tha Tun Aye, both lawyers and U Khin Maung Gyce, a trader, were allegedly arrested in March and beaten before being sent to Sittwe Prison, Rakhine state. The three, all members of the Arakan League for Democracy, an opposition political party, were detained awaiting trial at the end of the year.
◻ Pastor Gracey, an ethnic Chin Baptist minister, was arrested in February and sentenced in July to two years' hard labour after being convicted of passing information to the Chin National Front, an armed opposition group. She was transferred later the same month to a prison camp in Sagaing Division, amid concerns about her health.

Some 1,600 political prisoners, including hundreds of members of the NLD and other political parties, were held during 2001. Among those who remained imprisoned were U Win Htein, chief aide to Aung San Suu Kyi; U Win Tin, founding NLD leader; and Paw U Tun alias Min Ko Naing, a prominent student leader. At least 52 prisoners, including Paw U Tun, remained imprisoned after completing their sentences. At least 150 student activists remained in jail. Seventeen NLD members of parliament-elect remained in prison.
◻ Saw Naing Naing, an NLD member of parliament-elect who had been rearrested and sentenced to 21 years' imprisonment in 2000 in connection with an NLD

statement calling for the lifting of restrictions on the party, remained in prison at the end of 2001.

▫ U Aye Tha Aung, a prisoner of conscience and leader of the Arakan League for Democracy, sentenced to 21 years' imprisonment in April 2000, remained in poor health.

▫ Zaw Min, who had been arrested in July 1989, remained imprisoned in Mandalay Prison. He was reported to be suffering from severe mental health problems. Having already served his 10-year sentence, he continued to be held under the administrative detention provisions of the 1975 State Protection Law.

▫ Prisoners of conscience Nai Ngwe Thein, Min Soe Lin, and Min Kyi Win, three leaders of the Mon National Democratic Front, an opposition political party, remained in prison. They had been arrested in September 1998 for their alleged support for an NLD call to convene parliament. Min Kyi Win and Min Soe Lin, who were sentenced to seven years' imprisonment, were held in Mawlamyaine Prison, Mon state. Nai Ngwe Thein, aged 76, was held in Insein Prison.

The majority of the people released during the year had completed their sentences or had been held without charge or trial. Scores of those released were people who had been detained in September 2000 at the Yangon train station when Aung San Suu Kyi, who was attempting to go to Mandalay, was placed under *de facto* house arrest. Thirty-nine members of parliament-elect who had been detained without charge or trial since September 1998 for attempting to meet in Yangon were released.

Among those released in July were: the writer Daw San San Nwe, who had been arrested in 1994 and sentenced to 10 years' imprisonment for having contact with foreigners; and comedians U Pa Pa Lay and U Lu Zaw, who had been arrested in 1996 and sentenced to seven years' imprisonment in connection with a comedy performance.

Prison conditions

Prison conditions were believed to have improved since the International Committee for the Red Cross (ICRC), began to visit prisons in 1999. However, concerns about overcrowding and medical care remained. In 1997 the SPDC reportedly issued 11 instructions about the treatment of prisoners which were also said to have resulted in some improvements, although the regulations were not publicly available. At least 64 political prisoners had died in custody since 1988.

▫ Khin Maung Myint, an NLD youth leader, died of unknown causes in Kalay Prison in July. He had been arrested in 1997 and sentenced to eight years' imprisonment after attempting to organize a meeting with NLD youth activists and Aung San Suu Kyi. He had been in good health at the time of arrest.

Forced labour

The military continued to compel civilians to perform forced labour in the seven ethnic minority states. In Rakhine state, forced labour of Rohingyas, a Muslim ethnic minority group, continued in Maungdaw and Buthidaung townships, although there were reports of people being paid for their labour and of decreases in demands for forced labour in some areas. Forced labour also continued in some areas of the Kayin, Mon, and Shan states, and in the Tanintharyi Division in the east. The practice, which included carrying supplies for patrolling troops, and working on military farms and bases, was associated with the army's counter-insurgency activities against ethnic minority armed opposition groups in these regions. Prisoners convicted of criminal offences and sentenced to work in labour camps were also used as forced labour. Deaths from exhaustion and lack of medical care continued to be reported.

▫ A member of the Mon ethnic minority from Chaung Pya, Yebyu township, Tanintharyi Division, was forced by Light Infantry Battalion 273 to carry 60mm mortar shells for five days until his escape in January. He was kicked in the back for walking too slowly.

Extrajudicial executions

Extrajudicial executions of ethnic minority civilians taking no active part in the hostilities continued to be reported, particularly in the context of the army's counter-insurgency activities, when civilians were punished for alleged contacts with armed opposition groups.

▫ Sa Ti Ya, a 45-year-old Shan traditional healer and farmer, was taken from his house in Tun Hing, Murngnai township, Shan state, by SPDC Unit 99, and accused of being a member of the SSA-South. After being beaten he was reportedly shot in the back of the head twice and died instantly.

International initiatives

In April the UN Commission on Human Rights adopted by consensus its 10th resolution extending the mandate of the Special Rapporteur on Myanmar for another year. The resolution expressed concern about the high level of human rights violations, while welcoming some improvements. In November a similar resolution was adopted by consensus at the UN General Assembly.

In July the UN Economic and Social Council (ECOSOC) met and took note of ILO action on forced labour in Myanmar and requested that it be kept informed of future developments.

In November the ILO's High Level Team submitted its report to the ILO's Governing Body. The report concluded that forced labour of civilians was continuing, particularly near military camps, in spite of the SPDC's new decree, issued in October 2000 — SPDC Order Supplementing Order 1/99 — which reinforced the prohibition of forced labour by providing for punishments for both civilian and military authorities found responsible for the practice. The report acknowledged that progress had been made by the SPDC in halting the practice, but that in counter-insurgency areas it was an ongoing problem. The report recommended that there be a long-term ILO presence in the country to receive complaints about forced labour and to provide assistance to the government in eradicating the practice. The SPDC responded by stating that while they were ready to receive ILO visits, they were not in a position to accept a long-term presence.

In May the USA renewed limited economic sanctions against Myanmar. The European Union (EU) Common Position, which included the freezing of SPDC members' funds in EU countries, was renewed in April, and again in October when renewal was accompanied by a first package of modest but significant gestures in recognition of the slight improvement in the political situation. An EU troika visit took place in January.

The UN Special Envoy for Myanmar visited the country four times. He urged the SPDC to release political prisoners, with priority for members of parliament elected in the 1990 general elections but never allowed to take up office; the elderly; women; and those who had completed their sentences. The SPDC said that releases were being considered on a case-by-case basis.

Australia continued to sponsor a series of human rights training sessions for Myanmar government officials, including police and army personnel. The sessions took place in July, September and October.

AI country reports/visits
Reports
- Myanmar: Min Ko Naing – student leader and prisoner of conscience (AI Index: ASA 16/001/2001)
- Myanmar: U Win Tin – journalist and prisoner of conscience (AI Index: ASA 16/005/2001)
- Myanmar: Prisoners of political repression (AI Index: ASA 16/006/2001)
- Myanmar: Ethnic minorities – targets of repression (AI Index: ASA 16/014/2001)
- Myanmar: Torture of ethnic minority women (AI Index: ASA 16/017/2001)

NAMIBIA

REPUBLIC OF NAMIBIA
Head of state: Samuel Nujoma
Head of government: Hage Geingob
Capital: Windhoek
Population: 1.8 million
Death penalty: abolitionist for all crimes

Reports continued of "disappearances", torture and intimidation by the security forces in the Caprivi and Kavango provinces. Almost 130 detainees, most of them prisoners of conscience, remained in custody. The government sought to impose restrictions on freedom of expression. Gays and lesbians were harassed and assaulted by the police following inflammatory statements by the authorities.

Background
The Namibian Defence Force (NDF) launched several cross-border operations in support of the Angolan army into territory in southern Angola held by the opposition *União Nacional para a Independência Total de Angola* (UNITA), National Union for the Total Independence of Angola. Large numbers of Angolan refugees continued to flee the conflict to Namibia. In West Caprivi, Namibian police and armed forces reportedly participated in their forcible return to Angola. There were continuing concerns that government plans to relocate thousands of refugees to rural areas would disrupt marginalized indigenous ethnic San communities.

Violations on the border with Angola
NDF troops were responsible for human rights violations in Caprivi and Kavango provinces bordering Angola. Many inhabitants fled the area to neighbouring Botswana, particularly members of the Kxoe San community. Soldiers reportedly threatened them, and assaulted and detained them for violating a ban on their traditional livelihoods of collecting firewood, grass and wild-growing foodstuffs. The military denied harassing them and said the restrictions on their movements were for their own protection.

In July, a High Court application was filed for the release of 15 members of a Kxoe San community from Mutc'iku in West Caprivi. The 15 "disappeared" after they were arrested by the Namibian security forces in August 2000 on suspicion of collaborating with UNITA insurgents. The military told the court that they had escaped custody to Angola, despite earlier denials by both military and police that they had ever been in custody. Police officials said in court that they had only learned of the arrests and alleged escapes in August 2001. Evidence before the court raised serious doubts about the men's whereabouts. One detainee, Sandre Dikoro, had sent a note to his wife asking for cigarettes from a military detention centre six days after he was said to have escaped. In October a soldier told the court that he had seen another detainee in a detention centre some days after it was alleged he had escaped. In December, the court ruled that it could not be proved that the 15 were still in government hands and dismissed the application.

◻ Also in July, the NDF arrested five Kxoe San men on suspicion of hiding arms on an island in the Kavango river. Soldiers shot dead one of the men — Hans Dikuwa — near Bagani Military Base. The military said he was shot while trying to escape. A military autopsy concluded that he died from drowning. Eyewitnesses, however, alleged he was extrajudicially executed by soldiers. In September, the four remaining detainees were released on bail. They said that for 10 days soldiers had tortured them, including by forcing them to dig their own graves and lie in them, then firing rifles near their heads.

Delay in trial of Caprivi detainees
By the end of 2001, most of a group of 128 detainees had been awaiting trial for more than two years. They were among more than 300 people arrested following an attack in 1999 on a military base in northeastern Caprivi by members of an armed separatist group. At least 70 appeared to be prisoners of conscience. The 128 faced more than 200 charges ranging from murder and attempted murder to unauthorized crossing of the border. Investigations by the government into allegations that most had been tortured failed to lead to any prosecutions in 2001; as a result, several police officers named in torture allegations remained on active duty. Some of the 128 detainees alleged that police threatened and ill-treated them, and in one case offered a bribe, when taking them outside the prison in connection with continuing police investigations into the charges against them. In December, the High Court ordered that legal aid be provided for the 128 accused. The government's appeal to the Supreme Court against the ruling had not been heard by the end of 2001.

Freedom of expression
There were moves to restrict freedom of expression. Senior officials censured the press and non-governmental organizations, withdrawing state advertising from *The Namibian* newspaper after it criticized government policies and asking the civil service not to purchase the paper.

In September, the government introduced a draft Defence bill in the National Assembly that contained vague, broad and possibly unconstitutional infringements on the freedom of the press in the name of protecting national security. The bill would make the disclosure of "unauthorized information" deemed likely to endanger national security punishable by up to five years' imprisonment. It would also permit the military to seize journalists' photographs, film, negatives, sketches, plans, models or notes taken of any area under military control. By the end of 2001, the bill had not been debated.

Gays and lesbians
In March, addressing students at the University of Namibia in Windhoek, President Nujoma said police must arrest, imprison and deport homosexuals. This followed other statements that the government would deport foreign gays and lesbians. Homosexuality is not a criminal offence in law and homosexual acts were last prosecuted in the late 1980s as an "unnatural sex crime" under common law.

In May, officers of the paramilitary Special Field Force detained and assaulted Namibian men suspected of being gay. The government subsequently announced that disciplinary action would be instituted against officers involved in harassment.

Rule of law
Senior officials criticized the judiciary after rulings unfavourable to the government. In February the High Court retrospectively found the Minister of Home Affairs, Jerry Ekandjo, in contempt of court after the authorities had ignored a High Court order in October 2000 to release detainee José Sikunda. The police only released him in November 2000 when the High Court warned it would hold the Minister in contempt.

AI country reports/visits
Visit
AI delegates visited Namibia in November and were granted access to prisons in Windhoek and Grootfontein.

NEPAL

KINGDOM OF NEPAL
Head of state: King Gyanendra Bir Bikram Shah Dev (replaced King Birendra Bir Bikram Shah Dev in June)
Head of government: Sher Bahadur Deuba (replaced Girija Prasad Koirala in July)
Capital: Kathmandu
Population: 23.6 million
Official language: Nepali
Death penalty: abolitionist for all crimes
2001 treaty ratifications/signatures: Optional Protocol to the UN Women's Convention

Unlawful killings, "disappearances", torture and arbitrary arrest and detention by police and army were reported in the context of the "people's war" declared by the Communist Party of Nepal (Maoist) (CPN-Maoist) in 1996. The CPN-Maoist was responsible for deliberate killings, hostage-taking, execution-style killings and torture. The killing of the royal family in June provoked a period of political instability but there was a marked improvement from July when both sides maintained a cease-fire.

However, the human rights situation deteriorated sharply in November after the CPN-Maoist broke the cease-fire and a state of emergency was declared and the army was deployed to combat the CPN-Maoist. Impunity remained a concern.

Background
In the early part of the year, there was major political instability, including a stand-off between the Nepal Congress (NC) government and the Communist Party of Nepal (United Marxist Leninist) (CPN-UML), the main parliamentary opposition, over allegations of corruption and the government's handling of the CPN-Maoist "people's war". The CPN-Maoist increased attacks on police stations. In April they organized elections in several mid-western districts. By October, they had set up 21 "people's governments" running parallel to the government's local administration at district level. Similar bodies were set up at ward and village level in many other districts.

Constitutional crisis and aftermath
On 1 June, King Birendra Bir Bikram Shah, the Queen and eight other members of the royal family were killed, reportedly by Crown Prince Dipendra. Immediately after the massacre, Prince Dipendra was pronounced King, and Prince Gyanendra, King Birendra's brother, was appointed regent. However, after King Dipendra died on 4 June, Prince Gyanendra was pronounced King. After a period of instability in the immediate aftermath of the massacre, with many people doubting the official version about the killings, a realignment of political forces took place. While the CPN-Maoist initially pushed its longstanding demand for the establishment of a republic in the wake of the killings, mainstream political parties confirmed their commitment to constitutional monarchy.

On 13 July the army was for the first time directly deployed against the CPN-Maoist. Soldiers were sent to Holeri and Nuwagoan Village Development Committees (VDCs) in Rolpa district with instructions to obtain the release of 69 police officers and two civilians, who had been abducted by the CPN-Maoist on the previous day during an attack on Holeri police post. Reports of what happened in this remote area were unclear. There was apparently no engagement in combat, and the army withdrew after several days. Prime Minister Girija Prasad Koirala resigned shortly afterwards.

The newly appointed Prime Minister Sher Bahadur Deuba and the CPN-Maoist swiftly agreed a cease-fire on 23 July. Three rounds of talks were held between delegations from the government and the CPN-Maoist. However, negotiations broke down over the political demands of the CPN-Maoist, including the establishment of an interim government, constitutional assembly and republic.

State of emergency
On 23 November, the CPN-Maoist broke the cease-fire and attacked army, police and public property in 42 districts. Three days later, a state of emergency was declared, and a Terrorist and Disruptive Activities (Prevention and Control) Ordinance (TADO) was promulgated. The CPN-Maoist were declared "terrorists" and the army was fully deployed.

The imposition of the state of emergency was accompanied by the suspension of several fundamental rights, including the right to constitutional remedy (apart from habeas corpus), the right to assembly, the right to freedom of thought and expression and the right not to be held in preventive detention without sufficient grounds. There was concern that the unspecific definition of "terrorist" under TADO would give wide powers allowing for detainees to be held in preventive detention for up to 90 days, with an extension of up to 180 days on the consent of the Home Ministry, and could lead to people being detained for expressing peaceful political views.

Changes to the legal and institutional framework
In January, changes in the legal and institutional framework were introduced via Ordinances, including the creation of a paramilitary police force (so-called Armed Police Force) and the granting of additional powers to "maintain or arrange for maintaining peace, security and order within the region" to the administrators of the five developmental regions. The government also formed a Special Court under the Special Court Act to hear cases against people charged under the Anti-State Crimes and Penalties Act, 1989. In August the Ordinances were approved by parliament and became law.

The government introduced amendments to the rules issued under the Public Security Act in June, to widen the grounds for detention. Although the amendments were withdrawn in November, political activists continued to be repeatedly rearrested under the Act, despite court orders for their release.

Extrajudicial executions
In the first weeks after its deployment in November, the army was accused of killing civilians during "cordon and search" operations, and shootings from helicopters at alleged Maoists. In one incident at Bargadi, Dang district, on 28 November, 11 farmers were shot dead by an army patrol. Although some of them may have been sympathizers of the CPN-Maoist, eyewitnesses claimed that none of them were armed and that soldiers deliberately shot them.

On 3 and 4 June, police reportedly shot dead three people and wounded scores of demonstrators who had taken to the streets after the killings of the royal family.

In April the UN Special Rapporteur on extrajudicial, summary or arbitrary executions reported on her visit to Nepal in February 2000 to the UN Commission on Human Rights. She stressed the "urgent need to put in place strong, independent and credible mechanisms to investigate and prosecute alleged human rights abuses".

'Disappearances'/ unacknowledged detention
A number of cases of "disappearance" were reported during the year. Further evidence emerged that

prisoners were held by police in secret detention. More than 5,000 people arrested under the TADO were held in unacknowledged detention by police and army, sometimes for several weeks. Sixteen students arrested in Kathmandu in December 2000 were held in incommunicado detention for a month. In March, the government published a list of 282 people held in custody for their alleged involvement in "terrorist activities" and 12 others said to have been held in solitary confinement. Among them was Ishwari Dahal whose whereabouts had been unknown since he was arrested in September 2000. The list contained only three of the 73 CPN-Maoists whose whereabouts the CPN-Maoist leadership had urged the government to clarify.

▭ Shiva Prasad Sharma, aged 31, "disappeared" after he was reportedly taken away in a vehicle on 24 February near Paraspur, Nepalgunj, Banke district, by three men in plain clothes, believed to be police officers.

Torture and ill-treatment
There were several reports of torture, including rape, by police. The army was also responsible for torture, including subjecting prisoners to mock executions.

▭ Padam Bahadur Magar, a 46-year-old businessman from Ward No 4, Kalika VDC, Kanchanpur district, and an active member of the *Rastriya Jana Morcha*, a communist political party, was reportedly tortured after he was arrested on 23 March on suspicion of being a member of the CPN-Maoist. He alleged that while in custody at the District Police Office in Kanchanpur, police punched, kicked and beat him with a stick all over his body, including on his genitals, and also threatened to kill him.

▭ In June, a 14-year-old girl was raped at Pattharkot VDC-3, Sarlahi district. The police officer allegedly responsible was transferred from the area, but no other action was taken against him.

Arbitrary arrest and detention
▭ The arrests on 6 June of Yubaraj Ghimirey, editor-in-chief of the main Nepali newspaper *Kantipur*, and his colleagues, Binod Raj Gyawali and Kailash Sirohiya, were seen as a warning to the media to refrain from commenting adversely on the massacre of the royal family. Their arrests were connected to the publication in *Kantipur* of an opinion piece by Baburam Bhattarai, a CPN-Maoist leader, in which he accused India and the USA of being behind the royal massacre and urged army personnel not to support the new King. Amid widespread protests, they were released on bail on 15 June. The case against them was subsequently withdrawn.

▭ Krishna Sen was rearrested soon after he was released from jail on 10 March on the orders of a full bench of the Supreme Court, including the Chief Justice, and "disappeared" for five days afterwards. He was released amid widespread protests.

▭ Several human rights defenders and more than 30 journalists were among more than 5,000 people arrested by army and police under the TADO.

Abuses by the CPN-Maoist
Several members of mainstream political parties, particularly of the NC and the CPN-UML, were killed by the CPN-Maoist. The abduction of civilians and police, and the linking of their release to certain conditions, became a prominent feature of the "people's war".

▭ Members of the CPN-Maoist were responsible for the execution-style killing of eight police officers who were among 28 who had surrendered to them at Toli, Dailekh district, on 7 April.

▭ Mukti Prasad Sharma, president of the Pyuthan District Committee of the NC and former member of parliament, was abducted on 22 May from his home at Tikuri, Bijuwar VDC, Pyuthan district. The next day, *Jana Ahwan*, a weekly magazine known to be supportive of the CPN-Maoists, reported that the leadership of the CPN-Maoist had demanded the release of five of its members in prison or reported as "disappeared", in return for the release of Mukti Prasad Sharma. He was allowed to return home on 12 July. The next day, Lokendra Bista, one of the five CPN-Maoists who had been imprisoned since 1996, was released.

▭ During a press conference on 18 October, a CPN-Maoist leader admitted that 11 people taken captive had been killed. Among those known to have been "sentenced to death" and "executed" was Bhadra Sanjyal, a woman from Ward No. 2, Siuna VDC, Kalikot district. She was killed in mid-July after she was found guilty by the "people's court" of passing information to the police.

Impunity
Despite some moves in isolated cases to provide redress to victims of human rights violations, official accountability was widely lacking. An assistant sub-inspector attached to the district police office in Sindhuli district was sentenced in February to four years' imprisonment for raping an 18-year-old woman, Himali Gole, in early 2000. The court also ordered that half of his property be transferred to the victim.

Eight police officers charged with the murder of Suk Bahadur Lama, who had died in custody in 1999, were acquitted by the Nawalparasi district court in November. The family was given Rs50,000 (US$657) in financial assistance by the government — the first time the government had provided such assistance to relatives of someone who had died in police custody.

National Human Rights Commission (NHRC)
The effective functioning of the NHRC was hampered by insufficient financing and staffing. The government allocated only 5 million rupees against the 25 million rupees requested by the Commission for the year. There was a lack of cooperation from the civil service, particularly the home ministry and police.

AI country reports/ visits
Reports
- Nepal: Make torture a crime (AI Index: ASA 31/002/2001)
- Nepal: State of emergency may go too far (AI Index: ASA 31/014/2001)

NEW ZEALAND

NEW ZEALAND
Head of state: Queen Elizabeth II, represented by Michael Hardie Boys
Head of government: Helen Clark
Capital: Wellington
Population: 3.8 million
Official language: English
Death penalty: abolitionist for all crimes
2001 treaty ratifications/signatures: Optional Protocol to the UN Children's Convention on the involvement of children in armed conflict

An inquest into a fatal police shooting during 2000 began but was postponed indefinitely. Immigration officials expanded their powers to detain asylum-seekers.

Background
The government started to implement a program of improvements to New Zealand's system of human rights protection and promotion, especially on discrimination. In September, human rights were made a central criterion and a priority goal for New Zealand's program of overseas aid.

In December, parliament passed the Human Rights Amendment Act, based on a long-term review into New Zealand's compliance with its international obligations, called "Consistency 2000".

Under the new legislation, the government was obliged to comply fully with human rights standards, including those on discrimination based on age, disability or sexual orientation. The Act clarified and extended government responsibilities, reformed the national Human Rights Commission and strengthened human rights dispute resolution mechanisms and made them more accessible.

New bodies were established, including an Office for Human Rights Proceedings, with powers to pursue litigation in cases not resolved through mediation, and a Human Rights Review Tribunal, whose decisions are legally binding. The law also gave the Human Rights Commission limited monitoring and inquiry powers on government decisions affecting immigration, including the rights of asylum-seekers and refugees.

Police shooting inquest
In June, the Coroner's inquest into the fatal police shooting of Steven Wallace at Waitara in 2000 was adjourned, and in September indefinitely postponed, because his family started a private murder prosecution against a police officer. Under New Zealand law, inquests can only resume after the completion of such private prosecution. The shooting had prompted public debate about police use of lethal force and an inquiry was held, headed by a retired judge. In April, he recommended greater investigative powers for the Police Complaints Authority in serious cases, so that its investigations become less dependent on the police itself. An internal police review commissioned in June in response to Steven Wallace's death reportedly warned of an increasing reliance of officers on their guns.

Asylum-seekers
In August, Prime Minister Helen Clark committed New Zealand to accept up to 150 mostly Afghan refugees who had been rescued from an Indonesian boat by a Norwegian ship and denied the right to claim asylum in Australia. After their registration by the UN High Commissioner for Refugees on the Pacific island of Nauru, where they had been taken by the Australian authorities, New Zealand officials transferred 131 men, women and children to the Mangere Refugee Centre at Auckland, where they were held until granted refugee status in December.

In September, the immigration service increased its powers to detain asylum-seekers, including children and juveniles, for prolonged periods — possibly beyond those permissible under international norms. They appeared to be in conflict with the government's public assertions that the detention of asylum-seekers was not a solution to concerns about refugee applicants expressed by some politicians following the attacks in the USA of 11 September.

NICARAGUA

REPUBLIC OF NICARAGUA
Head of state and government: Arnoldo Alemán Lacayo
Capital: Managua
Population: 5.2 million
Official language: Spanish
Death penalty: abolitionist for all crimes

Human rights defenders faced threats and harassment. The National Police used excessive force against demonstrators and people in their custody.

Background
A general election was held in November. Enrique Bolaños, of the ruling *Partido Liberal Constitucionalista* (PLC), Constitutionalist Liberal Party, was elected President and was due to take office in January 2002. Changes to the electoral rules agreed in 1999 between the PLC and the opposition *Frente Sandinista de Liberación Nacional* (FSLN), Sandinista National Liberation Front, prevented smaller parties from presenting candidates or, if they did not gain a specified percentage of votes in the election, forced them to disband. The agreement also guaranteed seats in the National Assembly for outgoing President Arnoldo

Alemán — ensuring impunity for human rights violations or accusations of corruption during his term in office — and for the candidate who came second, FSLN leader Daniel Ortega.

Human rights defenders
Threats against and harassment of human rights defenders continued.

☐ The government continued to harass Dorothy Granada, a US nurse in her 70s. It had alleged in 2000 that the clinic where she worked had, among other things, carried out abortions and treated members of an armed group of ex-soldiers, the *Frente Unido Andrés Castro* (FUAC), Andrés Castro United Front. Despite repeated defeats before the courts and a resolution in her support by the Human Rights Procurator's Office, the government continued accusing her of unlawful activities and attempting to deport her. In February she came out of hiding after a deportation order against her was lifted. However, a Supreme Court ruling was still pending — on the government's appeal against a December 2000 court decision that she was a legal resident — when her residence permit expired in September and she had to leave the country.

☐ The government intensified its smear campaign against Vilma Núñez de Escorcia, president of the *Centro Nicaragüense de Derechos Humanos* (CENIDH), Nicaraguan Centre for Human Rights. Police investigations into repeated telephone death threats against her were reportedly inadequate. The authorities repeated claims that CENIDH had links with FUAC. However, in May the Attorney General officially dismissed the government's claims as unfounded.

National police
Actions by National Police officers during demonstrations and other police operations were reported to be unnecessarily violent.

☐ In February Carlos Adolfo García Berríos was reported to have been arbitrarily detained and beaten, while handcuffed, in a police vehicle. He suffered cuts to his face and head.

☐ In May, villagers from Mulukukú denounced excessive use of force during police operations following community disturbances in April in which a policeman was killed. According to reports, riot police entered the community before daybreak, firing tear gas, forcing people out of their homes and beating them. A number of children were said to have been severely affected by tear gas.

AI country reports/ visits
Report
- Nicaragua: Open letter to presidential candidates (AI Index: AMR 43/004/2001)

NIGER

REPUBLIC OF THE NIGER
Head of state: Mamadou Tandja
Head of government: Hama Amadou
Capital: Niamey
Population: 11.2 million
Official language: French
Death penalty: abolitionist in practice

A number of students were detained without trial for several weeks or months and two were still held at the end of 2001. Journalists were detained, harassed and threatened. There was continuing concern at the failure to investigate serious human rights violations, including the 1999 killing of former President Ibrahim Baré Maïnassara, by members of the presidential guard.

Detention without trial of students
At least 10 students, including Ousmane Abdelmoumine, secretary general of the *Union des étudiants nigériens de l'Université de Niamey*, Union of Nigerian Students at Niamey University, were held without trial for up to several months following clashes in February with security forces in Niamey in which a gendarme was killed and several students were wounded. The students were charged with "assaulting security forces" and "participating in violent protests". Most were released but two, including the secretary general of the students' union, remained in detention at the end of 2001.

Impunity
Despite public protests, no investigations were begun into serious human rights violations during the period of military rule from 1996 to 1999.

☐ The party of former President Baré Maïnassara, the *Rassemblement pour la démocratie et le progrès*, Rally for Democracy and Progress, continued to press for an international inquiry into his death in a military coup in April 1999. In April 2001 the party sought an amendment to the July 1999 Constitution, which included an amnesty for all those involved in the April 1999 coup. The National Assembly rejected the proposal.

☐ In May, six military officers arrested on suspicion of kidnapping and torturing Major Djibrilla Hamidou Hima, spokesperson for the former military government, were provisionally released. No reason was given by the court. It was not clear whether they had been formally charged.

Harassment of journalists
Several journalists were harassed by the police during the year.

☐ Traoré Daouda Amadou, publishing manager of the privately owned weekly newspaper *Matinfo*, was charged with "disseminating false news" after the publication of an article alleging that President Mamadou Tandja had gone to Morocco for medical treatment. Traoré Daouda Amadou complained that he was harassed and intimidated by the authorities, who offered to withdraw the complaint if he published a denial. Hours before the opening of the trial in May, the President dropped the charges.

NIGERIA

FEDERAL REPUBLIC OF NIGERIA
Head of state and government: Olusegun Obasanjo
Capital: Abuja
Population: 116.9 million
Official language: English
Death penalty: retentionist
2001 treaty ratifications/signatures: UN Convention against Torture; Rome Statute of the International Criminal Court; African Charter on the Rights and Welfare of the Child

The security forces continued to act with impunity. They were reported to have extrajudicially executed more than 130 people in one reprisal attack on civilians. At least one person was shot dead by the paramilitary police in the Niger Delta in a reportedly unlawful killing. No one was brought to justice for killings perpetrated by the security forces in previous years. At least four death sentences were passed by High Courts and 24 upheld on appeal. Under new penal codes and laws of criminal procedure inspired by *Sharia* (Islamic law), which extended the application of cruel, inhuman and degrading punishments, three people were sentenced to death, two by stoning; they were not executed. Several people were sentenced to having their hands amputated, and several floggings were carried out. Vigilante groups, some with explicit backing by state authorities, continued to be responsible for acts of unlawful detention, torture and killings, especially in the southeast. Members of politically active groups were repeatedly detained without trial.

Background

Violent intercommunal clashes increased, leaving hundreds dead and displacing tens of thousands of people internally. Some of the clashes, especially in Kaduna, Kano and Jos, were linked to tensions between Christians and Muslims.

The Human Rights Violations Investigation Commission, known as the Oputa Panel, continued to hear testimonies from witnesses to human rights violations committed between 1966 and the return to civilian rule in May 1999, including during the civil war of 1967 to 1970. Although President Olusegun Obasanjo appeared several times before the Commission, some former military heads of state repeatedly refused to respond to summonses issued by the Commission in its attempts to investigate high-profile cases such as the death in 1986 of journalist Dele Giwa or the 1995 trial and execution of writer Ken Saro-Wiwa and eight other Ogoni activists.

Oil and gas spills in the oil-rich Niger Delta area, often blamed by companies on deliberate damage to equipment such as well-heads and pipelines, frequently led to explosions and fires which killed and injured numerous people. In a number of incidents, gangs of young men attacked and took hostage company employees in Delta and Rivers States. Although some disputes were resolved peaceably through negotiations by company management and the security forces, some provoked intercommunal violence. The root causes of continuing human rights violations in the oil producing areas of Nigeria remained largely unaddressed.

The Minister of Justice and Attorney-General of the Federation, Chief Bola Ige, was murdered in December, apparently in a political assassination.

Killings by the security forces

Nigerian security forces continued to act with impunity and were responsible for at least one extrajudicial execution in the Niger Delta area and large-scale killings in Benue State. No independent investigations were carried out into allegations of excessive use of force or extrajudicial executions made in connection with these incidents, or into other killings by the security forces since the return to civilian rule in May 1999, including in Odi in 1999.

In June, Friday Nwiido, aged 29, was shot by the paramilitary Mobile Police in Baen, Rivers State, in the Niger Delta area and died during transport to health facilities. He had been in dispute about pay with his former employer, the Shell Petroleum Development Company of Nigeria (SPDC), and the police were looking for him after he was accused of using a company vehicle without permission. He was reportedly unarmed and did not constitute a threat when he was shot as he responded to a request to report to the police.

On 22 October army officers went to the area around the town of Zaki Biam in Benue State, close to the Taraba State border in central Nigeria, where 19 soldiers had been killed two weeks earlier. They were seeking those responsible and to recover stolen weapons. Soldiers had been based in the area to quell intercommunal violence between the Tiv and Jukun ethnic communities. Over the next few days, more than 130 civilians — women and children among them — were deliberately shot dead or killed as a result of indiscriminate shelling, apparently in reprisal for the killing of the soldiers. Men in several villages in the area were reportedly assembled before being summarily shot. Contradicting early army denials of involvement, officials in Benue and Taraba States, senior police officers, members of the National

Assembly, and Nigerian and international human rights organizations, all denounced the killings as extrajudicial executions. The National Assembly set up an inquiry into the killings, but no results had been made public by the end of 2001.

Death penalty

After no death sentences in 2000, at least four death sentences were passed by High Courts and 24 were confirmed on appeal by the Supreme Court. Most followed convictions for murder and some dated back for more than a decade.

At least three death sentences were passed by lower courts under new penal legislation and codes, including new codes of criminal procedure, recently introduced in several states in northern Nigeria and based on *Sharia*.

The new laws introduced a mandatory death penalty for adultery not previously punishable by death and allowed the application of the death penalty for other sexual offences on a discretionary basis. In some states legislation initially made no requirement for defendants in capital cases to be legally represented in court. Although they are punishable offences, sexual intercourse between members of the same sex, child abuse and adultery do not attract the death penalty under the federal Penal Code for Northern Nigeria, which remains applicable to non-Muslims.

So-called *Sharia* courts, lower courts in the hierarchy of the Nigerian judicial system, were given jurisdiction to hand down death sentences, a power formerly reserved to the High Courts. Previously, the lower courts used *Sharia* legal concepts only to determine cases in civil and personal matters. It was unclear to what extent the new legislation guaranteed constitutional rights of appeal to the higher federal courts. Rules of evidence and procedure used in criminal matters in the *Sharia* courts differed from those applied in the Magistrates' Courts, and discriminated against women.

◻ Attahiru Umar, aged in his thirties, was sentenced to death by stoning in Kebbi State in September. He was convicted on charges of homosexuality in connection with the sexual abuse of a young boy. No appeal was known to have been made to a higher court. The sentence was not known to have been carried out by the end of 2001.

◻ In October Safiya Yakubu Hussaini, aged 30, was sentenced to death by stoning in Sokoto State after being convicted of adultery, under a law which violates international standards of human rights. At her first trial she suffered discrimination on the grounds of her gender: she was convicted on the basis of inadequate evidence, including that she was pregnant while reportedly no longer married; however, the court did not investigate the child's paternity or her allegation that she had been raped by a married man. In November she was granted leave to appeal and subsequently appealed to the Sokoto State *Sharia* Court of Appeal. In December the Federal Minister of Justice publicly declared that she would not be executed. By the end of 2001 no decision had been given on her appeal.

◻ Sani Yakubu Rodi was convicted of murder in Katsina in November and sentenced to death by hanging. He pleaded not guilty at an initial hearing in July but changed his plea to guilty in September. He did not lodge an appeal.

Cruel, inhuman and degrading punishments

The new laws applicable to Muslims in northern Nigeria also introduced cruel, inhuman or degrading punishments, including amputation of limbs and flogging, for offences such as consumption of alcohol.

Many of those convicted and punished under the new legislation were from an economically deprived background, had received little if any formal education and were unaware of their legal rights of representation and appeal. Provisions for the protection of minors under the Penal Code for Northern Nigeria were not matched in the new penal codes.

Several people were sentenced to have hands amputated for theft or armed robbery. They included at least one child whose sentence was not carried out. At least three amputations took place. Several men and women were sentenced to floggings, mostly following convictions for sexual offences or for the consumption or sale of alcohol. Floggings were routinely carried out, sometimes within hours of conviction.

◻ In January Bariya Ibrahima Magazu, a teenage mother reportedly under 17 years old, was flogged 100 times with a cane in Zamfara State, after being convicted of pre-marital sexual intercourse in September 2000. She was not legally represented at her trial, and defence lawyers she appointed to lodge an appeal were told by court officials that the sentence would not be carried out before her appeal was heard by a higher court. However, the sentence was carried out before her rights of appeal had been exhausted and before the date given to her lawyers by court officials. Different standards of evidence were applied to her and to the three men she accused of coercing her into having sex with them. The men, all of them married, were not charged, tried or punished.

◻ In July, 15-year-old Ali Abubakar was convicted of theft in Kebbi State and sentenced to amputation of his hand, despite being a minor. It was unclear whether he had legal representation at his trial. In August, the Special Rapporteur on Women of Nigeria's National Human Rights Commission was given assurances by officials in Kebbi State that the punishment would not be carried out.

Vigilante brutality and killings

Throughout the year vigilante groups were responsible for unlawful detention, acts of violence, torture and killings. In some northern states of Nigeria, local *Sharia* enforcement committees, also known as *Hizba* committees, reported alleged offenders of the new penal codes to the police and directly to the new *Sharia* courts. Their legal status and relationship with the courts remained unclear. In southwest Nigeria, the Oodua People's Congress, an organization promoting Yoruba ethnic interests, was banned in April after members were accused of fomenting violence in which dozens of people died, mostly northerners and including some police officers. In the southeast, some state governments reportedly endorsed the activities of vigilante groups in the fight against crime.

◻ Members of the so-called Bakassi Boys, legally recognized as the Anambra Vigilante Service and logistically supported by the Anambra State administration, publicly killed four people in January, one person in May and 36 in late June in Onitsha, the state capital. The Anambra State authorities took no action to investigate the killings or to clarify the relationship of the vigilante group with the security forces and the state authorities. Several officers of the police, a federal agency, reportedly died in action against members of the Bakassi Boys.

Political imprisonment

Leading members and supporters of the Oodua People's Congress and the Movement for the Actualisation of the Sovereign State of Biafra (MASSOB), two politically active groups campaigning for greater autonomy for their ethnic and territorial constituencies, were arrested on a regular basis, often to be released without trial. Neither organization has clarified its position on the use and advocacy of violence in their political campaigns.

◻ MASSOB leader Ralph Uwazuruike was arrested several times, the latest in August after he attended a meeting in Lagos. Three other members of the organization were also arrested. They were detained for two weeks before being released without charge or trial.

◻ Frederick Fasehun and Ganiyu Adams, leaders of two factions of the Oodua People's Congress, were arrested on several occasions. Following the arrests of Frederick Fasehun in September and Ganiyu Adams in October, they were charged with unlawful possession of arms and instigating violence. Both were released on bail and charges were withdrawn in November.

AI country reports/ visits
Statement
- Nigeria: Reported reprisal killings by government soldiers must be investigated (AI Index: AFR 44/006/2001)

Visit
An AI delegation visited Nigeria in August to meet government officials and undertake research in Lagos, Abuja and northern Nigeria.

OMAN

THE SULTANATE OF OMAN
Head of state and government: Sultan Qaboos bin Said
Capital: Muscat
Population: 2.3 million
Official language: Arabic
Death penalty: retentionist

At least 15 men were executed. At least two others were sentenced to death.

Background
The government announced a number of judicial and legislative changes with potentially positive effects on human rights. The UN Committee on the Rights of the Child issued a number of recommendations urging legal and institutional changes designed to protect children.

Death penalty
At least 15 men, including four foreign nationals, were executed. All were convicted on charges of murder or drug trafficking after trial procedures which may have fallen short of international standards for fair trial. There were concerns that the defendants may not have been able to exercise their rights to defence and appeal. Most of the executions were carried out in the presence of the relatives of the murder victims.

◻ Two men, Hatem 'Ali Nour Baksh and 'Abdul Rahman Murad Mohammed, both Pakistan nationals, were reportedly sentenced to death in April on drug trafficking and firearms charges. No information was available regarding their trial proceedings and they remained at risk of execution at the end of the year.

◻ Mohama Abdullah Angeles, a Philippine worker sentenced to death in 1999 for murder, was pardoned by Sultan Qaboos bin Said in December.

Judicial and legal reforms
Judicial and legal reforms with a potentially positive impact on human rights in the country were announced. In the context of implementation of the 1999 Judicial Authority Law, the government announced a number of measures to restructure the justice system. They included the establishment of a Supreme Court, five new appeal courts, up to 40 courts of first instance, and the appointment of up to 100 new judges. In addition, a Royal Decree was issued stipulating the establishment of a Supreme Judicial Council.

Amendments to the penal code and code of penal procedures were announced restricting the permitted length of pre-trial detention to six months, and permitting the imposition of the death penalty after unanimous verdicts only.

The new laws also included a new press and publications law. The draft of this law had been referred to Sultan Qaboos bin Said for final approval in October 2000, after it was approved by the Consultative

Council. According to press reports, the draft law contained some provisions with a potentially positive impact on the right to freedom of expression and the protection of journalists.

In June, Oman acceded to International Labour Organisation Convention No. 182 and the government submitted a draft for a new Labour Law for study by a committee of the Consultative Council and subsequent debate and approval by the Council. No date was given as to when the draft would become law. In the meantime, up to 10,000 alleged illegal immigrants were deported. It was not known what procedures were followed in their cases or whether any were subjected to violations of their human rights.

Children

In October, Oman appeared for the first time before a human rights treaty body, the UN Committee on the Rights of the Child. The Committee considered the government's initial report on the implementation of the UN Children's Convention and made a number of recommendations. These included a request for the lifting of reservations placed by Oman on several articles of the Convention and reviews of laws and practices with the aim of bringing these into line with the Convention.

PAKISTAN

ISLAMIC REPUBLIC OF PAKISTAN
Head of state: Pervez Musharraf (replaced Mohammad Rafiq Tarar in June)
Head of government: Pervez Musharraf
Capital: Islamabad
Population: 145 million
Official languages: English and Urdu
Death penalty: retentionist
2001 treaty ratifications/signatures: Optional Protocol to the UN Children's Convention on the involvement of children in armed conflict

The military government completed phased elections to local bodies in August and continued the crackdown on corruption. The ban on public political activities enacted in 2000 remained in force and restricted the activities of political parties; hundreds of people were detained for contravening the ban. Political violence increased after the Pakistan government decided to support military action in Afghanistan by the USA and its allies. Islamist groups responded to this decision with violent demonstrations. Women and members of religious minorities continued to face high levels of violence throughout the year. The death penalty continued to be imposed and at least 13 people were executed.

Background

In June, General Pervez Musharraf, the Chief Executive since 1999, replaced Mohammad Rafiq Tarar as President. A meeting in Agra, India, in July between the Indian Prime Minister and President Musharraf failed to produce a joint statement because of President Musharraf's insistence that Kashmir was a central issue in bilateral relations.

The separation of the judiciary from the executive was completed in August when the office of district commissioner/district magistrate was eliminated. Its judicial functions were transferred to judicial magistrates working under the supervision of district judges. However, under an ordinance issued in August, some functions were transferred to the police, and confessions made before police officers were made admissible in court.

'Anti-terrorism' legislation

In August, the Anti-Terrorism Ordinance of 1997 was amended to empower the government to ban organizations "involved in terrorism" and to ban media distribution of materials "conducive to terrorism". It also provided for trials behind closed doors and required religious organizations to disclose their funding.

In September, a state of emergency was declared giving the government sweeping powers to maintain law and order.

Political arrests and detention

The ban on public political rallies continued to be enforced. Hundreds of political activists were arrested for breaking the ban; most were released within hours or days. Some Islamist leaders were held in preventive detention under the Maintenance of Public Order Ordinance (MPO) which allows for up to three months' detention without trial.

▫ In April, several hundred people, including women and children, were arbitrarily detained for a short period of time for peacefully demonstrating in Lahore and Karachi against water shortages.

▫ In October, dozens of Islamist protesters, including many Afghan refugees, were arrested during violent protests against Pakistan's support for US military action in Afghanistan. Several Islamist leaders including Fazlur Rahman of *Jamiat-e-Ulema-Islam* and Qazi Hussain of the *Jamaat-e-Islami*, were placed under house arrest under the MPO.

Freedom of expression

Several journalists were detained solely for their work.
▫ In June, four journalists at the daily newspaper *Mohasib* of Abbotabad in Punjab province were arrested on charges of blasphemy. The charges related to the publication of an article discussing whether pious Muslim men must wear beards. They were released on bail in mid-July.

Anti-corruption trials

In April, following protests by national and international human rights organizations, the Supreme

Court of Pakistan struck down several provisions of the 1999 National Accountability Bureau (NAB) Ordinance. Among the changes were the shortening of the permitted period of detention by NAB from 90 to 15 days and the easing of bail restrictions. By August, 356 corruption cases had been filed, of which 148 had led to convictions.

In April, the Supreme Court set aside the conviction for corruption in 1999 of former Prime Minister Benazir Bhutto and Asif Zardari and ordered a retrial, ruling that the judge had been biased. In May, a court ordered Benazir Bhutto's arrest to stand trial and one month later sentenced her to three years' imprisonment for failing to appear before it.

Torture and deaths in custody

In April, police officials acknowledged that torture, particularly of members of disadvantaged groups, continued to be practised. In May, Law Minister Shahida Jamil criticized the previous governments' failure to invest in police training, stating that police frequently had no other investigative techniques but the use of force to extract confessions. Several attempts were made to outlaw torture. In October, the Sindh Inspector General of Police issued standing orders not to use torture and stated that he would hold senior police officers criminally responsible for torture and deaths in custody in their jurisdiction.

Prolonged solitary confinement was sometimes unlawfully used to punish detainees or extort money. Several detainees in Faisalabad Central Prison were reportedly held in continuous solitary confinement for several months longer than the three-month maximum permitted in Pakistan law; one had reportedly been held in solitary confinement for three years.

Deaths in custody

In the first three months of the year, nine detainees died in Faisalabad Central Prison when health care was denied despite instructions by the prison doctor.

At least 40 people died in police custody or in prison as a result of torture during 2001. In the first nine months of the year, 12 deaths in custody were recorded in Lahore alone. According to police officials, about a dozen police officers were suspended and charged with criminal offences in connection with the deaths. At the end of the year, no details were available about charges or arrests.

☐ In October, Mian Arshad, a businessman detained at the beginning of October, died in the custody of the NAB in Lahore. He had been interrogated in connection with an allegation of corruption against a leader of the Pakistan People's Party. NAB officials stated that Mian Arshad had died of heart failure. However, the autopsy report listed four injuries to his body, along with bruises and swellings. Police delayed registering a complaint filed by relatives. An investigation was ordered but its findings were not known at the end of the year.

Freedom of religion

Several cases of blasphemy were reported, both against members of religious minorities and Muslims.

☐ A Christian teacher, Pervez Masih, was charged with blasphemy in April. He said that police officers beat him with rifle butts and kicked him until he almost lost consciousness. His trial began in May.

☐ In August, Yunus Sheikh, a doctor and lecturer, was convicted of blasphemy and sentenced to death in Rawalpindi. His appeal was pending at the end of the year.

The government failed to provide adequate protection to religious minorities against attacks by Islamist groups. In particular Shi'a professionals were openly and with impunity targeted by Sunni militants in Karachi. Few of those responsible for sectarian killings were prosecuted as witnesses and the families of victims feared revenge attacks, and judges were afraid to convict.

☐ In October, the government ordered a judicial inquiry and payment of compensation after 17 Christians were shot dead in a church in Bahawalpur by unidentified Islamists.

Women

The state failed to take adequate measures to protect women from abuse. Several hundred girls and women were killed for allegedly shaming their families. Their supposedly immoral behaviour included marrying men of their own choice or seeking a divorce. The non-governmental Human Rights Commission of Pakistan reported that 62 women had been killed in such "honour" crimes in the first quarter of 2001 in Sindh Province alone. Although widely reported, abuses were routinely ignored by the state.

☐ In April, 21-year-old Fakhra Younus had acid thrown in her face by her husband, a well-known former parliamentarian. Her face, shoulders and chest were extensively burned, her lips were fused together and one eye was damaged. Although her family managed to register a complaint, her husband was not arrested. The authorities reportedly refused to issue her with travel documents when she sought reconstructive surgery abroad. She eventually left the country in July.

The authorities also continued to ignore practices resembling slavery.

☐ In June, a *jirga* (tribal council) in Thatta district, Sindh Province, handed over two girls to "settle" a tribal feud arising from a murder. The 11-year-old daughter of the accused was forced to marry the 46-year-old father of the murder victim and the six-year-old daughter of the other accused was married to the eight-year-old brother of the victim. Although the arrangement was reported in the local media the authorities took no action to rescue the children.

Children

Over 4,000 juvenile detainees were held during the year. Many were detained for minor offences such as vagrancy and theft. They were often detained awaiting trial for longer than the maximum possible sentence for the alleged offence. Despite the requirement of the Juvenile Justice System Ordinance 2000, legal aid was not provided to all juveniles. As most prisons did not have separate cells for juveniles, many young detainees were held with adult suspects or convicts. Special courts to try juveniles were not set up, but regular courts were empowered to act as special courts.

Refugees
In May, the authorities closed the border with Afghanistan to refugees. Afghans seeking refuge who managed to enter Pakistan faced *refoulement*, arbitrary arrest, intimidation and deportation, particularly in the North West Frontier Province.

☐ In June, an Afghan refugee, Sallahuddin Samadi, was picked up by police in Islamabad. When the police discovered that neither he nor his relatives could pay the bribe they demanded, Sallahuddin Samadi was thrown from the moving car. He died 12 days later of his injuries. Two police officers were reportedly arrested and charged with criminal offences and an investigation was announced into the incident. It was not known if anyone had been brought to trial by the end of the year.

At the end of the year, the border remained closed to all those without valid visas. As a result, thousands of Afghans seeking refuge from the US-led military strikes in Afghanistan which began in October were forced to try to enter Pakistan at isolated points on the porous border.

During a meeting with AI's Secretary General in Islamabad in December, General Musharraf gave assurances that no Afghan refugee would be forcibly returned to Afghanistan.

Death penalty
At least 50 people were sentenced to death during 2001, some after apparently unfair trials. At least 13 people were executed.

☐ In July, an Afghan tribesman was executed after a tribal council in North Waziristan, a designated tribal area, found him guilty of murder. The father of the victim shot the Afghan dead in front of thousands of tribesmen.

☐ In November, Sher Ali was hanged in Timergarah for a murder committed in 1993 when he was 13 years old. The Supreme Court had earlier rejected an appeal which argued that in 1993 the death penalty could not be imposed in the Provincially Administered Tribal Areas where he had lived.

During a meeting with AI's Secretary General in Islamabad in December, General Musharraf announced the commutation of death sentences of juveniles imposed before the death penalty for children was abolished in July 2000.

AI country reports/ visits
Reports
- Pakistan: Insufficient protection of religious minorities (AI Index: ASA 33/008/2001)
- Pakistan: Freedom of assembly should not be curtailed again on 1 May (AI Index: ASA 33/009/2001)

Visits
AI delegates visited Pakistan in April and December.

PALESTINIAN AUTHORITY

PALESTINIAN AUTHORITY
President: Yasser 'Arafat
Official language: Arabic
Death penalty: retentionist

Hundreds of people, including prisoners of conscience, were arrested for political reasons during 2001. Those arrested included people suspected of "collaborating" with the Israeli authorities and suspected members of armed opposition groups. Reports of torture and ill-treatment were widespread. Three people died in custody. Twelve people were sentenced to death and two people were executed.

Background
The *al-Aqsa intifada* (uprising), which started on 29 September 2000, continued throughout 2001. More than 460 Palestinians were killed by the Israeli security forces, the vast majority of them unlawfully, when no lives were in danger. A total of 187 Israelis, including 154 civilians, were killed by Palestinian armed groups and individuals. Thousands of other people were wounded; many were maimed for life. (See also Israel and the Occupied Territories entry.)

Palestinian members of armed groups attacked Israeli military personnel and civilians, including children. Armed groups and individuals arbitrarily killed 65 Israeli civilians in the Occupied Territories and 89 Israeli civilians within Israel. The main armed groups involved in attacks on Israelis were *Fatah*, *Hamas* and Islamic *Jihad*. The Popular Front for the Liberation of Palestine (PFLP) and the Democratic Front for the Liberation of Palestine (DFLP) also carried out attacks on civilians. Other civilians were killed by new groups whose political organization remained vague or by individual Palestinians unconnected with armed groups. It is unclear how much control the Palestinian Authority (PA) has over any of these groups.

Arbitrary arrest and detention
Hundreds of suspected "collaborators" with Israel were arrested. Most were held in prolonged incommunicado detention and reportedly tortured. Scores of alleged members of *Hamas*, Islamic *Jihad* and *Fatah* were arrested. After the assassination of Israeli Tourism Minister Rehavam Ze'evi by members of the PFLP on 17 October, more than 60 suspected members of the PFLP were arrested. Some of those arrested may have been prisoners of conscience.

☐ Attorney Yunis al-Jarru, former deputy head of the Palestinian Bar Association in Gaza, and Dr Rabah Muhanna, the Gaza Director of the Union of Health Work Committees, were arrested on 18 October. Both were members of PFLP. On 27 October the Palestinian

High Court of Justice ordered the prosecutor to explain the reasons for their arrest. On 4 November the Palestinian Attorney General stated that they were detained under the jurisdiction of the State Security Court, charged with "damaging the interests of the state". On 7 November, the Palestinian High Court of Justice rejected this argument and ordered their immediate release. They were eventually released on 15 November.

☐ Yusra Fayek, aged 29 and the mother of six children, was arrested on 1 June 2001 by the *mukhabarat* (General Intelligence) in Khan Younis. She was two months pregnant when arrested, and had reportedly told the interrogator that this was the case. She was beaten, lost consciousness, woke up in hospital and realized that she had miscarried. Reportedly, the *mukhabarat* wanted her to be a witness in a case against two alleged "collaborators" who were also in detention. Yusra Fayek remained in detention at the end of 2001.

☐ Jawid al-Ghussein, a 70-year-old businessman, was forcibly taken in April from the United Arab Emirates to Gaza, where he was held incommunicado in a presidential guesthouse for several weeks. He was ostensibly being pursued for US$6.5 million dollars, which he was said to have borrowed or taken to invest in 1991. However, he was never charged or brought to trial and AI believes that he may have been detained on account of past criticisms of leading members of the PA. In October his health deteriorated and he was placed under house arrest with his family in Gaza. In November he was transferred to hospital in Cairo where he remained at the end of the year, apparently under armed Palestinian guard, unable to travel as his passport was held by the PA.

Torture and ill-treatment

Reports of torture and ill-treatment by various Palestinian security forces remained widespread. Methods used included beatings, suspension from a height and burning with cigarettes. Many of the reports of torture concerned those detained on suspicion of "collaboration" with the Israeli authorities.

☐ Mohammed Lahloh, aged 25, was arrested on 3 September in Jenin and held in solitary confinement until around 20 October. He stated that he was tortured throughout his detention. He was reportedly beaten and burned with cigarettes and had nails driven into his knees. He had some access to his family, but was not examined by a doctor and was denied access to his lawyer until 20 October. He was eventually released without charge on 7 November.

Deaths in custody

Three men died in custody in circumstances which suggested that torture or ill-treatment may have caused or contributed to their deaths. One Palestinian sentenced to death was killed, allegedly while trying to escape.

☐ Sulayman 'Awad Muhammad Abu 'Amra, aged 38, from Deir al-Balah, the father of eight children, was arrested on 8 August in Gaza by the *istikhbarat* (Military Intelligence). He was held incommunicado in the *istikhbarat* detention centre. His family was informed on 15 August that he had died the previous day. An autopsy was performed and revealed that death resulted from "several injuries in the body and sensitive parts, such as the abdomen and scrotum, caused by repeated blows by solid objects. All the wounds were recent and took place one week prior to death." President 'Arafat ordered an official inquiry into the death of Sulayman Abu 'Amra. The results of this inquiry had not been made public by the end of the year and no one was known to have been arrested in connection with his death.

Unlawful killings

Three demonstrators, including a 14-year-old boy, were killed in Gaza on 8 October by Palestinian police when hundreds of unarmed demonstrators took to the streets to protest against the bombing in Afghanistan by the USA and its allies.

Extrajudicial executions

More than 20 Palestinians suspected of "collaboration" with the Israeli authorities were killed or found dead in circumstances which suggested that they had been extrajudicially executed. Some extrajudicial executions were said to have been carried out by members of Palestinian security services, others by members of armed groups or individuals. The PA consistently failed to investigate these killings. Even when eyewitnesses said that they had seen the alleged killer, no investigations were believed to have been carried out and no one was brought to justice.

☐ On 27 January, Samir al-Bakri, a 46-year-old shop owner, was shot nine times by unidentified persons who knocked on the door of his home in Nablus at 5am. He died before reaching the hospital. He was said to have been suspected of "collaborating" with Israel in the past. No investigation is known to have been initiated into his death.

Death penalty

Twelve people were sentenced to death after unfair and summary trials in Higher State Security Courts or Military Courts. Most of those sentenced to death were accused of treason and "collaboration" with the Israeli authorities. Two Palestinians were executed in January; one was executed by firing squad the day after his trial. Those sentenced to death by the State Security Court were not entitled to appeal against their sentence. Their sentences had not been ratified by President 'Arafat by the end of the year.

☐ 'Alan Bani 'Odeh was executed by firing squad in Nablus on 13 January. He had been sentenced to death by the Higher State Security Court in December 2000 after an unfair trial which lasted less than three hours. He was convicted of "collaborating" with the Israeli security services in the killing of his cousin, Ibrahim Bani 'Odeh, who was killed by a car bomb on 23 November 2000. 'Alan Bani 'Odeh was not given the opportunity to appeal to a higher court against his conviction and death sentence.

including minors; and in the context of land disputes. The authorities frequently failed to initiate criminal investigations into killings in the context of social disputes.

◻ Interior Minister Julio César Fanego defended the possible excessive use of force by police who killed five men allegedly carrying out a robbery in March.

◻ On 9 March, it was reported that eight teachers participating in a demonstration were seriously injured and approximately 100 others injured when police used force to break up the demonstrators in the J. Eulogio Estigarribia district of Caaguazú department.

◻ On 28 July landless peasant farmer Nicolás Amarilla was killed in the course of land demonstrations in San Rafael del Paraná, Itapúa department. Information received indicated that judicial investigations into this killing had not been initiated by the end of the year.

AI country reports/ visits
Reports
- Paraguay: Conscription – recruitment of children, routine ill-treatment and unexplained deaths (AI Index: AMR 45/002/2001)
- Paraguay: Panchito López Juvenile Detention Centre – an opportunity for the Government of Paraguay to meet its promises (AI Index: AMR 45/004/2001)

Visit
AI delegates visited Paraguay in April.

PERU

REPUBLIC OF PERU
Head of state and government: Alejandro Toledo (replaced Valentín Paniagua in July)
Capital: Lima
Population: 26.1 million
Official languages: Spanish, Quechua, Aymara
Death penalty: abolitionist for ordinary crimes
2001 treaty ratifications/signatures: Optional Protocol to the UN Women's Convention; Rome Statute of the International Criminal Court; Inter-American Convention on Forced Disappearance of Persons

Scores of prisoners of conscience and possible prisoners of conscience remained imprisoned. Torture and ill-treatment remained a concern. A Truth and Reconciliation Commission to investigate human rights violations committed between 1980 and 2000 was established. People charged with treason under anti-terrorism legislation continued to be tried by military courts.

Background
President Alejandro Toledo took office on 28 July. Throughout his election campaign and in his inaugural speech he pledged to fight impunity and to protect and promote human rights. For the first time in recent Peruvian history, a civilian was appointed as Minister of Defence.

During his first months in office President Alejandro Toledo convened meetings with several political parties to reach a National Agreement on Governance. The agenda of the Agreement included constitutional reform, reform of the armed forces, security, decentralization and education. In addition, President Alejandro Toledo's government pledged free health care for everybody by the end of its mandate.

There were reports that the Shining Path armed opposition group continued to be active in the departments of Ayacucho, Junin, Huanuco and San Martín. In October there were reports that at least three people died when Shining Path members attacked an Ashaninka Indian community in the department of Junin. There were also reports that at least three Shining Path members had been detained that same month in the department of Huanuco.

Abuses by the former government
Vladimiro Montesinos, intelligence adviser to former president Alberto Fujimori, was detained in Venezuela in June and sent back to Peru where he faced charges of human rights violations, including aggravated injuries and homicide, money laundering and corruption. At the end of the year he was detained awaiting trial at the Callao Naval Base prison where leaders of the two armed opposition groups, Shining Path and the *Movimiento Revolucionario Túpac Amaru*, Túpac Amaru Revolutionary Movement, were also being held.

Scores of military officers who had been members of the cabinet, parliamentarians and other government officials and public servants during Alberto Fujimori's term of office were charged with fraud, corruption and money laundering. Some remained in prison awaiting trial; others were released on bail.

Alberto Fujimori, who had fled to Japan in November 2000, had his Japanese citizenship confirmed. In September, the Attorney General formally charged Alberto Fujimori with the murder of 15 people in 1991 at Barrios Altos, Lima, and with the forced disappearance and murder of nine students and a professor at La Cantuta University in Lima in 1992. In September, a judge of the Supreme Court of Justice ordered Alberto Fujimori's detention, alleging that there was strong evidence to suggest that Alberto Fujimori had full knowledge of the existence of the *Grupo Colina* "death squad" attached to Peru's Intelligence Service and believed to be responsible for these crimes. By the end of the year, Peru had not filed an extradition petition. However, the Japanese authorities insisted that no Japanese citizen could be extradited.

Impunity

In March the Inter-American Court of Human Rights ruled that the 1995 amnesty laws contravened the American Convention on Human Rights and therefore had no legal effect in all cases in which the rights enshrined in the Convention have been violated. In September the Inter-American Court of Human Rights stated that it was the duty of the Peruvian authorities to abide by this ruling and ensure that all human rights violations committed between 1980 and 1995 were investigated and those responsible brought to justice.

In June the transitional government of Valentín Paniagua issued a decree creating a Truth Commission to establish the circumstances surrounding human rights violations committed by the state and abuses committed by armed opposition groups between May 1980 and November 2000. The decree stated that once the commissioners had been appointed they would have 90 days to prepare the necessary formal rules by which their work would be guided. The government of Alejandro Toledo changed the title of the Commission to the Truth and Reconciliation Commission and expanded the number of commissioners to 12. By September all 12 commissioners had been appointed and at the end of October the Commission published its Rules on Organization and Functions which established that the Commission would have access to all official files in the hands of the judiciary, public ministries and the military justice system. However, there were concerns that the Commission would not be granted enough human and material resources to enable it to carry out an in-depth, effective, swift and country-wide examination of evidence related to cases of alleged violations submitted to it.

Mass graves

Dozens of mass graves were discovered during 2001 in the departments of Ancash, San Martín, Huancavelica, Apurimac, Ayacucho and Lima. Reports indicated that the mass graves dated from 1980 to the mid-1990s. During this 15-year period, thousands of people "disappeared" and were extrajudicially executed by members of the security forces, and armed opposition groups committed grave human rights abuses. There were concerns from the Ombudsman and from domestic human rights organizations that the investigations into the hundreds of bodies found in these graves were at risk because the evidence had been interfered with, in part because the authorities had failed to properly protect the sites and provide them with adequate security.

Prisoners of conscience

At least 200 prisoners of conscience and possible prisoners of conscience, all charged under anti-terrorism legislation (see below), were released. However, at least a further 100 prisoners of conscience and possible prisoners of conscience charged with similar offences remained incarcerated. Most of the prisoners of conscience and possible prisoners of conscience who remained in jail had spent over five years in prison on false charges, a legacy of the Alberto Fujimori government. However, there were concerns that these cases had not been dealt with swiftly by the new administration.

Political prisoners and the anti-terrorism legislation

The anti-terrorism legislation which came into effect in 1992 permitting trial on charges of treason in military courts had not yet been brought into line with international standards for fair trials. Since 1992, hundreds of political prisoners had been convicted of treason under this legislation by military courts which were neither independent nor impartial. In a handful of cases those tried by military courts had their sentences annulled and their cases transferred to the civilian jurisdiction.

◻ In 2001, Lori Berenson, a US citizen, was sentenced by a civilian court to 20 years in prison under the anti-terrorism legislation. She had been sentenced to life imprisonment by a military court in 1996, but this sentence had been annulled in 2000 by the Supreme Council of Military Justice which referred her case to the civilian courts. An appeal against her conviction by the civilian court was pending at the end of 2001.

◻ The case of four Chileans – Jaime Castillo, Laurato Mellado, María Concepción Pincheira and Alejandro Astorga – sentenced by a military court in 1994, was transferred to the civilian courts. The Inter-American Court of Human Rights had ruled in 1999 that the four Chileans had received an unfair trial and should be retried. The trial was continuing at the end of 2001.

Torture and ill-treatment

There were reports of torture and ill-treatment, in at least one case resulting in death. There were serious concerns that complaints of torture and ill-treatment did not result in those responsible being brought to justice or the victims receiving compensation. Legislation criminalizing torture came into effect in

1998. However, since then, torturers have been convicted under this legislation in only two cases. In addition, there were concerns that victims, their relatives and witnesses were intimidated and harassed; some complaints of torture or ill-treatment were dropped as a result.

☐ Jenard Lee Rivera San Roque was detained in May by police officers from the Cruz Blanca station, Huaura, Lima department, on suspicion of theft. He was taken home by nine officers, eight of them wearing plain clothes, where he was severely beaten with a chain and then taken to the backyard where he was forced to dig; the officers alleged that Jenard Lee Rivera had hidden the stolen goods in his patio. Jenard Lee Rivera was subsequently taken to the police station, where he was later found dead in his cell. According to the police, he had hanged himself. However, he had injuries on his face and body which were consistent with torture. His family lodged a complaint of torture on 22 June, since when the family has reported repeated harassment and intimidation. The case was under judicial investigation at the end of the year.

Prison conditions remained harsh and in some circumstances amounted to cruel, inhuman and degrading punishment. Challapalca prison remained operational despite calls from the Inter-American Commission on Human Rights that it be closed permanently. The prison, in Puno department, is more than 4,600 metres above sea level, and is extremely cold. The inaccessibility of the prison seriously limits the prisoners' right to maintain contact with the outside world, including relatives, lawyers and doctors. In September some 30 political prisoners who had taken control of a wing in the high-security prison of Yanamayo in Puno department were transferred to Challapalca prison. According to reports, the prisoners had refused to be transferred to other prisons for a few months while the Yanamayo prison was refurbished. By the end of year they had not been transferred back to Yanamayo or to other prisons.

Women
In July, the then Minister for Women's Affairs launched a National Plan against Violence against Women. According to reports, under the Plan women's refuges will be created and more resources will be allocated during the next five-year period for legal and psychological assistance for women filing complaints in police stations.

In September, women's organizations and human rights defenders urged the authorities to investigate allegations by the Health Minister that former President Alberto Fujimori was directly involved in planning the forced sterilization of women. During 1996 and 1997, the Latin American and Caribbean Committee for the Defence of Women's Rights studied the incidence of violence against women in the public health sector. They discovered evidence that the poorest women, as well as those who lived in rural areas, had been forcibly sterilized under false pretences, threats, intimidation and coercion. Some of these women reportedly died as a result of the medical intervention. The Committee reported that health-care workers, in an effort to meet government imposed sterilization quotas, took advantage of poor rural women. Between 1998 and 2000 the Office of the Ombudsman received scores of complaints of women who had been forcibly sterilized.

AI country reports/ visits
Reports
- Peru/Japan: Alberto Fujimori ex-president of Peru must be brought to justice (AI Index: AMR 46/017/2001)
- Peru: Amnesty International's recommendations to the Truth Commission (AI Index: AMR 46/020/2001)

Visit
In April, AI delegates visited Peru. They were not received by the two presidential candidates, Alejandro Toledo and Alan Garcia. The delegation met with members of the transitional government of Valentín Paniagua.

PHILIPPINES

REPUBLIC OF THE PHILIPPINES
Head of state and government: Gloria Macapagal Arroyo (replaced Joseph Estrada in January)
Capital: Manila
Population: 77.1 million
Official languages: Pilipino, English
Death penalty: retentionist

Defects in the administration of justice were highlighted by reports of torture and ill-treatment of criminal suspects by police to extract confessions and of extrajudicial executions of suspected drug dealers and others. Women in custody were vulnerable to rape and sexual abuse. Complaints procedures, investigations and criminal prosecution of suspected perpetrators of human rights violations failed repeatedly to provide effective redress. Arbitrary arrests, torture, extrajudicial executions and "disappearances" were reported in the context of military counter-insurgency operations. Armed political groups were responsible for grave abuses, including killings, torture and hostage-taking.

Background
In January, aborted Senate impeachment proceedings against former President Joseph Estrada on corruption charges sparked large-scale peaceful demonstrations calling for his resignation. Following a withdrawal of support by key military and political figures, President Estrada vacated the Presidency and was replaced by Vice-President Gloria Macapagal Arroyo. In May,

Estrada loyalists attempted to storm the presidential palace after former President Estrada was arrested and charged with plunder. President Arroyo declared a state of rebellion, temporarily suspending some civil liberties and filing rebellion charges, later withdrawn, against senior opposition figures. Nationwide congressional and local elections were held and supporters of the administration gained a majority in Congress. President Arroyo resumed peace negotiations with major armed political groups.

Communist insurgency

Peace negotiations, suspended since 1999, between the government and the National Democratic Front (NDF), representing the Communist Party of the Philippines (CPP) and its armed wing the New People's Army (NPA), resumed in Norway in April. Discussions continued regarding the implementation of a 1998 agreement on human rights and international humanitarian law, but negotiations were suspended in June after the NPA assassinated two congressmen, one a former prominent military intelligence officer accused of human rights violations. Confidence-building measures, including government pledges to release at least 49 of over 200 political prisoners, were undermined by continued armed clashes between units of the Armed Forces of the Philippines (AFP) and the NPA, and reports of human rights violations by military personnel. By December at least 25 political prisoners were reported released and formal peace negotiations had not resumed.

☐ In June, seven indigenous farmers were arrested by soldiers in Tamogan, Davao, accused of being NPA sympathizers. After being interrogated about supplying food to insurgents, four of the farmers reported that they were tortured, including being beaten, strangled and burned with cigarettes.

Armed conflict in Mindanao
Moro National Liberation Front (MNLF)

In line with the 1996 peace agreement with the MNLF, a regional plebiscite on the expansion of the four-province Autonomous Region of Muslim Mindanao (ARMM) was held in August. Of the provinces polled, only the Muslim majority island of Basilan voted to join the ARMM. MNLF founder and outgoing ARMM governor Nur Misuari opposed the timing of the plebiscite, and in the run-up to ARMM elections in November MNLF units loyal to him attacked AFP installations in Zamboanga and Jolo island. Over 140 people were reported killed. Nur Misuari was arrested on entering Sabah, Malaysia.

Moro Islamic Liberation Front (MILF)

Peace negotiations with the MILF, which collapsed in 2000 following a series of military offensives launched by the Estrada administration against MILF bases and communities in central Mindanao, were revived. Talks held in Libya and Malaysia led to the signing of a cease-fire in August. Despite periodic cease-fire violations, substantive negotiations on the scope of a formal peace agreement continued through late 2001. Twenty-four alleged MILF members, detained on suspicion of involvement in bomb attacks in Manila in 2000, were released. MILF members, some of whom were also members of renegade units, were responsible for abuses including the deliberate and arbitrary killing of civilians and hostage-taking.

Abu Sayyaf

Military operations against *Abu Sayyaf*, a Muslim separatist armed group involved primarily in kidnapping for ransom, continued throughout the year mainly on Jolo and Basilan islands. In May, group members kidnapped 17 Filipinos and three US citizens from a tourist resort in Palawan and transported them to Basilan. Amid further kidnappings, ransom payments and periodic releases, at least 15 hostages were reported murdered. By the end of the year two US citizens and a Filipina remained captive. There were reports of arbitrary arrests, extrajudicial executions and torture, by military and paramilitary personnel, of civilians suspected of being *Abu Sayyaf* members or sympathizers.

Impunity and the administration of justice

Emphasizing a commitment to upholding the rule of law, the government pursued criminal charges, including plunder and perjury, against former President Estrada. Concerns remained that, despite an extensive range of procedural safeguards, complaints mechanisms and legal sanctions, suspected perpetrators of serious human rights violations were rarely brought to justice and that a climate of impunity persisted.

Failures in the proper administration of justice derived repeatedly from unjustified use of arrests without warrant, mainly against ordinary criminal suspects but including suspected insurgents. After arrest, during unlawfully extended periods of "investigative" detention before the filing of charges, suspects were subjected to torture or ill-treatment by police or military personnel to extract confessions or information.

The right of victims of torture and other human rights violations to receive prompt, impartial and thorough investigations of their complaints continued to be severely curtailed, and public confidence in existing complaints bodies, including the Commission on Human Rights and the Office of the Ombudsman, remained low. Prolonged trial proceedings placed excessive burdens on those seeking judicial remedies, especially victims from poor or marginalized communities, and convictions in such cases were rare.

☐ Having investigated for over five years complaints of torture made by five suspects convicted and sentenced to death for the 1996 murder of Rolando Abadilla, the Department of Justice resolved in August not to file charges against police officers accused of torture on the grounds that a Supreme Court review, automatic in all death penalty cases, was continuing.

Vulnerability of marginalized groups
Indigenous people

Instances of deliberate and arbitrary killings were reported in the context of land disputes. Abuses were reportedly carried out by private security guards or gunmen reportedly hired by local land-owning interests with the apparent collusion of local officials and police. Investigations into such abuses often appeared ineffective.

Women and children in conflict with the law
Cases of rape and sexual abuse of women in custody continued to be reported. These involved women from marginalized groups such as suspected prostitutes, drug users and poor people arrested for minor crimes. Both women and minors in detention continued to be vulnerable to other physical assaults including slaps, punches or kicks. Officials announced plans to improve protection of women in custody from sexual abuse, but concerns persisted. In addition, reports continued of alleged drugs dealers, including street children, being shot dead in the community by suspected police officers or other armed men.

A woman held in Talavera Jail, Nueva Ecija, on charges of embezzlement was allegedly raped four times by a jail warden and threatened with death. Officials ordered the suspension of the accused pending investigations.

Death penalty
Declaring his intention to commute all death sentences and to support congressional repeal of the death penalty, former President Estrada signed commutation orders for 103 death-row inmates whose sentences had been confirmed by the Supreme Court. The new administration signalled that it would maintain an unofficial moratorium on executions and President Arroyo commuted 18 sentences. However, in October the President announced that she would support the execution of at least 95 convicted kidnappers following confirmation of their sentences. Over 1,800 people, including nine minors, have been sentenced to death, and seven men executed, since capital punishment was restored in 1994.

AI country reports/visits
Report
- Philippines: Fear, shame and impunity – rape and sexual abuse of women in custody (AI Index: ASA 35/001/2001)

Visit
In March, an AI delegate carried out research into the torture of detainees in Manila, and visited central Mindanao to assess reported violations of human rights and international humanitarian law in the context of armed conflict.

POLAND

REPUBLIC OF POLAND
Head of state: Aleksander Kwaśniewski
Head of government: Leszek Miller (replaced Jerzy Buzek in October)
Capital: Warsaw
Population: 38.6 million
Official language: Polish
Death penalty: abolitionist for all crimes
2001 treaty ratifications/signatures: Rome Statute of the International Criminal Court

There were reports of racist attacks in which the police failed to protect the victims adequately. Some investigations into such attacks did not appear to have been conducted thoroughly and impartially.

Racist violence
There were reports of incidents of racially motivated violence in which the police authorities failed in their duty to protect the victims adequately.

In August, 20 Roma who were staying in a hotel in Koszelówka, near Plock, were attacked by 40 young men wielding clubs and stones. The attack followed an incident in a local discotheque in which a Romani youth had allegedly committed a theft. The mob, shouting threats and racist abuse, reportedly forced open the gate to the hotel yard and threw bricks through the windows, which were secured by metal bars. They broke car windshields and threw burning wood inside the vehicles. Apparently two police officers who were at the scene of the attack did not intervene to stop the violence. The mob dispersed when three police patrol cars arrived. One Romani man who was hit in the face with a brick was hospitalized while several others received treatment for lesser injuries. The police detained three men and subsequently charged nine for participating in a fight and causing damage to property. A police spokesman denied that the assault was racially motivated and claimed that the two officers present at the scene of the attack were unable to intervene.

In June, Simon Moleke Njie, a refugee from Cameroon, and his visitor, a Senegalese national, described how they were beaten by four men, one of whom had a wooden bat, while standing at a bus stop in Warsaw. The four men punched Simon Moleke Njie and shouted racist abuse at him. The two victims managed to escape in a taxi and went to a police station which was only 200m away. One of the three officers standing in front of the station reportedly laughed when he saw Simon Moleke Njie's head injury. Another officer asked him for his passport. The officers refused to call an ambulance or to take contact details for the taxi driver, who had witnessed some of the assault.

Investigations into some racially motivated incidents appeared not to be thorough and impartial and, as a result, those responsible for racist violence were not brought to justice.

📄 In May, Florence Balagiza, an 18-year-old asylum-seeker from Rwanda, was reportedly attacked and racially abused by three men, one of whom was armed with a knife, near the refugee camp at Dąbak. When she returned to the refugee camp and called the police she was told that they were busy. The police came the following day. Florence Balagiza explained that she was unable to pay for a forensic examination of the injuries she had suffered in the attack and was reportedly told that the police could not offer her any assistance "because it was not their business". In August she received the Pruszków Public Prosecutor's decision to terminate the investigation because it was not possible to establish the identity of the perpetrator. This document, which contained a detailed description of the incident which was described as "robbery with the use of a knife", failed to note the racist nature of the assault. Officials in the Public Prosecutor's Office did not question the victim.

AI country reports/visits
Report
- Concerns in Europe, January-June 2001: Poland (AI Index: EUR 01/003/2001)

PORTUGAL

PORTUGUESE REPUBLIC
Head of state: Jorge Fernando Branco de Sampaio
Head of government: António Manuel de Oliveira Guterres
Capital: Lisbon
Population: 10 million
Official language: Portuguese
Death penalty: abolitionist for all crimes

The excessive length of criminal, administrative or disciplinary inquiries into allegations that police officers had ill-treated, or used disproportionate force against, suspects continued to cause concern. Some sentences handed down failed to reflect the seriousness of the crimes committed and raised doubts about the ability of the judicial system to deal effectively with cases of torture, ill-treatment and excessive use of force by law enforcement officers. Several deaths in prisons were being investigated. Claims of possible prison guard involvement in some killings were also being examined. Allegations persisted about acts of violence by custodial staff, and cruel, inhuman and degrading treatment in prisons. Some new reports were received about ill-treatment in police custody.

CPT report
In July, the European Committee for the Prevention of Torture and Inhuman or Degrading Treatment or Punishment (CPT) published its report on a visit carried out in April 1999 to several police establishments and to the prisons of Coimbra, Leiria, Lisbon and Oporto. Regarding prisons, the CPT concluded that, although it had received fewer allegations of ill-treatment of prisoners by staff than on previous occasions, allegations continued to be made about verbal abuse, rough treatment and the removal of inmates from their cells during the night by prison officers, who then struck them with batons. The CPT also received many accounts of ill-treatment by fellow inmates, including physical assault and intimidation. It remained concerned about the continuing level of inter-prisoner violence in general and in Oporto Central Prison (Custóias) in particular – a problem it considered "far from being resolved". The report described drugs-related problems there as "dramatic" and as constituting a "veritable marketplace of drugs as part of the daily routine".

The CPT also commented that there were fewer allegations of police ill-treatment than formerly, but that the "persistence of some allegations of ill-treatment by the police" (kicks, blows with fists, truncheons and other objects), particularly at the time of arrest, underlined the need for the authorities to remain vigilant.

Deaths and ill-treatment in prison
In October, two prisoners were killed at the penitentiary of Vale de Judeus (Alcoentre), reportedly by two fellow inmates. One of those killed, Augusto Morgado Fernandes, was reported to have been involved in a dispute with the prison authorities, and to have complained to the Ombudsman about persecution by custodial staff. He was allegedly stabbed 14 times with the end of a spoon that had been worked into a knife. Part of his skull was then crushed with an iron bar. The alleged killers were placed under investigation by the Judicial Police. Some reports implicated custodial staff in the killings, at least through negligence, particularly by allowing cell doors to be left open at night. However, the Ministry of Justice subsequently assured AI that the deaths did not occur "at an hour of the night when the cells should have been closed". It was generally recognized that the situation at Vale de Judeus had been tense for some time. Other violent incidents, including another killing, had taken place in recent months.

New reports reinforced the concern earlier expressed by the CPT about the situation at Custóias. One report, received in August, described continuing abuse of power by custodial staff, who delivered habitual and arbitrary beatings. It also referred to the inaction of prison guards in relation to serious inter-prisoner violence, to the daily and systematic sale of drugs and to the general lack of hygiene. Replying to AI's expression of concern about allegations that prison guards were physically ill-treating inmates at Linhó Prison (Sintra) and that conditions in the prison were inhuman and degrading, the Director General of Prison Services stated that in many cases the prisoner had been subjected to disciplinary measures for violent or disruptive acts, but little or no information had been received that would substantiate allegations of violence by guards. However, in the case of Nélio Henrique Sá who was assaulted by the deputy chief prison officer in Linhó Prison in April 2000, the officer had been issued with a written reprimand for inappropriate conduct. The Director General also stated that Linhó Prison was being comprehensively renovated and that improved sanitary facilities were being introduced. After the deaths at Vale de Judeus penitentiary, new security measures were announced. However, there was some concern that any possible withdrawal of rights, such as those affecting work, telephone access or relative freedom of movement within wings, could further heighten tension.

Police ill-treatment

There were some new reports of police ill-treatment and abuse of authority, particularly at the time of arrest. Investigations were carried out by the Interior Ministry's police oversight agency, the General Inspectorate of Internal Administration (IGAI) into 11 of the more serious allegations. In November, the IGAI informed AI that disciplinary action had been taken against police officers in three of these cases.

In November, a judicial investigation was opened into two joint complaints against Public Security Police (PSP) officers in Portimão. French nationals Nathalie Julien and her brother, Didier Julien, alleged that they were assaulted by five officers following an argument in a bar. They claimed that they were beaten with truncheons and kicked. Didier Julien suffered a fractured collar bone, allegedly caused by a blow delivered after he was handcuffed. Both had bruises and haematoma.

Effective impunity

Judicial inquiries into ill-treatment or excessive use of force by the police continued to make unacceptably slow progress. By the end of the year a number of judicial proceedings were still continuing after several years.

Rui Matias Oliveira, suspected of theft, was shot dead by a PSP officer in May 1990 during a car pursuit in Lisbon. He was unarmed. One of the three shots pierced Rui Oliveira's skull. The bullet was never recovered from the car, which had allegedly been emptied of contents and cleaned by officers of the same PSP division. In March 2001, 11 years later, the officer who fired the fatal shot was sentenced by the Court of Boa Hora to a suspended two-year prison term for negligent homicide.

Updates on deaths in custody

A judicial inquiry continued into the death of Paulo Silva, who died of internal injuries in January 2000 after complaining that he had been badly beaten while in the custody of PSP officers in Oporto. An appeal against the 2001 decision to close, without further action, the case of the death in custody in 2000 of Álvaro Rosa Cardoso was still pending. In July a follow-up report of the Portuguese government in response to the CPT report stated that, in the case of António Mendes dos Santos, who died in 2000 after being held in police custody for 10 days in Coimbra, there was "a suspicion" that he had died as a result of police ill-treatment. The prosecutor nevertheless advised that the case be closed owing to lack of evidence of police responsibility, but the victim's family requested a continuation of the judicial inquiry, which was proceeding at the end of the year.

Update: Anadia case

The IGAI informed AI that it had established that seven officers from an investigation unit of the paramilitary National Republican Guard in Anadia had either direct or indirect responsibility for the ill-treatment or illegal detention of several individuals. Disciplinary measures were being taken. The IGAI had informed the Attorney General's Office so that a judicial inquiry could be opened, but a prosecutor had decided that the inquiry should be assigned instead to the Military Tribunal of Coimbra.

AI action

AI was in correspondence with the government on the subject of prisons and individual cases of police ill-treatment. A report originally submitted to the UN Committee against Torture was updated and published in July. The report summarized AI's concerns about prisons and policing over several years. While welcoming the establishment and work of the IGAI, the report noted that there was no independent police oversight agency. AI urged that all allegations of torture, ill-treatment or other abuse by police officers be automatically investigated as "public crimes", where the filing of a judicial complaint was automatic.

AI country reports/ visits
Report
- Portugal: "Small problems ...?" A summary of concerns (AI Index: EUR 38/002/2001)

Visit

An AI delegate visited Portugal in December to gather information.

PUERTO RICO

COMMONWEALTH OF PUERTO RICO
Head of state: George Walker Bush (replaced William Jefferson Clinton in January)
Head of government: Sila María Calderón Serra
Capital: San Juan
Population: 4 million
Official languages: Spanish, English
Death penalty: abolitionist

There were allegations that US Navy personnel used excessive force against peaceful protesters and reports of ill-treatment by the Puerto Rican police.

Background
Vieques, a small island off the east coast of Puerto Rico, has been the scene of frequent demonstrations by the local population, civil rights activists and environmentalists protesting against the use of the island for some 60 years by US forces as a military training ground. In April 1999 a civilian worker was killed by an errant bomb, since when the US Navy has used inert bombs.

In June, the US administration ordered that the Navy pull out of Vieques by 1 May 2003. A non-binding referendum in July returned an overwhelming vote for an end to the bombing and for the immediate withdrawal of the US Navy. An official referendum, due to be held in January 2002 to decide whether the Navy should stay or go, was cancelled following the attacks on 11 September in the USA. In December, legislation was passed by US Congress stipulating that the Navy could not close its training range in Vieques until it found a suitable replacement. The Navy stated that it would resume using live ammunition in Vieques during its next training exercises.

Allegations of excessive force
During protests against US military exercises at Camp García on Vieques at the end of April and the beginning of May, a number of peaceful demonstrators, including elderly people and children, were reported to have been sprayed indiscriminately by US Navy personnel with large quantities of chemicals and pepper spray. Rubber bullets and pellet weapons were allegedly fired at them. Many reported being ill-treated in custody following arrest. They alleged that they were sprayed in the face with tear gas and pepper spray while kneeling and handcuffed from behind; that they were made to kneel for hours on rocky terrain and to spend long periods in the sun without water; and that they were subjected to humiliating procedures during clothed body searches, such as having their breasts or testicles squeezed. Others complained of being denied food, water, medication and phone calls for long periods. Most only had access to a lawyer after they had been brought before a judge after two or three days in detention. Several detainees on hunger strike were allegedly denied adequate quantities of water, causing severe risk to their health. It was alleged that the Navy continued to fire its inert bombs after activists, holding white flags and flares, penetrated the bombing range. The US Navy refuted the allegations and noted that the actions used by navy personnel during the protests were legitimate law enforcement procedures.

Ill-treatment
Four homeless men alleged they were ill-treated by police officers after being picked up in Bayamón in March and taken to another town where they were left on the street. They alleged that they were beaten on various parts of the body, sprayed in the face with an irritant and hit in the mouth with a police radio. The authorities claimed that the police were trying to identify those who might benefit from a rehabilitation program. However, it was alleged that the four were among a wider group of homeless people who were said to have been arbitrarily removed as part of an operation to clear the streets of homeless people. An investigation into the case was undertaken by the *Cuerpo de Investigaciones Criminales,* Criminal Investigations Office, but the outcome was not known at the end of the year.

AI country reports/visits
Statement
- US Navy must use restraint against protesters in Vieques, Puerto Rico (AI index: AMR 51/082/2001)

Visit
An AI delegate visited Vieques in May.

QATAR

STATE OF QATAR
Head of state: al-Shaikh Hamad Ibn Khalifa Al-Thani
Head of government: al-Shaikh Abdullah Ibn Khalifa Al-Thani
Capital: Doha
Population: 0.6 million
Official language: Arabic
Death penalty: retentionist

Restrictions on freedom of expression continued to be enforced. At least one possible prisoner of conscience was sentenced to a prison term. The Court of Appeal increased the sentences of 19 political prisoners from life imprisonment to capital punishment. Past allegations of torture remained without investigation and there were new allegations.

Restrictions on freedom of expression
In June three men related to the ruling family attacked Ahmad Ali, the editor of *Al Watan* newspaper, leaving him injured and unconscious. The assault took place after his newspaper published articles criticizing government policies. The attackers were arrested by the police but released a few days later, reportedly after a settlement was reached between them and the victim.

Despite earlier assurances that no one would be prevented from entering Qatar to demonstrate peacefully, representatives of several non-governmental organizations were reportedly denied visas at the time of a World Trade Organization ministerial conference there in November. Those who were given visas to travel to Qatar complained that they were denied access to conference delegates and their right to demonstrate was limited.

A draft law on publishing, still before the Consultative Council (*Majlis al-Shura*) at the end of 2001, reportedly contained clauses stipulating harsh punishments, including imprisonment, for vaguely worded offences and failed to provide safeguards for freedom of expression.

Possible prisoner of conscience
'Abd al-Rahman bin 'Amir al-Na'imi, detained without charge or trial since June 1998, was released in April. He had been arrested after he criticized aspects of government policy in a petition to the Consultative Council.

Torture
Investigations did not take place into allegations of torture made by prisoners in previous years, including those sentenced in connection with a failed coup attempt in 1996.

In March Lu'ay Muhammad Abdullah, a US national of Palestinian origin and a possible prisoner of conscience, was sentenced by Qatar City Court to two years' imprisonment on charges of "publicly insulting the ruler". The court found that he had "insulted the leaders of Qatar" on a website. He was allegedly beaten and forced to stand on one foot with his hands raised during interrogation. The sentence was upheld by the Court of Appeal in June.

Death penalty
In May the Court of Appeal increased the sentences from life imprisonment to capital punishment on 19 prisoners convicted following the 1996 coup attempt. At least 20 others had prison sentences increased to life imprisonment and 28 had their convictions overturned. The prosecution had appealed after the trial before a lower court ended in February 2000. The 19 included a Saudi Arabian national who had been acquitted at the trial.

Committee on the Rights of the Child
In October the UN Committee on the Rights of the Child considered Qatar's initial report on the implementation of the UN Children's Convention. It expressed concern about the inconsistencies of the juvenile justice system with the Convention. It also raised concerns about the trafficking of children for the purposes of camel racing and the health risks involved. In its recommendations, the Committee requested that Qatar withdraw its reservations on several articles of the Convention and review laws and practices to bring them into line with the Convention.

ROMANIA

ROMANIA
Head of state: Ion Iliescu
Head of government: Adrian Năstase
Capital: Bucharest
Population: 22.5 million
Official language: Romanian
Death penalty: abolitionist for all crimes
2001 treaty ratifications/signatures: Optional Protocol to the UN Children's Convention on the involvement of children in armed conflict

Police ill-treatment, sometimes amounting to torture, was widespread. There were numerous reports of police shootings in disputed circumstances. Provisions in the Penal Code criminalizing homosexuality were abolished, but a long-delayed comprehensive reform of the Penal Code and of the laws concerning the police force was again postponed. Conscientious objectors to military service were threatened with imprisonment.

Background

The ruling Party of Social Democracy of Romania, which changed its name during the year to the Party of Social Democracy, showed little respect for the rule of law. It instructed judges how to rule in certain cases and made partisan dismissals from and appointments to the judiciary. New parliamentary procedures, particularly the provision to keep committee meetings closed to the public, restricted the ability of non-governmental organizations (NGOs) to influence the debate on new legislation.

Corruption continued to be widespread and to undermine the legal system, the economy and public confidence in government. In May, for example, an unpublished report of the European Parliament alleged that not only did the government fail to resolve the problem of abandoned children but its officials were implicated in irregularities in international adoptions which placed children at risk of trafficking and other forms of abuse. In June the authorities suspended for at least a year the registration of new foreign families requesting international adoption.

Torture and ill-treatment

The number of reported incidents of police ill-treatment, in certain cases amounting to torture, increased. Some of the police officers involved had not been disciplined following earlier complaints of ill-treatment.

At least two people died in custody, reportedly as a result of torture or ill-treatment. A criminal investigation into one death in custody was initiated almost four months after the event, after public protests and repeated appeals from NGOs. The lack of adequate medical treatment in police lock-ups apparently contributed to the death in February of a man who was reportedly suffering from drug dependency. One reported victim of police torture, a 20-year-old man, committed suicide in January on the eve of a second interrogation.

Safeguards to prevent torture and ill-treatment were routinely ignored. Police often questioned suspects in the absence of a lawyer. Minors were questioned without their parents or a representative of an authority responsible for the social welfare of children being present. Most of those who alleged they were ill-treated were not allowed to contact their family and were denied medical treatment while in custody.

As in previous years, some of the victims who complained of police ill-treatment were subsequently charged with "assaulting a public official" and, in at least one case, detained. These charges appeared to be fabricated in order to put pressure on the victims to withdraw their complaints. In October, a representative of the General Police Inspectorate stated that in the first nine months of 2001, 137 people who were charged with "assaulting a public official" had allegedly made "insults, threats or affronts", which apparently did not involve any physical violence.

☐ In October, 350 gendarmes and special police officers reportedly attacked a village of around 1,300 inhabitants, apparently in reprisal for an alleged attack earlier that day on guards working for an oil pipeline company by a group of villagers. Dozens of villagers were indiscriminately beaten and their property was damaged or destroyed.

☐ In July Dumitru Grigoraş, a 35-year-old father of four children, was arrested by two police officers, following a complaint that he had been violent to his wife. A man living opposite the police station alleged that later that evening he heard screams from the police station and one of the officers shouting, "Tell me! By morning I will have killed you anyway". Early the next morning the body of Dumitru Grigoraş was taken to a local doctor's surgery. Police claimed that he had become ill while making a statement. Two days later Dumitru Grigoraş's wife and father were allowed to see the body. They refused to take the body for burial because it was covered in bruises and other injuries and demanded a second autopsy. In October it was reported that two police officers were detained pending an investigation into Dumitru Grigoraş's death; the result of the investigation was not known at the end of the year.

☐ In March, 14-year-old Vasile Dănuţ Moise was taken to the local police station in Vlădeşti for questioning by two police officers and a farmer whose cow had allegedly been stolen. Vasile Dănuţ Moise later described how the police officers beat him on the palms of his hands and on the back with a "shepherd's staff" (a wooden rod about one metre long) and with a truncheon. A third officer hit him on the head with a lever-arch file, making him fall against a stove. That evening Vasile Dănuţ Moise was taken to a paediatric hospital suffering from psychological trauma and injuries to his head, eye and back.

Investigations into complaints of torture or ill-treatment were rarely thorough and impartial. Some preliminary investigations were apparently prolonged in order to impede complainants from seeking redress.

Unlawful use of firearms by the police

At least one person was shot dead and several others were injured by police officers who used firearms in breach of international human rights standards. Victims were often shot during attempted thefts or while running away, when they did not pose an immediate threat to either the officers or passers-by. The vast majority of the shootings were perpetrated by officers of the Public Order Services. Investigations into such cases were not thorough and impartial. In March the Ministry of Justice stated in a letter to AI that the investigation into the killing of Radu Marian in October 1999 established that although warning shots had been fired by the police officer, the suspect "kept running zigzag, on an uneven field, so that although the police officer aimed at the feet, the bullet entered the back of Radu Marian's head and he died".

☐ In April, Alexandru Mihai Dombi was stopped by the traffic police on the outskirts of Oradea. When he failed to present his driving licence he was asked to leave his identity card with the officers. He and his two companions then continued the journey into town. However, their car broke down and they then walked to the nearby railway station. At the crowded station,

Alexandru Mihai Dombi started to run after spotting a large number of police officers. One of the officers reportedly ordered him to stop and then shot at Alexandru Mihai Dombi, hitting him in the head. According to reports, other officers also fired shots in the station which had been surrounded by the police. According to the police, after their first encounter with Alexandru Mihai Dombi they had discovered that he was wanted to serve a four-year sentence for fraud.

Reform of the Penal Code and police
In June the government adopted an emergency ordinance which abolished Article 200, which dealt with, among other things, homosexual consensual relations and under which prisoners of conscience had been held. The Article had also made it an offence punishable by between one and five years' imprisonment "to entice or seduce a person to practise same-sex acts, as well as to form propaganda associations, or to engage in other forms of proselytizing with the same aim".

However, the government apparently abandoned a draft which attempted to revise the Penal Code comprehensively. The draft had been adopted by the Chamber of Deputies in June 2000. The government introduced a new proposal to the Senate which retained excessive restrictions on the right to freedom of expression.

Attempts to reform the police force also faltered. Two draft laws were before parliament, under emergency procedures, which were intended to demilitarize the police and introduce limited monitoring of police by the local community. There was concern that these laws contained provisions on the use of firearms which were in breach of the UN Basic Principles on the Use of Force and Firearms by Law Enforcement Officials. However, on 12 September, the Ministry of the Interior reportedly asked the Senate to postpone its debate as the drafts had to be reconsidered in light of "new security requirements".

In November the European Commission in its 2001 report on Romania's progress towards accession to the European Union made extensive recommendations to the government, including further reform of the Penal Code, particularly of the provisions relating to freedom of expression, and increasing the accountability of police officers.

Conscientious objectors
Conscientious objectors were threatened with imprisonment.

In March the Military Court of Appeal reviewed court decisions in the cases of 16 conscientious objectors sentenced in 1999 and 2000. The 16 were Jehovah's Witnesses and had refused to carry out alternative service because they had reservations about its length and nature, and on the grounds that the law exempts from military service ordained ministers of recognized churches. In 13 cases the Court overturned their convictions and acquitted them of all charges. In the remaining three cases, the Court confirmed their earlier acquittal by the Bucharest Military Tribunal.

Fourteen conscientious objectors, who were convicted in 2000 and given suspended sentences, appealed to the Prosecutor General of Romania to file on their behalf an extraordinary appeal to annul their convictions. However, the Prosecutor General filed a different type of appeal, asking the Supreme Court to establish that the Military Court of Appeals interpreted the law correctly when it sentenced the 14. In October 2001 the Supreme Court rejected the Prosecutor General's appeal. An appeal by the 14 was before the European Court of Human Rights at the end of the year.

The civilian alternative to military service remained punitive in length; the grounds on which it was granted continued to be limited and the restrictions on when applications for alternative service may be submitted were unchanged.

AI country reports/visits
Reports
- Romania: Alleged torture of a 14-year-old boy by police (AI Index: EUR 39/005/2001)
- Romania: Penal Code reform – a step back (AI Index: EUR 39/008/2001)
- Romania: Alleged ill-treatment of a 15-year-old girl by a police officer (AI Index: EUR 39/009/2001)
- Romania: Alleged police ill-treatment of youths in Sighișoara (AI Index: EUR 39/011/2001)

RUSSIAN FEDERATION

RUSSIAN FEDERATION
Head of state: Vladimir Putin
Head of government: Mikhail Kasyanov
Capital: Moscow
Population: 144.7 million
Official language: Russian
Death penalty: abolitionist in practice
2001 treaty ratifications/signatures: Optional Protocol to the UN Women's Convention; Optional Protocol to the UN Children's Convention on the involvement of children in armed conflict

Russian and Chechen armed forces committed serious human rights violations and breached international humanitarian law during 2001 in the continuing conflict in the Chechen Republic (Chechnya). An estimated 160,000 internally displaced people, the majority women and children, remained in overcrowded refugee camps in Chechnya and neighbouring Ingushetia with inadequate

shelter and sanitation. Council of Europe delegates visiting the region in December stated that conditions for refugees in Chechnya were "terrible" and getting worse. Human rights abuses reported included arbitrary detention; torture, including rape; ill-treatment; "disappearances"; extrajudicial executions; and the use of unofficial secret detention centres that often amounted to little more than pits in the ground. Criminal investigations by Russian federal authorities into human rights violations by military and police forces in Chechnya were inadequate and ineffective; few of those responsible for grave violations were known to have been brought to trial in 2001. Elsewhere in the Russian Federation there were continuing reports of torture and ill-treatment in police custody and of cruel, inhuman and degrading prison conditions. Refugees and asylum-seekers were at risk of being sent back to countries where they could face human rights violations. Conscientious objectors to military service faced forcible conscription and imprisonment.

Background

In November, the *Duma* (parliament) approved a new Code of Criminal Procedure which sanctioned the introduction of jury trials from January 2003 in all regional courts for trials involving serious offences such as murder and rape. A 1999 ruling by the Constitutional Court had banned the imposition of death sentences until the jury trial system had been introduced throughout the Federation; jury trials at the time were available in only nine of the Federation's 89 regions. Despite the President's outspoken opposition to the death penalty, the introduction of jury trials in regional courts raised questions of whether this moratorium on executions would continue.

President Putin condemned the attacks in the USA on 11 September and sought to justify Russian policy in Chechnya by reiterating assertions that Chechen armed groups were linked to Osama bin Laden.

The Chechnya conflict

Both sides to the conflict in Chechnya continued to commit serious human rights abuses and to breach international humanitarian law. Violations committed by Russian forces during 2001 included arbitrary detention in secret detention centres and pits in the ground, torture and ill-treatment, "disappearances", and extrajudicial executions. Chechen forces attacked civilians working in the local administration in Chechnya, failed to take steps to minimize civilian casualties during attacks and ill-treated and unlawfully killed captured Russian soldiers.

In January, the Parliamentary Assembly of the Council of Europe voted in favour of ratifying the credentials of the new Russian delegation, which in effect restored the voting rights of the Russian delegation (suspended in April 2000), despite continuing reports of serious and widespread violations of human rights and international humanitarian law.

☐ On 20 February, Russian forces detained Anna Politkovskaya, a journalist investigating reports of torture, including the rape of detainees in Russian custody in Chechnya, for not having official permission to work in the region. She alleged that while in detention she was questioned about her work and that her life was threatened. She was released without charge on 22 February.

Prisoners of conscience

On 24 May, Russian forces detained Dik Altemirov, former Minister for Tourism and Sport in the Chechen government and a former Vice-President of the Chechen Republic, for two days on suspicion of involvement in Chechen armed groups. Dik Altemirov had advocated Chechen independence by peaceful means and supported the work of the Organization for Security and Co-operation in Europe (OSCE) Assistance Group in Grozny.

Impunity

The Russian federal authorities failed to investigate adequately widespread reports of human rights violations in Chechnya.

☐ In February, at least 51 bodies were found in Dachny village. However, no autopsies were performed and the authorities rushed to bury bodies that had not been identified, rather than preserve them for the purposes of further investigations.

In April the UN Commission on Human Rights adopted a resolution condemning the continuing abuses of human rights and breaches of humanitarian law and called on all parties to the conflict to take measures to protect civilians and aimed at ensuring accountability. Russian officials rejected the resolution, terming it "biased", while officials from the Russian Ministry of Foreign Affairs stated that the Russian government did not feel obliged to implement the Commission's recommendations. The Commission also reiterated its request that the relevant thematic special rapporteurs and special mechanisms visit Chechnya without delay, and urged the government to respond favourably to their requests for visits.

Arbitrary arrests and 'disappearances'

Russian forces continued to arbitrarily detain civilians during raids on towns and villages in Chechnya. Detainees were reportedly ill-treated or tortured while held incommunicado. Bribes were so commonly extorted from relatives to secure detainees' release that the act of detention itself often appeared to be motivated by financial gain. Hundreds of people "disappeared" after being taken into custody; the mutilated bodies of some were later found, along with the bodies of other unidentified individuals, in more than a dozen dumping grounds and mass graves throughout Chechnya.

☐ In June Russian soldiers in the village of Mayrtup, Kurchaloy district, arbitrarily detained between 20 and 30 men, including Said-Khasan Salamov and Said Magomed Bakhaev. According to reports, soldiers took eight of the group to the outskirts of the village, beat them and unleashed trained attack dogs on them. Four of the men were later transferred to a Russian military base and two others were released five days later. Said

Magomed Bakhaev was last seen, unconscious and badly beaten, being taken to a Russian military base. The fate and whereabouts of Said Magomed Bakhaev and Said-Khasan Salamov remained unknown at the end of 2001.

Torture and ill-treatment
There were widespread reports of torture and ill-treatment during military raids.

In June, Russian soldiers surrounded the village of Chernorechye, detained about 200 men, including boys as young as 14, and took them to a disused medical centre near the Grozny water reservoir. The detainees alleged that the soldiers blindfolded and beat them on the way to the medical centre and threatened to kill them. At the medical centre, interrogators reportedly burned the detainees with cigarettes and subjected them to electric shocks. By the end of the year, no prosecutions were known to have taken place in connection with this or any other allegation of torture of detainees by Russian forces in Chechnya.

Abuses by Chechen fighters
There were reports of human rights abuses against civilians by Chechen fighters, including hostage-taking and the unlawful killing of members of Russian armed forces taken prisoner. Chechen fighters engaged in frequent armed attacks against civilian members of the pro-Moscow Chechen administration, resulting in dozens of fatalities and serious injuries.

Prisoner of conscience
On 25 December Grigory Pasko was sentenced to four years in a labour camp for intending to distribute information that "would harm the battle readiness of the Pacific Fleet". The re-trial of Grigory Pasko on treason charges, which began in July, was held behind closed doors before the Military Court of the Pacific Fleet. Grigory Pasko, a journalist and naval captain, had been arrested in 1997 after exposing the Russian navy's illegal dumping of nuclear waste; he was accused of passing classified documents to Japanese news media. The retrial was ordered by the Military Collegium of Russia's Supreme Court following Grigory Pasko's release under a general amnesty in 1999.

Freedom of expression
In December, a Belgorod court convicted Olga Kitova, an investigative journalist at the newspaper *Belgorodskaya Pravda* and a member of the Belgorod parliament, on charges of slander and insulting or threatening an official. The trial followed the publication of articles she had written in which she alleged official corruption surrounding a rape case. In the articles, she alleged that law enforcement officials had falsified a rape charge against six students. The family of the victim brought the prosecution.

Olga Kitova was first detained in March, reportedly for failing to respond to a summons for questioning on charges of interfering in a criminal investigation, slander and defamation. She alleged that police officers who took her to the local procurator's office beat her. Hospital doctors treated her later that day for high blood pressure, bruises and other injuries to her head and arms.

Olga Kitova was again arrested in May and additionally charged with insulting and using force against, or threatening, an official. She was immediately hospitalized until 8 June. Her trial on charges of slander and insulting and using force against, or threatening, an official began in October after the Belgorod parliament voted to strip her of her parliamentary immunity. On 20 December she was given a suspended sentence of two and a half years, banned from seeking public office for three years, fined and ordered to pay moral damages to the family of the rape victim.

Conscientious objectors
Although the right to conscientious objection is enshrined in the Constitution, in practice courts continued to imprison objectors. There was no law authorizing alternative civilian service and courts were often inconsistent in their support for applications from men seeking a civilian alternative to compulsory military service.

Ilya Baryshnikov, a 19-year-old metal worker from the Nizhegorodskoy region, had attempted to enlist for alternative service in October 2000. His application had been refused in December 2000, and in February 2001 a criminal case was opened against him for refusing to serve. In March, a local court sentenced him to six months in a labour colony.

In August, Jehovah's Witness Maxim Tambovtsev from Pavlovsk, Voronezh region, successfully appealed to the Pavlovsk district court against a call-up by the conscription commission on grounds of conscientious objection. The court ordered the commission to provide him with an alternative civilian service. In September, the conscription commission appealed against this decision to the Voronezh regional court which sent the case back for further investigation. In November, the Pavlovsk court repeated its earlier verdict, supporting Maxim Tambovtsev. The conscription commission appealed against this decision to the Voronezh court and a decision was pending at the end of the year.

Torture and ill-treatment
Police reportedly continued to torture and ill-treat detainees in their custody in order to extract confessions. Detainees were also said to have been tortured during pre-trial detention.

In April, police in Elista, the capital of the Russian Republic of Kalmykia, allegedly beat Nadezhda Ubushaeva, a former schoolteacher. Nadezhda Ubushaeva and her family had gone to the main square to protest peacefully outside the parliament building against their forcible eviction from their apartment earlier that day. She alleged that approximately five police officers, led by a police colonel, arrived and dragged her to a police car, beating her with a hard instrument. On 13 April, doctors recorded injuries to Nadezhda Ubushaeva's hips, shoulders and face consistent with these allegations. She was held in the police station for about two hours. No investigation was known to have been initiated into these allegations.

Conditions in detention

There was no improvement in conditions in penitentiaries and pre-trial detention centres. Up to a million people were held in overcrowded conditions that often constituted cruel, inhuman or degrading treatment. An estimated five million people enter and leave the prison system annually. Medical care was generally inadequate; according to reports, 10,000 inmates die annually. Over 100,000 inmates were believed to suffer from tuberculosis, and HIV infection was also reportedly widespread. In April the Russian human rights commissioner stated in his annual report that conditions in the penal system were "horrible", describing pre-trial detention centres as "hotbeds of epidemics". He criticized the imposition of lengthy prison sentences for relatively minor offences, citing a case where a man received a four-year prison sentence for stealing two chickens.

President Vladimir Putin refused to grant clemency to prisoners to help alleviate overcrowding in prisons. However, in November, the *Duma* approved an amnesty for child offenders and women convicted of petty crimes, which it was estimated would cover some 10,000 children and 14,000 women. The amnesty applied to those who were under 18 years of age when the offence was committed, first-time offenders, those sentenced to less than six years' imprisonment, and those who have served over half of their sentence. Pregnant women, single mothers, women prisoners with disabilities, widows and women over the age of 50 were also eligible under the amnesty provisions.

Children

Children were often held in conditions that amounted to cruel, inhuman or degrading treatment. Child offenders were particularly vulnerable in a criminal justice system which serves to punish rather than rehabilitate children found to have infringed the criminal law; there was no separate justice system for children.

In June, Ministry of Justice officials announced that over 17,000 children were serving prison terms in 64 special colonies for adolescents; 10 colonies had recently opened in former army and Interior Ministry troops' barracks that were transferred to the Ministry of Justice's jurisdiction.

Refoulement

Legal provisions for asylum-seekers remained inadequate. Many asylum-seekers were subjected to *refoulement* (forcible return) to countries where they were at risk of grave human rights violations, before their claims for asylum had been fully considered.

▫ On 29 March an Iranian asylum-seeker, who had been arrested on 21 February at Moscow's Sheremetevo airport, was forcibly returned to Iran, where it was believed he risked imprisonment and ill-treatment. The deportation was carried out despite a pending court procedure on his asylum claim. The Ministry of Foreign Affairs, the state agency responsible for ensuring compliance with international obligations, reportedly tried in vain to prevent the deportation.

AI country reports/visits

Reports
- Russian Federation (Chechnya): The Council of Europe must act to stop further abuses (AI Index: EUR 46/003/2001)
- Russian Federation (Chechnya): Only an international investigation will end impunity – the UN Commission on Human Rights must act now (AI Index: EUR 46/007/2001)
- Russian Federation: FSB vs. environmental activist Grigory Pasko – punishment without a crime (AI Index: EUR 46/009/2001)

Visits
AI delegates visited the Russian Federation, including Moscow and the Republics of Kalmykia, Tatarstan, and Ingushetia, in February, July, September, October, November and December.

RWANDA

RWANDESE REPUBLIC
Head of state: Major-General Paul Kagame
Head of government: Bernard Makuza
Capital: Kigali
Population: 7.9 million
Official languages: Kinyarwanda, French, English
Death penalty: retentionist
2001 treaty ratifications/signatures: African Charter on the Rights and Welfare of the Child

Killings of unarmed civilians, "disappearances", arbitrary arrests, unlawful detentions and torture or ill-treatment of detainees were reported. Tens of thousands of Rwandese sought refuge in neighbouring countries. At least 120 people were sentenced to death for crimes committed during the 1994 genocide, some after unfair trials; no executions took place. An estimated 110,000 people continued to be detained, 95 per cent of them accused of taking part in the 1994 genocide. Many were held for prolonged periods without charge or trial in conditions amounting to cruel, inhuman or degrading treatment. Trials of genocide suspects continued at the International Criminal Tribunal for Rwanda (ICTR) in Tanzania. In eastern Democratic Republic of the Congo (DRC), Rwandese military and allied forces were responsible for the deaths of civilians; torture, including rape; "disappearances"; and the systematic harassment of human rights defenders. Most perpetrators of human rights violations continued to benefit from impunity.

Background

Rwandese troops thwarted incursions by armed opposition groups from the DRC into northwestern Rwanda between May and July, and there were skirmishes in southwestern Rwanda between September and December. Relations with neighbouring Uganda deteriorated and in March the Ugandan authorities declared Rwanda a "hostile nation". Both governments accused the other of harbouring, mobilizing and training "anti-government dissidents".

Local elections were held in March. Although there were no reports of malpractice, members of the National Electoral Commission, which vetted candidates, were nominated by government officials and campaigning by political parties was not allowed. As a result, 45 per cent of the electoral contests had a single candidate and 81 per cent of those elected were incumbents previously appointed by the government.

Dozens of former government officials and officers in the armed forces were harassed and forced into exile for criticizing the government over its human rights record, restrictions on political opposition and corruption.

The government established a Judicial and Constitutional Commission with the task of drafting a new constitution by 2003. The commission began to educate and consult with Rwandese during the constitution drafting process.

"Villagization" schemes, under which over one million rural Rwandese had been resettled in new "villages" between 1997 and 2000, came to a virtual stop with the withdrawal of international funding. The schemes had in many cases resulted in hardship, insecurity and increased communal violence.

Over 20,000 refugees returned to Rwanda, approximately the same number as in 2000. Most came from the DRC, the rest from Tanzania. By the end of the year, Rwanda was close to adopting refugee legislation that established procedures for determining refugee status in accordance with international standards.

Killings of civilians

The killing of civilians declined with a reduction in the number of incursions by armed opposition groups. Armed groups based in the DRC looted civilian property, wounding and killing at least five of their victims in the process, and government installations, particularly medical centres, in the northwest. At least 15 civilians who threatened to alert the Rwandese authorities were also killed. Unlike previous years, counter-insurgency operations by Rwandese forces suppressed the attacks without indiscriminately attacking the civilian population. Nonetheless, at least a dozen people were killed in crossfire between government forces and armed opposition groups. Rwandese forces also killed non-combatants, such as porters, who accompanied armed opposition groups.

Elements of the Local Defence Forces (LDF), a citizen's militia organized and armed by the government, and the Rwandese Patriotic Army (RPA), sometimes with the complicity of local government authorities, also killed civilians.

◻ In June, members of the LDF killed a 58-year-old woman in Gasiza district, Gisenyi province, after robbing her. Although arrested, they were released within a few days by the local authorities.

'Disappearances'

A number of "disappearances" were reported. Many of the "disappeared" were former or serving military officers, government officials and prominent members of civil society. No independent investigations of these reports were carried out.

◻ On 7 April, retired Major Alex Ruzindana, a demobilized army officer, "disappeared" while driving to Cyangugu with a serving army officer who subsequently returned to Kigali and informed Major Ruzindana's family that he had fled to Uganda. Senior government and military officials were alleged to have been involved in planning the "disappearance" and it was widely believed that Major Ruzindana had been killed because of his suspected opposition to the government.

Arbitrary detention

The rights of individuals to be informed of the reason for their arrest, to be issued a provisional arrest warrant and to have the benefit of a pre-trial detention hearing were restored in July when a law suspending portions of the Code of Criminal Procedure expired. Another result was that the detention of tens of thousands of individuals on suspicion of involvement in the 1994 genocide was effectively rendered illegal. The Public Prosecutor's Office continued the process begun in October 2000 of bringing such detainees before their local communities in order to gather testimony for prosecution before *gacaca* tribunals (see below).

Several people suspected of criticizing the government, or being associated with critics of the government, were detained without charge or trial. Some individuals were reportedly held for refusing to testify against genocide suspects.

◻ Six people — including Emmanuel Mudenge, Alfred Bandora and Kalim Tushabe, who worked for provincial public prosecution offices — were arrested in April and unlawfully detained for a month before being released without charge. They appeared to have been detained because of suspected links with Rwandese dissidents in Uganda.

Torture and ill-treatment

Many detainees were beaten following arrest, particularly those in district detention centres. Most were detained in desperately overcrowded and insanitary conditions, amounting to cruel, inhuman or degrading treatment. Several detainees and prisoners died as a result. Men, women and children were usually held in the same facilities. Women and child detainees were subjected to violence and sexual abuse. Rwandese prisons housed 10 times as many prisoners as they were designed to hold.

There were several allegations of rape by LDF or RPA forces, which were not known to have been investigated by the authorities.

☐ On 18 June, an LDF member reportedly raped a young widow in Mutura district, Gisenyi province. He was arrested but subsequently released. On 29 June he and others from the LDF allegedly raped at gunpoint and killed a 14-year-old girl in the same district. No one was detained.

Genocide trials

Approximately 1,300 people were tried in connection with the 1994 genocide during the year, about half the number tried in 2000. By the end of 2001, the Specialized Chambers established in August 1996 had tried less than six per cent of those detained for genocide-related offences. In many cases, trials did not meet international standards of fairness. At least 120 defendants were sentenced to death. There were no judicial executions.

The reduction in the number of trials in part resulted from reduced funding and the lack of judicial independence.

☐ The Public Prosecutor's Office in Butare refused to release eight people acquitted in December 2000, including Zacharie Banyangiriki, a former parliamentarian, on the grounds that "new facts" had come to light. The State Prosecutor ignored protests by the district Appeals Court and the Supreme Court of Rwanda. Zacharie Banyangiriki died in prison in November. His seven co-accused were still in prison at the end of the year. No ruling had been given on their appeal by the end of 2001.

Gacaca

In March, the government, faced with a judicial backlog, promulgated a law establishing a community-based system of justice known as *gacaca*, which from 2002 would begin trying lesser charges related to the 1994 genocide. In October, 260,000 *gacaca* tribunal lay magistrates were elected by popular vote. No trials had taken place by the end of 2001.

Concerns that *gacaca* is seriously flawed and that most aspects of the tribunals fall short of international standards of fairness remained unaddressed. There is no provision for legal counsel for the accused. There are serious questions regarding the legal competence, partiality and independence of the elected judges, and fears that pressure groups would subvert the communal debate supposed to determine the innocence or guilt of genocide suspects.

International Criminal Tribunal for Rwanda

Trials of leading genocide suspects continued at the International Criminal Tribunal for Rwanda (ICTR) in Arusha, Tanzania. Fifty-two suspects were detained awaiting trial at the end of 2001. One defendant was acquitted and released in June. Seven on-going trials involving 17 defendants, three of which had begun in 2000, had not been completed by the end of 2001. The ICTR Appeals Court rejected appeals by three prisoners in June. One appeal was pending at the end of the year. In December, six people convicted of genocide were transferred to Mali to serve their sentences.

Switzerland, the Netherlands, Belgium, Senegal, Mali, Tanzania and Kenya arrested 10 suspects and transferred seven of them for trial before the ICTR (see Belgium entry). The authorities in Italy refused to implement an international warrant issued by the ICTR in July for the arrest of a Roman Catholic priest alleged to have participated in the genocide, on the grounds that under Italy's domestic legislation there was no legal basis to proceed with the arrest (see Italy entry).

In March, the UN Office of Internal Oversight Services pointed to a number of abuses, foremost among them a fee-splitting arrangement between defence lawyers and their clients. In May, the Chief Prosecutor dismissed seven senior attorneys, citing "professional incompetence". Two defence team investigators were indicted for genocide-related crimes in May and December, and the contracts of three were terminated in July and August for suspected involvement in the genocide.

In early 2001, the Rwandese Patriotic Front (RPF)-led government agreed to cooperate with the ICTR's investigation into crimes against humanity allegedly committed by members of the RPF in 1994.

International justice

Foreign states tried a number of Rwandese accused of genocide under their national jurisdictions.

☐ In April, a Canadian court discharged one defendant who had been charged in 1996 with "inciting violence and ethnic hatred" in Rwanda in the early 1990s.

☐ In April, a Swiss military court of appeal confirmed a 14-year prison sentence passed in May 2000 on a Rwandese local government official for war crimes.

☐ Four people were convicted in Belgium in June and sentenced to prison terms of between 12 and 20 years. Two Roman Catholic nuns, a university professor and a businessman were convicted of war crimes.

Freedom of association and assembly

Leaders of political parties came under increasing pressure.

☐ Theobald Rwaka, Vice-President of the *Parti Démocratique Chrétien*, Christian Democratic Party, lost his ministerial post in March and fled the country in April following accusations of treason.

A number of new political parties were formed in early 2001, most of them outside Rwanda because of the government's ban on new political parties during the nine-year transition period ending in 2003.

☐ Former President Pasteur Bizimungu was placed under house arrest in May after launching the *Parti Démocratique pour le Renouveau*, Democratic Party for Renewal. Journalists who interviewed him were interrogated, threatened by the military authorities, and forced to surrender tape recordings. After restrictions on him were lifted in June, he was harassed and assaulted by unidentified assailants.

Abuses in the Democratic Republic of the Congo

The RPA and the Rwandese-backed Congolese armed opposition group, *Rassemblement congolais pour la démocratie-Goma* (RCD-Goma), Congolese Rally for Democracy-Goma, controlled large areas of the eastern DRC, in opposition to the DRC government and armed political groups which included Rwandese insurgents.

All the forces involved were responsible for unlawful killings of unarmed civilians; acts of torture, including rape; "disappearances"; and other serious human rights abuses. Both RCD-Goma and the forces opposing them used child soldiers, many of them forcibly recruited. Torture and ill-treatment regularly occurred in RPA detention facilities and military camps. Human rights defenders and civil society activists were subjected to harassment, detention and ill-treatment. (See Democratic Republic of the Congo entry.)

Intergovernmental organizations

In April, the UN Commission on Human Rights ended the mandate of the Special Representative for Rwanda.

The UN Expert Panel on the Illegal Exploitation of Natural Resources and Other Forms of Wealth of the DRC released its report in April. The report detailed widespread looting by the RPA and the role played by RPA commanders, businessmen and government structures in the systematic exploitation of DRC resources.

AI country reports/visits
Report
- Democratic Republic of the Congo: Rwandese-controlled east – devastating human toll (AI Index: AFR 62/011/2001)

Visit
AI delegates visited Rwanda in May and June.

SAINT LUCIA

SAINT LUCIA
Head of state: Queen Elizabeth II, represented by Pearlette Louisy
Head of government: Kenneth Anthony
Capital: Castries
Population: 0.15 million
Official language: English
Death penalty: retentionist

There were reports of police brutality and excessive use of force. At least one death sentence was passed in 2001, and at least two men remained under sentence of death at the end of the year.

Background
In elections held in December, the ruling Labour Party was returned to office with a slightly reduced majority.

Prison conditions
There were reports that prison conditions amounted to cruel, inhuman or degrading treatment. Sanitation was poor, with an open pit for all prisoners to use as a latrine. Severe overcrowding was exacerbated by the large number of remand prisoners awaiting trial.

In February the government announced it would address unsatisfactory prison conditions by constructing a new prison in which "an emphasis will be placed on the rehabilitation of prisoners, rather than on the punishment of criminals". The government also claimed to be increasing the number of magistrates in order to reduce the time between arrest and trial.

▫ In March, the High Court overturned a July 2000 court order that shackles be removed from Alfred Harding, who had been kept continuously shackled for nearly a year, and the order granting him compensation. The High Court ruled that the original motion was "misconceived" and should have been dismissed by the original trial judge.

Police brutality
There were reports of police brutality and excessive use of force. No police officers were charged in connection with allegations of extrajudicial executions or the use of excessive lethal force in previous years.

▫ In February, 23-year-old Randy Blanchard alleged that he was beaten by three police officers. One of the officers also cut off his dreadlocks with a cutlass, cutting his head in the process. He was taken to a mental hospital by police officers and held there for a week; he had no record of mental illness. A police officer was charged with unlawful wounding, but had not been tried by the end of the year.

▫ In November, 39-year-old Lucious Maurice was shot dead by police officers in disputed circumstances. Officers claimed they shot him after he threatened them with a cutlass. However, members of Lucious Maurice's immediate family, who witnessed his death, claimed he was not posing any threat when a police officer shot him twice. According to media reports, an investigation into the allegations was initiated, but the outcome was not known by the end of the year.

▫ Coroners' inquests were ordered into the deaths of Paul Hamilton and Alfred Harding who were shot dead by police in 2000. Paul Hamilton was reportedly shot in the back following a chase. Alfred Harding was shot dead after escaping from custody. He was reportedly shot twice after being told to lie down by a police officer and was denied medical attention. However, the progress of the inquests and of inquiries into the killings was extremely slow and had not been completed by the end of 2001.

Death penalty
At least two men were held under sentence of death at the end of 2001. No executions took place.

Human rights defenders
At least one lawyer was subjected to death threats and intimidation because of her activities as a defence lawyer.

Government responses
In February, the Prime Minister wrote to AI stating his government's commitment to the protection of human

rights and expressing concern that AI sought to undermine "the integrity of governments which share your concern for the rule of law, justice and human rights". The Prime Minister did not reply to subsequent correspondence from AI.

SAUDI ARABIA

KINGDOM OF SAUDI ARABIA
Head of state and government: King Fahd Bin 'Abdul'Aziz Al-Saud
Capital: Riyadh
Population: 19 million
Official language: Arabic
Death penalty: retentionist

Grave and widespread human rights violations continued to be reported. They were perpetuated by the strictly secretive criminal justice system and the government policy of barring political parties, trade unions and independent human rights organizations; international non-governmental human rights organizations were not allowed access to the country. The government failed to respond to any of the concerns raised by AI during the year. Hundreds of teenagers were flogged. Women continued to face severe discrimination. Arrests of suspected political and religious activists continued and the legal status of those held from previous years remained shrouded in secrecy. New information came to light on the torture of detainees in previous years. At least 79 people were executed. Over 5,000 Iraqi refugees continued to live in Rafha camp as virtual prisoners, denied the right to seek asylum in Saudi Arabia.

Background
While the human rights situation remained grave, there were two major developments which had the potential for a positive impact: the government announced new legislation and its human rights record was subjected to unprecedented public scrutiny by UN mechanisms.

In October the government announced that it had introduced, for the first time, a code of criminal procedure and a law regulating the legal profession. The two laws had not been made public by the end of the year and it was therefore not possible to assess their impact on human rights. For example, it was not known whether the new legislation would introduce legal safeguards against arbitrary arrest, lengthy incommunicado detention and secret trial proceedings or guarantee defendants the right to legal assistance throughout the judicial process and the right to effective appeal. However, Saudi Arabian lawyers and the media welcomed both measures as positive steps towards the recognition of the need for clear safeguards to protect the rights of defendants, and of the valuable role of lawyers.

The country's human rights record was subjected to unprecedented public scrutiny by the Committee on the Rights of the Child and the Commission on Human Rights. Both UN mechanisms expressed strong concern about the human rights situation in the country and called for redress. For example, the Committee on the Rights of the Child concluded that: "[n]oting the universal values of equality and tolerance inherent in Islam, the Committee observes that narrow interpretation of Islamic texts by State authorities are impeding the enjoyment of many rights protected under the Convention".

The government also submitted its initial report on the implementation of the UN Convention against Torture and was scheduled to appear before the Committee against Torture in November. However, the government withdrew at short notice and, as a result, its hearing before the Committee was postponed to a later date. AI drew the Committee's attention to Saudi Arabia's failure in its initial report to provide adequate information on torture, which remained rife in the country.

Women
Media coverage of women's issues, which began in 2000, continued into 2001, but no concrete steps were taken by the government to tackle the issue of discrimination in law and in practice. In December, the government announced that it had issued some women with identity cards. However, in April, when asked about a study into the issue of allowing women to drive and providing them with identity cards, the Minister of the Interior had reportedly replied: "It is not possible, and there are no studies on the subject at all... As I have said before, everything comes in its own time..." Similarly, when he was asked about women's representation in the *Majlis al-Shura* (Consultative Council) he reportedly dismissed this by stating: "Why make women a political issue... women are not a political issue, but a social subject..." Membership of the Consultative Council was increased during 2001 from 90 to 120, all men appointed by the King.

Major Martha McSally, a female fighter pilot in the US Air Force, challenged the dress code imposed by the US Air Force on female military personnel stationed in Saudi Arabia when off duty, on the grounds that it was discriminatory.

Torture and ill-treatment
Flogging of children
In January the Committee on the Rights of the Child recommended that Saudi Arabia "take all necessary steps to end the imposition of corporal punishment including flogging and all forms of cruel, inhuman and degrading punishment to persons who may have committed crimes while under 18..."

The response of the governorates (regional authorities) across the country was to wage campaigns of extrajudicial and summary floggings, targeting teenagers suspected of harassing women and other behaviour deemed immoral. Such behaviour included talking to women, whistling at them, trying to pass telephone numbers to them, and wearing transparent or women's-style clothes. By the end of the year, hundreds of teenagers had been flogged, most of them in public places where the alleged offences had taken place. Their cases were widely publicized in the media.

☐ Three youths were given 15 lashes each in the al-Rashid Shopping Mall in al-Khobar in the Eastern Province, where they had allegedly committed the offences. The flogging was described in the press as follows: "Officials announced the punishment several times over the mall's loudspeaker system, delaying its implementation to give shoppers time to gather... The flogging caused such a scene that shopping at the... mall... came to a standstill as the three were punished."

The campaign was spearheaded by the religious police, the Committee for the Propagation of Virtue and Prevention of Vice (CPVPV). In some regions the CPVPV was assisted by a committee composed of representatives from the office of the respective governorate, police, and the Prosecution and Investigation Department. In a press statement to the *al-Jazirah* newspaper, the Deputy Head of the CPVPV explained in response to questions about the legality of the campaign that: "...the case of harassment is not referred to the judiciary because it is considered expeditious matter for which the statute of the CPVPV prescribes 15 lashes. This is one of the prerogatives given to the CPVPV after agreement by the governorate..."

Torture in detention

As a result of the systematic practice of incommunicado detention, no detailed accounts of torture during 2001 were received. All those arrested during the year were subjected to incommunicado detention and when they were allowed access to families, or consular representatives in the case of foreign workers, this took place under strict supervision by prison officers and strict orders not to talk about detainees' treatment or the case concerning them. However, new information came to light on torture in previous years, and the press reported cases of domestic violence.

☐ Kalesh, an Indian national who was accused of theft and held in incommunicado detention, stated following his release in December 2000: "There were three people in civilian dress...They had a big stick with ropes at each end... I was asked to sit on the floor... At this time I am handcuffed and chained in my legs. The stick with the ropes was inserted through the folding of my knees...and the ropes were tied to my handcuffed hands. I became like a football... I was sitting/lying on the floor and these three devils... started kicking and beating me brutally with the rod... There are still marks... of that day on my body..."

Domestic violence

Severe discrimination against women continued to put women at increased risk of domestic violence. Foreign domestic workers were particularly vulnerable to such abuses. In March, an official from the Ministry of Labour was reported in the press as having revealed that around 19,000 foreign maids had run away from their employers. One of the main reasons cited was domestic violence against them.

In January, the Committee on the Rights of the Child expressed concern about domestic violence and the harm it inflicts on children. It recommended that Saudi Arabia "establishes hotlines and shelters staffed by women, for the protection of women and children at risk of or fleeing abuse". However, cases of domestic violence continued to be reported in the Saudi Arabian media.

☐ In May a journalist writing in the newspaper *Okaz* revealed that the neighbour of a 16-year-old girl who was locked up in the toilet by her father and stepmother for six months had informed the police of the girl's plight and constant crying, but the police did nothing.

Judicial corporal punishment

In addition to its use as extrajudicial punishment against children, flogging remained widely practised as a judicial corporal punishment handed down by judges as a main or additional punishment after unfair trials.

☐ A military officer was given 20 lashes in March after a court of expedient matters found him guilty of using a mobile phone while in flight with the Saudi Arabian Airlines.

☐ Muhammad al-Dawsari, Sa'id al-Subay'i and Muhammad al-Hadithi were sentenced in June to 1,500 lashes each, in addition to 15 years' imprisonment. All were convicted in connection with drugs charges. Four others tried with them in the same case were sentenced to death and executed. The floggings were scheduled to be carried out at a rate of 50 lashes every six months for the whole duration of the 15 years.

Prisoners of conscience and political prisoners

Arrests of suspected political and religious activists continued during 2001. Those arrested during the year were mainly members of the Shi'a and Christian communities, most of whom were released without trial after weeks or months of detention. In addition, there were unconfirmed reports that hundreds of people were rounded up in the wake of the 11 September attacks in the USA, but no details were available. It was not known how many remained in detention at the end of the year.

☐ Sheikh Muhammad al-Amri, a Shi'a religious scholar aged about 90, was arrested on 9 March and held for about two weeks before being released without charge. He was reportedly detained because he was visited by some Iranian Shi'a Muslims on pilgrimage (*Hajj*) in Saudi Arabia.

☐ Kamil Abbas al-Ahmad, aged 30, was arrested on 13 September at his home in Safwa and was detained at Safwa police station. The government did not provide any information as to the reason for his arrest, but it may have been related to his political activities. He had previously been detained on such grounds from July 1996 until June 1999, during which time he was allegedly tortured. He remained in detention at the end of the year.

The legal status and conditions of detention of those held from previous years remained shrouded in secrecy.

Sheikh Ali bin Ali al-Ghanim, who had been in detention since August 2000, was reportedly sentenced to five years' imprisonment and 500 lashes after a secret trial in prison. He was also reported to have been subjected to torture which allegedly included beating all over the body and sleep deprivation.

Death penalty
At least 79 people were executed. All were sentenced to death after unfair trials. They were convicted on charges which included murder, rape, or drug trafficking. The government continued to keep secret information on people under sentence of death and at risk of execution. The 79 included 23 foreign nationals, including seven Indian nationals and four Pakistani nationals. They also included two Saudi Arabian women, Badria al-Azizi and her mother, who were executed in connection with the murder of the father.

Refugees
Over 5,000 Iraqi refugees spent their 10th successive year as virtual prisoners in the Rafha military camp in the northern desert near the border with Iraq. The government continued to refuse them the opportunity to seek asylum in Saudi Arabia. They were among some 33,000 refugees originally housed in the camp. About 25,000 were resettled by the UN High Commissioner for Refugees (UNHCR) in Europe, North America, and Australia. The 5,000 remaining in Saudi Arabia continued to live in the camp under military guard with no right of movement beyond the perimeter fences.

AI country reports/visits
Report
- Saudi Arabia: Defying world trends – Saudi Arabia's extensive use of capital punishment (AI Index: MDE 23/015/2001)

Visits
AI renewed its request to send a delegation to Saudi Arabia following a statement to the press in December by the Director General of Prisons announcing that the government had invited AI to visit the country. However, by the end of the year, AI had not received a response to this request or other communications.

SENEGAL

REPUBLIC OF SENEGAL
Head of state: Abdoulaye Wade
Head of government: Mame Madior Boye (replaced Moustapha Niasse in March)
Capital: Dakar
Population: 9.7 million
Official language: French
Death penalty: abolitionist in practice

Despite two peace agreements and a notable reduction in the level of human rights violations committed by the security forces in the disputed region of Casamance, unrest and fighting did not stop. Abuses against civilians by armed opposition forces in Casamance continued throughout the year, particularly against people with "non-Casamance" names. Although the government made a commitment that past human rights violations by the military would be investigated, no inquiry had been set up by the end of 2001. The government also agreed to consider any future request for extradition from Senegal of the former President of Chad on charges of crimes against humanity.

Background
There was a notable reduction in reports of extrajudicial executions, "disappearances" and torture by the security forces as compared to the period before the present government came to power in April 2000.

Two peace accords were signed in March in order to end two decades of armed conflict between government forces and members of the *Mouvement des forces démocratiques de Casamance* (MFDC), Democratic Forces of Casamance Movement, an armed opposition group seeking independence for Casamance. The agreements provided for the release of all prisoners on both sides, the return of refugees from neighbouring countries, the clearance of mines, disarmament of MFDC armed groups, and the return of the military to barracks. However, these agreements could not be implemented because of continuing insecurity in the region, mainly as a result of fighting between rival armed groups within the MFDC. In addition to the armed conflict between MFDC armed factions, a leadership struggle led in November to a split between the supporters and opponents of Father Diamacoune Senghor, long-time Secretary General of the MFDC, who was named as President of the MFDC in August. These divisions prevented the MFDC from adopting a common position for negotiations with the government.

President Wade's *Parti démocratique sénégalais*, Senegalese Democratic Party, won an outright victory in the April legislative elections.

Deliberate and arbitrary killings by the MFDC
Alleged members of one of the MFDC's armed wings launched several attacks against civilians during the

year. The two most serious incidents took place in February and March when 20 unarmed civilians were shot dead after reportedly being identified by their "non-Casamance" names.

◻ On 16 February, 20 alleged members of the MFDC attacked a group of hauliers near Niahoump, some 70km northeast of the regional capital, Ziguinchor. They checked the identity cards of the truckers and shot dead all those with "non-Casamance" names. Thirteen people died immediately and another person died in hospital.

Prisoners of conscience

In March President Wade asked the judicial authorities to release all detainees held in connection with the Casamance conflict. Sixteen people were released in Kolda, Casamance, but several others remained in detention at the end of the year. Most had been held for months or years without trial.

◻ Michel Pereira, one of the last three Casamance detainees still held at the Rebeuss prison in Dakar, was believed to be suffering from mental illness. He had been held without trial since 1997, accused of threatening state security. Despite repeated requests and appeals, he remained in prison at the end of 2001.

Threats to freedom of expression

Journalists continued to be harassed and intimidated.

◻ In July, Alioune Fall, editor of the newspaper *Le Matin*, was detained for one day by the police *Division des investigations criminelles*, Division of Criminal Investigations, for publishing an article written by one of his journalists about escapes by several prisoners and discontent within the police force because the investigation into the incident was assigned to the gendarmerie rather than the police. In August, he was charged with "publishing false information", but no trial had taken place by the end of 2001.

◻ In August, Alioune Tine, head of the human rights organization *Rencontre africaine pour la défense des droits de l'homme* (RADDHO), African Human Rights Rally, was briefly detained for interrogation after declaring publicly that President Wade's view that reparations for slavery would be "absurd and insulting" was "scandalous and inopportune". Three days later, President Wade received Alioune Tine and said that his brief detention was a "mistake".

Impunity

Despite formal commitments by the authorities, no investigations were initiated in 2001 into past human rights violations.

◻ In January, student Balla Gaye was shot dead in clashes between demonstrators and the police near the University of Dakar. President Wade immediately ordered an investigation which concluded in November that the police may have been responsible for this death. A policeman was subsequently charged and detained.

Hissein Habré

In September, President Wade publicly announced his readiness to hand over former Chadian President Hissein Habré to stand trial in a third country for gross human rights abuses. This statement was a welcome contrast to a statement made by the President in April — following a Court of Cassation decision in March that the Senegalese courts had no jurisdiction to try him — that Hissein Habré had one month to leave Senegal. (See Chad entry.)

AI country reports/visits
Visits

In June an AI delegation visited Senegal and met President Wade and Father Diamacoune Senghor, then Secretary General of the MFDC. In August, AI held its biennial International Council Meeting in Senegal. In November, AI organized a human rights workshop in Dakar with victims of torture and relatives of people who "disappeared" in Casamance.

SIERRA LEONE

REPUBLIC OF SIERRA LEONE
Head of state and government: Ahmad Tejan Kabbah
Capital: Freetown
Population: 4.6 million
Official language: English
Death penalty: retentionist
2001 treaty ratifications/signatures: UN Convention against Torture

Continued attacks by rebel forces on Sierra Leonean refugees in Guinea drove them back into rebel-held areas of Sierra Leone where they were killed, raped and harassed. Rebel fighters and government-assisted militia forces killed dozens of civilians in attacks in northern Sierra Leone. The Guinean armed forces indiscriminately bombarded border areas of Sierra Leone, killing civilians. Most high-ranking rebel leaders were released from detention, while other rebel prisoners remained held without charge or trial. At least 10 died in custody, reportedly from medical neglect. Efforts to establish mechanisms to fight impunity continued.

Background

The November 2000 Abuja cease-fire agreed by the government and the opposition Revolutionary United Front (RUF) was maintained within Sierra Leone and the security, political and humanitarian situation improved. By the end of the year a total of 17,500 troops of the UN Mission in Sierra Leone (UNAMSIL) were successfully deployed throughout the country, including in RUF-held areas. They facilitated the disarming and demobilization of approximately 48,000 combatants including over 3,000 child combatants, the majority of whom were members of the RUF and the government-assisted militia, the Civil Defence Forces (CDF). United Kingdom (UK) troops, deployed in 2000 under a bilateral arrangement between the UK and the government in order to secure Freetown and its airport and to train the Sierra Leone Army, were reduced from 1,000 to 360 by the end of 2001. During the year the government and humanitarian agencies gained access to parts of the country previously controlled by the RUF, except for parts of Koinadugu district in Northern Province and parts of Kono and Kailahun districts in Eastern Province. By the end of the year, the government had declared all districts in the south, and several in the north and east, safe for return by civilians.

In the early part of the year there was continuing conflict along the border between Sierra Leone and Guinea, with intermittent attacks by RUF forces on refugee camps in Guinea and air bombardments by the Guinean armed forces on the RUF in Sierra Leone. Large numbers of civilians were displaced from districts in Northern Province to areas near Freetown. Fighting continued between the RUF and the CDF. A meeting chaired by the UN in May in Abuja, Nigeria, marked a renewed commitment to peace and the disarmament and demobilization process in Sierra Leone by the warring parties. In June and July further skirmishes between RUF and CDF forces disrupted the peace process temporarily. Along the border with Liberia, RUF forces continued to provide arms, ammunition and combatants to fight alongside the Liberian armed forces against Liberian armed opposition groups based in Guinea. In August an official process of consultation began between the governments of Sierra Leone, Liberia and Guinea, to address security concerns in the region. Meetings between the three countries, with the support of the Economic Community of West African States and the UN, continued to the end of the year.

Presidential elections intended to be held in November were postponed to May 2002. In October the RUF set up a political party, the Revolutionary United Front Party (RUF-P), and opened an office in Freetown.

By the end of the year the UNAMSIL human rights section had opened regional offices in Makeni, Magburaka, Kenema, and Port Loko. A high-level visit by the UN High Commissioner for Refugees (UNHCR) brought greater attention and action to address the situation of refugees and people who had been internally displaced within the country.

By the end of 2001 over 80,000 Sierra Leonean refugees had returned from Guinea and Liberia. The majority had been driven out by attacks by the armed forces, the local civilian population and civil defence groups in Guinea. Some 60,000 returned with the assistance of UNHCR, the remainder spontaneously on foot. A significant number returned to areas previously under RUF control. Approximately 7,000 refugees returned from Liberia, owing to increasing insecurity there, when the border between the two countries reopened late in the year. Many were resettled in, or assisted to return to, areas deemed safe in the south and in some parts of the north and east. Some also returned to RUF-held areas, including the diamond districts of Kono and Kailahun.

Throughout the year several thousand Guinean and Liberian refugees fled to Sierra Leone to escape armed conflict in Liberia, or were abducted by the RUF in Guinea and brought to Sierra Leone. Some were registered and assisted by UNHCR, but thousands of others were believed to be in the border areas of Kailahun district and inaccessible to humanitarian agencies.

Abuses by the Revolutionary United Front

RUF forces continued to kill, torture and abduct civilians and returned refugees in the areas which remained under their control. They forcibly recruited civilians to fight or labour for them, and raped women and girls. Looting was widespread.

Scores of killings and abductions of civilians by the RUF occurred in March and April, and again in June and July when the CDF attacked RUF positions in Kono and Koinadugu districts. RUF fighters raided communities suspected of backing the CDF militias. Torture, including rape, also continued.

▫ According to reports, early in the year several girls and women in Koidu, in Kono district, were forced to become "wives" to a single RUF combatant, and women from a group of 80 refugees returning to Koinadugu district from Guinea were assigned to RUF combatants and raped.

Throughout the year civilians, mostly men, continued to be forcibly recruited.

▫ In April, 500 men in Jagbwema, in Eastern Province, were reportedly captured by the RUF for training as combatants.

In Koidu the RUF reportedly forced young men to mine diamonds for them. At least two people were alleged to have been beaten to death by RUF combatants, a woman for mining without permission and a man for allegedly swallowing diamonds in an attempt to hide them.

In several instances, the RUF were reported to have abducted Guinean women and children in attacks on Guinea and brought them to Sierra Leone. Following such abductions, the women were reportedly gang-raped, forced to work for RUF combatants, held in harsh conditions and deprived of food. In several cases UNHCR negotiated their release and they were returned to Guinea.

Violations by government forces

Throughout the year CDF forces continued intermittently to kill and torture captured and suspected rebels, and to recruit children into their fighting forces. They harassed civilians and humanitarian agency personnel.

▫ In June and July, a CDF militia known as the *Donzos* was reportedly responsible for deliberately burning and looting villages and killing and injuring civilians suspected of supporting the RUF in Kono and Koinadugu districts.

No action was taken by government to hold the CDF to account for violations.

Indiscriminate bombardment by Guinean security forces

During the first half of the year, in response to increased tensions within the region and cross-border incursions into Guinea by armed groups, including the RUF, the Guinean armed forces mounted aerial military operations in Sierra Leonean territory. They targeted Kambia district in Northern Province in particular, but also other areas of Northern Province such as Bombali and Koinadugu districts. The attacks from helicopter gun ships resulted in scores of civilian casualties, massive displacement of people and destruction of property. Guinean ground forces also crossed the border into Kambia district to attack RUF forces, coerced civilians to carry loot for them and forcibly recruited men into their fighting forces.

The attacks did not appear to have been targeted at RUF military bases with any degree of care or accuracy or with regard for civilian lives. Witnesses said that, while civilians suffered greatly, there were few RUF casualties and little damage to its bases or equipment.

▭ In January helicopter gun ships reportedly attacked Yelibuya in Kambia district resulting in at least 20 civilian casualties, both wounded and dead. At least 300 homes were destroyed.

▭ Kamakwie, Bombali district, was attacked on 26 January and at least 12 civilians were killed. Although a significant number of RUF combatants were present in Kamakwie, their base and personnel were untouched.

▭ In April civilians were severely injured in attacks by Guinean forces near the towns of Kassiri and Rokupr and the villages of Kychom, Rokon and Sino in Kambia district.

Military assistance to rebel forces and the diamond trade

The international community and the Sierra Leone government continued to take steps to prevent the trade in diamonds being used to finance military assistance to the RUF. In May the UN Security Council imposed a ban on the export of rough diamonds from Liberia, accused of trading in diamonds with the RUF and providing military assistance in return. A UN-approved diamond export certification system introduced by the Sierra Leone government in October 2000 continued to function. By not making a distinction between diamonds by origin, it failed to prevent the trade in diamonds from RUF areas. In July, the Sierra Leone government, the RUF and the UN agreed to a ban on diamond mining in the eastern Kono district but this was not implemented or monitored and proved ineffective. In October, a UN Panel of Experts reported that RUF diamonds were being traded through the government system and recommended better monitoring. Throughout the year, governments and the international diamond industry continued to work towards agreeing an international diamond certification system.

Release of political detainees

As part of the peace process, most senior RUF detainees were released during the year, with the exception of former RUF leader Foday Sankoh. Between 80 and 100 remained detained without charge or trial, some held since the renewal of conflict in May 2000. They included members of the West Side Boys, a group of renegade soldiers responsible for serious human rights abuses until their arrest in September 2000. There were reportedly 10 deaths in custody among this group as a result of harsh detention conditions and poor medical care.

Impunity

Some progress was made on mechanisms to combat impunity. However, by the end of 2001 there were still insufficient funds for the Special Court for Sierra Leone which the UN Security Council decided in August 2000 should try crimes against humanity, war crimes and other serious violations of international humanitarian law. A lack of adequate resources could affect the number of cases which the court could try and therefore its ability to ensure a balance of cases which could be effectively investigated and prosecuted and therefore the perception of its independence and impartiality. Issues which remained unresolved included whether the court would have jurisdiction over crimes committed since the civil conflict began in 1991 or only from 1996, ensuring an independent prosecution policy was maintained, and its relationship with a planned Truth and Reconciliation Commission. Little attention was given to improving the domestic judicial system.

AI country reports/visits

Reports
- Guinea and Sierra Leone: No place of refuge (AI Index: AFR 05/006/2001)
- Sierra Leone: Renewed commitment needed to end impunity (AI Index: AFR/51/007/2001)

Visits

AI delegates visited Sierra Leone in April to carry out research, and to meet government officials and representatives of armed groups. A further visit in November to eastern Sierra Leone focused on the situation of refugees and internally displaced people.

SINGAPORE

REPUBLIC OF SINGAPORE
Head of state: S.R. Nathan
Head of government: Goh Chok Tong
Capital: Singapore City
Population: 4.1 million
Official languages: Chinese, Malay, Tamil, English
Death penalty: retentionist

Freedom of expression continued to be curbed by restrictive legislation and by the effects of civil defamation suits against political opponents. Peaceful demonstrators also faced penalties. At least 24 Jehovah's Witnesses were imprisoned during the year. Death sentences continued to be imposed and at least two executions were known to have been carried out. Criminal offenders were sentenced to caning.

Background
The ruling People's Action Party (PAP) continued its domination of the political scene, winning 82 out of 84 parliamentary seats in elections in November. On the opening day of the election campaign the PAP's control was confirmed when opposition candidates contested only 29 of the seats. The small and poorly funded opposition parties complained that constituency changes and a range of regulations imposed by the PAP made it more difficult for them to win votes. The Parliamentary Elections Act was amended, curbing the use of the Internet for political campaigning and banning the publication of opinion polls during elections.

Curbs on freedom of expression
The threats of potentially ruinous civil defamation suits against opponents of the PAP continued to inhibit political life and engendered a climate of self-censorship. The Internal Security Act (ISA) and other restrictive legislation remained in place, thus continuing to allow for indefinite detention without trial and undermining the rights to freedom of expression and assembly. Government controls imposed on the press and civil society organizations also curbed freedom of expression and were an obstacle to the independent monitoring of human rights. Two non-governmental civil society groups, the Think Centre and the Open Singapore Centre, were classified by the government as political associations, thereby making them ineligible for foreign funding and subjecting them to other restrictions. In April a law was passed empowering the government to restrict or suspend foreign broadcast services considered to be engaging in domestic politics. Foreign print media were already subject to similar restrictions.

Curbs on freedom of assembly
Fifteen members of the *Falun Gong* spiritual group were arrested for holding a vigil in memory of group members who had died in custody in China. In March seven of them were sentenced to four weeks in prison, reportedly for refusal to disperse during the vigil. Another eight were fined for holding a rally without a police permit. Under Singaporean law all assemblies of five or more people in public require a police permit.

In early 2001, two activists from the Think Centre and the Open Singapore Centre were questioned by police in connection with a peaceful rally they had organized to mark international human rights day. Participants at the rally had called for greater political freedoms and abolition of the ISA. The activists had also planned a marathon run for human rights, but were refused a police permit. Opposition groups criticized the procedures for applying for permits as arbitrary and lacking in transparency.

Civil defamation suits
Opposition figures continued to face politically motivated civil defamation suits which carried the threat of financial ruin. While the government claimed that PAP leaders had a legitimate right to defend their reputation, there were grave concerns that their real motive was to silence selected opposition figures and remove them from public life.

◻ J.B. Jeyaretnam, aged 75, a vocal government critic and former leader of the opposition Workers' Party, was declared bankrupt in January after being one day late in paying an instalment of libel damages. The proceedings stemmed from a defamation payment awarded against him, as the editor of the Workers' Party newsletter, for allegedly defaming members of the ethnic Tamil community in an article written by a colleague in 1995. After losing his court appeal against the bankruptcy order in July, he was expelled from parliament, barred from practising as a lawyer and prevented from standing as a candidate or from taking any active part in the subsequent elections. He continued to face separate defamation suits lodged against him in 1997 by Senior Minister Lee Kuan Yew and other leading PAP members.

◻ In November, the Prime Minister and Senior Minister lodged a defamation suit against Chee Soon Juan, leader of the opposition Singapore Democratic Party, after he publicly questioned them during the election campaign about a multi-billion dollar loan previously offered to former President Suharto of Indonesia. Chee Soon Juan apologized to the Ministers, but subsequently withdrew his apology and filed a suit against them for allegedly defaming him.

Conscientious objectors
At least 24 conscientious objectors to military service were imprisoned during the year. All were members of the banned Jehovah's Witnesses religious group. There was no alternative civilian service for conscientious objectors to military service.

Detention without trial
In December, 15 men were detained without trial under the ISA. They were accused by the authorities of having links to the *al-Qa'ida* network and of plotting to bomb

the US embassy and other targets in Singapore. During the police investigation they were held incommunicado, raising concerns that they could be subjected to torture or ill-treatment.

Death penalty
The death penalty was mandatory for drug trafficking, murder, treason and certain firearms offences. At least two executions for drug trafficking were recorded but the true number was believed to be higher. Zulfikar Bin Mustaffah and Thiru Selvam were hanged in September for drug trafficking. Thiru Selvam was reportedly sentenced to death on the basis of the testimony of another man who had been found in possession of marijuana. The judge had reportedly offered Thiru Selvam a prison sentence if he confessed. Between 1991 and 2000, 340 people were hanged, giving Singapore probably one of the highest execution rates in the world, relative to its population.

Cruel judicial punishment
Caning, which constitutes cruel, inhuman or degrading punishment, remained mandatory for some 30 crimes, including attempted murder, rape, armed robbery, drug trafficking, illegal immigration offences and vandalism. It was not known how many sentences were carried out during the year. Under the law, caning may be imposed on juvenile offenders.

AI country reports/ visits
Reports
- Singapore: International trial observer to attend Court of Appeal as former opposition leader J.B. Jeyaretnam faces possible expulsion from parliament (AI Index: ASA 36/005/2001)
- Singapore: Defamation suits threaten Chee Soon Juan and erode freedom of expression (AI Index: ASA 36/010/2001)

Visit
In July a representative of AI and Lawyers' Rights Watch Canada attended two Court of Appeal hearings related to the libel actions against J.B. Jeyaretnam

SLOVAKIA

SLOVAK REPUBLIC
Head of state: Rudolf Schuster
Head of government: Mikuláš Dzurinda
Capital: Bratislava
Population: 5.4 million
Official language: Slovak
Death penalty: abolitionist for all crimes
2001 treaty ratifications/ signatures: Optional Protocol to the UN Children's Convention on the involvement of children in armed conflict

There were reports of torture and ill-treatment of Roma by police officers and one Romani man died in custody in suspicious circumstances. The authorities failed to provide information to human rights monitors about investigations into these incidents. Information received from a non-governmental organization (NGO) raised questions about the standard of the investigation into the killing in 1999 of Ľubomír Šarišský. A lawyer defending Romani victims was inadequately protected by the police from racist violence.

Roma
In May the UN Committee against Torture, having considered Slovakia's initial report concerning the implementation of the provisions of the UN Convention against Torture, expressed concern about reported instances of police ill-treatment of Roma as well as allegations that police failed to provide adequate protection to Roma against racially motivated attacks by skinheads. The Committee also expressed concern that the authorities had failed to carry out prompt, impartial and thorough investigations into such incidents, or to prosecute and punish those responsible. It recommended that prompt measures be adopted to address its concerns. AI repeatedly requested information from the Slovak authorities regarding investigations into human rights violations against Roma but none was forthcoming.

◻ Karol Sendrei died on 6 July while detained in Revúca police station with his two adult sons. They had been arrested the previous day in Magnezitovce after they had complained that a police officer had assaulted one of the sons. The three Roma were reportedly tied to a radiator at the police station and beaten by officers. Karol Sendrei was beaten so severely that he lost consciousness and a doctor was called but he could not revive him. An autopsy established that he died as a result of shock caused by a ruptured liver, internal bleeding, and fractures to the jaw, ribs and sternum. One son, Peter Sendrei, was admitted for treatment to the local hospital with severe bruising all over his body. In October, seven police officers were arrested and charged with torture and inhuman and degrading treatment.

◻ In October the findings were made public of an investigation by the NGO European Roma Rights

Center (ERRC) into the death in August 1999 of 21-year-old Ľubomír Šarišský, who had been shot in the abdomen during interrogation in police custody in Poprad. In March 2000 Ladislav Pittner, then Minister of the Interior, stated that an official investigation had established that the detainee had attacked the officer and then shot himself accidentally with the officer's gun. The ERRC concluded that the official investigation and the trial of the officer responsible had not been prompt, thorough and impartial. Although an autopsy had revealed injuries which were consistent with allegations that Ľubomír Šarišský had been beaten at the time of arrest and during questioning, and two investigations failed to confirm the officer's version of the shooting incident, he was charged only with "causing injury to health through negligence in the course of duty". The negligence consisted in failing to properly secure his weapon. He was sentenced in October 2000 to a suspended sentence of one year's imprisonment after a trial which was conducted in a summary procedure. The lawyer for the victim's family was not informed that the trial was taking place.

Harassment of a human rights defender
In October, Columbus Igboanusi, an international human rights lawyer representing Romani victims of police ill-treatment and racist violence, was threatened in two separate incidents by a group of armed people in front of his apartment in Bratislava. A leaflet had been circulated by skinheads describing him as a defender of the Roma and a threat to Slovakia. When Columbus Igboanusi, a Nigerian national, sought police protection, he was questioned about his residency in Slovakia and the NGO he was representing. The following day a Bratislava newspaper published an article stating that Columbus Igboanusi had refused police protection.

AI country reports/ visits
Report
- Concerns in Europe, January-June 2001: Slovak Republic (AI Index: EUR 01/003/2001)

SOLOMON ISLANDS

SOLOMON ISLANDS
Head of state: Queen Elizabeth II, represented by John Ini Lapli
Head of government: Allan Kemakeza (replaced Manasseh Sogavare in December)
Capital: Honiara
Population: 0.5 million
Official languages: Solomon Islands Pidgin, English
Death penalty: abolitionist for all crimes

Police officers and former members of armed groups continued to enjoy impunity for human rights abuses. There was a widespread lack of confidence in the criminal justice system, which failed to investigate and bring to justice those responsible for ethnic violence, including killings, or torture in previous years. Former members of armed groups were recruited into the police and prison services. Many refused to give up their illegal guns and were accused of using them to commit human rights abuses. The UN High Commissioner for Human Rights initiated a human rights program.

Background
In February, representatives of rebel groups and of national and provincial governments signed the Marau Peace Agreement which covers an area excluded from a previous peace accord. Formal talks to review the 2000 Townsville Peace Accord failed in September after what appeared to be a political killing. Implementation of these two peace agreements was hampered by the refusal of many former militants and police officers to surrender guns, a pre-condition for immunity from prosecution.

The government appeared to be powerless to stop shootings, beatings, extortion and intimidation by suspected former members of armed ethnic groups, particularly in the period before elections in December. Villagers in Guadalcanal, Malaita and Western provinces complained of frequent threats of violence by so-called former "militants" with access to illegal guns.

Elections were held in December after civil society groups protested against attempts by the Manasseh Sogavare government to delay elections. Allan Kemakeza was elected Prime Minister. Alex Bartlett, a former leader of one of the armed ethnic groups, the Malaita Eagle Force, was appointed as Foreign Minister.

Prime Minister Kemakeza promised to implement a rehabilitation program for former militants to induce them to give up more than 500 high-powered guns found to be missing from the police armoury by the Peace Monitoring Council.

SOMALIA

SOMALIA
Head of state: Abdiqasim Salad Hassan
Head of transitional national government: Hassan Abshir Farah (replaced Ali Khalif Gelayadh in November)
Head of Somaliland Republic: Mohamed Ibrahim Egal
Head of Puntland Regional State: Jama Ali Jama (replaced Yusuf Haji Nur in November, who replaced Abdullahi Yusuf Ahmed in June)
Capital: Mogadishu
Population: 9.2 million
Official language: Somali
Death penalty: retentionist

Hundreds of people, including civilians, were killed and injured in fighting, mainly in the south, between clan-based militias linked to political factions, and between government militias and these clan-based militias. Death sentences were passed by Islamic courts and executions were reported. Islamic courts continued to operate although they did not comply with international standards for fair trial. Freedom of expression was curtailed resulting in the detention of prisoners of conscience.

Background

The transitional national government (TNG), based in Mogadishu, established in October 2000 following the internationally supported Arta Peace Conference in Djibouti, was still recognized in only a fraction of the south of the country. It continued to face opposition from the self-proclaimed governments of Somaliland and Puntland, and from armed factions which controlled parts of Mogadishu and the south. Fighting continued for control of territory between factions and the TNG, and among factions in the southern part of the country. Some faction militias began to be integrated into the police force and the army.

In March, a number of faction leaders, opposed to the TNG, met in Ethiopia and formed the Somali Reconciliation and Restoration Council (SRRC). Their stated aim was to hold a conference in 2002 that would lead to the establishment of a "representative Transitional Government of National Unity".

In a national referendum in Somaliland in June, voters endorsed the new Constitution which declared Somaliland's independence as a state. The referendum was opposed by the TNG and Puntland regional authority.

The term of Puntland leader Abdullahi Yusuf Ahmed came to an end in June. Under the Puntland Charter he was replaced temporarily by the President of the Supreme Court, Yusuf Haji Nur. Abdullahi Yusuf Ahmed refused to acknowledge his replacement, and supporters of both sides clashed in August in Bosasso, where around 40 people were killed. In November Jama Ali Jama was appointed by elders as the next leader, although this decision was again rejected by Abdullahi

Yusuf Ahmed. Fighting between supporters of both sides broke out in November and December in Garowe, resulting in the deaths of at least 13 people.

In October, the TNG lost a vote of no-confidence and the government was dismissed. A new Prime Minister, Hassan Abshir Farah, was appointed in November.

Reconciliation

Several attempts at reconciliation were made during 2001. In March the League of Arab States adopted a resolution urging support within Somalia for the TNG. In May the TNG announced it was appointing a 25-member National Commission for Reconciliation and Property Settlement. However, the Chair resigned in July citing a lack of government support. In December the Kenyan government hosted a conference attended by the President of the TNG and a number of faction leaders with the aim of reconciling both sides. The subsequent resolution reportedly called for the creation of "an all-inclusive government" in Somalia. However, key faction leaders within the SRRC boycotted the talks and rejected the outcome. In December, fighting in Mogadishu between supporters of faction leader Musa Sudi Yalahow and one of his officials, who had attended the Nairobi meeting, resulted in the deaths of 19 civilians.

In December delegates from the Inter-Governmental Authority on Development met in Mogadishu with officials from the TNG National Anti-Terrorism Task Force and discussed the reconciliation process and the "fight against terrorism".

A new UN Independent Expert on the situation of human rights in Somalia was appointed and visited in August and September.

Response to the 11 September attacks in the USA

The TNG and Puntland authorities swiftly and continually denied reports that *al-Qa'ida* training camps were present in Somalia, and the TNG established a National Anti-Terrorism Task Force in September. *al-Itihad*, an Islamist group based in Somalia, was included in a list of banned organizations issued by the US government.

Severe economic repercussions were felt by thousands of Somalis after the foreign assets of *Al-Barakat*, the major remittance bank in Somalia, were frozen by the US government which claimed that *Al-Barakat* was diverting funds to *al-Qa'ida*.

Tensions grew in late 2001 following reports that Somalia had been identified by the US government as a possible target for "anti-terrorist" action. In December, delegations from the US government and the UN visited Somalia to discuss security concerns with TNG and Somaliland officials.

Civilian victims of armed conflict

Fighting between rival clans and factions continued throughout 2001. Hundreds of civilians were killed in outbreaks during which indiscriminate force was used. Incidents took place mainly in the Mogadishu area and in the south and reportedly also involved Ethiopian troops supporting the Rahanwein Resistance Army. Scores of civilians were indiscriminately killed during fighting between rival clans and factions in May and July in Mogadishu. In October, 30 people were killed in Mogadishu in fighting between government forces and militia linked to political factions. There were killings and reprisal killings of clan opponents, expulsions of members of other clans, cases of kidnapping as well as detention, and torture or ill-treatment of prisoners. Women and minorities were particularly vulnerable to abuses. None of the factions respected the principles of international humanitarian law which regulate the conduct of armed conflict and protect civilians.

◻ In November, 18 students were reportedly shot dead by armed factions at their school near Buulo Barde in Hiran region.

◻ In March gunmen in Mogadishu abducted four UN staff members and three from the non-governmental organization *Médecins sans frontières*. All were released unharmed several days later.

Rule of law

A process to gradually bring Islamic courts, established by faction leaders, into the national judicial system began in Mogadishu. However, there was concern that they did not meet recognized standards of fair trial and judicial competence. Several death sentences were imposed by such courts, which were reportedly immediately carried out. Concern continued that judicial administrations and police forces in Somaliland and Puntland displayed inconsistent respect for legal rights. Reports persisted by human rights defenders in Somaliland of arbitrary detentions, unfair trials, poor prison conditions and cases of torture and unlawful killing by police.

Freedom of expression

Freedom of expression was very limited in all areas of the country, with little tolerance by government authorities or armed factions of criticism by individuals or the media. Scores of journalists and others were arrested and detained without charge for days or weeks. Many were prisoners of conscience. Human rights groups continued to urge the government and factions to respect human rights.

◻ In February, Safiyo Abdi Haji Garweyne, an 18-year-old woman, was killed and others injured when police reportedly opened fire on a crowd protesting at the arrest of a number of people following a peaceful demonstration in Bosasso, Puntland.

◻ Suleiman Mohamed Gaal, a former Somaliland presidential candidate, was arrested in May in Hargeisa, Somaliland, and held for two weeks. He was accused of supporting the TNG. He remained on bail without charge at the end of 2001.

SOUTH AFRICA

REPUBLIC OF SOUTH AFRICA
Head of state and government: Thabo Mbeki
Capital: Pretoria
Population: 43.8 million
Official languages: Afrikaans, English, Ndebele, Pedi, Sotho, Swazi, Tsonga, Tswana, Venda, Xhosa, Zulu
Death Penalty: abolitionist for all crimes

Torture, excessive force and the misuse of lethal force by the police continued to be reported. Prisoners awaiting trial were released to reduce severe overcrowding. The Truth and Reconciliation Commission completed its hearing of amnesty applications. Despite measures to increase police effectiveness, many victims of continuing high levels of rape and other sexual violence remained without protection or redress. A court ruling ordered the government to make anti-retroviral drugs available to HIV-positive pregnant women. In some provinces, the authorities took action to prevent rape survivors being given such drugs. The government sought the return of two suspects handed over to Botswana without formal extradition proceedings or assurances that they would not be sentenced to death; the Constitutional Court ruled unlawful the return of an asylum-seeker to the USA in 1999 under similar circumstances.

Background

In March the Pharmaceutical Manufacturers' Association (PMA) reached an out-of-court settlement with the government in its case to declare illegal new legislation intended to increase access to cheaper anti-retroviral drugs for South Africans with HIV/AIDS. A tenth of the population has the disease. The Treatment Action Campaign and other organizations, which had pressured the PMA to withdraw its case, also criticized the government for disputing publicly the cause of AIDS and failing to implement clear plans to address the crisis.

In April the Minister of Safety and Security, Steve Tshwete, announced that three leading members of the ruling African National Congress (ANC) were under police investigation in connection with an alleged plot against President Mbeki. However, the allegation appeared to be based on suspect intelligence information and the Minister later conceded that those named were innocent.

In October a senior ANC official, Tony Yengeni, was arrested and charged with corruption and perjury after an investigation by statutory and parliamentary bodies into a government multi-billion dollar arms deal with European companies.

There were increasing tensions between the ANC and its "tripartite alliance" partners, the Congress of South African Trade Unions and the South African Communist Party, over their involvement in strikes and public protests and the direction of government policies.

The government remained under pressure to address public concern about high levels of violent crime. Anti-crime vigilante groups carried out violent attacks on criminal suspects. The authorities implemented reforms to increase the effectiveness of investigations and the conviction rate, including improving training in "intelligence-led" investigations and extending court hours. Proposals for a Victims Charter, including financial compensation to crime victims, were developed in cooperation with the South African Human Rights Commission and non-governmental organizations (NGOs).

Human rights violations by the security forces

Incidents of torture, ill-treatment and suspected misuse of lethal force continued to be reported. The Independent Complaints Directorate (ICD) told parliament that they were investigating 266 reports of deaths in police custody and as a result of police action received between April and September, as well as 36 complaints of torture and 123 complaints of serious assault and attempted murder. One case involved members of the Umtata Murder and Robbery Unit who, in May, when interrogating a suspect, allegedly poured acid over his genitals. Following ICD investigations, police officers in Gauteng Province were arrested and charged after allegedly assaulting suspected illegal immigrants in incidents in March and August.

There were other reported incidents of such abuses.

◻ In November, two men required hospital treatment after being severely beaten, allegedly with pick handles, by police in the Pietersburg area, Northern Province. One of them, Benjamin Pootona, required emergency treatment for renal failure as well as bone fractures.

◻ In a possible racially-motivated death in police custody, in February the body of Bheki Zikhali was found in a forest in the Mbazwana area, Northern KwaZulu Natal, a day after he was arrested. The body reportedly bore signs of torture. According to witness testimony, Bheki Zikhali had been told by the white officer who arrested him that he was being taken to Mbazwana police station, but family members later found no trace of him there. An independent post-mortem examination was ordered. In April, four men, including two police officers, were arrested, charged with kidnapping and murder, and released on bail to await trial. The trial proceedings had not concluded by the end of the year.

◻ On 23 April Zakhele Mabhida was shot dead in the offices of the Durban Murder and Robbery Unit, shortly after he had handed himself over to the police in connection with an investigation into the killing of two police officers earlier in the year. Preliminary investigations indicated that he posed no threat to the police when shot.

There were a number of incidents in which police used excessive force.

◻ In February, when police were attempting to control a student protest at the University of the North in Sovenga, a police officer reportedly fired rubber bullets at student Mahlane Lazarus Letselane, injuring his eye, although he was posing no threat according to witness and film evidence.

In November, four police officers, accused of deliberately inciting police dogs to attack three defenceless Mozambican detainees in 1998, were convicted and sentenced to an effective four to five years' imprisonment.

The Ministry of Justice and human rights organizations sought an order from the Constitutional Court in November effectively to compel the police to implement a 1998 reform of the Criminal Procedure Act which limited the use of deadly force to situations where lives were under threat.

Prison conditions

The government took steps to improve prison conditions. The Judicial Inspectorate of Prisons had reported at the end of 2000 that prisons were severely overcrowded, with some at 200 per cent occupancy rate, and that a third of the prison population who were awaiting trial were detained under inhumane conditions and in breach of national law and international standards.

The Departments of Correctional Services and Justice authorized the release of some of these prisoners, many of whom had been unable to pay bail money owing to poverty. The Judicial Matters Amendment Act in December allowed prison directors to apply to court for the release of certain categories of unconvicted prisoners where overcrowding imminently threatened their health or safety. The Correctional Services Amendment Act in December amended provisions on the use of force and weapons, to ensure their use was proportionate to threats to life and safety.

Impunity

The trial continued in the Pretoria High Court of the former head of the chemical and biological warfare program, Dr Wouter Basson, on charges including murder and attempted murder of opponents of the apartheid government. In June the court acquitted the accused of 15 of the original 64 charges, including nine charges of murder, attempted murder, conspiracy to murder and assault. From July the accused testified and was under cross-examination for nine weeks concerning the remaining charges against him. Dr Basson only admitted to supplying non-lethal "substances" for use during cross-border operations including abductions of enemies of the state in the 1980s. He denied knowledge of the identities of these targets, except that they were from the ANC and the South West African People's Organization (SWAPO).

By June the Amnesty Committee of the Truth and Reconciliation Commission (TRC) completed its work with hearings and decisions on some 120 remaining applications for amnesties from perpetrators of human rights violations.

◻ The Committee granted amnesty to Eugene de Kock and eight other members of the former Vlakplaas police death squad for the "culpable homicide" in 1991 of the human rights lawyer, Bheki Mlangeni. The explosive device which killed him had been intended for the former Vlakplaas commander, Dirk Coetzee, who had exposed the death squad's operations. The Committee accepted that the applicants had acted under orders and for a political objective.

◻ In a case involving former Vlakplaas and Durban security police officers, the Committee refused amnesty to four applicants for the abduction and death in 1987 of a government opponent, Ntombikayise Priscilla Khubeka. Evidence provided to the Committee by independent forensic doctors confirmed that she had been shot dead and had not died from a heart attack as claimed by the applicants.

The court case brought against the TRC by Inkatha Freedom Party leader, Chief Mangosuthu Buthelezi, to compel it to reverse its finding that he was complicit in large-scale human rights abuses had not concluded by the end of the year.

In August the Minister of Justice told parliament that the government had committed funds for "final reparations" for victims of human rights violations, but that the details would not be discussed in parliament until the President received the final TRC report. The report had not been completed by the end of 2001.

Violations of the rights of women and children

High levels of violence, including sexual violence, against women and children continued. According to police statistics, from January to September there were nearly 38,000 reported rapes and attempted rapes. Just over 40 per cent involved victims younger than 18 years of age.

Government bodies, including the Sexual Offences and Community Affairs Unit of the National Directorate of Public Prosecutions, implemented programs to train police and criminal justice officials on the Domestic Violence Act. They took steps to improve facilities for victims of sexual violence at police stations and health clinics and to increase the effectiveness of the investigation and prosecution of the crime of rape. However, the shortage of police and prosecution resources and of infrastructure such as shelters, as well as prejudiced or unsympathetic attitudes towards complainants, particularly in rural areas, left many victims without protection or redress.

Access to health care

In December the Pretoria High Court ordered the government to make available an anti-retroviral drug to HIV-positive women giving birth in public health facilities and to their babies. The applicants, local NGOs and paediatricians, took the national and provincial health ministers to court because of concern at the high number of babies, about 70,000, who were infected each year through mother-to-child transmission. The court found the government in breach of its constitutional obligation to achieve the "progressive realisation of the right to health care" and that its restriction of access to the drug was discriminatory. The government lodged an appeal.

In Mpumalanga and the Northern Cape provinces, at least two doctors in public health facilities were suspended and others subjected to disciplinary proceedings because they provided anti-retroviral drugs to rape survivors to reduce the possibility of HIV transmission. The provincial Minister of Health in Mpumalanga applied for a court order to evict an NGO, the Greater Nelspruit Rape Intervention Project, from Rob Ferreira Hospital, apparently because it provided financial assistance for patients who were unable to afford the drugs.

Refugee and extradition concerns

In March, Kagiso Sebi, a South African and Benson Keganne, a national of Botswana, were unlawfully handed over to the Botswanan authorities by South African police officers to face murder charges. No extradition hearing had taken place and no assurances had been sought from the Botswanan government that the death penalty would not be used. The South African government requested their return. By the end of 2001, the Botswanan authorities were reportedly refusing to comply with the request.

In May the Constitutional Court ruled that government authorities had acted without any basis in law when, in October 1999, they handed over an asylum-seeker, Khalfan Khamis Mohamed, to US officials for trial in connection with the 1998 bombings of US embassies in Kenya and Tanzania. The Court also ruled that his constitutional rights to dignity, life and not to be punished in a cruel, inhuman or degrading way had been violated by the authorities' failure to seek assurances from the US government that he would not be sentenced to death.

Correspondence with government

AI raised concerns with the government about the care and treatment of rape survivors, human rights violations by the security forces, South African citizens at risk of execution abroad and the regional and international protection of human rights through the government's foreign policy.

AI country reports/visits
Visits
AI delegates visited South Africa on four occasions to undertake research on a range of human rights issues, and to participate in a workshop assessing the ethical implications of scientists' involvement in the covert chemical and biological warfare program of the 1980s and in a conference on crime investigation and human rights.

SPAIN

KINGDOM OF SPAIN
Head of state: King Juan Carlos I de Borbón
Head of government: José María Aznar López
Capital: Madrid
Population: 39.9 million
Official languages: Castilian Spanish, Catalan, Basque, Galician
Death penalty: abolitionist for all crimes
2001 treaty signatures/ratifications: Optional Protocol to the UN Women's Convention

The armed Basque group *Euskadi Ta Askatasuna* (ETA), Basque Homeland and Freedom, continued its campaign of bombings and shootings. A new extradition agreement with France allowed for the temporary return to Spain for trial of ETA suspects serving custodial sentences in France. There were numerous allegations that Civil Guards or police officers tortured detainees held incommunicado, and also reports about ill-treatment by prison guards. Known or convicted former torturers were pardoned and even honoured. North African children were expelled and effectively abandoned on the Moroccan border. Allegations were received about ill-treatment in police custody; immigrants and foreign nationals were among those who said they were victims. There were also allegations of police brutality during a demonstration in Barcelona, which was reportedly infiltrated by police officers, and claims of police brutality during a student demonstration in Las Palmas de Gran Canaria.

ETA killings

Fifteen people, including eight civilians, were killed by ETA. The continuing campaign of killings by ETA met with an intensified response at political, police and judicial levels. An agreement, signed in Perpignan, France, in October between the governments of France and Spain, allowed for the temporary extradition of ETA suspects serving sentences in France so that they could also be tried for crimes committed on Spanish territory. In December the French government agreed to a four-month handover of ETA member José Javier Arizkuren Ruiz ("Kantauri") so that he could be put on trial by the National Court on charges which included attempted regicide. Several judicial proceedings were continuing against members of Basque nationalist groups with alleged links with ETA. There were concerns that in some cases the authorities had interpreted a commitment to the concept of Basque sovereignty as support for, or membership of, ETA.

Santiago Oleaga, financial director of the newspaper *Diario Vasco*, was shot dead in San Sebastián, Guipúzcoa, in May and José María Lidón, a judge of the Court of Vizcaya, was shot dead in Getxo, Vizcaya, in November. Many other people were injured.

Alleged torture of ETA suspects

There were allegations that ETA suspects were being tortured by Civil Guards or police officers while being held incommunicado under "anti-terrorist" legislation. Reports described sexual assault, beatings, particularly on the head, the placing of plastic bags over the head, blindfolding, sleep deprivation and practices inducing physical exhaustion, such as being forced to stand for hours in certain positions. In July a delegation of the European Committee for the Prevention of Torture and Inhuman or Degrading Treatment or Punishment carried out its seventh visit to Spain. Its main purpose was to examine the efficacy in practice of the formal legal safeguards against ill-treatment available to detainees. The delegation interviewed a number of people who had recently been detained by the National Police or Civil Guard and who alleged that they had been tortured.

☐ Iratxe Sorzabal Diez, who worked for a Basque prisoner support group, *Gestoras pro Amnistía*, had been expelled from France to Spain in 1999, after being imprisoned in France. She was arrested in Hernani, Guipúzcoa, in March on suspicion of belonging to an armed group and involvement in a series of killings, and taken to the Civil Guard headquarters in Madrid. After arrest she was held incommunicado for the full five days permitted by law. She alleged that she was beaten during the journey to Madrid and that she was also subjected to electric shocks. After arriving in Madrid, she was beaten by six or seven officers and was thereafter repeatedly beaten around the head with hands, a telephone directory or a rolled-up magazine. She reportedly had a plastic bag placed over her head; another plastic bag was pushed into her mouth as far as her throat while her nose was covered, causing her to vomit. She was forced to undress, stand in the middle of a circle of officers and to repeatedly bend up and down or raise and lower her arms while being beaten. She alleged that she was touched on her breast, buttocks and genital area, threatened with rape and made to kneel on all fours on a blanket and punched. She was seen daily by a doctor, but the use of foam rubber or blankets during her ill-treatment had prevented any visible markings from the beatings. On 31 March she was taken to San Carlos Hospital in Madrid for medical tests on the orders of the forensic doctor attached to the National Court. A complaint was lodged with the National Court. She was released in September, reportedly because of lack of evidence against her.

☐ Unai Romano was arrested by Civil Guards in Vitoria-Gasteiz in September and subsequently transferred to Civil Guard headquarters in Madrid. He alleged that he was subjected to torture, including electric shocks to the testicles and ear lobes. The day after his arrest he was taken to Carlos III Hospital after apparent attempts at self-mutilation while he was in a cell, and his face and head had reportedly begun to swell to such an extent that he could not see. A complaint was lodged with an investigating judge at Vitoria. Unai Romano was subsequently imprisoned at Soto del Real in Madrid, where he reportedly began to recover his vision.

Pardons and awards for torturers

Eleven National Police officers and three Civil Guards who had been convicted of torture were included in a mass award of pardons to mark the millennium. Shortly afterwards a posthumous medal, intended to honour victims of politically motivated violence, was awarded to Melitón Manzanas, the victim of an ETA attack in August 1968. Melitón Manzanas had been responsible for the torture of hundreds of Basques during the rule of General Franco.

There were concerns that the granting of pardons and honours, the lax enforcement of sentences, poor standards of forensic medical reporting and the perpetuation of incommunicado detention, all contributed to a climate of impunity. There was also concern that the continuing failure to prosecute a number of those responsible for crimes waged by the *Grupos Antiterroristas de Liberación* (GAL), Anti-terrorist Liberation Groups, during the 1980s' "dirty war" against ETA was sending torturers a similar message.

Segundo Marey appeal

In March the Constitutional Court rejected an appeal made by 11 of the 12 people who were convicted by the Supreme Court in 1998 for the abduction and illegal detention of French businessman Segundo Marey — part of the "dirty war". Among the 11 were former Minister of the Interior José Barrionuevo and former Secretary of State for Security Rafael Vera. The Constitutional Court's decision meant that the prison sentences of the two officials were definitively reduced to three years and four months. However, on 30 May they, and three other high-ranking officials of the Ministry of the Interior, were allowed to leave prison after only nine hours and are not expected to serve any further prison term.

Alleged ill-treatment and forcible expulsion of children

There was continued concern that the autonomous cities of Ceuta and Melilla were renewing, or seeking to renew, the practice of expelling Moroccan children to Morocco for "family regroupment". There was a series of expulsions of unaccompanied children who had residence permits, had been living in Melilla for several years and were attending school. Some children were expelled repeatedly. None had reportedly received legal assistance before or at the time of their expulsion and none had found families waiting for them at the border. In December a nine-year-old child, Karim Bouitali, was reportedly among other children taken from reception centres in Melilla and, without the benefit of legal assistance, escorted to the frontier by armed police officers. He was later seen alone, clinging to the border fence, weeping, numbed with cold and drenched with rain. Many children who returned to Melilla alleged they had been beaten by Moroccan police at Beni Enzar police station before being thrown onto the street.

There were also earlier allegations that one child had been "slapped around hard" by Spanish police officers and that another had been punched in the eye while handcuffed. In 1998, after three Ceuta police officers filed a judicial complaint claiming serious irregularities in the detention of Moroccan children by the local police, as well as alleging physical ill-treatment, the Attorney General ordered that such expulsions be stopped. However, the three officers' complaint was still languishing in the courts, while they themselves became the target of legal proceedings and were subjected to a continuing campaign of harassment and vilification.

In July AI reminded the Spanish authorities of their obligations under the UN Children's Convention and urged them to examine the case of each child thoroughly before any decision was taken to remove that child from Spain. It also urged the government to ensure that courageous police officers and others who sought to defend human rights were not subjected to harassment and persecution by colleagues or government administrations.

Alleged ill-treatment of foreign nationals

There were several allegations of ill-treatment in police custody, including of foreign nationals.

Abdelhak Archani, a Moroccan national living in Badalona, Catalonia, reported that in July he had been abducted and beaten by three plainclothes police officers. He alleged that, after seeking to lodge a complaint about the theft of a passport, he was forced into a car and taken onto the hard shoulder of a motorway, where he was beaten with truncheons and subjected to racist abuse. He was then abandoned on the motorway. He was subsequently treated for his injuries at the Hospital de L'Esperit Sant at Santa Coloma de Gramenet. Abdelhak Archani's allegations were denied by the officers, who reportedly stated that they had found him drunk in the street and had simply taken him home. Judicial and internal police inquiries were under way at the end of the year.

Alleged police brutality during a demonstration

In July a large number of different associations and trade unions filed a complaint with the High Court of Catalonia, stating that police officers used excessive and indiscriminate violence during an anti-globalization demonstration of between 20,000 and 50,000 people in Barcelona in June, held to protest against the policies of the World Bank. There were allegations that, towards the end of a demonstration that had been peaceful, police officers stood by while a small group of about 50 to 100 hooded people, unattached to the main body of the demonstration, attacked shops, banks and telephone cabins. Shortly after a small, unidentified group of people started to argue with the demonstrators, there was a police charge. Over 20 people were arrested, mainly by plainclothes officers, and over 30 people were injured. Some arrests were carried out by plainclothes officers who reportedly wore handkerchiefs portraying the Catalan independence flag and carried extendable truncheons, plastic handcuffs, baseball bats or iron bars. A number of witnesses reported that undercover police officers had themselves carried out some of the acts of violence. The Ministry of the Interior reportedly admitted that about 100 police officers had infiltrated the demonstration but denied that they had been involved in violence. In July a Barcelona judge exonerated those arrested of a charge of public disorder. Preliminary inquiries were continuing into other charges in a number of cases. In November a number of students alleged that they had been the victims of excessive force by police officers during a demonstration in Las Palmas de Gran Canaria. A judicial inquiry was opened into the allegations, made by a students' union.

Update: António Fonseca

In March the judge investigating the death in custody in Arrecife, Lanzarote, in May 2000 of Guinea-Bissau national António Fonseca, closed the case, reportedly concluding that his death could not be attributed to a third party. No charges were brought against the National Police officers who had arrested him, taken him to the police station and allegedly severely beaten him. The judge reportedly rejected as incomplete the findings of a forensic expert, who had conducted a second autopsy on the body and had concluded unequivocally that he had been fatally injured by a "blow with a blunt instrument" to the right side of the neck. The judge also rejected the testimony of an alleged eyewitness as unreliable. The judge's decision left open a number of questions relating to numerous contradictions in the testimony. An appeal against the judge's decision was filed by António Fonseca's family but has not so far been granted.

AI country reports/ visits
Report
- Concerns in Europe, January-June 2001: Spain (AI Index: EUR 01/003/2001)

Visit
An AI delegate visited Spain in May to gather information.

SRI LANKA

DEMOCRATIC SOCIALIST REPUBLIC OF SRI LANKA
Head of state: Chandrika Bandaranaike Kumaratunga
Capital: Colombo
Population: 19.1 million
Official languages: Sinhala, Tamil, English
Death penalty: abolitionist in practice

An increase in human rights abuses was noted from May in the context of the protracted armed conflict between the security forces and the Liberation Tigers of Tamil Eelam (LTTE). Amid political instability and increased military activity, police and security forces were responsible for arbitrary arrest and detention, torture, "disappearances" and extrajudicial executions. There was a marked rise in allegations of rape by police, army and navy personnel, although the number of "disappearances" decreased in comparison with previous years. There was continuing concern about a possible resumption of executions after the government's decision in 1999 to end a long-term practice of automatic commutation of death sentences. Members of the LTTE were responsible for hostage-taking and widespread recruitment of children as combatants. There was a marked decrease in the number of LTTE attacks on civilians. Impunity remained a major concern.

Background

A unilateral cease-fire, declared by the LTTE in late December 2000 amid attempts by the Norwegian government to facilitate a dialogue between the government and the LTTE for a solution to the conflict, was called off by the LTTE in April. Intensified fighting culminated on 24 July with a massive attack by LTTE members on the main military airbase and the adjoining international airport north of Colombo, in which eight military and three commercial aircraft were destroyed. No civilians were killed, although several, including tourists, were injured.

Major political instability developed in late June. Members of the Sri Lanka Muslim Congress left the coalition government and a no-confidence motion was filed in parliament. In response President Chandrika Bandaranaike Kumaratunga suspended parliament for two months in July, a step which, although constitutionally permissible, was widely denounced as undemocratic. In early September, the opposition Janatha Vimukthi Peramuna (JVP) party reached an agreement to support the government for one year on a "probationary" basis.

A constitutional amendment was passed in September providing for the setting up of a 10-member Constitutional Council and independent commissions to oversee elections as well as to examine the police force, the judiciary and public services. Efforts to initiate these were halted when the President, faced with further defections and a second motion of no-confidence, dissolved parliament on 10 October and called elections. There was a very violent election campaign, with 47 murders reported. The United National Party (UNP) won and formed a new coalition government in December. It reciprocated a cease-fire declared by the LTTE and announced other measures aimed at reviving the dialogue with the LTTE with the assistance of the Norwegian government.

In the midst of the political crisis, the President allowed the longstanding state of emergency in the country to lapse on 4 July rather than risk losing a mandatory vote in parliament over its monthly extension. She invoked separate provisions of the Public Security Ordinance and the Prevention of Terrorism Act (PTA) granting wide powers to the security forces to arrest and detain people suspected of being members of or sympathizers with the LTTE. There was concern that safeguards for the protection of detainees were eroded as a result. With effect from 1 November, a central police registry of people arrested under the PTA and emergency regulations started functioning to allow relatives to obtain information such as the arresting authority and the place of detention. This measure to prevent "disappearances" was one of several recommended by the UN Working Group on Enforced or Involuntary Disappearances after its first visit to the country in 1991.

Killings of civilians

The failures of both sides in the conflict to take adequate measures to avoid civilian casualties resulted in many deaths. There were allegations that civilians were killed during bombing by the air force. In one such incident reported on 21 March from Nallathanithoduvai, Mullaitivu district, four civilians, including two women, were killed during bombing and shelling. The attacks followed the sinking of a navy gunboat by the LTTE earlier that day.

▫ Achinte Perera and Manjula Prasad, both supporters of the UNP, were shot dead while participating in a demonstration called by a coalition of opposition parties in Colombo on 19 July. The use of live ammunition against participants in a largely peaceful protest constituted an apparent use of excessive force by the police.

'Disappearances'

There were several reports of "disappearances", five of which remained unresolved at the end of the year. This represented a decline from the number reported in previous years. Cases occurred in Batticaloa and Vavuniya district.

▫ Murugesu Anandarasa, a 30-year-old shop worker from Maharambaikulam, Vavuniya district, was last seen on 23 April when a friend saw him being questioned by military intelligence officers outside the army's town camp.

Concern remained at the practice of holding detainees in secret detention, particularly by the Terrorist Investigation Department (TID) in Colombo and by the army and members of the People's Liberation Organization of Tamil Eelam (PLOTE) in

Vavuniya. TID officers were also reportedly responsible for denying prisoners access to representatives of the National Human Rights Commission.

Death in custody
◻ Kandaiyan Udayakumaran, aged 42, a displaced person from Jaffna, was taken into custody in Savakadu, Mannar, by navy personnel on 28 February. Officers returned to his home the following day and told his daughter that he had been taken for questioning and transferred into the custody of the Mannar police. On 1 March, navy personnel delivered his body to Mannar base hospital. According to the post-mortem report, he had died due to "hypoxia following strangulation of the neck".

Torture and ill-treatment
Torture continued to be reported on an almost daily basis. There were several reports of rape by security forces from various districts, including Mannar, Batticaloa, Colombo and Jaffna. These gave rise to fears that safeguards to protect women in custody, contained in presidential directives for the welfare of detainees issued in 1997, were being ignored. Complaints of torture, including rape, were often not dealt with effectively by police, magistrates and doctors.
◻ Sinnathamby Sivamany, aged 24, and Ehamparam Wijikala, aged 22, were arrested by navy personnel accompanied by members of the police Special Investigation Unit (SIU) in Mannar on 19 March. They were allegedly raped by navy and SIU personnel at the office of the police Counter-Subversive Unit.

Impunity
Lack of accountability for the perpetrators of human rights violations remained a serious concern. A circular, issued in January by a senior deputy inspector general of police which reinstated all police officers who had been suspended while criminal investigations continued into their alleged involvement in past "disappearances", was seen as a sign of the lack of commitment in the police department to hold its members accountable.

Death penalty
Following the departure from a longstanding practice of automatic commutation of death sentences, concern continued that people sentenced to death after March 1999 would be executed. In May the then Minister of Justice indicated his interest in conducting an in-depth study to "increase understanding of the actual situation of criminality in the country" before resuming executions.

Human rights abuses by the LTTE
There was a marked decrease in the number of civilians killed during attacks attributed to LTTE members. The LTTE "executed" several people it said were responsible for treason, rape or other crimes. There were also reports of abductions of Muslim and Sinhalese civilians, particularly in Batticaloa and Trincomalee districts. Many were released after their families paid ransom money.

◻ Sundaramoorthy Jeevanthamoorthy, a candidate in the parliamentary elections for the Eelam People's Revolutionary Liberation Front (Perumal Wing), was killed by members of the LTTE in the early morning of 28 October at Valaichenai, Batticaloa district. Two civilians were indiscriminately killed in the only suicide bomb attack of the year in Colombo on 29 October.

Child soldiers
An intensive recruitment drive starting in August by the LTTE confirmed fears that children were recruited as combatants. Scores of children were recruited in Batticaloa district, particularly in the divisions of Vakarai, Vavunativu, Pattipalai, Porativu, Eravurpattu and Koralaipattu. Some were as young as 10. Reports also indicated that many families who refused were compelled to leave their homes and were displaced to other parts of the district. There were also reports of intensified recruitment in the Vanni, the area to the south of the Jaffna peninsula largely controlled by the LTTE.

PLOTE members recruited children as young as 12 in the Vavuniya area in early 2001. An inquiry by the Criminal Investigation Department later found three children being trained at a PLOTE camp. They were returned to their parents. Several others known to have been recruited by the PLOTE remained unaccounted for.

SUDAN

REPUBLIC OF THE SUDAN
Head of state and government: Omar Hassan Ahmad al-Bashir
Capital: Khartoum
Population: 31.8 million
Official language: Arabic
Death penalty: retentionist

Unarmed civilians continued to be killed in the 18-year conflict between government and allied forces and the Sudan People's Liberation Army (SPLA) and other armed opposition groups, many as a result of indiscriminate bombing or direct attack by government forces and allied militias. Human rights abuses in war zones were committed with impunity by all parties to the conflict, including summary and arbitrary executions, torture, abductions and sexual violence against women and forcible recruitment of children into fighting forces. Tens of thousands were displaced and faced starvation, with relief supplies

disrupted by insecurity. In government-controlled territory, the security forces reportedly tortured detainees and used excessive force against demonstrators which resulted in deaths. Political opponents were arbitrarily detained without charge or trial for long periods, and lawyers, journalists and human rights defenders harassed and intimidated. Restrictions on freedom of association, assembly and expression remained in force. At least three executions were carried out; as many as 26 death sentences were reported to have been passed.

Background

The civil war continued to be driven by competition for control of oil fields in the Upper Nile and Southern Blue Nile regions. The SPLA attacked government-backed oil installations, while government forces increased aerial bombing and pro-government militias attacked civilians, apparently to displace them from areas of oil activities. The government and the SPLA continued to arm and support militias from the Nuer community, increasing interfactional fighting, ethnic tensions and attacks on civilians. In May, there was a split in the main Nuer armed group, the Sudan People's Democratic Front/Defence Force, as some commanders signed a memorandum of understanding with the SPLA.

Sudan gained wider acceptance on the international scene. The European Union continued its dialogue with the authorities and Sudan was voted onto the UN Commission on Human Rights in May. The government condemned the 11 September attacks in the USA and reportedly arrested suspects in Sudan at the request of the US authorities. On 28 September, the UN Security Council lifted sanctions on Sudan. The US government did not veto the lifting of UN sanctions, but extended for a year bilateral sanctions imposed since 1989. It initiated new moves to bring the parties to the internal conflict to peace negotiations.

Indiscriminate bombing of civilians

More than 100 incidents of air force bombings were reported in the regions of the Upper Nile, Southern Blue Nile, Bahr-el-Ghazal, Southern Kordofan and Equatoria, resulting in deaths and injuries of civilians. Soldiers dropped bombs manually from the back of gun ships and high-altitude planes, and there appeared to be no attempt to distinguish between military and civilian targets. Houses and health centres were destroyed, and relief operations were hampered.

▫ In January and February, areas under SPLA control in Southern Blue Nile were bombed. Four bombs were dropped on Kurmuk on 11 January, killing three civilians, damaging a hospital and resulting in the temporary evacuation of humanitarian staff. On the same day, three civilians were killed and a women's compound damaged in Yabus where 12 bombs were dropped.

▫ On 26 November government forces reportedly dropped six bombs on Malual Kon, killing two civilians, and three bombs between Malhualbai and Madhol, east of Malual Kon, killing two more.

Unlawful killings

Both government and armed opposition forces carried out unlawful killings of civilians.

▫ In January, four villages near Guelguk in Southern Blue Nile were reportedly attacked by pro-government forces to displace the population and allow a new oil concession to be developed. At least 11 civilians in Dhowanywa and 12 in Tenykak were reportedly killed, including six elders and seven children. The attackers allegedly pursued and shot dead residents who fled.

▫ Government forces reportedly launched aerial and ground attacks on civilian settlements in a major offensive on SPLA-held areas of the Nuba Mountains in May. Civilians were reported killed in three villages near Heiban, homes and crops burned and property looted. In Karda, soldiers reportedly burned to death two elderly people in their home.

▫ In November, Judge Mulana Agustinho al Nur Shamila was killed in his house in Kumo, reportedly by the paramilitary Popular Defence Forces (PDF).

Internal displacement

Tens of thousands of people fled direct attacks by government and rebel forces in Upper Nile and Bahr-el-Ghazal, and government offensives in the Nuba Mountains and Southern Blue Nile. Many were inaccessible to relief agencies because of the conflict or because the government obstructed relief flights to disputed territory.

In the contested oil-rich areas of Upper Nile and Southern Blue Nile, tens of thousands of inhabitants fled attacks by government and rebel forces. With their relatives dead or injured, homes and crops destroyed, and cattle stolen or killed, many were unable to support themselves.

▫ In May and June, SPLA attacks on the government-controlled towns of Raga and Deim Zubeir in Bahr-el-Ghazal displaced up to 50,000 people, according to UN estimates. Many fled to Southern Darfur, a region already affected by drought. Others remained in surrounding areas, at risk of bombings and attacks. In October, in a government counter-offensive, the air force bombed Mangayath, halting international aid deliveries to 20,000 displaced people, forcing them to flee again.

Abuses against women and children

Women and children were reportedly abducted and raped, and boys forcibly recruited to fight, by all forces involved in the conflict.

Soldiers reportedly abducted and gang-raped women and girls travelling by foot along roads in Upper Nile between April and June. A climate of fear and lack of mechanisms for handling rape allegations meant that most rapes were not reported. The PDF and government-allied *Muraheleen* militias drawn from the Baggara tribes reportedly kept women and children, captured in raids, in slavery-like conditions, using them for domestic and field labour. Thousands of women and children abducted during the 18-year conflict reportedly remained unaccounted for, despite the existence since 1999 of a governmental Committee for the Eradication of Abduction of Women and Children, mandated to trace and reunite them with their families. SPLA and allied forces allegedly abducted and raped women and girls.

◻ In November, the abduction of a Kenyan relief worker by PDF troops near Niamlel in Bahr-el-Ghazal highlighted continuing abductions by the PDF and *Muraheleen* along the railway line from Babanusa to Wau. She was released two weeks later.

Women's rights
In January, the President was reported as saying that Sudan would not sign the UN Women's Convention because it was contrary to Sudanese family values. Also in January the government amended the Labour Law by decree to prohibit women from working in physically demanding jobs. By the end of 2001, the Constitutional Court had not ruled on the constitutionality of a 2000 decree banning women from working in public places in Khartoum which had been challenged in the courts and subsequently suspended.

Women in Khartoum State continued to be harassed and ill-treated by police enforcing the Public Order Law, which restricts women's freedom of movement and regulates their behaviour and dress under threat of summary trial, flogging and imprisonment.

Torture and cruel punishment
The security forces tortured people suspected of opposing the government.

◻ Following his arrest in July in Rodom, Southern Darfur, Sebit Hassan Ramada was reportedly beaten every day for 16 days while in incommunicado detention in Buram. According to reports, Haggar Sesingere, also arrested in July in Rodom, was beaten and had his fingernails pulled out while in incommunicado detention for six weeks.

The courts handed down harsh punishments after unfair and summary trials.

◻ Five men had their right hands and left legs amputated on 25 and 27 January in Kober prison, Khartoum, after being convicted of armed robbery. The same sentences of "cross-amputation", imposed on another 19 men at the same time, had not been carried out by the end of 2001.

◻ In April, six women and three children were among a group of 56 Christians given 15 to 20 lashes each after being convicted of public disorder in a summary trial in Khartoum at which they were refused legal representation. They were arrested at a meeting in a church, and police used tear gas and live ammunition to disperse the crowd gathered inside.

Death penalty
Three men were executed and as many as 26 death sentences were passed in Darfur in December.

◻ Abok Alfa Akok, a non-Muslim, was convicted of adultery and sentenced to death by stoning by a court in Southern Darfur which tried her under Islamic law. The trial failed to meet international standards. An appeal against the sentence was planned.

Excessive use of force
The police and the security services used live ammunition, tear gas and beatings with sticks during arrests and to break up public meetings and demonstrations, resulting in deaths and injuries.

◻ No investigation was known to have taken place into the killings by armed police and the security services at Al-Gezira university in Medani in August. Two students, Mutasim Mohamed El Hassan and Yahia El Hussain, were shot dead and 16 others injured in clashes between students and armed police after violent unrest between students of different political affiliations.

◻ On 24 May, Ali Ahmed al Bashir, a member of the Popular National Congress (PNC) party, was shot dead near his house by security officers. Following a public outcry, the government ordered an investigation into the killing and three officers were suspended from duty, charged with murder and went on trial in September. Three further officers were subsequently also charged with murder.

Political detentions
The authorities detained political opponents, lawyers, journalists and human rights defenders under a December 2000 amendment to the 1999 National Security Act. The amendment allowed the security services to detain without charge or trial anyone suspected of "conspiracy against the state" for renewable periods of 123 days. The amendment specifically denied detainees judicial recourse. Some political detainees were released and charges against them withdrawn in October.

◻ Eight detained members of the National Democratic Alliance (NDA), an alliance of opposition parties, were charged with "conspiracy against the state" in March. They had been arrested in December 2000 while meeting a US diplomat. They were released in October after the President publicly announced that charges against them were withdrawn. Lawyers Ali Mahmoud Hasanain and Ghazi Suleiman, arrested in December 2000 for protesting against the NDA arrests, were released without charge in February.

◻ Several PNC leaders and supporters were arrested in February and over the following months. The leaders were accused of "conspiracy against the state" but not formally charged. On 1 October the government announced that the accusations against them were dismissed and they were all released except for leading member Hassan al-Turabi. At least 13 PNC supporters were rearrested on 2 October at a political meeting, and remained in detention without charge or trial at the end of the year.

◻ Nageeb Nagmeldin el Toum, Director of the Amal Centre for Rehabilitation of Victims of Physical and Mental Trauma, was detained for more than two weeks in March and property and medical files seized. Faisal el Bagir, a staff member at the Centre, was detained incommunicado for 12 days. Both were released uncharged. The Centre's files and property were returned in December.

☐ In October, Communist Party members Youseif Husein and Abbas Mohamed al Tahir were detained and were still held, incommunicado, at the end of 2001.

The security services detained and threatened journalists critical of the war or government policies, and submitted privately owned print media to censorship before publication.

☐ Albino Okieny, Chief Editor of the privately owned newspaper *Khartoum Monitor*, and journalists Alfred Taban and Nhyal Bohl were briefly detained for questioning several times. In October and November they were detained for questioning about articles critical of the government before being released on bail to await trial on charges of "inciting hatred against the state". The trial had not begun by the end of 2001.

AI country visits/ reports
Statements
- Sudan: Church shootings and arrests must be investigated (AI Index: AFR 54/009/2001)
- Sudan: Talisman Energy must do more to protect human rights (AI Index: AFR 54/010/2001)

SURINAME

REPUBLIC OF SURINAME
Head of state: Ronald Venetiaan
Head of government: Jules Ajodhia
Capital: Paramaribo
Population: 0.4 million
Official language: Dutch
Death penalty: abolitionist in practice

Impunity continued to be a major issue in 2001. Conditions of detention contributed to several prison riots. The authorities announced investigations into reports of ill-treatment. In the follow-up to the UN World Conference against Racism in September, the Netherlands government expressed regret for past slavery in Suriname, its former colony.

Impunity
In January, Dutch courts opened an inquiry, based on the UN Convention against Torture, into the 1982 "December murders" in which 15 journalists, academics and labour leaders were extrajudicially executed at Fort Zeelandia, an army centre in Paramaribo. However, in September the Dutch Supreme Court ruled that the case could not proceed, in part on the grounds that the crime was committed before the Convention was ratified and became binding in the Netherlands. Prosecution efforts continued in Suriname. Trade unionist and political leader Fred Derby, sole survivor of the massacre who had implicated former military leader Desi Bouterse in the events, died in May.

Conditions of detention
Conditions of detention, including severe overcrowding, remained a cause for concern. Riots prompted by overcrowding took place in police stations in January and March. In August, the death of a detainee in Keizerstraat police station, apparently of illness, contributed to a revolt among other detainees against overcrowding and poor conditions. The most serious riot took place in August in Duisburglaan prison, in which inmates set fire to cells. The Minister of Justice and Police ordered an investigation. At the same prison in April, an inmate had been shot dead by a prison guard during an escape attempt.

In February government authorities announced the allocation of funds to rehabilitate the prison system and relieve overcrowding.

Ill-treatment
In June the Minister of Justice and Police ordered an investigation into alleged police misconduct. He announced in July that police skills training would include education in human rights.

SWAZILAND

KINGDOM OF SWAZILAND
Head of state: King Mswati III
Head of government: Barnabus Sibusiso Dlamini
Capital: Mbabane
Population: 0.9 million
Official languages: English, Siswati
Death penalty: retentionist

The rights to freedom of association, peaceful assembly and expression remained restricted. Government actions threatened the independence of the judiciary and undermined court rulings. There were reports of torture and ill-treatment. Government opponents were subjected to arbitrary detention and politically motivated trial proceedings. The King commuted four death sentences; no executions were carried out. Violations of women's rights remained systematic.

Background
In August the King made public the report of the Constitutional Review Commission appointed in 1996. The report recommended, among other things,

strengthening the executive powers of the King, maintaining the ban on political parties, and ensuring that any "rights and freedoms" which may be part of any agreement with other states or international bodies did not conflict with Swazi "customs and traditions". The formation of a committee to draft a new constitution was announced in December.

Threats to the rule of law

On 22 June the King issued a law, Decree No. 2, which further restricted the exercise of fundamental rights. It reversed the effect of rulings by the High Court and Court of Appeal against the banning of news publications and against police actions resulting in the removal at gunpoint from their homes of members of two rural communities protesting against the imposition of a Chief. The Decree prohibited any further legal challenges in court to these matters. The Decree also confirmed that the King had sole discretion in the appointment of judges.

On 24 July, after widespread criticism of the law nationally and internationally, the Decree was repealed and replaced by Decree No.3. This Decree validated any actions taken by ministers or officials prior to 24 July and removed them from challenge in court. The new law also reinstated a 1993 law — Non-Bailable Offences Order No.14 — under which the courts are obliged to deny bail to any person charged with any of a number of scheduled offences. In June the Court of Appeal had ruled that the 1993 law was a "draconian" law and "inconsistent with the presumption of innocence". In June, some 1,000 people were reported to be in custody after being denied bail. Some of them had been awaiting trial for more than two years.

Violations of freedoms of assembly, association and expression

Fundamental rights to freedom of assembly, association and expression continued to be restricted. Police prevented a number of gatherings deemed to be political. Several journalists were harassed by police in the course of their work. A number of publications were banned and, towards the end of 2001, the government threatened to reintroduce a Media Council Bill to tighten restrictions on journalists and publications.

◻ On 19 October police broke up a news conference organized by members and affiliates of the Swaziland Democratic Alliance (SDA) to protest against the detention of an opposition leader, Mario Masuku, as well as other grievances. Armed police prevented the SDA organizers from entering the planned venue in Manzini, claiming that the event was illegal. When the organizers attempted to conduct the news conference at a second venue, the police, backed by heavily armed paramilitary police, forced their way in and pushed the organizers and journalists out of the building. *The Times* journalist Thulasizwe Mkhabela was assaulted, allegedly by a senior police officer. He lodged a complaint of assault later that day; he was compelled to lay his charge at the same police station where the officer involved worked.

◻ In August the High Court ruled that the authorities had unlawfully banned the *Guardian* newspaper in May. However, the paper was unable to resume publication because a government appeal against the ruling had not been heard by the end of the year.

Political trials

On 4 October, Mario Masuku, President of the People's United Democratic Movement, was rearrested. He had been arrested on charges of sedition in November 2000 and released under restrictive bail conditions. In early October he refused to continue to observe his bail conditions, which required him to report daily to the police regional headquarters in Mbabane, to obtain the permission of the Commissioner of Police to address any public gathering and to obtain the permission of the High Court to travel abroad. He was remanded in custody pending trial on the original sedition charges. He required treatment in hospital as a consequence of poor prison conditions which exacerbated his existing health problems of diabetes and hypertension. In December a trial date was set for early 2002.

On 24 September, six trade union leaders were acquitted by the Mbabane magistrates' court of charges of contempt of court. The defendants had been charged in connection with their participation in a strike in November 2000. When giving his ruling the magistrate criticized the police witnesses for the "contradictory" evidence they had given during the trial. An appeal against the acquittals was pending at the end of the year.

Torture and deaths in police custody

There were a number of reports of torture or ill-treatment by police. The Prime Minister ordered an inquiry into a number of deaths in police custody.

◻ Edison Makhanya and Sibusiso Jele died within hours of their arrest by police on 20 March. The police had arrived at the home of the Jele family where the two youths were sleeping. They ordered them to dress and took them away, handcuffed together, apparently in connection with a criminal investigation. Family members were told later the same day by police officials that the detainees had committed suicide by swallowing poison. Their deaths created a public outcry and, unusually, the government ordered the Chief Magistrate to hold a coroner's inquest. The inquest was held in open court. However, the inquiry was hampered by the conflicting evidence of police witnesses, the obstruction by police of the independent forensic pathologist representing the families at the post-mortem examinations, and the police failure to provide the inquest magistrate with the results of toxicology tests. Consequently the inquest court had been unable to deliver conclusive findings by the end of the year.

Death penalty

By the end of the year there were 11 prisoners under sentence of death at Matsapha Maximum Security Prison; all had been convicted of murder. Officials publicly confirmed the government's intention to employ an executioner.

In November the Appeal Court overturned the death sentence imposed on a South African national, Bongani Mkhwanazi, on the basis that there were extenuating circumstances. His sentence was commuted to 25 years' imprisonment.

Violence against women
Women and girls remained vulnerable to violence, including sexual violence and the risk of HIV infection, as a result of discriminatory national law and customary practices. Victims of rape continued to face prejudice from police and criminal justice officials.

AI country reports/visits
Statement
- Swaziland: New decree endangers fundamental rights and the rule of law (AI Index: AFR 55/002/2001)

Visit
AI delegates visited Swaziland in May.

SWEDEN

KINGDOM OF SWEDEN
Head of state: King Carl XVI Gustaf
Head of government: Goran Persson
Capital: Stockholm
Population: 8.9 million
Official language: Swedish
Death penalty: abolitionist for all crimes
2001 treaty ratifications/signatures: Rome Statute of the International Criminal Court

During the European Union (EU) summit in Gothenburg in June police reportedly used excessive force against anti-globalization demonstrators. Investigations continued into past deaths in police custody and one asylum-seeker was shot dead by police.

Deaths in police custody
Osmo Vallo
The commission of inquiry, established by the government to examine the procedures used to investigate the controversial death in May 1995 in police custody of Osmo Vallo, began its work in January. The commission was due to complete its inquiry in 2002. In January AI delegates briefed members of the commission about AI's concerns. In March the Supreme Court rejected the appeal by Osmo Vallo's mother for a new trial of the officers allegedly involved, stating that there was no new evidence to justify it.

Peter Andersson
In March the Prosecutor General decided to reopen the preliminary investigation into the death of Peter Andersson because the cause of death had not been sufficiently investigated. Peter Andersson died on 3 November 2000 in Örebro after being restrained by four policemen during arrest and subsequently in hospital. At the hospital, he was examined by a doctor and then transferred, lying on his stomach, strapped down on a trolley and handcuffed, from the emergency ward to the psychiatric clinic. It was reported that during this transfer one of the officers knelt on his back. Peter Andersson subsequently became lifeless and attempts to resuscitate him failed.

The shooting of Idris Demir
Idris Demir, a 27-year-old Kurdish asylum-seeker, was shot dead by a policeman in Jönköping on 9 March. Police officers stated that they followed Idris Demir to his apartment to check his driving licence, unaware that he had been ordered to leave Sweden following the rejection of his asylum claim. They alleged that Idris Demir grabbed a knife, held it to his own throat, and threatened to kill himself before running out of the apartment. They claimed that Idris Demir, when confronted by one policeman, attacked the officer with a knife. A second policeman then fired his gun, reportedly in self-defence. However, a friend of Idris Demir who witnessed the killing alleged that Idris Demir did not attack the police, but was shot in the back on his way down the stairs while trying to run away. In May, the Chief Prosecutor in charge of the investigation brought a prosecution against the police officer who shot Idris Demir on two counts: gross assault and causing another person's death. The officer was acquitted by the district court in November.

EU summit in Gothenburg
During the EU summit in Gothenburg between 14 and 16 June police reportedly used excessive force against anti-globalization demonstrators. Some of the demonstrations became violent with resulting injuries to people and significant damage to property. It was reported that 118 people were injured, including 56 police officers.

According to reports, about 500 people were initially detained or arrested by police during the EU summit; charges were subsequently not brought against 388 people. Prosecutions were brought against 46 people, 40 of whom had been tried by the end of the year. Thirty-two people were subsequently convicted of charges relating to the riots; some claimed that they were wrongly convicted on the basis of inadequate evidence. At least one person's conviction was overturned on appeal.

Shootings by police officers
On 15 June the police fired live ammunition at demonstrators, wounding three people. It was alleged that no warning was given before police opened fire. The government informed AI in September that an official committee had been established to consider policing issues in relation to demonstrations, as well as to analyse the police actions in Gothenburg. The committee was expected to report its findings in May 2002. The government also stated that the police force

was carrying out an internal review of the police actions in Gothenburg.

The Prosecutor General decided in October to review a decision taken by the Chief Prosecutor to close the preliminary investigation and not to bring any charges against the officers involved in the shootings.

Allegations of ill-treatment
It was reported that police used excessive force, including beatings with batons, against demonstrators who were not involved in violent protest. There were also allegations that police officers kicked or beat people with batons after they had been detained and, in some instances, while they were restrained with their hands tied behind their backs and lying down on the ground. Furthermore, it was reported that people were detained arbitrarily without charge, in some instances for many hours, during police actions at two schools, Hvitfeldska and Schillerska. About 150 complaints were lodged against the police and other authorities, including for ill-treatment or illegal detention.

Refugees
Two Egyptian asylum-seekers, Muhammad Muhammad Suleiman Ibrahim El-Zari and Ahmed Hussein Mustafa Kamil Agiza, were forcibly returned to Egypt in December after their asylum claims had been rejected in an unfair procedure. There was concern that in Egypt they would be at grave risk of torture and unfair trial. In addition, Ahmed Hussein Mustafa Kamil Agiza's wife and five children were denied refugee status in Sweden in an unfair procedure and remained at risk of forcible return.

The government recognized both men as having a well-founded fear of persecution, but excluded them from protection on the basis of their alleged connections to organizations which had been responsible for acts of "terrorism". The decision was based on secret evidence provided by the Swedish Security Police which was not disclosed in full to the men and their legal counsel.

The Swedish government held that the men would not be at risk of serious human rights violations in Egypt, on the basis of written guarantees from the Egyptian authorities.

AI country reports/visits
Report
- Concerns in Europe, January-June 2001: Sweden (AI Index: EUR 01/003/2001)

Visit
An AI delegate visited Sweden in January.

SWITZERLAND

SWISS CONFEDERATION
Head of state and government: Moritz Leuenberger
Capital: Bern
Population: 7.2 million
Official languages: German, French, Italian, Romansh
Death penalty: abolitionist for all crimes
2001 treaty ratifications/signatures: Rome Statute of the International Criminal Court

Allegations of police ill-treatment, often of foreign nationals, persisted, as did the use of dangerous methods of restraint and excessive force by police, notably during forcible deportation operations. One man died during deportation. An unarmed man was shot dead in disputed circumstances during a cross-border chase by police. Restrictions were placed on the rights of peaceful assembly and freedom of expression during the annual meeting of the World Economic Forum (WEF).

WEF policing operation
In January hundreds of people gathered to demonstrate against the annual WEF held in Davos, and some demonstrators and participants in meetings organized there by non-governmental organizations (NGOs) were prevented from entering the country or reaching Davos, in the east of the country, where a planned demonstration was banned. Many demonstrators were turned back at a nearby village and violent clashes took place between some demonstrators and police, both there and in Zurich.

Sixteen NGOs taking part in the WEF, including AI, wrote to the government recognizing the authorities' responsibility to ensure the security of WEF participants, but expressing concern about restrictions placed on the rights to peaceful assembly and freedom of expression, guaranteed under international human rights standards and the federal constitution. They called for a review of the WEF policing strategy in order to safeguard such rights in the future.

The government expressed regret about the restrictions imposed but said that "security measures were necessary" because the planned demonstrations, they claimed, threatened both the WEF participants' safety and their freedom of assembly and expression, and indicated that the courts would determine any infringement of constitutional rights. Official analyses of issues surrounding the WEF policing operation were initiated at the federal and cantonal level. In September the Federal Court ruled that the ban on the Davos demonstration had not violated constitutional rights of freedom of assembly and expression, given the risk of violence, but said that the authorities should have examined other options.

Ill-treatment on arrest
There were reports of ill-treatment and excessive force by police, often accompanied by racist abuse. Some

official investigations into such allegations were unsatisfactory. The text of a draft code of penal procedure unifying the existing 26 cantonal codes of penal procedure and three federal laws on penal procedure was issued in June, opening a consultation process due to end in February 2002. It included improved safeguards against ill-treatment of detainees in police custody, such as possibilities of earlier access to a lawyer and of having a third party immediately informed of the detention.

A video recording made by neighbours of Cemal Gömeç, a Turkish-Kurd refugee with a history of psychiatric illness, showed Bern Municipal Police officers striking him some 15 times with batons at the end of a four-hour standoff at his apartment during which he had threatened officers with a knife. Uniformed officers repeatedly fired rubber bullets and irritant sprays at him, and used a stun grenade and batons to overcome him and pin him to the ground. After a doctor injected him with a sedative he lost consciousness and suffered a cardiac arrest. He died in hospital four days later. The findings of initial forensic examinations included injuries caused by a blunt instrument to his face, head, torso and limbs, and fractures to his face. An investigation by the Bern Cantonal Police, under the direction of an investigating magistrate, was opened to establish the precise cause of death and whether charges of causing bodily harm and death through negligence should be brought against municipal police officers.

Ill-treatment during forcible deportation

Several criminal proceedings were under way in connection with use of excessive force, and dangerous and degrading methods of restraint during deportations under police escort. Two had resulted in death.

In July a court sentenced a doctor to five months' suspended imprisonment for causing the death through negligence of Khaled Abuzarifa, a Palestinian, at Zurich-Kloten airport in 1999. In preparation for deportation he was given a sedative and had his mouth sealed with adhesive tape (an officially-sanctioned restraint method at the time), was bound hand and foot, and strapped into a wheelchair. He died of asphyxia. The judge said that the doctor, who appealed against the sentence, had shown negligence in his misdiagnosis of Khaled Abuzarifa's breathing problems, which he had dismissed as a pretence, and failed in his professional obligations by agreeing to the taping of the prisoner's mouth but refusing to accompany him and the police officers to the plane. The court acquitted two of the escorting officers, but returned the case of the third to the public prosecutor for further investigation.

In July an autopsy concluded that the death of Samson Chukwu, a Nigerian asylum-seeker, in a detention centre in the Canton of Valais in May, at the start of a forcible deportation operation, could be attributed to positional asphyxia, resulting from dangerous restraint methods used by two police officers. They had lain him face-down on the floor, with his hands bound behind his back and an officer lying on top of him. In September the investigating magistrate decided that no criminal investigation should be opened against the officers, concluding that they had not violated standard procedures, and had not been trained in and were unaware of the dangers of the restraint methods they had used. Samson Chukwu's family lodged an appeal questioning these conclusions.

It was reported that a working group on deportations formed in December 2000, involving cantonal and federal authorities, was progressing towards the establishment of common guidelines on the execution of deportation operations and a pool of specially-trained officers. In June AI called on all cantonal governments to review, as an urgent priority, police restraint techniques and the relevant guidelines and training for police and medical personnel involved in deportation operations. AI made a number of recommendations for the safe implementation of deportation procedures, including the banning of methods of restraint impeding respiration and appropriate guidelines to minimize the risk of positional asphyxia. The working group was apparently taking AI's recommendations into account.

UN Human Rights Committee

In November, following its consideration of Switzerland's second periodic report on its compliance with the International Covenant on Civil and Political Rights, the Human Rights Committee welcomed progress made since the initial report but found failings in a number of areas, including reports of police brutality. Many of these concerns had been raised by AI.

The Committee instructed Switzerland to establish in all cantons "independent bodies" to "receive and investigate effectively all complaints of excessive use of force and other abuses of power by the police". It said that their powers "should be sufficient to ensure that those responsible are brought to justice or, as appropriate, subject to disciplinary sanctions sufficient to deter future abuses and that the victims are adequately compensated". It emphasized that "the possibility of resort to court action cannot serve as a substitute for such mechanisms".

The Committee also instructed Switzerland to ensure that all forcible deportations be carried out in a manner compatible with the Covenant and underlined that "it should ensure that restraint methods do not affect the life and physical integrity of persons concerned". It asked the government to report back within 12 months on the implementation of its recommendations on this issue.

AI country reports/visits
Reports
- Concerns in Europe, January-June 2001: Switzerland (AI Index: EUR 01/003/2001)
- Switzerland: Alleged use of excessive force by officers of the Bern Municipal Police – the case of Cemal Gömeç (AI Index: EUR 43/007/2001)
- Switzerland: Death during forcible deportation: an exchange of correspondence following the death of Samson Chukwu (AI Index: EUR 43/005/2001)

- Switzerland: The fatal shooting of Michel Hercouët by officers of the Basel-Stadt Cantonal Police (AI Index: EUR 43/009/2001)

Visit
An AI delegate visited Switzerland in March to carry out research.

SYRIA

SYRIAN ARAB REPUBLIC
Head of state: Bashar al-Assad
Head of government: Muhammad Mustafa Miro
Capital: Damascus
Population: 16.6 million
Official language: Arabic
Death penalty: retentionist

Scores of political prisoners, including prisoners of conscience, were released during 2001, most as a result of a presidential amnesty. Dozens of people, including prisoners of conscience, were arrested during the year on political grounds. Hundreds of political prisoners, including prisoners of conscience, continued to be held, most following unfair trials before the Supreme State Security Court (SSSC) and Field Military Courts. Torture and ill-treatment continued to be used against political prisoners, especially during incommunicado detention. There were reports that the health of prisoners of conscience and political prisoners was deteriorating as a result of lack of medical care. At least one person died in custody.

Background
Restrictions were imposed during 2001 on pro-democracy movements which emerged in 2000 following President Bashar al-Assad's assumption of office and advocated political participation and freedom of expression in Syria. The authorities accused these groups of defying government guidelines and stipulated that such groups must obtain an official licence.

There were reports that all political prisoners were transferred from Tadmur Military Prison to other prisons, including Sednaya Prison, and that the civilian section of the prison had been closed down.

2001 also witnessed an increasing demand for respect for human rights and for political and legal reform. A new human rights group, the Human Rights Association in Syria, was established during the year.

A legislative decree issued by President Bashar al-Assad in September restricted press coverage of a range of loosely defined topics including national security, national unity, security of the army, and the country's dignity and prestige. Following changes in laws governing the ownership and publication of newspapers, new newspapers were launched by junior members of the ruling Progressive National Front and the first privately owned newspaper was published.

The UN Human Rights Committee examined the second periodic report on Syria's implementation of the International Covenant on Civil and Political Rights, which had been due in 1984. The Committee called on the Syrian authorities to, among other things, investigate allegations of extrajudicial executions, torture, and "disappearances".

Prisoner releases
Scores of political prisoners were released, most as a result of a presidential amnesty issued in November. They included nine prisoners of conscience, mostly leading members of the unauthorized Party for Communist Action (PCA) who had been detained since 1987; dozens of political prisoners who had been held since the early 1980s in connection with their involvement with the unauthorized Muslim Brotherhood organization; and Jordanians and Palestinians who had been imprisoned for over 15 years in connection with the Palestinian *Fatah* movement.

Human rights defenders
Syrian human rights organizations and civil society groups stepped up their campaign against human rights violations in the country, despite restrictions imposed by the authorities in February outlawing any activities carried out without a prior licence from the authorities.

▢ Human rights defender Nizar Nayyuf was released in May and subsequently allowed to travel to France to seek medical treatment after restrictions imposed on his movements were lifted. He had spent nine years in detention as a prisoner of conscience in connection with the unauthorized Committees for the Defence of Democratic Freedoms and Human Rights in Syria. However, as a result of statements critical of the Syrian government which he made to the media, the authorities issued a warrant for his arrest if and when he returned home. He was charged with, among other things, disseminating false information abroad and seeking to change the Constitution by illegal means. One of his brothers was reportedly dismissed from his job and other members of his family were intimidated and reportedly threatened with exile by the Syrian authorities.

There were reports of physical assault and intimidation of members of emerging civil society groups and intellectuals.

▢ Nabil Sulayman, a novelist and founder of the Cultural Forum, a civil society group, was attacked by unidentified assailants in January in Latakia and hospitalized as a result. Nabil Sulayman, who along with other intellectuals had been calling for the lifting of the state of emergency and the release of political prisoners, said the attack was "aimed against all critical thinking and cultural activities which are pushing for change". No investigation was known to have been carried out and there were reports that members of the security forces may have been involved in the assault.

Arrests

Dozens of people were arrested during the year for their alleged involvement in anti-government activities. Most were members of unauthorized political parties or emerging civil society groups. Among those arrested in August and September were doctors, lawyers, teachers and businesspeople. At least 10 prisoners of conscience were arrested during 2001 and brought to trial before courts whose procedures fell short of international fair trial standards (see below). Most were initially held incommunicado at 'Adra Prison.

Kurdish political activists continued to be intimidated, threatened and detained. Among them were prisoners of conscience detained solely for exercising their rights to freedom of expression including distribution of Kurdish literature and involvement in Kurdish cultural activities.

◻ Muhammad Hammu, the owner of a Kurdish bookshop in Aleppo, was detained from 27 August to 3 September. He was released without charge but was threatened that his bookshop would be closed unless he "cooperated" with the authorities.

◻ At least 25 Kurdish political activists were detained in June, apparently following violent confrontations with the security forces who reportedly used excessive force to disperse a rally in the city of Aleppo in support of Abdullah Öcalan, leader of the Kurdistan Workers' Party (PKK), who remained under sentence of death in Turkey. The activists were charged with "resisting the socialist system". They remained detained pending trial at the end of the year.

Exiled Syrian nationals returning home voluntarily continued to risk detention and prolonged interrogation.

Prisoners of conscience

Ten prisoners of conscience were referred for trial during the year before the Criminal Court and the SSSC. They included two parliamentarians whose trials before the Criminal Court fell short of international fair trial standards. They were charged with, among other things, seeking to change the Constitution by illegal means, insulting the authorities, and inciting sectarian strife. Their lawyers said there were serious flaws in the trial procedures, including during the arrest and interrogation stages, and dismissed the charges as "null and void". They called for the immediate release of the defendants as their detention was "unconstitutional", but this was rejected by the court which ordered the detainees to be remanded in custody.

◻ Riad al-Turk, a lawyer and first secretary of the unauthorized Communist Party-Political Bureau, was arrested in September and held incommunicado during the first month of his detention at 'Adra Prison, where he remained at the end of the year. There were concerns about his health as he was suffering from heart disease and diabetes and had undergone major heart surgery two years earlier. Riad al-Turk was a former prisoner of conscience who had been detained without charge or trial, mostly incommunicado, between 1980 and 1998.

Dozens of prisoners of conscience, belonging to various unauthorized political groups, continued to be detained without trial or after unfair trials by the SSSC.

◻ 'Abd al-'Aziz al-Khayyir, a leading member of the PCA, remained in detention. He had been excluded from the presidential amnesty which led to the release of all other members of the PCA. He was serving a 22-year prison sentence, the longest sentence known to have been handed down by the SSSC, imposed after an unfair trial on charges of membership of the PCA. A medical doctor, he was arrested in Damascus on 1 February 1992 by members of Military Intelligence and subsequently tortured and ill-treated while being held incommunicado. While he was being sought by the Syrian authorities prior to his arrest, his wife had been arrested and detained from August 1987 until December 1991. She was held without charge or trial and was a prisoner of conscience.

Political prisoners

Hundreds of political prisoners arrested in the early 1980s in connection with their involvement with the unauthorized Muslim Brotherhood organization remained in detention serving long sentences, mostly handed down by Field Military Courts after unfair trials.

Scores of other political prisoners continued to be held. They included members of the Islamic Liberation Party, the Democratic Ba'th Party and the Arab Communist Organization; Kurdish political activists and Palestinians; and Jordanian and Lebanese nationals. Some had been held for more than two decades.

Dozens of seriously sick political prisoners remained without adequate medical care in conditions amounting to cruel, inhuman and degrading treatment.

News came to light during 2001 of the execution by the Syrian authorities in the early 1990s of Yusuf 'Abd al-Khaliq Mustafa Shahada, a Jordanian teacher with two children, for his involvement with the Muslim Brotherhood.

Torture and ill-treatment

Torture and ill-treatment continued to be inflicted routinely on political prisoners, especially during incommunicado detention at the Palestine Branch and Military Interrogation Branch detention centres.

◻ Sisters 'Ayisha and Asma Taleb and their father, an Iraqi family resident in Syria, had been held incommunicado at the Palestine Branch detention centre since the second half of 2000. 'Ayisha Taleb and her father were arrested following a dawn raid on a house in Hama by members of Military Intelligence who reportedly beat the father in front of his children before taking him and 'Ayisha Taleb away. Four months later a younger daughter, Asma Taleb, was arrested. The family's arrest was apparently connected to the father's alleged involvement with unauthorized Islamist groups. He was reportedly subjected to torture in the "German Chair", a metal chair with moving parts which stretches the spine and causes severe pressure on the neck and legs; given electric shocks; and beaten with cables while held in solitary confinement. On one occasion he was reportedly left naked during the winter in freezing conditions. 'Ayisha Taleb, who was pregnant at the time of her arrest, was reportedly severely beaten and as a result suffered a miscarriage. She was said to have suffered from severe pain as a result but no medical care was provided despite her pleas for help. Asma Taleb was detained in a solitary cell in the men's section of the Palestine Branch detention centre where she was said to have been repeatedly beaten and ill-treated. All three remained in incommunicado detention at the end of the year.

No investigations were known to have been carried out into recent or past allegations of torture.

Death in custody
At least one person died in custody in circumstances suggesting torture may have contributed to his death.

▫ Muhammad Shukri 'Allush, an 18-year-old Syrian Kurd, died in Jandrays police station on 2 May. Muhammad Shukri 'Allush was arrested at his home in Jandrays in 'Afreen earlier the same day and taken to the local police station for questioning, reportedly in connection with a theft. About four hours later his family was asked to report to the police station where they were told that he had committed suicide and ordered to collect his body. According to reports, there were visible injuries and bruises on his body and it was feared that torture may have contributed to his death. According to the authorities, Muhammad Shukri 'Allush "hanged himself inside the police station using his shirt which he fastened to the door of the lavatory".

AI country reports/ visits
Reports
- Syrian Arab Republic: Briefing to the Human Rights Committee 71st session – March 2001 (AI Index: MDE 24/001/2001)
- Syria: Torture, despair and dehumanization in Tadmur Military Prison (AI Index: MDE 24/014/2001)

Visits
Repeated communications to the Syrian authorities asking for AI to be allowed to visit the country to conduct talks with officials and carry out research were ignored.

TAIWAN

TAIWAN
President: Chen Shui-bian
Head of government: Chang Chun-hsiung
Capital: Taipei
Population: 22.5 million
Official language: Mandarin Chinese
Death penalty: retentionist

Despite its promises to improve the human rights situation, the government implemented few reforms. The death penalty continued to be imposed and 10 people were executed. Torture continued to be used as a means to force confessions, which were then used as evidence in court. Although some 20 Tibetan asylum-seekers were granted asylum, there was concern that immigration procedures were inadequate and lacked transparency.

Background
In the legislative elections held in December the ruling Democratic Progressive Party won 87 seats and became the largest political party in the 225-member legislature. The *Kuomintang* lost a majority in the legislature for the first time in Taiwan's history.

Economic difficulties, such as rising unemployment, and economic relations, including financial cooperation with China, were high on the political agenda. Taiwan became a signatory to the World Trade Organization in November and was expected to ratify its membership by January 2002. It was hoped that increased support for the ruling party would help to reverse economic decline; in the three months to September, Taiwan's Gross Domestic Product suffered its biggest quarterly fall in 26 years.

Torture and ill-treatment
Torture remained a serious and often unreported problem. It was reported in March that in a study conducted in 2000 by the Chinese Association for Human Rights, some 1,700 prisoners alleged that police officers tortured suspects to extract confessions. Lawyers and human rights activists feared that confessions obtained under torture were used by the police as evidence in court.

Death penalty
Ten people were executed during 2001. While executions continued, the government made legislative changes which reduced the number of crimes under the Military Criminal Code carrying a mandatory death penalty.

▫ The retrial which began in November 2000 at the Taipei High Court of Su Chien-ho, Liu Bin-lang and Chuang Lin-hsun, known as the "Hsichih trio", continued until the second half of the year. Despite President Chen Shui-bian's promises to consider a pardon from the death penalty for the three men, they remained on death row where they have been since 1992. AI had earlier urged the government to institute a thorough, impartial and independent investigation into reports that the three men were tortured while in police custody and confessed under duress, and called for a retrial. A former cellmate of Su Chien-ho testified in May that when Su Chien-ho returned to their cell after an interrogation session, his lips were bloody and he was unable to stand without help. The cellmate stated that Su Chien-ho's genitals were badly swollen. Another witness had earlier stated that he had seen Su Chien-ho tied to a chair while a wooden pole was used to beat the soles of his feet, an electric cattle prod was used to apply shocks to Liu Bin-lang's genitals, and Chuang Lin-hsun was hit on the head.

Promises of human rights reform

According to Prime Minister Chang Chun-hsiung, initial moves were being undertaken to ratify the International Covenant on Civil and Political Rights and the International Covenant on Economic, Social and Cultural Rights. The government was conducting a comprehensive review of current domestic laws to ensure that they were in line with international human rights conventions. In December, President Chen Shui-bian announced that in 2002 the government would issue a report and a white paper on human rights policies. He also stated that the draft plan to establish a national human rights commission would be reviewed, that international standards would be incorporated into domestic legislation, and that a basic law on human rights protection was being drafted.

Arms trade

There was concern that Taiwan was a leading manufacturer and supplier of electro-shock equipment, including stun guns, and that there were few or no restrictions on their sale and use.

TAJIKISTAN

REPUBLIC OF TAJIKISTAN
Head of state: Imomali Rakhmonov
Head of government: Akil Akilov
Capital: Dushanbe
Population: 6.1 million
Official language: Tajik
Death penalty: retentionist

At least 74 people were sentenced to death and at least five men were executed. There were reports of torture and ill-treatment of detainees. The government put on hold a plan to remove Afghan refugees from Dushanbe. Tajikistan continued to keep its borders closed to those fleeing fighting in Afghanistan.

Background

The level of political violence remained high throughout the year. Among prominent politicians assassinated in 2001 were the Deputy Interior Minister, a presidential adviser on foreign policy, and the Minister of Culture.

In June, at least 19 people were taken hostage in two separate incidents by former commanders of the United Tajik Opposition (UTO). The UTO had fought against government forces during the Tajik civil war that formally ended in 1997. The former UTO commanders demanded the release of UTO supporters they believed were held in custody on fabricated charges. The hostages were released unharmed a week later. On 22 June, government forces launched a retaliatory military attack against former UTO fighters in the outskirts of Dushanbe. There were allegations that civilians were killed in the attack.

Tajikistan offered the USA and its allies the use of its airspace and military bases for military attacks in Afghanistan.

Despite repeated calls throughout the year to open Tajikistan's border with Afghanistan to civilians fleeing fighting in Afghanistan, the border remained closed.

Death penalty

At least 74 people were reportedly sentenced to death in 2001. Five executions were confirmed, but the real figure was believed to be much higher. Two death sentences were known to have been commuted in 2001; at least 51 appeals for clemency were reportedly turned down by the President. The authorities failed to publish comprehensive statistics on the use of the death penalty.

There were reports that some of those sentenced to death had not received fair trials; some alleged that they had been tortured and ill-treated in pre-trial detention. No investigations were known to have been carried out into these allegations.

▭ Gaybullojon Saidov was reportedly executed on 4 April despite a request from the UN Human Rights

Committee that he not be executed while the Committee was examining his case. Gaybullojon Saidov's co-defendant, Andrey Rebrikov, was reportedly executed the same day. Both men had been sentenced to death by the military board of the Supreme Court of Tajikistan on 24 December 1999, after being convicted of supporting former Popular Front commander and warlord Makhmud Khudoyberdiyev who had allegedly tried to seize power in one area in 1998. There were reports that Gaybullojon Saidov was not allowed to choose his legal counsel or to meet his lawyer regularly, and that he was ill-treated in pre-trial detention.

Afghan refugees
Harassment and ill-treatment
A number of Afghan refugees alleged that they were beaten by police, in many cases reportedly to extort bribes. Several refugees were reportedly detained and ill-treated after they complained or sought to complain about police brutality. Fear of police retaliation reportedly stopped eyewitnesses from giving testimony to the relevant authorities in a number of cases.
Relocation
An order to remove Afghan refugees from Dushanbe by 31 July was put on hold. In July 2000, the President had decreed that refugees were not permitted to live in a number of towns and regions of Tajikistan to "ensure security and public order." Following the decree, Dushanbe's mayor had originally ordered all refugees to leave the city by 31 July 2001. There were concerns that access to employment, education and housing would be difficult for relocated refugees and that the government might not be able to ensure their safety.

AI country reports/ visits
Report
- Concerns in Europe, January-June 2001: Tajikistan (AI Index: EUR 01/003/2001)
Visit
AI delegates visited Tajikistan in June.

TANZANIA

UNITED REPUBLIC OF TANZANIA
Head of state: Benjamin Mkapa
Head of government: Frederick Sumaye
Capital: Dar es Salaam
Population: 36 million
Official languages: Kiswahili, English
Death penalty: retentionist

Security forces shot dead at least 22 people during demonstrations in circumstances suggesting unlawful use of lethal force. Torture, including rape, and ill-treatment were widely reported. Hundreds of political prisoners, including prisoners of conscience, were detained. Two opposition leaders were held as prisoners of conscience for eight months. Courts continued to pass death sentences.

Background
A political impasse surrounding disputed election results in 2000 and the brutal suppression of demonstrations in January 2001 continued until October when a political accord was signed between the ruling *Chama Cha Mapinduzi* (CCM), Party of the Revolution, and the main opposition party, the Civic United Front (CUF). It restated the unimplemented 1999 agreement on reconciliation and democratic reform. It also identified measures to address human rights concerns stemming from the events of January 2001; these included the establishment of an independent commission of inquiry to investigate the January unrest and measures to assist the victims and their families. No details as to the time-frame for implementation of these and other measures were available by the end of the year.

Parliament passed a bill in March to establish a Commission on Human Rights and Good Governance. No appointments were known to have been made by the end of the year.

January demonstrations
On 27 January demonstrations organized by the CUF were held in Zanzibar town, three towns on Pemba island and in Dar es Salaam and other mainland towns. They had been organized to protest against the election results of 2000 and the government's refusal to hold new elections in Zanzibar. Killings, large-scale arrests, beatings and torture of CUF officials and supporters occurred before, during and after the demonstrations, which were declared illegal by the government. Hundreds fled to neighbouring Kenya following the violence.
Unlawful killings
In Pemba security forces, reportedly armed with pistols, rifles and sub-machine guns, shot dead at least 22 demonstrators, in circumstances suggesting unlawful use of lethal force.

In Micheweni, Pemba island, security forces used tear gas against demonstrators, reportedly followed by indiscriminate use of live ammunition without advance warning. Police chased and tried to arrest demonstrators, reportedly shooting some in nearby swamps and from a helicopter.

Imprisonment
Hundreds of people, among them possible prisoners of conscience, were arrested and held without access to lawyers or families. Most were released on bail shortly afterwards. Following the CCM-CUF political accord, charges were dropped against all those accused of participating in an illegal demonstration.

Ibrahim Lipumba, CUF Chairperson, was among nearly 50 CUF officials and supporters arrested during a meeting on 25 January and beaten by armed riot police. Forty-four of those arrested were charged with holding an illegal meeting and released on bail. The case against them was dismissed in December.

In Pemba 18 people were arrested and charged in connection with the murder of a police officer, Haji Muslim Simai, during the demonstrations. All except one were released in May after the Attorney General dismissed the charges against them.

Juma Duni Haji and Machano Khamis Ali, leading members of the CUF, were arrested on 23 February on charges of participating in an illegal demonstration. They were released the following day but immediately rearrested and charged with murdering Haji Muslim Simai, bringing to 20 the number of people charged in connection with the murder (see previous case). The two men remained in Zanzibar Central Prison until 15 October when, following the CCM-CUF agreement, charges against them were withdrawn and they were released. They were among 18 prisoners of conscience who had been held on charges of treason from 1997 to 2000.

In January CUF Secretary General Seif Sharif Hamad and 39 others were arrested and charged with armed conspiracy and theft of weapons, and released on bail. AI believed the charges may have been politically motivated. The trial was adjourned several times. Charges against Seif Hamad and at least 10 others remained pending at the end of the year.

Torture and ill-treatment
Methods of torture used against hundreds of the demonstrators included beatings with long wooden batons and canes, and *kichura* (being made to squat and "jump like a frog"). Women were beaten, raped and otherwise sexually abused by police after the demonstrations in Zanzibar. In May police were reported to have set up an investigation into the beating of five CUF supporters in Pemba. No details as to the outcome of this investigation were available at the end of the year.

Police in Zanzibar town reportedly gang-raped a five-months pregnant woman and her two teenage daughters in front of each other after they entered their house searching for male demonstrators in January.

Freedom of expression
Journalists and others were detained for carrying out their professional duties or for the non-violent expression of their views.

A magistrates' court sentenced Khamis Rajab Dibagula, a Muslim preacher, to 18 months' imprisonment in July under Section 129 of the Penal Code on charges of insulting Christianity. In August, the same day as demonstrations organized by Muslims to protest against his imprisonment, the High Court ruled the sentence unlawful and ordered his release.

In November Augustine Mrema, National Chairman of the Tanzanian Labour Party, and Rugemeleze Nshala, President of the Lawyers' Environmental Action Team, were briefly detained after security officers searched their properties, reportedly for materials about alleged deaths at Bulyanhulu goldmine in 1996.

AI country reports/ visits
Statement
- Tanzania: Inquiry into Zanzibar killings must be prompt, independent and impartial (AI Index: AFR 56/013/2001)

Visit
An AI delegation visited Kenya and Tanzania in February and March to investigate reports of human rights violations during the January demonstrations and to interview refugees. Its findings were addressed to the government in November.

THAILAND

KINGDOM OF THAILAND
Head of state: King Bhumibol Adulyadej
Head of government: Thaksin Shinawatra (replaced Chuan Leekpai in January)
Capital: Bangkok
Population: 60.6 million
Official language: Thai
Death penalty: retentionist

Ten people were executed by machine-gun fire and at least 72 people were sentenced to death in 2001. At the end of the year some 300 people remained under sentence of death. Poor prison conditions and ill-treatment of prisoners and detainees, including severe beatings, continued to be reported. By the end of the year, more than 120,000 Karen and Karenni refugees were living in refugee camps at the border. The government refused a request from Shan asylum-seekers from Myanmar for the establishment of camps and denied them access to existing camps.

Background
Following elections in January, Thaksin Shinawatra was appointed Prime Minister and his *Thai Rak Thai* party

formed a coalition government. In August the Constitutional Court dismissed charges by the National Counter Corruption Commission that Thaksin Shinawatra had concealed personal assets. The last two National Human Rights Commissioners were appointed in June, but at the end of the year the Commissioners had still not been paid a salary. Also in June the 1952 Anti-Communist Act, which gave the military sweeping powers to arrest and detain suspected members of the Communist Party, was repealed. No new security legislation had been enacted to replace the Act by the end of 2001.

Death penalty

Ten people were executed, seven for drugs offences, in Bangkwang Maximum Security Prison, Nonthaburi Province. The government continued to assert that execution was an effective means of deterring drug traffickers. The execution of six people on 18 April provoked widespread public debate and condemnation from some groups. The cabinet approved the use of lethal injection instead of firing squads as a method of execution, although executions were not carried out using the new method during 2001.

Torture and ill-treatment in prisons

Conditions in many prisons and police lock-ups continued to constitute cruel, inhuman or degrading treatment. For example, death-row prisoners were kept in heavy shackles for prolonged periods. Five inmates were reportedly beaten to death by prison guards in April when they attempted to escape from Klong Prem Prison north of Bangkok. Beatings of African and Burmese prisoners by other prisoners under the supervision of guards were reported in Lard Yao Prison in Nonthaburi Province.

Migrant workers, refugees and asylum-seekers

In January, 17 members of ethnic Karen armed opposition group God's Army, including its twin teenaged leaders Johnny and Luther Htoo, crossed the border from Myanmar and surrendered to the Thai authorities. The authorities provided protection from forcible return to all 17 members of the group.

In December the authorities closed Maneloy camp, Raatchburi Province, where ethnic Burman dissidents and others were living while awaiting resettlement to a third country. Since January 1999, 2,373 people had been resettled from the camp. Following its closure Myanmar asylum-seekers, except the Shan, were obliged to attempt to enter a camp on the border. Those not in camps risk arrest and deportation.

More than 100,000 Shan asylum-seekers who had fled human rights violations in Myanmar continued to be denied access to refugee camps and were treated by the Thai authorities as migrant workers with no legal right to seek asylum.

Asylum-seekers from other countries continued to be arrested for "illegal entry" and detained for long periods at immigration detention centres.

In September and October the authorities registered almost 560,000 migrant workers from neighbouring countries. Migrant workers who were not registered continued to face arrest and deportation.

Forcible return

☐ Khaing Kaung Zan, a Myanmar asylum-seeker, who had been forcibly returned to Myanmar from Thailand in December 2000, was arrested, allegedly tortured, and sentenced to 10 years' imprisonment in January 2001.

☐ There was no information about the fate of some 50 male Karen asylum-seekers who had been arrested by the army in January 2000. It was feared that they had been forced across the border to Myanmar and killed by the Myanmar army.

☐ In November, 63 Karen asylum-seekers were forcibly returned by the 9th Infantry Division of the Royal Thai Army in Raatchburi Province to Htee Wah Doh, a settlement for internally displaced people in Myanmar. Later that month the Myanmar army destroyed the settlement, forcing all its residents to flee.

Prisoners of conscience

☐ Sok Yoeun, a Cambodian refugee and prisoner of conscience who was arrested in Thailand in 1999 for "illegal immigration", continued to be detained throughout the year. Court hearings of his case were ongoing, pending possible extradition to Cambodia. The Cambodian government accused him of involvement in a rocket attack on the Prime Minister's motorcade in September 1998, but there was no evidence linking him to the attack. Sok Yoeun suffered from a heart condition and tuberculosis.

☐ Ramlek Nilnuan, a land rights activist and prisoner of conscience, was released on bail in April. He had been arrested in July 2000 for trespassing in a national park.

Extrajudicial executions

In July, the Police Chief of Region 4 stated that police-backed "death squads" had killed over 300 suspected drug traffickers and that he expected some 1,000 people in total to be extrajudicially executed in his region during 2001 as a means of solving the proliferation of illegal drugs. Police shot dead many suspected drug traffickers in 2001, claiming that the suspects fired first, but lack of witnesses made it impossible to verify these claims. In October the Prime Minister gave an award to Loei Province police because 66 suspected drug traffickers had died during arrest so far in the year; police denied having extrajudicially executed them.

Impunity

☐ Six environmental activists were killed during the year. Among them was Jurin Rachapal, who was killed in January. He had been involved in protests against the destruction of mangrove forests by prawn farming in Phuket Province. Senators and local non-governmental organizations criticized the lack of progress in the murder investigations and insufficient government protection of potential victims.

☐ In September the government appointed a new committee to investigate the military crackdown against pro-democracy demonstrators in May 1992, which resulted in over 30 "disappearances", more than 50 deaths, and hundreds of injuries. However, by the end of

the year no one had been brought to justice and there was no information about the fate of the "disappeared".
▫ Ten years after Thailand's most prominent labour leader, Tanong Pho-arn, "disappeared" in the aftermath of the February 1991 coup there was still no progress in tracing him or establishing who was responsible for his "disappearance".

AI country reports/visits
Report
- Thailand: The "disappearance" of labour leader Tanong Pho-arn, 19 June 1991 (AI Index: ASA 39/007/2001)

Visit
AI delegates visited Thailand in January, February and March.

TOGO

TOGOLESE REPUBLIC
Head of state: Gnassingbé Eyadéma
Head of government: Gabriel Messan Agbeyome Kodjo
Capital: Lomé
Population: 4.7 million
Official language: French
Death penalty: abolitionist in practice
2001 treaty ratifications/signatures: Optional Protocol to the UN Children's Convention on the involvement of children in armed conflict

Freedom of expression continued to be threatened. Prisoners of conscience were sentenced to prison terms after unfair political trials. Impunity for those responsible for human rights violations in the last two decades continued. A joint commission of inquiry by the UN and Organization of African Unity (OAU) reported on widespread human rights violations and confirmed that bodies had been found at sea and on the beaches of neighbouring Benin at the time of the 1998 presidential elections. It called for the appointment of a UN Special Rapporteur on Togo to maintain international scrutiny of the human rights situation.

Background
Initially planned for October, legislative elections were postponed to March 2002 by the *Commission électorale nationale indépendante* (CENI), Independent National Electoral Commission. After the opposition boycotted the March 1999 legislative elections, international mediators, including governments from the European Union (EU) and the Francophonie group of states, assisted the Togolese government and the political parties in reaching agreement in July 1999 for new legislative elections.

The postponement came amid pressures from supporters of President Eyadéma to amend the Constitution to enable him to serve a third term as President beyond 2003. The Constitution allows for only two five-year presidential terms. President Eyadéma came to power in a military coup in 1967, and was subsequently elected President in 1993 and 1998 in elections marred by extrajudicial executions, torture and detentions of opposition supporters.

In September the European Parliament condemned any attempt to amend the Constitution, and called on the Togolese authorities to hold free and transparent elections as soon as possible. It also called for an end to the climate of impunity in Togo and for those responsible for human rights violations to be brought to justice.

Torture and ill-treatment
Torture and ill-treatment by the security forces was reported to continue in places of detention and prisons. Several students and members of opposition political parties were among the victims.
▫ After his release from five days' detention by the gendarmerie in September, Houndjo Mawudzro, a prisoner of conscience and student activist, described being whipped with a cord and beaten on the legs and soles of his feet. He was accused of incitement to rebellion but was not formally charged. In November he was briefly re-detained for a few days, apparently in reprisal for his public statement about the torture he had suffered in detention.

Political imprisonment
At least eight political prisoners were still in prison at the end of 2001, one of whom had been convicted after an unfair trial.

In political trials in July and August, two opposition leaders were sentenced to prison terms after trials which failed to meet international standards. The presiding judge was a leading member of the ruling party and could not therefore be considered independent.
▫ In August Yaowvi Agboyibo, Chairman of the opposition *Comité d'action pour le renouveau* (CAR), Action Committee for the Renewal, was convicted of defamation of character for alleging that a person close to the ruling party supported militias responsible for human rights violations between 1996 and 1998. Yaowvi Agboyibo was sentenced to six months' imprisonment and a fine. In September, while still in prison, investigations were opened into new charges against him of criminal conspiracy. He appeared to have been imprisoned to discourage questioning of Togo's human rights record and to prevent him contesting the legislative elections.

Prison conditions
Throughout the country conditions of detention were so harsh as to amount to cruel, inhuman and degrading treatment.

The civil prison in Lomé was severely overcrowded, holding 1,200 inmates in a prison designed to accommodate a much smaller number. According to reports an average of 90 people shared a cell measuring 4m x 6m, without electric light or windows. As punishment, for example for infringing prison regulations, prisoners were beaten or put in a cell measuring 1m x 2m with 15 others. Sanitary provisions were practically non-existent. Prisoners had to pay for access to only two showers and two lavatories for the whole prison.

In February Nyabledji John reportedly died in prison in Kara, northern Togo. He was believed to have died as a result of medical neglect, lack of food, and harsh, insanitary conditions. He was the second prisoner to have died out of a group of nine Togolese refugees arrested in December 1997 in Ghana and handed back to the Togolese authorities. Most were members of the *Comité togolais pour la résistance*, Togolese Resistance Committee, an opposition party in exile. After being transferred to Togo, they were severely beaten at the civil prison in Lomé, with the result that they could not walk and had difficulties breathing. Nyabledji John was allegedly forced to eat sand and then refused water. In July 1998, they were transferred to prison in Kara, where conditions were life-threatening. They were still detained without charge or trial at the end of 2001 and were reported to be held in a cell without any natural light.

International Commission of Inquiry on Togo
In February an International Commission of Inquiry on Togo, set up by the UN and the OAU to verify allegations made by AI in 1999 of hundreds of extrajudicial executions in Togo at the time of presidential elections in 1998, published its report. It confirmed that local fishermen had seen a large number of bodies in the sea and on the beaches of Benin during and after presidential elections in Togo in 1998.

It concluded that those killed were mostly opposition supporters but also included criminal suspects, and that "various accounts seem to indicate that [the perpetrators] are individuals associated with the security forces, the gendarmerie and the militias that operate in tandem with the authorities. In addition to extrajudicial, summary and arbitrary executions, these elements have engaged in torture and ill-treatment of detainees, and the rape and abduction of women in certain areas." It also referred to allegations of human rights violations committed by militias which reportedly enjoy the support and encouragement of the government.

Despite assurances given to the Commission by the Togolese authorities that they would guarantee the security of witnesses, at least a dozen of those who testified before the Commission were victims of intimidation and harassment during its visit and after publication of its report. Some had to seek refuge outside Togo. Others in Benin went into hiding.

Freedom of expression and assembly
There were continued violations of the right to freedom of expression, particularly of journalists who were imprisoned as prisoners of conscience and harassed in an attempt to silence them.

Restrictions on freedom of assembly worsened after June when tensions rose during political trials. The security forces dispersed non-violent demonstrations with tear gas on several occasions. Demonstrators were arrested and in some cases detained for a few hours. Some were reportedly beaten at the time of arrest.

◻ In June journalist Lucien Messan was sentenced to 18 months' imprisonment, with six months suspended, for forgery in relation to a communiqué released by the *Association togolaise des éditeurs de presse privée*, Togolese Association of Private Press Editors. He was pardoned and released in October. The communiqué was critical of a statement made by the Prime Minister to the UN Commission on Human Rights in March.

◻ In October journalists Nevame Klu, Ganiou Bawa and Rigobert Bassadou were briefly detained on charges of defamation and spreading false information after they published articles critical of a member of the ruling party and a local government official. The cases against them had not proceeded by the end of 2001.

AI country reports/ visits
Report
- Togo: The time for accountability has finally arrived (AI Index: AFR 57/006/2001)

Visit
In October and November, AI delegates visited Benin and Ghana to meet Togolese victims of human rights abuses.

TRINIDAD AND TOBAGO

REPUBLIC OF TRINIDAD AND TOBAGO
Head of state: Arthur Napoleon Raymond Robinson
Head of government: Patrick Manning (replaced Basdeo Panday in December)
Capital: Port-of-Spain
Population: 1.3 million
Official language: English
Death penalty: retentionist
2001 treaty ratifications/ signatures: Protocol Additional to the Geneva Conventions of 12 August 1949, and relating to the Protection of Victims of International Armed Conflicts (Protocol I); Protocol Additional to the Geneva Conventions of 12 August 1949, and relating to the Protection of Victims of Non-International Armed Conflicts (Protocol II)

Death sentences continued to be imposed but no executions were carried out. Reports of torture and ill-treatment by police persisted and abuses in detention continued to cause grave concern.

Background

In October, parliament was suspended when the government lost its working majority after three of the ruling United National Congress Party members of parliament refused to vote with the government. Elections in December did not result in either major political party having a majority in parliament.

Death penalty

There were at least 55 men and four women on death row at the end of 2001. There were no executions and no death warrants were issued during the year. Courts continued to impose death sentences at an alarming rate, with 12 people sentenced to death in a one-week period in August alone. In June, the government announced its intention to introduce legislation to lessen the legal safeguards available to condemned prisoners and so facilitate the resumption of executions. This appeared to be a reaction to recent court rulings that increased the legal rights of condemned prisoners. However, the Constitution (Amendment) Bill required the support of the opposition and had not been passed by the end of the year.

Abuses in detention

Conditions in places of detention continued to cause grave concern. There were reports of brutality by prison guards, in one case resulting in death.

The naked body of Anton Cooper was found in a cell at Golden Grove Prison on 26 June. According to the autopsy report, Anton Cooper, who was described as being in good health when he was taken into custody the previous week, died of "asphyxia associated with multiple blunt traumatic injuries". Other prisoners at the institution told the media that Anton Cooper had been severely beaten by approximately nine prison guards. According to their statements, after being beaten, he complained of severe pain and requested to see a doctor, whereupon the guards returned and beat him again.

In June, judges freed former death-row inmate George Moore, aged 75, after his murder conviction had been reduced to manslaughter on mental health grounds and the appeal court found he had served a sufficient prison term since 1987. The appeal court judges were severely critical of the medical care he had received in prison, describing the treatment available as "pathetically bad based on the experience of this appellant." George Moore had become partially blind while in prison because of a lack of treatment for cataracts, a situation the judges described as "unforgivable".

Abuses by police

Torture and ill-treatment by police continued to be reported. In July, the Prime Minister announced the establishment of a Police Management Authority in order to improve discipline in the police. At least four people received compensation after filing cases alleging police abuse.

In March, Siewchand Ramanoop won undisclosed damages from the state after a judge ruled that his constitutional rights had been violated by the police. Siewchand Ramanoop had been arrested on 1 November 2000 after he got into an argument with an off-duty police officer. The officer and one of his colleagues later confronted Siewchand Ramanoop, handcuffed him and beat him. Siewchand Ramanoop was then taken to Gasparillo Police Station and beaten again.

In April, Titus Fox, who was shot in the leg by a police officer and then arrested and charged with two offences which had been dismissed in 1991, was awarded TT$133,400 (approximately US$22,200) for assault and false imprisonment.

In May a police sergeant was arrested and charged with the rape of a teenage girl in San Fernando Police Station. According to reports, the girl had gone to the station with her mother to report an incident of domestic violence. The girl was later taken back to the station and assaulted.

In May, Joseph Reyes, who had been detained awaiting trial for four years, was freed by magistrates who ruled that his constitutional rights had been violated, thereby invalidating his confession to murder. Joseph Reyes had been denied access to a lawyer, handcuffed and denied food and water for long periods, and denied access to a toilet for eight days. He also alleged that he was beaten.

In November, a Special Reserve Police Constable was charged with murder in connection with the fatal shooting of 17-year-old Anisha Neptune in May outside the Four Roads Police Station.

TUNISIA

REPUBLIC OF TUNISIA
Head of state: Zine El 'Abidine Ben 'Ali
Head of government: Mohamed Ghannouchi
Capital: Tunis
Population: 9.6 million
Official language: Arabic
Death penalty: retentionist

Up to 1,000 political prisoners, most of them prisoners of conscience, remained in prison. Several had been held for more than a decade. The families of prisoners often faced harassment and denial of their basic rights. The authorities used various means to prevent former prisoners from resuming a normal life after their release. Several political opponents of the government were imprisoned during 2001. They included several political opponents, or alleged opponents, resident abroad who were arrested when they returned to Tunisia and faced unfair trials before military courts. The authorities once again stepped up their repression of human rights defenders.

Torture and ill-treatment by the security forces continued to be reported both in police stations and in prisons, in a general context of impunity.

Background

The ruling *Rassemblement Constitutionnel Démocratique*, Constitutional Democratic Movement, led a campaign calling for President Ben 'Ali to be re-elected in 2004 for a fourth term. President Ben 'Ali seized power on 7 November 1987 and in July 1988 introduced a constitutional law stipulating that the president can serve a maximum of three consecutive terms of office. President Ben 'Ali was elected in 1999 for a third term. During 2001, those who dared to speak out against the possible further re-election of President Ben 'Ali faced reprisals.

In July, a new political party, the *Congrès pour la République*, Republican Congress, was created and headed by human rights defender Moncef Marzouki. The party, which had not been recognized by the end of the year, called for civil and political freedoms and reform of the political system.

In the aftermath of the 11 September attacks in the USA, the authorities used the so-called struggle against "terrorism" to justify systematic repression during the previous decade, and to further toughen measures against human rights defenders, political opponents and political prisoners.

Human rights defenders

The authorities further increased repressive measures against human rights defenders in an attempt to curb their peaceful activities. The measures included arrest and imprisonment, judicial proceedings, ill-treatment by security agents, police surveillance and harassment. Several human rights defenders were banned from leaving the country or saw their movements arbitrarily restricted. Means of communication, including phone and fax lines and Internet connections, were cut.

The two main domestic human rights organizations continued to face tremendous difficulties.

Judicial proceedings against the *Ligue tunisienne des droits de l'homme* (LTDH), Tunisian Human Rights League, continued. In February, the court annulled the results of the LTDH's general assembly of October 2000, including the election of the new leadership; an AI delegate observed the trial. In June the Appeal Court in Tunis ruled that new elections for the leadership of the LTDH should be organized. The authorities initiated judicial proceedings in January and March against the newly elected leaders Slaheddine Jourchi and Mokhtar Trifi, Vice-President and President respectively of the LTDH, for having signed an LTDH communiqué denouncing human rights violations.

Measures were taken to curtail the activities of the *Conseil national pour les libertés en Tunisie* (CNLT), National Council for Liberties in Tunisia. The CNLT had been created in December 1998, but had still not been registered by the authorities at the end of 2001. On several occasions, members were prevented from gathering and were ill-treated by the security forces. Judicial proceedings were initiated against leading figures of the CNLT.

On 26 June, Sihem Ben Sedrine, a journalist and spokesperson for the CNLT, was arrested when she arrived at Tunis airport; an AI delegate observed the hearing before the examining judge on 5 July. Sihem Ben Sedrine was released on 11 August by presidential decision, pending judicial proceedings on charges of defamation. The charges related to comments on the lack of independence of the judiciary she had made in June on *Al Mustakillah*, a private television channel, based in London, United Kingdom.

Intergovernmental organizations

In January, the UN Special Representative on human rights defenders stated in her report to the UN Commission on Human Rights that she had received no reply from the Tunisian authorities to the urgent appeals sent in November 2000 concerning Moncef Marzouki as well as the suspension of the new executive of the LTDH. In May, the African Commission on Human and Peoples' Rights passed a resolution on the situation of human rights defenders in Tunisia and expressed concern about the government's decision in November 2000 to suspend the activities of the LTDH.

International human rights organizations

In a continued attempt to prevent international human rights organizations from monitoring human rights in the country, their representatives were either expelled or denied access to the country. Some were assaulted by members of the security forces.

Although the Human Rights Minister Slaheddine Maaoui had stated in an interview in the French daily newspaper *Le Monde* on 6 April 2001 that the two representatives of the *Fédération internationale des ligues des droits de l'homme* (FIDH), International Federation of Human Rights, and AI who had been banned from Tunisia since 1995 and 1994 would be welcome in the country, the proposal by the two organizations to conduct a joint visit to the country did not result in a favourable response, despite repeated attempts to follow up the request.

In September, during an official visit to Tunisia, two AI delegates were detained at night and ill-treated by plainclothes agents of the security forces. Equipment and documents relating to human rights issues were stolen. When the delegates attended a meeting with the Human Rights Minister, scheduled prior to their arrival in Tunis, the authorities failed to acknowledge the severity of the assault or to allay AI's concerns regarding the security of human rights defenders in the country. At least one person reported having received overt death threats from security agents to dissuade him from meeting with the AI delegates.

Torture and ill-treatment

Political prisoners, including prisoners of conscience, and common law prisoners continued to be subjected to torture and ill-treatment. Although in at least one case prison guards were charged and sentenced to four years' imprisonment for inflicting torture, the 1999 law making torture a criminal offence continued to be largely disregarded. At least one person was reported to have died in custody as a result of torture in 2001.

On 9 March, 25-year-old Abderrahman Jhinnaoui died in prison. He had been arrested on 12 January on suspicion of theft, and was reportedly tortured by the police in order to make him confess. After 54 days on hunger strike to protest his innocence, Abderrahman Jhinnaoui was allegedly tortured by agents of the prison administration. He died a few days later. Although the investigation into his death had not been completed by the end of the year, the authorities denied that the death resulted from torture. The authorities also exerted strong pressure on the family to take legal action to put a stop to the campaign by Tunisian human rights defenders for an investigation into Abderrahman Jhinnaoui's death.

Political prisoners, including prisoners of conscience, were held in extremely poor conditions and several were ill-treated when they protested, usually by hunger strikes, at these conditions. A new law on prison administration adopted in May was largely disregarded.

Abdelatif Bouhajila, a 31-year-old political prisoner sentenced to 17 years' imprisonment after an unfair trial in November 2000, began a hunger strike in Borj Erroumi prison in Bizerte in May to protest about poor prison conditions. Abdelatif Bouhajila, who suffers from asthma, kidney disease and a blood-clotting disorder, was placed in an overcrowded cell, forced to sleep on the floor and denied medical care. In July, he was transferred to the 9 April Civil Prison in Tunis following ill-treatment by a member of the prison staff.

Prisoners of conscience

Known or suspected opponents of the government from across the political spectrum continued to face detention and imprisonment for exercising their right to freedom of expression.

In June, 64-year-old Mohamed Mouadda, a former leader of the opposition *Mouvement des Démocrates Socialistes* (MDS), Movement of Socialist Democrats, was put back in prison to serve his remaining sentence. Mohamed Mouadda, a prisoner of conscience, had been arrested in October 1995 and sentenced to 11 years' imprisonment after an unfair trial. He had been conditionally released in December 1996. In March 2001, Mohamed Mouadda had signed a joint manifesto with Rached Ghannouchi, exiled leader of the unauthorized Islamist movement *al-Nahda* (Renaissance), in which they rejected the possible candidacy of President Ben 'Ali for the next presidential elections in 2004.

Harassment of prisoners' families and former prisoners

Various measures continued to be used to exert pressure on relatives of political prisoners. Some were denied access to medical care or had difficulty finding employment or keeping their jobs. Their homes were kept under surveillance and their phone lines were cut.

Measures were also taken to prevent former political prisoners from resuming a normal life. Hundreds of former political prisoners were deprived of their right to enrol at a university, dismissed from their jobs and denied medical care. Some were subjected to rearrest without notification of the charges; police surveillance; administrative control which required them to obtain authorization in order to move within the country; and arbitrary decisions obliging them to register daily, or sometimes several times a day, at local police stations during working hours.

Irregularities in the administration of justice

Unfair trials and impunity remained a pattern in the country. Several civilians were tried before military courts where procedures fell short of international standards. Allegations of torture were usually not investigated or prosecuted. Complaints lodged against the security forces or the prison administration for ill-treatment were rarely investigated. In some cases, the police refused to register the complaints of victims or their relatives. Human rights lawyers were subjected to harassment and intimidation and their clients were also harassed in an attempt to curtail the lawyers' activities.

On 6 July, Judge Mokhtar Yahiaoui, President of the 10th Court at the First Instance Court in Tunis, sent an open letter to President Ben 'Ali in which he criticized a situation where magistrates were forced to comply with executive decisions on the outcome of investigations and trials. He requested the implementation and guarantee of the constitutional principle of independence of the judiciary. Mokhtar Yahiaoui was thereafter suspended from his position, summoned before a disciplinary body, but restored to a post as President of the 5th Court just before the date set for the hearing, following a national and international solidarity campaign. In July, the UN Special Rapporteur on the independence of judges and lawyers sent an urgent appeal to the Tunisian authorities seeking clarification regarding the case, to which the government responded in November. At the end of the year, Judge Yahiaoui was summoned again before a disciplinary council. The council convened on 29 December and decided to dismiss him, apparently on charges that the content of the 6 July letter constituted in itself a breach of his professional duties. This decision coincided with the creation of an association for the independence of the judiciary of which Judge Yahiaoui was expected to become president.

Communications with the authorities

The authorities denied the existence of repression against human rights defenders and considered "null and void" the concerns expressed by AI on the administration of justice. There were no responses to concerns raised by AI on individual cases.

AI country reports/ visits
Report
- Tunisia: Joint report on the continuing deterioration of the human rights situation in Tunisia (AI Index: MDE 30/031/2001)

Visit
Two AI delegates visited Tunisia in September (see above).

TURKEY

REPUBLIC OF TURKEY
Head of state: Ahmet Necdet Sezer
Head of government: Bülent Ecevit
Capital: Ankara
Population: 67.6 million
Official language: Turkish
Death penalty: abolitionist in practice
2001 treaty ratifications/signatures: Protocol No. 12 to the European Convention on Human Rights

Thousands of prisoners were held in conditions of prolonged isolation which could amount to cruel, inhuman or degrading treatment, while the debate surrounding the high security "F-type" prisons intensified. The pressure on human rights defenders increased: they faced harassment, death threats, arrests and prosecution, and branches of human rights associations were closed. Many people were imprisoned for exercising their right to freedom of expression, particularly when they expressed opinions on the Kurdish question, the "F-type" prisons or the role of Islam. Torture in police custody remained widespread and was practised systematically, while the perpetrators were rarely brought to justice. Two Kurdish politicians "disappeared" in gendarmerie custody. Dozens of political killings were reported, some of which may have been extrajudicial executions. The *de facto* moratorium on executions was upheld.

Background

In March, Turkey outlined a national program of steps to be taken to meet the conditions set out in December 2000 for starting negotiations to join the European Union. Turkey decided to give priority to a review of the 1982 Constitution, which was adopted when the country was under military rule. While some restrictions on fundamental human rights were lifted, new restrictions were introduced that fell short of Turkey's international obligations. The amendment did not include significant safeguards against torture, and the death penalty was abolished for some offences only. A number of promised legal reforms were initiated. New governmental human rights bodies were established. However, there was no major improvement in the human rights record.

The armed conflict between government forces and the Kurdistan Workers' Party (PKK) effectively came to an end in 1999, but there were still some clashes between the Turkish army and PKK groups. Repression of political parties and organizations in the mainly Kurdish southeast continued. Numerous representatives of the legal pro-Kurdish People's Democracy Party (HADEP) were arrested and put on trial. People were restricted from publicly expressing their Kurdish identity. Demonstrations, meetings and other public events were banned, increasingly so following the attacks in the USA on 11 September. Numerous media outlets were closed temporarily. The Islamic-oriented *Fazilet Partisi* (Virtue Party) was banned in June.

Torture and ill-treatment

Torture was widespread and practised systematically. There were numerous reports of torture and ill-treatment of men, women and children, mainly from western cities, the southeast and the region around Adana in the south. Many of the victims were political activists including supporters of leftist, pro-Kurdish and Islamist groups. Despite intimidation and fear of reprisals, several allegations of torture were made by people arrested on criminal charges. Other alleged victims of torture and ill-treatment included Kurdish villagers, relatives of political activists and trade unionists. Allegations were also received from people alleged to be leading figures in organized crime. Reports indicated that those suspected of theft and burglary – among them many children – continued to be systematically beaten in detention. In some cases torture appeared to be linked to discrimination on the basis of sex, sexual orientation or ethnicity.

Torture and ill-treatment occurred mainly in police and gendarmerie stations during the days immediately after arrest. The most frequently reported methods included severe beatings, blindfolding, suspension by the arms or wrists, electric shocks, sexual abuse, and food and sleep deprivation.

 Eleven villagers who were held by the gendarmerie in the western province of Uşak during the night of 23/24 January reported that they were beaten while blindfolded and handcuffed from the moment of their arrest. At the gendarmerie station they were forced to sit on a cold concrete floor, having been stripped of their lower clothing. Two of them also reported that they had been subjected to *falaka* (beating on the soles of the feet), and that their genitals had been squeezed. The villagers reported that when they were taken to the local state hospital on the morning after their arrest, still blindfolded and handcuffed, the doctors did not examine them properly and did not note their complaints. After their release the men filed formal complaints against the gendarmerie officers and the doctors. The men had been arrested following an anonymous complaint that they had stolen sheep five years earlier.

 An 11-year-old Kurdish girl, Gazal Berü, was attacked by dogs in front of the gendarmerie station in Yiğitler village, in the southeastern province of Bingöl, on 19 March and bitten to death. Her sister reported that the soldier standing next to the girls ordered the dogs to "get them". Villagers testified that the dogs belonged to the gendarmerie and that there had been repeated but unanswered complaints about them since 1994.

High security prisons

Isolation in prisons continued to be a subject of intense debate. The authorities continued to build 11 "F-type" prisons and new wings to existing prisons in which dormitories were replaced with smaller cells.

Thousands of inmates of six "F-type" prisons already in use were kept in prolonged solitary confinement or small group isolation which could amount to cruel, inhuman or degrading treatment. Although Article 16 of the Anti-Terror Law was amended in early May to allow prisoners to receive unobstructed visits and to participate in communal activities, the law did not ensure that prisoners spent adequate time in communal areas. AI received numerous reports of ill-treatment in "F-type" prisons, but they were difficult to verify because of the restricted access to these prisons. By the end of the year, 42 people had died as a result of a hunger strike against these prisons.

Rape in custody

Reports of rape and sexual assault by members of the security forces continued. During incommunicado detention in police or gendarmerie custody, women and men were routinely stripped naked. Methods of sexual abuse reportedly included rape, electric shocks and beating on the genitals and women's breasts. By the end of 2001, 147 women, 112 of them Kurds, had sought help from a legal aid project in Istanbul set up in 1997 to bring perpetrators to justice. Fifty-one of the women alleged they had been raped; the rest reported other forms of sexual torture. The suspected perpetrators were overwhelmingly police officers, although allegations were also made against gendarmes, soldiers and village guards. Only one was convicted.

☐ After a demonstration on 1 May, several women were taken to police headquarters in Izmir. Two of them gave similar reports that police officers tried to recruit them as informers. During the night each woman was reportedly taken to a separate room and blindfolded, beaten, stripped naked and sexually abused. Both were reportedly raped by police officers. The women were released the following day without having seen a prosecutor or a judge.

Prolonged police custody

There were increasing numbers of reports about police and gendarmerie detention of political activists in Diyarbakır for several weeks or months, although the maximum permitted in Turkish law was seven days (10 under the state of emergency). Alleged members of the armed Islamist organization *Hizbullah*, and from October alleged PKK supporters, were returned to custody after having been remanded in prison.

☐ Tekin Ülsen was taken to the anti-terror branch of the police headquarters in Diyarbakır on 23 June and questioned about alleged links with *Hizbullah*. While in unacknowledged detention Tekin Ülsen reported that he was tortured with electric shocks, hosed with cold water, had his wrist cut and his testicles squeezed. Despite a judge's order on 19 July that Tekin Ülsen be remanded in prison, he was returned to police headquarters and was finally moved to Diyarbakır prison on 20 July.

Impunity

Officers accused of torture were rarely suspended from duty, and in some cases received promotions. Detainees who alleged that they had been tortured were almost invariably blindfolded. Medical evidence of torture was frequently suppressed. Doctors who documented torture were often harassed. The intimidation of victims and witnesses and a generalized climate of fear also contributed to impunity, as did prosecutors' reluctance to investigate security officials. Statements reportedly extracted under torture were placed in court records and judges often refused to investigate allegations of torture.

☐ Sait Dönmüş and Mehmet Ali Kaplan were arrested in Diyarbakır on 30 June 2000 on suspicion of supporting the PKK and held at Silvan gendarmerie headquarters for six days before being brought before a prosecutor and released. They were reportedly stripped naked and blindfolded, and were then tortured with electric shocks, beaten and had their testicles squeezed. The following day they were examined at Diyarbakır State Hospital where doctors recorded that their injuries were consistent with torture. After the gendarmes complained about the medical report, the deputy health director attempted to persuade the doctors to change it. When they refused to do this, the gendarmes reportedly destroyed the original report and obtained a substitute which stated that no signs of torture had been found. Following a successful appeal against attempts to prevent prosecution proceedings, the deputy health director was convicted of abuse of his professional role in November 2001, but his sentence was suspended. In a second trial, two gendarmes accused of having tortured Mehmet Ali Kaplan and Sait Dönmüş were acquitted on 27 April 2001. According to the statements of the plaintiffs, the accused were not the officers who had tortured them. The court ruled that the prosecution should reopen the case to identify the perpetrators.

Two HADEP politicians 'disappeared'

☐ Serdar Tanış and Ebubekir Deniz, both representatives of HADEP, "disappeared" after being summoned on 25 January to the gendarmerie station in Silopi, Şırnak province. After initially claiming that the two men had not been detained, the authorities later stated that they had been released after 30 minutes. In March the authorities announced that they had confiscated a letter indicating that the two men had been abducted by the PKK and were being held in a camp in northern Iraq. There were grave doubts about the authenticity of the letter and its account of events. Before his "disappearance", Serdar Tanış had been threatened repeatedly by the local gendarmerie commander and warned to give up his party activities.

Increased pressure on human rights defenders

Human rights defenders continued to face harassment and intimidation. On 7 September the authorities raided the Diyarbakır office of the Human Rights Foundation of Turkey, one of five treatment and rehabilitation centres for torture victims around the country. Items confiscated and held for a month included all patient files, computers and details of doctors who supported the Foundation. It was suspected that the reason for the raid was the work carried out by the Foundation in preparing documentary evidence of torture.

AI's application to open a branch in Turkey was rejected by the Council of Ministers in November.

Branches of the Human Rights Association (IHD) remained forcibly closed indefinitely and others were closed temporarily. Members of staff were detained for short periods.

◻ Lawyer and human rights defender Eren Keskin, head of the IHD branch in Istanbul and a founder of the Legal Aid Project for sexually tortured women, went on trial for "insulting the Turkish army", after her description of the sexual torture suffered by members of a Kurdish women's group known as the Peace Mothers was published in the newspaper *Yeni Gündem* (New Agenda). The death threats made against Eren Keskin increased after she travelled to Silopi as part of the delegation investigating the "disappearance" of the two HADEP representatives (see above).

Prisoners of conscience

Many people, including writers, journalists, trade unionists, local and national politicians, religious leaders and human rights defenders, continued to be imprisoned or tried for exercising their right to freedom of expression, particularly on issues related to the Kurdish question, the "F-type" prisons or the role of Islam. Some of them benefited from a law on conditional releases, but others were excluded.

◻ Dr Fikret Başkaya, founder and chairman of the Turkey and Middle East Forum Foundation, began a 16-month sentence in Kalecik prison on 29 June. He had been convicted and sentenced under Article 8/1 of the Anti-Terror Act for "disseminating separatist propaganda through the press". The conviction followed the publication in June 1999 of an article he wrote in the daily newspaper *Özgür Bakış* questioning the validity of Turkey's approach on the Kurdish issue following the arrest of Abdullah Öcalan, leader of the PKK.

Death penalty

The *de facto* moratorium on executions was upheld. However, at least 24 death sentences were passed in 2001; four were later commuted to prison terms. The constitutional amendment on 3 October stated that the death penalty "cannot be imposed except in times of war, imminent threat of war and for terrorist crimes". Of the 117 prisoners whose death sentences had been upheld by the Appeal Court and who can be executed upon parliamentary approval, at least 73 were sentenced under "anti-terror" legislation.

Political killings

Dozens of killings by security officers were reported; some may have been extrajudicial executions.

◻ Burhan Koçkar, a HADEP member and municipal police officer in Doğubeyazit in the eastern province of Ağrı, was shot dead during the night of 31 October by masked special team police officers. They had mistaken his flat for that of his brother Nedim, who was among the 13 HADEP members arrested that night. Burhan Koçkar's relatives and employer rejected claims by the police that he was armed.

Some deliberate and arbitrary killings of dissidents were attributed to armed political groups such as the leftist Revolutionary People's Liberation Party-Front (DHKP-C) and the Islamist *Hizbullah*.

AI country reports/ visits
Reports
- Turkey: "F-type" prisons – isolation and allegations of torture or ill-treatment (AI Index: EUR 44/025/2001)
- Turkey: The "Amnesty Law" – an ambiguous step (AI Index: EUR 44/052/2001)
- Turkey: An end to torture and impunity is overdue! (AI Index: EUR 44/072/2001)

Visits

AI delegates visited Turkey in January, May, June and November to research human rights violations. AI trial observers visited in February and March.

TURKMENISTAN

TURKMENISTAN
Head of state and government: Saparmurad Niyazov
Capital: Ashgabat
Population: 4.8 million
Official language: Turkmen
Death penalty: abolitionist for all crimes

Conscientious objectors continued to be detained or imprisoned and some were reported to have been tortured. Reports persisted that members of unregistered religious denominations and their families were frequently harassed by the authorities and subjected to short-term detentions, confiscation of property and destruction of religious materials, and deportation.

Background

Despite having been made president for life in 1999, President Saparmurad Niyazov announced in February that he would step down in 2010 and that there would be elections to determine his successor. In May there were calls by some supporters to declare President Niyazov a prophet, based on the new national spiritual and moral code, the *Rukhnama* (Book of the Soul), which he had drafted and reportedly declared to be of the same importance as the Bible and the Koran. The *Rukhnama* was adopted by parliament on 19 October.

Torture of conscientious objector

In May Dmitry Melnichenko, an 18-year-old Baptist, was detained and tortured by officers of the National Security Committee in Serdar after conscientiously refusing to carry arms and swear an oath of military allegiance. According to the non-governmental organization *Missionswerk Friedensstimme*, Voice of Peace Mission, he was beaten on the head, knees and buttocks with a truncheon, as well as being insulted and humiliated. When Dmitry Melnichenko continued to refuse to swear the oath, officers used wires from a field telephone to administer electric shocks to his ears. A hood was placed over his head while he continued to undergo beatings to the face and neck. On 1 June Dmitry Melnichenko was reportedly told that criminal charges would be brought against him if he did not swear the oath by 10 June. However, following international pressure no charges were brought, and he was subsequently permitted to serve in a medical unit where he was not required to carry arms.

Possible prisoner of conscience

Concerns for the safety of Shagildy Atakov, a Baptist, were heightened in February following reports that he had been treated so harshly in prison that he was in imminent danger of dying. He had allegedly been beaten repeatedly by prison guards and had been inappropriately administered psychotropic drugs, apparently in order to punish him for his religious beliefs.

According to his wife who visited him in Seydi labour camp, Shagildy Atakov was suffering from jaundice, hardly able to walk, was bruised and had abdominal pains, and frequently lost consciousness. Shagildy Atakov reportedly told his wife that he was being treated with psychotropic drugs and that he had been given no explanation why he needed this treatment. In February and March he was moved to various locations, including a prison hospital, but was finally transferred some 800km across Turkmenistan to a maximum security prison in the Caspian port of Turkmenbashi. The authorities proposed to delete the remainder of Shagildy Atakov's sentence if he agreed to emigrate to the USA with his family, which he refused to do.

Persecution of religious minorities

Human rights violations by law enforcement officials against religious believers continued to be reported. Peaceful meetings in private homes were broken up and the participants fined or detained for short periods; religious materials were confiscated and places of worship closed down; religious believers were physically and verbally abused; and a number of foreign missionaries and their families were deported.

Artygul Atakova, the wife of Shagildy Atakov (see above), and their five children continued to be harassed by the authorities. According to *Missionswerk Friedensstimme*, the family, all Baptists, were threatened with reprisals, including loss of parental rights, by religious leaders and other officials in the village of Kaakhka, where they live in internal exile, if they did not convert to Islam.

AI country reports/visits
Report
- Concerns in Europe, January-June 2001: Turkmenistan (AI Index: EUR 01/003/2001)

UGANDA

REPUBLIC OF UGANDA
Head of state: Yoweri Museveni
Head of government: Apollo Nsibambi
Capital: Kampala
Population: 24 million
Official language: English
Death penalty: retentionist

Presidential and parliamentary elections were marred by violence, arbitrary arrests and unlawful detention. Armed opposition groups continued to commit gross human rights abuses, including the abduction, maiming and killing of civilians. At least 23 people were sentenced to death; no one was executed.

Background

A Constitutional Review Commission was established in February to review the Constitution and issues of concern including freedom of association and the abolition of the death penalty.

Relations between Uganda and Rwanda continued to deteriorate throughout 2001. The two governments exchanged accusations of "harbouring terrorists" on their territory. Two Ugandan army officers were arrested on charges of treason, but were subsequently released. One fled to Rwanda and began recruiting others dissatisfied with the Ugandan government.

Uganda withdrew most of its troops from the Democratic Republic of the Congo (DRC), in accordance with the 1999 Lusaka peace agreement. However, a small contingent of Ugandan troops remained in the border area and in some border towns. The government said that this was to prevent incursions by the rebels from the Allied Democratic Front, based in the DRC, into Uganda. (See Democratic Republic of the Congo entry.)

The 1999 Amnesty Act, which offers an amnesty to all rebel fighters who surrender, remained in force at the end of 2001. The Amnesty Commission, which oversees the implementation of the Act, opened an office in Gulu, a town in northern Uganda which had been the target of many attacks by the Lord's Resistance Army (LRA), an armed opposition group based in Sudan. Steps were taken to improve relations between Sudan and Uganda, as agreed after the signing of a bilateral peace agreement in 1999, and Uganda established a diplomatic presence in Sudan.

The debate on homosexuality continued throughout 2001, particularly in the media, and in May the Archbishop of the Church of Uganda banned the retired Bishop of West Buganda from preaching in any Anglican church in Uganda because of his support for the gay community in Uganda.

Elections

Presidential and parliamentary elections were held in 2001. In March President Yoweri Museveni was re-elected for a second and final five-year term with over 69.3 per cent of the votes. Parliamentary elections were held in June under President Museveni's "Movement" system, which does not allow political parties to contest elections; individual candidates are required to stand on their own merits. The elections again returned a "Movement"-dominated government headed by President Museveni.

There were criticisms in relation to both elections as regards the process of voter registration and reports of intimidation, bribery and arbitrary arrests. In January, during the presidential election campaign, police used excessive force to break up a demonstration in a suburb of Kampala. The demonstrators were protesting against the disqualification of presidential candidate Nasser Sebaggala because of a lack of appropriate educational qualifications. The police beat and used tear gas against the demonstrators. A number of individuals were arbitrarily arrested and held for a short period of time.

Shortly after President Museveni's re-election was announced, four bombs exploded in and around Kampala. One bomb exploded in central Kampala, killing at least two people. A second bomb exploded on a road south of Kampala, injuring a number of people. The third and fourth bombs exploded on 16 March, killing one person and injuring several others. No group claimed responsibility for these attacks.

Candidates in both elections submitted petitions raising concerns of vote-rigging and allegations of intimidation and malpractice; the majority were dismissed by the courts.

Torture and arbitrary detention

There were reports that several opposition candidates in both the presidential and parliamentary elections and their supporters were harassed and arbitrarily detained.

☐ Former Major Okwir Rabwoni, a Member of Parliament (MP) and a leading campaign official for the main opposition presidential candidate, retired Colonel Kizza Besigye, was arrested on 20 February at Entebbe Airport. The military reportedly used excessive force in making the arrest, and Okwir Rabwoni was subsequently detained without charge at the military intelligence headquarters in Kampala for two days before being released.

Although the parliamentary elections were conducted in an atmosphere of relative calm, there were allegations of election-related violence, harassment and intimidation by state agents, particularly in the north and west of the country. Opposition candidates were reportedly harassed by state agents in Mbarara, Rukingiri and Gulu districts.

There were also reports from Ibanda North in Mbarara district indicating that soldiers from nearby barracks beat up voters on the eve of polling day.

Harassment of the opposition

Some outspoken opposition figures were systematically harassed during the year.

☐ Winnie Byanyima, MP for Mbarara Municipality and wife of presidential candidate retired Colonel Besigye, was detained by the police and charged with sedition in April. The charges related to remarks she had made that the Ugandan authorities were training militia to fight in Rwanda. She was released on bail shortly afterwards and was awaiting trial at the end of the year. In September she was briefly detained again and charged with unlawful possession of an unlicensed weapon. She was released on bail and was awaiting trial at the end of the year.

☐ Retired Colonel Kizza Besigye was subjected to a sustained campaign of harassment by the security forces during and after the presidential election. For example, on 17 March he was prevented from travelling to South Africa by the military and on 20 March he was taken in for questioning by the Directorate of Criminal Investigations, reportedly in connection with charges of sedition and treason. On 30 June he was briefly detained by police on the Masaka road while he was travelling to Rukingiri to attend the victory party of his wife, Winnie Byanyima. In September Kizza Besigye fled to the USA after expressing fears for his safety.

Abuses by armed opposition groups
Allied Democratic Front

Abuses committed by the Allied Democratic Front, based in the DRC, continued in western Uganda throughout 2001. These included the abduction, maiming and killing of civilians.

☐ On 17 March members of the Allied Democratic Front reportedly attacked Kasese town, western Uganda, and killed at least 10 people and wounded several others.

Lord's Resistance Army

The Lord's Resistance Army (LRA) continued to commit abuses against the civilian population of northern Uganda, primarily in the districts of Gulu and Kitgum, during 2001. Despite ongoing talks between the government and junior officials of the LRA on a possible peace agreement, the LRA continued to abduct, maim and kill civilians. Children were among their victims. In accordance with the 1999 peace agreement between Uganda and Sudan, Ugandan children abducted by the LRA and held in LRA camps in Sudan continued to be returned and resettled in Uganda throughout 2001. At least 357 children escaped from the LRA or were repatriated from Sudan during 2001.

UKRAINE

UKRAINE
Head of state: Leonid Kuchma
Head of government: Anatoliy Kinakh (replaced Viktor Yushchenko in May)
Capital: Kiev
Population: 49.1 million
Official language: Ukrainian
Death penalty: abolitionist for all crimes

Ukraine was criticized by a number of intergovernmental organizations for human rights violations, including persistent allegations of torture and ill-treatment of detainees by police officers, and restrictions on press freedom. No progress was made in bringing to justice those responsible for the possible "disappearance" of journalist Georgiy Gongadze in 2000. Several journalists were attacked by unknown assailants; at least one died as a result.

Background

In June and July, after several years of debate, the Ukrainian parliament adopted a package of 10 laws on judicial and legal reforms. The new legislation, which was intended to bring Ukraine's legislation into conformity with Council of Europe standards, included a new Criminal Code and Code of Criminal Procedure as well as a series of laws which amended existing legislation relating to the judiciary, the procuracy, the police and pre-trial detention.

Torture and ill-treatment

Allegations of torture and ill-treatment of detainees by law enforcement officials persisted and appeared to be widespread. Allegations were frequently accompanied by reports that detainees were refused prompt access to legal representation and were not allowed to inform family members of their detention. Concern about alleged torture and ill-treatment was expressed by several intergovernmental organizations which, in the latter half of 2001, considered periodic reports submitted by Ukraine.

In August the UN Committee on the Elimination of Racial Discrimination expressed concern about reports of police brutality against the Roma population, including arbitrary arrest and illegal detention, and recommended that Ukraine take immediate steps to stop such abuses.

In October the UN Human Rights Committee expressed concern, during its consideration of Ukraine's fifth periodic report, about "the persistence of widespread use of torture". It urged Ukraine to ensure that all allegations of torture were effectively investigated by an independent body, that those responsible for torture be prosecuted and that victims be given adequate compensation.

In November the UN Committee against Torture echoed similar concerns during its consideration of Ukraine's fourth periodic report, recommending that Ukraine "[t]ake effective measures to prevent acts of torture and ill-treatment in its territory, in view of the persistent reports that torture is still regularly practised".

Armed forces

Reports of the torture and ill-treatment of young conscripts were received in relation to Ukraine's armed forces where soldier on soldier violence persisted in the form of hazing. In October and November respectively the UN Human Rights Committee and the UN Committee against Torture urged Ukraine to strengthen measures to end hazing, prosecute offenders and undertake training and educational activities to eradicate the culture which encouraged its practice in the armed forces.

Harsh prison conditions

Conditions in prisons and pre-trial detention centres continued to fall below international minimum standards. Prisoners were poorly fed, received inadequate medical care and were held in poorly heated and ventilated conditions in overcrowded cells, despite efforts to reduce the prison population through ongoing prison amnesties.

Possible 'disappearance'

No progress was made in determining who was responsible for the abduction and apparent killing of the independent journalist Georgiy Gongadze who failed to return to his home in the city of Kiev on 16 September 2000. A decapitated body which was believed to be that of Georgiy Gongadze was found several weeks later in a shallow grave in woodland on the outskirts of Kiev. The alleged involvement of President Leonid Kuchma and two other senior state officials in the abduction of the then 31-year-old editor of the Internet newspaper *Ukrayinskaya Pravda* resulted in a wave of protests throughout the country. Various international bodies expressed concern about the promptness and impartiality of the investigation into Georgiy Gongadze's "disappearance".

Freedom of expression

Press freedom continued to come under pressure from the Ukrainian authorities. Editors of privately owned newspapers and television companies complained of being repeatedly subjected to a number of administrative checks by the authorities in an apparent attempt to stifle their journalistic activities. The charge of criminal libel, though later decriminalized, was resorted to by state officials on a number of occasions in order to silence critical journalism. There were also reports of journalists being physically attacked by unknown assailants; at least one died as a result. The circumstances surrounding these attacks remained unclear and those responsible were rarely brought to justice.

◻ Igor Alexandrov, head of the *TOR* television station in the town of Slavyansk, died on 7 July of injuries to his head sustained during an attack by unknown assailants wielding baseball bats four days earlier as he arrived at work. Colleagues believed that his murder was related to *TOR*'s coverage of alleged government corruption and organized crime.

AI country reports/visits
Reports
- Ukraine before the United Nations Human Rights Committee (AI Index: EUR 50/001/2001)
- Concerns in Europe, January-June 2001: Ukraine (AI Index: EUR 01/003/2001)

UNITED ARAB EMIRATES

UNITED ARAB EMIRATES
Head of state: Al-Sheikh Zayed bin Sultan Al-Nahyan
Head of government: Al-Sheikh Maktum bin Rashid al-Maktum
Capital: Abu Dhabi
Population: 2.7 million
Official language: Arabic
Death penalty: retentionist

Death sentences were reportedly handed down and flogging was imposed as a judicial punishment. No executions were carried out. Reports of death in custody, forcible return, torture and ill-treatment were received.

Death sentences and cruel judicial punishments
At least two people were sentenced to death by *Shari'a* (Islamic) courts in Fujairah and Dubai. Both men had been convicted of murder.

At least 18 flogging sentences were passed during the year, all allegedly for adultery and all but two were passed on foreign nationals by *Shari'a* courts in Fujairah and Dubai.

Death in custody and 'disappearance'
Between May and August, five Libyan nationals were arrested. All five men had escaped from Libya several years earlier, fearing arrest in connection with their political or religious activities. One of the five, 'Abdullah Abu al-Qasim al-Ghazal, was arrested in 'Ajman on 31 August. His wife was summoned to al-Khalidiya Police Station in Abu Dhabi on 6 September and was informed that he had committed suicide. She refused to collect his body and asked for an autopsy to be carried out on the grounds that there were marks on his body and that the official notification papers for his death reportedly stated the cause of death as "unknown". No information was available regarding any investigation into the death of 'Abdullah Abu al-Qasim al-Ghazal or the current whereabouts and status of the other four men.

Political arrests
In the aftermath of the 11 September attacks in the USA and military intervention by the USA and its allies in Afghanistan, scores of nationals of the United Arab Emirates (UAE) were arrested throughout the Emirates between September and November. They were arrested at their places of work, homes or a local mosque. Dozens had been released by the end of the year. However, there were fears that others might be held incommunicado and could be at risk of human rights violations including torture or ill-treatment.

Forcible return
Jawid al-Ghussein, a 70-year-old Palestinian businessman, was forcibly returned to areas under the jurisdiction of the Palestinian Authority on 22 April, where he was held incommunicado in a presidential guesthouse for several weeks. (See Palestinian Authority entry.)

Intergovernmental organizations
In June, the UAE acceded to International Labour Organisation Conventions No. 111 on Discrimination (Employment and Occupation) and No. 182 on Worst Forms of Child Labour. In November, press reports stated that the Ministry of Labour and Social Affairs was studying proposed amendments to the UAE Labour Law. Although the law prohibits child labour in the UAE, children from Asia and Africa are often trafficked to the UAE to work as jockeys in camel races. They endure extremely poor conditions and are often abused.

Freedom of expression
In September 2000, an unidentified individual claiming to represent the Ministry of Information reportedly contacted newspapers, including *al-Khaleej*, and television shows in the UAE, informing them that approximately 15 presenters and writers could no longer appear in their respective media. This alleged ban appeared to remain in force at the end of 2001.

In March, three US nationals were arrested in Dubai for promoting Christianity by distributing Christian religious materials on busy streets. They were released on bail in early April, and press reports of 11 April quoted US embassy sources stating that all three had been deported.

UNITED KINGDOM

UNITED KINGDOM OF GREAT BRITAIN AND NORTHERN IRELAND
Head of state: Queen Elizabeth II
Head of government: Tony Blair
Capital: London
Population: 59.5 million
Official language: English
Death penalty: abolitionist for all crimes
2001 treaty ratifications/signatures: Rome Statute of the International Criminal Court

New security legislation, in the wake of the 11 September attacks in the USA, opened the door to human rights violations. The European Court of Human Rights ruled that the United Kingdom (UK) had violated the right to life in Northern Ireland. There was an increase in paramilitary killings and shootings in Northern Ireland. The authorities failed to bring prosecutions in a number of controversial cases of deaths in custody in England. There were inadequate safeguards to prevent the suicide of young people in prisons.

Background

Paramilitary violence, in the form of shootings, beatings and sectarian attacks, increased in Northern Ireland. A complete breakdown in the peace process was averted in August when the UK and Irish governments proposed a package of measures to the political parties in Northern Ireland. The UK government announced in October that it no longer accepted that one of the main Loyalist paramilitary organizations, the Ulster Defence Association (UDA), was observing a cease-fire.

In the wake of Britain's worst race riots and disturbances since 1985, which took place in several cities in England, AI warned that the government must actively tackle racism at all levels of society. AI had documented cases of discriminatory practices in relation to deaths in police custody, detention, ill-treatment, investigations into racist killings and attacks, and other aspects of the criminal justice system. The Director General of the Prison Service referred in January to "blatant malicious pockets of racism" within prisons. In April the Racial and Violent Crimes Unit of the Metropolitan Police said that racist attacks increased whenever politicians made inflammatory statements about asylum-seekers.

In March a review of the coroner system was announced, which will extend to the procedures for investigation and certification of deaths, including post-mortem examinations and inquests.

In October the UN Human Rights Committee examined the UK's fifth periodic report on its implementation of obligations under the International Covenant on Civil and Political Rights (ICCPR). While noting improvements, the Committee identified concerns, including the failure to carry out fully independent and comprehensive investigations into a number of murders in Northern Ireland; racially motivated violence, including within the justice system; and the detention of asylum-seekers in prisons.

Response to the 11 September attacks

In the aftermath of the 11 September attacks in the USA, racist attacks on individuals and mosques were reported.

The UK government assumed a political leadership role in the US-led coalition that on 7 October began a bombing campaign in Afghanistan. In November AI called on the USA, UK and the United Islamic Front for the Salvation of Afghanistan (United Front) to conduct an inquiry into the deaths of hundreds of *Taleban* prisoners and others at Qala-i-Jhangi fort, after an uprising by some *Taleban* captives was put down by bombing by US warplanes and United Front artillery. (See Afghanistan entry.) The UK rejected the call for an inquiry.

The Anti-terrorism, Crime and Security Act 2001 was passed in December after less than a month of parliamentary and public scrutiny. The UK derogated from Article 5(1) of the European Convention on Human Rights and Article 9 of the ICCPR in order to allow for indefinite administrative detention. Under the Act, the Secretary of State may order such detention, without charge or trial and without recourse to judicial review, of any non-UK national deemed a "suspected international terrorist and national security risk" on the basis of reasonable suspicion. The evidence would not be subject to public scrutiny or effective challenge. Among other measures, the Act also denies asylum-seekers labelled as "terrorists" the right to have the merits of their claim individually assessed. In December, eight people were detained under the new legislation.

Northern Ireland

European Court of Human Rights

The European Court of Human Rights concluded in May that the UK had violated the right to life in four cases brought by the families of 12 people, 11 killed by the security forces and one by an armed Loyalist group with the alleged collusion of the security forces. The Court found that procedures for investigating the use of lethal force by the security forces failed to meet the requirements of the European Convention on Human Rights. It criticized the lack of independence of the investigating police officers from the officers implicated; the lack of reasons given for failure to prosecute; the lack of public scrutiny; the lack of information provided to the victims' families by the authorities; and defects in the inquest procedure, including lack of verdicts and the failure to compel security force members to give evidence.

▫ In February David Wright, the father of the murdered Loyalist leader Billy Wright, obtained a ruling by the High Court that he should be given witness statements relating to his son's death. Billy Wright was shot dead in the Maze prison in December 1997 by two Irish National Liberation Army (INLA) prisoners. His father claimed collusion between prison officers and

Amnesty International Report 2002

the Republican prisoners and called for a public inquiry into the shooting.

🗀 In April the UN Special Rapporteur on the independence of judges and lawyers called again for an independent judicial inquiry into the Loyalist murders of human rights lawyers Patrick Finucane and Rosemary Nelson. Although police investigations continued in both cases, no one was successfully prosecuted.

🗀 The trial of William Stobie — a former member of the UDA and the only person charged in connection with the 1989 murder of Patrick Finucane — collapsed in November after the prosecution was abandoned. Two weeks later William Stobie was killed in a shooting claimed by the Red Hand Defenders, a Loyalist armed group. William Stobie said that, before the killing of Patrick Finucane, he had warned Special Branch, the security police, of a planned killing but no action was taken. Johnston Brown, a former police officer, alleged in May that Special Branch had failed to provide the police investigation into Patrick Finucane's death with a 1991 tape recorded confession by a Loyalist to the killing, and that a decision to pursue the investigation had been blocked at a high level.

🗀 In August the UK and Irish governments proposed, as part of a package to break the political deadlock in Northern Ireland, that an international judge investigate six killings in which the security forces had allegedly colluded. The cases were: Patrick Finucane; Rosemary Nelson; Robert Hamill; Harry Breen and Bob Buchanan, two police officers; Lord Justice Maurice and Lady Cecily Gibson; and Billy Wright.

Ill-treatment
The remaining interrogation centre, Gough Barracks, where ill-treatment had previously been reported, was closed down in September. People arrested under the Terrorism Act 2000 during the year were detained and questioned at designated police stations, in the presence of their lawyers.

In May the European Committee for the Prevention of Torture (CPT) reported on its 1999 visit to Northern Ireland. Its delegation heard allegations of ill-treatment in holding centres and prisons. It saw video evidence of a detainee at Castlereagh interrogation centre in 1999 being thrown against a wall and struck with a desk. The government informed the CPT that the complaint had been investigated and rejected.

🗀 Bernard Griffin was awarded £100,000 (US$141,700) in an out-of-court settlement. He alleged that he had been beaten by police officers in 1998.

Killings, shootings and beatings by armed groups
The number of shootings and bombings by armed groups increased markedly. There were reportedly 19 killings by armed groups during the year, of which 14 were by Loyalists and five by Republicans. There was an upsurge in sectarian attacks, including petrol bomb attacks on people's homes. A prolonged Loyalist protest at Holy Cross School in north Belfast, resulting in the violent intimidation of young schoolgirls, highlighted the growing polarization between loyalists and nationalists within parts of Northern Ireland.

🗀 The Red Hand Defenders claimed responsibility for a number of killings, including of Martin O'Hagan, a well-known Catholic journalist, in September, and 18-year-old Gavin Brett, a Protestant mistaken for a Catholic, in August.

🗀 In November the INLA reportedly killed Charles Folliard, a Protestant.

There was also an increase in the number of "punishment" shootings and beatings by armed groups of people within their own communities. According to police figures, 331 such attacks were carried out in 2001. Loyalists reportedly carried out 121 shootings and 91 assaults, and Republicans carried out 66 and 53 respectively. Many of the victims were young men; some were children under the age of 18. Hundreds of people were forced, under threat of paramilitary violence, to flee Northern Ireland.

🗀 Jim Lismore was reportedly "punished" by Republicans by being shot through both hands, feet and elbows in April.

Police shootings
Police shot dead several people in disputed circumstances during 2001, including one who reportedly was mentally ill.

Updates
🗀 In May all prosecutions collapsed against Sussex police officers involved in an armed raid which resulted in the killing of James Ashley. He was shot dead, while naked and unarmed, by police in his home in Hastings, Sussex, in 1998. An investigation by Kent police, supervised by the Police Complaints Authority, concluded that the police raid was based on deliberately false intelligence. In June the Chief Constable of Sussex resigned and in December it was announced that three police officers involved in planning the raid would face disciplinary charges.

🗀 In December the Crown Prosecution Service (CPS) decided, after a second review of the case, not to prosecute two police officers for the killing of Harry Stanley in 1999.

Past deaths in police custody
🗀 In October the CPS announced that it had reviewed new evidence in the case of Christopher Alder and that five police officers would face manslaughter charges. The new evidence suggested that Christopher Alder, who died in April 1998 in a police station, might have survived had he been given immediate medical assistance.

🗀 In May the High Court postponed until after the inquest a judicial review of the CPS decision not to prosecute any of the eight London police officers allegedly involved in the restraint of Roger Sylvester, aged 30. Detained under the Mental Health Act in January 1999, he died after being restrained. The inquest was pending at the end of the year.

Past deaths in prison
🗀 In June the CPS announced, for the third time since 1996, that it would not prosecute any prison officer in connection with the death of Alton Manning, who died in December 1995 after being restrained in prison.

◻ In October the High Court ruled that there should be a public and independent investigation into the "systemic" failures which led to the murder of Zahid Mubarek in his prison cell by a violent and racist cellmate in March 2000. A government appeal against the decision had not been heard by the end of the year.

Suicides in prison

There were inadequate safeguards to prevent prisoners from committing suicide. In April the European Court of Human Rights found that the UK had violated provisions of the European Convention on Human Rights in the case of Mark Keenan who had committed suicide in prison in 1993. It found that he had not been provided with the treatment required for a mentally ill person and that the inquest into his death did not provide a remedy for determining the liability of the authorities for any alleged mistreatment or for providing compensation.

◻ In April an inquest into the suicide of Kevin Henson, aged 17, heard that medical records had not been communicated to prison staff and that he had therefore not been regarded as "at risk".

◻ Internal inquiries were opened into the deaths in October of two youths who reportedly hanged themselves in institutions for young offenders: 19-year-old Luke Cortezo-Malone and 16-year-old Kevin Jacobs.

Ill-treatment and racism in prisons

Prisoners continued to allege ill-treatment and racist abuse within prisons, and to complain about an inadequate system to investigate their allegations.

◻ In September, three prison officers were convicted of ill-treating prisoners in Wormwood Scrubs Prison, London, during the 1990s. Three other officers had previously been convicted on similar charges. AI urged the government to carry out an independent inquiry into what appeared to be a pattern of systematic abuse in the prison.

Refugees

In September the High Court ruled that the detention of four Iraqi Kurdish asylum-seekers was unlawful because it violated their rights under the European Convention on Human Rights. The judge ruled that the detention was being used solely to facilitate quick decision-making. This ruling was overturned in October in the Court of Appeal. Leave was given to appeal further to the House of Lords.

In October the Home Secretary announced plans to overhaul radically the asylum system.

Child soldiers

By the end of 2001, the UK had not ratified the UN Optional Protocol to the UN Children's Convention on the involvement of children in armed conflict. Under-18s were deployed to Macedonia and during the military intervention in Afghanistan.

◻ In June a verdict of accidental death was returned at the inquest into the death of Wayne Richards, a 17-year-old recruit shot dead while training in March 2000.

Samar Alami and Jawad Botmeh

In November the Court of Appeal rejected an appeal against conviction and sentencing by Samar Alami and Jawad Botmeh. They had been sentenced in 1996 to 20 years' imprisonment after being convicted of conspiracy to cause explosions in 1994 at the Israeli Embassy and Balfour House in London. AI believes their convictions were unsafe and that they were denied their right to a fair trial.

Freedom of expression

◻ In April the preliminary hearing in the trial of David Shayler started. The former intelligence agent was charged under the Official Secrets Act after alleging misconduct by security and intelligence agencies. The defence argued that the Official Secrets Act was inconsistent with the Human Rights Act. The court ruled that the defence could not argue that his actions had been in the public interest, a ruling upheld by the Court of Appeal.

AI country reports/ visits

Reports
- United Kingdom: Northern Ireland – an inclusive Bill of Rights for all (AI Index: EUR 45/006/2001)
- United Kingdom: Creating a shadow criminal justice system in the name of "fighting international terrorism" (AI Index: EUR 45/019/2001)
- United Kingdom: Summary of concerns raised with the Human Rights Committee (AI Index: EUR 45/024/2001)
- United Kingdom: Strengthening proposals for the Northern Ireland Bill of Rights (AI Index: EUR 45/025/2001)

Visits
AI delegates visited Northern Ireland in April and September. Delegates observed hearings in David Shayler's case in April and July, and the appeal hearing in October in the case of Samar Alami and Jawad Botmeh.

UNITED STATES OF AMERICA

UNITED STATES OF AMERICA
Head of state and government: George Walker Bush (replaced William Jefferson Clinton in January)
Capital: Washington D.C.
Population: 285.9 million
Official language: English
Death penalty: retentionist

The death penalty continued to be used extensively. There were reports of police brutality and unjustified police shootings and of ill-treatment in prisons and jails. Human rights groups and others voiced concern at the lack of public information given about the circumstances under which more than 1,200 people, mainly foreign nationals, were detained during investigations into the 11 September attacks on the Pentagon and World Trade Center. Some detainees were held incommunicado in the initial stages of arrest. Congress passed wide-ranging "anti-terrorist" legislation, aspects of which were of concern to AI and other human rights groups. In November President Bush passed an order establishing special military commissions to try non-US citizens suspected of involvement in "international terrorism" which would bypass international fair trial norms. AI called for inquiries into several incidents involving the killing of civilians by US and allied forces during military action in Afghanistan and into the killing of hundreds of prisoners in Qala-i-Jhangi fort following an uprising.

Background

The attacks on the Pentagon and World Trade Center in the USA on 11 September, involving the hijacking of civilian aircraft and the murder of at least 3,000 people, led the government to announce a "war on terrorism", involving legislative and other measures. AI condemned the 11 September attacks and called for those responsible to be brought to justice in accordance with international human rights standards. On 7 October the USA and its allies launched military action in Afghanistan, including extensive air strikes against training camps operated by the *al-Qa'ida* network and Osama bin Laden — named by the US government as the "prime suspect" in the 11 September attacks — and other targets.

Aftermath of 11 September attacks
Legislation

In October, Congress passed the Patriot Act, whose provisions included new government powers to detain foreign nationals suspected of involvement in "terrorism" or "any other activity that endangers the national security of the United States" for up to seven days without charge. The Act authorized the Attorney General to continue to detain indefinitely on national security grounds foreign nationals charged with immigration violations, whose removal was "unlikely in the reasonably foreseeable future". Civil liberties organizations expressed concern about these and other provisions under the Act, including the broad definition of "terrorist activity" for which foreign nationals could be deported or detained.

Arrests

More than 1,200 people, mainly non-US nationals of South Asian or Middle Eastern origin, were taken into custody during investigations into the 11 September attacks. Civil rights advocates expressed concern at the unprecedented levels of official secrecy surrounding the detentions and at reports that some detainees were denied prompt access to attorneys and relatives during the initial stages of detention. There were reports of Muslim detainees suffering physical or verbal abuse from guards or other inmates while held in local jails and of cruel conditions of confinement, including prolonged solitary confinement, inadequate exercise and the wearing of shackles during non-contact visits.

In late November, the Attorney General released partial data on the arrests, revealing that 104 people had been charged with various criminal offences, many of them minor and none directly related to 11 September, of whom half remained in custody. Another 548 unidentified individuals were held on immigration charges. The authorities failed to give information on where the detainees were held or whether those facing deportation on immigration charges, who included asylum-seekers, had adequate access to legal representation.

AI's concerns relating to measures following the 11 September attacks included reports of incommunicado detention, ill-treatment in custody, government powers to detain foreign nationals indefinitely on the basis of mere suspicion of involvement in "terrorism", new powers to monitor communications between lawyers and detained clients on national security grounds, and the potential use of secret evidence.

Special military commissions

In November President Bush signed a Military Order allowing for non-US citizens suspected of involvement in "international terrorism" to be tried by special military commissions which would expressly bypass the normal rules of evidence and safeguards prevailing in the US criminal justice system. Under the Order, the commissions could operate in secret and pass death sentences, and their decisions could not be appealed to a higher court. Trials before such courts would violate the principle of non-discrimination and international fair trial standards.

Possible violations of international humanitarian law by US forces in Afghanistan

An as yet unknown number of Afghan civilians were killed or injured or had their homes or property destroyed during the US-led coalition bombing which began on 7 October and continued for the rest of the year. AI raised concerns with US authorities about specific attacks in which civilians were killed and civilian objects were destroyed, urged that investigations be conducted into possible violations of international humanitarian law and called for a moratorium on the use of cluster weapons. In November, AI called on the USA, the United Islamic Front for the Salvation of Afghanistan (United Front), and the United Kingdom to conduct an inquiry into the deaths of hundreds of *Taleban* prisoners and others at Qala-i-Jhangi fort, after an uprising by some *Taleban* captives was put down by bombing by US warplanes and United Front artillery.

Police brutality

Police brutality and disputed police shootings continued to be reported, mainly involving members of ethnic minority groups. The Justice Department investigated a number of police departments for alleged patterns of civil rights violations, including racism and excessive force. Several police officers were tried on criminal charges relating to deaths or assaults in custody.

◻ In April, in Cincinnati, three days of civil unrest were sparked by the police fatal shooting of an unarmed black man. Timothy Thomas, aged 19, was killed while fleeing from a white officer. He was the fourth black man killed by Cincinnati police in five months. The officer's subsequent acquittal by a judge of misdemeanour charges set off further unrest in September. The US Justice Department issued a preliminary report on the Cincinnati Police Department in October, which recommended sweeping changes to the department's use of force policies and improvements in the investigation of complaints.

◻ In December, a police officer from Prince George's County Police Department, Maryland, was sentenced to a 10-year prison term for violating an unresisting man's civil rights when she released her police dog on him. She was released on bail pending appeal. A police sergeant was sentenced to 15 months' imprisonment in September for his role in the incident. This was one of several cases where the county police had set dogs on suspects who were members of ethnic minorities. In July AI sponsored the first of three meetings in which alleged victims of police brutality in Prince George's County gave testimony to federal Justice Department investigators conducting an ongoing "pattern and practice" inquiry into civil rights violations in the department.

Torture and ill-treatment in prisons and jails

Abuses, including excessive force and misuse of stun weapons, chemical sprays and restraints, were reported in various adult and juvenile facilities. At least three people died after being placed in restraint chairs. More than 20,000 prisoners continued to be held in conditions of extreme isolation in supermaximum security prisons.

◻ In July, Kevin Coleman died in the Wade Correctional Center, Louisiana, after three days in a four-point restraint chair. He had a history of disturbed behaviour and had been forcibly removed by a five person "extraction team" when he refused to leave his cell. Both pepper spray and an electro-shock shield were applied to him before he was strapped into the restraint chair.

◻ In February the National Prison Project and the American Civil Liberties Union (ACLU) of Connecticut filed a lawsuit charging that Connecticut prisoners housed under contract in Wallens Ridge State Prison (WRSP), a supermaximum security facility in Virginia, were subjected to "cruel and unusual punishment" by being placed in five-point mechanical restraints for prolonged periods. The lawsuit also claimed that inmates were zapped with stun guns and had pellets fired at them for trivial offences. In July the Connecticut Department of Corrections announced that it would remove all 133 of its prisoners remaining at WRSP. In May the Virginia Department of Corrections suspended the use of the Ultron II stun gun after an autopsy suggested it played a role in the death of Lawrence Frazier, a Connecticut inmate in WRSP who died in 2000 after being zapped repeatedly with a stun gun and placed in restraints.

◻ In October a US district judge ordered the removal of all seriously mentally ill prisoners from Wisconsin's supermaximum security prison in Boscobel, ruling that the conditions of extreme isolation could exacerbate their illness. The ruling was part of a wide-ranging lawsuit challenging conditions in the prison. In September the State Governor signed a bill banning inmates who were under 18 from being housed in the prison, one of the concerns highlighted by AI during a visit to Wisconsin in June.

Juvenile detainees

◻ There were reports that Native American children in the Pine Hills School Youth Correctional Facility, aged from 14 to 17, were subjected to frequent bouts of pepper spray by staff. Documentation revealed during court proceedings in February showed that some youths at the facility, including several with histories of mental illness, had been sprayed as many as 15 times each.

◻ There were allegations that girls held at the Chalkville Campus, a juvenile facility for girls operated by the Department of Youth Services in Alabama, were tortured and ill-treated. Allegations levelled against the authorities included rape, resulting in at least two girls becoming pregnant; pressure on girls to have abortions; sexual abuse and assault of inmates; beatings; punitive solitary confinement; and lack of adequate medical care.

The USA continued to use life imprisonment without the possibility of parole against defendants who were under 18 at the time of the crime, in violation of international law.

◻ In March, Lionel Tate, a 14-year-old African American boy, was sentenced to life without parole after being convicted of the first-degree murder of his six-year-old playmate. Lionel Tate was 12 years old at the time of Tiffany Eunick's death.

Death penalty

In 2001, 63 men and 3 women were executed, bringing to 749 the total number of prisoners put to death since the US Supreme Court lifted a moratorium on executions in 1976. The USA continued to violate international standards by using the death penalty against the mentally impaired, individuals who were under 18 at the time of the crime, and those who had received inadequate legal representation.

The moratorium on executions in Illinois, announced by the state governor in January 2000, was still in force at the end of 2001. Executions continued elsewhere, however, with Oklahoma executing 18 prisoners, more than in any year since its records began in 1915. New Mexico executed for the first time since 1960. Georgia carried out its first executions since June 1998. In October the Georgia state Supreme Court had ruled that the use of the electric chair was unconstitutional, clearing the way for Georgia to begin executing by lethal injection. Politicians in several states proposed reintroducing the death penalty or expanding its scope in the aftermath of the 11 September attacks in Washington and New York.

In one of his last acts before he left office on 20 January, President Clinton commuted the death sentence of federal death-row prisoner David Ronald Chandler because of doubts over his guilt. Within the first six months of the new administration, two federal prisoners, Timothy McVeigh and Juan Raul Garza, had been executed, the first federal executions since 1963. In Juan Garza's case, the Inter-American Commission on Human Rights had called for his death sentence to be commuted on the grounds that he had received an unfair trial. Arguing for the jury to pass a death sentence, the US government had introduced evidence of unsolved crimes in Mexico for which Juan Garza had neither been charged nor prosecuted.

On 27 June, the International Court of Justice issued a landmark judgment in a case involving two German nationals, brothers Karl and Walter LaGrand, who were put to death in Arizona in 1999. The Court found that the USA had "breached its obligations to Germany and to the LaGrand brothers under the Vienna Convention on Consular Relations" by failing to promptly inform the brothers upon arrest of their right to communicate with their consulate. More than 100 foreign nationals remained on death row in the USA at the end of 2001. In the majority of cases, their consular rights had been violated. Two foreign nationals were executed during the year, one Iraqi and one South African.

Gerald Mitchell was executed in Texas in October for a murder committed when he was 17 years old. Two other juvenile offenders — Napoleon Beazley in Texas and Antonio Richardson in Missouri — came within four hours of execution before courts issued last-minute stays. Prosecutors continued to seek death sentences against defendants who were under 18 at the time of the crime. More than 80 juvenile offenders remained on death row at the end of the year.

Jay Scott, who had exhibited serious mental illness in recent years and had been diagnosed as suffering from schizophrenia, was executed in Ohio in June. It was his third execution date in two months. On the previous two occasions he had been less than an hour from execution when court stays were announced. On the second occasion, catheters had already been put in his arms in preparation for the lethal injection when the execution was called off.

Updates

In May, the Ninth Circuit Court of Appeals overturned an injunction barring the use of the stun belt in Los Angeles County, California, imposed after a lawsuit was filed in the case of Ronnie Hawkins, a prisoner who was zapped with a stun belt after verbally interrupting court proceedings. The Appeals Court ruled that activating the remote control stun belt for verbal outbursts in court was unconstitutional but said that the belt could be used as a security device.

Mazen Al-Najjar, a Muslim cleric, was rearrested in November after being issued with a final deportation order for overstaying his student visa. He was placed in solitary confinement in a maximum security prison, with restrictions on visits with his family. Mazen Al-Najjar had previously been detained for more than three and a half years on the basis of secret evidence while appealing against the deportation order, but a judge had ordered his release in December 2000 after finding there were "no bona fide reasons to conclude that [he] is a threat to national security". As a stateless Palestinian with no country to return to, Mazen Al-Najjar risked being detained indefinitely under the provisions of the Patriot Act (see above).

AI country reports/visits
Reports
- USA: Allegations of homophobic abuse by Chicago police officers (AI Index: AMR 51/022/2001)
- USA: Women asylum-seekers punished for state's failure to protect them (AI Index: AMR 51/028/2001)
- USA: The illusion of control — "consensual" executions, the impending death of Timothy McVeigh, and the brutalizing futility of capital punishment (AI Index: AMR 51/053/2001)
- USA: Old Habits Die Hard — the death penalty in Oklahoma (AI Index: AMR 51/055/2001)
- USA: Abuses continue unabated — cruel and inhuman treatment at Virginia supermaximum security prisons (AI Index: AMR 51/065/2001)
- USA: Too young to vote, old enough to be executed — Texas set to kill another child offender (AI Index: AMR 51/105/2001)
- USA: A time for action — protecting the consular rights of foreign nationals facing the death penalty (AI Index: AMR 51/106/2001)
- USA: Memorandum to the US Attorney General — Amnesty International's concerns relating to the post 11 September investigations (AI Index: AMR 51/170/2001)
- USA: No return to execution — the US death penalty as a barrier to extradition (AI Index: AMR 51/171/2001).

Visits
AI delegates visited the USA in April, June and September.

URUGUAY

EASTERN REPUBLIC OF URUGUAY
Head of state and government: Jorge Batlle
Capital: Montevideo
Population: 3.4 million
Official language: Spanish
Death penalty: abolitionist for all crimes
2001 treaty ratifications/signatures: Optional Protocol to the UN Women's Convention

The Peace Commission established the fate of 20 Uruguayans who "disappeared" in Uruguay and Argentina between 1973 and 1985. Efforts to bring to justice those responsible were thwarted by the authorities.

Investigations into 'disappearances'
In August the Peace Commission, established in August 2000 to clarify the fate of Uruguayans who "disappeared" between 1973 and 1985, reported that it had shed light on the cases of 15 Uruguayans out of 34 who had been detained and had "disappeared" in Uruguay during this period. It established that they died in custody as a result of torture but that their bodies had not been found.

The Commission also uncovered information about five out of 100 Uruguayans who were detained and "disappeared" in neighbouring Argentina, and stated that legal steps were being taken to exhume and repatriate the remains to Uruguay. There were reports that the Commission would extend its working period until it had been able to clarify more cases.

However, the 1986 Expiry Law prevented perpetrators from being brought to justice. It granted exemption from punishment to police and military personnel for human rights violations committed for political motives or in fulfilment of orders before 1 March 1985. During a visit to Uruguay in October the UN High Commissioner for Human Rights expressed her concern about this law and the need for a just and long-lasting reconciliation to close wounds unhealed for three decades.

Efforts to combat impunity
In June a judge in Argentina indicted three Uruguayan former armed forces officers — José Nino Gavazzo, Jorge Silveira and Manuel Cordero — and a police officer, Hugo Campos Hermida, for their alleged involvement in the "disappearance" of more than 20 Uruguayan nationals in Argentina. The judge requested that they be preventively detained in Uruguay pending a request by Argentina to the Uruguayan authorities for their extradition.

In July the same judge requested the preventive detention in Uruguay, pending a request for extradition from Argentina, of former army commander Julio Vadora. He was allegedly involved in a conspiracy by military governments in Argentina, Bolivia, Brazil, Chile, Paraguay and Uruguay to return exiles to the countries they had fled and where many were subsequently tortured, had "disappeared" and were murdered.

The Uruguayan authorities refused to detain any of the officers. In September, the army awarded an honorary decoration to Jorge Silveira. Also in September, relatives of 12 Uruguayans who "disappeared" in Argentina in 1976, filed a complaint against 10 members of the Uruguayan security forces, including Jorge Silveira, for the crimes of deprivation of liberty, abduction of minors and conspiracy to commit an offence.

AI country reports/visits
Report
- Uruguay: The case of Simón Riquelo — a 25-year struggle for truth and justice (AI Index: AMR 52/001/2001)

UZBEKISTAN

REPUBLIC OF UZBEKISTAN
Head of state: Islam Karimov
Head of government: Otkir Sultanov
Capital: Tashkent
Population: 25.3 million
Official language: Uzbek
Death penalty: retentionist

Reports of ill-treatment and torture by law enforcement officials of alleged supporters of banned Islamist opposition parties and movements, such as *Hizb-ut-Tahrir*, continued unabated. Thousands of devout Muslims and dozens of members or supporters of the banned secular political opposition parties and movements *Erk* and *Birlik* were serving long prison sentences, convicted after unfair trials of membership of an illegal party, distribution of illegal religious literature and anti-state activities. Reports continued to be received that devout Muslim prisoners were singled out for particularly cruel, inhuman and degrading treatment in places of detention, particularly prison camps. Several prisoners, among them a prominent human rights defender, died in custody, allegedly as a result of torture. There were at least 22 death sentences, reportedly imposed after unfair trials, and at least four executions were carried out.

Background
In July police used excessive force to break up peaceful demonstrations by female relatives of imprisoned alleged members of the banned Islamist opposition movement *Hizb-ut-Tahrir* in Andizhan and Tashkent,

the capital. The women were protesting against the torture reportedly suffered by their male relatives. Dozens of the protesters were reportedly forcibly removed to detention centres.

Following the attacks in the USA on 11 September, and the subsequent bombing campaign in Afghanistan, there was concern that Uzbekistan might further clamp down on the country's internal opposition. Uzbekistan, which borders Afghanistan, was one of the main allies of the US-led coalition in the region and at least 1,000 US ground troops were based at the Khanabad military base in the south of the country.

At the end of September, nine suspected members of *Hizb-ut-Tahrir* were charged with membership of an illegal party and attempting to overthrow the constitutional order, and sentenced to long prison terms. They were also charged with "having links to Osama bin Laden", the first time such a charge had been used in court. Human rights observers at the trial said that no convincing evidence of such links had been produced by the prosecution and they expressed fear that the case set a dangerous precedent.

In November Muhammad Salih, the exiled leader of the banned opposition *Erk* Democratic Party, was detained by Czech police at Prague airport, Czech Republic. He was remanded in custody while an extradition request from Uzbekistan was being examined. In December he was released and returned to Norway, where he had received refugee status in 1999, after Prague City Court ruled against extradition to Uzbekistan.

In September President Karimov publicly stated that around 100 people were executed each year. In October the number of offences punishable by death was reduced to four.

Allegations of torture and ill-treatment

Reports of ill-treatment and torture by law enforcement officials of alleged supporters of banned Islamist opposition parties and movements, including women, continued unabated. Thousands of devout Muslims and dozens of members or supporters of the banned secular political opposition parties and movements *Erk* and *Birlik* were serving long prison sentences, convicted after unfair trials of membership of an illegal party, distribution of illegal religious literature and anti-state activities. The courts were reported to have systematically failed to investigate or take into account the defendants' allegations of torture. Defendants accused of non-political criminal activities were also reported to have been tortured and ill-treated in detention in attempts to coerce confessions.

☐ Reports continued to be received that devout Muslim prisoners were singled out for particularly cruel, inhuman and degrading treatment in places of detention, especially in strict regime prison camps. According to relatives and former prisoners, upon arrival at a prison camp, suspected so-called "Wahhabists" (members of independent Islamic congregations or followers of independent *imams* (religious leaders)) or suspected members or supporters of *Hizb-ut-Tahrir*, were separated from other prisoners and made to run between two lines of guards who beat them with truncheons as they passed. There were also allegations that devout Muslim prisoners were subjected to beatings, humiliation, forced labour and rape by other prisoners with the complicity of prison authorities. They were forced to sing the national anthem and were severely beaten if they refused to do so. There were consistent allegations that devout Muslim prisoners were punished if they were caught praying or reading the Koran, and that their beards were forcibly shaved.

Deaths in custody

Human rights groups reported several cases of deaths in custody as a result of torture or ill-treatment by law enforcement officers, including that of Emin Usman, a well-known Uzbek writer of ethnic Uighur origin.

☐ On 7 July, three weeks after his arbitrary detention by officers of the Kashkadarya Regional Department of the Ministry of Internal Affairs, police returned to his family the body of Shovruk Ruzimuradov, a former prisoner of conscience and head of the Kashkadarya branch of the non-governmental organization Human Rights Society of Uzbekistan. They claimed that he had hanged himself in his prison cell. It was believed that he had died as a result of torture; relatives discovered that the body was extensively bruised and that some internal organs had apparently been removed. Mourners trying to attend the funeral were impeded by cordons around the village. Human rights activists arriving for the funeral from Tashkent reported that they had been ordered to return to the capital after being questioned and threatened by the police. Supporters believed that Shovruk Ruzimuradov was arrested because of his recent human rights activities, especially his monitoring of the forcible deportation of thousands of mountain villagers accused by the Uzbek authorities of collaborating with the banned opposition Islamic Movement of Uzbekistan (IMU) (see below).

Trials of forcibly displaced villagers

In June, 73 ethnic Tajik mountain villagers were found guilty of collaborating with the IMU during their incursion into Uzbekistan in August 2000 and sentenced to between three and 18 years' imprisonment in four separate closed trials. This was despite earlier government assurances to the UN Human Rights Committee that the action to evacuate the villagers was taken in order to improve the living conditions of the people concerned and that no criminal cases would be opened against these forcibly displaced villagers. The group trials, which opened simultaneously and without prior notice at the end of May in Tashkent, were held in separate court buildings cordoned off by armed police. Relatives trying to gain access to the court proceedings were reportedly intimidated and attempts were made to force them to leave the city. Only one foreign observer, representing the non-governmental organization Human Rights Watch, obtained access to one of the trials. All others, including foreign diplomats, local human rights monitors and the media, were barred.

According to the Human Rights Watch observer, the prosecution failed to provide any substantive evidence to prove the defendants' guilt. All the defendants had allegedly been held incommunicado until their trial and had not been granted the right to be represented by a lawyer of their own choice. In court the defendants reportedly withdrew their confessions and alleged that they had been tortured in order to force them to confess to fabricated charges. They alleged that they had been forced to memorize and recite prepared confessions on film. Some of the men showed the court marks on their bodies allegedly caused by torture. The court, however, failed to take any of these allegations into consideration.

In August 2000 the Uzbek military had forcibly and without prior notice rounded up and resettled thousands of mostly ethnic Tajik inhabitants from mountain villages in the southern Surkhandarynsk region on the border with Tajikistan, reportedly because armed units of the IMU had infiltrated these villages. According to witness accounts, the villagers were forced into military helicopters at gunpoint, and their homes were then set on fire and bombed, and their livestock was killed. The villagers were eventually resettled in Sherobad district, into previously abandoned houses, in allegedly very poor conditions and with no drinking water. According to some reports, arbitrary arrests of male villagers over the age of 17 started around November 2000.

Prisoner of conscience Ismail Adylov

On 3 July Ismail Adylov, a member of the unregistered Independent Human Rights Organization of Uzbekistan, was unexpectedly released from prison after being granted a special presidential pardon. Ismail Adylov had been suffering from a chronic kidney disease, aggravated by harsh prison conditions, which made him extremely susceptible to infection. After his release Ismail Adylov said that he had been regularly and systematically beaten and ill-treated throughout his detention.

Ismail Adylov had been sentenced to six years' imprisonment on charges of attempting to overthrow the constitutional order, sabotage and possessing material constituting a threat to public security and order, after an unfair trial in September 1999. All the charges related to documents which were reportedly planted by police during a search of his home. He was believed to have been detained and sentenced because of his human rights work.

Possible prisoners of conscience

Scores of possible prisoners of conscience, including women, suspected by the authorities of being supporters of or sympathizers with Islamist opposition parties, were arbitrarily detained and charged with anti-state offences.

Rahima Akhmadalieva, aged 40, was sentenced to seven years' imprisonment on 21 September for "undermining the constitutional order of Uzbekistan". There was concern at reports that the charges against her were fabricated and that she had been imprisoned solely to punish her for not disclosing the whereabouts of her husband, independent imam Ruhiddin Faruddinov.

Rahima Akhmadalieva had been detained on 17 March by officers from the Ministry of Internal Affairs (MVD), who questioned her about her husband. Her 19-year-old daughter, Odina Makhsudova, was detained three days later when she searched for her mother at the MVD. Her mother told her that she had been prevented from sleeping to force her to reveal her husband's whereabouts. Odina Makhsudova was reportedly threatened and forced to watch the guards beating a detainee with rubber truncheons. Odina Makhsudova was later released, on condition that she kept silent about what had happened and that she helped to find her father. Her mother continued to be held without charge in a basement cell at the MVD for a further two months. During this time she was reportedly denied regular medication, which she needed for the treatment of a heart condition.

Death penalty
Sentences

Nigmatullo Fayzullayev and Maksim Strakhov were sentenced to death by Tashkent City Court on 18 April for premeditated aggravated murder. The Appeals Board of Tashkent City Court upheld their death sentences on 29 May.

Maksim Strakhov's mother reported that when her son was arrested in October 2000 he was severely beaten by law enforcement officers for more than three days. He had reportedly previously received psychiatric treatment for post-traumatic stress symptoms after military service in Chechnya. The Supreme Court reportedly decided on 21 June to put the execution of Maksim Strakhov on hold for three months while psychiatric tests were carried out to assess his mental health. At the end of October, Maksim Strakhov's lawyer was informed that the Appeals Committee of the Supreme Court had concluded that the execution could go ahead. Maksim Strakhov's mother reportedly appealed to the Supreme Court, calling for further medical tests as she believed that the first tests were not conducted properly. According to her son they had consisted only of an X-ray of his skull and a five-minute conversation with a doctor. The UN Human Rights Committee reportedly sent an urgent communication to the Uzbek authorities, requesting a stay of execution of Maksim Strakhov. Nigmatullo Fayzullayev was still believed to be in imminent danger of execution.

Executions

Gabdulrafik Akhmadullin was executed on 6 June in Tashkent Prison despite international appeals to commute his death sentence. On 29 May his wife had reportedly been told by a presidential adviser that her husband's appeal for clemency would be considered within two or three months.

AI country reports/visits
Reports

- Uzbekistan: The rhetoric of human rights protection – briefing for the UN Human Rights Committee (AI Index: EUR 62/006/2001)
- Central Asia: No excuses for escalating human rights violations (AI Index: EUR 04/002/2001)

VENEZUELA

BOLIVARIAN REPUBLIC OF VENEZUELA
Head of state and government: Hugo Chávez Frías
Capital: Caracas
Population: 24.6 million
Official language: Spanish
Death penalty: abolitionist for all crimes

At least 240 people were killed by police in circumstances suggesting they were victims of extrajudicial execution or excessive use of force. Allegations of torture and ill-treatment continued. Five people were reported to have "disappeared". Conditions in many prisons remained inhumane, and violence among inmates continued to claim many lives. There were threats to freedom of expression.

Background
Official and public concern about rising levels of violent crime continued to generate widespread debate, including calls within government circles for the imposition of a state of emergency. Human rights organizations identified the primary causes as the government's failure to address human rights violations, tackle widespread impunity and corruption, and deal with the country's deep-seated social and economic problems. There were serious institutional weaknesses in structures charged with safeguarding human rights, such as the judicial system, in which numerous dismissed judges had not been replaced. In August, the National Assembly approved a law on refugees and asylum-seekers. In December a one-day national strike was called in response to a series of controversial economic measures passed by presidential decree in the previous month.

Killings by police
Deaths in circumstances suggesting extrajudicial execution or the excessive use of force increased steeply in a number of states. In September, the Office of the Attorney General sent the National Guard to take over police stations in the state of Portuguesa following persistent allegations that a so-called "extermination group" was operating inside the state police force. Between September 2000 and May 2001, investigations had been opened into the deaths of 100 people reported to have been killed by the police. By the end of the year, a number of police officers were under investigation. In October, the Attorney General announced the appointment of a national attorney to look at complaints of killings by members of the security forces in eight states. Also in October, the Ombudsman produced a preliminary report into 239 complaints of killings by police in several states. According to the Ombudsman, operations by the security forces generally appeared to follow a similar pattern, including the simulation of armed confrontations, illegal raids and death threats to witnesses and relatives. Human rights defenders who publicly denounced killings by the police in the states of Portuguesa and Bolívar were threatened.

⌾ In February, 17-year-old Argenis Antonio González died after officers of the Metropolitan Police arrived at his workplace and opened fire indiscriminately. The police reportedly planted a weapon next to his body.

Torture and ill-treatment
There were continuing reports of torture and ill-treatment by members of the security forces. There was concern that police officers continued to abuse their power with impunity as the vast majority of cases failed to make any progress in the courts.

⌾ Silvano Castro, and one other, both members of the Pemón indigenous group who were campaigning against the construction of an electricity supply network in the Gran Sabana region, were beaten by soldiers in March during a protest held by the group. The incident was part of a pattern of harassment and intimidation against the Pemón.

'Disappearances'
Five new cases of "disappearance" were reported. Orlando José Castillo "disappeared" after he was detained by police officers on 20 January in the state of Yaracuy. In October it was announced that 10 police officers were under investigation in connection with the case.

Impunity
In October, plaintiffs for four people who "disappeared" after being detained in Vargas state in December 1999 rejected a proposal by the Inter-American Commission on Human Rights to facilitate a friendly settlement between the interested parties and asked for the normal process to continue. They expressed concern that the government was not acting with due speed, and stated that the state's continuing failure to address the problem of impunity had significantly contributed to the deteriorating human rights situation.

Prison conditions
Conditions in prisons continued to be extremely harsh. Although numbers were lower than in previous years, scores of prisoners were killed, mostly as a result of violence by fellow inmates. In June, inmates of El Rodeo Prison and their relatives staged a protest that included a demand for an investigation into ill-treatment by prison guards. The government acknowledged once again the crisis in the prison system and in August announced it was launching an emergency repair program to modernize the country's prisons.

Refugees
Colombians fleeing political violence continued to face difficulties in Venezuela despite the introduction in August of new legislation establishing the right to seek asylum and protecting the rights of refugees. In August, the UN High Commissioner for Refugees opened an office in San Cristóbal near the border with Colombia. Its representatives expressed concern in November about the number of people awaiting a decision on their application for refugee status.

VIET NAM

SOCIALIST REPUBLIC OF VIET NAM
Head of state: Tran Duc Luong
Head of government: Phan Van Khai
Capital: Ha Noi
Population: 79.2 million
Official language: Vietnamese
Death penalty: retentionist
2001 treaty ratifications/signatures: Optional Protocol to the UN Children's Convention on the involvement of children in armed conflict

The year saw renewed repression in Viet Nam, with dozens of people sentenced to long prison terms, some of whom were prisoners of conscience, and a crackdown on ethnic minority groups, and religious and political dissidents. The government continued to prevent independent human rights monitors from visiting the country, and denounced any criticism from outside as unacceptable interference. At least 55 people were sentenced to death and at least 10 executed, but the actual numbers were believed to be much higher.

Background

In February, unrest erupted in the Central Highlands provinces of Dac Lac and Gia Lai. Members of ethnic minority groups protested about the seizure of their land by Vietnamese settlers and about their lack of freedoms, including the rights to freedom of worship and to be educated in their own languages. The protests were quickly crushed and hundreds of refugees from the area fled across the border to Cambodia. At the ruling Communist Party's five-yearly congress in April, the General Secretary Le Kha Phieu left office and Nong Duc Manh was appointed to the post. The prevailing climate of political infighting and public dissent led to further restrictions on basic freedoms, and outspoken criticism of anyone who attempted to report on them. Diplomatic relations with the USA were soured, in spite of the granting of trade privileges to Viet Nam, because of a bill in the US Congress which called for aid and trade to be tied to progress on human rights protection.

Unrest in the Central Highlands

In February, thousands of people from the indigenous minorities protested in the Central Highlands provinces of Dac Lac and Gia Lai. Their grievances included anger at government confiscation of their ancestral forest homelands, an influx of lowland Vietnamese settlers taking their agricultural land, lack of freedom of worship for the many who are members of unauthorized evangelical Protestant churches, and denial of basic rights including education in native languages. Some protesters called for independence for the Central Highlands region. The authorities quickly closed off the area and prevented journalists and diplomats from travelling to the provinces to assess the situation. The Vietnamese authorities accused US-based opposition groups of fomenting the unrest. There were reports of dozens of arrests and, in the following weeks, several hundred people crossed the border to Cambodia as refugees (see Cambodia entry). The Vietnamese authorities asked the Cambodian authorities to return the refugees and more than 100 people were consequently forced back across the border to Viet Nam. At least one man was detained and beaten by Vietnamese police; unconfirmed reports allege others were tortured. An agreement between the Cambodian and Vietnamese governments and the UN High Commissioner for Refugees (UNHCR) to arrange the voluntary repatriation of the refugees foundered in July when the Vietnamese authorities refused to grant UNHCR access to the area to facilitate safe return.

In August, the UN Committee on the Elimination of Racial Discrimination considered Viet Nam's sixth to ninth periodic reports, and requested further information on how ethnic minorities in the country are able to exercise freedom of religion and other fundamental rights. It recommended the adoption of more specific anti-discrimination legislation.

◻ In September and October, 20 people were brought to trial in three separate cases relating to the February unrest. No foreign journalists or international observers were able to attend the trials, which lasted only two days. Trials in Viet Nam are routinely unfair, with defendants denied the right to call and question witnesses and defence lawyers permitted only to plead for clemency on their clients' behalf. The 20 people were charged with organizing illegal activities and inciting locals to cause social disorder and instability, and given sentences ranging from a term of three years (suspended) to 12 years' imprisonment. All those sentenced were possible prisoners of conscience. Following the trials, dozens more refugees fled to Cambodia.

Continued suppression of religious freedom

Religious dissidents from faiths including the Hoa Hao church, the Unified Buddhist Church of Viet Nam (UBCV), and the Roman Catholic and Protestant churches were subjected to harassment and detention for their peaceful religious activities.

◻ In May, Father Thadeus Nguyen Van Ly, a Catholic priest in the Hue diocese, was arrested at his church as he prepared to celebrate mass. A lifelong critic of government policy towards religion, Father Ly had previously been detained without trial for a year in 1977-78, and imprisoned for 10 years between 1983 and 1992. In October, the official media announced that Father Ly had been sentenced to 15 years' imprisonment for "undermining the unity policy" and "defying an administration order of confinement". He was a prisoner of conscience.

Harassment of government critics

The authorities continued to harass individuals who expressed unauthorized political views. Measures against dissidents included placing two prominent critics, Ha Si Phu and Mai Thai Linh, under house arrest in February. Similar action was taken against senior UBCV monk Thich Quang Do in June. The official media also carried critical commentaries against individuals with dissenting views. In August, a new regulation on residence prohibition and house arrest was issued, containing strict measures for the further punishment on release from prison of those convicted of certain crimes, including "violating national security". New regulations limiting the use of the Internet were also published.

Trials

In May, 37 people were sentenced to prison terms of up to 20 years for "terrorism against the state". All the accused were found guilty of plotting "terrorist acts", but it was not clear from the reported evidence that all of those on trial had used or advocated violence. Some were convicted of smuggling leaflets containing anti-communist writings, and possessing flags of the former South Viet Nam. Restrictions on access for human rights monitors made it impossible to monitor this and other trials.

Death penalty

As in previous years, the government did not make public full statistics on the death penalty. Fifty-five death sentences and 10 executions were recorded throughout the year, but the real figures were believed to be much higher. Executions were carried out by firing squad, sometimes in front of large crowds.

Denial of access

AI received no direct response from the government about the human rights situation, but a government spokesperson publicly criticized the organization on several occasions for alleged "interference in internal affairs". Domestic human rights monitoring was not permitted and access continued to be denied to independent international human rights monitors.

AI country reports/ visits
Reports
- Socialist Republic of Viet Nam: Religious intolerance – Recent arrests of Buddhists (AI Index: ASA 41/001/2001)
- Socialist Republic of Viet Nam: Father Thadeus Nguyen Van Ly – Prisoner of conscience (AI Index: ASA 41/005/2001)

YEMEN

REPUBLIC OF YEMEN
Head of state: 'Ali 'Abdullah Saleh
Head of government: 'Abdul Qader Bajammal (replaced 'Abd al-Karim 'Ali al-Iryani in March)
Capital: Sana'a
Population: 19.1 million
Official language: Arabic
Death penalty: retentionist

Arrests of political suspects and harassment of critics of the government took place in various parts of the country. At least two political trials were held. Torture and a death in custody were reported. At least 56 people were executed and scores, possibly hundreds, were under sentence of death at the end of 2001.

Background

While human rights gained unprecedented visibility in terms of both formal bureaucratic structures and grassroots activism, human rights violations were on the increase as compared with previous years.

In March a new government was sworn in and Wahiba Fare' was appointed as Minister of State for Human Rights. In August she held talks with the UN High Commissioner for Human Rights and agreed on technical cooperation and support in the field of human rights, particularly in relation to recommendations issued in 1999 by the UN Committee on the Rights of the Child. In August, the Office of the UN High Commissioner for Human Rights announced that it had appointed a human rights officer based in Sana'a, and that its program of cooperation included "assistance in the elaboration of regulatory procedures for dealing with children in conflict with the law, various seminars and training sessions, provision of training manuals on international human rights standards to law enforcement officials, and promoting the inclusion of children's rights in university curricula". The Minister was also reported to have agreed to cooperate with the association of journalists on initiatives aimed at spreading and consolidating a culture of respect for human rights.

Various seminars and workshops on human rights were organized by different organizations. These activities received wide media coverage highlighting issues such as discrimination and violence against women and prison conditions faced by women.

Political participation was expanded by the addition of a second chamber of parliament, the *Majlis al-Shura* (Consultative Council), and the introduction of elected local government assemblies. The Consultative Council, consisting of 111 members, was appointed by the President in May. The members included heads of political parties and tribal leaders chosen by the President. The term of office of the President was extended from five to seven years and that of parliament from four to five years.

However, in contrast to these positive developments, there were continuing clashes between government forces and tribal groups and violent inter-tribal conflicts in different parts of the country throughout the year. According to reports, scores of people were killed and more than 100 injured, including members of the security forces. The local elections in February were marked by a number of armed clashes caused by disputes between parties and candidates over registration and voting regulations. The elections were won by the General People's Congress, the main ruling party.

The attacks in the USA on 11 September increased political tension in Yemen which was placed under a *de facto* state of emergency with the Prime Minister reportedly declaring: "We have decided that investigations must be carried out into anyone who had any connection... [with] Afghanistan".

Arrests

Widespread arrests of political suspects were carried out in different parts of the country throughout the year, particularly in the aftermath of the 11 September attacks. Those arrested before 11 September included people detained after clashes between security forces and tribes, and following bombing incidents as well as people suspected of having links with armed Islamist organizations such as *al-Jihad* and the Aden-Abyan Army. They also included people detained after peaceful protests. Many were released after short periods of detention without trial. The exact number of those who remained held at the end of the year was not known although some of them were brought to trial during the year (see below).

Following the 11 September attacks in the USA, the government carried out widespread waves of arrests, reportedly after information was submitted by the US government on suspected supporters of Osama bin Laden. Those targeted for investigation and arrest included members of Islamist organizations and anyone who had aroused the suspicion of the authorities.

◻ Two people, 'Abdelsalam Nur al-Din, Director of the Institute of the Centre for Red Sea Studies (CRSS) at Exeter University in the United Kingdom, and his colleague, Ahmad Saif, were arrested without a judicial warrant at the end of October by members of the Political Security police in Sana'a. They were detained at the headquarters of the Political Security and interrogated on suspicion of being spies and of having connections with Osama bin Laden. They were held incommunicado for three days, during which time they were allegedly held in solitary confinement and beaten. They were released without charge only following the intervention of some government officials. Both were in Yemen on an official fact-finding visit to establish joint cooperation projects between the CRSS and Yemen University as well as other official institutions. Prior to their arrest they had meetings with different government officials, including ministers.

The exact number of people arrested in the wake of 11 September who remained in detention was not known; the government acknowledged 21 arrests while press reports indicated up to 500 were detained at the end of the year.

Harassment of journalists

In an address to members of the journalists' association in September, the Minister of State for Human Rights was reported to have said that "press freedom and human rights are two faces of one coin". However, this did not put an end to a pattern of harassment of journalists critical of the government or its policies who continued to face legal proceedings and arrest.

In November the editors of eight different newspapers and magazines were reportedly asked to appear before the West Sana'a Court to answer lawsuits brought against them. One involved a case brought by the Ministry of Information against the *al-Shura* newspaper for publishing excerpts from a novel which was "inconsistent with the Islamic religion". The outcome of the court hearing was not known at the end of the year.

◻ Hassan al-Zaidi, a journalist with the weekly newspaper the *Yemen Times*, was arrested twice, in June and September, and detained for up to three weeks each time by the Political Security in an undisclosed location. He was reportedly arrested for having interviewed a kidnapped German tourist being held hostage while security forces were trying to locate the kidnappers.

Political prisoners and unfair trials

At least two political trials involving people charged in connection with bombing incidents in 2000 were started during the year.

◻ Four people were tried in connection with the bombing of the British embassy in Sana'a on 13 October 2000 which damaged the building. In February, the defendants appeared before a criminal court which ruled that it was not competent to try the case and referred it to a special court. In June the case opened again before a special court which found the defendants guilty and sentenced them to prison terms ranging between four and 15 years, in addition to payment of the cost of damage caused to the embassy. An appeal by the defendants was pending at the end of the year.

◻ The trial opened in April of at least five alleged members of the Aden-Abyan Army suspected of carrying out the bombings that targeted a church, a hotel and the office of the *Saba* news agency in Aden on 13 October 2000. The exact number of defendants in the case was not known, but they were thought to include the four men tried in connection with the bombing of the British embassy. The defendants faced charges including the illegal possession of bombs, carrying out a bombing attack, disrupting public security and sabotage. However, lawyers for three of the defendants reportedly rejected the charges against their clients.

Torture and ill-treatment

Torture and ill-treatment were reported. There were allegations that people were beaten during interrogation, deprived of sleep or food, prevented from using the toilet, and kept shackled for long periods.

☐ Muhammad 'Abdulah Salem al-Yafi'i, who was serving a six-year sentence, died in prison in December 2000, allegedly as a result of torture. His relatives reportedly visited him a week before his death and stated that he was in good health at that time. No investigation was known to have been carried out into his death during 2001.

Flogging continued to be imposed as a judicial punishment throughout the country.

Death penalty

At least 56 people were executed in 2001. All were convicted on charges which included murder. Many were sentenced after trial proceedings which did not meet international safeguards for defendants facing capital charges. Although the exact number was not known, reports suggested that scores, possibly hundreds, of people were under sentence of death at the end of 2001.

☐ Hussein bin Hussein al-Ma'mari, who had been diagnosed as suffering from schizophrenia, was executed in August. During his trial in 1998, his lawyer produced strong medical evidence suggesting that he was mentally ill, but the court still convicted him of murder and sentenced him to death.

YUGOSLAVIA
(FEDERAL REPUBLIC OF)

FEDERAL REPUBLIC OF YUGOSLAVIA
Head of state: Vojislav Koštunica
Head of government: Dragica Pesić (replaced Zoran Žižić in July)
Capital: Belgrade
Population: 10.5 million
Official language: Serbian
Death penalty: abolitionist in practice
2001 treaty ratifications/signatures: First and Second Optional Protocols to the International Covenant on Civil and Political Rights; Optional Protocol to the UN Children's Convention on the involvement of children in armed conflict; Rome Statute of the International Criminal Court

Both Federal and Serbian governments took steps to address some outstanding human rights concerns, although limited progress was made towards reform of the military, police and judiciary. Apart from the transfer of former President Slobodan Milošević to the custody of the International Criminal Tribunal for the former Yugoslavia (Tribunal), the authorities largely failed to address impunity for alleged war crimes in Bosnia-Herzegovina, Croatia and Kosovo. An amnesty law provided immunity to conscientious objectors and deserters from the VJ (Yugoslav Army) and provided for the release of around 200 ethnic Albanians imprisoned in Serbia. Impunity for perpetrators of "disappearances" and abductions in Kosovo continued. An estimated 230,000 Serbs and Roma, internally displaced from Kosovo, remained in the Federal Republic of Yugoslavia (FRY), along with 390,000 refugees from Bosnia-Herzegovina and Croatia. In Kosovo ethnically motivated attacks on minorities continued and politically motivated attacks on moderate politicians occurred, particularly before the November elections, while tensions between Serb and Albanian communities resulted in abuses of human rights. The UN Mission in Kosovo (UNMIK) and the NATO-led peace-keeping Kosovo Force (KFOR) failed to fully protect and promote human rights, particularly those of detainees.

Background

Following the election of FRY President Vojislav Koštunica in October 2000 and a new Serbian government headed by Zoran Djindjić in January 2001, political instability, accusations of corruption and the potential fragmentation of the Federation discouraged external investment and hindered the resolution of outstanding human rights violations.

In Montenegro, President Dukanović announced in October that a referendum on independence would take place early in 2002. Increased demands for autonomy in Vojvodina province led to the drafting of a new constitution in November.

In southern Serbia, clashes between Serb security forces and the armed ethnic Albanian group, the Liberation Army of Preševo, Medvedje and Bujanovac (UÇPMB), continued until an agreement in May between FRY and Serb authorities, NATO and ethnic Albanian representatives. Under the agreement, the VJ and Serbian police returned to areas bordering Kosovo and the UÇPMB disbanded and disarmed under an amnesty brokered by KFOR. However, a political settlement was only partially implemented, and allegations of ill-treatment of ethnic Albanians by Serbian police continued.

In Kosovo, UNMIK promulgated in May a Constitutional Framework for Provisional Self Government which provided for an assembly with guaranteed representation for ethnic minorities and authority over domestic affairs. Powers were reserved for the Special Representative of the UN Secretary-General in Kosovo (SRSG) over major policy areas, including budgetary policy, law enforcement, the judiciary, external relations, and internal and border security, in conjunction with KFOR. November elections for the assembly were won by the Democratic League of Kosovo (LDK). Approximately 43 per cent of Serbs eligible to vote did so, encouraged by the signing on 5 November of the UNMIK-FRY Common Document, which sought to address their security and human rights concerns.

Serbia and Montenegro
Rule of law and administration of justice
Some progress was made to reform Federal and Serbian police forces but comprehensive measures, including human rights training, were not implemented. New appointment procedures for judges and prosecutors were approved in November. A report on prisons by the Organization for Security and Co-operation in Europe recommended complaints procedures, inspection mechanisms and human rights training of prison staff.

In Montenegro, the Podgorica High Court passed two death sentences for murder in October. In November, Serbia abolished the death penalty and the government in Montenegro announced their intention to abolish it.

In May the UN Committee against Torture concluded that the FRY had violated its obligations under the UN Convention against Torture in failing to promptly or fully investigate the death of Milan Ristić who allegedly died as a result of police ill-treatment in February 1995.

The courts awarded compensation in five of the 66 actions brought against the Serbian police alleging harassment, unlawful detention and ill-treatment of members of the opposition group *Otpor* (Resistance) between January and September 2000.

War crimes
Following extensive international pressure, on 23 June the Federal Government adopted by decree a bill on cooperation with the Tribunal. Following an appeal by lawyers acting for the former President Slobodan Milošević, the Constitutional Court froze the decree on 28 June, finally ruling it unlawful in November. The former President, who had been in custody on domestic charges of corruption since April, was transferred by the Serbian authorities to the Tribunal's custody on 28 June. In his first appearance before the Chamber in July, he refused to accept the jurisdiction of the Tribunal.

◻ Three other indicted suspects voluntarily surrendered to the Tribunal, while another five were arrested and transferred to the custody of the Tribunal. Police officers protested that they had been tricked into arresting two suspects in November in the absence of a law on cooperation with the Tribunal.

◻ On 19 December the European Court of Human Rights ruled inadmissible a complaint brought in October 1999 against 17 NATO member states by a survivor and five relatives of people killed in the bombing of Serbian television station RTS during NATO's military operation in 1999.

Identity-based violations
Racist attacks on Roma, Jewish, Albanian and other communities reportedly continued. Perpetrators were rarely brought to justice.

◻ In April two people were convicted at Niš District Court of incitement to racial, religious or national hatred following an attack on a 15-year-old Roma boy in April 2000.

◻ Police allegedly failed to provide adequate protection or to bring to justice those responsible for organizing violence in July when 40 civilians and eight police officers were injured after hundreds of supporters of nationalist organizations assaulted lesbians, gay men, journalists and bystanders and prevented the first Gay Pride celebration in the FRY.

Conscientious objectors and the Amnesty Law
In February, an Amnesty Law came into force providing immunity from prosecution to conscientious objectors and deserters who had refused to participate in wars between 1992 and 2000.

◻ In January, Srdjan "Sičko" Knežević, coordinator of the Network for Conscientious Objection, was arrested by military police at Belgrade airport and brought before Niš Military Court in connection with his alleged desertion from the VJ in 1999. He was subsequently released without charge. Despite the Amnesty Law, he was arrested four times between March and September while leaving the FRY to attend conferences abroad on conscientious objection.

A petition to the government in June by 30,000 voters seeking the provision of a genuine alternative civilian service was not debated in parliament as required by law. In December the Federal parliament passed a law reducing compulsory military service to nine months and alternative service in non-combatant sections of the military to 13 months.

Freedom of information and expression
Repressive provisions of the 1998 Information Law were ruled unconstitutional by the Federal Constitutional Court in January and repealed by the Serbian parliament in February. However, new regulations had not been adopted by the end of the year, and fines paid by, and equipment confiscated from, independent media under the previous government were not returned. Journalists critical of the government were reportedly called in for interview by the police.

YUG

Refugees and internally displaced persons
After a re-registration process, completed by June, approximately 390,000 refugees from the wars in Bosnia-Herzegovina and Croatia remained in the FRY. Following amendment of the citizenship law in February, refugees were not required to renounce their nationality to gain FRY citizenship. The Joint Committee on Returns to Kosovo identified areas to which some of the 230,000 displaced Serbs and Roma could return, although few returns took place.

An estimated 15,000 ethnic Albanians fled the fighting in southern Serbia to Kosovo; 5,500 had returned by the end of 2001. At least 65,000 ethnic Albanian refugees fled the conflict in Macedonia to Kosovo; another 11,000 fled to southern Serbia and elsewhere in the FRY.

Abductions and 'disappearances'
Little progress was made by either UNMIK or the FRY authorities respectively in investigating the alleged abductions of some 1,300 Serbs and Roma by the Kosovo Liberation Army (KLA) since 1999, or the "disappearance" of around 3,000 ethnic Albanians feared arrested by Serbian security forces in 1999. The UNMIK Police Missing Persons' Unit reported that they had closed some 591 files.

In Serbia, in June the Belgrade District Court ordered the exhumation of unmarked graves discovered at a police training base at Batajnica near Belgrade. By November, over 400 of the estimated 1,000 bodies buried there and in mass graves in Petrovo Selo and Bajina Basta had been exhumed under the observation of international and domestic monitors. The bodies were believed to be those of ethnic Albanians transported from Kosovo and re-buried in Serbia during the 1999 NATO Operation Allied Force. Investigations have been opened, but as yet no charges have been brought.

Ethnic Albanian prisoners
By June some 200 ethnic Albanians held in Serbian prisons since July 1999 had been released under the Amnesty Law. The Law did not cover those convicted of "terrorism", many of whom were reported to have been convicted after unfair trials.

☐ In April the Supreme Court ordered the release of the Djakovica (Gjakove) group of 143 men sentenced in May 2000 to between seven and 12 years' imprisonment for "terrorism", on the grounds that their trial had been marred by "serious violations of criminal procedure".

☐ In April the Niš District Court convicted Luan and Bekim Mazreku of "terrorism", reportedly on the basis of forced confessions, after a trial which failed to meet international standards of fairness.

In November, under the UNMIK-FRY Common Document, it was agreed that the remaining prisoners would be transferred to Kosovo after a review of their cases in Serbia. Some 201 ethnic Albanians remained in custody at the end of 2001.

Kosovo (Kosova)
UNMIK continued to administer Kosovo under UN Security Council Resolution 1244/99.

Rule of law and administration of justice
The police and judiciary failed to investigate and prosecute those responsible for human rights violations and to ensure international standards for fair trial.

UNMIK and KFOR failed to fully protect and promote human rights, particularly the rights of detainees, and AI and other organizations raised concerns about accountability, property rights and executive detention orders. There was inadequate training of the international civilian police force (CIVPOL) and a lack of resources for forensic investigation. UNMIK failed to guarantee detainees the assistance of legal counsel, including during interrogation. The failure to establish a comprehensive witness and victim protection program compromised CIVPOL's ability to conduct thorough investigations and prosecute those suspected of trafficking in women.

Detentions
In August UNMIK established a Detention Review Commission (DRC) to review administrative detentions authorized by the SRSG in violation of international standards. However, the DRC failed to provide detainees with the means to challenge their detention.

☐ After a remote-controlled bomb killed 10 Serb civilians and injured 40 others on a bus in a KFOR-escorted convoy of buses near Podujevo (Podujeve) on 16 February, four suspects were detained. This followed an earlier attack on 13 February on another convoy (see below). Despite an order by Pristina District Court for the release of three of them — Avdi Belhuli, Qele Gashi and Jusuf Veliu — the SRSG ordered their continued detention under successive Executive Orders from March until September, when their detentions were reviewed by the DRC. Following an *in camera* hearing the DRC authorized their continued detention until December. Their lawyer was excluded from the hearing and not provided with the evidence justifying their further detention. They were released in December by order of the Supreme Court.

Detentions without judicial authority were also authorized by the KFOR Commander. Detainees were not always informed of the reasons for their detention or their right to counsel, and were denied access to the courts to challenge the lawfulness of their detention.

Up to 1,500 men were believed to have been detained on suspicion of membership of an armed opposition group, unlawful border crossing or weapons possession following the UÇPMB amnesty in May and during the conflict in Macedonia between June and September. The majority of detainees were released within 24 hours, although others were detained for over 30 days. Most were believed to have been released without charge.

☐ In October, 10 men were convicted of unlawful possession of firearms at Gnjilane District Court — the only detainees known to have been brought to trial.

War crimes trials
Some court proceedings conducted against Serbs suspected of war crimes, including those presided over by international judges, failed to meet international standards.

◻ In October, the Supreme Court overturned the conviction of Miroslav Vucković, member of a Serb paramilitary group, sentenced in January to 14 years' imprisonment for genocide by a panel of one international and four Albanian judges. The Supreme Court ruled that there was insufficient evidence to support such a conviction for genocide, and returned the case to the Mitrovica (Mitrovice) District Court for retrial on arson and aggravated theft charges.

The UNMIK-FRY Common Document included a commitment to review proceedings conducted by members of the ethnic Albanian judiciary in which Serbs had been convicted for serious crimes.

Minorities
Violent crimes against Serbs, Roma, Muslims and other minorities remained disproportionately high, and few perpetrators were brought to justice.

◻ On 13 February a KFOR-escorted convoy of buses between Strpce (Shterpce) and Serbia came under sniper-fire; a driver was killed and several passengers injured.

◻ Inter-ethnic human rights abuses in the divided town of Mitrovica resulted in violent disturbances in which members of the international community and KFOR troops were among those targeted. KFOR responded on some occasions with excessive use of force.

A lack of security and freedom of movement, the absence of an impartial judiciary and outstanding cases of missing persons continued to affect minorities and prevented return. The UNMIK-FRY Common Document committed UNMIK to establishing an Office for Return, to improve the processing of property claims for returning displaced persons and to address other human rights concerns expressed by Kosovo Serbs.

AI country reports/visits
Statements
- FRY (Kosovo): Amnesty International protests the unlawful detention of Afrim Zeqiri (AI Index: EUR 70/004/2001)
- Federal Republic of Yugoslavia: Milošević must be transferred to The Hague (AI Index: EUR 70/005/2001)
- FRY (Kosovo): Amnesty International calls for an end to Executive Orders of detention (AI Index: EUR 70/017/2001)
- Federal Republic of Yugoslavia: Kosovo elections: Time to right the wrongs (AI Index: EUR 70/018/2001)

ZAMBIA

REPUBLIC OF ZAMBIA
Head of state and government: Levy Mwanawasa (replaced Frederick Chiluba in December)
Capital: Lusaka
Population: 10.6 million
Official language: English
Death penalty: retentionist

At least 20 people were shot dead by police. Torture of criminal suspects was extremely common. Freedom of expression and assembly were repressed. The number of people unlawfully detained for prolonged periods increased. There was also a rise in the number of people, especially women, abducted by police because they were related to suspects. At least 10 people were sentenced to death; no executions were carried out.

Background
Shortly before the 1998 World Bank Consultative Group meeting in Paris, the Zambian government had pledged to implement major policing reforms, including human rights training and the establishment of a Police Complaints Authority. However, by the end of 2001, there was little evidence these reforms have been carried out.

During 2001, public debate focused on whether the Constitution should be changed to allow President Frederick Chiluba to run for a third term, with police repressing demonstrations by those opposed. In April, dozens of parliamentarians and senior cabinet officials left the ruling party, the Movement for Multiparty Democracy. In May President Chiluba announced he would not seek re-election.

The long-awaited "tri-partite" elections for president, parliament and local office were held in December, and Levy Mwanawasa was sworn in as president amid allegations by local civil society and European Union observers that the election was not fair.

Police shootings
By the end of the year, the number of fatal police shootings was rising steadily. Some shootings took place in front of eyewitnesses, apparently on the assumption that officers would not be investigated, disciplined or charged with homicide. At least three children under two years of age and a five-year-old girl were shot, apparently accidentally, by police.

◻ A paramilitary police officer on security duty at the Lusaka home of Gibson Zimba, the financial administrator in the President's Office, shot dead three secondary school teachers — Fumu Chimuonga, Edon Mupenda and Kelvin Nyirongo — on 7 September in suspicious circumstances. Police later alleged that the three were part of an armed group of five burglars trying to break into the house, but no gun was found on the bodies. Post-mortems indicated that the victims were shot in the head and body several times with more than one firearm. The police officer involved remained on active duty during a police investigation into the deaths. An inquest was scheduled for January 2002.

Torture and intimidation by police
In November, the UN Committee against Torture expressed concern at allegations of continuing, widespread use of torture and apparent impunity for perpetrators. The Committee noted that the government agreed in November at the Committee meeting to incorporate the crime of torture into the Criminal Code, and had enacted measures to protect and monitor people in custody. Yet police routinely tortured suspects in criminal cases; family members and witnesses were also at risk. Torture was apparently more frequent, but rarely reported, in remote rural areas. Most civil suits against police for torture were settled for small amounts of compensation. Most complaints did not result in disciplinary action against the officers involved.

Cairo Daka was arrested in Lusaka in September, accused of stealing from his employer, and tortured to death by police. Officers allegedly used a long iron bar to beat him during interrogation. His wife alleged that, in two separate incidents, police abducted her, undressed her, beat her with a whip and then tied her to an electrical pole and threatened to shoot her. Two officers were arrested and charged with murder, but had not been tried by the end of 2001.

Freedom of expression and assembly
Hundreds of demonstrators were arrested from February onwards in the context of the continuing controversy over a third term for President Chiluba. Police frequently demanded that protest organizers obtain a police permit, although this was no longer required by law. Two separate High Court rulings in April stated that such police actions were unconstitutional and "in bad faith". Nevertheless, police continued to use tear gas, beatings and arrests to break up opposition rallies that did not have a permit, calling them unlawful. Police continued to break up peaceful public events and even threatened to arrest anyone honking their car horn on Fridays, seen at the time as an expression of opposition to a third term for President Chiluba.

Women
A victims support unit, based in police stations, set up in 1996 continued to assist women victims of domestic violence and sexual assault, although its budget remained inadequate.

There was a worrying pattern of police abductions of family members in order to force criminal suspects to "voluntarily" surrender themselves.

Following a public protest in June by some 100 schoolgirls at Chinsali Girls' Secondary School, police arrested all 100 of the girls and held most of them in jail for a week after a magistrate denied many of them bail. Police subsequently dropped all charges but later threatened to arrest, charge and imprison the girls should they ever demonstrate publicly again.

Death penalty
At least 10 people were sentenced to death; no one was executed during the year.

Mabvuto Jere, aged 27, was sentenced to death for stealing a bicycle. The death sentence is mandatory in Zambia for armed robbery and he had threatened to assault the owner of the bicycle.

AI country reports/visits
Visit
AI delegates visited Zambia in February and July.

ZIMBABWE

REPUBLIC OF ZIMBABWE
Head of state and government: Robert Mugabe
Capital: Harare
Population: 12.9 million
Official language: English
Death penalty: retentionist

The human rights situation steadily deteriorated in 2001 as violence escalated in the run-up to the 2002 presidential elections. There were numerous and consistent reports of forced evictions, arbitrary arrests, beatings, torture and political killings, amounting to a pattern of deliberate, state-sponsored repression of opposition to the government or its policies. Abuses were reported to be widespread throughout the country, but intensified in the run-up to by-elections and during farm occupations. Most were carried out by the so-called "war veterans" — groups armed and supported by the police and army — and other supporters of the ruling Zimbabwe African National Union-Patriotic Front (ZANU-PF), who were able to act with impunity. There were growing reports that the police not only stood by and failed to intervene in assaults by "war veterans", but also actively took part in a number of attacks alongside ZANU-PF supporters. Freedom of expression came under increasing restrictions during the year. Journalists and lawyers were arbitrarily detained, beaten, tortured and threatened for reporting on political or human rights issues or representing the victims of human rights violations.

Background
Reports emerged during the year that the Zimbabwean government was planning the biggest ever logging operation — 81.5 million acres — in the tropical rainforests of the Democratic Republic of the Congo

(DRC). The rights to the rainforest were conceded by the DRC government in return for Zimbabwe's military aid, including an estimated 1,000 troops, in the continuing conflict with rebel forces in eastern DRC.

In September the Zimbabwean government reached agreement with Commonwealth governments in Abuja, Nigeria, to renew its commitment to the 1991 Harare Declaration. This calls on all Commonwealth governments to work for "the protection and promotion of the fundamental political values of the Commonwealth" including the rule of law and fundamental human rights. Continued reports of land seizures and human rights violations indicated the agreement was not honoured.

At the end of 2001 the Zimbabwean government was in the process of introducing legislation to create a new crime of "terrorism", punishable by death; to punish with terms of imprisonment non-violent civil disobedience, criticism of the President and disturbing the peace; and to criminalize all journalism by those not licensed by the state.

Elections

By-elections in three constituencies following the deaths of sitting Members of Parliament were the catalyst for a series of politically motivated attacks, assaults and abductions. The victims included candidates for the opposition Movement for Democratic Change (MDC), MDC activists and supporters, and voters with no apparent political affiliations.

Although some violent clashes reportedly involved both ruling party and opposition supporters, the vast majority of victims appeared to be opposition supporters.

☐ In April an MDC supporter was allegedly abducted from his home in the Harare suburb of Dzivaresekwa. He was taken to the outskirts of the town by assailants who burned an "X" on his back with red-hot chains and threatened to kill him. He was believed to have been attacked because he had distributed MDC party cards. He said that he did not report the assault to the police because he feared reprisals from his attackers.

☐ Douglas Chapoterera, the MDC's vice-chairperson for the Makoni West constituency, his wife, niece, and four children, narrowly escaped death in August when their house in Dewedzo was reportedly set on fire by ZANU-PF supporters. A group of about 50 ZANU-PF supporters reportedly arrived at the house just before midnight brandishing pickaxe handles and sticks. They reportedly smashed the windows and front door before dousing the house in petrol and setting it alight. Douglas Chapoterera's wife required hospital treatment for injuries she sustained when she fought her way past the attackers and back into the burning house to rescue her baby son. The attack was reported to the police. However, by the end of the year the police had taken no action; no one had been arrested and no evidence gathered.

Farm occupations

Up to 70,000 black farm workers were estimated to have been assaulted and forced to abandon their homes by state-sponsored militia composed of "war veterans" and other ZANU-PF supporters. Many were destitute after losing both their livelihoods and all their belongings when their houses were razed to the ground. Farm invasions were stepped up during 2001 and reports indicated that 90 per cent of the commercial farms in the country were on a government list of farms for acquisition. In Mashonaland West Province, for example, some 7,000 farm workers were reported to have been forcibly evicted from their homes in August alone. There were increasingly grave warnings of a looming crisis in the country when staple crops ran out.

The police evicted some 1,000 illegal settlers from a farm belonging to a wealthy British long-standing supporter of ZANU-PF. However, this was in sharp contrast to the authorities' failure to evict illegal settlers elsewhere in the country. State complicity in these occupations was clear. Senior police officers failed to implement court orders to evict illegal settlers and there were reports that in some instances police vehicles were used by "war veterans" coordinating illegal occupations.

The majority of the victims of assaults by "war veterans" were black farm workers, although white commercial farmers and business people, and journalists were also the victims of politically motivated attacks.

☐ In June, Zondiwa Dumukani, a 32-year-old driver working at the Blackfordby farm in Waterfalls on the outskirts of Harare, was reportedly beaten to death by a group of eight "war veterans" and ZANU-PF youths. According to reports, police officers in the area ignored the assault and did not try to intervene. Fellow farm workers said that the attackers wanted all farm employees to see the farm owner being forced to leave and that Zondiwa Dumukani was killed because he went in search of his son and was accused of running away by the ZANU-PF supporters. No one had been arrested or charged in connection with the killing. However, the farm owner and around 30 employees were arrested following Zondiwa Dumukani's death and charged with assaulting the "war veterans" and ZANU-PF supporters.

Police involvement in abuses

Police officers were directly implicated in some instances of beatings and torture and reportedly used excessive force to disperse peaceful protesters. The police also consistently failed to take adequate steps to prevent incidents of violence and intimidation and to arrest those responsible. In some cases they reportedly arrested opposition party activists to prevent them from campaigning in rural by-elections. In addition, roadblocks manned jointly by the police, security forces and ZANU-PF supporters were reportedly used to stop and search travellers for evidence of their support for the MDC. As a result, journalists, election monitors, opposition activists and others involved in activities connected to by-elections, had their freedom of movement restricted.

☐ Tawanda Hondora, Chairperson of Zimbabwe Lawyers for Human Rights, was attacked in April in

Chikomba constituency, Mashonaland East Province. He alleged that he was kicked, beaten and whipped by ZANU-PF supporters armed with stones and axes. He alleged that police officers stood by and watched the assault without attempting to intervene. He and two lawyers with him lodged a complaint at the Sadza police station, where his request for a medical examination was refused and the three lawyers were searched and interrogated about their suspected affiliation to the MDC. A complaint was later lodged with the police in Harare, but Sadza police officials denied that the incident ever took place. Tawanda Hondora had gone to Chikomba with the two other lawyers to investigate allegations of intimidation and assault of witnesses in cases where election procedures were being challenged in the High Court.

☐ Police detained some 18 MDC officials and staff following the 5 November abduction and murder of ruling party supporter Cain Nkala, a leading member of the Zimbabwe National Liberation War Veterans Association. At the time of his death, Cain Nkala had been awaiting trial on charges of abducting MDC organizer Patrick Nabanyama, who "disappeared" after being abducted by "war veterans" in June 2000. Members of Parliament Fletcher Dulini Ncube and Moses Mzila Ndlovu, and MDC adviser Simon Spooner were among the MDC officials subsequently charged with abduction and murder. The Court failed to act on allegations by four detainees — Kethani Sibanda, Remember Moyo, Sazini Mpofu and Gilbert Moyo — that they had been held in unlawfully prolonged incommunicado detention, tortured, threatened at gunpoint unless they signed confessions already written for them, and forced to implicate themselves and other detained MDC officials. The detentions appeared to be politically motivated. Reacting to the news of Cain Nkala's abduction, Vice-President Joseph Msika threatened the MDC with a "bloodbath". President Mugabe repeated accusations against the MDC, calling the killing a "terrorist provocation" and naming Simon Spooner as the culprit.

In the area of Chimanimani, state-sponsored militia coordinated by the Central Intelligence Organization (CIO), the security police, systematically beat and intimidated residents, who were represented in Parliament by an opposition party politician.

☐ In November, CIO officers, "war veterans" and ZANU-PF supporters allegedly abducted two men and urinated in their faces, threw sand in their eyes, threatened to kill them and beat them unconscious with whips, electric cable and rocks while questioning them about MDC activities. The CIO officer in charge had allegedly been involved in the death of Tichaona Chiminya and Talent Mabika, two MDC activists burned to death in a petrol bomb attack in April 2000. Although the High Court issued a summons in April 2000 to the officer to answer murder charges, police said that they did not know his whereabouts and failed to arrest him.

Students

☐ In April police action to end protests by students over reductions in college grants at the University of Zimbabwe campus in Harare left one student dead and at least 28 others injured. The police said that Batanai Hadzidzi died after being trampled to death by students who were fleeing in panic after riot police fired tear gas into their accommodation. However, eyewitnesses stated that he was not actively involved in the protests and was beaten to death by riot police using truncheons on 8 April. No investigation is known to have been carried out into this death or into the wounding of several students the next day when police fired live ammunition to break up a non-violent protest march against police brutality.

Attacks on journalists

More than 40 journalists from privately owned newspapers who tried to report on political or human rights issues, or who filed reports critical of the government, were harassed, beaten and threatened. In some cases criminal charges were also brought against journalists in an attempt to hinder them from carrying out their work.

☐ Geoff Nyarota, editor-in-chief of *The Daily News*, was arrested in August with three journalist colleagues over an article containing allegations of police complicity in a wave of looting on commercial farms in Chinhoyi, Doma and Mhangura in Mashonaland West Province. The report alleged that attackers had used police vans to move looted goods. The three journalists were held for several hours before being released by court order after charges against them were dismissed. Geoff Nyarota was released after a judge ruled that the charge against him of "publishing false news" was unlawful. The printing press of *The Daily News* had been bombed in January, days after President Mugabe accused the paper of being a mouthpiece for the opposition.

☐ The government deported three foreign journalists, branding others as "terrorists", banned the BBC from entering the country and blocked CNN broadcasts. In November it published the Access to Information and Protection of Privacy Bill, which would require Zimbabwean journalists to apply annually to a government-controlled panel for a licence to write, impose jail sentences for breaches of a strict code of conduct and restrict entry for foreign journalists to the country.

The judiciary under pressure

The government continued its attempts to undermine the impartiality of the judiciary. On several occasions the government refused to comply with Supreme Court judgments. Four senior judges resigned during the year, apparently as a result of harassment or government pressure.

☐ Anthony Gubbay, Chief Justice of the Supreme Court, took early retirement in March, reportedly after receiving a series of threats. On at least one occasion "war veterans" forced their way into the High Court in Harare armed with steel rods and threatened him. His resignation reportedly came after he received assurances from the government that it would not put pressure on other judges to resign; he received no assurances that his safety would be protected. Esmael Chatikobo, a High Court judge, resigned in May. He had reportedly angered ZANU-PF officials by issuing a restraining order in 2000 to prevent police from raiding the private radio station *Capital Radio*. Another judge, James Devittie, resigned in June, a few days after handing down three judgments against ZANU-PF and in favour of the opposition in electoral petitions challenging election results filed by the MDC.

AI country reports/ visits
Reports
- Zimbabwe: International community must take action now (AI Index: AFR 46/003/2001)
- Zimbabwe: Appeal to the European Union and the Commonwealth (AI Index: AFR 46/010/2001)

Visits
AI delegates visited Zimbabwe in May, November and December.

AI REPORT 2002
PART 3

WHAT IS AI?

Germany Amnesty International, 53108 Bonn
e-mail: info@amnesty.de
http://www.amnesty.de
Ghana Amnesty International, Private Mail Bag, Kokomlemle, Accra - North
e-mail: aghana@sections.amnesty.org
Greece Amnesty International, 30 Sina Street, 106 72 Athens
e-mail: info@amnesty.gr
http://www.amnesty.gr
Guyana Amnesty International, PO Box 101679, Palm Court Building, 35 Main Street, Georgetown
Hong Kong Amnesty International, Unit B, 3/F, Best-O-Best Commercial Centre, 32-36 Ferry Street, Kowloon
e-mail: admin-hk@amnesty.org
http://www.amnesty.org.hk
Iceland Amnesty International, PO Box 618, 121 Reykjavík
e-mail: amnesty@rhi.hi.is
http://www.amnesty.is
Ireland Amnesty International, Sean MacBride House, 48 Fleet Street, Dublin 2
e-mail: info@amnesty.iol.ie
http://www.amnesty.ie
Israel Amnesty International, PO Box 14179, Tel Aviv 61141
e-mail: amnesty@netvision.net.il
http://www.amnesty.org.il
Italy Amnesty International, Via Giovanni Battista De Rossi 10, 00161 Roma
e-mail: info@amnesty.it
http://www.amnesty.it
Japan Amnesty International, Sky Esta 2F, 2-18-23 Nishi Waseda, Shinjuku-ku, Tokyo 169
e-mail: amnesty@mri.biglobe.ne.jp
http://www.amnesty.or.jp
Korea (Republic of) Amnesty International, Kyeong Buk RCO Box 36, Daegu 706-600
e-mail: admin-ko@amnesty.org
http://www.amnesty.or.kr
Luxembourg Amnesty International, Boîte Postale 1914, 1019 Luxembourg
e-mail: e-mail@amnesty.lu
http://www.amnesty.lu
Mauritius Amnesty International, BP 69, Rose-Hill
e-mail: amnesty@intnet.mu
Mexico Amnistía Internacional, Calle Patricio Sanz 1104, Departamento 14, Colonia del Valle, Mexico D.F. - CP 03100
e-mail: adm-mx@amnesty.org
Morocco Amnesty International, Place d'Angleterre, Rue Souissra, Immeuble No. 11, Appt No. 1, Rabat - l'Océan
e-mail: admin-ma@amnesty.org
Nepal Amnesty International, PO Box 135, Bagbazar, Kathmandu
e-mail: ain@ccsl.com.np
Netherlands Amnesty International, PO Box 1968, 1000 BZ, Amsterdam
e-mail: amnesty@amnesty.nl
http://www.amnesty.nl

New Zealand Amnesty International, PO Box 793, Wellington
e-mail: campaign@amnesty.org.nz
http://www.amnesty.org.nz
Nigeria Amnesty International, PMB 3061, Suru Lere, Lagos
e-mail: ainigeria@yahoo.co.uk
Norway Amnesty International, PO Box 702 Sentrum, 0106 Oslo
e-mail: info@amnesty.no
http://www.amnesty.no
Peru Señores, Casilla 659, Lima 18
e-mail: admin-pe@amnesty.org
Philippines Amnesty International, Room 305 CRM Building II, 116 Kamia Road, 1101 Quezon City
e-mail: amnestypilipinas@meridiantelekoms.net
Portugal Amnistia Internacional, Rua Fialho de Almeida 13-1, PT-1070-128 Lisboa
e-mail: aisp@ip.pt
http://www.amnistia-internacional.pt
Puerto Rico Amnistía Internacional, Calle El Roble No. 54-Altos, Oficina 11, Río Piedras, Puerto Rico 00925
e-mail: amnistiaPR@yahoo.com
Senegal Amnesty International, BP 21910, Dakar
e-mail: aisenegal@sentoo.sn
Sierra Leone Amnesty International, PMB 1021, Freetown
e-mail: aislf@sierratel.sl
Slovenia Amnesty International, Komenskega 7, 1000 Ljubljana
e-mail: amnesty.slo@guest.arnes.si
http://www.ljudmila.org/ai-slo
Spain Amnistía Internacional, Apdo 50318, 28080 Madrid
e-mail: amnistia.internacional@a-i.es
http://www.a-i.es
Sweden Amnesty International, PO Box 4719, SE-116 92 Stockholm
e-mail: info@amnesty.se
http://www.amnesty.se
Switzerland Amnesty International, Postfach CH-3001, Bern
e-mail: info@amnesty.ch
http://www.amnesty.ch
Taiwan Amnesty International, No. 89, 7th floor #1, Chung Cheng Two Road, Kaohsiung
e-mail: aitaiwan@seed.net.tw
http://www.aitaiwan.org.tw
Tanzania Amnesty International, Luther House, 3rd Floor, PO Box 4331, Dar es Salaam
e-mail: aitanz@simbanet.net
Togo CCNP, BP 20013, Lomé
e-mail: aitogo@cafe.tg
Tunisia Amnesty International, 67 rue Oum Kalthoum, 3ème étage, Escalier B, 1000 Tunis
e-mail: admin-tn@amnesty.org
United Kingdom Amnesty International, 99-119 Rosebery Avenue, London EC1R 4RE
e-mail: info@amnesty.org.uk
http://www.amnesty.org.uk

WHAT IS AI?

United States of America Amnesty International, 322 8th Ave, New York, NY 10001
e-mail: admin-us@aiusa.org
http://www.amnestyusa.org
Uruguay Amnistía Internacional, Tristan Narvaja 1624, Ap 1, CP 11200, Montevideo
e-mail: amnistia@chasque.apc.org
Venezuela Amnistía Internacional, Apartado Postal 5110, Carmelitas, 1010 A Caracas
e-mail: admin-ve@amnesty.org
http://www.amnistia.int.ve

AI coordinating structures

Bolivia Amnistía Internacional, Casilla 10607, La Paz
Burkina Faso Amnesty International, 08 BP 11344, Ouagadougou
e-mail: aburkina@sections.amnesty.org
Caribbean Regional Office Amnesty International C.R.O., PO Box 1912, Grenada, West Indies
e-mail: amnestycro@caribsurf.com
Croatia Amnesty International, Martičeva 24, 10000 Zagreb
e-mail: admin@amnesty.hr
Curaçao Amnesty International, PO Box 3676, Curaçao, Netherlands Antilles
Czech Republic Amnesty International, Palackého 9, 110 00 Praha 1
e-mail: amnesty@amnesty.cz
http://www.amnesty.cz
Gambia Amnesty International, PO Box 1935, Banjul
e-mail: amnesty@gamtel.gm
India Amnesty International, G13 First Floor, Hauz Khas Main Market, New Delhi, 110016
e-mail: admin-in@amnesty.org
Hungary Amnesty International, 1399 Budapest, PF 701/343
e-mail: amnesty.hun@axelero.hu
Malaysia Amnesty International, Pro-tem Committee, 43A, Jalan SS 15/4, 47500 Subang Jaya Selangor Darul Ehsan
e-mail: amnesty@tm.net.my
http://www.crosswinds.net/~aimalaysia
Mali Amnesty International, BP E 3885, Bamako
e-mail: amnesty-mli@spider.toolnet.org
e-mail: amali@sections.amnesty.org
Mongolia Amnesty International, Ulaanbaatar 21 0648, PO Box 180
e-mail: aimncc@magicnet.mn
Pakistan Amnesty International, NEC, B-12, Shelozon Centre, Gulsan-E-Iqbal, Block 15, University Road, Karachi - 75300
e-mail: amnesty@cyber.net.pk
http://www.geocities.com/amnestypakistan
Palestinian Authority Amnesty International, PO Box 543, Khalaf Building, Racheed Street, Gaza City, South Remal via Israel
e-mail: admin-pa@amnesty.org
Paraguay Amnistía Internacional, Calle Juan de Salazar 488 casi Boquerón, Asunción
e-mail: ai-info@amnistia.org.py
http://www.amnistia.org.py

Poland Amnesty International, ul. Jaśkowa Dolina 4, 80-252 Gdańsk
e-mail: amnesty@amnesty.org.pl
http://www.amnesty.org.pl
Slovakia Amnesty International, Staromestská 6, 811 03 Bratislava
e-mail: amnesty@internet.sk
http://www.internet.sk/amnesty
South Africa Amnesty International, PO Box 29083, Sunnyside 0132, Pretoria, Gauteng
e-mail: info@amnesty.org.za
Thailand Amnesty International, 125/4 Sukhumvit Soi 89, Bangjak, Phrakhanong, Bangkok 10250
e-mail: admin-th@amnesty.org
http://www.thailand.amnesty.com
Turkey Amnesty International, Muradiye Bayiri Sok. Acarman ap. 50/1, Tesvikiye 80200, Istanbul
e-mail: amnesty@superonline.com
Uganda Amnesty International groups, PO Box 23966, Kampala
e-mail: augamnesty@yahoo.com
Ukraine Amnesty International, Maydan Rynok 6, Drohobych, 82100
e-mail: officeai@dr.lv.ukrtel.net
Zambia Amnesty International, Private Bag 3, Kitwe Main PO, Kitwe
e-mail: mjmusonda@hotmail.com
e-mail: JMusonda@comesa.int
Zimbabwe Amnesty International, 25 E Bible House, 99 Mbuya Nehanda Street, Harare
e-mail: amnestyzimbabwe@yahoo.com

AI groups
There are also AI groups in:
Albania, Angola, Aruba, Azerbaijan, Bahamas, Barbados, Belarus, Bosnia-Herzegovina, Botswana, Cameroon, Chad, Dominican Republic, Egypt, Estonia, Grenada, Jamaica, Jordan, Kenya, Kuwait, Kyrgyzstan, Lebanon, Liberia, Lithuania, Macedonia, Malta, Moldova, Mozambique, Romania, Russian Federation, Yemen, Yugoslavia (Federal Republic of)

AI IN ACTION

"I have been struck by the courage of the people. Families whose homes were bombed in Kabul and who fled with nothing are bravely putting their lives together. Children, dirty and half-starved, still smile and play in the dust. Women who have suffered repression for the past 20 years are full of ideas of how they will rebuild a better, more equal society for themselves. Their courage is so inspiring that I wanted to share this experience with you. This is what makes our work meaningful. So, let's take the opportunity today to celebrate the work of all human rights defenders and the courage of all victims."

AI's Secretary General, Irene Khan, speaking at a refugee camp in Pakistan on Human Rights Day, 10 December 2001

The attacks in the USA on 11 September gave the AI movement one of the strongest challenges of its 40-year history. An immediate yet considered response by human rights organizations was vital in the wake of the attacks. This section of the *Amnesty International Report 2002* gives an overview of work undertaken by AI members throughout the year in response to 11 September and in their upholding of commitments to programs of work previously in place.

AI's strength reflects the quality of the materials it produces and the meticulous research on which its campaigning activities are based. During 2001, AI delegates visited more than 75 countries and territories to meet victims of human rights violations, observe trials, and interview local human rights activists and officials.

AI's activities range from public demonstrations to letter-writing, from human rights education to fundraising concerts, from targeted appeals on behalf of a single individual to global campaigns on a specific country or issue, from approaches to local authorities to lobbying intergovernmental organizations.

AI confronts governments with its findings by issuing detailed reports and by publicizing its concerns in leaflets, posters, advertisements, newsletters and on the Internet. AI information is available on countless websites worldwide.

AI campaigns to change government attitudes and unjust laws. One of the ways it does this is by feeding a constant stream of information to the media, to governments and to the UN, urging them to take action.

The organization also strives to promote awareness and strengthen the protection of human rights. It appeals to international organizations to intervene when a crisis appears likely to develop. It seeks the protection of refugees fleeing persecution and it works with local human rights workers who are subjected to harassment or who are under threat of attack.

Long- and medium-term actions

The number of AI's local groups, youth and student groups and networks participating in actions continued to grow throughout the year. Based in more than 100 countries, members took action on 2,813 named individuals, including prisoners of conscience and other victims of human rights violations. A total of 818 long-term Action Files were running, and were assigned to 2,742 groups who used a variety of campaigning techniques including letter-writing and public events. A total of 72 new Action Files were produced and allocated during the year, while 184 were closed in the same period.

The year saw AI activists responding to an increasing number of requests for action. One such Action File concerned the treatment of youth and student groups in Belarus, especially an opposition youth movement known as ZUBR, a new country-wide grouping of students and young people. Concerns included the arbitrary detention of ZUBR activists for peacefully exercising their rights to freedom of assembly and association, and the alleged ill-treatment of ZUBR members by the police. Other files included one on behalf of political prisoners held in Drapchi prison in Tibet, and one each on the Indian states of Jammu and Kashmir and West Bengal.

Local groups were also involved in Regional Action Networks (RANs), which generate ongoing campaign work on a specific group of countries. During the year a total of 1,796 groups were assigned to 23 RANs and they took part in 181 actions.

Youth and students

Youth and students make up approximately half of the AI membership worldwide and are organized into about 3,500 groups in 60 different sections and structures. In 2001 they campaigned energetically and creatively on all AI concerns. In March students from 15 countries participated in an International Week of Student Action to raise awareness about the widespread use of torture in Peru. Although the event was tailored for the youth and student network, other AI activists also became involved, particularly as the timing of the presidential elections in Peru afforded a good opportunity for raising AI's concerns.

Youth camps took place in different regions. Among these was the first AI international youth camp in Europe, held in Slovenia, where 70 participants from 28 European countries met to discuss human rights, develop their campaigning skills and take practical action. This gathering produced a lively debate about further enhancing the role of youth and student groups in AI.

Urgent Actions

If urgent action is needed on behalf of people in imminent danger of serious human rights violations, volunteers around the world are alerted, and they send thousands of letters, faxes and e-mails within days.

During 2001, AI initiated 408 such appeals to the Urgent Action network. There were also 404 updates to previous urgent action appeals; 117 of these recorded good news about the case, and 235 asked for further appeals to be sent. These actions were issued on behalf of people in 81 countries and territories, who were either at risk of or had suffered human rights violations

AI IN ACTION

including torture, "disappearance", the death penalty, death in custody, or forcible return to countries where they would be in danger of human rights violations.

Crisis response

The scale and nature of the 11 September attacks in the USA required an immediate response from human rights activists. At least 3,000 people from more than 60 countries were killed, causing trauma and grief in every region on earth. AI condemned the attacks unreservedly. AI members worldwide offered their condolences and expressed their solidarity to the victims and their relatives. Under the slogan *Justice not revenge*, AI called for the perpetrators of the attacks to be brought to justice, in line with international human rights standards.

A US-led coalition began bombing in Afghanistan on 7 October and continued for the rest of the year. An as yet unknown number of Afghan civilians were killed or injured or had their homes or property destroyed. AI raised concerns with US authorities about specific attacks in which civilians were killed and civilian objects were destroyed, urged that investigations be conducted into possible violations of international humanitarian law and called for a moratorium on the use of cluster weapons. In November AI called on the USA, the United Islamic Front for the Salvation of Afghanistan (United Front), and the United Kingdom (UK) to conduct an inquiry into the deaths of hundreds of *Taleban* prisoners and others at Qala-i-Jhangi fort, after an uprising by some *Taleban* captives was put down by bombing by US warplanes and United Front artillery.

AI members tackled the serious human rights concerns raised in this crisis through campaigning and publicity work. One of the most pressing issues was how to deal with the spate of attacks against Muslim, Asian, Middle Eastern and other minority communities in many countries. Another urgent concern was how to react to the introduction or tightening up of security and anti-terrorism legislation in many countries around the world in ways which undermined human rights protection. AI sections joined coalitions and worked with other non-governmental organizations (NGOs) in calling for restraint and respect for human rights by all parties in the armed conflict in Afghanistan and surrounding countries.

AI highlighted its concerns in its report, *The backlash: Human rights at risk throughout the world* (AI Index: ACT 30/027/2001), which AI members used to lobby their governments to take strong action against perpetrators of racist attacks in their countries. It enabled AI members to raise concerns about the treatment of refugees and asylum seekers, as well as about limits to civil liberties and basic freedoms which were being felt in all regions of the world. The US authorities were challenged about the introduction of special military commissions; on the detention without basic human rights safeguards of mainly non-US nationals; and on the debate regarding the possible use of "pressure techniques" by US security forces to elicit information from detainees during interrogation.

Part of the aim of the crisis response was to draw attention to human rights violations taking place in countries not immediately involved in the conflict but where abuses were taking place following the 11 September attacks; these included campaigning and mass letter-writing on cases in Malaysia and Nepal, among others.

After 11 September a number of countries introduced or amended their legislation in ways which had a direct impact on human rights. High-profile lobbying was done by AI's European Union (EU) office and within sections in the EU. Initiatives were undertaken by AI sections in Canada, India and the UK. AI members in the UK sent "greetings cards" to their members of parliament condemning draconian measures being introduced in the UK government's emergency legislation, the Anti-terrorism, Crime and Security Act. The section was joined by other NGOs, as well as UK Muslim community groups, in a vigil outside Parliament on Human Rights Day, 10 December, to protest against the measures under the slogan "No to detention without trial".

AI Spain mobilized more than 1,000 members to actively work on the crisis response, some of whom participated in demonstrations held all over the country. The section successfully lobbied the Spanish government to commit funds to the UN High Commissioner for Refugees (UNHCR), and collected 10,000 signatures for letters to the US authorities.

The International Secretariat (IS) set up a website page entitled *Justice not revenge*, which was used as an active campaigning tool in providing fast and accessible information to the public as well as to AI members. Website actions were prepared on Central Asia and on Afghanistan; the latter, the *Human rights agenda for Afghanistan*, was also translated into Pashtu and Dari for use in Afghanistan, as well as into Sindhi and Urdu. Other sections, including Belgium and Canada, used Internet campaigning to reach wide audiences.

Many AI sections joined with other NGOs and also held their own events around the *Justice not revenge* theme. AI Switzerland used the image of a lottery ticket to convey the message that human rights should not be a lottery. In Morocco, the section took the opportunity of an annual youth camp event attended by 25 youth organizations to draw attention to AI's crisis response. AI sections in Belgium and Sweden focused on AI's concerns about the rights of women in Afghanistan. In addition, a number of AI sections lobbied their own governments to put pressure on the UK, US and Russian governments not to supply or use cluster bombs or other arms which would be used to violate human rights.

AI members in Pakistan undertook campaigning actions in difficult circumstances. Members held a vigil in October and their efforts were rewarded with some success in obtaining media coverage of AI's information. They played a key role in translating materials into Urdu and Sindhi. Much of the section's work focused on refugees, including preparation for and participating in the December visit of AI's Secretary General.

On Human Rights Day, many AI sections held candlelight vigils and related activities, and some sections lit 30 candles to represent each of the articles of the Universal Declaration of Human Rights. This symbol was used by AI's Secretary General, Irene Khan, at an event held in a refugee camp in Pakistan which she was visiting. A major focus of attention was the presentation to the UN Secretary-General Kofi Annan of the Nobel Peace Prize in Oslo, Norway. The attention of the world's media on this event afforded AI Norway an excellent opportunity to organize activities around the country, as well as a letter and website petition. These were presented to Kofi Annan on 9 December.

AI's global website petition for Human Rights Day — *Act Now for Human Rights!* — called on all governments to address human rights both at home and internationally, and to ensure that justice and human rights standards not be undermined in the aftermath of 11 September. The petition was signed by thousands of people, from Austria to South Africa. Some sections chose different symbols. AI New Zealand's message "Give human rights a hand" was used to collect handprints of people wishing to express their commitment to human rights. AI Belgium's 10 December petition addressed to the UN Secretary-General was sent by e-mail to 2,000 members and generated 1,000 signatures within four days. From Bermuda to Uruguay, Nepal to Poland, AI sections and members campaigned on the crisis response in dynamic and varied ways.

Human rights defenders

Human rights defenders play a vital role in holding states to account in respect of their promises and obligations to protect the rights of their citizens. In many countries around the world human rights defenders face constant persecution on account of their efforts to support the victims of human rights violations and to expose the abuses committed by state agents. Work to strengthen and protect human rights defenders continued to be one of AI's priorities.

In Latin America, AI's special program of protection mechanisms for human rights defenders at risk works closely with local and international organizations to develop and apply national programs of protection for defenders. This work includes a program of national and international internships, as well as various initiatives to enable human rights defenders facing imminent danger, including witnesses, to be accompanied. Members of the electronic Human Rights Defenders Network for Latin America took special action on behalf of threatened human rights defenders in Colombia, Dominican Republic, Guatemala and Mexico.

In June AI supported a consultation held in Mexico between human rights defenders from Latin America and the Caribbean and the UN Special Representative on human rights defenders, to discuss the Special Representative's mandate and brief her on obstacles faced by defenders in the region. In October the Special Representative visited Colombia to raise with the authorities the urgent needs of defenders, more than 30 of whom were killed in the previous five years.

Also in June, AI published a report, *Colombia: Robust measures urgently needed to protect human rights defenders* (AI Index: AMR 23/023/2001), outlining the systematic persecution of members of ASFADDES, an organization working on behalf of the "disappeared", and calling for the Colombian authorities to adopt concrete measures to protect them. In December AI published a report, *Mexico: Daring to raise their voices* (AI Index: AMR 41/040/2001), and launched a campaign on behalf of Mexican human rights defenders whose work the authorities often attempted to undermine by portraying them as criminals or subversives. The report documented continued harassment of human rights defenders in Mexico, despite a change of government in December 2000 after more than 70 consecutive years of one-party rule, and emphasized the authorities' duty to investigate these and past cases.

In South Asia, AI has facilitated gatherings of human rights defenders since 1999 to discuss mutual concerns about their work, encourage interaction as a means of support, and develop concrete protection mechanisms. This work continued in 2001 with a series of workshops for human rights defenders in India to discuss the UN human rights system and how it can be used by human rights defenders to support their work.

The work of human rights defenders in West Africa was promoted in a successful campaign launched in April in Senegal. It was followed by a workshop on protection mechanisms with the UN Special Representative on human rights defenders. Innovative campaign activities included publicizing the work of human rights defenders in the media as well as lobbying governments in West Africa and intergovernmental organizations. The campaign led to the establishment of coalitions of human rights defenders in many West African countries, and the formation of a subregional network for their promotion and protection.

In July a subregional workshop was organized in Mali for women human rights defenders in West Africa to highlight the difficult environment in which they work, and to develop appropriate protection mechanisms. Work continued in developing a placement project whereby human rights defenders forced to flee their country would be enabled to continue their work within the region in collaboration with human rights NGOs.

Human rights defenders in the Middle East continued to face difficulties in their work. In Tunisia, judicial proceedings against the *Ligue tunisienne des droits de l'homme*, Tunisian Human Rights League, continued, and measures were taken to curtail the activities of the *Conseil national pour les libertés en Tunisie* (CNLT), National Council for Liberties in Tunisia. On several occasions, members were prevented from gathering and were ill-treated by security forces. Judicial proceedings were initiated against leading figures of the CNLT.

In September, during an official visit to Tunisia, two AI delegates were detained at night and ill-treated by plainclothes agents of the security forces. Equipment and documents relating to human rights were stolen.

AI IN ACTION

At least one person reported having received overt death threats from security agents to dissuade him from meeting with the AI delegates.

Worldwide campaigns

Intensive work continued on AI's worldwide campaign *Take a step to stamp out torture*, begun in October 2000 and focusing on three key themes: the means of preventing torture; the role of discrimination in the torture inflicted on certain groups; and putting an end to the impunity which has shielded so many people responsible for torture. The campaign has had a significant impact in several important areas: individual cases of people at risk of torture and ill-treatment (see example below); and developing a wider understanding and awareness of torture, discrimination and impunity. In addition, AI members worked hard to press governments to observe international treaties. By the end of the year, the torture campaign website, www.stoptorture.org, had received around 32,790 subscribers from 188 countries willing to take action on urgent cases by sending appeals.

Campaigning for an individual

AI took worldwide action in November on behalf of Houndjo Mawudzro, a student leader and human rights activist in Togo who had been detained and tortured in September. There were fears that he would be tortured again when he was rearrested on 7 November and charged with "defamation of character and false accusation" because of a press statement he issued giving details of the torture he suffered when first detained in September. An urgent appeal issued on his behalf was posted on AI's website www.stoptorture.org, and a press release was issued to coincide with the visit of the President of Togo to France. 10,900 appeals were sent on his behalf. Houndjo Mawudzro was released on 28 November, after being summoned to the prosecutor. Houndjo Mawudzro thanked his supporters and said that he had been aware of AI's campaign on his behalf.

Campaigning on intergovernmental action

There were also achievements on broader issues.

Following the adoption of the Rome Statute of the International Criminal Court on 17 July 1998, AI launched a worldwide campaign for all governments to ratify the Statute. The Court, which will bring to justice those accused of genocide, crimes against humanity and war crimes, will be created when 60 states have ratified the Statute. At the end of 2001, 48 states had ratified, and it was expected that the number will reach 60 in the first half of 2002. Almost all AI sections and structures around the world lobbied their governments to ratify, and in many countries led the national campaign, in most cases in close coordination with other national NGOs.

Campaigning by AI activists contributed to four countries ratifying the UN Convention against Torture during the year, and a number of government leaders and officials made commitments to adopt legislation to prevent torture in their countries. In moves widely acknowledged as significant, the UN Commission on Human Rights adopted AI's recommendations for governments to take measures to stop the production and transfer of torture equipment, and the EU adopted guidelines for the prevention and eradication of torture in other countries.

Child rights

For the 2001 Child Rights Action, AI's activists continued the work against the torture and ill-treatment of children. Featuring cases from Albania, Chechnya, Democratic Republic of the Congo and Egypt, AI highlighted concern about children tortured by police and during armed conflicts. Material was produced especially for younger children between the ages of 10 and 12.

AI's child rights activists, together with the movement's activists on intergovernmental organizations, worked towards the UN General Assembly Special Session on Children (UNGASS). AI focused on three main areas: ratification of international instruments; child soldiers and juvenile justice, particularly the imposition of the death penalty for persons under 18 years of age; and torture and cruel, inhuman or degrading treatment. UNGASS was postponed following the attacks in the USA on 11 September, but AI's lobbying for child rights continued.

AI's activists, in close cooperation with the International Coalition to Stop the Use of Child Soldiers, continued to lobby for the Optional Protocol to the UN Children's Convention on the involvement of children in armed conflict. On 12 November, New Zealand became the 10th state to ratify the Protocol, thus allowing it to enter into force on 12 February 2002.

The risks faced by children in areas of armed conflict were addressed in an action on the torture and routine ill-treatment of conscripts by their superiors. An action was also issued on the deaths of conscripts in the armed forces and national police in Paraguay. AI activists continued to campaign against the recruitment and deployment of child soldiers by the UK armed forces, including in NATO's Operation "Essential Harvest" in Macedonia and in military operations in Afghanistan in the wake of the attacks in the USA on 11 September.

AI continued to receive and act on cases of violence against children by police officers. One concerned the alleged beating on the face and body of a 15-year-old-girl by police in Romania. AI was also concerned that the child was held and questioned at the police station without any legal and other appropriate assistance. AI members also campaigned on the grossly inadequate conditions at Panchito López juvenile detention centre in Paraguay, where ill-treatment, sometimes amounting to torture, was endemic.

Women's rights

AI's worldwide campaign against torture, *Take a step to stamp out torture*, signalled another major landmark in the organization's work on women's rights. Its report *Broken bodies, shattered minds: Torture and ill-treatment of women* (AI Index: ACT 40/001/2001) was published on International Women's Day, 8 March, and attracted huge media and public attention across the world. AI presented detailed recommendations to governments, including public condemnation and criminalizing of violence against women, investigating all allegations, and prosecuting and punishing the perpetrators.

AI sections in more than 40 countries in five global regions took part in the international campaign which accompanied the launch of the report. Their campaigning activities focused on developing links with women's movements in their countries and raising public awareness on the interrelationship between torture and violence against women.

Some key events that took place during the campaign were:
- AI Norway worked with a national network of women's shelters to expose the lack of proper protection and support for battered and raped women in the country, despite strong commitments by the Norwegian government on the issue of violence against women;
- in Thailand, the section organized a series of meetings with women's NGOs working on behalf of women in the sex industry. A seminar was held examining the underlying discrimination facing women sex workers and the need for strong legal reform in Thailand to protect their rights. This initiative was followed by a one-day human rights education conference for sex workers, and a high-level meeting with the Senate (Parliament) Commission of Women, Youth and Elderly Affairs;
- AI local and student groups in the USA were involved in organizing a speakers' tour covering eight cities by local activists working on behalf of women in prison in the USA and women asylum-seekers in the country. The tour prompted the launch of a manual to protect female prison inmates in the USA and a campaign to support women asylum seekers fleeing gender-based persecution;
- AI Philippines focused on the climate of state impunity as the impediment in addressing torture and violence against women, and worked with its growing network of women's NGO partners to press Congress to pass legislation protecting women from such abuses;
- AI Palestine and AI Morocco worked with women's NGOs, producing manuals for workshops and outreach, to enhance making women's rights a reality.

AI sections took the opportunity offered by AI's campaign against torture to connect with women's movements in their countries to raise the profile of the new Optional Protocol to the UN Women's Convention, which provides for an individual complaint procedure and an inquiry procedure into violations of women's human rights. Paraguay became the fourth country to ratify the Optional Protocol, a step which it took on International Women's Day. In Mongolia, AI members joined a prominent women's network in a public event acknowledging the importance of the UN Women's Convention. In Bermuda, the AI section worked with women's NGOs to urge that the UK's ratification of the UN Women's Convention be extended to Bermuda.

A series of country reports containing evidence of violence against women was produced during the year. Specific information included rape or other sexual abuse of women in custody in Jamaica, Lebanon, the Philippines, Turkey and the USA; and torture, including rape, and gender-oriented violence within different communities in India.

The rights of lesbian, gay, bisexual and transgender (LGBT) people

2001 was a highly successful year for LGBT activism. In June, as part of the ongoing campaign against torture, AI launched its report, *Crimes of hate, conspiracy of silence: Torture and ill-treatment based on sexual identity* (AI Index: ACT 40/016/2001). This was the first time an LGBT-themed report had featured in an international AI campaign, and it was enthusiastically received by LGBT rights activists.

The report, launched in Argentina at a gathering of representatives of NGOs and the national and international press, highlighted the cases of many torture victims targeted because of their real or perceived sexual identity. The international launch of the report was matched by many national launches and actions. AIUSA held events in Chicago, New York, San Francisco and Washington. AI Philippines produced placards, banners, stickers and temporary tattoos for a gay pride march in Manila, at which AI activists distributed the report and news release. AI Poland held a conference with a local gay and lesbian association. In El Salvador, the report was launched at a public presentation attended and covered by national newspapers and television and radio stations. At an event in Israel at the Association for LGBT Individuals, a board member of AI Israel gave a lecture on torture and sexual identity. AI Netherlands organized the sending of thousands of telephone text messages to the authorities in Namibia on the issue of hate crimes. In the UK, the event to launch the report was dedicated to the memory of Poliyana Mangwiro, also known as Tsitsi Tiripano, a Zimbabwean LGBT rights activist who was closely associated with AI and who died shortly before the report was published. The launch received press coverage in 23 countries.

The year saw several challenges to the freedom of expression and association of LGBT activists and organizations around the world, as well as numerous cases of people harassed or attacked because of their sexual identity. An AI delegation visiting Honduras expressed concern about the refusal by Honduran authorities over seven years to grant legal status to local NGOs working on LGBT issues. AI expressed concern to the authorities in the Federal Republic of Yugoslavia about the failure of the Belgrade police to protect participants in Serbia's first gay pride celebration from assault by anti-gay individuals and organizations. AI protested against the exclusion of the International Lesbian and Gay Association (ILGA) from participation in the UN World Conference against Racism.

In May, some 60 men were arrested and detained in Egypt, allegedly in connection with their sexual orientation. Fifty-two of them were brought to trial in July. Twenty-two men and one juvenile were adopted

AI IN ACTION

by AI as prisoners of conscience following their convictions and sentences of between one and five years' imprisonment. Members of the LGBT worldwide network were at the forefront of AI's campaigning on this issue. On 15 August, to mark one of the hearings in this case, AI activists from all five global regions demonstrated in support of the men. Two examples of the many activities undertaken by AI sections were: AI Switzerland, together with other NGOs, demonstrated about the case in front of UN buildings in Geneva in August; and AI Sweden joined a demonstration organized by the Swedish Federation for Lesbian, Gay, Bisexual and Transgender Rights (RFSL) at the Egyptian embassy in Stockholm. After the latter demonstration, the RFSL president and the coordinator of the AI Sweden group for LGBT issues were invited to a meeting with Egypt's Chargé d'Affaires to discuss the case. AI sections in Asia joined a region-wide public outcry against Egypt's ill-treatment of the arrested men.

There was good news for AI's LGBT rights campaigners. In June the Romanian government adopted an emergency ordinance which abolished Article 200 of the Penal Code, which dealt with, among other things, homosexual consensual relations, and under which prisoners of conscience had been held.

Other LGBT work continued throughout the year. In August AI made a statement on identity-based discrimination to the UN Sub-Commission on the Promotion and Protection of Human Rights.

Alongside increased activism during the year, several new LGBT groups, structures and networks were set up, and improvements to the international network of LGBT groups and structures were initiated. In October an AI delegation attended the 23rd ILGA European Regional Conference in the Netherlands. The Conference allowed LGBT groups and organizations in Europe to share their experiences and expertise.

Military, security and police (MSP) transfers

Throughout 2001, AI members continued to campaign for effective controls on the transfer of arms and security assistance in order to prevent these being used for grave human rights abuses. It campaigned for a worldwide ban on the production, promotion and trading of any security equipment used for inherently cruel, inhuman or degrading purposes, and for their suspension in the case of questionable equipment such as electro-shock weapons.

Concerted lobbying and publicity by AI members worldwide surrounded the publication of the report, *Stopping the torture trade* (AI Index: ACT 40/002/2001), issued as part of AI's campaign against torture. In Nigeria, for example, a press conference was held, and letters were sent to the Minister of Foreign Affairs, the Minister of Defence and members of the Nigerian legislature. In Ireland, AI groups and health professionals undertook extensive lobbying of politicians on this issue. In Germany, AI called on the government to suspend the trade in electro-shock weapons, and in Spain AI members contributed to efforts which succeeded in exposing a company involved in trafficking leg-irons and other security equipment. Also in Spain, the government agreed to ban the sale of leg-irons and belly-chains. Action by AIUK led to an official review of police equipment, including electro-shock weapons.

AI welcomed the adoption in April of a resolution by the UN Commission on Human Rights calling on all governments to take appropriate measures to prevent the production, use and export of equipment designed to inflict torture or other cruel, inhuman or degrading treatment. The Commission requested the UN Special Rapporteur on torture to find ways to prohibit the trade in such equipment, and to combat its proliferation. The Commission also called on the UN High Commissioner for Human Rights to provide support to governments in the training of law enforcement officers to prevent torture and ill-treatment. Lobbying by AIUSA contributed to the move by the US Congress in September to begin preparing a ban on the export of crime control equipment to countries where the government has repeatedly engaged in acts of torture, and for a total export ban on equipment used for torture.

The first-ever UN Conference on the Illicit Trade in Small Arms and Light Weapons, held in New York, USA, in July, provided AI with other opportunities to raise public awareness and put pressure on governments to work towards a legally binding international convention to control arms exports. AI sections used the event to publicize the issue. In France a video on small arms featuring a World Cup football player (Lilian Thuram) was broadcast on television and in cinemas from July to November. AI Italy led the Italian Coalition on Small Arms in presenting to the Italian government a research paper on the production and export of small arms from Italy. AIUSA helped organize an international rally at the Conference, which brought together families of victims of gun violence with human rights activists from around the world.

Although delegates from Canada, Norway and the EU pressed for clear agreements that small arms not be exported to countries where there is a clear risk that they will be used to violate human rights, the move was blocked by several countries, including China, the Russian Federation and the USA and countries in Asia and the Middle East. AI's delegation to the UN Conference worked with the International Action Network on Small Arms (IANSA), an alliance of over 300 NGOs. AI continued to campaign for human rights controls on arms and helped organize an international conference in November in Nairobi, Kenya, of over 100 NGO representatives.

AIUSA helped lobby the US Congress to suspend military aid for Colombia in the Fiscal Year 2002 Foreign Operations Appropriations Bill as a result of the Colombian government's failure to ensure that human rights conditions were met. Work by the section with a coalition of organizations resulted in a decrease in the amount of money that was approved for the armed forces in Colombia, and in the maintaining of human rights conditions on aid to Colombia in the final version of that Bill.

AI also campaigned for the strengthening of the EU Code of Conduct on Arms Transfers. To more fully protect human rights, AI advocated that the EU Code must be made legally binding, and its implementation subject to accountability and scrutiny in national parliaments and in the European Parliament. Citing cases of arms trafficking to West and Central Africa, as well as to Indonesia, Israel and Saudi Arabia, AI pressed for the EU Code to include control of the activities of brokers and carriers, as well as the distribution of licensed products and the establishment of strict mechanisms for their use.

Following the 11 September attacks in the USA, AI sections in the EU, USA and other arms-exporting countries pressed their home governments to impose a moratorium on the use of cluster bombs and to refrain from sending arms into Afghanistan which could be used to commit human rights abuses. AI also urged them to use their influence to stop the use of child soldiers and landmines, and to promote concrete measures to end impunity and ensure compliance with the Geneva Conventions. AI also approached the governments of the Russian Federation and Pakistan and called on other neighbouring governments to take steps to protect human rights.

To further promote the central relevance of international law in underpinning effective arms control, especially international human rights and humanitarian law, AI helped develop a draft "Framework Convention on International Arms Transfers", codifying existing law. A number of AI sections, including AI Canada and AIUK, lobbied their home governments to support the Convention. In support of this work, a further edition of the campaign newsletter *Terror Trade Times* (AI Index: ACT 31/002/2001) was produced by the IS, providing AI sections with information on cases of gross human rights abuse with small arms and security equipment, and was used as a campaigning tool by sections.

An increasing number of AI sections strengthened their work on outreach to police on human rights issues. The IS began to develop a series of expert training workshops for staff and section representatives covering key issues related to the control of small arms and security equipment, and also the training and accountability of police and law enforcement officers. Variations of these workshops were held in the Czech Republic, Kenya, Malawi, Poland, South Africa and the UK and helped to strengthen the network of 60 MSP coordinators and groups.

Human rights education (HRE)

Human rights education is now a major component of the work of many AI sections and structures around the world. At the 2nd International HRE Forum, held in October in Belfast, Northern Ireland, 70 AI delegates and invited guests from 41 countries were able to share their experiences, ideas, HRE programs and materials.

The event was held in Northern Ireland in the context of the ongoing peace process. The Chief Commissioner for the Northern Ireland Human Rights Commission gave the opening address, and AI Ireland and AI Northern Ireland presented their "Cross Border Primary School Human Rights Education Peace Initiative". AI's Secretary General, Irene Khan, spoke strongly in support of HRE as an important tool in preventing human rights violations.

Following the attacks in the USA on 11 September, the AIUSA HRE team developed a Crisis Response Guide for teachers. The Guide included lessons and activities to assist in introducing a human rights perspective into people's reactions to the attacks and to reassert the validity of human rights. The Guide is used extensively in schools and also in the wider community.

Regional HRE strategies were developed with AI sections. These were consistent with AI's international policy on HRE and reflected the regional needs and human rights environment. A regional consultation took place in Morocco in April for AI members from the Middle East and North Africa. In March a regional consultation for Asia was held in Thailand.

In Asia, AI Mongolia worked with a local project to produce a range of education programs for the AI membership and also government officials. AI Philippines conducted HRE for new members. AI Malaysia used theatre effectively as part of its HRE program, and AI Nepal continued its work with a network of 25 educators who conducted programs in rural areas for women and youth and were re-evaluating their work with the police.

As part of AI Israel's program of work in schools, a container of toys donated by schoolchildren was sent to AI Sierra Leone. AI Palestine conducted programs with women and children on awareness of women's and children's rights. Together with the Lebanese Ministry of Education, AI organized a HRE workshop in Lebanon, where key workers in the formal education system discussed methods for delivering HRE as part of the curriculum. A workshop for newly authorized human rights groups including women's rights NGOs was held in Bahrain in November.

In March, AI Slovenia and the IS organized the annual conference for the HRE Central and Eastern Europe project in Bled, northern Slovenia. Attended by 30 HRE coordinators and other HRE activists from 15 countries, the agenda included program development, HRE materials and techniques for fundraising. AI Ireland and AI Netherlands gave a presentation on human rights education and the police. A range of innovative HRE programs were also implemented by sections and structures in the Americas.

The Rights-Education-Action-Program (REAP), funded and administered by AI Norway and focusing on long-term projects in specific countries, played a major role in strengthening AI's approach to HRE. AI Mexico and AI Morocco were the first AI sections to receive funding from REAP.

Refugees

One of the effects of the attacks in the USA on 11 September was to further erode basic principles of refugee protection. Several commentators, including AI and the UN High Commissioner for Refugees, warned

AI IN ACTION

about statements and practices equating refugees with criminals or "terrorists". AI called on governments to protect refugees and asylum-seekers, and to ensure that any security measures put in place after 11 September would not prevent those displaced by conflict or persecution from receiving protection.

AI called on the US authorities to provide information on the hundreds of foreigners taken into custody in the USA after 11 September. Many sections lobbied against new anti-terrorism measures which could have a negative effect on the rights of asylum-seekers and refugees. AIUK members took action on the newly-proposed measures in the Anti-terrorism, Crime and Security Act. AI members campaigned for states neighbouring Afghanistan to keep their borders open, and urged that Afghans elsewhere not be denied access to the asylum process.

Despite worldwide events to mark the 50th anniversary of the UN Refugee Convention, core principles of refugee protection were challenged in 2001. In August the Australian government refused to allow more than 400 shipwrecked asylum-seekers on the Norwegian freighter, the *Tampa*, to disembark on to Australian territory. AI and other NGOs urged the Australian government to allow the passengers to apply for asylum in Australia, but this was refused and they were eventually sent to the Pacific island republic of Nauru and to New Zealand to have their asylum claims examined. AI Australia voiced its opposition to this and to many other measures forming the so-called "Pacific Solution" which would prevent asylum-seekers from gaining access to Australia. AI Spain also undertook a thorough analysis of the Spanish asylum system and published a comprehensive report in September.

AI sections around the world continued to work against narrow interpretations of the UN Refugee Convention. AI Germany successfully campaigned to ensure that people fleeing persecution by non-state actors should be eligible for refugee status in cases where the government in the country of origin was unable or unwilling to provide protection. Work undertaken by AI Sweden led to indications that the government would review current Swedish legislation giving only subsidiary protection to people fleeing persecution on the basis of gender or sexual orientation. AI Japan and AI Norway also worked on individual cases of people fleeing persecution for reasons of their sexual orientation.

AI's work for fair and satisfactory asylum procedures continued to be one of the main areas of campaigning and lobbying. The EU was examining a number of proposals affecting refugee protection in all EU states, including on asylum procedures. AI's EU Association highlighted a number of issues such as the right of asylum-seekers to remain in the country while their appeals were being considered. In December the EU summit undertook a review of the implementation of the conclusions of the 1999 summit which was one of the foundations of the establishment of a common EU asylum system. AI New Zealand campaigned against a marked increase in detention of asylum-seekers. AI Netherlands campaigned against an accelerated procedure to examine asylum claims in the Netherlands which did not contain necessary safeguards. AI Uganda worked to ensure that proposed asylum legislation in Uganda was in line with international standards.

AI sections and structures continued to assist individuals around the world by providing asylum-seekers, legal counsel and decision-makers with human rights information about asylum-seekers' countries of origin. AI also opposed the forcible return of many asylum-seekers to countries where they might risk serious human rights abuses. In November an Uzbek opposition leader, Muhammad Salih, who had refugee status in Norway, was arrested in the Czech Republic and threatened with extradition to Uzbekistan, where he would have been at grave risk of torture. After the intervention of AI and other organizations he was allowed to return to Norway. AI members also took action on the forcible return from Bosnia-Herzegovina and Sweden of Egyptians suspected of membership of armed Islamist groups. AI believed the men to be at grave risk of torture in Egypt.

INTERNATIONAL AND REGIONAL ORGANIZATIONS

Intergovernmental organizations play an important role in the protection and promotion of human rights worldwide. Throughout 2001, AI continued its efforts to further its human rights work by seeking to influence international and regional organizations, by both campaigning against human rights abuses and promoting international standards for the protection of human rights. It lobbied the institutions directly and individual member states through AI sections in those states.

Below are some of the highlights of AI's work with these organizations.

UN Headquarters, New York

Following the 11 September attacks in the USA, AI urged the **Security Council** to ensure that the UN Charter, international human rights and humanitarian law provide the framework for action it proposed to counteract "terrorism". Security Council Resolution 1373 called for wide-ranging measures to combat "terrorism" and established a "Counter-Terrorism Committee" to implement its provisions. The Committee can seek expert advice on how to implement the resolution but, in the absence of plans to include human rights experts, AI insisted that such expertise be provided. This is especially important since implementation of the resolution could adversely affect human rights protection, notably in areas of immigration, asylum and law enforcement. AI also urged that the Committee's guidance on implementation be amended to ensure that action taken conforms with international human rights standards.

The Security Council gave particular attention to the situation in Afghanistan following the attacks by the US-led coalition in the country. AI contributed to this debate by providing information on the human rights situation and briefed senior officials. AI made recommendations to promote a human rights agenda for Afghanistan in its report, *Afghanistan: Making human rights the agenda* (AI Index: ASA 11/023/2001). Specific proposals included ending impunity and ruling out an amnesty for grave abuses of human rights in any political settlement; protection of the rights of women, minorities, refugees and internally displaced persons; and the building of human rights institutions. AI pressed for the establishment of an expert committee to tackle impunity and advise on rebuilding the justice system.

AI participated in informal briefings arranged by the Security Council on the human rights situation in the Democratic Republic of the Congo (DRC) and Liberia and on "Women, Peace and Security". On the DRC, AI highlighted the use of child soldiers in the armed conflict, the need to address the impunity enjoyed by perpetrators of human rights abuses and to rebuild the judicial system, and the deployment of human rights monitors. In the briefing on Liberia, AI focused on the protection of refugees and internally displaced persons, and advocated deploying UN human rights monitors throughout the country to report on the human rights situation. AI is part of the Non-Governmental Organization (NGO) Working Group which contributes to the implementation of Security Council Resolution 1325 on women, peace and security. In briefing the Security Council, the Working Group stressed the need to involve women at all levels when negotiating peace and reconstruction, and its willingness to contribute to the UN Secretary-General's study on the implementation of Resolution 1325.

AI used the **General Assembly** as an opportunity to campaign for governments to ratify human rights treaties, including the Optional Protocol to the Convention on the Elimination of All Forms of Discrimination against Women and the Optional Protocol to the Convention on the Rights of the Child on the involvement of children in armed conflict. It also urged governments to support the draft optional protocol to the Convention against Torture and Other Cruel, Inhuman or Degrading Treatment or Punishment.

AI paid particular attention to resolutions dealing with Afghanistan, Iran, "terrorism" and refugees. The attacks of 11 September gave added focus to the General Assembly debate on "terrorism" and impetus to complete the draft comprehensive convention on international terrorism. AI expressed concerns about the very broad definition of "terrorism" in the draft convention, the failure to protect the right to seek asylum and the lack of fair trial guarantees in a statement, *Draft comprehensive convention on international terrorism: A threat to human rights standards*.

The General Assembly Special Session on Children was postponed to May 2002 following the attacks in the USA. AI had three main concerns which it wanted discussed at this session: ratification of human rights treaties; child soldiers and juvenile justice, in particular, the imposition of the death penalty on persons under 18 years of age at the time the crime was committed; and torture and cruel, inhuman or degrading treatment. As part of its campaign against the recruitment and use of children as soldiers, AI urged governments to ratify the Optional Protocol to the Convention on the Rights of the Child on the involvement of children in armed conflict.

UN Geneva

At the 2001 **Commission on Human Rights**, AI focused its campaigning on the human rights abuses in Colombia, Indonesia, Russian Federation, Saudi Arabia, Sierra Leone and Togo. It spotlighted abolition of the death penalty, in particular for those under 18 years at the time the crime was committed; the draft convention on "disappearances"; and the draft optional protocol to

INTERNATIONAL AND REGIONAL ORGANIZATIONS

the Convention against Torture. AI also called upon all states to extend open invitations to the UN thematic special rapporteurs and working groups, and during 2001 provided information and briefings to such mechanisms, including the Working Group on Enforced or Involuntary Disappearances, the Special Rapporteur on torture and the Special Representative of the Secretary-General on human rights defenders. In addition AI submitted information under the confidential "1503 procedure" about the human rights situation in Indonesia and Saudi Arabia.

At the **Sub-Commission on the Promotion and Protection of Human Rights**, AI drew attention to the torture and ill-treatment of people targeted because of their identity, such as race, gender or sexual orientation. In June AI published a report entitled *Crimes of hate, conspiracy of silence: Torture and ill-treatment based on sexual identity* (AI Index: ACT 40/016/2001). In a public statement AI called on the Sub-Commission to play a pioneering role in breaking the conspiracy of silence about abuses against lesbian, gay, bisexual and transgender people.

AI was an active participant in the preparations for the **World Conference against Racism** in Durban, South Africa, in August and September. It sought to draw attention at the Conference to racism in criminal justice systems, including in the use of the death penalty, and discrimination against refugees and asylum-seekers. AI also supported efforts to bring to light multiple forms of discrimination such as those relating to race and gender, sexual orientation and caste. As a contribution to the Conference, AI produced two reports, *A handbook: Using the international human rights system to combat racial discrimination* and *Racism and the administration of justice*.

2001 marked the 50th anniversary of the 1951 **Convention relating to the Status of Refugees** (Refugee Convention). AI highlighted its continued importance and advocated that those countries who had not yet acceded to these instruments did so (see *50th Anniversary of the Refugee Convention: Amnesty International appeals for further accession*, AI Index: IOR 51/003/2001). During 2001, the **Global Consultations on International Refugee Protection**, a process initiated by the UN High Commissioner for Refugees and aimed at revitalizing refugee protection, culminated in a Ministerial Meeting of States Parties to the Refugee Convention and/or its 1967 Protocol, held in Geneva in December. At the meeting, a declaration was adopted expressing the continued commitment of states to the full and effective implementation of the Convention and its Protocol. AI stressed the importance of developing a more effective system for monitoring the implementation in its statement to the meeting, *Refugee protection is human rights protection* (AI Index: IOR 51/011/2001).

AI continued to provide **UN treaty-monitoring bodies** with human rights information on states' reports. During 2001 AI gave information to the Human Rights Committee and the Committee against Torture on countries including Afghanistan, Azerbaijan, Bolivia, Brazil, Georgia, Indonesia, Israel, Democratic People's Republic of Korea, Switzerland, Ukraine and the United Kingdom. Information was also provided to the Committee on the Rights of the Child about Saudi Arabia and the recruitment of child soldiers in Paraguay, and to the Committee on the Elimination of Racial Discrimination before its consideration of China's periodic report. AI also made a written submission to the Human Rights Committee for its consideration when drafting a General Comment on Article 4 of the International Covenant on Civil and Political Rights. This deals with derogations under the Covenant regarding the protection of rights under states of emergency.

As in previous years AI participated in the **International Labour Conference** and raised concerns about the situation in Colombia under International Labour Organisation Conventions No. 87 on Freedom of Association and Protection of the Right to Organise and No. 98 on the Right to Organise and Collective Bargaining, and the situation in Myanmar under Conventions No. 29 on Forced Labour and No. 87. AI also called on states to ratify Convention No. 182 on the Worst Forms of Child Labour, which includes an explicit reference to child soldiering (Article 3).

Regional intergovernmental organizations

AI continued its campaign for member states of the **Organization of African Unity** to ratify the African Charter on the Rights and Welfare of the Child. At sessions of the **African Commission on Human and Peoples' Rights**, AI drew attention to violations of the right to freedom of expression in North Africa and attacks on human rights defenders throughout Africa. AI established first contacts with the newly appointed African Committee of Experts which will monitor state party compliance with the African Charter on the Rights and Welfare of the Child.

AI continued to press the **European Union** (EU) to develop a more comprehensive human rights policy that encompassed not only its relations with countries outside the EU but also addressed human rights problems within its own borders. AI's proposals for guidelines on torture for use in relations with other countries met with a swift response from the Council of Ministers, which in April adopted guidelines modelled on those operating successfully on the death penalty since 1998. AI consistently raised its concerns, including through a publicity campaign, about the impact of European integration in the field of asylum. It drew attention to the torture and ill-treatment of members of minority groups, including asylum-seekers, and called for systematic monitoring and accountability at national and EU level, particularly in view of the forthcoming enlargement of the Union by up to a dozen new member states. The 11 September attacks in the USA gave new significance to the need to ensure refugee protection. AI criticized the EU for pursuing a single-minded security agenda which risked compromising basic human rights standards. In discussions with the Belgian EU Presidency and in an open letter in November, AI Secretary General Irene

INTERNATIONAL AND REGIONAL ORGANIZATIONS

Khan called for governments to make certain that the aim of security would not undermine the very rights the EU seeks to safeguard, and that the principles and values on which it was founded would not be compromised.

AI campaigned for **Council of Europe** (CoE) member states to ratify Protocol No. 12 to the European Convention for the Protection of Human Rights and Fundamental Freedoms, which provides a guarantee against discrimination. It also pushed for the CoE to adopt draft Protocol No. 13 to the Convention, which abolishes the death penalty in all circumstances. After the 11 September attacks, AI raised its concerns about anti-terrorism legislation and legislative proposals in CoE member states. With the aim of ensuring that the human rights of all people within CoE member states were respected and protected in the course of measures taken to enhance security, AI made recommendations to strengthen guidelines being prepared within the CoE in its submission, *A human rights framework for the protection of security*. AI also raised concerns about proposals to reform the European Court of Human Rights that might reduce an individual's right to redress before the court.

AI raised concerns about the continued resort to the death penalty at the Human Dimension Implementation Meeting, the annual human rights conference of the **Organization for Security and Co-operation in Europe** (OSCE), in particular in relation to Belarus, Kazakstan, Tajikistan, Uzbekistan and the USA. In a statement on the prevention of torture, AI urged that the OSCE Office for Democratic Institutions and Human Rights compile an annual report on torture, identifying specific factors leading to torture, ill-treatment and impunity, and potential remedies. AI called for the OSCE to examine more fully the issue of violence against women, and to reaffirm the right to conscientious objection to military service (see *OSCE Human Dimension Implementation Meeting 2001: Statements issued by Amnesty International*, AI Index: IOR 30/001/2001). In a consultation meeting on human rights defenders, AI expressed concern about their ill-treatment in a number of OSCE countries and called for the principles of the UN Declaration on Human Rights Defenders to be incorporated into national laws and implemented (see *OSCE Supplementary Human Dimension Meeting: Human rights – advocacy and defenders*, AI Index: IOR 30/002/2001).

In February AI chaired an NGO hearing on human rights defenders at the **Inter-American Commission on Human Rights**, where the creation of an Inter-American Special Rapporteur on human rights defenders was proposed. AI, in cooperation with other NGOs, urged governments participating in the third Summit of the Americas of the **Organization of American States** (OAS) in April to prioritize human rights over commercial or economic issues, to strengthen the inter-American human rights system, and to support and protect human rights defenders throughout the continent (see *Americas: Putting human rights on the agenda – summary of Amnesty International's concerns on the Americas*, AI Index:

AMR 01/001/2001). Several resolutions adopted at the OAS General Assembly in June reflected AI's concerns and recommendations, including the request for the Inter-American Commission on Human Rights to study the situation of human rights defenders in the Americas; the call for the OAS Permanent Council to consider drafting an inter-American convention against racism and all forms of discrimination and intolerance; and the appeal to OAS member states that have not already done so to ratify the Rome Statute of the International Criminal Court and the UN Convention on the Rights of the Child and its Optional Protocol on the involvement of children in armed conflict.

In advance of the **Association of South-East Asian Nations** (ASEAN) Regional Forum in June, AI called on participating governments to ensure that their agenda included the deteriorating human rights situation in Aceh, Indonesia, its implications for regional peace and security and, in particular, threats against human rights defenders. AI attended the **Asia Pacific Forum of National Human Rights Institutions** in Sri Lanka and presented recommended standards for the establishment and functioning of such bodies in the document, *National human rights institutions: Amnesty International's recommendations for effective protection and promotion of human rights*. In a region without an intergovernmental human rights body, AI believes that this forum is an important vehicle for discussion and promotion of human rights within the region.

Developing international human rights law

Throughout 2001 AI campaigned for a strong and effective **Optional Protocol to the (UN) Convention against Torture** and participated in the negotiations. The aim of this Protocol is to establish an international body of experts in, for example, human rights, penal management and health, which would make visits to places of detention within the jurisdiction of states parties, to facilitate states' compliance with the provisions of the Convention against Torture. Negotiations to reach agreement on the text were difficult and the Working Group session in 2001 ended with three separate proposals on the table – all of which need substantial work if the Optional Protocol is to be a success. For further details, see AI's report, *Optional Protocol to the Convention against Torture: Time to take a stand on the prevention of torture*.

Impunity: the International Criminal Court

As one of the more than 1,000 members of the NGO Coalition for an International Criminal Court, AI campaigned for states to ratify the Rome Statute of the International Criminal Court through its national sections and structures in more than 60 countries. During 2001, 21 states ratified the Rome Statute. By the end of 2001, a total of 48 states had ratified it. For the Statute to enter into force, 12 more ratifications are required, following which the Court will be established. AI commented on draft implementing legislation for Argentina, Croatia and the United Kingdom.

INTERNATIONAL AND REGIONAL ORGANIZATIONS

As part of its work on universal jurisdiction, AI produced *Universal jurisdiction: The duty of states to enact and implement legislation* on CD ROM. The document contains over 750 pages of information that will resource a forthcoming worldwide action for AI sections and structures to lobby their governments to enact legislation on universal jurisdiction.

Selected AI reports
- Universal jurisdiction: The duty of states to enact and implement legislation (AI Index: IOR 53/002/2001 to IOR 53/018/2001) on CD ROM
- Optional Protocol to the Convention against Torture: Time to take a stand on the prevention of torture (AI Index: IOR 51/006/2001)
- A human rights framework for the protection of security (AI Index: IOR 61/005/2001)
- Claiming women's rights: The Optional Protocol to the UN Women's Convention (AI Index: IOR 51/001/2001)
- United Nations General Assembly, 56th Session 2001, Draft comprehensive convention on international terrorism: A threat to human rights standards (AI Index: IOR 51/009/2001)
- A handbook: Using the international human rights system to combat racial discrimination (AI Index: IOR 80/001/2001)
- Racism and the administration of justice (AI Index: ACT 40/020/2001)
- National human rights institutions: Amnesty International's recommendations for effective protection and promotion of human rights (AI Index: IOR 40/007/2001)

EU Office
(available on website: www.amnesty-eu.org)
- Putting human rights into practice – AI Memorandum to the Belgian Presidency of the EU (EU Office, July 2001)
- The asylum crisis: A human rights challenge for the EU (EU Office, September 2001)
- Security, refugee protection and the human rights agenda after 11 September: AI's concerns regarding EU policies (EU Office, November 2001)
- The Human Rights Agenda for the EU in 2002 – AI memorandum to the Spanish Presidency (EU Office, November 2001)

SELECTED INTERNATIONAL HUMAN RIGHTS TREATIES

Selected international human rights treaties
(AT 31 DECEMBER 2001)

States which have ratified or acceded to a convention are party to the treaty and are bound to observe its provisions. States which have signed but not yet ratified have expressed their intention to become a party at some future date; meanwhile they are obliged to refrain from acts which would defeat the object and purpose of the treaty.

Country	ICCPR	(first) OP to ICCPR	2nd OP to ICCPR (death penalty)	ICESCR	CEDAW	OP to CEDAW	CRC	OP to CRC (children in armed conflict)	ICERD	Refugee Convention (1951)	Refugee Protocol	Rome Statute of ICC[+]	Convention against Torture
Afghanistan	○			○	D		○		○				○[28]
Albania	○			○	○		○		○	○	○	D	○
Algeria	○	○		○	○		○		○	○	○	D	[22]○
Andorra					○	▶	○	●				●	
Angola	○	○		○	○		○			○	○	D	
Antigua and Barbuda					○		○		○	○	○	●	○
Argentina	○	○		○	○	D	○	D	○	○	○	●	[22]○
Armenia	○	○		○	○		○		○	○	○	D	○
Australia	○	○	○	○	○		○		○	○	○	D	[22]○
Austria	○	○	○	○	○	○	○	D	○	○	○	○	[22]○
Azerbaijan	○	●	○	○	○	●	○	D	○	○	○		○
Bahamas					○		○		○	○	○	D	
Bahrain					○		○		○			D	○
Bangladesh	○			○	○	○	○	○	○			D	○
Barbados	○	○		○	○		○		○	○	○	D	
Belarus	○	○		○	○		○		○	●	●		○
Belgium	○	○	○	○	○	D	○	D	○	○	○	○	[22]○
Belize	○				D		○	D	●	○	○	○	
Benin	○	○		○	○	D	○	▶	●	○	○	D	○
Bhutan					○		○			D			
Bolivia	○	○		○	○		○		○	○	○	○	○
Bosnia and Herzegovina	○	○	●	○	○	D	○	D	○	○	○	D	○
Botswana	○				○		○		○	○	○	○	○
Brazil	○			○	○	▶	○	D	○	○	○	D	○
Brunei Darussalam							○						
Bulgaria	○	○	○	○	○	D	○	▶	○	○	○	D	[22]○
Burkina Faso	○	○		○	○	▶	○	▶	○	○	○	D	○
Burundi	○			○	○	▶	○	▶	○	○	○	D	○
Cambodia	○			○	○	▶	○	D	○	○	○	D	○
Cameroon	○	○		○	○		○	▶	○	○	○	D	[22]○
Canada	○	○	○	○	○		○	○	○	○	○	○	[22]○
Cape Verde	○	○	○	○	○		○		○			D	○
Central African Republic	○	○		○	○		○		○	○	○	●	
Chad	○	○		○	○		○		○	○	○	D	○
Chile	○	○	▶	○	○	D	○	▶	○	○	○	D	○
China	D			●	○		○	▶	○	○	○		○[28]

Legend:
- \+ not yet in force
- ● became a state party in 2001
- ○ state is a party
- ▶ signed in 2001
- D signed but not yet ratified
- 22 Countries making a declaration under Article 22 recognize the competence of the Committee against Torture to consider individual complaints
- 28 Countries making a reservation under Article 28 do not recognize the competence of the Committee against Torture to undertake confidential inquiries into allegations of systematic torture if warranted

Amnesty International Report 2002

295

SELECTED INTERNATIONAL HUMAN RIGHTS TREATIES

	International Covenant on Civil and Political Rights (ICCPR)	(first) Optional Protocol to the ICCPR	Second Optional Protocol to the ICCPR, aiming at the abolition of the death penalty	International Covenant on Economic, Social and Cultural Rights	Convention on the Elimination of All Forms of Discrimination against Women (CEDAW)	Optional Protocol to CEDAW	Convention on the Rights of the Child (CRC)	Optional Protocol to the CRC on the involvement of children in armed conflict	International Convention on the Elimination of All Forms of Racial Discrimination	Convention relating to the Status of Refugees (1951)	Protocol relating to the Status of Refugees	Rome Statute of the International Criminal Court+	Convention against Torture and Other Cruel, Inhuman or Degrading Treatment or Punishment
Colombia	○	○	○	○	○	D	○	D	○	○	○	D	○
Comoros					○		○		D			D	D
Congo (Democratic Republic of the)	○	○		○	○		○	●	○	○	○	D	
Congo (Republic of the)	○	○			○		○		○	○	○		
Cook Islands							○						
Costa Rica	○	○	○	○	○	●	○	D	○	○	○	●	○
Côte d'Ivoire	○	○		○	○		○		○	○	○	D	○
Croatia	○	○	○	○	○	●	○		○	○	○	●	22○
Cuba					○	D	○	D	○				
Cyprus	○	○	○	○	○	▶	○		○	○	○	D	22○
Czech Republic	○	○		○	○	●	○	●	○	○	○	D	22○
Denmark	○	○	○	○	○	○	○	D	○	○	○	●	22○
Djibouti					○		○			○	○	D	
Dominica	○			○	○		○			○	○	●	
Dominican Republic	○	○		○	○	●	○		○	○	○	D	D
Ecuador	○	○	○	○	○	D	○	D	○	○	○	D	22○
Egypt	○			○	○		○		○	○	○	D	○
El Salvador	○	○		○	○	▶	○	D	○	○	○		○
Equatorial Guinea	○	○		○	○		○			○	○		
Eritrea				●	○		○		●			D	
Estonia	○	○		○	○		○		○	○	○	D	○
Ethiopia	○			○	○		○		○	○	○		○
Fiji					○		○		○	○	○	○	
Finland	○	○	○	○	○	○	○	D	○	○	○	○	22○
France	○	○	○	○	○		○	D	○	○	○	○	22○
Gabon	○			○	○		○		○	○	○	○	○
Gambia	○	○		○	○		○	D	○	○	○	D	D
Georgia	○	○	○	○	○		○		○	○	○	D	○
Germany	○	○	○	○	○	D	○	D	○	○	○	○	22○
Ghana	○	○		○	○		○	D	○	○	○	○	22○
Greece	○	○	○	○	○	D	○	D	○	○	○	D	22○
Grenada	○			○	○		○			D			
Guatemala	○	○		○	○	D	○	D	○	○	○		○
Guinea	○	○		○	○		○		○	○	○	D	○
Guinea-Bissau	D	D	D	○	○	D	○	D	○	○	○	D	D
Guyana	○	○		○	○		○		○			D	○
Haiti	○				○		○		○	○	○	D	
Holy See							○	●	○	○	○		
Honduras	○	D	D	○	○		○			○	○	D	○
Hungary	○	○	○	○	○	○	○		○	○	○	●	22○
Iceland	○	○	○	○	○	●	○	●	○	○	○	○	22○
India	○			○	○		○		○				D
Indonesia					○	D	○	▶	○				○
Iran (Islamic Republic of)	○			○			○		○	○	○	D	
Iraq	○			○	○		○		○				
Ireland	○	○	○	○	○		○	D	○	○	○	D	○
Israel	○			○	○		○	▶	○	○	○	D	○28
Italy		○	○		○		○	D	○	○	○	○	22○

+ not yet in force
● became a state party in 2001
○ state is a party
▶ signed in 2001
D signed but not yet ratified

22 Countries making a declaration under Article 22 recognize the competence of the Committee against Torture to consider individual complaints

28 Countries making a reservation under Article 28 do not recognize the competence of the Committee against Torture to undertake confidential inquiries into allegations of systematic torture if warranted

SELECTED INTERNATIONAL HUMAN RIGHTS TREATIES

	International Covenant on Civil and Political Rights (ICCPR)	(first) Optional Protocol to the ICCPR	Second Optional Protocol to the ICCPR, aiming at the abolition of the death penalty	International Covenant on Economic, Social and Cultural Rights	Convention on the Elimination of All Forms of Discrimination against Women (CEDAW)	Optional Protocol to CEDAW	Convention on the Rights of the Child (CRC)	Optional Protocol to the CRC on the involvement of children in armed conflict	International Convention on the Elimination of All Forms of Racial Discrimination	Convention relating to the Status of Refugees (1951)	Protocol relating to the Status of Refugees	Rome Statute of the International Criminal Court+	Convention against Torture and Other Cruel, Inhuman or degrading Treatment or Punishment
Jamaica	○			○	○		○	D	○	○	○	D	
Japan	○			○	○		○		○	○	○		○
Jordan	○			○	○		○	D	○			D	○
Kazakstan				○	●		○	D	○	○	○		○
Kenya	○			○	○		○	D	●	○	○	D	○
Kiribati							○						
Korea (Democratic People's Republic of)	○			○	●		○						
Korea (Republic of)	○	○		○	○		○	○	○	○	○	D	○
Kuwait	○			○	○		○		○			D	○[28]
Kyrgyzstan	○	○		○	○		○		○	○	○	D	○
Lao People's Democratic Republic	D			D	○		○		○				
Latvia	○	○		○	○		○		○	○	○	D	○
Lebanon	○			○	○		○		○				○
Lesotho	○	○		○	○	D	○		D	○	○	○	●
Liberia	D			D	○		○		○	○	○	D	
Libyan Arab Jamahiriya	○	○		○	○		○		○				○
Liechtenstein	○	○	○	○	○	●	○	D	○	○	○	●	[22]○
Lithuania	○	○	D	○	○	D	○		○	○	○	D	○
Luxembourg	○	○	○	○	○	D	○	D	○	○	○	○	[22]○
Macedonia (former Yugoslav Republic of)	○	○	○	○	○	D	○	▶	○	○	○	D	○
Madagascar	○	○		○	○	D	○		○	○	○	D	▶
Malawi	○	○		○	○	D	○	D	○	○	○	D	○
Malaysia					○		○						
Maldives					○		○		○				
Mali	○	●		○	○		○	D	○	○	○	○	○
Malta	○	○	○	○	○		○	D	○	○	○	D	[22]○
Marshall Islands							○					○	
Mauritania					●		○		○	○	○		
Mauritius	○	○		○	○	▶	○	▶	○			D	○
Mexico	○			○	○	D	○		○			D	○
Micronesia (Federated States of)							○						
Moldova	○			○	○		○		○			D	○
Monaco	○		○	○			○	●	○			D	[22]○
Mongolia	○	○		○	○	D	○	▶	○			D	
Morocco	○			○	○		○		○	○	○	D	○[28]
Mozambique	○		○		○		○			○	○	D	○
Myanmar					○		○						
Namibia	○	○	○	○	○	○	○		D	○	○	D	○
Nauru	▶	▶					○	D	▶			●	▶
Nepal	○	○	○	○	○	▶	○	D	○				○
Netherlands	○	○	○	○	○	D	○	D	○	○	○	●	[22]○
New Zealand	○	○	○	○	○	○	○	●	○	○	○	○	[22]○
Nicaragua	○	○	D	○	○		○		○	○	○		D
Niger	○	○		○	○		○		○	○	○	D	○
Nigeria	○			○	○	D	○	D	○	○	○	●	●
Niue							○						
Norway	○	○	○	○	○	D	○	D	○	○	○	○	[22]○
Oman					○		○					D	
Pakistan				○	○		○	▶	○				

+ not yet in force
● became a state party in 2001
○ state is a party
▶ signed in 2001
D signed but not yet ratified

[22] Countries making a declaration under Article 22 recognize the competence of the Committee against Torture to consider individual complaints

[28] Countries making a reservation under Article 28 do not recognize the competence of the Committee against Torture to undertake confidential inquiries into allegations of systematic torture if warranted

Amnesty International Report 2002

297

SELECTED INTERNATIONAL HUMAN RIGHTS TREATIES

	International Covenant on Civil and Political Rights (ICCPR)	(first) Optional Protocol to the ICCPR	Second Optional Protocol to the ICCPR, aiming at the abolition of the death penalty	International Covenant on Economic, Social and Cultural Rights	Convention on the Elimination of All Forms of Discrimination against Women (CEDAW)	Optional Protocol to CEDAW	Convention on the Rights of the Child (CRC)	Optional Protocol to the CRC on the involvement of children in armed conflict	International Convention on the Elimination of All Forms of Racial Discrimination	Convention relating to the Status of Refugees (1951)	Protocol relating to the Status of Refugees	Rome Statute of the International Criminal Court[+]	Convention against Torture and Other Cruel, Inhuman or Degrading Treatment or Punishment
Palau							○						
Panama	○	○	○	○	○	●	○	●	○	○	○	D	○
Papua New Guinea					○		○		○	○	○		
Paraguay	○	○		○	○	●	○	D	D	○	○	●	○
Peru	○	○		○	○	●	○	D	○	○	○	●	○
Philippines	○	○		○	○	D	○	D	○	○	○	D	○
Poland	○	○	D	○	○		○		○	○	○	●	[22]○[28]
Portugal	○	○	○	○	○	D	○	D	○	○	○	D	[22]○
Qatar							○		○				○
Romania	○	○	○	○	○	D	○	●	○	○	○	D	○
Russian Federation	○	○		○	○	▶	○	▶	○	○	○	D	[22]○
Rwanda	○			○	○		○		○	○	○		
Saint Kitts and Nevis					○		○						
Saint Lucia					○		○		○			D	
Saint Vincent and the Grenadines	○	○		○	○		○		○	○	○		●
Samoa					○		○			○	○	D	
San Marino	○	○		○			○	D	▶			○	
Sao Tome and Principe	D	D	D	D	○		○		D	○	○	D	D
Saudi Arabia					○		○		○				○[28]
Senegal	○	○		○	○		○	D	○	○	○	○	[22]○
Seychelles	○	○	○	○	○		○	▶	○	○	○	D	[22]○
Sierra Leone	○	○		○	○	D	○	D	○	○	○	○	●
Singapore					○		○	D					
Slovakia	○	○	○	○	○	○	○	▶	○	○	○	D	[22]○
Slovenia	○	○	○	○	○	D	○	D	○	○	○	●	[22]○
Solomon Islands				○			○		○	○	○	D	
Somalia	○	○		○					○	○	○		○
South Africa	○			D	○		○		○	○	○	○	[22]○
Spain	○	○	○	○	○	●	○	D	○	○	○	○	[22]○
Sri Lanka	○	○		○	○		○	○	○				○
Sudan	○			○			○		○	○	○	D	D
Suriname	○	○		○	○		○		○				
Swaziland					○		○		○	○	○		
Sweden	○	○	○	○	○	D	○	D	○	○	○	●	[22]○
Switzerland	○		○	○	○		○	D	○	○	○	●	[22]○
Syrian Arab Republic	○			○			○		○			D	
Tajikistan	○	○		○	○	D	○		○	○	○	○	○
Tanzania	○			○	○		○		○	○	○	D	
Thailand	○			○	○	D	○					D	
Togo	○	○		○	○		○	▶	○	○	○		[22]○
Tonga							○		○				
Trinidad and Tobago	○			○	○		○		○	○	○	○	
Tunisia	○			○	○		○		○	○	○		[22]○
Turkey	D			D	○	D	○	D	D	○	○		[22]○
Turkmenistan	○	○	○	○	○		○		○	○	○		○
Tuvalu					○		○			○	○		
Uganda	○	○		○	○		○		○	○	○	D	○
Ukraine	○	○		○	○	D	○	D	○	○	○	D	○[28]
United Arab Emirates					○		○		○			D	

+ not yet in force
● became a state party in 2001
○ state is a party
▶ signed in 2001
D signed but not yet ratified

[22] Countries making a declaration under Article 22 recognize the competence of the Committee against Torture to consider individual complaints

[28] Countries making a reservation under Article 28 do not recognize the competence of the Committee against Torture to undertake confidential inquiries into allegations of systematic torture if warranted

SELECTED INTERNATIONAL HUMAN RIGHTS TREATIES

	International Covenant on Civil and Political Rights (ICCPR)	(first) Optional Protocol to the ICCPR	Second Optional Protocol to the ICCPR, aiming at the abolition of the death penalty	International Covenant on Economic, Social and Cultural Rights	Convention on the Elimination of All Forms of Discrimination against Women (CEDAW)	Optional Protocol to CEDAW	Convention on the Rights of the Child (CRC)	Optional Protocol to the CRC on the involvement of children in armed conflict	International Convention on the Elimination of All Forms of Racial Discrimination	Convention relating to the Status of Refugees (1951)	Protocol relating to the Status of Refugees	Rome Statute of the International Criminal Court[+]	Convention against Torture and Other Cruel, Inhuman or Degrading Treatment or Punishment
United Kingdom	○		○	○	○		○	D	○	○	○	●	○
United States of America	○			D	D		D	D	○		○	D	○
Uruguay	○	○	○	○	○	●	○	D	○	○	○	D	[22]○
Uzbekistan	○	○		○	○		○		○			D	○
Vanuatu					○		○						
Venezuela	○	○	○	○	○	D	○	D	○		○	○	[22]○
Viet Nam	○			○	○		○	●	○				
Yemen	○			○	○		○		○	○	○	D	○
Yugoslavia (Federal Republic of)	○	●	●	○	○		○	▶	○	○	○	●	[22]○
Zambia	○	○		○	○		○		○	○	○	D	○
Zimbabwe	○			○	○		○		○	○	○	D	

+ not yet in force
● became a state party in 2001
○ state is a party
▶ signed in 2001
D signed but not yet ratified

22 Countries making a declaration under Article 22 recognize the competence of the Committee against Torture to consider individual complaints

28 Countries making a reservation under Article 28 do not recognize the competence of the Committee against Torture to undertake confidential inquiries into allegations of systematic torture if warranted

SELECTED REGIONAL HUMAN RIGHTS TREATIES

Selected regional human rights treaties
(AT 31 DECEMBER 2001)

Organization of African Unity (OAU)

States which have ratified or acceded to a convention are party to the treaty and are bound to observe its provisions. States which have signed but not yet ratified have expressed their intention to become a party at some future date; meanwhile they are obliged to refrain from acts which would defeat the object and purpose of the treaty.

This chart lists countries which were members of the OAU at the end of 2001.

- ● became a state party in 2001
- ○ state is a party
- ▶ signed in 2001
- D signed but not yet ratified

	African Charter on Human and Peoples' Rights (1981)	African Charter on the Rights and Welfare of the Child
Algeria	○	D
Angola	○	○
Benin	○	○
Botswana	○	●
Burkina Faso	○	○
Burundi	○	
Cameroon	○	○
Cape Verde	○	○
Central African Republic	○	
Chad	○	○
Comoros	○	
Congo (Democratic Republic of the)	○	
Congo (Republic of the)	○	D
Côte d'Ivoire	○	
Djibouti	○	D
Egypt	○	●
Equatorial Guinea	○	
Eritrea	○	○
Ethiopia	○	
Gabon	○	D
Gambia	○	●
Ghana	○	D
Guinea	○	○
Guinea-Bissau	○	
Kenya	○	○
Lesotho	○	○
Liberia	○	D
Libya	○	○
Madagascar	○	D
Malawi	○	○
Mali	○	○
Mauritania	○	
Mauritius	○	○
Mozambique	○	○
Namibia	○	D
Niger	○	○
Nigeria	○	▶
Rwanda	○	●
Sahrawi Arab Democratic Republic	○	D
Sao Tome and Principe	○	
Senegal	○	○
Seychelles	○	○

SELECTED REGIONAL HUMAN RIGHTS TREATIES

		African Charter on Human and Peoples' Rights (1981)	African Charter on the Rights and Welfare of the Child
● became a state party in 2001	Sierra Leone	○	D
○ state is a party	Somalia	○	D
▶ signed in 2001	South Africa	○	○
	Sudan	○	
D signed but not yet ratified	Swaziland	○	D
	Tanzania	○	D
	Togo	○	○
	Tunisia	○	D
	Uganda	○	○
	Zambia	○	D
	Zimbabwe	○	○

SELECTED REGIONAL HUMAN RIGHTS TREATIES

Organization of American States (OAS)

States which have ratified or acceded to a convention are party to the treaty and are bound to observe its provisions. States which have signed but not yet ratified have expressed their intention to become a party at some future date; meanwhile they are obliged to refrain from acts which would defeat the object and purpose of the treaty.

This chart lists countries which were members of the OAS at the end of 2001.

	American Convention on Human Rights (1969)	Protocol to the American Convention on Human Rights to Abolish the Death Penalty	Inter-American Convention to Prevent and Punish Torture (1985)	Inter-American Convention on Forced Disappearance of Persons (1994)
Antigua and Barbuda				
Argentina	○ 62		○	○
Bahamas				
Barbados	○ 62			
Belize				
Bolivia	○ 62		D	○
Brazil	○ 62	○	○	D
Canada				
Chile	○ 62	●	○	D
Colombia	○ 62		○	D
Costa Rica	○ 62	○	○	○
Cuba*				
Dominica	○			
Dominican Republic	○ 62		○	
Ecuador	○ 62	○	○	D
El Salvador	○ 62		○	
Grenada	○			
Guatemala	○ 62		○	○
Guyana				
Haiti	○ 62		D	
Honduras	○ 62		D	D
Jamaica	○			
Mexico	○ 62		○	●
Nicaragua	○ 62	○	D	D
Panama	○ 62	○	○	○
Paraguay	○ 62	○	○	○
Peru	○ 62		○	●
Saint Kitts and Nevis				
Saint Lucia				
Saint Vincent and the Grenadines				
Suriname	○ 62		○	
Trinidad and Tobago				
United States of America	D			
Uruguay	○ 62	○	○	○
Venezuela	○ 62	○	○	○

● became a state party in 2001
○ state is a party
● signed in 2001
D signed but not yet ratified

62 Countries making a Declaration under Article 62 recognize as binding the jurisdiction of the Inter-American Court of Human Rights (on all matters relating to the interpretation or application of the American Convention)

* In 1962 the VIII Meeting of Consultation of Ministers of Foreign Affairs decided to exclude Cuba from participating in the Inter-American system.

SELECTED REGIONAL HUMAN RIGHTS TREATIES

Council of Europe

States which have ratified or acceded to a convention are party to the treaty and are bound to observe its provisions. States which have signed but not yet ratified have expressed their intention to become a party at some future date; meanwhile they are obliged to refrain from acts which would defeat the object and purpose of the treaty.

This chart lists countries which were members of the Council of Europe at the end of 2001.

● became a state party in 2001
○ state is a party
◗ signed in 2001
D signed but not yet ratified

* Protocol No. 6 to the Convention for the Protection of Human Rights and Fundamental Freedoms concerning the abolition of the death penalty in times of peace (1983)

** Protocol No. 12 to the Convention for the Protection of Human Rights and Fundamental Freedoms concerning the general prohibition of discrimination (2000). The Protocol will enter into force after 10 ratifications.

Country	Convention for the Protection of Human Rights and Fundamental Freedoms (1950)	Protocol No. 6*	Protocol No. 12**	European Convention for the Prevention of Torture and Inhuman or Degrading Treatment or Punishment (1987)
Albania	○	○		○
Andorra	○	○		○
Armenia	◗	◗		◗
Austria	○	○	D	○
Azerbaijan	◗	◗		◗
Belgium	○	○	D	○
Bulgaria	○	○		○
Croatia	○	○		○
Cyprus	○	○	D	○
Czech Republic	○	○	D	○
Denmark	○	○		○
Estonia	○	○	D	○
Finland	○	○	D	○
France	○	○		○
Georgia	○	○	●	○
Germany	○	○	D	○
Greece	○	○	D	○
Hungary	○	○	D	○
Iceland	○	○	D	○
Ireland	○	○	D	○
Italy	○	○	D	○
Latvia	○	○	D	○
Liechtenstein	○	○	D	○
Lithuania	○	○		○
Luxembourg	○	○	D	○
Macedonia	○	○	D	○
Malta	○	○		○
Moldova	○	○	D	○
Netherlands	○	○	D	○
Norway	○	○		○
Poland	○	○		○
Portugal	○	○	D	○
Romania	○	○	D	○
Russian Federation	○	D	D	○
San Marino	○	○	D	○
Slovakia	○	○	D	○
Slovenia	○	○	◗	○
Spain	○	○		○
Sweden	○	○		○
Switzerland	○	○		○
Turkey	○	◗		○
Ukraine	○	○	D	○
United Kingdom	○	○		○

The Geneva Conventions and their Additional Protocols
(AT 31 DECEMBER 2001)

The four Geneva Conventions of 12 August 1949 were ratified collectively by states. They are: the Geneva Convention for the Amelioration of the Condition of the Wounded and Sick in Armed Forces in the Field (First Geneva Convention); the Geneva Convention for the Amelioration of the Condition of Wounded, Sick and Shipwrecked Members of Armed Forces at Sea (Second Geneva Convention); the Geneva Convention relative to the Treatment of Prisoners of War (Third Geneva Convention); and the Geneva Convention relative to the Protection of Civilian Persons in Time of War (Fourth Geneva Convention).

● became a state party in 2001
○ state is a party

	Geneva Conventions of 12 August 1949	Protocol Additional to the Geneva Conventions of 12 August 1949, and relating to the Protection of Victims of International Armed Conflicts (Protocol I)	Protocol Additional to the Geneva Conventions of 12 August 1949, and relating to the Protection of Victims of Non-International Armed Conflicts (Protocol II)
Afghanistan	○		
Albania	○	○	○
Algeria	○	○	○
Andorra	○		
Angola	○	○	
Antigua and Barbuda	○	○	○
Argentina	○	○	○
Armenia	○	○	○
Australia	○	○	○
Austria	○	○	○
Azerbaijan	○		
Bahamas	○	○	○
Bahrain	○	○	○
Bangladesh	○	○	○
Barbados	○	○	○
Belarus	○	○	○
Belgium	○	○	○
Belize	○	○	○
Benin	○	○	○
Bhutan	○		
Bolivia	○	○	○
Bosnia and Herzegovina	○	○	○
Botswana	○	○	○
Brazil	○	○	○
Brunei Darussalam	○	○	○
Bulgaria	○	○	○
Burkina Faso	○	○	○
Burundi	○	○	○
Cambodia	○	○	○
Cameroon	○	○	○
Canada	○	○	○
Cape Verde	○	○	○
Central African Republic	○	○	○
Chad	○	○	○
Chile	○	○	○
China	○	○	○
Colombia	○	○	○
Comoros	○	○	○
Congo (Democratic Republic of the)	○	○	
Congo (Republic of the)	○	○	○
Costa Rica	○	○	○

GENEVA CONVENTIONS AND THEIR ADDITIONAL PROTOCOLS

● became a state party in 2001
○ state is a party

	Geneva Conventions of 12 August 1949	Protocol Additional to the Geneva Conventions of 12 August 1949, and relating to the Protection of Victims of International Armed Conflicts (Protocol I)	Protocol Additional to the Geneva Conventions of 12 August 1949, and relating to the Protection of Victims of Non-International Armed Conflicts (Protocol II)
Côte d'Ivoire	○	○	○
Croatia	○	○	○
Cuba	○	○	○
Cyprus	○	○	○
Czech Republic	○	○	○
Denmark	○	○	○
Djibouti	○	○	○
Dominica	○	○	○
Dominican Republic	○	○	○
Ecuador	○	○	○
Egypt	○	○	○
El Salvador	○	○	○
Equatorial Guinea	○	○	○
Eritrea	○		
Estonia	○	○	○
Ethiopia	○	○	○
Fiji	○		
Finland	○	○	○
France	○	●	○
Gabon	○	○	○
Gambia	○	○	○
Georgia	○	○	○
Germany	○	○	○
Ghana	○	○	○
Greece	○	○	○
Grenada	○	○	○
Guatemala	○	○	○
Guinea	○	○	○
Guinea-Bissau	○	○	○
Guyana	○	○	○
Haiti	○		
Holy See	○	○	○
Honduras	○	○	○
Hungary	○	○	○
Iceland	○	○	○
India	○		
Indonesia	○		
Iran (Islamic Republic of)	○		
Iraq	○		
Ireland	○	○	○
Israel	○		
Italy	○	○	○
Jamaica	○	○	○
Japan	○		
Jordan	○	○	○
Kazakhstan	○	○	○
Kenya	○	○	○
Kiribati	○		
Korea (Democratic People's Republic of)	○	○	
Korea (Republic of)	○	○	○

Amnesty International Report 2002

GENEVA CONVENTIONS AND THEIR ADDITIONAL PROTOCOLS

	Geneva Conventions of 12 August 1949	Protocol Additional to the Geneva Conventions of 12 August 1949, and relating to the Protection of Victims of International Armed Conflicts (Protocol I)	Protocol Additional to the Geneva Conventions of 12 August 1949, and relating to the Protection of Victims of Non-International Armed Conflicts (Protocol II)
Kuwait	○	○	○
Kyrgyzstan	○	○	○
Lao People's Democratic Republic	○	○	○
Latvia	○	○	○
Lebanon	○	○	○
Lesotho	○	○	○
Liberia	○	○	○
Libyan Arab Jamahiriya	○	○	○
Liechtenstein	○	○	○
Lithuania	○	○	○
Luxembourg	○	○	○
Macedonia (former Yugoslav Republic of)	○	○	○
Madagascar	○	○	○
Malawi	○	○	○
Malaysia	○		
Maldives	○	○	○
Mali	○	○	○
Malta	○	○	○
Marshall Islands			
Mauritania	○	○	○
Mauritius	○	○	○
Mexico	○	○	
Micronesia (Federated States of)	○	○	○
Moldova	○	○	○
Monaco	○	○	○
Mongolia	○	○	○
Morocco	○		
Mozambique	○	○	
Myanmar	○		
Namibia	○	○	○
Nauru			
Nepal	○		
Netherlands	○	○	○
New Zealand	○	○	○
Nicaragua	○	○	○
Niger	○	○	○
Nigeria	○	○	○
Norway	○	○	○
Oman	○	○	○
Pakistan	○		
Palau	○	○	○
Panama	○	○	○
Papua New Guinea	○		
Paraguay	○	○	○
Peru	○	○	○
Philippines	○		○
Poland	○	○	○
Portugal	○	○	○
Qatar	○	○	
Romania	○	○	○
Russian Federation	○	○	○

● became a state party in 2001
○ state is a party

GENEVA CONVENTIONS AND THEIR ADDITIONAL PROTOCOLS

- ● became a state party in 2001
- ○ state is a party

Country	Geneva Conventions of 12 August 1949	Protocol Additional to the Geneva Conventions of 12 August 1949, and relating to the Protection of Victims of International Armed Conflicts (Protocol I)	Protocol Additional to the Geneva Conventions of 12 August 1949, and relating to the Protection of Victims of Non-International Armed Conflicts (Protocol II)
Rwanda	○	○	○
Saint Kitts and Nevis	○	○	○
Saint Lucia	○	○	○
Saint Vincent and the Grenadines	○	○	○
Samoa	○	○	○
San Marino	○	○	○
Sao Tome and Principe	○	○	○
Saudi Arabia	○	○	
Senegal	○	○	○
Seychelles	○	○	○
Sierra Leone	○	○	○
Singapore	○		
Slovakia	○	○	○
Slovenia	○	○	○
Solomon Islands	○	○	○
Somalia	○		
South Africa	○	○	○
Spain	○	○	○
Sri Lanka	○		
Sudan	○		
Suriname	○	○	○
Swaziland	○	○	○
Sweden	○	○	○
Switzerland	○	○	○
Syrian Arab Republic	○	○	
Tajikistan	○	○	○
Tanzania	○	○	○
Thailand	○		
Togo	○	○	○
Tonga	○		
Trinidad and Tobago	○	●	●
Tunisia	○	○	○
Turkey	○		
Turkmenistan	○	○	○
Tuvalu	○		
Uganda	○	○	○
Ukraine	○	○	○
United Arab Emirates	○	○	○
United Kingdom	○	○	○
United States of America	○		
Uruguay	○	○	○
Uzbekistan	○	○	○
Vanuatu	○	○	○
Venezuela	○	○	○
Viet Nam	○	○	
Yemen	○	○	○
Yugoslavia (Federal Republic of)	○	○	○
Zambia	○	○	○
Zimbabwe	○	○	○

Amnesty International Report 2002